WASSERSTROM

Fourth Edition

P9-DTB-842

JUDAISM
Development and Life

LEO TREPP

Wadsworth Publishing Company
I(T)P® An International Thomson Publishing Company

Belmont, CA • Albany, NY • Boston • Cincinnati • Detroit • Johannesburg
London • Madrid • Melbourne • Mexico City • New York
Pacific Grove, CA • Scottsdale, AZ • Singapore • Tokyo • Toronto

Religion Editor: *Peter Adams*
Assistant Editor: *Kerri Abdinoor*
Editorial Assistant: *Mindy Newfarmer*
Marketing Manager: *Dave Garrison*
Print Buyer: *Stacey Weinberger*
Permissions Editor: *Susan Walters*

Production: *Matrix Productions Inc.*
Interior Design: *Adriane Bosworth*
Copy Editor: *Patti Law*
Cover Design and Image: *Andrew Ogus*
Compositor: *Scratchgravel Publishing Services*
Printer: *Webcom Limited*

Printed in Canada
2   3   4   5   6   7   8   9   10

Wadsworth Publishing Company
10 Davis Drive
Belmont, CA 94002

International Thomson Editores
Seneca, 53
Colonia Polanco
11560 México D. F. México

International Thomson Publishing Europe
Berkshire House
168-173 High Holborn
London WC1V 7AA, United Kingdom

International Thomson Publishing Asia
60 Albert Street #15-01
Albert Complex
Singapore 189969

Nelson ITP, Australia
102 Dodds Street
South Melbourne
Victoria 3205 Australia

International Thomson Publishing Japan
Hirakawa-cho Kyowa Building, 3F
2-2-1 Hirakawa-cho, Chiyoda-ku
Tokyo 102, Japan

Nelson Canada
1120 Birchmount Road
Scarborough, Ontario
Canada M1K 5G4

International Thomson Publishing
Southern Africa
Building 18, Constantia Square
138 Sixteenth Road, P.O. Box 2459
Halfway House, 1685 South Africa

Library of Congress Cataloging-in-Publication Data

Trepp, Leo.
    Judaism : development and life / Leo Trepp. — 4th ed.
        p.   cm.
    Includes bibliographical references and index.
    ISBN 0-534-54634-X
    1. Judaism.   I. Title
BM561.T7   IN PROCESS
296—dc21   98-54468

This book is printed on acid-free recycled paper.

CONTENTS

Chapter 5   Jewish Mysticism, Hasidism, and Modern Jewry   94

Chapter 6   Emancipation and the Modern Age in Western Europe   109

Chapter 7   The American Destiny   125

Chapter 8   Zionism and the State of Israel   157

Chapter 9   The Holocaust   177

Chapter 10   Jews outside Israel and North America   186

In memory of my parents,
Maier and Selma Trepp ז״ל
foremost of my teachers,
who sealed their faith by their lives.

PREFACE

This introduction to Judaism is intended for both Jews and non-Jews. It wishes to contribute to mutual understanding and love, based on open dialogue. It does not presuppose any previous knowledge of Judaism. It replaces my book which, for close to three decades, has widely served as a text of instruction and reference. During these years Judaism has evolved; history has unfolded and society has changed. Jewish thought and lifestyles have been transformed, the religious life has been transmuted through many schools and in numerous directions, and scholars have given us new insights. Such changes have been considered, while the basic concepts and intentions on which the work has been grounded from the beginning have remained. I hope that readers will find this new version equally useful.

As an introduction, the work is necessarily of limited length and general character and does not attempt to address the nuances of some concepts. The presentation is self-contained; additional material should not be required for its understanding. However, the Bible should be consulted. The bibliography is intended to lead the reader farther into subject matter of particular interest.

It is my hope that this work may convey an understanding of Judaism as a living faith, give a feeling for its scope and sway, and an awareness of its abiding contribution to humanity. I regard Judaism as an organism in evolution and have myself experienced the life-sustaining strength stemming from its traditions. My approach has generally been conservative-traditional, without overlooking scholarly and scientific research. This approach, I hope, may show how Jews throughout the centuries have seen themselves and how they presently see their heritage in light of the insights revealed by scholarly investigations. I regard all denominations in contemporary Judaism as legitimate expressions of the Jewish mind and have taken no position favoring any of them. The presentation and interpretation is my responsibility; Judaism has no official body granting imprimaturs.

Historical knowledge is essential for understanding an evolving historical religion such as Judaism. The book opens with a definition of the Jew and the fabric from which Judaism is woven. Then it sketches the essential developments of Jewish history (Chapters 2 through 6) including the impact of Christianity (Chapter 3). Current interest in mysticism prompted inclusion of a separate chapter (5). The student who is interested in a survey of Jewish history should turn to these chapters and, for a fuller understanding, should also consult the chapters on Tanakh and Oral Torah.

Emphasis has been placed on Zionism and the State of Israel (Chapter 8) and on the Holocaust (Chapter 9). The Holocaust is the greatest tragedy in the history of the Jewish people since the fall of the Second Temple. Zionism and the rebirth of the sovereign State of Israel mark the Jews' reentry into active history. These events have deeply affected Jews, individually and collectively, in self-perception, spirit, and action. Chapter 11 is devoted to the relationship between Christianity and Judaism in contemporary life. The Second Vatican Council transformed Christian hostility toward Judaism and Jews into a spirit of brotherly love and open dialogue. Chapters 12 and 13 briefly analyze the wellsprings of the Jewish spirit, especially Torah, Talmud, and Codes. Chapters 14 and 15 briefly describe the concepts, beliefs, practices, symbols, and theology that have sprung from these sources. Chapters 16 through 21 discuss contemporary expressions of Judaism in worship and life. Chapter 16 deals particularly with the attempts to come to grips theologically with the Holocaust. Chapter 22 reviews the changing place of women in Jewish history and their contemporary struggle for equality. Chapter 23 ventures into offering some prospects. The Glossary explains important terms that appear in the text.

In the endeavor to emphasize the equality of the sexes, the generic use of the word "man" has been changed to the plural "we," as this term encompasses both men and women, and, at the same time, does not impede the flow of the presentation. "We" therefore stands for "men and women"; it does not only include the author or the reader, nor does it intend to direct the reader's behavior in any way. For example: "Structured prayer expresses *man's* feelings better than *he* could in *his* own words" (p. 326), has been changed to "Structured prayer expresses *our* feelings better than *we* could in *our* own words." The attempt to be gender-neutral has not been wholly successful, due to the difficulties of the language, but the intent is there.

Major insights have come to me from my teaching at the University of Mainz and the close contacts with my colleagues and students. I feel most grateful to Dr. Günter Mayer, head of the Institute of Jewish Studies for his friendship and ideas and Dr. Michael Tilly for his assistance. They have also kept me abreast of developments in Protestant–Jewish relations. From the outset, I received valuable continuing information on the ecumenical movement from the Vatican, the Secretariat for Catholic-Jewish Relations in the United States, and Catholic bishops in the United States and Germany. Bishop Karl Lehmann of Mainz, Chairman of the German Catholic Bishops Conference, has shown me great courtesies, offered suggestions, and carried my own critical observations to the Vatican. I express my thanks to The American Jewish Committee for providing me with material.

Permission to quote is gratefully acknowledged. *The Tanakh—A New Translation of The Holy Scriptures* (Philadelphia: Jewish Publication Society, 1962–1982) is generally used for Bible translations, except where I chose my own. Judah Halevi's "Ode to Zion" is quoted in the Nina Salaman translation from *A Book of Jewish Thoughts* (New York: Block Publishing Company, 1943). Reinhold Niebuhr is quoted from his work *Pious and Secular America* (New York: Charles Scribners Sons, 1948, pp. 107ff. and 111ff.).

Appreciation is expressed to the following publishers and authors for permission to quote from copyrighted material: N. N. Glatzer, *The Dynamics of Emancipation* (Boston: Beacon Press, 1965), © 1965 by Nahum N. Glatzer; D. R. Cutler (ed.), *The Religious Situation 1968* (Boston: Beacon Press, 1968), essay by E. Fackenheim; Richard Rubenstein, *Arer Auschwitz. Radical Theology and Contemporary Judaism* (Indianapolis: The Bobbs-Merrill Company, Inc., 1966), © 1966 by Richard L. Rubenstein; Anne Frank, *Diary of a Young Girl* (Garden City, New York: Doubleday & Company, Inc. 1952); Friedrich Wilhelm Marquardt, Erwählung *und Normalität* (Emuna Köln/Frankfurt, Germany: Geschaftsführender Vorstand des deutschen Coordinierungsrats, February 1969); Martin Buber, *Eclipse of God* (New York: Harper & Row, 1952); Paul Tillich, *Dynamics of Faith* (New York: Harper & Row, 1957); Wm. G. McLaughlin & Robert N. Bellah (eds.), *Religion in America* (Boston: Houghton Mifflin Company, 1968), essay by R. Rubenstein and responses, © 1966, 1968 by the American Academy of Arts and Sciences.

Permission to quote from the following copyrighted material is also gratefully acknowledged: Msgr. Antonius C. Remselaar, *Land Israel, Diaspora und die Christen* (München, Germany: Chr. Kaiser Verlag, 1970); J. R. Marcus, *The Jews in the Medieval World* (New York and Philadelphia: Meridian Books, and Jewish Publication Society of America, 1960), © 1938 by Union of American Hebrew Congregations; *Three Jewish Philosophers* (New York and Philadelphia: Meridian Books, and Jewish Publication Society of America, September 1960, first printing August 1960, all rights reserved, reprinted by arrangement with The East & West Library, London); Arthur Hertzberg, *The Zionist Idea* (New York and Philadelphia: Meridian Books, Inc., and Jewish Publication Society of America, 1960), © 1959 by Arthur Hertzberg; *The Oxford Annotated Bible, Revised Standard Version* (New York: Oxford University Press, 1962); Leo Baeck, *The Essence of Judaism* (New York and Berlin: Schocken Books, 1948, fourth printing 1967, German edition 1932); Franz Rosenzweig, *Der Stern der Erlösung* (New York and Berlin, Schocken Books, 1930); Alexander Altmann, *More Newuchim* (New York and Berlin: Schocken Books, Inc., 1935); Benno Jacob, *Das Erste Buch der Torah, Genesis* (New York and Berlin: Schocken Books, Inc., 1934); Martin Buber, *Kdnigtum Gottes* (New York and Berlin: Schocken Books, Inc., 1934); In G. Plaut, *The Rise of Reform Judaism* (New York: World Union for Progressive Judaism, 1963); Hans Küng, *The Church* (London: Search Press, successor to Burns and Oates, © Search Press, 1967); A. Roy Eckardt, *Elder and Younger Brothers* (New York: Schocken Books, 1973; © A. Roy Eckardt); *Informationen Zur Politischen Bildung*, Nrs. 140, 149, Bundeszentrale ftir politische Bildung, Bonn, Germany, Tables on Jewish population development, CCAR Yearbooks for excerpts of the "platforms" with permission by Rabbi Joseph B. Glaser, Executive Vice-President. *American Jewish Yearbook*, The American Jewish Committee and J. P. S. 1972 has been used for population statistics. *Ten Principles for Reform Judaism*, Central Conference of American Rabbis, August 1998.

My special gratitude is expressed to the institutions that permitted me to photograph, or granted me the use of photographs of, sacred objects in their possession. The reproductions were deliberately chosen from items in public institutions within metropolitan areas to encourage readers to continue Jewish studies by visiting these institutions and their outstanding collections. I am grateful to the Skirball Museum of the Hebrew Union College—Jewish Institute of Religion, Los Angeles campus, and Ms. Nancy Berman, former curator, for permission to reproduce the Chair of Elijah. I wish to express my appreciation to the Judah L. Magnes Museum (Jewish Museum of the West) and Mr. Seymour Fromer, former curator, for permission to reproduce the Sukkah Plate, the painting of Mendelssohn and friends, the Mezuzah, Hanukkah Menorahs, Seder plate, Havdalah set, German breastplate, Torah curtain, and Torah ornaments. I am grateful to Kathie Minami, professional photographer, who took most of these pictures. To the government of the State of Israel I express sincere thanks for providing me with pictures of Dead Sea manuscripts and the Shrine of the Book in Jerusalem.

I extend my thanks to Congregation Emanu-El and the late Rabbi Joseph Asher of San Francisco, who permitted me to reproduce their sanctuary, Ark, and Torah scrolls. I wish to thank Phyllis Friedman, the photographer who captured the crowd on the way to the synagogue for festival prayer service. My special gratitude is expressed to Mr. Robert McKenzie, who photographed the sounding of the Shofar. All other pictures are my own.

I gratefully acknowledge the suggestions and comments made by my colleagues who saw all or part of the manuscript: Rabbi Theodore S. Levy, Temple Society of Concord; Franklyn D. Josselyn, formerly of Occidental College; Francis J. Buckley, S.J., University of San Francisco; C. Allyn Russell, Boston University; and Joel Relzburg, LaSalle College.

My most heartfelt thanks go to my publisher, Wadsworth Publishing Company. Peter Adams, Philosophy Editor, and Mindy Newfarmer, Editorial Assistant, have led the new work to fruition. Peter's support, friendship, and encouragement have been invaluable. I am most grateful to him; to my production editor, Jerry Holloway; my designer, Adriane Bosworth; and my copy editor, Patti Law.

Finally, I am most grateful to all who have used the book in its earlier form and found it instructive. I hope the new version will serve them even better.

This work is dedicated to the memory of my parents. My mother perished in a Nazi extermination camp. I was also confined in a concentration camp for some time before I came to America. I feel a deep emotional attachment to the heritage of Judaism. I am proud and grateful to be an American. I have earnestly tried to retain the scholarly detachment that a work of this type demands. If at times my own feelings inadvertently break through, I wish to be forgiven.

Leo Trepp

CHAPTER 1

Introduction:
The Jews and the
Fabric of Judaism

THE SINGULAR CHARACTER of the Jews is revealed in the very problem of definition. At best they may be defined as individuals who consider themselves Jews, having cast their lot with that of the Jewish people. But how shall we define the Jewish people? They are not a race. Innumerable racial components are found among Jews: there are Caucasian Jews, black Jews, and Japanese Jews. From the beginning of Jewish history there has been a constant influx of the most variegated racial groups. Some of the leading Jewish personalities—as far back as the most ancient past and including ancient Israel's greatest king, David—can trace their ancestry back to non-Jews. This mixture of races continues to our own day.

Are the Jews a nation? In Israel they proudly call themselves a nation. In the former USSR they were so regarded and, as a nation with "foreign ideology," were condemned to second-class citizenship. Harassed in their desire to maintain their faith and traditions, they were to be wiped out by attrition. With the dissolution of the USSR they have become officially free to rebuild Jewish life and institutions. The successor "Commonwealth of Republics" remains unstable, however, and anti-Jewish propaganda and actions resting on age-old prejudices and finding expression under the new freedom of speech have reemerged. Uncertainty has motivated large numbers of Jews to avail themselves of the newly granted right to emigrate and find new homes in Israel and Western countries where they can freely affirm their identity.

American Jewry in contrast considers itself primarily a religious group, of ethnic character but certainly not a national group. But religion also fails as a clear-cut definition because it does not take into account the deep sense of responsibility Jews feel for their brothers and sisters all over the world and overlooks their pride in the State of Israel. What then are the Jews?

The Scripture speaks of the Jewish people as a "household," *Bet Yisrael*, the House of Israel. We may well accept this definition. A household creates a

1

specific atmosphere through the love its members hold for one another, the common tradition that molds them, and the experiences they share. This spirit encompasses those who dwell within the family home and those abroad, those born into it as well as those who join it. A family has certain common ways of expressing this spirit in custom and practice; but even those who may not share the forms of expression partake of the spirit, the love, even the conflicts and "family" quarrels, and are tied to each other by a sense of kinship, which is not the same as a political union.

In good times and in hard times throughout their history the Jews have felt upheld by a divine Covenant. In daily morning prayer the Jew affirmed,

> But we are Your people, children of Your Covenant, children of Abraham . . . descendants of Isaac . . . the congregation of Jacob, whom You called Israel. . . . Therefore it is our duty to praise You . . . and to sanctify Your Name. . . . How good our lot . . . how beautiful our heritage . . . twice daily we affirm, 'Hear, O Israel, the Lord is our God, the Lord is One!

The *Covenant* bound its children to their God and to one another. Under God and the Covenant they were brothers and sisters. The Covenant called for a response to God; it was a duty and was expressed in Mitzvot (singular: Mitzvah, the deed in response to God's commanding voice; which includes religious obligations and general good deeds). But duty was no burden, it was grace: Sanctification of God's Name bestowed joy on the performance of every commandment, on life under Mitzvah as a whole. The Jews saw their lot and heritage as beautiful and pleasant, a beauty that transcended all sufferings. The Covenant gave meaning to life and inspired survival in the face of denial of meaning by the outside world. Under it, Torah became their constitution, Mitzvot was a response, Land a laboratory, dispersion a testing ground. The convert who accepted the Covenant became a full-fledged member of the people.

In our time, among average Jews, the Covenant awareness may be vague, even unconscious. Yet it may well be a source of the spirit of mutual responsibility among Jews.

THE TORAH

Torah is the instrument and living record of this Covenant, and the character of the Jewish people has been fashioned by its tradition. "Moses commanded Torah; it is the heritage of the congregation of Jacob" (Deuteronomy 33:4). These words are learned by Jews in early childhood and recited daily. They reveal the meaning of Torah. The word itself means "instruction," for the Torah is more than law; it is the compendium of instruction, the guide for life. In the narrowest sense, Torah applies to the Scroll of the Five Books of Moses found in every synagogue. In a wider sense Torah refers to the teachings contained in the Five Books of Moses and in the remaining books that comprise the Hebrew Scriptures.

From the beginning, explanation accompanied the written word. In the minds of the rabbis such explanation rested on a divine instruction, one not written down but transmitted verbally. This was *Oral Torah*. Some of it was later laid down in the Talmud (see below) by masters who were regarded as being endowed with the "Holy Spirit." Torah continues to evolve right down to the present. It therefore stands for the evolving body of Jewish teachings; it is the heritage.

Torah addresses the needs of every generation of the congregation of Jacob (see Deuteronomy 33:4), and each generation adds to it out of its own experiences. Thus, Torah mirrors the whole Jewish destiny; it has guided it, and with every Jewish child it is being enlarged. "Moses commanded Torah to us" with it—Moses, who the Jews considered the greatest of teachers, but was still a human being. Torah is both divine and human: Out of human experience, in humanity's confrontation with God, Torah evolves. Out of Jewish history, God is made manifest.

At the same time, the actual text of Torah, the Five Books of Moses (Genesis, Exodus, Leviticus, Numbers, and Deuteronomy; also called the Pentateuch in Greek) and the entire *Tanakh* (the Hebrew Scriptures) is of fundamental significance. In their explanation of the Written Torah the masters and rabbis considered every word, and even every letter to be of the greatest importance, forming the link between Written and Oral Torah. In this manner the *Talmud* is linked to Torah. In talmudic discussions we can note minute attention given by the rabbis to every detail in the text of Written Torah to discover its intended meaning. To the modern Jew, knowingly and unknowingly, Written Torah is understood in the light of Oral Torah, which may lead, quite unconsciously, to an interpretation or understanding different from those suggested by a simple reading of the text. We may find that interpretation in this book. Indeed, we have a living Torah. A creative tension has been fashioned between God the Giver and people the respondents, who, in responding, fashion it. Jewish tradition trace the Torah back to the desert, to Mount Sinai, which was no-man's land. Thus it is tied to no specific territory, but is eternal, universal, applying to all lands and conditions. It is the heritage of the "congregation," wherever it may be found. It also has fashioned the congregation.

GOD

The Torah speaks of God. God is one and there is no other. The Jew affirms this daily: "Hear O Israel, The Lord is our God, the Lord is One" (Deuteronomy 6:4). God is the Creator of the Universe, with which He made a Covenant to sustain it. God appointed humanity to be stewards of nature (Genesis 2:15) and made a Covenant with humanity, appointing its members to be His coworkers in nature and in history (Genesis 9:8–17). God is Master of history. Humanity, under the Covenant, stands above nature as its steward but under God as its Lord.

Ultimately, God's essence remains hidden from the human mind. But God becomes manifest in nature in the events of life. That God lives and reigns is made clear to the Jews as they consider above all their survival amidst the events of history. Torah relates that Moses, who wished to see God's "face," was told, "You cannot see My face, for man may not see Me and live . . . . You will see My back [that which God has wrought, God's presence in history], but My face must not be seen" (Exodus 33:20, 23). Then God recites His divine attributes to Moses. He is "compassionate and gracious, slow to anger, rich in steadfast kindness, extending kindness to the thousandth generation, forgiving iniquity, transgression, and sin; *but* clearing the guilty, *He will not do* (Exodus 34:6–7). The rabbis interpreted this passage in such fashion that the words shown in italics here were not included; making God the acquitter even of the guilty. More is revealed in this change than merely an example of an evolving Torah. The rabbis meant to say that God, who is unfathomable, is to be understood and found in imitation. This includes acquitting those who have wronged us. In this manner they wish human relations and history to evolve.

Torah itself speaks of God in anthropomorphic terms. It mentions God's eyes, His outstretched arm, etc. In doing so it "speaks the language of average individuals" (B. Yev.71a; Baba Metzia 31b; etc.) [1] who "can conceive of Being only if it can be thought of as bodily being" (see Maimonides; Guide 1; 26). This personification allowed the Jews to see God as the loving Father in Heaven, their King, their Judge. In His "hands" they placed their body and their spirit (e.g., Psalm 95:4; 2 Samuel 24:14). An awareness of God's personal concern and love could thus be implanted, and a personal relationship between the individual Jew and God established. Love could be asked for and given. A loving God could plead, "You shall love the Lord your God" (Deuteronomy 6:5). God was their shield and buckler, Sustainer and Redeemer. To the average Jew, God's presence was both the source of being and the rationale for survival. Yet, being all of these, God remained infinitely more, beyond human understanding and comprehension.

Being more, He can never be less; hence He can never be portrayed in any form. Form is static; God is dynamic. Form is temporal; God is eternal. Form destroys the divine unity, for form is composed of many parts. The Jewish concept of God thus disagrees with the Christian concept of God assuming human form in the person of Jesus.

Under the impact of the surrounding world—its thoughts and pressures, the philosophy of Aristotle and the theology of Christianity, the Crusades, the expulsion of the Jews from Spain, the Holocaust and the thrust of modern life—Jewish thinkers in various ages endeavored to shed light on the being and essence of God. They offered various interpretations. All of these are human efforts to pierce into the unfathomable otherness of the immutable God and, rather than diminishing Him, throw light upon some of the facets and effects of His being. We shall consider some of them in discussing Jewish theology.

THE LAND

The Land was regarded as the laboratory of the Covenant. In Jewish consciousness, Jewish destiny was inextricably linked to the Land of Israel. To the Jews, their history starts as Abraham is bidden to migrate to the Promised Land, for only there can he fulfill himself as the servant and herald of God. The Land is promised to his descendants (Genesis 13:14–17; 15:18–20), the Israelites. Actually they never left it entirely at any time in history, neither during the centuries that the children of Israel sojourned in Egypt nor after the Romans destroyed the Second Temple. The Land of Israel always remained the Promised Land, where Torah could be translated into the life of the nation.

The ethical pronouncements of the prophets actually had power because they were proclaimed from the independent Land of Israel. Rooted in the soil of their land, among free and sovereign people the prophets issued their call for social justice. They spoke not to their own people alone but to all of humanity in their rebuke, and in the comfort and hope they offered under the divine Covenant. This is significant. Had they pleaded for universal ethical conduct and principles when the Jews were homeless, their voice might not have been sincere, nor would it have been so recognized. It might have been held that, being dependent on others, they were pleading for understanding and compassion. But speaking as citizens of a free people on their own soil, the prophets rebuked the chauvinism to which independent nations (including Israel) can fall prey. By sharing their insights with the entire human community and by including humanity among the beloved of God, they showed true magnanimity and fellowship.

When the Land was taken away it forced the people to find new justifications for their continued existence. People on their own soil need only to live; people removed from it must find a rationale for survival. One rationale for the Jews was that they would return to the Land when it was God's will; hence they must deepen their religious life in order to survive and to be worthy of a return. The evolution of normative Judaism, including synagogue and liturgy, stands under this impact. This hope of freely living on their land and shaping their destiny under God gave impetus to the messianic ideal: ultimate realization of the Covenant. Convinced of the certainty of their return, which was enshrined and expressed in every prayer, they found the strength to endure centuries of humiliation and persecution. Through the Land, unity was forged among the community of the House of Israel spread throughout the world. The polarity of land and *Diaspora* (the Jewish community dispersed throughout the rest of the world) stimulated creative thought in philosophy and poetry, for ever the meaning both of dispersion and of their land had to be made clear.

In the nineteenth and twentieth centuries, religious yearning for the coming of messianic times was translated into concrete and political terms. Only a minority of persecuted Jews were given the opportunity to find shelter in the Land. Still, millions were saved who would have otherwise died. For the rest of Jewry, the Land is the center of Jewish spirit. Some Israelis today want all Jews to return, and the State of Israel has therefore opposed the immigration of Russian Jews to any other country. However, for the Land to hold the entire Jewish population of the world is a physical impossibility. Nor is this desire shared by Jews living in free countries, especially the United States. American Jews feel proudly American, but they also feel a kinship with the reborn State of Israel and look on it with pride. It has become a source of self-affirmation and hope. To many Jews it appeared that, with the restoration of the State of Israel, their God who seemed to have averted His face at Auschwitz had turned it again to the Jewish people.

MITZVAH

Mitzvah is the response to God under the Covenant. It is an action response. *Mitzvah* means "commandment." It presupposes a Commander, namely God, addressing the human being; it implies action. Through Mitzvah the Jew responds to God. At Mount Sinai, at the moment when the Covenant was established, the people promised, "All that the Lord has spoken we will do and hear [understand] it" (Exodus 24:7). Understanding comes in the act, provided it is performed as a service to God and undergirded by the true intent of the heart, *Kavanah*. Empty performance carries little value, as does the affirmation of faith alone. Only faith and action together constitute service, as Kavanah enters every thought, prayer, and act. In living, we become God's coworkers.

There are two kinds of Mitzvot (plural of Mitzvah) in Torah: those of ritual observance (between a person and God), and those between one person and another. Tradition makes no distinction between them. But through Mitzvot relating human beings to each other and establishing social justice, God enters all human relationships. "Love your neighbor as yourself" (Leviticus 19:18) is the basic Mitzvah and was rightly proclaimed by the Sages as the cornerstone of Judaism.

Through Mitzvah, Jews attain self-identification. But they must know the source and intent of the Mitzvah; hence the study of Torah (instrument of the Covenant) in itself becomes a Mitzvah. Here lies the foundation of the Jew's concern with education: Study is Mitzvah, and in all study God is somehow made evident; it is His creation to be contemplated and penetrated.

Of the 613 Mitzvot traditionally seen as handed down to the Jews, 365 are prohibitions and 248 are calls to action. The number of prohibitions supposedly corresponds to the days of the year; every day's activity must be limited and must be confined within God's domain. The number of positive actions was said to correspond to the parts of the human body, every one of which must be ready for duty in promoting His Kingdom.

Many Mitzvot were related to the Land, to sanctify it and the people who dwelt on it. When the Land was taken away, new rules and the conscientious performance of the other Mitzvot were substituted to unify the people. What has resulted is a proliferation of injunctions, a psychological defense against spiritual and physical erosion. In the sixteenth century, Rabbi Joseph Karo, searching for a unifying bond that would forever keep the people together, decided on a Code of Mitzvot, the *Shulhan Arukh*, which became the authoritative work.

THE MESSIAH

Time and circumstances might prevent the people from full performance of Mitzvot, but it has been hoped that the day would come when both Israel, on its own free land, and all humanity might no longer be impeded from freely fulfilling God's bidding in liberty, love, and justice toward each other, redeemed from war and persecution. This was the time of the Messiah.

The Messiah, from the Hebrew *Mashee-ah*, the Anointed, is the redeemer sent by God at the end of days. He will emerge from the dynasty of David. In biblical times kings were anointed with oil. As a young lad, David, on God's behest, was anointed by Samuel (1 Samuel 16:13). He was promised that the kingship of his offspring and his royal throne would be established forever (2 Samuel 7:12–13). The Psalmist repeats the promise in Psalm 89:

> I have made a covenant with My chosen one.
> I have sworn to My servant David:
> I will establish your offspring forever,
> I will firmly build your throne for all generations. (vv. 4–5)
> I have found My servant David,
> with My sacred oil have I anointed him. (v. 21)
> I will establish his offspring forever,
> his throne as long as the heavens last. (v. 30)
> I will not violate My covenant,
> or change what I have uttered.
> This I have sworn by My Holiness once and for all,
> I will not be false to David.
> His offspring shall be forever,
> and his throne like the sun before Me. (vv. 35–38)

In biblical times the people originally took these words as assuring the stability of the ruling dynasty of David. Gradually, however, as pressures from conquering powers grew, messianic fulfillment was placed in the future. Redemption would come at the "end of days" (Isaiah 2:2–5). This concern with the end days is called eschatology. Isaiah describes it as a never-ending time of peace for all humanity, when "they will beat their swords into plowshares" (Isaiah 2:4; also Micah 4:1–6). Then,

> a shoot shall grow out of the stump of Jesse [David's father]. . . . The spirit of God shall rest on him . . . he shall judge the poor with equity. . . . The wolf will dwell with the lamb. . . . In that day the stock of Jesse . . . shall become a standard to peoples—nations shall seek his counsel. . . . He will . . . gather the dispersed of Judah from the four corners of the earth. (Isaiah 11:1–12)

The Messiah of the future is a human being, but is divinely inspired.

Additional concepts came to be woven into the messianic expectation. We find them, for instance, in the Book of Daniel. The messianic time will be preceded by a period of terrifying wars and conflicts, and the dead will be resurrected and put to judgment (Daniel 12). These beliefs gave strength to the Jews in periods of persecution. They saw in them the era of "the birth pangs of the Messiah." The victims of the Holocaust went to the gas chambers with the words of Maimonides on their lips: "I believe with a perfect faith in the coming of the Messiah, and though he tarry, I shall keep believing."

The Zionist movement has one of its roots in messianic hope. "We will not wait for the redemption of Zion through a Messiah, we shall ourselves prepare the way."

Orthodox Jews believe in the coming of a personal Messiah, a man who, on God's behest, will set the world aright and restore Israel to land, liberty, and full performance of Mitzvot. Non-Orthodox Jews, including those who no longer regard themselves as being bound by all the injunctions of the Shulhan Arukh, see in the Messiah the symbol of "messianic times" in the sense that they hope for the day when, in the words of a daily prayer, "God will restore ([le-takken] the world under God's rule," and commit themselves to work for *Tikkun Olam*, the restoration of the world, in justice and universal peace. It will be a time which will also bring freedom from discrimination and persecution to the Jews.

THE COVENANT: INTERACTION OF ELEMENTS

These major forces of Torah, God, Land, and Israel interact, each of them evolving from the other, each of them leading to the other. We cannot separate them. On this basis the Jews understand their relationship with God: They are bound together with God by a Covenant. To be in the world as His fighter or His suffering servant is the mission of the Jews. Moses prophesied about this Covenant:

> Now if you listen and listen again to My voice [in study of Torah], and keep My Covenant [in action], you shall be My treasured possession among all the peoples. Indeed, all the earth is Mine [as the universal God], but you shall be to Me a kingdom of priests [in fulfillment of His commandments testifying to God] and a holy people [in setting an example among all the peoples, that they may follow Him as well]. (Exodus 19:5–6)

Later the prophet Jeremiah speaks of a new covenant God will enter with the Jewish people. It will be unlike the previous one God made with them at the exodus from Egypt. Then, Torah had been imposed upon them. Now,

> I shall place my Torah in their innermost being, inscribe it upon their heart. I shall be their God, and they shall be my people. (Jeremiah 31:31–32)

To the Jew, the Covenant is a call to service, not an election to privilege. The inadequacy of Jewish obedience will be removed in messianic times. In the Covenant, God and the individual are the two axes around which all life revolves. Judaism therefore speaks of two covenants in the past: the Covenant with Noah, which encompasses all of humanity, calls all human beings to service and assures them of God's redeeming love. The additional Covenant with Israel imposes additional obligations on the Jew.

Covenant and the Messiah are interwoven. Judaism sees the proof of the Messiah in the fulfillment of Isaiah's exchatological prophecies. This time has not yet come. Therefore Judaism disagrees with Christianity.

Christianity believes that in Christ (the Anointed, i.e., Messiah) the Messiah has already come, and regards itself as "The New Covenant." It also believes in "The Second Coming" of Christ. Over the centuries Christianity has held that, with Christ, the Covenant with Israel had been fulfilled by God. However, the Vatican Council affirmed that while Christianity stands under "The New Covenant," the Covenant with Israel is not fulfilled by God and never will be. The majority of Protestant churches subsequently adopted the same affirmation. Thus, in different ways, Jews and Christians look to a future when the world will be ultimately redeemed.

Note

1. The references are to the tractates of the Talmud. There are two versions of the Talmud: the Babylonian Talmud and the Jerusalem Talmud. If a quote is taken from the Babylonian Talmud, this is indicated by a "B"; if it is taken from the Jerusalem Talmud, this is indicated by a "J." Our quotes in the text are taken from the Babylonian Talmud (B) Tractate Yevamot, page 71a and Baba Metzia page 31b. See the discussion of the Talmud in Chapter 13.

CHAPTER 2

The Biblical, Hellenistic, and Talmudic Periods

TO MANY THEOLOGIANS, Jewish history reflects the effort of the Jewish people to fulfill the Covenant under ever-changing conditions. During the greater part of their historical existence, the Jews had to demonstrate their trust in the Covenant—their faith—by their will to survive for the sake of the ultimate future, the Messianic Age. Adjusting to physical as well as cultural and religious pressures, they became God's "suffering servants." Jewish history resulted in the evolution of Judaism. The two are inseparable.

To write even an outline of Jewish history would go beyond the framework of this book. In the following pages we will trace the evolution of Jewish history as a guide and framework for those who are not acquainted with it. It may enable them to put people and ideas into their historical setting and to follow the evolving tapestry of Judaism as the Jewish people weave the elements of God–Torah–Land–Mitzvot into ever-new patterns.

BIBLICAL HISTORY

Israelite history, from its beginnings to the time of Ezra (about 444 or possibly 397 B.C.E.[1]), is recorded in Holy Scriptures, the Tanakh. Here we are given a picture of the interaction of political events and spiritual evolution during the formative years of the Jewish people. To the authors of the Tanakh, the spiritual element is of paramount importance, and historical facts are at times adjusted to reflect the spiritual. The Tanakh is one of the "wellsprings of the Jewish spirit" (see Chapter 12). It will be useful therefore to read Chapter 12 on the Tanakh in conjunction with this historical survey. For the sake of simplicity and unity, the historical elements of Israelite history will be summarized on the following pages. As a rapid survey based generally on biblical accounts, it condenses events into a whole that may give them a more unified character than this history actually possessed.

Contemporary archaeology has found that much of the historical record of the Tanakh is accurate; some parts of this record may not be exactly verifiable, but their veracity is probable in view of the accurate picture they give of the general conditions of the period with which they deal. Other parts have been slanted in line with the theological position of the writers and the message they wished to convey. There are portions that may have to be regarded as myths and demythologized in order to interpret their spiritual message for today.

Early History

Patriarchs, Slavery, and Liberation

Toward the first quarter of the second millennium, Abraham migrated from "Ur of the Chaldees" (Genesis 11:31) to Canaan. This event may be called the beginning of Hebrew history. Abraham made a Covenant with the one God, which does not necessarily mean that he rejected the existence of other gods, but for him there was only one God, "the God of Abraham" to whom he gave allegiance and in whom he put his trust. The description of conditions in the period of Abraham and the sharp contours of his personality that Scripture draws, permit us to assume that Abraham was a real person, not merely a hero-figure. In obedience to God, Abraham moved to Canaan and, in turn, was promised the Land as the perennial possession of his descendants. The Jewish claim to the Land is based on this promise.

We read in Torah that Abraham was willing to sacrifice his son Isaac as God commanded (Genesis 22:1–18). When God saw Abraham's faith, He stopped the sacrifice; Abraham's intention was sufficient to witness to his trust in God. Perhaps the event is recorded to point out that human life is inviolable and can never be a means to the fulfillment of a command, even a divine one.

Abraham had a second son, Ishmael, whom he loved but excluded from the succession. The Arabs consider Ishmael their ancestor. In this sense, Arabs and Jews are "cousins." Since Christians consider Abraham their spiritual father (see Romans 4:11 ff.), the three great religions converge in his person.

Isaac's son Jacob, who came to be called "Israel," was the recognized bearer of the family heritage. He had twelve sons. During his time, a severe famine forced most of Jacob's family to migrate to Egypt; the rest remained in Israel. Those in Egypt were soon enslaved as enemy aliens and forced to build garrison cities for Pharaoh, king of Egypt. In spite of oppression, they multiplied into a people. Each of the twelve sons' families developed into a tribe, according to the Scripture.

After many years of servitude, the Hebrews were freed, and, under the leadership of MOSES, they departed from Egypt around 1280 B.C.E. Moses became their teacher, gave them Torah, founded their faith, kept them in the desert for forty years to transform them from a group of slaves into a free people, and led them to the borders of their Promised Land. He died before entering the Land.

The People in Their Land: Judges and Kings

The Land had to be conquered and settled. The people's leader was Joshua. He achieved some victories over the native population, but the settlement was a slow process. Joshua and his successors had the task of building a confederacy of the twelve tribes that constituted the people at the time. These tribes were fiercely individualistic and fusion was difficult. The confederation was to be developed by centering all the tribes spiritually and politically in the Covenant with God at Sinai and in ancient traditions. Physically they were to be bound together by a national sanctuary; each tribe was in charge of the sanctuary for one month a year.

The spirit was to unite the people. However the culture of the Canaanites, among whom the people dwelt, was more developed than that of the Hebrews and was a powerful distraction. The Canaanites followed a heathen cult. As the Hebrews embraced the cult, their unity dissolved, they became politically weak, and they were repeatedly attacked and subjugated by stronger neighbors. In moments of severe distress, they united, selected an outstanding leader, jointly took up arms against their enemies, and overcame them. The leader then remained the people's guide for the rest of his (in Deborah's case, her) life; he became a judge, deepening the spirit of unity among the people. The influence of the judge vanished with his death, and the whole chain of events was repeated with tragic monotony. Some of the judges were great and heroic personalities, most of them were "minor judges." Their work actually held the confederation together (see Judges 10:1–5; 12:7–15).

The people failed to realize that their strength lay in their spirit, and that in recognizing God as their ruler they would find unity and strength. Instead, they chose another expedient: a hereditary monarchy, which they hoped would guarantee perpetual leadership. Around 1020 B.C.E. they chose SAUL as their king. Saul was a striking man and a brilliant military leader. His son Jonathan was equally gifted. The king, at times with the aid of his son, was able to rid the people of their enemies. Soon, however, a young man named David began to gain popularity by his charismatic personality and his military abilities. At first Saul tried to take David under his wing, even giving him his daughter Michal for his wife. But very soon he found that David was rapidly replacing him in popular favor. Even Jonathan became David's close friend. Saul, who had shown signs of moodiness and depression, now began to fear for the future of his dynasty, and henceforth devoted his energies to capturing and destroying his rival, David. In the end he paid a bitter price for this waste of time and resources. He lost his life while battling the Philistines, and carried his people to destruction as well.

The Philistines were a warrior nation who probably originated on Crete. They were great navigators who had settled on the coastal strip of Canaan. Eventually, they gave their name to the land: Palestine. Because they had iron weapons while the Israelites had only bronze, they were able to subdue the people. Furthermore, the Philistines were united in purpose; the Israelites were disunited.

When Saul died around 1000 B.C.E. DAVID became king. He reversed the tide. David was both a general and a poet, a shrewd administrator and a tender-hearted lyricist. He had every human shortcoming, but he also had the greatness to admit error, accept its consequences, and remedy his faults. He became Israel's ideal king; he conquered Jerusalem and made it his capital and led the nation to strength. He enlarged the Land and responded in psalm and in action to the command and rebuke of God. Thus he set the image of the anointed, the Messiah, a man of his seed and his wisdom, who would bring Israel and humanity to the age of abiding peace.

David effected a thorough reorganization of Israel. In order to expand his kingdom, David had to maintain a standing army; in order to weaken tribal allegiances, he reorganized the land in administrative districts that deliberately cut across tribal frontiers; in order to centralize his power, he established his residence in Jerusalem, a city that belonged to none of the tribes, having been taken recently from the Jebusites. There David established a sanctuary and an elaborate pattern of worship; there, too, adjacent to the sanctuary, was the king's palace, the focal point of royal power.

David was unable to complete his projects. When he died his son SOLOMON carried them through. Solomon built the Temple, one of the wonders of the ancient world. He expanded trade and commerce, but to do so he had to conscript forced labor and extract heavy taxes. Married to an Egyptian princess, Solomon was inclined to see himself as an Oriental monarch. He was considered the wisest of men, probably because he surrounded himself with wise counselors. Actually, it seems he lacked the psychological insight needed to unite the people in allegiance to the king over their tribe. Only a satisfied population could be expected to abide with the royal house. But the people were dissatisfied and restless.

The Two Kingdoms

When Solomon died they approached his successor, REHOBOAM, for a redress of grievances and were scornfully rebuked. As a result, ten of the twelve tribes of Israel seceded to form the kingdom of Israel in the north; only the tribe of the royal house, Judah, and the tribe of Benjamin remained with David's family in the kingdom of Judah.

Both kingdoms had a checkered history. In the kingdom of Israel, royal dynasties underwent frequent changes. The kingdom of Judah was ruled by the House of David. In both, the character of the reigning king determined the nature and complexion of internal and external affairs. The kingdom of Judah possessed the national sanctuary at Jerusalem and, in general, a greater awareness of its purpose under God. The northern kingdom was willing to exchange integrity for expediency. This period, beginning in the eighth century B.C.E. and stretching into the fifth century B.C.E., marks the ministry of the great literary prophets. The portions of their works that we still possess belong to the greatest documents of the human spirit. The *prophets* preached, rebuked, and called to task, but they also comforted. Their message constitutes one of the fountain heads of the Jewish spirit.

The kingdom owed its strength under David and Solomon to a lull in the power struggle between the great forces that resided at its borders, the kingdoms of the Tigris and Euphrates valleys to the east and Egypt to the west. Now the struggle for power was resumed between the giants, and the now-divided

Israelite state lay between them, a traffic artery for commerce and for armies. Israel became enmeshed and was defeated.

In 722 B.C.E., the kingdom of Israel was destroyed by the Assyrians and its ten tribes lost. The kingdom of Judah, submitting to Assyrian overlordship, survived. From then on, there remained only the descendants of Judah—the Jews.

Chastened by the fate of their brothers in the north and the ever-present threat of their own destruction, some of Judah's kings were ready for religious reform. King HEZEKIAH (715–687 B.C.E.), miraculously saved from the Assyrian armies that had destroyed the northern kingdom, saw the restoration of full allegiance to God as the way to preservation. Pagan shrines were destroyed and its worship wiped out, and observance of holy days which had fallen into neglect, such as Passover, was restored. But Hezekiah's son and successor MANASSEH, who ruled for fifty-five years, reverted the nation to pagan worship. His son, JOSIAH (c. 640–609 B.C.E.), once again reversed the trend: He purified the Temple of idols, restored its worship, and had the idolatrous priests put to death.

This latter religious revival was prompted by the discovery of a book in the recesses of the Temple. The book, found in 622 B.C.E., contained major parts of the Book of Deuteronomy. The work may have been written at that time, or it may have been written at the time of Hezekiah and hidden during Manasseh's rule; some of its material may have been of even earlier origin. Josiah's reforms, based on the newly discovered book, restored the people's spiritual strength. It was sorely needed, for Judah's end was near, and only observation of the Covenant could hold the people together after the Babylonians destroyed it in 586 B.C.E.

An Evaluative Summary

We must recognize that the Bible's report contains a great deal of legendary material and shows the bias of the writers. To them undivided allegiance to God brings peace and prosperity, divided allegiance inevitably leads to calamity and disaster. Nevertheless the basic trend is unmistakable. The period from the leadership of Moses to the end of the two kingdoms is a time filled with grave inner tensions and struggles between competing forces in Israel. There existed the compelling need and striving for unity and a strengthening of the spirit of kinship. Against it stood tribal allegiances, popular desires, the striving toward acculturation to the surrounding world and strong individualism. Powerful counterforces were in constant tension. This tension can be recognized in subsequent Jewish history. The emphasis through the centuries that Torah alone was the unifying power thus becomes understandable. Within it conflicts needed not be detrimental; the dialogues created by such controversies could be creative and provide evolution of faith and people.

Excursion: Some Ancient Biblical
Personalities in Contemporary Life

Certain Bible personalities have left a strong imprint on the life of the modern society. ABRAHAM is recognized by Jews, Christians and Muslims as their ancestor. ISHMAEL is revered by the Muslims as their ancestor. JACOB had his name changed to ISRAEL (Genesis 32:29), the name of the modern Jewish state. Moses is universally known as liberator, leader and lawgiver of the Hebrews. The first five books of the Torah are called "The Five Books of Moses." Among the Jews Moses is revered as "Mosheh Rabbenu," "Moses our Master," who teaches Torah to all generations.

JOSHUA is remembered for having "fought the battle of Jericho," bringing about the miraculous collapse of the walls of the city without attack, only with the help of God (Joshua 7:1–20). Actually, by the time of Joshua's conquest, the city had long been destroyed. GIDEON is remembered as God's valiant warrior, who fought the vast army of his enemy with a deliberately small force to make it evident that the victory belonged to God alone (Judges 7). (There is a Christian organization called The Gideons that distributes Bibles.) SAMSON is known as the giant hero of incredible exploits of strength who could not curb his sex drive and, in the end, is defeated by Delilah, whom he loved imprudently (Judges 13–16). His love affair with the temptress Delilah and his subsequent defeat were even made into an opera, "Samson and Delilah" by Charles Saint-Saens.

DAVID is universally remembered as the ancestor of the Messiah. SOLOMON, referred to in the Bible as the wisest man on Earth, gave proof of his wisdom in the judgment he rendered in a conflict between two women. Both had given birth to a child but one of the newborns died. Both women claimed to be the mother of the living child. Solomon ordered both children to be cut in half and each mother receive a half and then watched what happened. Prompted by mother love, the real mother surrendered her son to her contestant rather than lose her child (1 Kings 3:16–28). Today we sometimes speak of "Solomonic wisdom" or "a Solomonic judgment."

SARAH, an outstanding beauty (Genesis 12:11, 14), also established the dominion of the woman in the home, which Jewish women have subsequently held. MIRIAM, Moses sister, saved his life. As a baby, he was set adrift in the river Nile because Pharaoh had commanded that all Hebrew boys be put to death. His mother had placed him in a little basket which floated on the water. Miriam kept watch over him until a royal princess of Egypt found and adopted him. Miriam was also a prophetess (Exodus 15:20). The name Maria is the latinized form of Miriam.

DEBORAH was so outstanding a personality that the Israelites did not hesitate to choose her, a woman, to be their judge, general, and head of state. The people came to her with their litigations and she rendered the decisions. She could see that the time was ripe for a counterattack against the Canaanites and developed the strategy that led to victory. Her victory hymn of thanks to God reviews in poetic form the events of the battle. Under Deborah's leadership "the land was tranquil for forty years" (Judges 4:1–5:31). Her accomplishments were so significant that even the male chroniclers of the biblical events could not pass her over in their report.

Babylonian Exile

During the years 598–586 B.C.E., the Babylonians, having supplanted the Assyrians as the great power of the East, conquered Judah and destroyed the

Temple. The ruling elite was taken into exile in Babylonia. One part of the community fled to Egypt, the rest of the Jewish people remained in the Land. Having lost physical possession of the Land, they refined their faith during the crucible of exile.

Apart from feeling themselves exiles, the Jews found their lives pleasant. They were given their own jurisdiction in internal affairs, and some of their members rose to high positions at the royal court. Babylonia became a spiritual workshop. The Land and its redemption were transformed into hope and aspiration. Torah was at the center of life, and worship took the place of Temple sacrifices; Mitzvot were both a response to God and the link which bound the House of Israel together. Seeds for the eventual unfolding of Synagogue and liturgy may have been planted.

In spite of the Jews' adaptation to life in Babylonia, expulsion from their homeland to exile was a profoundly traumatic experience. Psalm 137 reflects their shock and a rather unworthy feeling of vengefulness born out of hopelessness and impotence.

> By the rivers of Babylon, there we sat, sat and wept, as we thought of Zion. . . .
> If I forget you, O Jerusalem, let my right hand wither; let my tongue stick to my palate if I cease to think of you, if I do not keep Jerusalem in memory even at my happiest hours. . . . Fair Babylon, you predator, a blessing on him who repays you in kind what you have inflicted on us, a blessing on his who seizes your babies and dashes them against the rocks. (Psalm 137)

As they emerged from the numbness of despair, two questions came to their minds: Why did it happen, and how long 's it going to last? The immediate answer was: It happened because we have sinned by breaking the Covenant. Was it going to be a short sojourn? The prophet Jeremiah made it clear to them that their sojourn among the nations might well be of long duration. He advised them to settle down.

> Thus said the Lord of Hosts, the God of Israel, to the whole community which I exiled from Jerusalem to Babylon: Build houses and live in them, plant gardens and eat their fruit. Take wives and beget sons and daughters; and take wives for your sons and give your daughters to husbands, that they may bear sons and daughters. Multiply there and do not decrease. And seek the Shalom [welfare] of the city to which I have exiled you and pray to the Lord in its behalf; for in its Shalom you will find Shalom. (Jeremiah 29:4–7)

Dwelling among the nations, they must do more than simply come to terms with their fate, rather "seek the welfare of the city . . . and pray to the Lord for it," for in its prosperity they would prosper. Good citizenship thus became a religious duty. Jews were to look at the country of their homes and birth as a permanent dwelling place. The distrust of others, preached up till now to the unique people dwelling within a heathen world, was to be replaced by heartfelt concern for the welfare of the nation and its citizens, its inner and outward peace, expressed in prayer and in active participation. From this time on, we shall find

Jews filled with earnest desire to promote the welfare of the countries of their dispersion.

Under these circumstances, the first question had to be taken up again: Was life in dispersion to be regarded as punishment for sin, or perhaps as a task? A long exile as a result of sin would actually punish the children for the faults of their fathers. The prophets Jeremiah and Ezekiel both addressed the problem:

> 'Fathers have eaten sour grapes and the children's teeth are blunted.' This proverb shall no longer be current in Israel. . . . If a man be just, he shall surely live. . . . If he begets a son that is a robber . . . he shall not live, having done all these abominations. . . . If he begets a son that sees all his father's sins . . . but has taken heed and has not imitated them . . . he shall not die for the iniquity of his father; he shall surely live. (Ezekiel 18:2–17; compare Jeremiah 31:29–30)

The impact and implication of these statements are fundamental and far-reaching. The Babylonian Jewish community and all of their descendants were told that their sufferings were not caused by the sins of their ancestors. They were advised that they dwelt among people of other religious convictions because God had willed that they be torchbearers of monotheism among the pagans and creatively participate in the upbuilding of a good society. They were responsible, however, for their own conduct. Living uprightly, their persecution could then be seen, not as the result of their sins, but as a divine test. The Jews, as a minority, would be tested to show the strength of their faith and challenged to show the spirit of godliness. If the majority of a nation failed to deal graciously with the Jewish or any minority, then this failure pointed to its own shortcoming in thwarting the divine will. The suffering of the Jews would thus illuminate the world's failure to acquit itself before God.

The search for the meaning of their exile led to general discussion of suffering and sin in post-Exilic Jewish literature. Isaiah in his parable of the Suffering Servant (chapter 53) demonstrates that the steadfast faith of the sufferer sets an example from which future generations may learn and profit. The legend of Job (an inhabitant of a non-Jewish environment) dwells in great detail on the suffering the just will bear. People must accept suffering as a test of faith, and, in accepting, they will find insight and strength. God Himself justifies Job.

According to a rabbinic view (B.Makkot 24a), Ezekiel's statement boldly overrides a principle enshrined in the Ten Commandments; namely, that God visits the iniquities of the fathers upon the children (Exodus 20:5). This reveals the deeper insight the Jews acquired in the course of the generations: There is no inherited guilt, there is only personal responsibility for every individual and for those he or she may influence. This remains the Jews' conviction.

Having understood the permanence of their position among other peoples, the Jews had to put their religious life on new foundations. The Land could now serve as spiritual inspiration. The Temple was no more; no sacrifices could henceforth be offered; the priestly caste (the family of Aaron) had lost its function. The adjustment, begun in Babylonia, continued and found its fruition in the centuries after the return of part of the people to their homeland. It was so ingenious that other religions have followed it.

Developments in Early History (1250–550 B.C.E.)

Hebrew Independence in Canaan

1250 1200 1150 1100 1050 1000 950 900

Philistines settle in Canaan

IRON AGE I 1200–900

Song of Deborah 1125

Gideon Jephthah Samson

Period of Judges 1150–1020

Fall of Shiloh

Samuel

Saul

Saul 1020–

1002

Hebrew Monarchy

David 1002–962

Solomon 962–922

IRON AGE I 1200–900

The Kingdoms of Israel and Judah

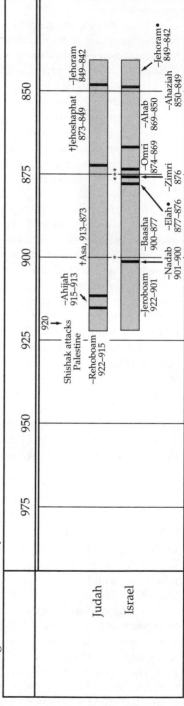

975 950 925 900 875 850

Judah

Israel

Rehoboam 922–915

Shishak attacks Palestine — 920

Abijah 915–913

†Asa, 913–873

†Jehoshaphat 873–849

Jehoram 849–842

Jeroboam 922–901

Nadab 901–900

Baasha 900–877

Elah 877–876

Zimri 876

Omri 874–869

Ahab 869–850

Ahaziah 850–849

Jehoram 849–842

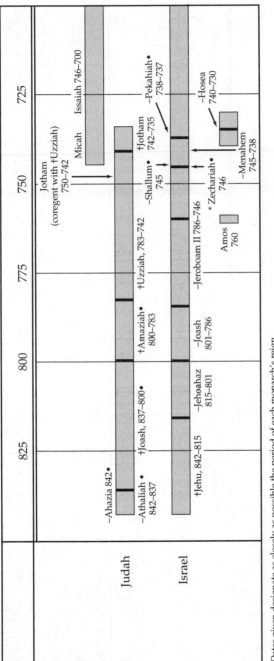

Dates given designate as closely as possible the period of each monarch's reign.

● Time of flowering
* Old dynasty overthrown, new dynasty established
† Kings approved of by author of *Kings*
– Kings disapproved of by author of *Kings*
• Assassinated

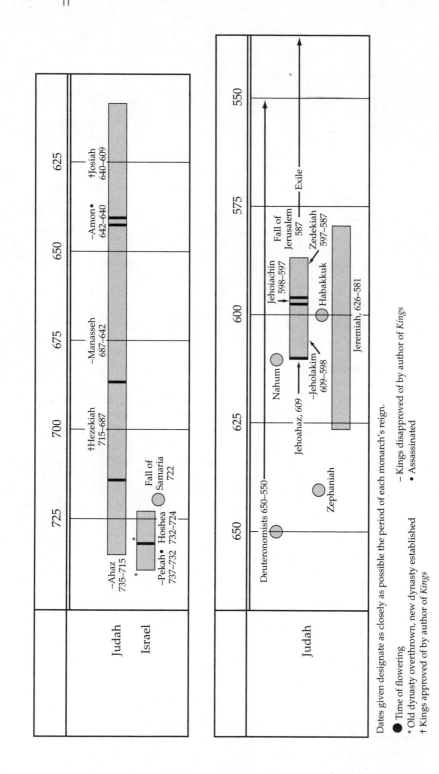

Dates given designate as closely as possible the period of each monarch's reign.

● Time of flowering   – Kings disapproved of by author of *Kings*
* Old dynasty overthrown, new dynasty established   • Assassinated
+ Kings approved of by author of *Kings*

Source: Adapted from *The Old Testament* by H. Keith Beebe. Copyright © 1970 by Dickenson Publishing Company, Inc. Reprinted by permission of Wadsworth Publishing Company, Belmont, California 94002.

We may perhaps recognize some of the religious practices of Babylonian Jewry in the gatherings Ezra convened upon his return to the homeland (Nehemiah 8, 9).Torah and Mitzvot were strengthened to compensate for the physical loss of the Land, and on the return to assure its possession. The word of Torah was to be read to the people and explained, interpreted, and studied. Thus the foundations were laid for the house of meeting, which also became the house of prayer. The national sanctuary at Jerusalem (like all the temples of antiquity) had been not so much a place of popular assembly as a dwelling place of God; the people had been primarily spectators at a set ritual. Now the meeting house evolved and the people were participants (which continued after the building of the second Temple). In later periods permanent synagogues were built. Here lay the seeds of the form of the House of God in Western religions. Torah would now be the center of worship and life. The recital of Torah was surrounded by prayer and psalm and made meaningful by explanation. A pattern of worship emerged to be fully developed over many centuries. It again was followed by many Western religions: Scripture reading, sermon, prayer, and hymn.

Return from Exile: Home-Born and Convert

In 538 B.C.E., Cyrus, conqueror of Babylonia, permitted the Jews to return to their homeland. He was sure that in gratitude for this favor they would become a stable element in this outpost of his realm. He permitted the building of a new Temple at Jerusalem, which was completed under Darius, one of his later successors (515 B.C.E.).

About ninety years after the return of the Jews, Nehemiah and Ezra, two leading members of the strong Jewish community remaining in Babylonia and high officials at the royal court, came to Jerusalem. Ezra assembled the people and read the Torah to them from a high pulpit (Nehemiah 8:4). From this "tower" the central elevated desk for the reading of the Torah in traditional synagogues may be derived. It is called *bimah* (or *almemor*). Ezra renewed the Covenant and accepted the commitment of the people to repent their ways (444 B.C.E.). Insisting on the strictest family purity, Ezra and Nehemiah even compelled the settlers to divorce their wives of non-Jewish birth. Their rationale was that Jewish kinship had to be deepened and all alien influences had to be eliminated in order to assure the people's unconditional commitment and obedience to God and Torah, the only safeguards of Jewish survival. They believed that only families who were uncompromisingly obedient to Torah and Mitzvot and brought up in them for generations could safeguard the Jewish future. The Samaritans, a people of Jewish and non-Jewish ancestry with a syncretistic religious practices, were rejected.

From Ezra's council "The Great Assembly" may have developed, to which some of the last prophets were said to have belonged. Mentioned in the Talmud we have no other historical information about its creation.

Historical Consequences of Ezra's Ruling

Due to the impact of external forces, the Jews' attitude toward converts underwent changes. During their early settlement, Jews had been hospitable to converts. They were willing to receive the stranger who desired to join them. Isaiah extended a divinely inspired welcome to "the foreigners who attach themselves to the Lord" (Isaiah 65:6–8). The Book of Ruth is a charming testimony to this hospitality. Ruth, a Jewish convert, was lovingly accepted and became the ancestress of King David. However, in the face of possible religious erosion, Ezra now put up a barrier.

Since those days the Jewish attitude toward conversion has remained ambivalent. At times (e.g., during the period of the Roman principate), conversion activity was widespread. At the height of Jewish conversions, which includes the period of the emergence of Christianity, a very broad outlook prevailed. "God fearers" who were not prepared to accept all of the Jewish laws—above all, circumcision—would be accepted as "associate members." The God fearer became a *ger toshav*, a resident alien, entitled to enjoy the full measure of the sustaining brotherhood of the Jewish people, though restricted in religious privileges. If he or she so desired, a non-Jew could, of course, convert fully to Judaism and, as *ger tzedek*, become a Jew in the full sense of the word, enjoying all the rights and privileges as well as bearing all the obligations. The feeling was: If people were looking for spiritual guidance and Judaism can give it, then it must be offered. Later, efforts at conversion became minimal, partly as a result of the Christian prohibition against it. At present, a more liberal outlook exists, at least among non-orthodox Jews.

RESTORATION AND THE BEGINNING OF POST-BIBLICAL HISTORY

Restoration

Ezra may be credited with editing substantial amounts of the Pentateuch (the Greek term for the Five Books of Moses). He reorganized the people's life by the norms of Torah. The second Temple became once again the center of the nation's religious life. The priestly cult and, with it, priestly power were restored.

The arrival of Alexander the Great of Macedonia on the stage of history opened the flood gates to the influence of Greek culture (Hellenism). Conquering the known world (336–323 B.C.E.), Alexander entered Jerusalem and was so gracious to the Jews that many named their sons after him. Upon Alexander's early death, Judah fell under the rule of the Ptolemies of Egypt (the first Ptolemy was one of the generals who had divided up Alexander's empire). So strong was the influence of Hellenism that many pious Jews in Egypt never learned Hebrew. Consequently, Torah was translated into Greek to remain the guide for those Jews. This early translation is known to us as the *Septuagint,* from the Latin word for "seventy," because it is supposedly the work of seventy scholars.

Fighting for Freedom and the Temptation of Power

Soon, however, Judah became attached to the kingdom of Syria, the House of the Seleucids. One of their kings, Antiochus IV, Epiphanes, desirous of unifying his empire by means of Greek worship and thought, but also appeased by Jewish Hellenists, endeavored to suppress Jewish religion. In 167 B.C.E., this brought on a rebellion, led by Judah Maccabee (Judas Maccabaeus, the Hammerer) of the House of *Hasmon*, not for independence but for freedom of religion. It resulted in complete independence. The victory is celebrated in the festival of Hanukkah (see p. 362).

The Hasmoneans traced their descent to Aaron the high priest; they were, therefore, members of the priestly caste, the only group entitled to conduct the service in the Temple and to provide the high priest. The Hasmoneans now assumed the power of the royal purple as kings, adding to it the office of high priest. Their power was truly absolute and soon became corrupt. Possessed by political and dynastic ambitions, the rulers had forgotten that they were the guardians of the Covenant.

New Spiritual Leaders: The Rabbis

Societal conflicts arose that gradually, but with ever-growing momentum, gave the spiritual leadership to the *Pharisees*, a group that emerged from an unknown origin. They were ambitious to become the people's leaders in competition with the priesthood. For a while, they employed political means to reach their goal, which brought them into conflict with the rulers. Eventually they changed their outlook and their method. True power, they realized, rested on ethical leadership, based on the teachings of Torah, as they interpreted it. They were highly successful in attaining this leadership.

Torah and Mitzvot in daily life and worship became central. Their explication was undertaken by the *rabbis*, the teachers, not the priests. A rabbi could be a priest or a layman, rich or poor, of noble ancestry or a recent convert, but he had to be upright in character, searching for knowledge, and dedicated to his task. His work could be carried out anywhere and at any time; all he needed was a group of students and a shelter against the elements. During the next centuries these rabbis were devoted to consolidating and expanding the knowledge and spirit of Torah. They saved Judaism, for when the Temple was again destroyed, this time by the Romans, the center of Jewish life could be immediately shifted to the house of study.

Roman Domination

Herod the Great

Locked in bitter struggle for the kingship, two brothers of the House of Hasmon, Hyrcanus and Aristobulus, called on Rome to be the arbiter of their claims. In 63 B.C.E. Pompey gave the power to the weaker of the two brothers,

Hyrcanus, and assigned him an advisor—actually a supervisor—who would see to it that Rome retained the power that had fallen into its lap. The advisor was Antipater, an Idumaean, son of a people who had been forcibly annexed and converted to Judaism by the Hasmoneans. Antipater's son, for whom the father prepared the way to the throne, was HEROD THE GREAT (37–4 B.C.E.). He nearly wiped out the Hasmonean family, although he had married into the house, dealt harshly with the people, and tried everything to please the Roman overlord. He left his mark by his numerous buildings. Ever suspicious of plots against his life, he built for himself the fortified palaces of Masadah and the Herodion in remote parts of the land. They offered him comfort and defense. He also renovated and expanded the Temple in such splendor that it became known for its majestic beauty.

After Herod's death the Romans no longer ruled in an indirect manner, namely as "advisors" to the Jewish rulers; they assumed power openly, governing as overlord through administrative agents called *procurators*. Many of these men were cruel and venal, having been sent to the province with the understanding that they might enrich themselves. In Judaea, one of their methods was to taunt the people by exhibiting the Roman eagle, a graven image abhorrent to the Jews. Arousing the spirit of rebellion, they would then cruelly suppress it, condemning hundreds to death by crucifixion and confiscating their belongings for their own pockets. Unrest grew, and the cry for freedom from intolerable oppression increased. The whole population was seething with rebellion.

PONTIUS PILATE stood out as one of the worst procurators. It is not surprising, therefore, that he saw Jesus' activities and messianic pronouncements as acts of rebellion and had him crucified as "King of the Jews" to show what would happen to anyone who wanted independence and to be a king. Crucifixion, the brutal Roman way of execution, was the lot of many Jews who despised Pontius Pilate and resisted him, preferring to die rather than give up their tradition.

Apocalyptism

During these tempestuous times *apocalyptism* gained increasing acceptance among the people. Apocalyptism has left us a vast literature. We find apocalyptic messages in the final chapters of the Book of Daniel. The apocalyptic preachers ascribed their message predicting the future to have been received from God by earlier biblical personalities, such as Enoch, Barukh, Ezra, and others. There is a difference, however, between a prophet and an apocalyptic. The prophet related God's message to the course of human history, the apocalyptic to cosmic events. The prophet proclaimed that disaster would come as a consequence of the people's sinfulness, but added that this disaster could be avoided if the people changed their way and returned to God. For the apocalyptic, the course of history was set; the *eschaton*, or end, was at hand and nothing could change it. A cosmic cataclysm would come and soon: Sinners would be wiped out, but the righteous would be saved, provided they separated themselves from the corrupt world and corrupt neighbors. The events of the time were seen as clear indications that the end was near, as corruption had become all encompassing. The fight against the forces of evil was a sacred duty. Roman domination and oppression was perceived in this light, and repentance was mandatory in view of the approaching end. This is the spirit in which JOHN THE BAPTIST called for repentance. His followers immersed themselves as a symbolic act of purification from their sins.

New Orientations

Eventually Pilate was too much even for Rome, and he was recalled. In 64 C.E., Florus, the last procurator, took office. He provoked the Jews to such a degree that they finally rose in armed rebellion. Florus could not quash it, and the Roman legions had to be called in under the command of the general Vespasian (later Roman emperor, 69–79 C.E.). After years of war, Titus, Vespasian's son, finally conquered Jerusalem (70 C.E.), destroyed it and burned the Temple.

The destruction of Jerusalem and the Temple were cataclysmic events in Jewish history. The loss of Jewish life has been estimated at one million, surpassed only by the Holocaust in the twentieth century. Judaism had to reorient itself.

By the time of the Temple's fall, new foundations for the survival of the Jewish people had already been established. The all-encompassing study of Torah would perpetuate the Jewish people in the spirit of the Covenant. HILLEL, a great rabbi, had founded an academy and raised outstanding disciples who could assume leadership. One of them, Yohanan ben Zaccai, had obtained Roman permission to establish a religious center in the little city of Javneh (Jamnia), in order that Torah could immediately take over as the central force, should the Temple fall. Torah was now the repository of the all-embracing Covenant and the guarantor of life. The reconstruction of Judaism along new forms began. Yohanan, however, was not regarded as equal to Moses, which meant that he could interpret and evolve the Torah of Moses but could not abrogate it.

Resistance and Martyrdom

The spirit of armed resistance had not been destroyed either. It led to several rebellions in an effort to reconquer the land and restore full Jewish sovereignty. A group of resisters barricaded themselves on the fortress of Masadah, holding the Roman legions at bay for years, but in the end they committed suicide rather than permit themselves to be captured.

The rebellion of Simon bar Koseba (reverently called Bar Kokhba, Son of the Stars, by his followers, and mockingly so by the Romans after his fall) in 132–135 C.E. was the last one. It failed, broken by the Roman Emperor Hadrian. Hadrian realized that the Jews could not be overcome as long as they had Torah and Mitzvot, and he therefore prohibited both. Jews became martyrs of faith. The province up to then still called Judea was renamed Palestine to deny the Jews the right of name and ownership. After Hadrian's death (138 C.E.), Jewish religion was again permitted. Palestine remained the vibrant center of Jewish life and the focal point of Jewry throughout the world. Jewish unity and cohesion were maintained by having a central religious and spiritual head, called the Patriarch.

He resided in Palestine and served as central authority for the Jewish Diaspora, which was widely spread into Babylonia, Egypt, and Roman provinces as far away as Germany.

Emerging Christianity

A more detailed discussion of Christianity will be found in Chapter 3. Only a brief historical presentation shall be given here. Early Christianity had emerged during the last decades of the Jewish Commonwealth out of the conviction of its adherents that the end of days was near. They linked themselves to Jesus of Nazareth. During the first generation its members remained within the Jewish faith and observed its commandments while at the same time accepting Jesus as the Christ, which means Messiah.

There exists no generally convincing historical evidence supporting a claim of the early Christians that theirs was a new dispensation that supplanted Judaism.

Through enthusiastic missionaries, especially Paul, Christianity spread throughout the Gentile world. The core of Paul's teaching was that Jesus, through his death at the cross, had atoned for all of humanity's sins. Salvation came through belief in Jesus the Christ; the observance of the Jewish commandments, he declared, was of no value as a way to salvation. Election (the choice by God of individuals for status and salvation) was by God's grace. It was therefore no longer necessary to convert to Judaism and join the Jewish nation, as all men were equal before God. With this theology Paul took the decisive step in separating Christianity from Judaism. The abolition of Mitzvot and of Jewish identity in favor of belief in Christ would have spelled the end of the Jewish people. Rabbis took countermeasures, calling above all for a complete separation from the followers of Christianity, especially Christians of Jewish origin who had stepped up their missionary activities among the Jews after the fall of the Temple. Christians interpreted the fall of the Temple as God's punishment for the Jews not having accepted Christ as Messiah; God had rejected the Jews. The Gospels, written after the destruction of the Temple, have Jesus predicting its destruction (Matthew 24:2; Mark 13:2; Luke 21:6).

Under the rule of Emperor CONSTANTINE (308–337), Christianity, now essentially the religion of the Gentiles, became the state religion of the Roman Empire (the Council of Nicaea in 325 was already a high point). Jews were now subjected to ever greater disabilities under Christian Rome; they were condemned as an accursed race. In 425 the Jewish office of Patriarch was abolished, and the Christian bishop of Jerusalem took the title of Patriarch. By that time, a center of Jewish life had been established in Babylonia, a non-Christian country, but Jewish life in Palestine remained active; only the crusades and the cruelty of the Crusaders put an end to Jewish creativity in Palestine, to be revived only after many centuries.

The Impact of Greek Thought

The Maccabees had fought against the intrusion of Hellenism into Judaism. In subsequent generations and history it became clear that Jews could not isolate themselves from the thought of the cultures that surrounded them and in which they lived. To what degree non-Jewish culture could and should be accepted or kept out became a matter of debate and has remained so. Large groups rejected it on principle, others felt that only a synthesis of tradition and non-Jewish thinking could assure Jewish survival, and that exposure to some achievements of the world might actually benefit Judaism. This meant sifting between non-Jewish ideas and practices that were considered valuable, even embodying some of them into the faith itself, and rejecting those that were regarded as detrimental. Over this issue minds remained divided.

Greek thought had a particularly strong and lasting influence. The prophets had not been systematic thinkers. They were moved by the spirit of God and spoke with emotional fervor. Under Greek influence, systematic thinking was introduced, to become a permanent feature of Jewish study. Plato, Aristotle, and the Stoics were taken seriously. The *Sanhedrin*, the ancient Jewish supreme court, is reminiscent of Greek legislative bodies in its function as innovator in law.

A good example of Greek influence is the attitude of Judaism to universal study of Torah. Plato had called for a universal system of public education. Aristotle had shown that the pursuit of knowledge spells true and greatest happiness, but admitted that this happiness would be denied to those who lacked the material means to afford the leisure of study. Combining these two elements with the injunction of Torah to teach diligently (Deuteronomy 6:7) and applying them to the study of Torah, the rabbis concluded that education must be universal and that people must do with the absolutely barest minimum of existence, if need be even self-deprivation, in order to find the happiness of study.

> Eat bread with salt, drink water in small measure, sleep on the ground, accept a life of deprivations, but toil in Torah. If you will do thus, hail unto you, good will be yours, hail unto you in this world, good will be yours in the world to come. (Mishnah Abot 6:4)

The Talmud tries to follow Aristotelian patterns of logic wherever possible. However, the Jews turned down the philosophy of Epicurus, who denied the existence of God or, at least, God's concern, and the future of the soul after death; the worst epithet that can be hurled against a Jew who has fallen away completely is Epicurean. Thus under the impact of worldly wisdom, Jewish philosophy emerged.

The Jewish philosopher PHILO, who lived in Egypt during the first pre-Christian century, offers an example of an attempted assimilation of Jewish tradition to Greek thought. Philo spoke and wrote Greek and conducted his own life in the spirit of the Stoics yet remained a deeply religious and observant Jew. Influenced by the Greek thinkers of his time, who interpreted Homer allegorically and as a guide to ethics, Philo undertook the same task in interpreting Torah. To Philo the events related in Torah point to deeper meanings of ethical significance; the Mitzvot are visible means by which God tries to make manifest eternal truths of reason. In studying Torah and performing the Mitzvot, Jews rehearse and reveal eternal and universal truths (see also below "Jewish Philosophy").

The Sects

The period from Ezra to about the end of the second century C.E. was one of great activity. Under the influence of Hellenism there emerged a number of sects, which remained in existence up to the destruction of the Temple. Each was concerned with the survival of Torah and people.

The *Sadducees* were religious conservatives who belonged to the aristocracy. The movement was led by the high priest and his family, descendants of Zadok who had once anointed Solomon as king of Israel (1 Kings 1:39), hence the name Zadokites, or Sadducees. As aristocrats, they had come in contact with Greek learning. The majority held that Torah could be preserved if it was understood literally and enforced with severity. The Written Torah had been codified; it was to be the *only* guide to life. No deviations from the written word, no new interpretations were to be permitted. Since Torah did not mention the immortality of the soul, they rejected it as alien thought. The Sadducees were severe judges.

A statement in the "Sayings of the Fathers," one of the tractates of the Mishnah, relating the ethical maxims of the Sages (see Chapter 13), may reflect Sadducean teachings at their noblest:

> Antigonus of Sokho . . . used to say: 'Be not like servants who serve the Master in order to receive a reward [in the hereafter], but be like servants who serve the Master without expecting a reward, and may the fear of Heaven [God] be upon you.' (Avot 1, 3)

The rabbi's name, Antigonus, was Greek and thus shows the influence of Hellenistic culture; he must have come from an acculturated family. He stressed that no reward was to be expected in a future world, as this was not found in Written Torah. He emphasized that the fear of God must be the guideline, keeping his disciples on the straight and narrow road of Torah observance. A few of the Sadducees came to feel, however, that they might as well enjoy their luxury, as there would be no reward for self-denial in any hereafter (Avot de Rabbi Nathan, chapter 5). They became hedonist and assimilationist.

Seeing the Temple as the safeguard of Jewish survival, the Sadducees were deeply concerned with Temple ritual, which had to follow the letter of the Written Torah. Caiaphas, the high priest appointed by Pilate, was a Sadducee, which may explain his rationale for his actions: If the activities of one man, Jesus, created suspicion in the Roman mind and endangered the future of the Temple, and thus the people, let him be sacrificed for the sake of the whole.

The *Essenes* believed that the apocalyptic end of the world was near and so cast off all worldly possessions. Some traveled about, calling the people to repentance; John the Baptist may have been an Essene. Others formed monasteries and lived a completely secluded group life dedicated only to God because they wished to have no contact with the world and its compromises. Then they would be the remnant to be saved on the final day of reckoning, the battle between "the sons of light and the sons of darkness."

In 1946 a number of scrolls were discovered in caves surrounding the Dead Sea, where they had been placed in clay jars and hidden from the Romans.

Among them are the oldest manuscripts of biblical books we possess. We also find psalms, which are like hymns. Others, like the Manual of Discipline, give new facts about the life among Jews in Judea in the period between the Old and the New Testament. They have shown an even closer relationship than had been known before between Jewish ways of life and thought and the early Christian Church. These scrolls, many of them now in a special shrine in the National Museum of Israel in Jerusalem, are called the *Dead Sea Scrolls.*

Based on these documents it was believed that the scrolls had been written by a group assumed to be an offshoot of the Essenes, a monastic group that had established itself at Qum-ran, on the shore of the Dead Sea. They followed a strict discipline; including the practice of frequent ritual purification, by immersing their bodies in water, prayed, read Scripture, and assembled for a ritual meal, breaking bread, sharing wine.

Most of the material was jealously guarded by the scholars entrusted with its restoration, and for over forty years no other scholars were permitted access to them. In result of worldwide protest, photocopies were finally published. With the rest of the documents now available to worldwide scholarship, new results may be expected, leading to new insights and possibly new conclusions about the character of the community in which they originated.

The *Zealots*, who were deeply religious, were prepared to do battle for the Lord against the heathen conqueror. Because Rome was the enemy of the "end of days," the only good Roman was a dead Roman. After Jerusalem fell in 70 C.E. some of the Zealots barricaded themselves in Masadah, a fortress built by Herod the Great for his security and pleasure. Masadah is located near the Dead Sea on

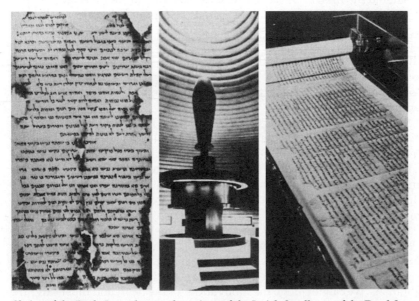

Shrine of the Book, Jerusalem, and portions of the Isaiah Scroll, one of the Dead Sea Scrolls. (Courtesy, Government of Israel.)

a steep rock jutting out 900 feet over the plain. In 66 C.E. a group of Zealots had taken the fortress from the Roman garrison that held it. Fueled by national and religious pride, they held it for almost three years after the fall of Jerusalem. The Roman army had to build special camps and assault ramps to retake Masadah in 72 C.E. But they could not take any captives. When resistance became impossible, the 967 men, women, and children holding Masadah took their own lives rather than fall into the hands of their enemy.

The fortress was excavated between 1963 and 1965 by the Israeli government and Hebrew University. It is now a place of pilgrimage for Israeli youth, and on its plateau officers of the armed services are sworn in and receive their commissions. Thus is the past linked to the present.

The memorials these sects have left us have acquired new importance and significance in our time and have given us new insights in the life of the Jews during the period between the two Testaments.

In contrast to these sects that disappeared with the fall of the Temple, the *Pharisees* by their example and teaching have had an enduring presence to this day. Historically, the Pharisees have been the most influential of the sects, and have had a basic and lasting impact on the evolution of Judaism. When the Temple fell, all the other sects vanished, but the heritage of the Pharisees endured. Our knowledge of this sect rests largely on the self-characterization of the rabbis in power after the Temple fell. These rabbis consciously saw themselves as heirs of the Pharisees and may have idealized them.

The term *Pharisees* comes from the Hebrew *Perushim*, or "separated ones." Originally, it may have been a pejorative designation given by their opponents. However, it became a term of distinction for the small group of perhaps 6,000 who considered themselves "elect" in the sense that they were to set an example. We are reminded of the New England Puritan concept of being elect, although the Pharisees did not regard themselves as being specially elected for salvation. They held the view that religion is a system of praxis that, by internal logic, raises the issue of where to draw the line. Frequently bold in interpretation, in order to adjust Torah to the people's need they were meticulous in their performance of Mitzvot. In this manner they influenced the future of Jewish religion and practice.

HILLEL was the central intellectual and spiritual figure in Jerusalem in the generations before the fall of the Temple. He expressed an ideal perception of the character a Pharisee should acquire and the way he should perform his duties. To him, love of God and humanity should undergird all actions, for the intent of the heart was what mattered, not the empty act. According to Hillel, the foundation of Judaism lay in the principle, "Do not do unto others what would be hateful to you were it done to you."

Because the Pharisees were highly respected, they attracted imitators who exhibited an exaggerated outward form of piety. The Talmud tells us in detail that the pharisaic leaders were well aware of these hypocrites and castigated them scathingly. But when asked why they did not remove them, the rabbis responded that, as humans, we cannot judge the motivations of the heart and must leave the judgment to God (B. Sota 20–22b). In accordance with pharisaic tradition, which was his own, Jesus equally rebuked some Pharisees. Through the centuries, Christians interpreted the words of Jesus to include *all* Pharisees, and thus branded them without exception as hypocrites or, at least, legal hairsplitters without a true spirit of faith. It is now understood that this was not a fair assessment.

The Sages: Heirs to the Pharisees

The Pharisees and their successors, the Sages of the Talmud, saw themselves as divinely ordained keepers of Torah and successors of the prophets in the chain of tradition.

> Moses received the Torah from Sinai and delivered it to Joshua, and Joshua to the Elders, and the Elders to the Prophets, and the Prophets delivered it to the Men of the Great Assembly [a body of Sages, including prophets (B. Megillah 17b), said to have been established by Ezra and forerunner of the talmudic masters]. These said three things: be deliberate in judgment, raise up many disciples, and make a fence around the Torah. (Avot 1.1)
> Simon the Zaddik was one of the survivors of the Great Assembly. He used to say: "The world rests on three things: on Torah, Service [Temple service, later interpreted as worship and Mitzvot] and acts of love." (Avot 1:2)

These examples reveal the mind of the Sages. Simon the Zaddik was a bridge between the Great Assembly and the later rabbinical body.

The Sages became bold innovators. Yohanan ben Zaccai, a Pharisee, was permitted by Vespasian to open an academy at Javneh. Seeing no hope for the rescue of the Temple and its offices, he took it upon himself to base the future of the Jews on the Covenant of Torah alone, to raise many disciples, ordain them, and install the rabbis as Torah's keepers. The changing times called for a radically new approach: The rabbis had to assume the power to legislate. The phrase "Deliberate in judgment" illustrates how they saw themselves empowered to dispense justice and make ordinances. They increased this power in subsequent centuries. As legislators, they had to be meticulous in observance of the Torah. However, they saw themselves not as innovators, but as interpreters. Their legislation was read *out* of Torah by being read *into* the text. It was Oral Torah equally regarded as divinely revealed. This called for painstaking analysis of every word of Scripture to show that the new interpretation was already in it. As every ordinance ultimately rested on the word of God revealed at Sinai, its promulgators had to be exact in its performance.

The rabbis felt empowered merely to put a fence around the Torah, similar to the fence Moses built around Mount Sinai so that the people might not encroach on the place of divine revelation (Exodus 19:12). Then it was meant literally; now it was understood figuratively; namely, to surround the commandments of Torah with additional injunctions, in order that the laws of Torah not be violated. In reality, rabbinical interpretation frequently gave new meaning to the words of Scripture and changed its laws from their literal meaning. The Sadducees recognized such "liberalism" and opposed it.

This process of evolutionary interpretation took place in the *Bet Midrash*, the House of Study. The rabbis passed their teachings from generation to generation by word of mouth, and each generation added to the body of this Oral Torah. However, in this form of transmission lay a twofold danger. The material became so voluminous that few could remember all of it, much less keep it in mind for discussion and decision making. Some rabbis, such as Rabbi Akiba and his disciple Rabbi Meir, saw themselves compelled to make lecture notes. In addition, the situation of the Jews frequently became precarious. After the abortive Bar Kokhba rebellion, for instance, Emperor Hadrian proscribed the teaching and practice of Jewish religion.

But if Torah was to be preserved, teaching had to continue. The leading rabbis and their disciples had no choice; they defied the edict. They were hunted by the Roman government and, when caught, were cruelly tortured and executed. The story of "Ten [Rabbis], Slain by the Government," is told annually in the worship of Yom Kippur to evoke the spirit of commitment to the Jewish heritage.

Among these Ten was RABBI AKIBA (50–132 C.E.). He had reached manhood as an ignorant shepherd, then fell in love with his rich employer's daughter Rachel, who returned his love but made him promise to study Torah. Her father, upon learning of her secret marriage to Akiba, cut off her support. Akiba studied for twenty-four years while his wife supported him by the toil of her hands. Eventually her father relented (B. Ketubot 62b/63a). Akiba became the master of his time. Finally, he was caught and put to death. But as his flesh was being torn from his body by red-hot pincers, he smiled. "Should I not be happy?" he asked his terrified students. "'You shall love the Lord your God with all . . . your soul,' even surrendering your life to Him. Now I can meet this supreme test of love, should I not rejoice?" (B. Berakhot 21b). With him and his colleagues, a wealth of knowledge perished.

The Mishnah

In view of the Jews' precarious situation, RABBI JUDAH, Patriarch of the Jewish community and friend of the Emperor Antoninus Pius (and perhaps also of his nephew, the emperor and philosopher Marcus Aurelius), decided that Oral Torah must be edited and written down. The Mishnah (Review), of which we shall say more later, was completed around 200 C.E. That was none too soon, since conditions became more difficult as Palestine fell under the power of the Christian state. The masters who speak in the Mishnah are called *Tannaim*, the Teachers, and are recognized by the title of Rabbi.

Babylonian Jewry

When two of Rabbi Judah's disciples went to Babylonia during the early years of the third century to establish there a center for Jewish learning, they did not take any great risk. Babylonian Jewry already had behind it a proud history extending over 800 years. As we saw, the prophet Jeremiah had written them at the beginning of their exile to consider their new dwelling place a permanent residence for many generations and to devote themselves faithfully to the tasks of good citizenship. As soon as Jerusalem had been resettled by their brethren, they considered it the spiritual and intellectual as well as physical core of Jewry, but they did not neglect the development of their own institutions. Thus Hillel had received his early training in Babylonia and migrated to Judea to complete his studies and eventually to lead. Now Abba Areka (Abba the Tall), a giant of a man both physically and intellectually, and his colleague Samuel set out to establish in Babylonia a second center of leadership.

Babylonian Jewry was happy, wealthy, and respected. The community was large, numbering several million. The Jews had all the rights of citizens and actually formed their own autonomous state within the kingdom, comparable to a state within the United States. At the head of it stood the RESH GALUTA, the Exilarch, a descendant of the House of David. A satrap of the empire, the splendor of his court reflected his high position. He was governor in the real sense of the word. Babylonian Jews were deeply religious and proud of their two leading academies in the cities of Sura and Nehardea. The presidents of these academies were the spiritual heads and Chief Justices of the Jews and bore the title *Gaon*, which means "Excellency." Abba Areka and Samuel became the presidents of these two schools. So great was Abba Areka's prestige that he became known simply as *Rav*, "the Master."

The Talmud

In an effort to evolve the Mishnah both in theory and in practice, an interesting system was adopted in Babylonia. In the Bet Midrash, the Academy, disciples devoted their days to study. A rigid order prevailed, even the seating was assigned according to the rank of the scholar. Additionally, in spring and fall the scholars would assemble for a whole month of discussion and debate; then they were given homework to study for the next assembly, or *Kallah*, while pursuing their regular ways of making a living. These debates, which closely followed the Mishnah, were recorded verbatim and formed the *Gemara*, "that which is learned from Tradition." Gemara is no dry code of laws. It breathes the living spirit of question and answer, legal analysis and homiletic exegesis, *bon mot* and jest; often it is rambling, following a free association of thoughts. The rabbis who speak in the Gemara were of lesser authority than those of the Mishnah. To indicate this they were called *Amoraim*, "Speakers," and given the title of Rav.

Eventually, the material became so voluminous that it had to be edited. Thus was the Talmud formed. Work on the Talmud went on in both Palestine and Babylonia. We therefore have *Yerushalmi*, the Jerusalem Talmud, and *Bavli*, the Babylonian Talmud. In 360 C.E., the academies of Palestine were forcibly closed by the Christian authorities, the Yerushalmi remained incomplete. Development of the Bavli continued and was finally edited around 500 C.E. The Talmud will be discussed in detail in Chapter 13.

The Gaonic Period

Being outside the Christian empire of Byzantium, Jewish life in Babylonia, which had fallen into the orbit of Islam (see p. 60), remained undisturbed.

Baghdad became a center of Jewish learning. The relationship between the two religions was good. After the completion of the Talmud, study and research went on under the leadership of the *Gaonim* (plural of *Gaon*), who made it their goal to establish themselves and the Babylonian Talmud as the exclusive authority in Judaism. In this they succeeded. Jews from all over the world directed their questions to them, and received authoritative *Responsa*. For example: While in Palestine Torah, the Five Books of Moses was read in a three-year cycle in public worship, the Babylonian authorities insisted that it be read in a one-year cycle, and prevailed. The Babylonian Talmud was henceforth *the* source of Jewish law. The Jerusalem Talmud was pushed into the background.

In response to an inquiry by Jews in Barcelona, Rav Amram Gaon, who held office from 857–875, was the first to issue an authorized text of the prayer book. Up to this time the content of the prayers was fixed but their formulation was left to the preceptor. From now on the text of the prayers were canonized.

The Gaon Saadia versus Islam, the Karaites, and Aristotle

By the ninth century a number of new spiritual problems arose. A Jewish sect called the *Karaites*, or "Scripturites," founded in the eighth century, denied the validity of the Talmud, based itself entirely on Scripture, and drew new deductions from it. It was feared that karaitic teaching, if it were allowed to prevail and spread, might destroy the organic evolution of Judaism that rested on shared rabbinic tradition, and so undermine the unity of the people. The movement had to be fought. Equally important was the challenge presented by the ever-increasing knowledge and study of Aristotle, whose conclusions, so logically developed, clashed with the teachings of Torah. The claims of Islam to be the only true religion had to be logically refuted as well.

The GAON SAADIA (882–942) addressed himself to all of these challenges. He stands out as the first Jewish "scholastic," making an effort to synthesize Aristotle and Jewish tradition whenever possible. Whatever was good in Aristotle—measured by the yardstick of Jewish tradition—had a right to be incorporated. When synthesis was impossible, Saadia refuted Aristotle by logic. In his *Book of Doctrines and Beliefs*, Gaon Saadia claimed Judaism as the religion of reason. We shall discuss his philosophy in Chapter 15.

Saadia likewise attacked the views of the Karaites in tract after tract. Since the Karaites maintained that Torah ordained complete avoidance of fire and light on the Sabbath, he ordained that lights be kindled on the eve of the Sabbath and a blessing be spoken, thanking God for having ordained the Sabbath lights. This blessing is offered over the lights in Jewish homes to this day. For the people, he translated the Bible into Arabic, compiled a Hebrew grammar, and issued a prayer book.

His life was stormy, but his mission was clear: The Torah, growing and evolving through rabbinic interpretation and injunctions, had to be preserved against the deadening outlook of Karaites and alien philosophical and religious thought. A small community of Karaites has survived to the present. It follows its own traditions, but considers itself a part of the Jewish people.

The Decline of Babylonian Leadership

Eventually, as disturbances and wars swept over the Near East, Babylonian Jewry lost its leadership position. By the eleventh century C.E., Spain and Germany had become centers of Jewry. In the twentieth century, the once vibrant Jewish community in Persia (modern Iran) and Iraq disappeared. Rising Islamic fundamentalism resulted in the emigration of most of the Jews from these countries to Israel, America, and other free countries.

Note

1. "B.C.E." stands for Before the Common Era. It is used to designate dates preceding the birth of Christ. "C.E." designates dates following the birth of Christ.

CHAPTER 3

The Impact
of Christianity

THE PERIOD whose events we have just traced witnessed the emergence and rise of Christianity. As we turn now to a brief discussion of Christianity's impact on Jewish history, non-Jewish readers should recognize it as an analysis of how Christianity has *appeared* to Jews. It may surprise and at times even disturb some Christian readers to find concepts and ideas being questioned which to them are self-evident. It is my belief that it is important to know and understand each position in order that fruitful dialogue may become a lasting reality.

The emergence of a genuine dialogue between the faiths may be one of the positive developments of our time. It holds great promise of true human fellowship and concern among the faithful of these two religions, as among all people. In spirit and in character, today's climate is totally different from the religious disputations convened by the Catholic Church during the Middle Ages, whose outcome was a foregone conclusion, and whose purpose was simply to prove to the rulers, the world, and the Jews the "error" of the Synagogue and the triumphant truth of the Church. The spirit of these disputations can still be noticed in the sculptures on great cathedrals, such as that at Strasbourg: the Synagogue in collapse, her eyes bandaged, her staff broken; the Church holding her banner aloft, with crowned head and proud eyes confidently viewing both time and eternity. Seen in this manner, and treated harshly on account of their "blindness," the Jews were naturally afraid of Christians.

The fortunate change that has come within our own time can be ascribed to a number of causes, among them the scientific temper of the twentieth century, the deepening of the democratic outlook which calls for freedom of religion, and the secularization of life in general. The spread of atheism and communism actually called for a spirit of cooperation among the religious forces in the struggle against God-denying ideologies and forces. The Holocaust, claiming millions of Jews as victims of the accumulated impact of centuries of anti-Semitism, weighed heavily upon the conscience of humanity. It aroused Christians to a profound self-examination, leading to a renewed commitment to world leadership in the true spirit of Christian ethics. In this spirit of love that binds Christians and Jews, we shall try to view briefly some of the impact of Christianity upon Judaism as seen by a Jew.

JESUS AND THE JEWS

Jesus in the Gospels

The life, passion, and resurrection of Jesus, the Christ, are related to us in the *Gospels*. They are documents of faith (as are the Hebrew Scriptures); they are not detached historical accounts. The historical Jesus is less their object than the Risen Christ. Piety permeates the story. It became subject to embroidery and error, as is the case in any oral tradition. The Gospels were written after the ministry of Paul and under the impact of his teaching. Paul's theology, as we shall point out, contrasts sharply with basic Jewish principles, and it subjected him to Jewish attacks during his lifetime. This antagonism is reflected in the Gospels.

Written in part by Jews and in part by non-Jews, the Gospels reflect the changing relationship between the Jewish community and the emerging Christian one. Jewish Christians, who became convinced that Jesus was the Messiah, regarded themselves as authentic Jews. They were filled with the deep desire to win over their brethren to the "good news." They endeavored to show that Jesus had spoken primarily and specifically to Jews, as is reflected in many passages of the Gospel of Matthew that are positively and specifically addressed to the Jewish community (e.g., 5:17ff.; 10:5; 15:17ff.; 15:24; 23:2). By and large, the Jews did not respond positively to this message. This must have been a deep disappointment to the new Christians, convincing them that their hope lay in the conversion of Gentiles. This frustration and shift is mirrored in passages of Matthew which have a universalist but anti-Jewish character (e.g., 2:43; 22:7; 28:18ff.).

The non-Jewish writers were antagonistic to Jews. They maintained that Judaism had now been superseded, an attitude not entirely surprising for people who had decided to choose one religion over another. The fall of the Temple in 70 C.E. was evidence to the Christians that God had punished the Jews for their refusal to accept Christ. Words of prophecy to that effect were ascribed to Jesus (Matthew 24:2; Mark 13:2; Luke 21:6). However, the Christian community itself was still in flux, and beliefs and doctrines clashed. The predominant faction might then characterize nonconformists pejoratively as "Jews." Such references in the Gospels need not be regarded as judgments on Jewish thought and action in general.

The Gospel writers had to whitewash the Roman government if Christianity was to be tolerated at all. Even Pilate, one of the most cruel and venal of procurators, was exonerated. As we have seen, he was so cruel that even Rome recalled him. But he is shown washing his hands (Matthew 27:24), which is a Jewish ceremony symbolically pleading for remission of sin in connection with the death of an innocent man. The ceremony as described in the Gospels shows that Pilate has misunderstood the original law. (See Deuteronomy 21:1–9, which deals with an unknown murder victim found at a crossroads in the countryside. The elders of the closest city wash their hands, symbolically expressing their innocence of this crime that resulted from a lack of protection and help extended within their territory. Then they ask divine forgiveness for the crime *having been* committed by unknown hands, not one they *are about* to sanction by consciously approving it.) We cannot assume Pilate suddenly adopting a Jewish practice, considering how deeply he hated the Jews and how determined he was to antagonize them by offending their religious beliefs. (Unless, of course, he had heard about the practice and repeated it in mockery, which throws an entirely different light on his action: It then becomes a blasphemous provocation of Jewish tradition.)

Within the Gospels we find contradictions regarding the year of Jesus' birth and crucifixion, and basic elements of his trial and conviction cannot be reconciled with Jewish life and practice. Jesus lived a simple life. The circle of those who knew him was small. His impact and that of his teaching was slow in emerging. Jesus himself may have passed through his lifetime without being known either personally or by his teaching to the overwhelming majority of his Jewish contemporaries in Judea or to the millions in the Diaspora. The Jewish historian JOSEPHUS, a meticulous chronicler of Jewish history during this period, does not mention Jesus. (A statement about Jesus in Josephus's work is generally considered to be a later addition by an unknown, possibly Christian, writer.) Josephus did, however, hold a strong bias in favor of Rome, which may have led to his silence. But the Jewish philosopher Philo, who lived in Egypt from about 25 B.C.E. to about 50 C.E. and was a spokesman for the Jews, does not mention Jesus either.

Jesus and the Pharisees

Jesus was true to the spirit of the Law that the Pharisees taught. By speaking of "the Pharisees," the Gospels make it appear that the pharisaic movement was monolithic. In fact it was a highly complex movement. Some of its members were harsh and strict in their interpretation of the commandments, others were lenient. Jesus was lenient to the limits of the law, so it is not unlikely that he may have made enemies among those who were strict. The hypocrites within the pharisaic group may also have hated him for his rebuke, which was in tune with the severe criticism of this group from other Pharisees. Jesus associated and ate with the Pharisees (Luke 14:1), and must have had friends among them.

To some Pharisees, Jesus' actions may have been too radical. He permitted his disciples to pluck corn on the Sabbath to still their hunger. To offended Pharisees who claimed that such action broke the Sabbath laws he offered precedence in history that the law may be broken when people are hungry (Matthew 12:1–8). When Jesus healed a man with a withered hand on the Sabbath, Pharisees "counseled to destroy him" (Matthew 12:10–14). To Jesus, living with a withered hand was not living. After healing a man of dropsy on the Sabbath Jesus asked whether this healing was legitimate, but the Pharisees stayed silent.

Jesus interpreted the law leniently but did not break it. When he saw human beings in need, he overruled the law in its strict interpretation. He did not wish to abolish the law; actually, Jewish law permitted the violation of commandments, including the laws of the Sabbath, when there was actual danger to life. (At one time, the rabbis "violated" Sabbath law when they found Hillel close to death on account of exposure to the elements and restored him to life.) One of the Pharisees even blessed Jesus (Luke 14:1–15). Was this a different group of Pharisees, or might these men have felt that, in this case, Jesus' action was justified? It seems Jesus' conflict with "the Pharisees" was a conflict with "some Pharisees."

The author of Acts, in his report on Rabban Gamaliel aids us to overcome the stereotype of "the Pharisee." Gamaliel, a Pharisee, pleads in behalf of the apostles, who, according to Acts, had been brought before the council and high priest accused of teaching in Christ's name. Gamaliel advised the court not to judge, but to let God be the judge of the truth of the apostles' message, and let the men go free. The apostles were flogged but not killed, a compromise decision between the Sadducee high priest, the "strict" Pharisees and the "lenient" ones (Acts 5:34–39).

Many Pharisees had no problems with Jesus' teachings. The idea of a messianic claimant, who lived as a Jew, obedient to law and tradition, and who was not a sinner, was acceptable to them. We never find a single case where a person was tried as a blasphemer for claiming to be the Messiah; in fact, Rabbi Akiba proclaimed Bar Kokhba as the Messiah one hundred years later. Jesus also believed in resurrection, as did the Pharisees. He based his own teaching on that of John the Baptist as described in Matthew 3:4–17, and we find no opposition to John's activity among any Jews. And, to the Pharisee who asked what was the greatest commandment in Torah, Jesus summarized the Torah's words of the twofold love: the commandment to love God (Deuteronomy 6:5) and the commandment to love one's neighbor (Leviticus 19:18), combining the commandments in simple sentences, as Jewish children of the time learned them in catechetical instruction (Matthew 23:37–39).

Jesus and the Essenes

Jesus implicitly rejected the teachings of the Essenes, who taught their followers to love one's neighbor and hate one's enemy, which contradicts the commandments of Torah (Matthew 5:43–44; compare Exodus 23:4–5; Leviticus 20:17ff.). The disciple who asked Jesus for a special, distinguishing prayer, just as John the Baptist had given his disciples a special prayer, was led to the simple prayer spoken by the common Jewish folk: "Our Father, who are in heaven . . ." (Luke 11:1–4).

Jesus and the Sadducees

Hostility against Jesus was more pronounced in the Sadducees. They did not believe in resurrection (Matthew 22:23–33). They saw the survival of the Jewish people inextricably linked to the Temple, its existence, and its ritual, yet Jesus reportedly attacked these. Pharisees could see a Jewish future without a Temple; the Sadducees could not.

We may assume that, faced with the possible destruction of the Temple and the whole people, Caiaphas, a Sadducee high priest, became alarmed and counseled that it was better for one man (Jesus) to die than for the whole people to perish (John 18:13). He may have been afraid that Jesus would endanger the whole people by his messianic claims. The Roman procurator did not understand the subtleties of such a claim. To him, "Messiah" was equivalent to "King." Jewish kings had always been anointed with oil. To Rome, then, a Messiah was an insurrectionist, bent on overthrowing the Roman rule. Rome's retaliation was inevitable, as Caiaphas saw it, and would spell destruction for the Jews. It might even lead to the razing of the Temple. In fact, most likely Pilate had to hear only the word *Messiah* to make up his mind. Mocked as "King of the Jews" by the inscription over his cross, Jesus was crucified.

Jesus' trial by a Jewish court is so difficult to explain that Samuel Sandmel writes after close study, "The entire trial business is legendary and tendentious" (*A Jewish Understanding of the New Testament*; Cincinnati: Hebrew Union College, 1957, p. 128). Unless we were to assume that Jewish court procedures in Jesus' time were completely different from those laid down later in the Mishnah (Sanhedrin), we have to approach the report with critical doubt. We find that the trial proceedings ran counter to all existing laws of procedures, evidence, and so on; in short, they flouted the entire body of legislation, which was strictly binding and permitted of no exceptions. The Sanhedrin met at appointed times, and was bound by Jewish law. Therefore, it never sat at night, never handed down a conviction in criminal matters on the day of the trial, and hence never held any trial sessions on the day before the Sabbath or any holiday. The trumped up charge was blasphemy, although according to Jewish law, Jesus had not committed blasphemy at all. With a death sentence handed down, he could have been executed, but not by crucifixion, a form of execution not permissible under Jewish law.

Jesus and the Romans

Now the Romans took over. Jesus was brought into Pilate's palace before a Jewish crowd, who knew of the accusation against him. "Trying to release him" (Matthew 27:15ff.; Mark 15:6ff.; Luke 23:16ff.; John 18:39ff.) indicates that Pilate placed the decision in the crowd's hands. Nowhere else do we find in Rome the practice of letting the people choose and decide. If we accept the occurrence, we have to ask: Was Pilate playing with them to get their reaction, intending to arrest them as well if they sided with Jesus? Perhaps they were afraid to respond honestly. It was better to affirm loyalty to Caesar and permit one innocent man to die, as Caiaphas had advised. Then the people might survive (see John 19).

Who were these people who, on the eve of Passover, when everybody was busy preparing for the holy day, assembled at the residence of Pilate, a man they despised? They may have been just rabble, or perhaps they were assigned to this task of representing "the voice of the populace" by the high priest, to prove to the procurator that the Jews wished to have no part in Jesus' insurrection. They were no more representative of the Jewish people than were the legionnaires representative of the entire Roman people, but for centuries "the Jews" as a whole were implicated in the conduct of these few. It is hard to assume that the Jews would suddenly adopt a new religious principle; namely, accepting guilt for their children and for future generations. This would run counter to the fundamental conviction of the Jews, so firmly instilled in them by the prophets, that there is no such thing as an inherited guilt (as we saw in the discussion of Jeremiah and Ezekiel).

The Romans treated Jesus as a political criminal. They crucified him, affixed a notification of his "crime" on his cross, and confiscated his clothes as a political offender. (The property of a non-political criminal was not subject to confiscation.) After Jesus had died, a Jew named Joseph of Arimathea pleaded with Pilate to release the body of Jesus, which was in Roman custody, in order that he might give it proper burial as Jewish tradition prescribed (Matthew 27:58ff.). This act, most likely mirrors the attitude of the average Jew toward Jesus: He was another martyr, put to death by a cruel Roman government. It must be remembered that the new sect of Nazarenes (the term *Christians* did not come until later), standing under the leadership of Peter, strictly obeyed and practiced Jewish law and expected converts to do the same as a condition of their admission.

PAUL AND THE PARTING OF WAYS

In the apostle Paul's emphasis on faith as opposed to Mitzvot we find the beginning of the dissent between the two faiths. Nevertheless, Paul himself was full of pride in his Jewish background and full of love for his Jewish brethren.

The strong foundations of Christianity's growth were laid by Paul's missionary work. It became widespread, powerful, and eventually the official religion of the Roman Empire. Non-Jews quickly outnumbered the Jewish Christians. The new religion saw Judaism as a rival faith, and engaged in widespread missionary activity. Antagonism developed. As a result of Paul's doctrines, Judaism and Christianity had to go their separate ways. For this reason the Jewish foundations of Paul's thoughts and actions deserve to be noted.

Paul's Background

Paul was a complex man. He grew up in a strictly observant Jewish family in the Diaspora. Diaspora Jewry outnumbered the community in the homeland by millions. The several million Jews of the dispersion were generally accepted and had the right to practice their religion, even when such practice interfered with the duties generally imposed on citizens. As observers of the Sabbath, for instance, they were exempt from military service. Paul was proud of his ancestry (2 Corinthians 11:22; Romans 11:1) and of his people's place in the world, for they were conscious of being God's people (Philippians 3:5).

Being God's people entailed duties and obligations. Isaiah had urged them to be "a light unto the nations" (Isaiah 42:6), and the prophets had made it clear that the convert was precious in the eyes of God (e.g., Isaiah 56:6–7). Many of the leading Pharisees therefore favored missionary activity. Hillel declared, "Be of the disciples of Aaron, loving peace, pursuing peace, loving all of God's creatures, drawing them to Torah" (Abot 12:1). All Gentiles had to be given the opportunity to accept Torah and cast their lot with the Jewish people in order to find salvation. Only then could they be held responsible for their idolatrous way of life (Pesikta Rabba 161a). Matthew 23:15 shows the pharisaic concern for the conversion of heathens.

Diaspora Jewry and Missionary Work

Diaspora Jewry engaged in widespread missionary work. As we saw, there were two categories of converts: the full convert who had undergone the full procedure as prescribed, and the "God-fearers" who had committed themselves to observe the Sabbath and other laws and to uphold Jewish ethics, but who had not undergone circumcision. Jewish missionaries were concerned to bring many people yearning for a spiritual faith under the wings of God and His salvation. Paul, as a youth, was a witness to these activities. They may have inspired him to go out himself as a missionary to save people.

Diaspora Jewry was strongly influenced by Hellenistic civilization. To the Jews in Palestine, Torah was instruction, the guide on their road of life; it contained the laws that were part of the Covenant that bound Israel and God. To many in the Diaspora community, Torah was *nomos*, or Law. Law was Covenant, a much narrower outlook that had resulted from the Septuagint translation of "Torah" as "nomos" and the impact of many other intellectual and philosophical forces stemming from Hellenistic civilization. At the same time, Jews such as the philosopher Philo interpreted Torah allegorically, seeing in the laws of Torah symbols showing the road toward the laws that God had *naturally implanted* in humanity. Philo's thinking affected Paul in two ways: Torah became for him just Law, and, if the human soul was sanctified, the divine Covenant might be found outside the Mitzvot of Torah.

Paul therefore stood under an inner compulsion that was Jewish: Humanity had to be saved. He started out as a Pharisee, and a zealous one, and called himself a Pharisee throughout his life (e.g., Philippians 3:5). As a Pharisee, he became a missionary, originally an uncompromisingly strict traditional one (Galatians 5:11 may refer to his earlier missionary attitude). Like many of the Pharisees, he earned his living by the toil of his hands; he was a tentmaker.

But Paul deviated from Jewish tradition partially as a result of his Diaspora experiences. He was a man of extremes, and the compromise solution of two types of converts was not for him. If the Law was to be observed, then all of it had to be observed, or the Law in its entirety was irrelevant as a means of salvation. He became a persecutor of those Jewish Christians who denied the validity of Law and tradition (Galatians 1:13; Philippians 3:6). He had no quarrel with the mother Church—the first church, presided over by Peter and central in prestige and authority—in Jerusalem, which demanded obedience to the Law in addition to faith in Christ. The mother Church took no notice of him at this stage of his career. Paul was convinced that the Law was holy and just and good, and he was to state even later that, "In my innermost self I delight in the law of God" (Romans 7:22). He became zealous for the law—until his outlook was suddenly transformed by the personal illumination that the law had been superseded by faith in Christ.

Paul's Revelation

Paul was sent to Damascus by the authorities to punish Jewish Christians who preached abandonment of the law (not to bring them back to Jerusalem, for the Jews no longer had that power; they could only inflict the punishments of the congregation, which included scourging). On his way, Paul had a vision of Christ, a revelation: With the coming of Christ, the Covenant of Law had been replaced by the Covenant of Christ. The Law no longer held any compelling power. Humanity comes to God through faith in Christ.

In a sense, Paul's conclusion rested logically on the thoughts advanced by the Hellenistic Jewish philosophers. To them, the Law was the instrument of education bringing humanity to obedience to God's *natural law.* But Paul's conclusion was radical: Through Christ, a new spirit would enter the souls of the faithful; obedience to natural law was the fruit of the spirit, not the Law. He came to understand the position of the Hellenistic Jews at Damascus, whom he had been sent to castigate. Paul's personal experience and his sense of spiritual renewal through this knowledge that Law had been abrogated were now to become the foundation of a fundamental and universal principle upon which he built his ministry and his missionary work.

Paul's Missionary Activity

Paul's stand caused controversy and conflict. Moved by the urgency of his task, Paul immediately set out on his missionary work. He did not feel it necessary to go to Jerusalem first in order to obtain authorization from the mother Church. He regarded himself as called by Christ and therefore of equal standing with the disciples. Although he probably had not known Jesus personally, he had received the vision of Christ, and it was Christ whom he was preaching, not the story of the man Jesus on earth. His vision, Paul felt, placed him in the same position as the prophets of old to whom God had granted His revelation. He saw his task as more pressing than theirs had been, for the end of days, he believed, was about to come, and as many as could be reached had to be brought to Christ before then.

Paul went abroad and made many converts. His success caused rejoicing among the leaders of the mother Church at Jerusalem. But Paul taught his non-Jewish audiences that the Law, including circumcision, not only was not necessary but actually was an impediment. He therefore had to defend himself before the leadership in Jerusalem. There he insisted that he had been authorized to teach that the Law, including circumcision, had been abolished and he would continue to preach this doctrine. Against the majority of the leadership of the Church he prevailed, at least to the point of being made the apostle to the Gentiles. Paul succeeded in convincing Peter to join the new Christians when Peter visited Antioch and ate with them—a breach of the dietary laws, we may assume (Galatians 2).

Paul traveled throughout the greater part of the civilized world of his time, frequently preaching in synagogues to Jewish and non-Jewish audiences. His teachings quite often caused severe trouble. Many Jews regarded his teachings as destructive, for they contradicted the law of Torah and abolished the Mitzvot. Penalties were invoked against him (2 Corinthians 11:24ff.).

In return Paul violently attacked the Jews (Romans 2:21–24), specifically their practice of circumcision (Galatians 5:12; Philippians 3:2). His utterances were frequently used against the Jews later in history. But we must understand them in context: Paul was incensed, and he responded to violent argument in his own violent manner. It was an internal squabble among Jews, Paul and his opponents. His words were motivated by the excitement of the moment. An intra-Jewish argument, an aside voiced perhaps to forestall questions, were later made into principles. Paul spoke as the moment bid him to do; he spoke to concrete situations. When his words were gathered and canonized they assumed the character of basic writings, and every word was considered of equal importance.

Essentially Paul was loyal to the Jews. His heart went out to his Jewish brothers, people of covenants, patriarchs, the Messiah (Romans 9:1–5); he regarded them as lost because they did not accept his teachings. Although he saw in the followers of Christ the new Israel, Paul loved his own people.

We have followed the life of Paul at some length because it is inseparable from his teachings. His theology springs from his life. Through it, the Church was given the means of growth; without it, Christianity might have remained a sect within Judaism. Non-Jews became its leaders and its faithful. By unifying the Church, Paul led it out of Judaism. In his preaching, however, Paul followed the pattern of Jewish exegesis; his sermons were discussions in the manner of Jewish study, and he drew his conclusions from the text of Scripture (see Romans 9). The Christian sermon, therefore, has followed the pattern of the Jewish sermon. At the same time, the "Old Testament" was seen as a prophecy of the coming of Christ. This has resulted in frequently divergent interpretations of the Hebrew Scriptures by Christians and Jews.

Paul's Basic Teachings

In his Epistle to the Romans (Romans 7) Paul gives us a report of the anxieties that led him to his conversion. "Taking delight in the Law of God" (7:22), he found that this same Law tempted him to break it. The Law said, "You shall not covet" and thereby aroused in him all kinds of desires. The seductive power of sin entered his heart through the commandment; its effect was to "kill" rather than quicken (7:7ff.). Many contemporary biblical scholars maintain that this report is not autobiographical, but rather a poetic illustration of the effects of the Law as Paul perceived them after his conversion. These scholars hold that Paul actually did not feel any distress in observing the Law during his earlier years, in spite of his own words, but, in looking back on his former state, he now felt that his life under the Law must have been distressing.

Paul found himself transformed by a personal revelation. This revelation raised to absolute conviction in him several fundamental truths by which his life henceforth was shaped. These truths—related to divine dispensation, and emerging from it his own calling—were: Jesus Christ is the Lord; through Jesus Christ, God has provided for the salvation of all believers; and Christ will return to bring about the end and consummation of history. Paul's own mission, ordained by God, rested on these truths. He was to be the apostle to the Gentiles.

From these convictions Paul drew several conclusions. That God sent salvation through Christ meant that God saw humanity's need of salvation. Christ's death revealed that the Law, hitherto regarded as the road to salvation, did not lead to salvation—Christ alone was the way. "If righteousness should come through the law, Christ died in vain" (Galatians 2:21). Obedience to the Law in the assumption that it led to salvation was therefore sin, for humanity cannot bring about its own salvation.

The Law did have a function, however: The Law quickened one's awareness of sin (Romans 7:7ff.). There was a form of righteousness in obedience to the Law because of its capacity to reveal its own deficiency, open the human mind and soul, and pave the way to true faith; namely, that Christ alone brings salvation (Philippians 3:4–12). Jewish righteousness came through the Law; hence Jews need not abandon it, but they must, through it, come to Christ. As far as the Gentiles were concerned, the Law had resulted in a separation between those who observed it and those who stood outside of it. This separation must be broken, for in Christ's Spirit all of humanity, Jews and Gentiles alike, had been freed from the powers of sin, death, and the Law (Romans 5–8). All human beings must form a union of equals with equal access to salvation; all are one body (1 Corinthians 12:12ff.). Paul therefore turned sharp words against those converts who wished to observe Jewish law, as this would create divisiveness (Galatians 3). Initially, the Law had been given by God as a means of education, but the tutorship of the Law had now ended.

The community of believers formed one body, an organic whole. One could not belong to it while, at the same time, participating in another one. Paul therefore equally warned his followers against any action that harmed the wholeness of a person's physical body: "The body is not for fornication, but for the Lord, and the Lord for the body" (1 Corinthians 6:13–20). This is not "law" but the result of the simple realization of the Christian's condition (1 Corinthians 6:12).

Without needing any Law but guided by the Spirit, Christians are under the compulsion to establish and follow those ethical principles that even the Gentiles follow by natural insight (Romans 2:14ff.; Galatians 5:19–26). In this manner Paul reinstated rules as fruits of the Spirit. Significantly, he drew the details of these ethical requirements from Hebrew Scriptures; as a Jew, he saw no need either to improve on them or to find new ones.

The difference between Paul and the Jewish outlook regarding ethical conduct may appear to be merely semantic. In Judaism, the rules of conduct are commandments, law; in Paul, they are fruits of the Spirit. But we should remember that Paul had been brought up on the methods of the rabbis (as we recognize them from Mishnah and Gemara) and had internalized them. For them, each separate term, even a nuance, found in Scripture may hold a new meaning and lead in different directions. Since Paul argued in a talmudic manner, the distinctions become basic.

Paul held that the miracles presented to the Jews and the commandments given in Torah were to be understood symbolically (1 Corinthians 9:9–12; 10:6). They led to that natural law by which the Spirit guides all humanity. The Christian should do that which is naturally and universally accepted: not give offense (1 Corinthians 10:32); promote unity; and, above all, love (1 Corinthians 13:1ff.). In this symbolic interpretation of the laws, and in Paul's reliance on natural law, implanted in humanity, we recognize the ideas of the Jewish philosopher Philo—with one difference: Philo insisted on faithful observance of the Mitzvot, giving them an additional, symbolic meaning; Paul saw no purpose in the observance of specific commandments.

There are both fundamental agreements and disagreements between Paul's teachings and Jewish doctrine. According to Judaism, salvation is assured to every Jew on the basis of belonging to the Covenant. "All of Israel, every one of them, have a share in the world to come [salvation], as it is stated: 'Your people, altogether they are righteous, they will forever inherit the earth' (Isaiah 60:21)" (B. Sanhedrin 104b). This salvation is attained by God's grace, not simply by the Law; humanity does not bring about its own salvation. For Paul, all of the newly covenanted people have a share in salvation on the basis of the Covenant of the body of Christ. According to Judaism, salvation is equally assured every righteous person among the Gentiles. "The righteous of the nations of the world, every one of them, have a share in the world to come" (Tosefta Sanhedrin 13). What makes them "righteous" is the observance of the Noahide commandments, which, according to rabbinic teaching, were imposed on Noah's descendants, the entire human race.

> The Rabbis taught: Seven laws were imposed upon the descendants of Noah: Civil justice [the establishment of just laws, to be administered through just courts], [the prohibition of] blasphemy (which includes perjury), [the prohibitions of] idolatry, of incest (including adultery and similar sexual offenses), the shedding of blood (murder), robbery (theft), the eating of a limb (flesh cut) from a living animal. (B. Sanhedrin 56a)

These laws are seen as basic elements of natural human morality. They are designed to establish a just society under God with respect for human life and family, for property, and for animals as God's creatures. Judaism has maintained that all non-Jews abiding by these laws are assured of salvation. Only those persons who undermine society by pursuing practices in willful violation of the Noahide commandments will be denied salvation.

Paul also expected observance of the Noahide commandments; Galatians 5:19ff. corresponds to them. However, he required faith in Christ as the condition for salvation. According to Judaism, Gentiles do attain salvation without entering the Covenant of Israel; it is not required of them. To Paul, it is necessary for Gentiles to enter and be under the Covenant of the body of Christ in order to attain salvation.

Why does humanity stand in need of salvation? Paul maintained that, with Adam's sin, death entered the world. Because Adam sinned, all his descendants—the entire human race—are in the throes of sin and death. The law kept humanity in check during a period of education. Ultimately, however, God graciously sent Christ into the world, and by his sacrificial death, he redeemed humanity from the Law, from sin attached to all humanity ever since Adam sinned, from that arising out of the Law, and from death. Through baptism, the old humankind is buried with Christ and reborn in Christ (Romans 5:1–15). Adam, who sinned, was the father of humanity so far; Christ is the beginning of a new humanity, saved through him.

Judaism, by contrast, has held that human beings sin not *because* Adam sinned but *as* Adam sinned. Each individual person will sin (Ecclesiastes 7:20), but by the grace of God will receive forgiveness as humanity returns to Him. Judaism sees sin as the result of the freedom God has given human beings. Nature must submit to God's law, humans are free to do so or not. All people are of limited strength in body and character. Their lives are short, therefore their vision is limited. They will err in judgment. "Who can possibly know what is best for a man to do in life—the few days of his fleeting life are like a shadow. Who can tell man what will happen to him later on under the sun?" (Ecclesiastes 6:12). "There is not one righteous man on earth who does what is good and does not miss the mark [sin]" (Ecclesiastes 7:20).

Human beings have drives; *yetzer ha-tov* is the drive to do good and *yetzer ha-ra* is the drive to sin. Everyone stands under the duty to do battle with his or her *yetzer ha-ra* and overcome it. "Sin crouches at the door, its urge is toward you, but you can master it" (Genesis 4:7). Returning to God, repentance (*teshuvah*), brings God's forgiveness. Victory in the battle against sin may then become a power for good.

In proving his point, that faith in Christ is the only way to salvation, Paul arrived at conclusions different from the teachings of Judaism but used methods typical of Jewish exegesis (Romans 4; Galatians 3:6). In Genesis 15:1–6, God promised Abraham, who was already very old, that he would have an heir and that his descendants would be as numerous as the stars in heaven. "And he had faith in the Lord, and He reckoned it to him as righteousness" (v. 6). Later, in chapter 17:9ff. God established the Covenant of circumcision with Abraham. Paul concluded, therefore, that Abraham was regarded as righteous before God even before he performed the Law of the Covenant, circumcision. Abraham was considered righteous because he had faith. The Hebrew word is *he-min*, "he trusted," which has the same root as "Amen." In spite of all indications to the contrary, Abraham trusted, had faith in God and was convinced that God would do whatever He promised. This same trust, or faith, must permeate the Christian; namely, that Christ is the Redeemer from sin. Then God "will reckon it to him as righteousness" and will justify him. "[Abraham] hoped against hope . . . that is why his faith was 'reckoned to him as righteousness'" (Romans 4:18, 22).

This faith was met by God's grace, and the faith of the Christians in Christ as Redeemer will result in God's grace too. Those who have faith are the children of God, the new Israel under the new Covenant. Through Christ, all powers that might separate humanity from the love of God are removed (Romans 8:38–39). Through Christ, God gave proof of His love and freely granted grace that does not depend on observance of the Law—in fact, would be hampered by it. Thus are the faithful justified and reconciled with God (Philippians 3:14). Death and corruption have no power over them, for Christ lives in them (Galatians 2:20). (Jewish interpretation, among others, holds that God rewarded Abraham for his trust expressed in the commandments he had already fulfilled: leaving his homeland on God's command, offering sacrifices, tithing himself, etc., as found in Genesis 12–14.)

Why was Christ sent, why did Christ undergo his passion? He was sent out of God's free-will grace, and not as reward for any good human deeds. Christ accepted his passion and his death freely in obedience to the will of his Father in Heaven for the salvation of humanity.

Paul and the Jews—Implications

How did Paul feel about the Jews who did not accept his message? God had not rejected His people; to him, they were merely blind. Yet this blindness could be a blessing for the world, to stir the Christian world to live in such a fashion that the Jews would be "jealous" (Romans 11). Israel was the root that sustains the plant. But now the Christians were being called to live in a way that the Jews would wish to emulate.

Commenting on these words, Hans Küng, the German Catholic theologian, writes regarding the Church and the Jews:

> Only one course of action is permitted to the Church on this common journey [with the Jews]—not "tolerating," not "missionizing," not "converting," but only "making Israel jealous" (Romans 11:11). The Church can make Israel jealous of the "salvation" it has received, in order to spur Israel to emulate it. But how? The church, in its whole existence, must be a token of the salvation it has received. In its whole existence, it must bear witness to the messianic fulfillment. In its whole existence it must vie with Israel in addressing itself to a world which has turned its back on God, and in demonstrating to it, with authority and love, the word that has been fulfilled, the righteousness that has been revealed, the mercy that has been accepted, the reign of God which has already begun. Its whole life, lived in a convincing way, would be a call to all men to believe the good news, to experience a change of heart and to unite themselves with its Messiah.
>
> This is how Israel and the Church must confront one another, not in theoretical debate, but in existential dialogue; not in an uncommitted battle of words, but in committed competition. By its whole life the Church must witness to the reality of redemption. Is this the case? Is this the witness of the Church? The Jews do not think so. The reality of redemption asserted by the

New Testament seems to them, particularly in the light of the Old Testament, to have been an illusion. (Hans Küng, *The Church*, London: Search Press Ltd., 1967, p. 149.)

Seen in this light, Paul's words about the Jews are, in fact, a challenge to the Church, and reveal how deeply he loved his people. He placed upon his Christians the heavy burden of promoting love and peace in the world with such commitment that the Jews would acknowledge it. In the twentieth century the French bishops, as we shall see, interpreted Paul's statement to mean that both Jews and Christians should become "jealous" of each other, Jews of Christians and Christians of Jews. Out of such a "competition" would come, not only the justification of Christianity in Jewish eyes, but, also the justification of Judaism in Christian eyes, and, above all, the Kingdom of God.

THE SPLIT WIDENS

Though Paul affirmed that a new Covenant had come into being, a new Israel had emerged, he also affirmed that the old Covenant was still in existence, and the promises made by God to the Jews had never been abrogated. The Jews denied the existence of a new Covenant, yet the early church dwelt and grew within the precincts of the Synagogue. In the Roman Empire, adherence to the state religion was required by law, and severe penalties were meted out to atheists. Exempt from this obligation were only the specially recognized, licit religions. Judaism was a licit religion; Christianity, being new, was not, but it could exist within the Synagogue.

Nevertheless, Paul's teachings created tensions. The Jewish leaders could see a danger in it: Jews might break away from Mitzvot, Jewish peoplehood might be weakened. This tension grew with the fall of the Temple in the year 70 C.E. because of the danger to survival in which the Jews found themselves. Barriers had to be established.

A public plea for the destruction of the sectarians, "Birkhat ha-Minim," was either introduced at this time, or at least given emphasis. Jews, who belonged to various sects, including but not exclusively, the Nazarenes, could not respond with "Amen." They were thereby recognized and prohibited from attending synagogue worship.

After the defeat of the Bar Kokhba rebellion, Hadrian proscribed the Jewish religion. Now the Christians, specifically the Gentiles among them, saw the need to distinguish themselves from the Jews: Their religion had nothing to do with Judaism. This may account for anti-Jewish expressions found in the New Testament. The Jews, on their part, discouraged the admission of converts, especially when they found informers among the newcomers. As Christians saw "Birkhat ha-Minim," directed exclusively against themselves, they used it to attack the Jews. Compared with the actions of the Church it was an insignificant, protective measure.

Christian Actions

Soon Christianity greatly surpassed Judaism in number and political power. To those in search of a spiritual religion, both faiths opened a road of salvation. They were competitors. To establish a faith that would unify the populace, Constantine elevated Christianity to the religion of the state. The now Christian state repressed Judaism, and the theologians provided the reasons and justifications for this action. The split was complete.

Claiming to have inherited political power from the pagan world and being the "spiritual Israel," the Church asserted its right to be both the political and spiritual leader. It did not exterminate the Jews because Augustine had taught that the Jews were permitted to survive in order to bear witness to the truth of Christianity. This meant, however, that they had to live in abject decrepitude and universal contempt. The Christian state did its utmost to keep them in this condition. Church Fathers preached hatred and contempt for the Jews and the monks spread it. Church councils and the emperors of the East Roman (Byzantine) Empire, using the most insulting language, enacted severe anti-Jewish degrees. The Jews were a "pernicious," "despicable" sect that met in "sacrilegious assemblies." Christians were to be excommunicated if they rested on the Sabbath, even if they observed Sunday as the day of rest. To make certain that Easter did not coincide with Passover, its date was changed. At the same time the rabbis were forbidden to proclaim the day of the New Moon and to send messengers to the Diaspora to inform them of the decision. The Patriarch Hillel II therefore created a fixed calendar (358) that has been followed by the Jews ever since. Palestine, where Christ had lived and undergone his passion, was claimed as a treasured possession of the Church. Christians were settled there; churches were erected. The prohibition against Jews to enter Jerusalem was renewed.

In Palestine and in Diaspora lands, Jews were from time to time attacked by armed bands inspired by Church leaders. Synagogues were razed, which was against the law of the state but the emperors had no power in this matter. When a mob, inflamed by their bishop, destroyed the synagogue of a city in Mesopotamia, the emperor Theodosius I commanded the bishop to rebuild it. At that moment Ambrosius, the bishop of Milan, forced the emperor to publicly withdraw this order. The Jews were forbidden to build new synagogues. Finally the Patriarchate was abolished by the state and the donations of Diaspora Jewry for its upkeep had from now on to be paid to the state treasury. The work on the Palestinian Talmud came to an end. The teaching of contempt against the Jews, extending over the centuries, implanted a hatred of the Jews in the minds of Christians, that must be regarded as a contributing factor to the Holocaust.

Jewish Reactions

Out of their experience of increasing oppression, the Jews came to cling with ever greater tenacity to their ancient conviction that the Messiah had not yet come. Had he come, there would be no more oppression and persecution. In affirmation of their will to survive, for their own sake and for the sake of the world and the coming of the Messiah, they held on to the laws of Torah with ever greater fervor and in joy of obedience.

As Leo Baeck, rabbi and leader of German Jewry during the time of Hitler, pointed out, the Jews did not see in the Law a burden; they saw in Judaism "the religion of . . . divine law . . . that tells man what God demands of him, granting him the right of determination and decision, demanding of him that he fulfill the will of God" (Leo Baeck, *The Essence of Judaism*, New York: Schocken, 1961; German edition, *Das Wesen des Judentums*, Frankfurt; Kaufmann, 1932, p. 296). This law was received by an act of divine grace. There existed no contradiction between law and grace; both were interwoven.

Differences and Common Values

Hillel had an intellectual opponent whose name was Shammai. Both men headed their own schools in Jerusalem. Hillel was lenient in interpreting and applying the commandments of Torah in the life of the people; Shammai was strict. The rabbis taught that a heavenly voice had instructed them that both opinions were be to be regarded as "the words of the living God." The decision was to follow Hillel because he was kinder to the people. Two opinions can therefore be simultaneously valid. Christianity, however, was influenced to a greater degree by Hellenistic thinking. The Greeks asked for definitions, and nothing could both be and not be at the same time. In this light, the Covenant of Faith and the Covenant of Law could not coexist as equals. Paul had to explain to his Gentile listeners that the new Covenant, the Covenant of Faith, had superseded the Covenant of Law. From this viewpoint, if living under faith was freedom, then living under the Law was being under a yoke. If Christianity was true, then Judaism was no longer true. If Christianity was accepted by God, then Judaism was repudiated. This either/or theology caused and sustained the split to the present; only now is it beginning to heal. Judaism, in contrast, is not bound by the either/or. Christianity as a world religion need not be a theological problem for it.

Modern Jewish theologians have placed Jesus within Judaism and the pharisaic tradition. Martin Buber calls him his brother. The Jews in Jesus' time, except for his close disciples, did not see in him the Messiah, for he had not brought about the predictions of the Jewish Scriptures regarding the time of the Messiah (e.g., Isaiah 11). Jews have firmly held to this conviction. For the Jew, the time of the Messiah is the time when God alone will rule in history and peace and universal love will have filled all of humanity. Additionally, the concept of the incarnation, of God becoming human, was and is contrary to the Jewish concept of God's absolute oneness and absolute transcendence.

With Paul the Church moved out of the confines of Judaism. This has led to two widely divergent forms of monotheism. Jewish monotheism is categorically unitarian; Christian monotheism is trinitarian (Father, Son, and Holy Spirit). Jews did not then and do not now consider themselves forerunners of a new, Christian dispensation. Jewish Scriptures held no hint of such an event; Christianity later read into them predictions of Christ's coming. In consequence, Jews and Christians may at times read the same words of the "Old Testament" and yet understand them differently. (Jews regard the term "Old Testament" as condescending, so some Christians, especially scholars, have replaced it with "Hebrew Scriptures.") Jews have held that the world is not redeemed but, in line with their messianic hope, it is redeemable, and humanity is God's co-worker in this task. Jews have felt that they have an abiding function in the world's redemption under God's plan.

Yet Jews regard Christianity as vital under God's will. This permits the possibility of dialogue—even a mutual covenantal relationship—if each partner sees the worth of the other. Jews believe that by its religious and ethical teachings, Christianity is of paramount importance in God's scheme for humanity's salvation. Maimonides, in the twelfth century, pointed this out. Accusing Jesus, that is Christianity, of causing "Israel to be destroyed by the sword, their remnant to be dispersed and humiliated," he yet affirms, "it is beyond the human mind to fathom the designs of the Creator . . . for Christianity and Islam have served to clear the way for King Messiah, to prepare the whole world to worship God with one accord. . . . Thus the Messianic hope, the Torah, and the commandments have become familiar topics . . . among [the inhabitants of] the far isles and of many peoples, uncircumcised of heart and flesh" (Kings, end of ch. 11). The text is found only in manuscripts that were not censored by Christian authorities who forced its elimination.

The twentieth-century Jewish thinker Franz Rosenzweig regarded Christianity and Judaism as actually dependent on each other. Martin Buber has pointed to the fact that Christian faith—*pistis*—is weighted toward renewal through the rebirth of the individual, whereas Jewish faith—*emunah*—is weighted toward renewal through the rebirth of nations. We may have reservations in regard to this sharp distinction, but we can accept Buber's conclusion that "the two religions may have things to say to each other as yet unsaid, and a help to give to one another whose blessed results cannot even be fully conceived at the present time" (*Two Types of Faith*, New York: Harper & Row, Harper Torch Books, 1961).

Common Values, Experiences, and Challenges

Our time has witnessed the resumption of the dialogue. As Jews and Christians equally draw their spiritual sustenance from the books of the Hebrew Bible, the dialogue can be based on the ideals which Christians and Jews share. Above all, there is the common faith in One God, who is the God of love and mercy. From the oneness of God as the Universal Father emerges the covenant of human fellowship. The two basic commandments of Torah, love of God and love of fellow human beings, are literally repeated in the New Testament (Deuteronomy 6:5 in Matthew 23:37 and Leviticus 19:18 in Matthew 23:39), thus creating a common obligation.

Both religions have experienced persecution and have produced saints and martyrs by whose example humanity can learn steadfastness in faith. Judaism does not have saints in the manner of the Catholic Church, but it accords this title to those who laid down their lives as martyrs "for the sanctification of God's Name." Jews and Christians have stood the test of defamation, persecution and martyrdom. Jews have borne it for longer periods than any other faith and people. By this experience, both religions can support the faithful of all religions, giving them steadfastness through faith in times of testing, whenever they may come. This was recognized by the Dalai Lama, who has been exiled by the Chinese from his home in Tibet. In 1990 he invited a group of Jewish leaders to his residence in India to learn from them the way of spiritual survival of a people in exile. In turn, these Jews learned much from him and his compassionate spirituality.

Christians have been under the temptation of power. Jews have been its special victims for almost two millennia. They now face a similar temptation in the State of Israel. The challenge for Christians and for Jews lies in the recognition and application of the fact that power may be the enemy of spirituality. Spirituality commands that all human beings be recognized and treated with justice and compassion as all were created in the image of God.

CHAPTER 4

The World of
"Jewish Middle Ages"

FROM THE AGE OF ROME TO THE AGE OF REASON

THE MEDIEVAL WORLD was divided into two religiously oriented spheres of influence. As we have seen, the Roman Empire extended through Western Europe as far as Britain and became Christianized beginning in the fourth century. In the seventh century Islamic influence spread from Arabia eastward to Babylonia and westward across North Africa into Spain. Migrating or being settled within these two spheres, the Jews developed a number of variant customs and practices, including different pronunciations of Hebrew. These differences still exist, though they have not affected Jewish unity.

One group, following the road of the Roman Legions, settled in Italy, France, Germany, Britain, and eventually Eastern Europe. They established great centers of learning, particularly in Germany, and later in Poland and Russia. They are called *Ashkenasim* because it was assumed that the term *Ashkenas* in the Bible (Genesis 10:3) referred to Germany. Their descendants constitute the majority of present-day Jewry.

The other group had settled in North Africa and Spain, and came under the rule of the expanding Islamic empire. In Spain it established a center of Jewish learning and a flourishing Jewish culture. This group is called *Sefardim*, the word *Sefarad* in the Bible being interpreted as referring to Spain. The Sefardic pronunciation of Hebrew has been adopted as the official one in the State of Israel and, as a result, will probably become universal among Jewry.

We shall return to these two groups in more detail after considering the relationship between Judaism and Islam.

The Impact of Islam

Islam, which means "submission" to God, emerged in the seventh century C.E. Its founder was MOHAMMED (c. 570–632 C.E.), one of the great ethical and religious personalities of history. He pondered deeply the lack of true religion and

54

morality he perceived among his people and felt the need to establish a new life for them on new religious foundations.

Mohammed was born in Mecca, in what is now Saudi Arabia, on the crossroads of trade between East and West. He had contact with both Jews and Christians and learned from them. Mohammed was also a visionary and a mystic. While contemplating in solitude, he received a revelation. God, through the angel Gabriel, appointed him to be His prophet. From then on, divine revelation was granted him over a long period of time, and the message he received, as dictated by Mohammed to a faithful disciple, became the *Quran*, the Book of Recitation. To this day, the Quran is recited in the form of a recitative, and faithful Muslims learn large portions of it by heart.

Immediately after his initial revelation, Mohammed began his ministry among the people of Mecca. But they did not listen to him; they jeered and persecuted him. He therefore decided to emigrate to the city of Medina. This migration, called *Hejra*, occurred in 622 C.E. and marks the first year in the Islamic calendar. In Medina Mohammed succeeded. He established himself as master of a large following, allowing him to create a military strike force. Persuasion was reinforced by military action; opponents were crushed. Eventually, Mohammed returned to Mecca, establishing it as the center of the new faith he had created.

Mohammed acknowledged his debt to Judaism and Christianity, both of which he regarded as genuine revelations of God, but for their own time. Both Jews and Christians had corrupted the will of God by their interpretation, and therefore, God had sent Mohammed to teach the true faith and set it down in the Quran as the final and unchangeable revelation, never to be surpassed. The fact that the Quran was revealed in Arabic was a sign that God's favor now rested on the Arabs. The faithful were instructed to spread the faith and to establish—even by means of war—an empire in which religion, political power, and society formed one indissoluble union.

As the Quran, its principles and laws, is the final and ultimate word of God, Islamic faith is not open to evolution in a measure similar to Judaism and Christianity. The "Oral Torah" reveals the continuing evolution of Judaism, and the councils and reformers that of Christianity (see Deuteronomy 17:8–11; Matthew 16:19). In Islam the Quran is final. The primary additional source of authoritative teaching outside the Quran is *Hadith*, the utterances and practices of Mohammed in his everyday life, as verified by authoritative tradition.

When Mohammed appeared on the scene of history, the Jews constituted a fully integrated community on the Arabian peninsula. Their style of life was the same as that of their neighbors (e.g., they may have introduced the cultivation of the date palm into Arabia); only their faith distinguished them from the rest of the population. Known as "the people of the book," the Jews were admired by their neighbors for their religious steadfastness.

Seeing himself as a new prophet, Mohammed expected to bring both Christians and Jews into his faith. He was convinced that the Jews would accept his teachings, especially as Arabs considered the Jews a kindred people; the belief had developed that the Arabs were the descendants of Ishmael, while the Jews were the descendants of Isaac, and both were sons of Abraham (Genesis 16, 21).

In his teachings Mohammed proclaimed many thoughts akin to Jewish and Christian principles of faith. Like Judaism (in contrast to trinitarian Christian monotheism), Islam affirmed an absolutely unitarian monotheism. Mohammed preached unity.

"O men, see, We [God] created you from one man and one woman, in order that you may know each other . . . . He who is greatest in reverence of God is the most honored of Allah [God] in your midst" (Quran, Sura [chapter] 49, entitled "The Chambers," verse 13).

He emphasized the link between the faiths.

"Speak you: We believe in Allah and His message to us, as He sent it to Abraham and Ishmael and Isaac and Jacob and the tribes, and as it was given to Moses and Jesus, and as it was given to the prophets from their Lord: We make no distinction among them" (2:136).

He proclaimed that Jews and Christians need not be afraid on the Day of judgment.

"The possessors of Scripture shall have nothing to fear on the Day of judgment" (2:59).

He declared the food of Jews to be lawful for Muslims, as both observe dietary laws. He permitted Muslim men to marry Jewish or Christian women (5). (However, a non-Muslim was not to marry a Muslim woman, for he would thereby attain dominance over her.) Converts were not to be won by force (2:257). In a Hadith we find Mohammed stating that he himself will speak up against those that unduly wrong the Jews or Christians and burden them (Balduri 162; Abbu Yussuf 71).

Mohammed's hopes of winning the Jews to his new faith were not to be realized. To his chagrin, the Jews steadfastly refused to give up their religion, in spite of the fact that Mohammed had incorporated many Jewish ideas and laws into the Quran. Consequently, he turned against them with great vigor, and proclaimed that both Jews and Christians would be severely judged and condemned on the Day of judgment (3:79).

We therefore find in the Quran an ambivalence in regard to both Jews and Christians. On the one hand it praises them for their adherence to the One God and His Scriptures, and, on the other hand, it rebukes them for their unwillingness to accept Islam as the final and highest divine revelation, in which the messages of Moses and Jesus were both contained and transcended. Abraham became for Mohammed "not a Jew nor a Christian but a Muslim" (Sura 3), a man "submissive to God."

Because Mohammed found the Jews actively hostile, his judgment of Judaism became harsher than his position on Christianity. To break their active resistance to his teachings he took action against them that resulted in massacres. Since

Mohammed regarded it as essential that Arabia and the Arabian people be united under one faith, the remainder of the Jews were expelled. Many went to Palestine. To this day Jews are not permitted to enter Saudi Arabia, even as visitors.

Originally, Mohammed had planned to make Jerusalem the center of his new faith as a symbol of the continuity-in-evolution with Judaism. When the Jews rejected Islam, Mohammed decided to emphasize the break between the religions and chose Mecca as the permanent center of Islam. He also chose Friday as the day of rest, in contrast to the Jewish Saturday and Christian Sunday.

The Struggle for Succession: Sunnites and Shi'ites

After Mohammed's death, a power struggle for the succession ensued that was to have religious significance. *The Sunnites,* "orthodox" Muslims, held that the Caliph, the "Successor" to Mohammed, should be elected by the community of the faithful. (The Sunnites were grounded in the principle of community consensus.) The choice fell on Abu Bakr, Mohammed's beloved friend and father-in-law. Another group insisted that the succession, the caliphate, should remain among Mohammed's descendants and, since the prophet had no sons, should go to his son-in-law Ali. They formed "Shi'a," "the party" of Ali, and have come to be known as Shi'ites. *The Shi'ites* rejected the principle of community consensus, and adopted the doctrine that in every age there was an infallible man, *Iman,* to whom God had entrusted the guidance of His servants. Divinely ordained as ruler and teacher, he had superhuman qualities granted him by God. The faithful had to believe in the Imans of all times but especially the one of their own.

The Shi'ites had a strong appeal to the non-Arab population in conquered countries, especially soldiers who fought in the Arab armies but retained an inferior status and received lower pay. These peoples had a higher culture, had taught the Arabs arts and skills, outnumbered the Arabs in towns and settlements, but suffered grave economic disabilities and were forbidden to marry Arab women. They longed for social justice. The Shi'ite movement, perhaps partly in response to their protests, developed a messianic character, a descendant of Ali would emerge and restore justice. He would usher in a time of everlasting peace.

The Shi'ites became dominant in Iran, Iraq and Pakistan; the rest of the Muslim world generally belongs to the Sunnites. The doctrines of these religious groups within Islam have had a powerful impact on the contemporary world.

The Expansion of Islam and the Position of the Jews

Moved by the divine imperative to spread the faith of Islam, Muslims created an empire over the next hundred years that extended from Spain to India. In this empire members of other religions were tolerated but never given equal rights as citizens. Rulers of the Islamic empire had to deal with numerous religious minorities (Christians had only one religious minority in their midst; namely, the Jews). Muslim rulers had to be deliberate in the treatment of these groups (Christians had free reign). The Jews in this ever-expanding sphere of

Islam were permitted to remain and hold their possessions, but merely as *dhimmi,* "protected people." They had to pay a poll tax and were subjected to restrictions. At times they were not permitted to ride on a horse because that would elevate them over Muslim pedestrians, and they could not bear arms. Jews were not permitted in the Islamic heartland of Arabia.

There were fewer theological conflicts between Muslims and Jews than between Christians and Jews. Both Islam and Judaism were strict unitarians, Christians were trinitarians. Both Judaism and Islam rested on law and its performance in life, whereas Christianity had abolished the law and was rooted in faith. Muslims could not accuse the Jews of deicide (murder of God), as Christ was not divine in Islamic tradition. The Talmud, completed before the Islam arose, was not considered a slanderous work against its faith as it was by the Christians.

The religious-political struggles within Islam resulted, beginning in 750, with the formation of a great empire centering in Iraq, whose Califs were more interested in their own aggrandizement than in being protectors of the faith. A court was formed that is mirrored in *The Arabian Nights.* Trade and commerce, science, art, and philosophy flourished. The Jewish internal autonomy, the Gaonate and its great yeshivot, were left untouched. Jews were permitted to settle once again in Jerusalem.

Baghdad in the ninth and tenth centuries was not merely a city of splendor, it was also a center of philosophy. Here Jewish, Christian, and Islamic thinkers exchanged philosophical ideas. Through their knowledge of Greek, Jews had been exposed to Greek philosophy and transmitted it to the Arabs. Jewish, Islamic, and Christian revelation had to be philosophically defended against Aristotle's thought and logical arguments and against each other. Arabic became the common language of the Jews and Jewish thinkers, such as Saadia and Maimonides, wrote their philosophical works in Arabic. Within a century the empire dissolved, and a great number of individual principalities took its place. The fate of the Jews therefore depended on the individual rulers.

Muslims were engaged in trade and therefore found the Jews, who were doing the same, valuable contributors to the wealth of society. For this reason Jews settled in large masses in the cities at the crossroads of trade, such as Baghdad and Kairouan.

The princes were frequently pragmatic. It was therefore possible for Jews to attain high offices and political leadership in state and society, if the rulers saw a personal gain in availing themselves of their services. Court bankers played a significant role and lived like the aristocracy. But uncertainty and tension never ceased. Frequently the masses reacted with fury against the elevation of the "degraded ones." In 1066 riots broke out in Granada, and the whole congregation was murdered, including its leader, Joseph Hanagid, son of Samuel Hanagid (see "Samuel the Prince" below).

The Shi'ite Caliph of Egypt, Al-Hakim, imposed harsh and degrading laws upon the Jews in 1008 ordaining that "the Jews shall hang from their neck the image of a calf as they did in the desert." (This was the first ordinance that forced Jews to wear a distinguishing mark on their garments.) Other ornaments were forbidden them. The Almohades, "Proclaimers of the Unity of Allah" (twelfth century), imposed such harsh treatments upon the Jews in North Africa and the

Spanish provinces they had taken from the Christians that Jews fled to the Christian part of the land. Others, like Maimonides, had to leave Spain to escape forcible conversion, to which the Jews of Yemen were equally exposed. Maimonides sent them a letter of guidance and comfort,

Islam has witnessed periods of great expansion, power, and wealth alternating with periods of withdrawal and societal stagnation. It saw in victory and success a sign of divine approval, in withdrawal and defeat a sign of divine disfavor and rebuke, a mandate to redress the situation. It reached its highest peak when political greatness led to cultural achievement. Moorish Spain from the tenth to the thirteenth centuries left us magnificent works of art. Generally speaking, the periods when Islamic political success was combined with intellectual and artistic achievements were good times for the Jews. They were valuable partners in an unfolding civilization, while, at the same time, Islamic fundamentalism was tempered by a more universalistic or pragmatic outlook that found room for non-Muslims.

Contemporary Islam and the Jews

Contemporary Islam has been confronted with problems quite similar to those the Jews have faced for centuries. Both, at one time or another, were thrust into the stream of life and thought of the surrounding world. For Islam, this transformation has been recent and traumatic. The same can be said of the Jews, except that the problem of coping with the thought and lifestyle of the world has been age-old. Like Judaism, Islam has today a large and growing diaspora in the West. Like Judaism, Islam has had to meet the challenge of preserving the faith of its adherents within the new environments in which they constitute a minority. In both religions, fundamentalistic movements have called for a return to strictest obedience to the law.

Ideally there could emerge out of the encounter between Islamic tradition and Western values a new and valuable Islam-inspired contribution to the cultures of the West, perhaps a two-way street opened between East and West. This has happened in the historical life of the Jews. Dialogue between the West and Islam needs to be sought. This applies specifically to dialogue between Islam and the Jews. According to tradition, Jews and Arabs share a common ancestry, both their faiths are unitarian, and Jews and Arabs have had to face similar historical problems and can teach each other. Jointly they can become a stronger force of peace than they can be individually. That this may be achieved may perhaps become evident by the example of Jewry in Moorish Spain, which we will discuss in the next section.

THE SEFARDIM

By the time the Muslims conquered Spain, Jews had lived there for centuries. They had gone there as traders. Under Roman rule they were free, prosperous, and respected. Their peaceful life was disrupted by the invasion of Spain by

Germanic peoples—first the Vandals and then the Visigoths, both of whom arrived in the fifth century. The Visigoths eventually became Christians and, with this change, the fate of the Jews turned from prosperity to persecution. But in the eighth century, the Arabs conquered the land, and brought the Jews relief from Christian oppression. They established a glittering civilization centering at Cordova. The royal court became the center of art and thought, and many learned Jews flocked to it.

As we have seen, Jews in the Islamic sphere were theoretically not considered equal to Muslims. In practice the Caliphs of the small Islamic principalities in Spain frequently granted Jews high status, promotions, and power. These rulers were vying with each other for wealth and prestige, and found in Jews personalities capable of raising the power, affluence, and prominence of their states. The Jews were free to participate in the fullness of political, social, cultural, and economic life. Commerce was the source of wealth for the Jews, but they were equally engaged in a great variety of crafts, and, in some regions, in agriculture. Among them were great merchants, shopkeepers, gold and silversmiths, tanners, shoemakers and many others. Medicine attracted many of them. A number of them rose to high office at the court of the Califs, and used their position to safeguard the position of their coreligionists.

Under Islamic rule in Spain the Jews were able to acculturate fully into the civilization in which they lived and, at the same time, retain their identity, develop a flourishing Jewish culture, and produce outstanding thinkers and leaders. The interaction of the two cultures actually enriched Jewish life and thought. Spain became a workshop of positive assimilation. The following brief sketches of some of these personalities offers a glimpse of the conditions of Spanish Jewry and of Jewish reaction to non-Jewish civilization.

Hasdai Ibn Shaprut: Builder of Foundations

The twelfth-century chronicler, Rabbi Abraham ibn Daud, tells us of "four captives," rabbinical emissaries sent from Babylonia who were captured by pirates. Each was ransomed by a different Jewish community, settled there, and developed it into a Torah center independent of Babylonia. One of these rabbis came to Spain. Thus Spain became an autonomous Torah center. It was to thrive due to the generous support Jewish leaders provided for sages, yeshivot, and poets.

The foundations were laid by Hasdai ibn Shaprut (912–975). With him Jewish culture began to flourish in Spain. Serving the Calif at Cordova as royal physician, adviser, and diplomat, he was equally a distinguished Jewish scholar in his own right and a translator from Greek. He had always lived in two cultures, and was concerned that Spanish Jewry had become deeply immersed in general culture but had not yet developed independent centers of Jewish learning from which it could draw its strength. Hasdai used his position and power at court to the benefit of his Jewish community, and his wealth and prestige within it to lay the foundations for a Jewish culture in Spain that was to synthesize Jewish heritage and the intellectual traditions of the Western world.

Hasdai sponsored the founding of yeshivot in Spain and supported them generously. He invited scholars to come to Spain and maintained them. The Babylonian authorities awarded him the title *Resh Kallah*, "Head of the Community"; Ibn Daud called him *Nasi*, the "prince" of the Jews. Thus was ushered in a period in Jewish history, lasting three centuries, which led Spanish Jewry to its greatest heights. The center of Jewish learning shifted from Babylonia to Spain.

At the time as later, the Jews were frequently told mockingly that all their power and independence had forever vanished. Jacob's prophesy, "the scepter shall not depart from Judah, nor the ruler's staff from between his feet" (Genesis 49:10) had been canceled out. No longer was there an independent Jewish state. When Hasdai learned that around 740 the king and the entire nation of the Chazars, a people dwelling on the western shores of the Black Sea, had been converted to Judaism and that this sovereign Jewish state was flourishing, he saw an opportunity to defeat the detractors of Judaism. He hoped to prove that Jewish sovereignty still existed. He sent a letter to the king of the Chazars and eventually received confirmation; it was indeed true. (The Chazars eventually intermarried with the rest of Jewry and disappeared as a distinct group.) Hasdai's discovery was to lead to a great theological work by Judah Halevi, *The Chuzari*, which is discussed below.

Samuel the Prince: Power in Creative Service

The work so auspiciously started by Hasdai was carried forward by Samuel ibn Nagrela. Like his predecessor, he never forgot his duty toward his fellow Jews.

Samuel, born in Cordova in 933, was still living in 1056. He was officially given the title *Nagid*, "Prince of the Jewish community." He acquired great wealth as an overseas trader, and lived in luxury. Some scholars believe that he built the Alhambra at Granada and lived in it. He rose to become the vizier of the Calif of Granada and served his master well. He gave the state an exceptional administration and headed the royal troops victoriously as a general in battle. It was said that he was at home in Greek philosophy and all branches of mathematics, knew everything about geometry and logic, and exceeded astronomers in his knowledge of the skies. Among the Jews he was recognized as an outstanding talmudic scholar. He wrote an introduction to the Talmud, a compendium of law, and interpretations of Scripture stressing that Torah and Mitzvot had to be established ever more firmly. Through correspondence with Jewry all over the world, including the Gaon Hai in Baghdad, he maintained the bond of kinship. Lavish gifts from Samuel went to scholars who needed them in Spain as well as abroad. These gifts permitted them to carry out their work undisturbed. As Samuel showed, it was possible to hold highest office in dedicated citizenship and, at the same time, be a Jew devoted to God–Torah–Mitzvot–People.

As master of his own talmudic academy, Samuel himself trained a generation of leaders to carry on his work. He may be said to have continued Hasdai's principles: Jews should live fully in the world and draw from its attainments. In scathing words he castigated those who wished to show their Jewishness by ostentatiously wearing their *Tzitzit* (fringes, see below) on the outside. He rebuked those who praised God for not having made them a woman, and opposed long Talmud explanations and debates of details because these external forms and behavior did not strengthen Jewish tradition. Torah and the Jewish faith stood above all other wisdom, but the Jew must equally be schooled in the wisdom of the Greeks and the learning of the Arabs.

Samuel felt at home as a Jew in Spain. He was convinced that Jews would never lose their identity as long as they followed his principles. Centuries later Western European Jewry, including Neo-Orthodoxy, was to adopt the same guidelines. Eastern European Jewry rejected them.

Solomon Ibn Gabirol: Philosopher and Poet

Among Samuel's friends was the poet and philosopher Solomon Ibn Gabirol (1021–1069). Like the poets of his society, he could sing of wine and joy, but he also wrote majestic liturgical poems which have graced the worship of the synagogue. Gabirol was also versed in general philosophy and wrote a philosophical work, *The Fountain of Life,* in which he saw all the world emanating from God (similar to the neo-Platonic view). The work was translated into Latin; so was the name of the author, from Gabirol to Avicebron. Up to the nineteenth century, the work was regarded as the writing of a non-Jewish scholar. Spanish Jewry had indeed effected a synthesis of general culture and Jewish tradition, of citizenship and deepest Jewish loyalty.

Judah Halevi: Philosopher, Singer of Zion, Pilgrim

Judah Halevi (1080–1140) was a tender soul. Born in Toledo, he was attracted to medicine, as so many Jews have been drawn to this profession which, in its entirety, is true Mitzvah, the healing of God's children. Eventually, he moved to Cordova. His life reveals a spiritual evolution. As a young man he may have devoted himself to Judaism and worldly culture in equal measure, but as he grew older Judaism gained priority in his thought and life, and in old age he came to negate diaspora living and migrated to the Holy Land.

He was a man of great charm, a poet who, in his youth, sang of spring and beautiful women. Growing older he found his true subject in his love for his people and his yearning for the Land of Israel:

Zion, wilt thou not ask if peace's wing
shadows the captives that ensue thy peace . . . ?
Lo, west and east and north and south—worldwide
all those from far and near, without surcease
salute thee, Peace and peace from every side.

To weep thy woe my cry is waxen strong,
but dreaming of thine own restored anew,
I am the harp to sound for thee thy song.
Thy God desired thee for a dwelling place

and happy is the man whom He shall choose,
and draw him nigh to rest within thy space.

Here was the call of the Land, with its power to form the spirit of its people—if not as a reality, then as hope and aspiration. Diaspora, even under the best of conditions, was exile. In old age, Halevi left the comforts of his home to make his pilgrimage to the Holy Land. Legend has it that he sank into the dust in adoration at the sight of the city of Jerusalem and a Bedouin galloping by crushed him under his horse's hoofs.

Halevi was also a philosopher and used his knowledge in defense of Judaism and the Jewish people. Taking the story of the Chazars as a framework for his discussion of Judaism, he wrote *The Chuzari—An Apology for a Despised Religion.* He related that the king of the Chazars, unhappy with his heathen religion, called in three sages, a Muslim, a Christian, and a Jew. The Jew convinced him of the value of Judaism, which offered Halevi the opportunity to expound the ideas of Judaism. The Jews are indeed God's chosen people, but chosen to serve humanity. They are the heart of humanity, beating for humanity as the heart beats within the body, according to the body's needs, suffering for it, and indispensable to it. Torah and Mitzvot are explained and the kinship of the people is strongly emphasized. To this sense of kinship Halevi—in poetry, life, and death—adds the Land of Israel as the force which, under God, has maintained the Jew as a guiding light and suffering servant of all humanity. (See also Chapter 15.)

Moses Maimonides: Universal Genius

The most famous of all Spanish Jews was Moses Maimonides (1135–1204), a universal genius of whom it has been said that "from Moses (the Master of Sinai) to Moses (Maimonides) there was no man like Moses." In him we see clearly the interplay of internal and external forces that have shaped Judaism and the Jews.

At the time he was born in Cordova, the Jews found themselves oppressed by the fanatic Almohades (see above) and placed before the choice either to accept Islam or to emigrate. For ten years Maimonides's family had to move from country to country, which gave the boy a chance to study under many masters. The Land of Israel drew Maimonides to spend some years there, but finally he settled in Fustat (Cairo), Egypt, where he was to become court physician and head of the Jewish community. In Cordova, city of his birth, a square bears his name, and a statue of recent date honors him; in Acre (Acco), Israel, the gate through which he entered is marked by a plaque. Legend has it that, after his death, his body was placed on a leaderless donkey, to let God, guiding the animal, decide where he should find his rest. The animal deposited the body in the land of Israel. Thus is marked his spiritual pilgrimage through the wisdom of Israel and the world. He became the master of Judaism and one of the world's great philosophers.

Maimonides's first concern was preservation of Torah. In its behalf, he wrote a commentary to Mishnah, synthesizing Jewish thinking and Aristotelian philosophy. His "Eight Chapters" in explanation of the Sayings of the Fathers are still widely studied in popular courses; they fuse Aristotle's ethics with Jewish tradition. Being a systematic thinker, he tried to condense basic Jewish beliefs in a form of creed. Maimonides's creed came under attack immediately after his death. His critics held that Judaism cannot and should not be creedally confined. They maintained that Maimonides had followed Islamic and Christian examples, perhaps in response to the desire by contemporary Jews for a Jewish creed, which they wanted since the other religions had creeds. This may be true. But it also rested on Maimonides's conviction that even the average person, not schooled in philosophy, needs to have an awareness of the essential principles of Judaism. Maimonides's creed is still followed by traditional Jewry. It was later rendered in the form of a poem, "Yigdal," which is widely used as a hymn in public worship.

Maimonides's creed is expressed in thirteen basic beliefs:

1. That God alone is the Creator.
2. That He is absolutely One.
3. That He has no body or bodily shape.
4. That He is the first and the last.
5. That only to Him may we pray and to no other.
6. That the words of the Prophets are true.
7. That the prophecy of Moses is true, and that he is the father of all prophets.
8. That the Torah, now found in our hands, was given to Moses.
9. That this Torah is not subject to change, and that there will never be another Torah from the Creator.
10. That the Creator knows all the thoughts and deeds of man.
11. That He rewards and punishes according to the deed.
12. That the Messiah will come; though he tarry, I will expect him daily.
13. That the dead will be resurrected.

The power of his statement of principles is exemplified by the fact that twentieth-century martyrs of the Warsaw ghetto went to their deaths with a hymn on their lips based on Maimonides's fundamentals of faith, "I believe in the coming of the Messiah. . . . " The eternal validity of Torah was thus impressed once again on the people.

Maimonides's second concern was Mitzvot. He underscored their social significance in addition to their spiritual one. Feeling that the law of the Talmud needed clarification and codification, he wrote a compendium of the entire Oral Torah, called *Mishneh Torah*, which he felt would enable anyone, especially a rabbi, to find authoritative answers quickly. It was a complete digest of Torah and Talmud, systematically arranged and rationally explained. There could be no doubt any more about the importance and practice of Mitzvot. His third work, *The Guide of the Perplexed,* shows the impact of his surroundings and his own conviction that philosophy is necessary to reinforce the faith. It will be discussed in Chapter 15.

Open to all influences, Maimonides built the structure of Jewish life and learning on a synthesis, believing that the inner forces he stressed—God–Torah–Mitzvot–Land—permitted admission of external ones if they can be assimilated. He was convinced that in the contest among Judaism, Christianity, and Islam, Judaism would emerge victorious, since it held the truth and did not, unlike the others, resort to coercion or seduction. He yearned for the coming of the Messiah, a man who had reached the pinnacle of wisdom and therefore become a true prophet.

Maimonides was attacked for his philosophical ideas. Many of the rabbis, exclusively devoted to the study of the Talmud, saw in him too much of a rationalist, standing too much under Aristotle's influence. Others came to his defense. The conflict, already underway at the time of his death, reached vast proportions immediately afterwards. Communities became divided. In scholarly circles, the debate is still going on: Was Maimonides of divided mind, traditionalist as author of Mishneh Torah, "Greek philosopher" as author of the "Guide" or was his work of one cast? Whatever the answer, his influence on Jewish and Christian philosophy—including that of St. Thomas Aquinas—has been profound.

There were other great minds, exegetes, poets, world travelers, and mystics who reached out to the divine beyond. The few we have mentioned offer a picture of the greatness that was Spanish Jewry's and its attempt to synthesize Jewish and worldly wisdom and to forge a distinct identity within Spanish culture.

Christian Conquest: the Inquisition

As Christians pushed slowly forward, dislodging the Moors, Spanish Jewry deteriorated. At first, Jews still served as royal counselors in the newly established Christian kingdoms, but the task of protecting their brothers and sisters became harder and harder. In 1233, the Inquisition was introduced in Aragon, directed by the newly created order of Dominicans. Officially it was subject to the pope's orders and supervision, but it acted independently of them and with excessive harshness.

In 1263, the leading rabbi of the time, MOSES NAHMANIDES, was compelled to engage, in the presence of king and court at Barcelona, in public disputation on the question "Has the Messiah come, or has he not yet come?" His opponent was the Dominican friar Pablo, a converted Jew. The argument was to be based on Scripture. Nahmanides demanded and obtained the right to free expression of his thoughts. He spoke without restraint and received a gift from the king. It was an expression of royal appreciation for his courageous and compelling defense of Judaism. But he knew that he was no longer safe in his beloved Spain, so he settled in Palestine. At a later disputation at Tortosa (1413–1414), the Jewish representatives knew that they could not be permitted to prevail; the cards were stacked against them. They even pleaded with their opponents to stop the event, from which they foresaw only evil for the Jewish people, but this was not permitted.

Expulsion from Spain—The Marranos

Coercion and seduction toward conversion grew with the years. Jews had to listen to Christian sermons even in their own synagogues, popular opinion turned against them, and the rabble rose. After combining the kingdoms of Castille and Aragon by their marriage, King Ferdinand and Queen Isabella expelled the last of the Moors from their united territory. In 1492 they decreed the expulsion of the last remnant of infidels in Spain, the Jews. The pleas of the Jews and their offer of a substantial monetary gift, were drowned out by the voice of the unbendingly hateful Grand Inquisitor Torquemada. In rickety ships they set out searching for new homes. (Estimates of the number expelled range from 100,000 to 800,000; the most generally accepted number is about 250,000.)

Only converts could remain; many Jews accepted Christianity as a veneer, practicing their faith in secret. This was extremely dangerous, for to have once accepted Christianity and turned from it was apostasy. On the slightest suspicion, the Inquisition would swoop down on those suspected of being secret Jews, extracted confessions through torture, and had them burned at the stake.

The people generally distrusted the converts, calling them *marranos,* "swine." Surviving in spite of it all, some of the descendants of the marranos in Spain reemerged openly as Jews only in the twentieth century. It has been claimed that even Columbus may have been a marrano, though the proofs are inconclusive. In any case, he speaks in his diaries with great compassion of the departing Jews, whose crammed boats he passed on his way toward a new world. His expedition left at the same time as the Jews, possibly because Columbus had Jews among his crew who had to get out of Spain.

A number of fugitive Jews went to Portugal by invitation of King Manuel, who recognized the benefits they could offer the country. In 1497 the king wished to marry a daughter of Ferdinand and Isabella, who insisted that there be no Jews in his country. Not wishing to lose the benefits of the Jews, the king had them converted by force. The exiled Jews eventually settled in Holland, Turkey, North Africa and other countries, all of which profited from their abilities. Some groups went to Palestine, others to the colonies of the new world.

Contemporary Spain

This was the end of Spanish Jewry, but the Spanish government today favors the return of the Sefardim, once Spanish citizens. They may claim their citizenship rights. Jewish congregations have been officially recognized ever since the days of the Spanish Republic. In the spirit of Vatican II, Spanish Jews have even engaged in some early stages of dialogue with the Church. The edict of 1492, which expelled the Jews and prohibited them from ever settling in Spain was officially revoked about 500 years after it was issued. The solemn service in the synagogue of Madrid, commemorating the 500th anniversary of the expulsion, was attended by the President of Israel and the King and Queen of Spain.

Unity through Law: Joseph Karo

Seeing the distress of a dispersed and persecuted Jewish community, a leading rabbi in Palestine established a central rabbinical body there, a Sanhedrin, to unite the people around Torah and Land. He failed, but one of his disciples, Joseph Karo (1488–1575), succeeded in a different way.

JOSEPH KARO, born in Spain, had experienced the expulsion of Spanish Jewry as a child. He grew up in Turkey where he eventually established a reputation as a talmudic scholar and attracted many disciples. Karo was also a mystic. The Mishnah became for him a person, speaking to him and guiding his daily actions. An "angelic mentor" made him settle in the Holy Land. Guided by this angelic mentor, he realized that Mitzvot were the unifying bond of the widely dispersed Jewish people. He wrote a code, the *Shulhan Arukh*, "The Well Prepared Table," outlining in detail all the minutiae of Jewish law. After MOSES ISSERLES (1530–1572) made additions and adjustments to Ashkenasic usage, it became and has remained the code of traditional Jewry.

THE ASHKENASIM

In the destiny of Ashkenasic Jewry we see the struggles and conflicts of kings and popes, of nationalism against the universal Church, of Renaissance, Reformation, and Enlightenment, of social unrest and political revolution.

Medieval Society: Its Spirit and the Jews

The destiny of the Jews in Northern Europe, the Ashkenasim, can be fully understood only against the background of medieval society as a whole. For the Jews, most of it was a time of great hardship. While we may speak of the Middle Ages as beginning with the collapse of the Roman Empire and ending with the Renaissance of the fifteenth and sixteenth centuries, Jewish condition in Western Europe remained "medieval" until the eighteenth century, the Age of the Enlightenment. In the East some conditions bore medieval character well into the twentieth century. "Jewish Middle Ages" is therefore not identical with the Middle Ages as commonly understood.

At the beginning of the Christian era, Rome held vast areas in Northern Europe, as far as Britain. It is possible that Jews reached Northern Europe either as Roman legionnaires or as providers for the armies. The Germanic warrior peoples, who worshiped heroism and heroic gods and were filled with strong tribal allegiances, chafed under the overlordship of Rome. They sought independence and, at the same time, were attracted to the south by its climate. As Rome weakened they pushed southward. During the first Christian centuries, the Roman Empire was able to contain the pressure of Nordic nations against its borders. Strong fortifications, from England to the Black Sea, kept the barbarians out. In the fourth century the pressure caused an avalanche. Pushed by the Huns who had come from the Far East, the Germanic tribes were on the move. In the great upheaval, Rome and its civilization collapsed. Up to around 800 C.E., Western Europe dwelt in a twilight zone politically and culturally. Cities disappeared, trade and commerce ceased, nations displaced one another, and warfare was universal.

Christianity made gradual inroads into the chaos; without it there would have been no culture at all. It gave the Nordics a new faith, resting on the suffering Christ and calling for humble submission without being able to eradicate the hero-worship rooted in their past. It proclaimed the universal church, without being able to eradicate their tribal allegiances and nationalism. It tried to fuse both elements. It created national states, such as the Holy Roman Empire of the German Nation, subject to the Pope. It established a Christian knighthood, and it called for crusades. The spirit of nationalism and of heroism were christianized. The Jews became the victims of both. When Europe emerged from these "dark ages" it was Christian except for Spain, which had been conquered and developed by the Moors.

Medieval society had several distinguishing features. It was saturated with Christianity; there was no action, object, or thought of an individual or of society as a whole that was not permeated by the Christian faith and correlated with Christ and salvation. Every person and group was neatly placed in categories according to the scheme of God. Kings were divinely ordained and, under the feudal system, stood at the head of a hierarchy of Christian princes, knights, and nobles; craft guilds were rigidly controlled and peasants remained poor, ignorant, and oppressed. Society was Christian and closed.

Yet the system did not work. The central power was too weak, especially in the Holy Roman Empire; the nationalistic ambitions of emperors and kings clashed with papal claims of superiority over secular rulers; knights fought each other and the kings for tribal allegiance and territorial gain. Consequently, there were incessant wars and endless power struggles.

Medieval people were generally uneducated and their thinking simple. They needed concreteness in every concept and idea, and saw all contrasts in black and white. For this reason the Church appealed to the senses and emotions in order to spread its message throughout this society. Everything in life became a symbol.

Up to the close of the eleventh century, while culture was still plastic, the life of Jews was comparatively undisturbed. The Church taught, then and later, that the Jews had to survive in a state of dejection in order to be witnesses to the Church's victory. Jews were accursed for having crucified Christ, but they would eventually accept Christ. Then, in the end, the curse would be removed from them. It would be removed immediately from any Jew at any time as soon as he or she accepted Christianity. The Jews therefore had a place in the scheme of the

Church. Their oppression was dogmatically founded, and pragmatically desirable to motivate them toward conversion. At the same time they demonstrated to Christians the fate of "the enemies of Christ."

The harsh principles of the Church's teaching were mitigated by the practical necessities of life. Many rulers, both spiritual and temporal, needed an element in society able and dedicated to promote trade and commerce. The nobility regarded engaging in trade as beneath its dignity and had no skill for it, the merchant class was undeveloped, and the peasantry was wholly uneducated. The Jews could read and write and could help their non-Jewish neighbors who lacked these skills. They could promote trade because they had international contacts with their coreligionists, with whom they could also communicate in a common language, Hebrew. Because they were equipped to fill these functions, Jews were frequently invited to settle in a kingdom or community and were even given privileges. Outside the Christian life but related to it, they had a definite place within society. They, in turn, adopted the language and customs of this society and often established friendly relationships with some of their Christian neighbors.

This was to change. The tenor of the times was violent; victims were numerous and varied, but the Jews were always among them. Degradation, sufferings and martyrdom reached peaks during the Crusades, beginning in 1096, the Ordinances of the Lateran Council of 1215, and the "Black Death" of 1349. During the Renaissance, ecclesiastical and temporal authorities felt that contact with Jews might further weaken the fabric of faith already frayed by Humanism and the Reformation.

It is remarkable that, in spite of these conditions, relationships between Christians and Jews were often friendly, and cultural ties of mutual influence existed.

The Fate of the Ashkenasic Jews

The first documentary proof of an established Jewish community, Cologne, goes back to 321 C.E. By the time of their extermination by the Germans under Hitler's rule, the Jews had lived in Germany longer than any other ethnic group. They presented to the German people an opportunity to establish a true spirit of justice, for these Jews demanded but one thing: to be permitted to live as human beings in the full expression of their religious tradition. That Germany failed to live up to this ethical challenge is one of its greatest tragedies.

In the beginning the Jews were treated well. When Charlemagne consolidated his empire (800–814), he treated them kindly. We find a Jew named Isaac among the delegation the emperor sent to Harun al-Rashid, the Calif of Baghdad. Isaac, the only one to return, having survived the rigors of the journey, brought back an elephant as a gift from the Calif to Charlemagne. The animal, previously unknown in Germany, created a sensation. A Jewish family in southern France that had allied itself with Charlemagne in his military action against Spain and rendered significant military assistance was knighted by the emperor and awarded a principality of its own. At that time the Jews were welcome in Germany, where they served as merchants, providing the link between the farmers and the nobility. This position they also held in other countries. Permitted to own real estate, they established stately homes when their means permitted it.

The famous Kalonymus family, from which great scholars, poets, mystics, and saints were to emerge, moved from Lucca (in Italy) to Mainz (probably between 917 and 990). The family was given permanent residence at Mainz and many privileges by the Emperor Otto II. A German chronicle relates that in a battle between the Emperor Otto II and the Saracenes in 982, the Jew Kalonymus of Lucca had saved the emperor's life and freedom by giving him his own battle horse, after the emperor's had been shot. The privileges given the family were the expression of the Emperor's gratitude.

From Mainz they settled in Worms, no later than 970. A letter of privileges, granted by Emperor Henry IV (1074) is addressed to the "Jews and the other citizens of Worms." Henry renewed their charter in 1090, only six years before the massacre of the Crusades. The bishop of Speyer expressed his satisfaction at having persuaded a group of Jews to move from Mainz to a suburb he had placed at their disposal. He felt they would benefit the city (1084). They were admitted to numerous other cities, but these three are important. These Rhenish cities of Speyer, Worms, Mainz, mother cities of Jewry, became the centers of Jewish learning.

During these centuries the relationships between the Jews and their Christian neighbors were generally good, although occasional excesses against them occurred. This was to change. A call for stricter enforcement of Church law and for a tightening of discipline emerged from a monastic order at Cluny, France (910). It led to the decline of Jewish status.

The *Crusades* marked a radical turning point in the fate of Jews in Germany and France. Thereafter they were oppressed. By the end of the eleventh century the infidel Turks were firmly in possession of the holy places of Christianity in Palestine. The Church called for an armed reconquest of the Holy Land under the sign of the cross. In this manner it hoped to harness the knights' love of war and heroism to Christian faith and obedience. The Church considered itself strong enough to assure them success.

In 1096, as the First Crusade began, religious fervor and emotions rose to fever pitch. Overheated imagination endowed the "enemies of Christ" with devilish traits—they had to be defeated. As a result the Jews became martyrs. They were the infidels within Christian lands, demons, the brood of Satan, an accursed race. Fiery sermons were preached against them from the pulpits of churches and cathedrals, and it was foretold by theologians that the person of the Antichrist would emerge from their midst. Many crusaders felt that, before going to the Holy Land to free it from the infidels, they might as well start with those who lived among them, the Jews. This also promised rich loot. The Jews of Mainz fought valiantly, but were overcome by the hordes. The Jews of Speyer and Worms were attacked while in prayer. Thousands of Jews immolated themselves and their children rather than accept baptism. All preferred to die rather than give up their faith.

The Second Crusade (1146) again claimed Jewish martyrs. In fiery appeals, Bernard of Clairveaux called the masses to join it. At the same time he sternly forbade Christians to attack, kill, or expel Jews. He made it clear that anyone who harmed a Jew was violating the body of Christ himself. But his words were not heeded.

This crusade also marked an economic turning point for the Jews. Christian merchants had long been jealous of Jewish trade both at home and worldwide. In the first crusade the Christians had taken Jerusalem, and wiped out the bulk of the Jewish people in Palestine. This victory of the crusaders convinced Christian merchants that the trade roads to the East would henceforth be firmly in Christian hands. It was the beginning of pushing the Jews out of all spheres of trade, finally permitting them only to lend money.

The lives of Jews became even more precarious with the decrees of the *Lateran Council* of 1215. Pope Innocent III, who saw himself as supreme head and arbiter of all Christianity, determined to plunge the Jews into shame, degradation, and despondency. As an accursed race, they had to place on their breasts the yellow badge of outcasts. As the devil's brood they had to wear on their heads a cone-shaped hat symbolizing the horn of the devil. This made them easy prey for tormentors. Seclusion and persecution were officially ordered.

Emperors and kings considered the Jews their personal property and forced them to engage in money lending. The Cluniac Reforms of 910 included a strong prohibition against Christians engaging in money trade. The Jews were therefore pressed into it, and increasingly excluded from other occupations. As money lenders, the Jews served the rulers as "sponges to be squeezed out." They might enrich themselves for a while; then their goods were expropriated. A ruler might give the Jews of a town as a "gift" to a vassal or a community, which meant that the Jews' belongings were surrendered to the receiver. They might even be driven out, naturally leaving everything behind. Or the debts that Christians owed them might be canceled by order of the ruler. As Christian businessmen gradually acquired the skill to engage in all branches of trade, they insisted that Jews be pushed out of them.

Forced to borrow from the Jews, and at high rates, the population naturally developed a deep animosity for them, often attacking them in mobs or expelling them. The rates were high because the risks were great. Funds had to be available for unexpected demands, and the rulers did not care how the Jews accomplished this, they merely insisted on having funds in full and immediately. Eventually, Christian bankers in many lands, among them the Fuggers in Augsburg, Germany and the Medici in Florence, Italy, began to ignore the prohibitions of the Church and set up money lending on a grand scale, taking even higher rates of interest. When Christian communities found out that they had been better off with the Jews, they invited those they had driven away to come back and settle, for a while. It was a sad merry-go-round. Eventually, the bankers succeeded in pushing the Jews out. They were permitted money lending only on the lowest level, or trade in old clothes; this was all that was left to them. The craft guilds, being Christian in character, never accepted them, which prevented them from pursuing crafts. Agriculture, once their main occupation, was closed to them. When they were no longer useful as money lenders, they were expelled from the country altogether.

The Jews learned to know the precariousness of worldly possessions. Every child from earliest youth had to recite: "The Torah [and the Torah alone] is the [assured] heritage of the congregation of Jacob" (Deuteronomy 33:4). Nothing else was secure. Such conditions knitted the Jews closely together. Wealthy Jews one day might be homeless fugitives the next; thus they would give hospitality to any Jew who knocked at their door.

Vicious slanders were spread about the Jews. One of the worst was the accusation that they were using the blood of Christian children for the Passover service. A similar accusation had been leveled against the early Christians by those who did not understand the character of the Mass, the transubstantiation of the wine into the blood of Christ (Christians had been accused of killing heathens to obtain their blood for communion). Now Christians used against the Jews the very slander from which they themselves had suffered so much. The popes raised their voices to proclaim the falseness of this accusation, and to prohibit it, but the mob would not listen. Jews were also accused of desecrating the sacred host, thus attacking Christ. It did not matter that the Jews did not believe in transubstantiation and the sanctity of the host, and that such a desecration, which implied acknowledgement of this sanctity, would be meaningless and never occur to them. The slander persisted and claimed its victims.

England, France, and Germany

Among the places where the accusation of using Christian blood in the Passover service was used to incite the population was Lincoln, England (1255). The relationship of king and people to the Jews became so hostile that in 1290, only a few years after the incident, the Jews were expelled from the country altogether.

It is not surprising that there were Jews who escaped by becoming Christians; in fact, it is remarkable that there were so few of them. Some of these converts, in order to justify their actions, now became rabid Jew-haters and ardent missionaries among Jews. Realizing that Torah was the source from which Jews renewed their strength, they vented their hatred against it (not against the Scriptures, which were shared by Christians, but against Oral Torah, the Talmud). The Talmud was accused of containing anti-Christian statements. One such accusation led to the public burning of carloads of precious manuscripts in Paris (ca. 1242). Singled out by this public condemnation of their holiest treasures and branded as bearers of a hostile outlook based on subversive teachings, the Jews came to be regarded by the people not only as anti-Christian but as enemies of the emerging nationalism. They were religious and national subverters of society.

As people in France rose against the burdens of taxation (induced, they felt, by Jewish money lenders with their alien spirit), the king appeased them by expelling the Jews from French soil (1394). Only in the papal province of Avignon were they permitted to remain. Expelled Jews sought homes in Germany and Poland.

A few years before the Jews' expulsion from France, a terrible fate befell the people of Europe. In 1349, the *Black Death,* bubonic plague caused by rats brought in by ships trading with the Orient, swept over Europe, leaving death and destruction in its wake. It roused the emotions of the masses to violence. The Jews became the scapegoats. They were accused of having poisoned the wells, and were brutally massacred throughout the land. Many of them left Germany forever to find a new haven in hospitable Poland, which needed their skills. This was the beginning of large-scale settlement there. They did not know how short-lived their peace was to be.

Some Jews remained in Germany, however. This was both possible and necessary. It was possible because "The Holy Roman Empire of the German Nation" was regarded as the continuation of the Roman Empire. In it the Jews had been citizens. They could therefore claim to have remained citizens. The claim was submerged but somehow kept awake in the minds of rulers and occasionally used by the Jews themselves. It was necessary because the Jews, being regarded as the personal property of the Emperor, were needed as an ever-ready and cheap source of money. It could be tapped whenever a ruler stood in need of it, which was most of the time. In 1356, the "Golden Bull" established the election procedures for the imperial office. Seven electors (the highest dignitaries of the Empire, both spiritual and temporal lords) had the right to elect the emperor. In this bull, the Jews residing in the territories of the electors were turned over to the electors as their "property" with full rights of exploitation.

After the Black Death, Jews were accepted back because it was lucrative to do so. For permission to live in a territory or city each Jew had to acquire and annually renew a Letter of Protection, which was very costly. Exorbitant taxes, both regular and special, were imposed on them. The congregation as a whole was responsible for their collection. From now on they also had to dwell within a separate district, a few small streets, entered through gates that were closed at night, the *ghetto*. Since this ghetto could not be enlarged with the growing population, story had to be built upon story in crowded quarters. Eventually the very light of the sun was practically excluded. The Jews' contact with nature had long been cut off.

Masters of the Ashkenasic Community

Like Sefardic Jewry, the Ashkenasim produced great masters. A few of them shall be discussed briefly because they are of abiding importance.

The work of the German masters reflects a concern with Jewish survival which was different from that of the Spanish masters. In Spain the Jews lived under conditions of freedom within the culture of their environment. In Germany they existed under conditions of ever-increasing segregation, isolation, and pressure toward conversion. Great inner strength was required to withstand the indignities imposed upon them. The Jewish community had to strengthen its conviction that it was the congregation of the Covenant and had to deepen its solidarity. Deeper immersion in Torah and Mitzvot were the answer. Philosophy was not part of the endeavor, not because Jews were isolated from the rest of the cultural world, but because they *wished* to remain isolated from its stream and influences. For this reason the outlook and work of the Ashkenasim differ from those of Spanish Jewry.

Synagogue at Worms, Germany, interior, originally built in 1034, destroyed by the Nazis in 1942 and reconstructed. Note the Bimah in the center of the room, the Ark and curtain on which the seven-branched Menorah is embroidered (of recent date), the candles of the Hanukkah candelabrum, the eternal light over the Ark. Some of the great Ashkenasic masters mentioned in this chapter prayed here. (Photo by the author.)

Each of the masters whom we shall mention may be regarded as a representative of the various facets in the total effort to arm Jewry against the forces of adversity and disintegration. Their common aim was to strengthen within it the awareness of being the Sons and Daughters of the Covenant. Under the leadership of these personalities, their disciples, and academies, the cities of Speyer, Worms, and Mainz now became the core of Talmud study and authoritative decisions for Western Jewry. The names of these three cities were abbreviated "Sh-U-M" to signify the unity of the three cities as teaching centers. Up to now the Gaonim and Yeshivot in Babylonia had been the arbiters of Jewish law for the Jews throughout the world. Their replacement for Western Jewry was a radically innovative step.

Rabbenu Gershom ben Judah: Master Mind and Legislator

Rabbenu "our Rabbi" Gershom ben Judah (960?–1028 C.E.), was head of the Academy of Mainz. With him, the center of Jewish learning came into being. So great was his prestige that he became known as the "Light of the Diaspora," and so great was the prestige of his school that its ordinances were accepted as binding by all of Western Jewry. He prohibited polygamy, a practice that had long been discarded by Western Jews but had not been outlawed by Torah. He ordained that no woman could be divorced against her will. This prohibition is not found in Torah. He was concerned that ethics be ever deeper rooted in the Jewish community. He decreed that no one could read a letter not addressed to him, even if the letter was open. A businessman was forbidden to lure away a customer from his competitor. Other ordinances dealt with the relationships of creditor and debtor. Rabbenu Gershom was aware of the trials of his community. A Jew who had taken baptism under pressure and then returned to his Jewish faith was not to be reminded of his grievous sin. (Gershom's son had converted by his own free will and never returned to Judaism, but when he died his father observed all the rites of mourning for him.) Rabbenu Gershom understood the ordeals and temptations to which his people were exposed and was concerned with the status and dignity of Jewish women. He is buried in the old Jewish cemetery at Mainz.

Rashi, the Giant: The Commentator
Who Unlocked Torah and Talmud

Out of Gershom's school and the academy of Worms emerged the most important of all medieval Jewish scholars, Rabbi Solomon ben Isaac, abbreviated Rashi (1040–1105). He opened for his people the treasure house of Torah and Talmud; without his commentary, the Talmud would be for us a closed book. Born at Troyes, France, he spent his youth studying in the cities along the Rhine. He returned home to vineyards and wine business that afforded him a comfortable living and allowed him to maintain his disciples at his academy without accepting any remuneration from them. Returning to France just in time to escape the massacre of the First Crusade, he died in the town of his birth.

In the simplest words and utter clarity of style, in succinct and illuminating presentation that reveal him as a truly great pedagogue, Rashi wrote a commentary to both the Bible and the Talmud. Following the text sentence by sentence, he clarified obscure passages, analyzed the text, elucidated its meaning. Sometimes he would even translate difficult words into the French spoken by the Jews, a sign of their adjustment to their surroundings. Unlike modern commentators, Rashi did not have at his disposal the results of critical scholarship or of archaeology and comparative linguistics. He saw Torah as the divine word and explained it often by referring to the Aramaic versions of the Scripture. Above all, he brought in the Aggadah and Midrash of the Talmud in simple, condensed form to elucidate the deeper meaning of the text as the rabbis had understood it. Torah was to be made accessible to all as their guide in life.

Recognizing the importance of Rashi, posterity has seen in his abbreviated name the achrostic of another three words: *Rabban shel Yisrael*, "the Teacher of Israel." His commentary was influential in Christian circles as well. NICHOLAS DE LYRA (ca. 1270–1340), no friend of the Jews, studied Rashi's Bible commentary extensively. De Lyra, a Franciscan, was professor of theology at the Sorbonne, and his fifty-volume work, *Postillae Perpetuae*, was a running commentary to all the books of the Old and New Testaments. He was widely read during the Middle Ages. De Lyra's commentary, in turn, became Luther's guide in his translation of Scripture. Rashi's clear explanation may well have put doubt in many minds regarding the interpretation of the Roman Catholic Church, thus contributing to the spirit that led to the Reformation.

Tosafot: Rashi's Descendants and Supercommentators

During the twelfth and thirteenth centuries, masters of the French schools, including Rashi's grandsons, wrote additional commentaries that were based on Rashi and analyzed specific points in the Talmud. These are called *Tosafot*, "additions." Every edition of the Talmud contains Rashi's commentary on the inside margin of each page and Tosafot on the outside margin.

The Kalonymus Family: Scholars, Poets, Martyrs, and Mystics

The house of Kalonymus, mentioned previously, used its wealth and prestige to develop academies of learning. One of its outstanding representatives, Rabbi Kalonymus Ben Meshullam (eleventh century) of Mainz, gave new poetic form to a liturgical poem originating in the Byzantine period and environment, *Unetane tokef kedushat ha-yom*, "Let us proclaim the holiness of the day." By the power of his poetry it has become universally adopted in the liturgy of the High Holy Days. It is regarded as one of the greatest liturgical poems in Jewish literature. It expresses the holiness of the Days of Awe and acclaims God as supreme judge, who decrees human destiny but is ever ready to accept repentance, prayer, and deeds of love in expiation of any sin (see also the reference on p. 81).

Kalonymus's son and grandson were given the right to settle in Speyer (1090), where they established a house of learning. Judah, another member of the family who arrived later from Italy, died at the height of the Crusades (1200). He lived both in Worms and Ratisbon, and moved in a somewhat different direction from the rest of his family, immersing himself in prayer and mysticism; his response to life was to escape into a world other than the one that was so unhappy. He was called *Judah Ha-Hasid*, Judah the Saint (mystic), and through him the mysticism of Hasidism (see p. 94ff.) found a foothold in Northern Europe. In later centuries it was transplanted and given new appeal by the Hasidim of Poland.

Rabbi Meir of Rothenburg: Thwarted Escape to the Holy Land

In 1286 Rabbi Meir ben Barukh of Rothenburg (1220–1293), who had cried out in bitter elegy at the burning of the Talmud in Paris, decided to emigrate to Palestine. There alone could Torah be developed, while in Germany there were only trials. Meir failed; he was recognized and captured during his journey and was imprisoned for ransom by order of the Emperor Rudolph von Hapsburg. The emperor could not tolerate the loss of a Jew, who, like all of them, was his property. Meir forbade his people to pay the ransom lest a precedent be established and more rabbis be captured. After seven years in confinement he died there. Then the ransom had to be paid anyway for his body. Alexander Wimpfen of Frankfurt sacrificed his entire fortune to ransom the master's body. He only wished to be buried next to him. Both men lie side by side in the ancient Jewish cemetery at Worms. Ashkenasic Jewry held a deep love and respect for its rabbis, which makes Wimpfen's action and wish understandable.

Martyr, Escape, and a Table Cloth for the "Well-Prepared Table"

Rabbi Meir's disciple, Rabbi Mordecai ben Hillel, decided that Mitzvot must be emphasized to provide stability among the physically rootless, and he proposed a code. He died a martyr's death at Nuremberg in 1289. Mordecai's colleague, RABBI ASHER BEN YEHIEL, succeeded in escaping to Spain, thus linking the Ashkenasic tradition to the Sefardic. Synthesizing the work of the German and Spanish masters, he and his son Jacob completed the proposed code. It was a four-volume work, which Rabbi Asher called *Turim*, "Rows," after the four rows of precious stones in the breastplate of the high priest; Mitzvot were the precious stones. Rabbi Joseph Karo based his *Shulhan Arukh* on both Maimonides and the Turim. Writing his work in Palestine Karo symbolized the unity of the Jewish people through Mitzvot and Land.

Customs and religious practices vary among Jews in various lands because they are based on the interaction of outward and inward forces of environment and tradition. RABBI MOSES ISSERLES of Cracow, Poland (c.1520–c.1572) therefore wrote a supplement to the *Shulhan Arukh* for Ashkenasic Jewry. He called his supplementary notes *Mappah*, "Tablecloth," for Karo's "well-prepared table."

Rabbi Jacob Moellin, Maharil, the Preservation of Minhagim and of Liturgical Song

For centuries individual congregations had developed their own local customs, *Minhagim*. Seeing the importance of these local customs, Rabbi Jacob Levi Moellin (also called in abbreviated form *Maharil*), who died in 1427, collected and established these Minhagim as abiding guides to practice. The persecutions at the time of the Black Death had wiped out many communities. New ones were arising in their stead. The customs of the previous congregation could give the members of the new one pride in the uniqueness of their community and identification with the Jewish past. Tradition was essential for the Ashkenaic community, which so often was uprooted.

Maharil was also an accomplished *cantor* (singer of liturgy) and ruled for the same reason that the traditional tunes, which expressed the yearnings of centuries, could not be changed—especially those of the high holy days, to which people had become accustomed. His own city of Mainz abided by this rule most faithfully, until it was wiped out by the Nazis. Transmitted orally, these songs were in danger of being lost. (I have tried to preserve them on tape as my memory allowed.) In 1998 transcriptions were made. Maharil is buried in the Jewish cemetery at Worms, where he had spent the last years of his life.

Jewish liturgical music like Minhagim was strongly influenced by the tastes of the surrounding world. A distinct difference developed in customs and Jewish liturgical song, between Western and Eastern European Jewry. The music of Western European Jewry was generally written in major keys and was joyful, for this Jewry had repeated periods of reasonable peace. The music of Eastern European Jewry was written in the minor keys in general and was melancholic, expressing the endless suffering of that community. These differences increased the difficulties between Western and Eastern European Jews when the latter began to settle in large numbers both in Western Europe and in America.

RENAISSANCE AND REFORMATION

The *Renaissance*, or "Rebirth," originated in Italy. Excavations brought many works of antiquity to light, works of naturalness, beauty, and proportion. This stood in sharp contrast to the works of the previous centuries, which people of the Renaissance called the "Middle Ages." The new spirit extended to all facets of life. It encouraged individualism, exploration, and nationalism. It made the human being the center of all thought and action, and thereby contrasted sharply with the spirit of the Middle Ages, which was God-centered. Renaissance men and women were filled with joy of life. Wishing to become immortal the opulent citizens sponsored great artists by whose work they themselves would be remembered through the centuries. Families such as the Medicis of Florence became rulers of the city and sponsors of art that has in fact perpetuated their name.

The Renaissance spread over all of Europe. It brought forth Humanists in the narrow sense of the term. These were scholars who studied the works of antiquity, written in Latin, Greek, and Hebrew. The Humanists were disgusted with the corrupted Latin written in medieval works and spoken by the clergy. The Renaissance was, however, confined to the elite. The little man in his toil felt little of it. It did not bring any significant change in the conditions of the Jews.

Italian Jews, from the distance of their ghetto, shared in the cultural revival of the time, and their ideas came to the attention of many influential scholars. The newly invented art of printing aided the spread of Jewish works, but the general position of Jewry on the continent did not improve. In fact, the ghetto in Italy was established at this time; the Jews were sequestered in a ghetto because the Catholic Church feared that the spirit of the Renaissance, which had led to the Reformation, might lead the faithful toward new heretical concepts out of their contacts with Judaism. The Jews had to be isolated. However, Pope Leo X, a humanist, ordered the printing of the Talmud because he felt that ancient literature ought to be preserved.

In Germany, as in Italy, the humanist movement sparked the interest of Christian scholars in Hebrew, the Hebrew Bible, and Jewish literature, including Jewish mysticism and especially the works of the Kabbalah. A courageous humanist, JOHANNES REUCHLIN (1455–1522) at great personal risk defended the books of postbiblical Jewish literature before Emperor Maximilian I against an accusation by Johannes Pfefferkorn, a Jewish convert to Christianity. Pfefferkorn asserted that these Jewish works, especially the Talmud, contained attacks against Christianity and should be burned. Reuchlin, who had some acquaintance with some of the Hebrew originals, refuted him by saying these books contained much material that could be of service to Christianity. It was a bitter struggle. Maintaining that the Jews should be converted to Christianity, Reuchlin nevertheless opposed persecution as the method for doing so, and proposed kindly persuasion instead. Reuchlin called for protection of the Jews, as they were citizens of the Holy Roman Empire; that is, the German empire. The Talmud was saved.

By his defense of the Jewish scriptures Reuchlin struck a blow against "the men of darkness," the scholastics, with their medieval pattern of thought and their corrupted Latin. The Jews had become catalysts in the battle of the humanists against outworn ideas. Reuchlin's thinking is reflected in that of Martin Luther, his contemporary.

Martin Luther and His Impact on Jewish History

Martin Luther (1483–1546), like Reuchlin, was a man of great courage, an individualist, ready to fight for his ideas and ideals, which he drew from the study of the original texts of Holy Scripture. He was both a Renaissance man and medievalist in his outlook. This is evident in his relationship to the Jews. The new spirit of the times is expressed in his pamphlet "Jesus Christ Was a Jew by Birth" (1523). In it he stated that the Jews had been treated so cruelly that they could not be expected to become Christians. Kindlier treatment, he felt, and kindly persuasion would bring them into the fold: "I hope that if Jews are treated in a friendly fashion and instructed from Holy Writ, many of them will become worthy Christians."

At the outset of his reformatory activity, Luther favored the Jews in expectation that they would join his movement, especially as he had purified and reformed Christianity. (Here we recognize a similarity to Mohammed.) When the Jews refused, Luther turned viciously against them, revealing a spirit of unbending medieval mercilessness. In his pamphlet "Of The Jews and Their Lies" (1546) he admonished the princes to "expel the hardened blasphemers." In "Sharp Compassion" he demanded:

> first, that we burn their synagogues with fire . . . secondly, it is necessary to uproot and destroy their houses in the same manner . . . and house them under some roof or in a cowshed . . . thirdly, that all their prayer books and their books of the Talmud be taken from them . . . fourthly, that their Rabbis be forbidden by pain of bodily punishment and death to teach henceforward . . . fifth, that the Jews be absolutely forbidden to move on the roads . . . sixth, that they

shall be forbidden their usurious transactions and all their precious belongings of silver and gold shall be taken from them . . . seventh, that young and healthy Jews shall be given mallets, hoes and spindles and shall be required to earn their bread by the sweat of their brow. . . . There is room for apprehension . . . that they are liable to harm us . . . if they should serve us or work for us. . . . Let us therefore use the simple wisdom of other peoples like those of France, Spain and Bohemia . . . and expel them from our land forever.

Luther's legacy is therefore contradictory. He launched a traditional interest of Protestants in the Bible and the Jewish roots of Christianity. He counseled kindness toward the Jews, and his contemporaries paid more heed to the Luther of 1523 than of 1546. But Luther also infused the body of his new doctrines with a spirit of hatred for the Jews, which later influenced the character of the German Lutheran Church. Luther's utterances could be and were used to justify anti-Semitism. They were a blueprint for Hitler's extermination program. This would have been abhorrent to Luther, for he wished Jews to live and hoped for their conversion.

Luther's theology and thought contained two elements that brought the greatest suffering to the Jews. The first were the abovementioned anti-Jewish utterances of his later years, which influenced many of his followers. The second was his insistence that only faith, not works, brings salvation, and that the Lutheran church in all temporal matters had to obey earthly rulers. In Nazi times, the Lutheran church therefore spoke up only when its own faith was threatened by the government and the faith of its people was being attacked. It did not take a stand against the unchristian, murderous actions of the Nazi rulers against the Jews, a stand that might have had some effect. This historical background may shed light on some facets of German anti-Semitism.

In 1934, while Nazi power was growing, a group of Protestant leaders met in convention at Barmen to declare that their allegiance was to Christ alone. At this synod the "Confessional Church" was organized in opposition to the official German Protestant-Lutheran Church, which had become nazified. The Confessional Church resisted the incursion of Nazi doctrine. Karl Barth, one of the greatest Protestant theologians of his time, drafted the platform. As late as 1967, Barth revealed that he had always reproached himself for not introducing "the Jewish question" as one of the planks, although he ruefully added that such a text would not have been accepted in 1934, considering the participants' outlook on the Jews.

To its honor, the Lutheran church has publicly confessed its error and called itself to repentance. It has repudiated Luther's anti-Jewish teachings. In large measure the church's contrition is due to Barth's influence.

England Opens Its Doors

Only in England do we find a decided change in the status of the Jews as a result of the Reformation. Oliver Cromwell, Puritan ruler of England, who had deposed and ordered the execution of King Charles I, became convinced in studying Scripture that Christ would not return until the Jews were spread out over all parts of the world; hence they had to come to England again. Negotiations with a Dutch Rabbi, Manasseh ben Israel, eventually led to the formal declaration by Parliament (1655) that there was nothing in English law preventing Jewish settlement on English soil. This marks the beginning of the modern Jewish community in Great Britain.

Jewish Life

In spite of their trials, the Jews kept their faith, their mental balance, their sense of humor, and even their contact with the world. At the same time, never knowing how long a family might remain together, they deepened their spirit. Never certain whether the precious manuscripts they owned might be burned, they immersed themselves in their contents, in the study of Torah. Never assured that their possessions might not be taken away at a moment's notice and they themselves uprooted overnight, they gave help and hospitality to fugitives from other areas. Through Torah and Mitzvot, in the fervent hope that the Messiah might come at any time to restore them to the freedom of their land, they retained their emotional equilibrium.

It would be a mistake to assume that, because Jewish life was uncertain, it was unrelieved sorrow. The conditions of Jewry varied with the principalities in which they lived and the attitude of the princes. When times were good, Jews enjoyed life: every community had its dance house, the women dressed in silk and satin (causing the issuance of dress ordinances), and card playing became a widespread addiction.

Although legal ordinances continued to isolate the Jews, cultural crosscurrents that influenced both Jews and Christians point to an interchange on the popular level. The Jews spoke the language of their environment (e.g., German, which, in Poland and Russia, developed into Yiddish; and French, as seen in the Rashi commentary, where the author translated difficult Hebrew words into the vernacular). Jewish mystics drew widely from Christian mystical thought. From the Church, the Jews took the Yahrzeit's light (the light kindled at the anniversary of a parent's death). From the Synagogue, the Church derived the *Dies Irae* of the Requiem Mass, which is based on the Jewish poem "*Unetane tokef*" of the Byzantine period. The same text inspired Rabbi Kalonymus's poem for Rosh Hashanah (see pp. 76 and 354). Because the Jews were excluded from the craft guilds, Christian architects built synagogues in the style of the period, and Christian artists fashioned the silver ornaments for the Torah and the valuable candlesticks and kiddush cups for religious use. The Jews could read and write, and this alone made them necessary agents in a society where usually only clerics mastered these skills.

In the thirteenth century, German Jews even produced a troubadour, *minnesinger*, Süsskind von Trimberg, who, like his most famous contemporary, Walter von der Vogelweide, traveled from court to court entertaining great lords and ladies with his songs of love and chivalry. In Venice the sermons of RABBI LEONE DE MODENA (1571–1648) drew all of society to the synagogue to hear him. Salomone di Rossi composed Jewish baroque music in Italy.

The Shtadlan—Rabbi Joselmann of Rosheim

German Jews, like Spanish Jewry, had intercessors, *Shtadlanim*, who represented them before emperors and princes, and pleaded for them among the leaders of the nation. The leading personality in the early sixteenth century was Joseph (Joselmann) of Rosheim in the Alsace (1478–1554). He was not a rabbi but was highly educated. Joselmann used his great wealth and energy to defend his people. During the restlessness that followed Luther's appearance, he traveled from place to place to obtain the annulment of anti-Jewish decrees. To Protestants, he brought proofs from the Bible that Luther was wrong. In Brandenburg he succeeded in having the expulsion edict against the Jews withdrawn. In public defense against a blood libel brought by a Catholic monk, he submitted all the papal bulls that refuted and forbade the dangerous slander. The accuser of the Jews was dismissed in disgrace.

Internally he regulated the economic activities of the Jews to silence any possible Christian complaints. Then he appeared at the meeting of the Reichstag (Diet) at Augsburg (1530) as "the Emissary of all the Jews" and submitted ordinances which the Jews themselves had enacted under his leadership. The Diet withdrew the anti-Jewish decrees it was about to pass. Joselmann's arguments rested on the principle that all human beings were created by God and therefore equal, especially before the law.

Joselmann enjoyed the respect and trust of Emperor Charles V, the same man who, as King of Spain, would not tolerate one single Jew in his kingdom. The Emperor granted far-reaching rights and privileges to the Jews, which were ratified by the Reichstag. In the conflict between Catholics and Protestants, Joselmann advised his people to exercise great caution in word and action. But being afraid of the designs of the Lutherans, he urged them to pray for the Catholic emperor and the success of his enterprises.

After World War II the slowly reemerging German Jewish community chose a similar method of inner arbitration and outward representation. At the head of its "Central Council" it placed an elected layperson.

EASTERN EUROPEAN JEWRY

The fate of Polish and Russian Jewry appears like a condensed version of Jewish destiny throughout history, ranging from well-being to abysmal suffering. Migration to Eastern Europe began with the Crusades and increased with subsequent peaks of persecution, such as during the Black Death. Jews in large numbers settled in Poland, Lithuania, Bohemia, Moravia, the Ukraine, and up to the borders of Russia, which was closed to them. The rulers welcomed them, although the Catholic Church disliked them intensely. Subsequent centuries saw the Jews as pawns in the struggle between kings and Church: If the Church found itself powerful enough to have its will prevail, the Jews suffered; if the king prevailed, opposing the Church in his own effort to retain absolute power, the lot of the Jews was happier.

With the rise of a Polish merchant class the Jews found themselves under attack and restricted in their economic activities. The Polish kings and nobility saw the economic advantages the Jews could bring to an undeveloped Poland, badly in need of a middle class of merchants. They took the Jews under their protection, allowed them to settle throughout the land next to the Christian inhabitants, and accorded them freedom of movement and of enterprise.

The Economic and Organizational Structure of Eastern European Jewry

In many ways the life of Eastern European Jewry differed from that of the Jews in the West. Being in a country whose native population had neither a sophisticated language nor culture, the Jews retained their German language, and transformed it into *Yiddish*. The garb of the German citizens became the *caftan*.

The Polish nobility hated the Jews but needed them. Deeply and continually in debt, noblemen left their estates in pledge to their Jewish money lenders. Jews rented large estates from the nobility with all they contained, including their mills, lodging houses and inns where they sold liquor, and made them prosper. They even leased royal mines. Eventually, Jews controlled agriculture, exported timber, and supplied foodstuffs to the armies in the West.

After the Reformation, Poland became a haven for Protestants. If they wished to be tolerated they had to show tolerance for the other religious minority, the Jews. Conditions became agreeable up to the Khmielnitski uprising in 1648.

Afraid of the brutality and ignorance of the civil magistrates, the Jewish community early in its history had pleaded for and obtained the right to self-government. Granting it, the princes insisted on a tight, centralized Jewish authority which would supervise the internal affairs and, above all, assure the regular and complete payment of taxes. The Jewish community came to form a body within the body of the state, sternly controlled and disciplined. Beginning in the sixteenth century the chief rabbis of the communities were recognized by the kings as Jewry's justices and chief administrators and given absolute authority, which may account for the abiding piety of Eastern European Jewry.

Each city had an elected council, *Kahal*, consisting of rabbis and wealthy laypersons. The surrounding rural districts were under its power. It formed an administrative unit, regulating every aspect of life, conduct, law, custom, and relations with the non-Jewish population. It appointed all officials, set their salaries and oversaw their performance in office. It represented, protected and defended the Jewish community and its members toward the outside world. Its rabbis ruled on the basis of halakhah. Above all, it assessed the taxes, of which almost three quarters went to the rulers. The local councils, in turn, stood under the authority of a central council, the "Council of the Four Lands," Poland, Lithuania, Bohemia and Moravia. It met regularly, allocated taxes, and represented Jewish interests before kings and princes.

Essentially, the Councils were oligarchic, which led to tensions between the wealthy and poor, city residents and itinerants, rabbis (for whom the Torah was the primary concern and directive) and the wealthy who had other interests. Those of its members who had access to the authorities by virtue of their wealth and influence carried great weight.

Khmielnitsky: Persecution Erupts into Pogroms, Jews Withdraw into Torah

Persecutions had sporadically occurred previously. In the seventeenth century the fury of the Jew haters was to engulf the Jews. The Khmielnitsky Massacres were the first in a long series of mass murders of Jews, the *pogroms*. Khmielnitsky was the head of a free-roaming band of warriors called the Cossacks. Professing Greek Orthodox faith, they rebelled against the Roman Catholic Polish nobility. Serfs, dissatisfied with their fate, joined the Cossacks. During the ensuing civil war the whole country was ravaged. The Jews were in the middle and were slaughtered by the tens of thousands with unspeakable brutality.

Following the Khmielnitski uprisings the status of the Jews deteriorated rapidly. Branded as aliens and regarded with suspicion, they were an easy target for the preachments of clergy against them, and, as the "error" of their being Jews was constantly impressed upon the Poles, they could serve as scapegoats in times of disaster or social unrest.

Sabbatai Zevi: False Messiah

Shortly after the Khmielnitsky pogroms news reached the Jews from the East that the Messiah had come. His name was Sabbatai Zevi. This news turned their grief into exaltation and ultimate expectation. The horrors they had endured could now be understood as the "birth pangs of the Messiah," the severe sufferings predicted for the Jews before his arrival. Now God had sent redemption to His people, the Messiah had come. He would liberate His people and bring them to the Promised Land.

Sabbatai Zevi (1626–1676), born in Smyrna (Turkey), had proclaimed himself the Messiah. He was a young, handsome, learned and highly charismatic man, who mesmerized the people. On his travels, which included Jerusalem, he had found a large and enthusiastic following. He established a court and claimed that his divine ordination permitted him to transform traditional performances prescribed by halkhah. He abolished the days of fasting, henceforth they were to be days of joy. The prophet Zechariah had so prophesied it for the time of redemption (Zechariah 8:18–19), and now this time had come. He even pronounced the name of God, YHVH, a name so holy that all Jews were and are forbidden to utter it. Only the high priest could speak it on Yom Kippur, and then the people hearing it prostrated themselves in awe and adoration. Sabbatai claimed this right by virtue of his call.

Enthralled by his personality and message thousands in the Diaspora, including Germany as well as Poland, sold their real estate at bargain prices, packed their belongings on wagons, and prepared to go to the Land of Israel in response to his summons. Some rabbis were skeptical and warned against Sabbatai. They were right. Sabbatai proved to be an imposter. He was most likely a manic-depressive, with moments of great but unsubstantiated elation followed by deep depression. Eventually he was captured by the Turks, and was given the choice to become a Muslim or be executed. He chose to convert to Islam.

The Jews sank into despair. Some of Sabbatai's followers were unwilling to accept the blow: He would surely arise again. An underground sabbatean movement continued in existence for a considerable time. But the lives of the people returned to the ancient pattern of poverty, insecurity, and suffering.

Jewish Spiritual Responses to Calamity

Among the Jews, the search for deliverance from their horrible sufferings moved in several directions. Deep immersion in the Talmud and Mitzvot grew ever more profound after the shattering event of Sabbatai's failure. Following it, and almost in response to it, a new movement emerged: Hasidism.

Immersion in Torah and Mitzvot resulted for many in a withdrawal from the world. Mitzvot became ever more embracing. Injunctions, such as the prohibition of cutting the corners of the beard (Leviticus 19:27), were taken literally, resulting in long earlocks never cut. Self-imposed seclusion was added to the enforced one. Mitzvot formed the wall of separation. The separation from the rest of the world and its lack of a comparable culture provided an external safeguard against corrosion. Immersion in the Talmud gave inner strength and conviction. Early on, printing establishments provided an abundance of books, the Bible in 1530; the Talmud (first printed in Lublin, Poland) in 1559. The Talmud opened an escape into a better world.

Pilpul, the Exacting Study of the Talmud

About a century before Sabbatai Zevi, Rabbi Shalom Shakna (1500–1559) developed a method of Talmud study that corresponded to the need of his people. It led to the most detailed analysis of every verse and word, and was designed to bring about basic "agreement" in the opinions of a variety of conflicting judgments and commentaries expressed by numerous authors in a variety of countries and different ages. This was necessary to preserve the link with the past. Each generation rested on the preceding ones, which were regarded as more learned and closer to the source. None of these early ones could be assumed to have been in error, even in a single case. The chain of tradition had to be without any weak links so the chain of conviction would be equally strong. Ways had to be found to link divergent opinions of different centuries and to bring all opinions into agreement. This was possible only by hair-splitting logic; it became a kind of mental gymnastic which sharpened the mind but was actually meaningless. This method of *pilpul* remains in some of the old-fashioned yeshivot.

Education was practically universal. Between the ages of three and five, a boy was taken to *cheder* (the schoolroom), where he studied Bible and Talmud from early morning until late at night, often under the guidance of a teacher who was far from being a pedagogue. Advanced students were sent to a *yeshivah* (academy) in the city where the people took turns providing them meals, having a different student every day. During this period, girls received only a basic education, which trained them to fulfill religious obligations, keep a kosher home, and influence their children through the home. In later times, some received a more thorough education.

Study became the young man's full vocation, deep into the night; the bloom of youth would fade from his cheeks. Many never emerged from this mode of life. When they married, their in-laws might provide for them or, if this was impossible, the wife would eke out a living for the rest of her days to afford uninterrupted study for her husband. The prestige of the learned was high; the great rabbis were revered and brilliant students were sought by the wealthy as the most suitable sons-in-law.

Hasidism

Another movement was Hasidism. Its founder was RABBI ISRAEL BEN ELIEZER, (1700–1760), who became known as *Baal Shem Tov,* abbreviated *Be-Sh-T, Master of the Good (Devine) Name.* He brought hope to the Jews, who mourned their beloved martyred in the Khmelnitzky massacres and were deeply distressed at the collapse of their messianic expectations which Sabbatai Zevi had stirred.

Born in Podolia of humble origin, Rabbi Israel began his active life as a synagogue sexton and assistant teacher. But he was also a miracle healer, a *Baal Shem,* Master of the Divine Name, which gave him power over the forces of nature. He applied it and distributed amulets and charms to cure people. He spent much of his time in solitary meditation, delved into the Kabbalah, established contact with mystics and possibly also with Sabbateans. On Rosh Hashanah of the year 1747 he had a mystical revelation, *hitgalut,* giving him a new vision and mission. It was revealed to him that the Messiah would come when the Baal Shem's teachings were known and followed by the Jewish masses. To spread his message therefore became his calling.

The Besht taught that God's presence filled the entire world and encompassed every aspect of it. *Devekut,* attachment and communion with God therefore gave human life meaning and holiness. Every human task, be it menial work or study or eating or drinking, could be a response to God if performed with *kavvanah,* attunement, in joyful service to Him. The Besht emphasized the *joy* of serving God. Sorrow and asceticism would only call forth God's severe justice under which the world could not survive, joy would call forth God's grace and love and lead to the coming of the Messiah. God should be served in song and dance, and even daily toil should be filled with the joy of being work for God and with Him.

All people, even the most unlearned—and perhaps they more than others—carried the calling of preparing the world for the messianic future. Every limb of one's body could become a tool in this service. The road to redemption was *devekut* combined with joy.

The common people, however, were not capable of attaining a complete *devekut*. They needed the leadership of the *Zaddik*. By their contact with the Zaddik and by imitation of his ways they could be raised closer to it. The term "Zaddik" as used by the Hasidim is difficult to translate. Generally, it means "the righteous," perhaps we may render it here as "he who is completely right in God's eyes." The Zaddik was "the foundation of the world" (Ecclesiastes 10:25). In his behalf God had created the world. The Zaddik lived in a perfect state of *devekut,* his every thought and action were filled with it. Therefore the Zaddik could change it, but only if he succeeded in making the common folk worthy of it. He had to abandon the solitariness of his study and go to the people to raise them up. He served as intermediary between God and the people, their role model, and he brought their petitions to God. He was responsible to God for them.

The Baal Shem himself went out to the people. Using the simple approach of parable and story, he gave them hope, encouragement, and inspiration. He taught them that God Himself needed redemption, for He, too, was in exile with His people as a result of the world's sinfulness. In order that the world be restored to the unity that it had lost by human sinfulness, God needed humanity's redemptive act. Every human being had a function in it. The Jew, however, had a major role to fulfill. The people of the Covenant had not lost its mission and its function. The Messiah had not come, but this was no reason for despair, for the task of preparing for redemption was placed by God in the heart and hand of every single Jew.

The people flocked to the Baal Shem. They would rouse themselves into ecstasy, their bodies swaying in worship to express with every bone and muscle their allegiance to God. They knew that prayer must pour forth out of the innermost soul to reach God and be expressed with the total personality of the worshiper. They would dance before God in joyful abandon. They had found new hope.

The message of the Baal Shem was carried forth by his disciples, some of them talmudic scholars, others simple folk and popular preachers, *Maggidim*. After the death of the BESHT R. DOV BAER (ca. 1710–1772), the *Maggid of Mezhirech* and Rovno, also a talmudic scholar, gave the movement firm foundations from which it expanded.

The leaders of the movement, the Zaddikim, were called *Rebbe* (in contrast to the talmudic rabbi, called *Rav*). They were believed by the people to have a deeper insight into the hidden meanings of Torah. Divine grace flowed into every word and action they performed. They were Masters of the Divine Name (*Baal Shem* in Hebrew), that creative Word by which the world had once been shaped and by which it could be influenced again. Thus, the people flocked to their leaders to get help in their individual needs. They hung on their lips, especially during the twilight hours of the Sabbath, for cryptic and mysterious words of revelation.

Worship was transformed. The Hasidim established their own synagogues, whose worship differed from the established ones and their rites. Prayer was regarded as more important than talmudic study, for it linked man to God. It became ecstatic, expressing in outcries and bodily action the attunement, *devekut*, of the worshiper to God. The prayer books followed based on the sefardic rite, as did those of the Kabbalists, and contained kabbalistic elements. Following kabbalistic tradition the Hasidim also chose especially sharpened knives for the slaughter of animals. By these practices they set themselves in opposition to the non-Hasidic community.

By the nineteenth century half of Eastern European Jewry had joined the movement, and its Rebbes exerted great influence in undermining the authority of the city rabbis. These were, for instance, not asked to give their imprimatur on the books published by the Hasidic movement. A split opened between the traditionalist, talmudic-oriented Jews and the Hasidim. Among the disciples of the Besht, numerous "dynasties" sprung up. Each Rebbe had his followers. He did not have to be of exceptional learning, for it was believed that he had inherited his gifts from his father. Each of them held court in princely fashion. Rivalries ensued. Only a few Hasidic groups survived the Holocaust and set themselves up in the free world, especially America.

Hasidism and Contemporary Jewry

The ideas of Hasidism have made themselves felt in our own time. From them stems the enthusiasm that fired the pioneers in Israel. They undertook the most back-breaking tasks in rebuilding the Land of Israel in the spirit of promoting redemption. Hasidism affected also those Jews who did not adhere to formal religion in doctrine and practice. They translated it into secular terms and applied it to the physical redemption of Land and people. The dances of the pioneers have one of their sources in Hasidic abandon.

Some Hasidic groups settled in the United States after the Holocaust. The most prominent among them are "the Lubavichers" who originated in Lubavich, Poland. Their charismatic and dynamic leader was the late Lubavicher Rebbe, RABBI MENACHEM M. SCHNEERSON (1902–1994). He established his headquarters in the Williamsburgh section of Brooklyn, New York. From there he developed a worldwide network of congregations and day schools. To promote cohesion and spread the spirit of Jewishness he availed himself of such modern technology as closed-circuit television. He trained and ordained a large number of rabbis. Uncompromising in their commitment to orthodox Judaism, these rabbis have founded synagogues and schools on every continent. They have reached out to non-Orthodox Jews with great love. Their aim has been to show these Jews the joys of orthodox living and bring them back to it as *"Baale Teshuva,"* Men of Return. Respected and revered by non-Jewish leaders in American life from presidents down, the Rebbe emphasized the public affirmation of Judaism. On his request, gigantic Hanukkah menorahs have been erected in central squares of many cities in America and in the world, including even Moscow, and their lights are kindled nightly during the festival by one of his rabbis. At the same time he exerted a profound influence on the political life in Israel, promoting Orthodoxy and repressing non-Orthodox movements. A residence for him was built in Israel which, however, he would not enter until the Messiah came. He expected his advent at any moment. Some of his followers considered him the Messiah, who would reveal himself when the world and the Jewish people were worthy. After his death some of his adherents expected his resurrection as the Messiah.

The cohesion among the Hasidim in the United States is very strong. They live together in a closed society and are uncompromisingly Orthodox. They follow the traditions of Eastern European Jewry and wear the garb of the Eastern European Hasid of the past. They deny their children a college education with its rewards to keep them true to their Jewish tradition. They have even established communities of their own, for instance in New Jersey, with complete internal autonomy.

Mitnagdim, Antagonists of the Hasidim

The Hasidic movement in Eastern Europe was strongly opposed by those Jews who saw in it a corruption of Judaism. The leader of these *Mitnagdim, Opponents,* was RABBI ELIJAH BEN SOLOMON (1720–1779) of Vilna (Vilnius) in Lithuania. He was one of the greatest Jewish scholars of all time, affectionately called by his people the *Gaon of Vilna.* Rabbi Elijah saw in the Hasidim, their worship and practices, a schismatic movement, that threatened Judaism. Their devaluation of Torah study violated halakhah, their adoration of the Zaddik as intermediary between God and the people was idolatry especially as many of the Rebbes were ignorant. Their way of life was heresy. He excommunicated the adherents of the Hasidic movement. The conflict between Mitnagdim and the Hasidim was bitter.

In contrast to Hasidism, he proposed a way based on reason and vision. He felt that Judaism had to be pulled back from either hair-splitting logic or mystical interpretation, and had to be brought back onto the highway of reason and rational ways of study. Even some secular knowledge was advisable as it improved the understanding of Talmud and Codes. Worship was to be made more meaningful and more "modern" in a modest way.

The Mussar Movement

Following his guidance the Lithuanian communities established great yeshivot, emphasizing the intellectual pursuit of talmudic studies. RABBI ISRAEL SALANTER (1819–1883), was convinced that study and Mitzvot had to be undergirded by a spirit of emotional fervor. He introduced the study of *Mussar,* Jewish Ethics, both in the yeshivah and among average Jews. It called for self-examination. While the Hasidim grounded their life of devotion in joy, the Mussar movement was rooted in a spirit of sorrow, of self scrutiny and recognition of the vanities of the world.

How the Rift Ended: Haskalah, the Common "Enemy"

Beginning with the eighteenth century, the Enlightenment took hold of the Western world. As we shall see, it transformed Jewry. Gradually, it also penetrated youthful elements in Eastern Jewish communities. The Hebrew term for

"Enlightenment" was *Haskalah.* In the light of reason the *Maskilim* (adherents of Haskalah) questioned and opposed many Jewish traditions, commandments, customs, and existing social conditions. Hasidim and Mitnagdim recognized that a new and dangerous adversary had arisen, attacking both. In defense of Jewish tradition they had to meet the new thoughts and their adherents by counterattack. This called for a unified front of traditional Jewry. Thus, Hasidim and Mitnagdim found their way to each other and to unity.

Life under the Russian Czars

Russia became a Christian state around 900. Its Eastern Orthodox religion was more fundamentalist than Western Christianity; the Reformation did not affect it. When Byzantium, the center of the faith, fell to the Turks in 1453, Moscow became the metropolis of the Orthodox Church. Actually, it was regarded as the center of Christianity by the Russians, who believed that Rome had forfeited this distinction on account of the Roman Church's many heretic teachings. Russia took the doctrine of the Jews as accursed people in all its literal harshness. In a spirit of religious purity, it did not permit Jews to settle within its borders.

In the course of the centuries, Russia carried out a program of imperialist expansionism of unparalleled success, a policy followed by the Soviet Union as well. The Russian empire grew from a small territory around Moscow into a world power by absorbing weaker countries at Russia's borders.

One of the independent states at Russia's border was Poland, which had become enfeebled by dissension among the various feudal lords. By the eighteenth century it had become impossible to unite Poland under a king of Polish descent, and a power vacuum developed. Russia would have liked to absorb Poland but there were two other powerful states at Poland's borders, Prussia and Austria, who were equally eager to expand their territory at the expense of their weaker neighbor. In the end, and as a result of three treaties (1774, 1793, 1795), the big powers divided Poland among themselves and wiped it off the map. After World War I, Poland reemerged.

The partitions of Poland brought one million Jews into the Russian empire. They were a most unwelcome addition, but it was impossible to expel so large a number of people, especially as no one was prepared to take them.

It became Russian policy to get rid of the Jews by forcing one third to emigrate, by pressuring another third into baptism, and by letting the last third starve to death. In the meanwhile they were to be confined within a strictly circumscribed, closed district, the *Pale.* They were no longer permitted to live in villages, only cities. Under the reign of Empress Katherine the Great, Jews from all over Russia were dumped into the Pale. Thousands lost their livelihood, contact with the world was cut off, and the Jews became desperately poor, sitting ducks for pogroms. By 1880 about four million Jews were crammed into it. The Pale continued up to the Russian Revolution in 1917.

The Napoleonic invasion of Russia in 1812 brought a glimpse of the spirit of Western Enlightenment and relief to Russian Jews. With the defeat of Napoleon, reaction set in all over Europe, and the pressure on Russian Jews increased. Under NICHOLAS I (1825–1855), a brutal autocrat, the Pale was narrowed, the Jews squeezed closer together, and new restrictive measures imposed. Even in the Pale Jews were not permitted to live in villages. For a while, a tax was placed on the wearing of the skull cap, the caftan and the streimel (fur hat). Men were forbidden to grow sidelocks. The ordinances could be subverted by bribing the local officials entrusted with their enforcement, who therefore exploited the Jews. Censorship of Hebrew books, including those imported from abroad, was imposed, and many presses forcibly closed. The *kahal* was abolished, thus Jewish communities lost their autonomy. The tax collector remained and became one of the most important personalities within the Jewish community. Jews were classified by occupation; merchants, artisans, and farmers were "useful," the rest was not.

To enforce conversion, Nicholas ordered the conscription of Jews (1827). A quota of conscripts was established for each community. Beginning at the age of eighteen they were to serve for twenty-five years without any opportunity for promotion unless they became Christians. In "preparation" for this service, children at the age of twelve and even earlier could be (and were) conscripted, dragged away from their homes, mistreated, and tortured to make them give up their faith. The burden fell mainly on the "useless" poor, who, by edict, had to provide three times as many recruits as the "useful." By order of the Church authorities, the priests serving the armed forces baptized whole groups by force. Many of these victims committed suicide rather than submit to baptism. Many others perished in heroic stubbornness.

Under the slogan "moral education" the government intervened in Jewish education. The Russian system of elementary education for Jews was to be enlarged at the expense of the yeshivot. A German rabbi, MAX LILIENTHAL (1815–1882), was called to direct the school system. He undertook the task believing that the Jews were to be acculturated. When he found that, in essence, he was to create an organization for the conversion of Jewish children, he fled in terror. Eventually, he had a distinguished career as one of the early rabbis in the United States.

While the most severe restrictions were removed with the death of Nicholas I, new pressures were applied later under Alexander III and Nicholas II. In the meanwhile a nationalistic, pan-slavistic movement emerged. It was influenced by Germany. The Russians believed that, since the Germans, leaders in cultural progress, had "scientifically" discovered that the Jews were their misfortune, the Jew hatred had a verifiable, scientific foundation. The anti-Jewish pan-Slavist nationalists stirred the people's slumbering animosity to action against the Jews, who could be held responsible for the people's misery. The movement was guided by the Czar's government, directed by a clandestine organization of courtiers, and incited by the press, especially anti-Semitic papers financed by the Czar.

The masses of Russia groaned under their yoke. To deflect the popular fury, pogroms against the Jews were instituted. In 1881 they ravaged over 100 communities. In 1903 a horrible pogrom accompanied by murder, rape, and torture took place at Kishinev. These pogroms shook the world by their extent and brutality and were denounced by Christians throughout the West. The economic situation of the Jews was equally hopeless. Migration to the United States now became a torrent.

In 1911, on inspiration by an association of the nobility, the blood libel was revived, and a poor Jew, Mendel Beilis of Kiev, brought to trial for it. He was acquitted, and the liberal press revealed that the trial had been initiated by the Minister of Justice, who reported daily to the Czar on its progress. Had Beilis been convicted, it would have served as a cause for "action" against all Jews.

A satirical pamphlet against the French Emperor Napoleon III, who had his finger in political developments worldwide, was changed by the Russian authorities. It now ascribed to the "Wise Men of Zion" a secret plot to undermine the existing states, incite them to war against each other, weaken them, and then assume world power for the Jews. This pernicious forgery, called "Protocols of the Wise Men of Zion" was to gain worldwide distribution and bring untold harm to the Jews. Its influence has not yet been entirely eliminated.

In Russia the routine never varied. It included discrimination, even against Jewish soldiers in World War I. As the fronts moved, Jews were transported at a moment's notice from one part of Russia to another. Pogroms followed. After the defeat of Russia in World War I it was discovered that Czar Nicholas II had actually expected to be victorious, and had prepared new harsh measures against the Jews after his "victory."

When the Russian Revolution came in 1917 the Jews thought that they were now free. They were mistaken; there were pogroms in the Ukraine. The Jews were now classified as members of the "middle class," which the Bolsheviks (1917) were determined to wipe out. They were equally hit by the war against religion. Stalin, as we shall relate, (Chapter 10) was a vicious anti-Semite who persecuted the Jews ruthlessly. Their persecution in the USSR ended officially with the dissolution of the USSR. Their condition improved but remained uncertain. The people's attitude, forged by centuries of indoctrination, was not predictable (see pp. 194–197).

Emigration and the Beginning of Zionism

The persecution of Jews led to emigration, especially to the United States, and the beginnings of the Zionist Movement. Many segments among the Jews, including the Maskilim, members of Haskalah, the Enlightenment, recognized that only a return to Zion could bring freedom to the Jews. A movement called *Ahavat Zion*, "Love of Zion," the Brotherhood of Zion Society, was founded in 1881 at St. Petersburg.

In 1882 Dr. LEON PINSKER (1821–1891) despaired of Jewish emancipation by the government and published his appeal for *Auto-Emancipation*. Migration to Palestine got under way. It was led by young Jews who called themselves BILU (an abbreviation of the Hebrew sentence, "O House of Jacob, come, and let us go!"). Zionism was on the march. Theodor Herzl was to give it its name and organization.

THE JEWS IN THE MIDDLE AGES:
THE BLENDING OF CULTURES

The history of the Jews during the Middle Ages was one of adversity. It is remarkable, therefore, to note how deeply they cast their roots in their new homelands. They learned to live in two civilizations, demonstrating to the world that humankind can live together and that cultures can preserve their individuality while sharing with each other the best that each has to offer. Yiddish, the language spoken by Ashkenasic Jews, and Ladino, the language of the Sefardim throughout the Middle Ages, are based on German and Spanish respectively. These languages are frequently used as a second tongue by many Jews even today. Similarly, the caftan, once the dress of the medieval burgher, became the "Jewish dress" in Eastern Europe. As frequent Church edicts calling for stricter separation of Jews from Christians reveal, contacts with friends were retained. But the Jews would not give up their faith, even though the door of the Church stood always open and baptism would wipe out all disabilities.

The Jews never lost their zest for life. This may be a source of that peculiar kind of Jewish humor, whimsical and tender, skeptical and optimistic, born of faith and love, critical of both God and humanity, yet encompassing all human foibles with amused compassion. This humor emerged from reflection on their fate as God's beloved yet who could barely subsist; His chosen people, yet they were totally insecure on earth. This was indeed "divine comedy." But who could doubt Him? Their optimism and their faith in God and humanity's ultimate goodness—evidenced even in Anne Frank's deeply moving diary—carried them through.

Yet scars remained. Their socioeconomic situation was completely abnormal. In the West, they were excluded from the soil they had so deeply loved. Known early in history for the kind of inventive craftsmanship which allowed for mass production, they were excluded from the guilds. Some of the scars are still visible in modern Jews, who are so recently removed from persecution that most of them have received eyewitness reports of it, if they were not its direct victims. In this manner, we must understand certain socioeconomic imbalances still existing. We may also understand the "exclusiveness" born of long inbred apprehension about their acceptance by the world at large, and their ambition for success and acceptance, a truly ambivalent position. Perhaps we may find in these conditions one explanation for the temptation felt by a number of Jews to escape from the dominance of religion into a general humanitarianism—this could be the first time that such an escape is possible without abandonment of Jewishness. Another reason for this may lie in the fact that only the humanistic Enlightenment gave Jews the rights of citizens that were withheld from them during the reign of religion.

Conditions, particularly in the United States, indicate that they are normalizing. Out of this change, new problems have arisen concerning the retention of Jewish identity in a civilization that is a great leveler. This new trend of events was slowly set in motion by the Emancipation, with which we shall deal in Chapter 6.

CHAPTER 5

Jewish Mysticism, Hasidism, and Modern Jewry

JEWISH MYSTICISM AND HASIDISM have become widely known in the twentieth century. Young people in particular have become fascinated by some of its aspects. This new interest was initiated by the work of two great masters. MARTIN BUBER (1878–1965) has given us a highly poetic interpretation of Eastern European Hasidism which attracted many readers, and GERSHOM SCHOLEM (1897–1982) devoted his life to the scientific study of Jewish mysticism. Nineteenth-century Jewish scholars regarded Jewish mysticism as superstition; Judaism was the "religion of reason." Scholem, who was professor of Jewish mysticism at the Hebrew University in Jerusalem, gave it respectability. He investigated it in rigorous scholarly fashion and opened the field to further exploration. His successors have based their work on his.

MYSTICISM

A mystic is one who seeks and finds a deeper understanding of God and a closer relationship with God than that granted to the average pious person in Torah, prayer, and Mitzvot. To Jewish mystics this meant a penetration in Torah. Torah, God's word, is absolute truth. It contains all knowledge and wisdom, but much of it is hidden to the average student. Deepest penetration into its secrets will reveal its innermost revelation.

Torah tells us of the mystical experiences granted to the prophets. In turbulent times "the doorposts shook" when Isaiah was given the vision of God. It was a reminder that He was Ruler of the universe, adored by the angels, who cried, "Holy, holy, holy . . ." (Isaiah 6:1–6). It made it equally clear that God is not confined to the Temple, His glory fills the universe. Ezekiel specified that his vision came to him in Babylonia, where king and nobility had already been taken into exile (Ezekiel 1:1–3). He thereby disclosed to them that God would reveal Himself to them wherever they were.

The great teachers of Judaism were essentially opposed to the idea of continuing revelation to individuals. Torah had been given at Sinai and revelations in the form of visions had been granted to the prophets; from then on, reason was the means by which Torah could be understood and explained. The masters also generally opposed mystical speculations on God, His essence, interaction with the universe and human beings in creation, history, revelation, redemption, and the end of days. They were afraid that mystical speculation might lead to heretical views. Nevertheless, mysticism has existed throughout Jewish history.

A number of talmudic rabbis were mystics. Being apprehensive that the subject might lead the uninitiated astray, they opened its recesses only to a few select disciples, those worthy of "special transmission," or *Kabbalah*, which eventually became the term for mystical works (B. Hagigah 11b–13a). The dangers and risks of such speculations were explained in the following passage of the Talmud. It warns that even great rabbis are not immune to the dangers of mystical contemplation.

> Four entered *Pardes* [the paradise of mystical speculations]: Ben Azzai, Ben Zoma, Aher, and Rabbi Akiba. Ben Azzai saw and died; Ben Zoma saw and lost his mind; Aher saw and lost his faith. Only Akiba entered and emerged in peace. (B. Hagigah 13–15)

Mystical speculations were restricted to a select group of men, who nevertheless stood in the mainstream of Jewish life. RABBI AKIBA, regarded as the greatest teacher of his time, was a mystic. He lived and died a martyr's death in the persecutions under Hadrian. Some of his teachings and institutions show his attempt to inspire his community to affirm God's reign publicly at a time when this affirmation was life-threatening. The *Kedushah*, "sanctification," in daily congregational prayer, in which Israel joins the angelic host in praise of God, emerged from the circle of mystics surrounding Rabbi Akiba.

Tracing the evolution of Jewish mysticism we find that each period built on the insights of the preceding ones. The mystical utterances in Torah gave rise to the mystical schools of the talmudic and gaonic periods. These, in turn, inspired those in German and Spain that flourished in the twelfth and thirteenth centuries. From the thirteenth to the fifteenth century Spain was the center of mystical speculations. When the Spanish Jews were expelled the center moved to Palestine. In the eighteenth century the mystical movement of Hasidism arose in Eastern Europe and has influenced Jewry ever since.

In periods of relative ease, such as in Spain, the mystics constituted an inner circle. They concerned themselves with the question of the divine essence. How did God relate to the world as its Creator and Sustainer, what was the place of Torah in the divine scheme of the universe, and what was the place of the Jews in history? In Germany and beginning with the expulsion from Spain, as Jewish life became more insecure, Jewish mysticism affected Jewish life and practice. Within the compass of this book we can sketch only a few outstanding periods, personalities, and works.

Early Works

During the talmudic and gaonic periods (third to seventh centuries) various small homiletic works appeared. *Hekhalot*, "Palaces," deals with the ascent of Rabbis Akiba and Ishmael through various heavenly palaces up to the "seventh heaven." There they beheld the vision of God's throne and God Himself. Both rabbis belonged to the Ten Martyrs who, according to tradition, were executed as a group by order of Emperor Hadrian. The story of their martyrdom is told in one of the books. *Merkavah*, "Chariot," deals with *Maaseh Merkavah*, the accounts of Ezekiel's vision of the heavenly chariot. It includes hymns heard by the mystics on their ascent. In all these treatises the distinction and importance of the Jew are emphasized. The works influenced the development of mysticism.

Sefer Yetzirah

Sefer Yetzirah, the Book of Creation, is the oldest mystical work the Jews know. Its authorship remains a mystery. In antiquity it was ascribed to the patriarch Abraham. According to *Sefer Yetzirah*, God "carved" (i.e., created) the universe by means of the numeric value of the letters in the Hebrew alphabet (each Hebrew letter has a numerical value). The term used for "number" is *Sefirot*. (Future mystics interpreted this term not as "number" but as "sphere.")
Possession of the creative power of these numbers gave power.

> As our father Abraham, peace be with him, came, he looked and pondered and saw, explored and understood, and chiseled and carved until he attained it, [namely, the power of creation,] as it is stated "the persons they made in Haran"(Gen.12:5). Then the Lord of All, His Name be blessed in eternity, revealed Himself to him, took him on His lap, kissed him on his head, called him "My friend" and made a Covenant with him and all his progeny through time. (Section 6; paragraph XV)

The words in Genesis 12:5 that are translated "the persons they had acquired [Hebrew, *asu*] in Haran" are understood literally as "made," or "created." Those therefore, who, like Abraham, understood the concealed power of the numbers in the letters, were *Zaddikim* in the sense of being free from sins that bar the access to God, and were endowed with creative power.

> Rava said: "If the 'Zadikim' so desired, they could create a world, for it is written, 'Your iniquities have been a barrier between you and your God' (Isa. 59:2)." Rava created a man and sent him to Rav Zera. The Rabbi spoke to him but he [the creature] did not answer. Said the Rabbi to him, "You must have been made [created] by the companions [of the academy], return to your dust." Every eve

of the Sabbath Rabbi Haninah and Rabbi Oshaya studied Sefer Yetzirah and created a calf, one-third of normal size, which they then ate (B. Sanhedrin 65b).

The uniqueness of the Jewish people and even of their alphabet are thus emphasized to a suffering community. To its Zaddikim is given the power of creation. The very existence of the world rests on them.

The Middle Ages

During the Middle Ages two centers of Jewish mysticism were established, one in southern France and northern Spain and the other in Germany. The Spanish school was headed by Nahmanides. Its mystics advanced the speculation about God, the world, and Israel. When the Jews were expelled from Spain this center was transferred to Israel. The mystics of Germany sought an explanation for the tragic fate of the Jews in the Rhineland. At the same time they were influenced by Christian ideas. We shall first turn to the German school, *Hasidei Ashkenas.*

Hasidei Ashkenas

In the twelfth and early thirteenth centuries the Hasidei Ashkenas, the pious, namely mystics, gave Jewry new direction. Their movement and teachings were a response to the traumatic impact of the devastating Crusades. The whole community had suffered bitterly and needed hope and guidance. These rabbis did not, therefore, regard themselves as an elite group but were concerned with their flock. They were accessible to the average person, whom they wished to give strength and guidance, for whom they prayed, and in whose behalf they hoped to perform miracles.

The first masters, KALONYMUS HA-HASID and JUDAH HA-HASID belonged to the Kalonymus family, which had brought the mystical traditions from the East via Lucca to the Rhineland. There they had raised distinguished disciples. Their speculations were essentially based on Hekhalot and Merkavah mysticism and on Sefer Yetzirah, on which they commented.

Seeing God anthropomorphically and expanding on this aspect, they described His powers: His revelation was granted to the prophets through visions, and their ascent to Him was given through prayer. The eternal and unfathomable God could not be conceived as entering human lives, but a divine power emanating from God; namely, *Kavod*, "the Glory," entered into communication with human beings and sustained them.

Prayer was vital. It rested on Torah and revelation and gave strength to the sorely tried. These mystics saw in every word of Torah and the prayerbook a divine message, a link between God and humanity. They added, subtracted, and compared *gematria*, the numerical value of words and verses, and insisted on unchanging and careful retention and pronunciation of every word and syllable. A changed letter could corrupt the hidden message and break the link to God.

All of life had to be placed under God. Ethics was of greatest importance. Rabbi Judah ha-Hasid wrote a work, *Sefer Hasidim*, which dealt with every aspect of human life. Through Mitzvot all of life to its smallest detail had to be placed under God. The more difficult a Mitzvah was the greater would be its spiritual reward. The ultimate Mitzvah was "the Sanctification of the Name," the surrender of life to Him, but in every Mitzvah lay a sanctification. It was a search for meaning in the trials of the Crusades that claimed so many martyrs. Looking at their surrounding world, the Hasidim severely condemned Christian knights for their wantonness, a warning to Jews to stay away from the customs of their neighbors. At the same time they admonished their folk to show the same complete allegiance to God that was demonstrated by these knights toward their liege lord, for whom they were prepared to lay down their lives. Such allegiance to God would preserve them, liberate them from their trials, and bring the days of the Messiah.

Influenced, perhaps by Christian asceticism to serve as mediators for their flock, they imposed upon themselves a severely ascetic way of life. Every moment was to testify to the denial of the world and its temptations and to become sanctified. The Hasid must be wholly detached from any desire, ask nothing for himself, accept scorn and vituperation with equanimity, never react or respond. In this manner, having no concerns for himself, he could pray for his fellow Jews and expect a divine reply. In similar manner all Jews must react to the world and retain their balance. This was response to the agonies of the Crusades.

The movement of the Hasidei Ashkenas was of relative short duration. Subsequent mystical studies found their centers in Southern France, Italy, and Spain, and eventually culminated in the Zohar.

The Zohar

Torah

The *Zohar*, "Book of Radiance," became for many Jews the most sacred book after Torah and Talmud. It is a homiletic commentary on the weekly Torah portions. By revealing the mysteries of the Torah, it emphasized its importance as the sustaining force of the universe and as protectress of the Jews. When the Yemenite Jews after centuries of persecution were rescued and brought to the State of Israel, they carried the Zohar next to the Torah in their arms. The book had uplifted them in their trials.

The Zohar was written toward the end of the thirteenth century by a Spanish Jewish mystic named Moses de Leon. Up to the time when Gershom Scholem uncovered its authorship, the work was erroneously ascribed to Rabbi Simeon ben Yohai, who lived in Palestine during the second century of the Christian era and, as an outspoken foe of the Roman occupiers of the land, had to hide for twelve years in a cave. There he and his son Eleazar studied Torah, obviously concentrating on mystical thoughts since they had no books. God miraculously sustained both men (B. Sabbat 33b).

The mystics had developed a special concept of Torah. Torah came to be seen as more than instruction and commandments, it was alive. God's Torah was with God from the beginning, was created even before the world was created. It contained the divine blueprint of creation, and remained God's consultant and coworker in creation and ever after. By equating "Wisdom" with Torah the mystics found proof in Proverbs.

> The Lord created me [wisdom, identified with Torah] at the beginning of His course, as the first of His works of old. At the start I was fashioned, at the beginning, the origin of the earth. There was still no deep when I was created. . . . Before the mountains were rooted . . . He had not yet made earth and fields. . . . I was there when He set the heavens into place. . . . When He assigned the sea its limits . . . when He fixed the foundations of the earth, I was with Him as a confidant, rejoicing before Him at all times, rejoicing in His inhabited world, finding delight with humanity. (Proverbs 8:22–31)

To some mystics, Torah was God's hidden Name. Torah as we possess it is an emanation of God's Name. Its text was an arrangement and rearrangement of the Name of God. Through this Name God created the universe. But when given to Israel the Name was "scrambled." Were we to decipher the scrambled text we possess and discover its true essence—that is, the Name of God—we would gain creative powers and creatively affect the world.

Torah and world form an organism. Through Torah, the universe was fashioned and maintained. The Torah was handed by God to Israel at Sinai; hence there exists an especially close relationship between Torah and Israel, that extends through both to the world. At Sinai, each of the 600,000 witnesses—the Israelites who left Egypt (see Exodus 12:37)—was given one letter of Torah, a mantra of his own; only in the days of the Messiah will each witness understand what it was and what it meant. But even now every Jew might affect the universe through his letter.

In history God arranges and rearranges primeval Torah, namely the letters of His Name, in accordance with His design for the world at every stage of its unfolding. This meant that, at every stage of history, the letters of Torah had a deeper, hidden meaning related to the times. The Jew who immerses himself in Torah, even one verse of Torah, may release forces that can liberate the world. Thus, more than mere study of Torah was called for; penetration into the depths of its hidden meanings was necessary.

The term *Pardes* was an acrostic for the methods of Torah study on ever deeper levels. *P* stands for *Pshat*, the literal meaning; *R* for *Remez*, the allegorical meaning; *D* for *Derash*, the talmudic interpretation; and *S* for *Sod*, the mystical interpretation. Because Torah was given to Israel, Israel had a special function in the world. Actually this method of scriptural interpretation on several levels corresponded to the methods of interpretation given by Christian interpreters, from whom it was probably taken.

The literal interpretation of Scripture was only a surface interpretation; the kabbalistic interpreter had to go ever deeper into the text and into himself. The student of the Zohar went into mystical depths.

The Sefirot

Penetrating into the depths of Torah, the Zohar developed the idea of the *Sefirot* found in Sefer Yetzirah. It explained: God Himself, the divine essence is forever hidden from us and unknowable to human beings. God is *En Sof*, the Infinite. God as unfathomable is affirmed.

At one time and for reasons known only to Himself, God decided to step out of His hiddenness and make Himself manifest through ten Sefirot, each lower than the preceding one. They reveal God to humanity and allow humans to relate to Him. These attributes emanating from En Sof, constitute the internal divine unfolding and, at the same time, these emanations constitute the unfolding of the world and are operative in the human being.

Each *Sefirah* (singular of Sefirot) has a name. Most widely used are the following:

1. *Keter*, Crown: God's supreme power, will, and thought
2. *Hokhmah*, Wisdom: God's blueprint for the world
3. *Binah*, Intelligence: the divine source of all existence
4. *Hesed*, Mercy: God's goodness
5. *Gevurah* or *Din*: God's power, justice, and punishment
6. *Tiferet* or *Rahamim*, Compassion: the divine quality balancing *Hesed* and *Din*
7. *Netzah*, Eternity: God's lasting endurance
8. *Hod*, Majesty: God's majesty
9. *Yesod*, Foundation: from which all operative forces in God flow into the world
10. *Malkhut*, Kingdom, or *Shekhinah*, Presence: a separate, feminine figure, that gathers all the elements of the nine other Sefirot, mirrors them, and carries them into the world. Malkhut is also described as Keneset Yisrael, the community of Israel, which is therefore the conduit from God to world.

These divine powers interact forming a tree, the tree of the world, whose root in En Sof cannot be known. They also form the figure of a man. Since humanity was created in the image of God, the Sefirot are also active in the human being.

A schematic representation may clarify and reveal additional meanings.

En Sof, inaccessible to us

1, 2, 3: *Keter–Binah–Hokhmah* are superior as they constitute God's head

4 *Hesed* is God's right arm, from which goodness flows

5 *Din* is God's left arm; it is judgment, but also the source of Evil

6 *Tiferet* or *Rahamim* balances 4 and 5; it is the divine heart

7 *Netzah* represents the right leg

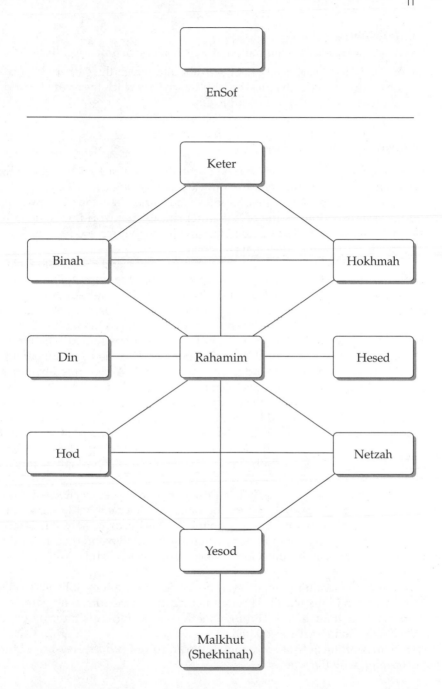

8 *Hod* represents the left leg

9 *Yesod* represents the Foundation in which all the Sefirot are gathered

10 *Malkhut –Shekhinah* is a special Sefirah, into which the gathered Sefirot are poured. It is the channel through which they reach the created world, and the world's prayers ascend to God.

The Meaning of the Sefirot

Our admittedly sketchy presentation of the Zohar reveals several basic elements. As *En Sof,* God is unfathomable. But God's unfolding in the Sefirot can be traced by human beings. *Keter,* the Crown, is God's brain; it is the divine will to create. *Hokhmah,* Wisdom, is the divine blueprint for the world. Hokhmah is identical with Torah. With *Binah,* Understanding (from the Hebrew, *beyn,* making distinction *between* things), the actual creation begins.

Hesed, Lovingkindness, is God's unlimited goodness and compassion. *Din,* Judgment, is God's judgment and punishment. It is also the source of Evil in the world, whose origin is thus placed in God Himself. Evil is the result of human sinfulness, but not exclusively. It did not come into the world because Adam's sinned, but was from the beginning woven into creation; it is in God Himself; it comes into being when God's power of judgment is unrestrained. The world could not endure however were it to be governed by *Din,* God's judgment, for human beings are too frail to be judged by strict justice. Were it ruled by *Hesed* alone humanity would not fear divine justice, it would become unrestrained in licentiousness and violence. These two Sefirot are therefore balanced by *Rahamim,* God's pity. It is placed between both, on the spine of the divine body; it is God's heart. God has a heart for His creation. *Netzah,* triumph, God's right leg (beneath Hesed), is the compassionate walk of God through His creation. *Hod,* Majesty, God's left leg beneath *Din,* is His majestic march through history as ruler and judge.

In *Yesod,* Foundation, all the Sefirot flow together. It is associated with the phallus and acquires importance, since the phallus is not merely the seat of desire, but of procreation and of circumcision that makes the drive holy. It is placed on the spine as medieval man believed that the sex drive emerged from the brain. It links God's will through God's heart to the creative, and therefore, holy act of humanity.

Shekhinah, the feminine, acquires importance because it establishes God's *Malkhut,* His reign in the world. Through her all the divine forces are gathered and transmitted to humankind. Through her the human pleas are transmitted to God. Shekhinah and Israel are equated.

The names of the Sefirot were mostly taken from David's blessing of the people opening with the words:

Yours, Lord, are greatness [*gedulah*], might [*gevurah*], splendor [*tiferet*] triumph [*netsah*] and majesty [hod]—yes all that is in heaven and on earth; to You belong kingship (mamlakhah=malkhut) and pre-eminence above all. (1 Chronicles 29:11)

The Zohar thus reveals the ways in which the God of Israel rules the universe. It created a cosmic panorama in which Israel under God's plan was indispensable to the world. To Israel belonged the Torah, the creative wisdom out of which God fashioned and maintained all of creation. Being identified with Shekhinah Israel became the conduit from God to world and world to God. Even Evil was explained as possibly originating in God; suffering therefore was to be accepted. It need not be the wages of sin. Eventually, God in *Rahamim* would redeem His people and in *Din* punish its persecutors. Israel had restorative power, leading through history to the coming of the Messiah.

The Ari

In 1492 the great Jewish community of Spain was destroyed and its members dispersed throughout the world. The *Ari* undertook to explain this tragedy and give the people ways of transcending it. RABBI ISAAC LURIA (1534–1572), born in Jerusalem of Ashkenasic descent, settled in the center of mystical thought, Safed, in what is now northern Israel. His disciples called him the ARI, meaning "lion," but it also was an acronym: *A* shkenasi *R* abbi *I* saac. He wrote very little; most of what is known of his beliefs has come through his disciples. His message rested on the Zohar but had to be adjusted to new conditions. An original thinker and charismatic personality, he introduced three basic teachings: *Tzimtzum, Shevirat Ha-Kelim,* and *Tikkun.*

Tzimtzum. In the beginning God completely filled the entire universe. But if there is nothing outside God, how can a world, God's creation, exist? In order to leave room for the world to exist, God withdrew into Himself, leaving room for creation. This was Tzimtzum. Without it there could have been no world, as God was All. By Tzimtzum God wished to achieve another purpose. Within God Himself various contrasting elements existed potentially, above all the dualism between good and evil. The divine withdrawal removed them from the Godhead. Their remnant remained however on the walls of the empty space as some water remains on the walls of a bucket, when its contents are poured out.

Shevirat Ha-Kelim. As God now proceeded to create the universe, a ray of the divine light emanated from Him into the now created space to assume the form of the Sefirot, the form of a man, as the Zohar had explained. To Luria *Adam Kadmon,* Man of the Beginning was actually a divine emanation. Now, going out from Adam Kadmon, all the Sefirot were to be filled with the divine light. Its rays were then to enter the world to be created, which would be wholly filled with the rays of the divine. But the vessels—except for those of the three supreme Sefirot, Keter, Hokhmah and Binah—could not contain the divine rays. Attacked by the Evil the vessels broke under the power of the divine light. Good and Evil were released.

Tikkun. With the "breaking of the vessels" the divine rays were dispersed and scattered into the darkest abysses of Evil. The forces of Evil found sustenance and strength for their destructive work from the divine emanations. The breaking of the vessels constituted the tragedy of history: God's Shekhinah, His indwelling in the world, had been dispersed; the sparks were scattered; the Shekhinah was in exile.

It now became the duty of all human beings to "gather the sparks," to mend the vessels, and return the sparks to the Shekhinah, the conduit to God. A life in full accord with the divine will could promote this task; then the world would be restored to unity and be filled with the divine. Humanity could thus redeem the world, redeem God Himself.

Had Adam not sinned he could have accomplished Tikkun. But he did sin, and the task therefore rested on humanity as a whole and on the Jews specifically. Had Israel not committed the sin of the golden calf it could have achieved Tikkun at Sinai. Now the duty rested on the Jewish community as the partner of God's Shekhinah, His indwelling in the universe and society. God's Shekhinah dwelt within the Jewish people. Since Israel, too, had been scattered and exiled, God was in double exile: exiled in a world of broken vessels and, again, with Israel, among the nations. Through obedience to Torah, Jews fulfilled their worldwide mission of gathering the sparks. With this gathering the Jewish exile and the divine exile come to an end.

Every Mitzvah Jews perform brings Tikkun closer, every transgression moves it farther away. Every action Jews carry out must lead them to ever deeper *Devekut*, cleaving to God. Every act must be filled with *Kavvanah*, the mystical intention to bring about the unification of God's Name and of the Shekhinah with God and the coming of the Messiah. The responsibility of the Jews for the entire human society is immense.

Acts and Symbols of Tikkun

After their exile from Spain, by which God Himself was again driven into a new exile, the Lurian circle expected the immediate arrival of the messianic times. This act of unification, of sacred marriage between Shekhinah and Israel, was symbolically reenacted by the mystics of Safed on various occasions, especially on the Sabbath.

According to general Jewish tradition, as Sabbath arrives, a second, higher, soul enters every Jew, and abides throughout the entire Sabbath. A sacred marriage takes place, of Jew and the Sabbath soul; the Sabbath is the bride. For mystics, the Shekhinah was represented in the Sabbath. Sabbath-Shekhinah was the Jew's bride. On the Sabbath, the Jew was united with the Shekhinah, the super soul.

The rabbis of talmudic times would go out into the fields on Friday evenings to welcome the Sabbath bride. The mystics of Safed would do the same, but now a mystical interpretation was added to the simple act of welcoming the Sabbath: the Shekhinah was welcomed. At dusk on Friday evening, dressed in white, they went out into the fields to welcome the Sabbath. They returned home singing the hymn, "Shalom aleikhem," Peace be with you, angels of God, may your coming, your blessing and your departure be unto peace. Like the talmudic rabbis, the mystics had marital intercourse during the night of the Sabbath (Betuvot 62b), but they gave this human union an added meaning: it reflected the mystical union of Shekhinah and the Jew. The Sabbath anticipated for a brief period the unification of God and universe. God therefore rejoiced as human beings creatively united in wedlock; He rejoiced doubly as they did so on the Sabbath. Sex acquires holiness.

Jewish mysticism frequently used sexual imagery. The asceticism of the Hasidei Ashkenas did not include abstinence from sex. It emerged as a required Mitzvah from the commandment "be fruitful and multiply" (Genesis 1:28). In the Sefirot, as we have seen, *Yesod*, Foundation, is equated with the phallus. Sex in wedlock and within the boundaries set by circumcision is rightful and human union may even reflect the sacred union between God and Israel.

Practices Based on the Mystics

Traces of the mystics' practice have remained to the present. At twilight on Friday evening, the congregation assembled in worship sings a hymn of welcome to the Sabbath about to enter. This hymn, "Lekha dodee," was composed by SOLOMON ALKABETZ (1488–1575), one of the mystics of Safed. The hymn begins with the following words, which also form the refrain after each strophe,

> Come, my beloved, the Bride to meet, the face of the Sabbath to receive and greet.

In traditional worship the congregation turns to the door while singing the final verse. It visualizes the entry of the Sabbath and welcomes the bride. The Congregation sings:

> Come then in peace, crown of Your Spouse,
> Come in joy and jubilation
> Into the midst of the faithful, the chosen folk.
> Come ye, O Bride, come ye, O Bride!

The hymn "Shalom aleikhem" has also become very popular. As children, we would sing it as the family, holding hands, marched around the Sabbath table. The Sabbath was the fullest expression of cleaving to God's Torah. The Sabbath provided a foretaste of Tikkun, the World of the Messiah. The Sabbath, ordained in the Ten Commandments, is basic among the Mitzvot and powerfully reminded the Jews that by observing Torah, they aided in Tikkun.

Under the influence of the Lurianic school and its call for *teshuvah*, a monthly minor Yom Kippur, was instituted in order to efface the sins of the past month that might retard Tikkun. Observed on the eve of the New Moon, it includes penitential prayers, Selihot, and, if ten men fasted, the Torah could be read. As a youth I regularly participated in this service in my hometown of Mainz.

Rabbi Solomon Alkabetz started the vigil on the eve of Shavuot, the feast of the giving of the Torah. It was held "to prepare the ornaments" of the "Bride Torah" to be "wed" anew to Israel on the following morning. The text consists of the opening and concluding passages of all the pericopes of Torah, all tractates of Mishnah and of selections from the Zohar. It is significantly called *Tikkun*. Today a lecture and discussion may take the place of the set text. A similar vigil is held on the eve of the seventh day of Sukkot. The day itself henceforth came to be regarded as a kind of Yom Kippur, a day of grace forgiveness of sins, and of God's judgment on the amount of water the world was to receive,

In the concluding Adoration after every service, we find the words

> We . . . hope in you, Eternal, our God soon to see Your splendor, sweeping idolatry away . . . perfecting—*le-takken*—the world by Your kingship so that all humanity will invoke Your name, bringing all the earth's wicked back to You.

In this sense, contemporary Jews have given the concept of Tikkun a modern meaning. Tikkun has come to mean participation in the restoration of the world through the promotion of social justice and universal peace. While Jews are standing under a special obligation, every human being is called upon and can contribute to Tikkun: the establishment of the world under the rule of God, the end of the exile, the building of a human universe that will be filled with divine radiance.

In this manner Rabbi Isaac Luria, by his teachings and his customs expanded the Zohar in accordance with the needs of his time. He explained to his contemporaries, the expellees from Spain, that their suffering had been ordained. They had to go to the uttermost depths in order to help "gather the sparks" dispersed there. The expulsion had a meaning under God's plan. Additionally, Rabbi Isaac initiated practical ways by which they could further promote Tikkun, and be comforted over their tragic fate. Mitzvot were the way. The Sabbath was a foretaste of the fulfillment. With it the Shekhinah entered their congregations and their homes and removed them and itself from exile to union. Torah, which was identical to Hokhmah, was equally the bride to be adorned through Mitzvot. Theshuvah was called for. Why God did not foresee and prevent the cosmic catastrophe that had occurred through the impact of Evil, was not explained. It had come to pass and now the Jews had to be the vanguard of Tikkun and suffer in steadfastness to redeem the world.

The messianic movement of Sabbatai Zevi had roots in Luria's theology. The sparks had been gathered, Tikkun had been achieved. When Sabbatai married a woman of doubtful background and character he proclaimed it as a union with the Shekhinah, whom he had redeemed.

Latter-Day Hasidism

We may now better understand the concepts of the latter day Hasidim, after the Khmelnitzky Massacres. They rested on tradition, which they evolved to meet existing conditions. The *Baal Shem*, Master of the Name, was Zaddik of whom the Talmud had already spoken. He was "the foundation of the world" and was capable of influencing God's actions. He was a person who was free of iniquities, who faced no barrier between himself and God and had creative powers. Like the Hasidei Ashkenas, he never asked anything for himself and was therefore able to intercede with God and perform miracles in behalf of others. He guided his flock in *Devekut*, the cleaving to God in every thought and act. Restoration of the unity of the Name, as Luria had taught, was to be the motivating force of every action. At times, we read in Hasidic prayer books, preceding a *Berakhah* (blessing), the words: "I am setting out to perform this holy act [initiated by the Berakhah] to unify the Name." Through study of Torah and performance of Mitzvot, but also through performance of daily pursuits, the redemption of God, humanity, and universe could be hastened; the messianic age could be brought nearer. This was reason for joy. The condition was that each of these actions were undergirded by *kavvanah*, the holy intent to unify the Name.

The Zaddik peered into the future; he had magical powers. He gave advice and counsel. He gathered his flock on special occasions, such as holy days. The Third Meal in the waning hours of the Sabbath, became a mystical gathering. The guests, permitted to partake of a morsel of the Rebbe's food, watched him awestruck, as he, peering into the ever-deepening darkness, spoke in cryptic words about deepest mysteries and predictions of the future. The Third Meal, adapted to modern changed conditions and feelings, was reintroduced in Israel by the poet Haim Nahman Byalik.

Adaptations in Modern Life—Mystical Search Is Renewed

HAIM NAHMAN BYALIK (1873–1934) inaugurated the Third Meal while living in Palestine, naming it *Oneg Shabbat*, "Sabbath Delight." Byalik was a poet, uniquely qualified to combine the cultures of the West with the heritage of the Jews. He was born and raised in Poland, where he received a thorough talmudic education. Coming to Berlin he was exposed to the West and its culture; in 1923, he settled in the Holy Land. In his poetry he gave expression to the soul of the Jewish people, and at the same time, demonstrated the power of the Hebrew language to express every shade of feeling and emotion. He came to be regarded as Israel's national poet. Under his inspiration the Third Meal became an hour of reunion and rededication for the members of the kibbutz. In word and song they shared their thoughts, hopes, and aspirations. In the atmosphere of the waning Sabbath they renewed their dedication to each other and to the Land of Israel, whose builders they were.

As a spiritual fellowship gathering, *Seudah shelishit*, the Third Meal has come to be observed among many Diaspora groups as well. The Hasidim celebrate it in its traditional form. *Oneg Shabbat* gatherings after worship, such as on Friday night, have adopted Byalik's term for the fellowship meetings on the Sabbath. Some of its spirit has entered other occasions of Jewish celebration.

The contemporary interest in Jewish mysticism may reflect the disillusionment of our postmodern society with Reason as the absolute validator of propositions. It did not bring enlightenment; it led to the Holocaust. The *Shoah*, the Holocaust itself, raised questions for which reason had no answer. Once again, conditions in Jewish life led to the attempt to find the way to God through mystical interpretations and actions. Their mission "to gather the shells" had forced Jews to go to the uttermost depths of hell. Thus mysticism might cast a ray of understanding of the mysteries of God's absence in the Holocaust and God's returned presence in the restoration of the State of Israel.

The Golem

Among the elements connected with mysticism, the *Golem*, "shapeless matter," artificial man, has held great fascination for writers, anthropologists, and people in general, Jews and non-Jews alike. According to Talmud and Sefer Yetzirah, rabbis supposedly did create humaniod beings that were devoid of speech. Abraham, according to Sefer Yetzirah, created persons, or *nefashot*. The term *nefesh* (singular from *nefashot*) is translated as "soul"; so is the word *neshamah*. But there is a difference between the two. *Nefesh* stands simply for "person," *neshamah* makes the person human by giving him a soul and endowing her with speech.

According to the Midrash, God created Adam, (Hebrew for "earth creature") first as a golem out of earth taken from all corners of the world, and then breathed His spirit into him, the *neshamah*, and he became a living and speaking human. The Hasidei Ashkenas were said to have used humanoids as their servants, bringing them to life when they needed them and turning them back to dust when their task was done. They came to life as the word *Emet*, "Truth," was written on their forehead, and reverted to earth when the first letter was erased; *Met* means "Death."

The last, said to have fashioned a golem was RABBI JUDAH LOEB of Prague (1520–1609), who was known for his scholarship and asceticism. As a mathematician Rabbi Loeb was a friend of Tycho Brahe, the astronomer, who was also an astrologer. Together with two disciples Rabbi Loeb brought a clay figure to life by placing a slip of paper with God's name on his forehead. He used this golem as servant during the week and as rescuer of Jews from the plots of Jew haters. But one Friday evening the golem went berserk and had to be destroyed. This occurred as the Sabbath was welcomed with the Sabbath Psalm (Psalm 92), which had to be interrupted and started over again after the golem had been returned to clay. To this day, the Psalm is recited twice in the venerable Altneuschul synagogue of Prague.

The creation of humanoids seems to have fascinated the media. Frankenstein was such a creature in the motion picture by that name. Its moods and actions were unpredictable. Following this film many others of the same type were produced and enjoyed wide appeal. The actions of Jewish mystics has come a long way.

CHAPTER 6

Emancipation and the Modern Age in Western Europe

WHAT IS EMANCIPATION?

The European Renaissance led to the Age of Reason in the seventeenth century, which in turn led to the Age of Enlightenment in the eighteenth century. The motto of these ages was Reason and Progress, and these two principles reigned supreme. In the light of reason, discrimination against any group on account of its religion was irrational, and therefore, unacceptable. Enlightened progress demanded the abolition of the disabilities imposed on the Jews on account of their faith.

Enlightenment led to the Emancipation, which means "setting free," granting freedom and civic equality to those who have been without it. For the Jews it moved from West to East. In the United States they obtained their civic equality from the beginning, in principle and without conditions. Under the impact of the Declaration of Independence and the Constitution the Western European countries could not withhold it. In England it was gradually attained and in Holland the last restrictions against Jews were removed. It was different in France and in Germany; there Emancipation had a twofold meaning. The Jews were to be given equal rights as citizens. In return, the Jews were to cast off their isolation; relinquish their internal jurisdiction; immerse themselves wholeheartedly in the society and culture of the countries in which they lived; and adapt to the majority in their education, their way of life, their cultural and aesthetic values, and their political allegiance. Above all, Jews had to identify fully with the countries of their newly granted citizenship and find there the emotional security of belonging they had hitherto experienced in their own peoplehood. Meanwhile, they were on probation. Society had to be won over from its long-held views and prejudices.

To these demands Western European Jews wholly agreed. Their upper classes had become widely acculturated and chafed under the dichotomy of being accepted in high society but legally cast out. They hoped the time of probation would be short if all the Jews adjusted quickly. This called for thorough reforms. Worship had to be modernized: Jewish law had to be reexamined and, in part, dismantled; Jewish tradition had to be reinterpreted. A new rationale for the survival of Jews had to be found. They had to abolish their internal autonomy and their sense of being a "nation" and reconstitute themselves as an exclusively religious body. Most of these goals were desirable for an evolving religion and its adherents; the ill lay in the fact that the motivation, to a large degree, came not from within but from the desire to please the non-Jewish world. This led a number of Jews to a complete negation of their heritage. They were baptized.

The Emancipation equally stimulated forces of value to Judaism. *The Science of Judaism* was created. Its founder was LEOPOLD ZUNZ (1794–1886). Hitherto Judaism had never been explored scientifically as were the other religions and cultures. If it were to become "respectable" and perhaps even find entrance as a subject matter to be taught in universities, its essence, origin, and evolution had to be scientifically researched. This new approach would also give modern Jews a new understanding and might increase their spirit of allegiance.

Exposed to general theology and philosophy—some of whose representatives were anti-Semitic—Jews had to engage in these disciplines. Their motivation lay not simply in defense, but in the earnest desire to give proof of their rightful equality as citizens by making valuable contributions in the fields of culture, art, science, and scholarship. Worship and religious practices were adjusted to the thinking and aesthetic taste of the time. This cut into traditional ways, but it kept many Jews within Judaism. Without these new forms they might have deserted it.

The adjustment was not entirely successful. The number of Christians of truly goodwill was limited. The majority had for centuries been indoctrinated with contempt for the Jews; fear of increased Jewish competition in business and professions also played a role. The majority remained antagonistic and the anti-Semitic undercurrent remained strong. In Germany, for instance, equality remained a mirage and full security was never attained.

Gaining Citizenship Rights

The *French Revolution,* inspired by the French Enlightenment philosophers and the American Revolution, proclaimed "The Rights of Man" equal rights for all men. It brought the Jews equality in France, with the proviso that it was granted to individuals only and not to the nation. Should the Jews have equal rights as citizens? "To Jews as individuals we shall give everything, to Jews as a nation, nothing" was the statement of Clermont Tonnère in the French Assembly during a debate on the enfranchisement of the Jews. Based on this principle, Jews were granted civil rights in 1791.

The impact of this regulation went deep. To be in accord with modern life and able to enjoy the blessings of citizenship, Jews had to remold their own thinking. Some of Judaism's age-old supports were thereby weakened. Others would have to be strengthened.

The French revolutionary armies carried the liberation of the Jews into the countries they conquered. Napoleon, who eventually emerged as absolute monarch, was a man of contrasting traits. He was a child of the Revolution. As such he liberated the Jews in the nations he had overpowered. He equally was an autocrat, who required absolute obedience in thought and action from all his subjects. To make certain the Jews would be truly obedient to him, he completely dismantled any internal jurisdiction. Instead he organized their congregations in regional consistories subject to the one in Paris, which was subject to him. He also called a group of leading rabbis to Paris to form a Sanhedrin, which had the difficult task of adjusting Jewish laws to Napoleon's desire without harming Jewish tradition.

Pressured by the state, but also motivated by the desire for active participation in the life of the nation as recognized citizens, the Sanhedrin had to walk a thin line. It held that

> ... the divine Law, the precious heritage of our ancestors, contains within itself dispositions which are political and dispositions which are religious ... the religious dispositions are, by their nature, absolute and independent of circumstances and of the age ... this does not hold true of the political dispositions ... which were taken for the government of the people of Israel in Palestine when it possessed its own kings, pontiffs and magistrates. ... (Quoted from N. N. Glatzer, *The Dynamics of Emancipation;* Boston: Beacon Press, 1965, p. 9)

The Sanhedrin could therefore proclaim that the Jews recognized no country but the one in which they held citizenship and for which they were willing to lay down their lives. French Jews saw all Frenchmen as their brothers. Interfaith marriage placed the rabbis in a dilemma. They had to yield to Napoleon's pressure but could not abrogate Jewish law. Eventually they declared that interfaith marriage, while inadmissible under religious law, was to be recognized by Jews as a valid marriage bond because it conformed to state law. A person who had entered such a marriage in a justice court would remain a Jew, but rabbis could not solemnize the bond.

Following Napoleon's example, the European states organized the Jewish communities as religious bodies, eliminating such rights as their internal self-government and the judicial powers of rabbis over family relations. Judaism was now a denomination. Given their citizenship rights, the Jews were willing to fight for their countries. In Prussia, hundreds volunteered in the war against Napoleon (1815). But when Napoleon had been beaten, the rights of the Jews were rescinded.

A new uphill struggle began. So harsh were the laws (for instance, in Bavaria, where marriages were restricted), that many Jews migrated to the United States. Efforts to unite Germany on a democratic basis led to revolutions in 1830 and 1848; both failed and forced many liberals and Jews to find a life of freedom in America.

Slowly the Jews obtained citizenship rights. In Germany, they were not granted full and unchallenged equality until 1918. Before then, with few exceptions, they could not be judges, civil servants, or army officers while maintaining their faith.

It had been the hope of the Jews that by exhibiting their patriotism they might show the world that they were deserving of full equality. Insecurity turned many into superpatriots, staying aloof from Eastern European Jews, whom they supported but from whom they kept apart. Yet the developments of the time did give hope that equality would emerge, and German Jews saw in Germany their home. After all, they had lived in it for close to 2,000 years, had fought for it in the wars of liberation from Napoleon and ever since, had taken their place in its cultural life, and had benefited it economically by their industry. They were a good, substantial middle class with all its virtues and faults. About a half million strong, they left 12,000 of their youths on the battlefields fighting for Germany in World War I.

Moses Mendelssohn

In MOSES MENDELSSOHN (1729–1786), German, and subsequently, all of Jewry found its great leader. A small, hunchbacked man, his early growth stunted by hunger and deprivation, he had a brilliant intellect, having immersed himself in both Jewish and non-Jewish philosophy. Liberal in thought, progressive in ideas, Mendelssohn was deeply religious and faithful in the performance of Mitzvot. As a young man, he won a prize for a work submitted to the Prussian Academy, his competitor being none other than Immanuel Kant.

Moving to Berlin he found in GOTTHOLD EPHRAIM LESSING a guide who helped him perfect his German style of writing. A deep friendship developed between the two men, and the grief over Lessing's early death shortened Mendelssohn's own life. Lessing (1729–1781) was indeed an exceptional man. The son of a Protestant pastor, he became an outspoken advocate of religious freedom in the spirit of the Enlightenment. An acclaimed poet, playwright, theater critic, and polemicist he was one of the few recognized intellectuals in Germany who actively fought for the Jews and against the deep-seated anti-Jewish prejudices existing in all German circles. His most enduring drama, *Nathan the Wise,* was a resounding call for religious equality. Its leading character was patterned after Moses Mendelssohn.

Mendelssohn's circle eventually included the leading minds in Berlin. For years, however, he could live in Berlin only as a "domestic employee" of a wealthy Jew. This man had been granted a residence permit by Frederick II (the Great), king of Prussia, because as a rich person he was "useful" to the king. Public opinion among the leading minds eventually forced the reluctant Frederick to grant Mendelssohn a residence permit in Berlin. Mendelssohn's election to the Prussian Academy of Sciences was vetoed by the king.

By his early philosophical writings Mendelssohn had become universally renowned as a leading representative of the Enlightenment. He was called the "German Socrates." Yet he remained a truly faithful Jew, defending his faith cou-

Mendelssohn, Lavater, and Lessing in Discussion, by Moritz Oppenheim. Fictional description of the three in friendly debate. Mendelssohn is sitting at the left of the table; Lessing is standing. Oppenheim was a nineteenth-century Jewish painter of family and religious life. (Photo by the author, courtesy of Judah L. Magnes Museum, Jewish Museum of the West, Berkeley, California.)

rageously. When Johann Caspar Lavater (1741–1801), a Swiss clergyman, challenged him either to validate Judaism against Christianity in the light of reason or to become a Christian, Mendelssohn proudly replied, "My examination . . . has strengthened me in the faith of my fathers, I hereby witness before the God of truth . . . that I shall abide by these my convictions as long as my soul shall not change its nature."

In his work *Jerusalem or About Religious Power and Judaism*, published in 1783, Mendelssohn rested his thoughts on those of the British philosopher John Locke and possibly the American Declaration of Independence. He explained that the State rested on a contract between the citizens and their ruler. State and ruler committed themselves to protect the life, liberty and property of the citizens. The State had the power to direct, supervise, and restrain their *actions* to prevent harm; it had no right, however, to judge their *conscience* and grant or withhold full equality from any citizen on account of his convictions and beliefs, including religious ones. Jews had a right to full equality.

As a man of the Enlightenment, Mendelssohn showed how the Enlightenment assumed that all humanity had equal access to the truth that brings salvation. The ethical ideals of religion could be found through reason, which was granted to all. He therefore had to explain the revelation at Sinai given only to the Jews. He held that the Jews at Sinai were given not ideals but a law. Judaism was revealed law; its core was Mitzvot. These were symbol actions. Their purpose was to strengthen in the Jews the commitment to the universal ethical obligations, found by reason and binding on all human beings. The mind of the Jew was not constrained by dogmas to be believed, but was free to follow reason into the fields of philosophy and science—in short, into general culture.

Having defended and explained the Jews and Judaism to the world, Mendelssohn regarded it as an equal duty to educate his fellow Jews and lead them to complete adjustment to their environment. It was their duty to contribute fully to the culture and thought of the countries of their citizenship. To guide them, he directed the translation of the Pentateuch into modern German and wrote a Hebrew commentary as well. Thus Jewry could acquire the vernacular language—the gateway to communication and participation—using its most sacred treasure, the Torah, as guide. In modern German, they would be called to the performance of Mitzvot as found in Torah. The Hebrew language of his commentary would elucidate, so that throughout life they might remain staunch adherents to the divine commandments.

Mendelssohn expected the Christian world to grant full recognition to its Jewish citizens and to respect their faith, even as Jews respected all faiths. This was a step toward Judaism as religion, pure and simple, even though Mendelssohn was unaware of it; the element of peoplehood was de-emphasized. Modernization began, and the Science of Judaism owes him its beginnings.

JEWISH RELIGION ADAPTS TO A NEW AGE

The religious communities, both Christian and Jewish, stood under the supervision of the state. The ruling kings and princes hoped that the Jews would eventually accept Christianity. This was to be accomplished by various means. The king of Prussia prohibited every innovation in Jewish worship, with the idea that it would eventually be so contrary to modern taste that Jews would turn to the Church instead. Others promoted reforms in Judaism, regarding them as stepping stones to Christianity. The traditional rabbis preferred the Prussian solution though for the opposite reason: They believed it would create a wall between Judaism and Christianity and thus guard against conversion. They regarded every form of modernization as dangerous, even if it was not contrary to Jewish law. There was opposition, for instance, to Mendelssohn's translation of the Bible on the grounds that it would draw readers to German literature, alienating them from Jewish learning and leading to religious decay. But new trends could not be stopped.

Denominations

The transformation of Judaism could not be avoided. From the outside came pressure from governments, from the inside the necessity of adjustments to keep Jews within the faith. The extent of the changes required in worship and practice divided rabbinical leaders, and denominations emerged within Judaism. Some rabbis saw the need for incisive changes and founded *Reform Judaism* (Abraham Geiger); more traditional rabbis founded *Conservatism* (Zacharias Frankel); and full traditionalists created *Neo-Orthodoxy* (Samson Raphael Hirsch). They all were agreed that rabbis had to be trained academically in universities and modern seminaries. Reform established the *Hochschule für die Wissenschaft des Judentums* (University for the Science of Judaism) at Berlin. Geiger was one of its teachers; Conservatism established the *Jüdisch Theologisches Seminar* (Jewish Theological Seminary) at Breslau, founded by Zacharias Frankel; and Neo-Orthodoxy created the *Rabbiner Seminar* (Rabbinical Seminary) at Berlin, founded by Esriel Hildesheimer.

Struggles: Internal and External

It may be helpful to explain the new Jewish movements in roughly Hegelian terms, particularly as some of the innovators, especially Hirsch, were consciously influenced by him. During the nineteenth century GEORG FRIEDERICH HEGEL (1770–1831) was the most influential philosopher of his time. Hegel saw history as the unfolding of the Absolute, God, through a pattern of thesis–antithesis–synthesis. He also saw the Prussian state as the ultimate of this evolution.

Old-time Judaism, pre-Mendelssohnian in spirit and action, denied an outward process of evolution in religion. God had revealed Himself. Torah had been laid down in written and oral law, Tanakh and Talmud. It was eternal in its formulations. Its view of Jewish historical destiny, however, might be explained in Hegelian terms. Thesis: God gave His Torah at Sinai; He placed the people into their land, where Torah could be the foundation of a society living as a sovereign nation. Antithesis, working upon thesis: Expelled from the land, the Jews were charged with the task of self-preservation in adversity; they were segregated. By means of a new commitment to Torah, and growing through steadfastness in adversity, they would purify themselves of the dross of their errors, specifically a disregard of Torah that had caused their exile. Synthesis, emerging from thesis and antithesis: In Messianic times, Israel, refined by trial, would be restored to its land forever to live on its own soil wholly true to God and guided exclusively by Torah.

Reform Judaism saw the unfolding of history from the perspective of the modern age. Thesis: the tradition based on Scripture and Talmud as understood in the past. Antithesis: biblical scholarship and the modern concept of ethics, reacting upon tradition and correcting it. Synthesis, emerging from both: a modern Judaism, retaining Jewish social ethics but unfolding within Western society through Jews who took seriously the newly obtained civic equality and the duties it entailed, and were fully immersed in the state.

Conservative Judaism saw the unfolding within the stream of internal Jewish history. Thesis: pre-Mendelssohnian Judaism that had become alienated from the world and its progression. Antithesis: Reform Judaism, too enthusiastically endorsing the new at the expense of emptying Judaism of content. Synthesis, embodying and transcending both: Judaism as the unfolding spirit of the Jewish people. It synthesizes old and new. Ever evolving out of its own inner resources and forces, it is attuned to both the past and the needs of changing times. The Jews were fully immersed in the state, but equally tied to the Jewish people.

Neo-Orthodoxy also rested on the principle that Jews had to be fully immersed in the state that had granted them citizenship rights, without giving up the commandments of Torah. *Thesis:* "Torah-true" Judaism, obedient in every way to the rules of the *Shulhan Arukh* but without contact to the world. Antithesis: Western culture. Synthesis: "Israel-Man," fully Jew and, within his Judaism (in Hirsch's view, *on account of* his Judaism), fully immersed in the society, the culture of the West. But this culture was only permitted to serve Judaism as a handmaiden. As long as it did not touch the core of tradition, and especially as it enhanced traditional Judaism, this culture was approved.

Although it is possible to analyze the developments in Judaism in Hegelian terms, the leaders of Judaism, with the exception of Hirsch, whose works and letters reveal his influence, may not have been conscious of Hegel's influence on their thinking. Orthodoxy would have rejected such an analysis. It rejects both any legitimate impact of non-Jewish philosophy and the legitimacy of any non-Orthodox Jewish movement. It therefore denies any possibility of having been influenced by them.

Reform Judaism

Reform Judaism was the first of the new movements to emerge. Its break with tradition was in conscious response to the perceived needs of the time, and a deliberate means to preserve the allegiance of modern Jews to their heritage. The Mitzvot, which for Mendelssohn had still been untouchable, now came under scrutiny. Modern biblical scholarship had to be applied to Torah, Talmud, and Halakhah, subjecting them to critical analysis. Questions regarding their origin and purpose had to be asked and answered. Additionally, the demands of the modern state and its society to whom the Jews were committed had to be considered. Did dogmas and principles relating to the Land and Jewish peoplehood still have a place in the religion of the modern Jew as a citizen of a Western European country? What about the Mitzvot expressing these principles, or those setting Jews apart from the rest of the population? A number of conferences were called (notably in Braunschweig in 1844 and Frankfurt in 1845) to examine Torah and Mitzvot scientifically and in view of new conditions. Particular individuals provided the driving force and affected the decisions.

ABRAHAM GEIGER (1810–1874) was the towering genius of Reform Judaism, essentially its founder. To him, as a rationalist the revelation at Sinai as historical fact was not proven since science offered no proof of any revelation. Mendelssohn had seen Judaism as revealed law; Geiger rejected this idea, as he rejected any revealed doctrines. He opposed the prayers for a return to the Land; the land of his citizenship was the land of the Jew. The Jewish hope for peace and equal rights, symbolized in the Messiah, had found its fulfillment through the emancipation. This was an attack on the validity of Torah, Mitzvot, the whole body of Halakhah, and the Land. What remained was the deep-seated sense of kinship with the Jewish people and a pride in its spiritual character. The genius of the people, "revelation" in a non-literal sense, served as rationale for its survival. As Geiger expressed it,

> *Is not the Jewish people . . . endowed with a genius, with a religious genius?* . . . an aboriginal power to understand more vividly, and feel more intensely the close relation between the spirit of man and the Supreme Spirit? . . . If this be so, we may speak of a close contact between the individual spirit and the Supreme Spirit . . . so that it could break through its confining limits: it is—let us not hesitate to pronounce the word—revelation, and this, too, as it was manifested in the whole people. . . . Nor does Judaism claim to be the work of single individuals, but that of the whole people. Judaism has grown from the people of revelation. . . . Judaism is a religion of truth, discovering, as it does the unchangeable and everlasting: This is its everlasting essence. (Quoted from Gunther Plaut, *The Rise of Reform Judaism*; New York: World Union for Progressive Judaism, I, 1963, pp. 126–27.)

Forms therefore change and evolve as the insight of the individual Jew directs. Torah becomes a source of ethics, performance of Mitzvot becomes a matter of individual decision, but not binding, the Talmud and Shulhan Arukh have no power of commitment, and the Messianic hope has been fulfilled in Jewish Emancipation that has allowed the Jews to be missionaries of ethics to humanity.

The genius of the Jewish people as teacher of ethics was strongly emphasized. The Hebrew language of prayer was to be retained, in part at least for its emotional appeal. Education, sermon, and worship now were to form Torah in this new interpretation, and Mitzvot were to be understood as the missionary ideal of spreading ethics throughout the world. For these the Jew must live. Geiger was both a dynamic personality and a scholar. His impact has been felt in all of modern Jewry. The effect of Geiger's Reform Judaism was strongest in the United States.

Conservative Judaism

Among the participants in the rabbinical conference at Frankfurt was ZACHARIAS FRANKEL (1801–1875), Chief Rabbi of Dresden. But he left it, convinced that its radical approach was a *negative* Judaism. He, too, was a man of science, who knew Jewish history as a process of evolution. Judaism had never stood still; hence its future development could be promoted on the basis of a "positive historical Judaism." The Torah, heritage of the congregation of Jacob, belongs to the people. Between its instructions and the changing conditions of life exists a constant creative tension. The people, in their inherent wisdom, slowly and gradually adjust Torah to life, the Talmud being a prime example of such an adjustment. The Torah is thus anchored not in an unchanging word of God but in the people, who, as His coworkers, develop it continually by common, unspoken consensus. "The positive forms of Judaism are organically integrated into its character and form a part of its life and, therefore, may not be coldly and heartlessly disposed of"(Plaut, *Rise of Reform Judaism*, p. 86).

This process is slow, but it retains Torah, Halakhah, Mitzvot (unless changed by the people), and the principles of Jewish peoplehood and of the Land and its redemption. The link with past and future is never broken. Study and education are essential, and, as in every living organism, cells will die and new ones will be fashioned. This is Conservative Judaism, particularly strong in Germany; we shall note its rise in America as well.

Neo-Orthodoxy

It is important to remember that Neo-Orthodoxy was a reform movement. Measured by contemporary standards, it was not a liberal one, though pre-Mendelssohnian Jews would have regarded it as very liberal. The German sermon, the rabbinical robe, and the decorum at worship were sternly enforced innovations and reforms.

SAMSON RAPHAEL HIRSCH (1808–1888) was the articulator of Neo-Orthodoxy. He was imbued with the ideas of Moses Mendelssohn. To Hirsch, written and oral Torah was literal divine revelation, both in law and in doctrines; hence it could never be changed. Yet Hirsch was also in tune with Geiger, whom he saw as his great adversary. The missionary ideal of which Geiger had spoken was also to be pursued. But to Hirsch this could be done only if Jews both studied Torah and lived by the Mitzvot in every detail. By setting an example of obedience to God in their religious conduct and in all human relationships Jews could set a standard. They had been sent into the Diaspora to show the way back to God to a world that had become estranged from Him through selfishness and materialism. The Jew should be *Israel–Man*: being a paragon of humanity by being a Jew. Mitzvot were explained as symbols enshrining this message and fortifying it in the observant Jew, making him "priest of humanity," teacher, leader in ethics. The performance of Mitzvot would set the Jews apart; beyond that they were to seek the friendship of their Christian neighbors.

> Practice justice and love as thy Torah teaches thee; be just in action, true in your word, bear love in thine heart toward thy non-Jewish brother, as thy Torah teaches thee; feed his hungry, clothe his naked, refresh his sick, comfort his sorrowers, advise his bewildered, hasten to his assistance with counsel and action in his need and danger, exhibit the whole, noble fullness of thine Israel-dom. (Samson Raphael Hirsch, *Nineteen Letters on Judaism*, Altona, 1837, fifteenth letter)

The Jews' obligation to immerse themselves fully in the state, the culture, and civilization of the Western world rested on Jeremiah's letter to the Jewish community of Babylonia. It was a duty to combine *Torah im Derekh Eretz*, "Torah with worldly culture." The aesthetic values of the West were also to be fully incorporated in life and religious worship, provided they did not disagree with Torah. The Land, whose redemption was not denied, had to take a secondary place. It would be redeemed in God's own good time and in conjunction with a transformation of all of humanity; prayer for its restoration under God's will was ordained, it entailed the plea for universal redemption, but to restore the Land through human action would be against God's will.

Orthodoxy according to Hirsch's definition was the best assurance for and foundation of the most dedicated citizenship. Rejecting any modification of the law, Hirsch never attended any of the rabbinical conferences at which such modifications were discussed. In his later congregation at Frankfurt, Hirsch eventually severed any contact with institutionalized non-Orthodox Jewry. His ideas, however, constituted reforms. His profound allegiance to the state and diaspora life forced him to the ingenious idea that the redemption of the Land would go with that of humanity as a whole at an as yet undetermined time. The Reformers rejected the expectation of a return. Hirsch combined it with the redemption of humanity, allowing him fully to endorse Jewish life in the Diaspora, especially Germany. This interpretation, commanding immersion in state and society and adoption of its ways as a permanent condition mirrored Reform, though it was combined with orthopraxis, the practice of traditional Orthodox laws.

Neo-Orthodoxy, strictly separating itself from all other religious groups, required a highly acculturated and educated Jewish community for its implementation. Initially small in America, its influence is being increasingly felt. A new generation of university-educated Orthodox Jews, no longer separated from the stream of Western culture, has found in Samson Raphael Hirsch and his works an articulate guide in its search for a synthesis of Orthodox Judaism and contemporary civilization. Hirsch's numerous works have been translated into English.

Nineteenth-Century Jewry

During the Emancipation period, the various branches of the House of Israel developed wide divergences. We can discern roughly four major groups. They were to become united again by the tragic events of the *Shoah* (Hebrew for "catastrophic" and the term for the Holocaust).

In Western Europe, where Jews enjoyed citizenship rights in varying degrees, Germany formed the ideological center. The Conservative outlook was predominant, Neo-Orthodox encompassed about one-fifth, and Reform was insignificant. English Jewry followed the general principles of Hirsch. French and Italian and, to a degree, Austrian urban Jews (in contrast to the rural population, which was Orthodox) were more inclined to follow Frankel's school of Conservatism. In all of these countries Judaism was seen by its own adherents and by the population in general as a religion.

Eastern European Jewry was primarily Orthodox in the pre-Mendelssohnian sense. It lived by itself in deep piety. There were some stirrings of "Haskalah-enlightenment" among intellectuals, but there was no understanding of the modern philosophies of Judaism and its practices among the Jewish populace. Emancipation in the political sense never truly occurred, and the Jews in their distress found strength in their traditions.

The *Yishuv* (Jewish community) in Palestine that was to become the State of Israel was influenced by socialism. To the pioneers, the Land was part of their living religion. Finally, there was American Jewry (discussed in Chapter 7), as yet amorphous but tending to be pragmatic in its approach.

THE IMPACT OF ANTI-SEMITISM

Anti-Semitism was far from dead, even in the West. Anti-Jewish sentiment was found among Christian teachings, and, for many, it had been so deeply instilled by these teachings and the events of history that it had become second nature. It broke out violently in France in connection with the Dreyfus case (discussed on p. 161). In Germany it permeated the religious, intellectual, and economic life, the court, the Church, the university, the army, and industry.

Why did Germany become the focal point of modern anti-Semitism? (Russian anti-Semitism was of the medieval type.) Because Jews had lived in Germany without interruption for close to two thousand years, there was a chance in Germany for the various forms of anti-Semitism to be piled on each other as history progressed. Jews had been expelled from England and France for many centuries and gradually been accepted again later. In Germany, prejudice against Jews became ingrained. Luther had legitimized it, and the Jews, as a prosperous but small minority, could therefore be used as scapegoats.

Medieval anti-Semitism had economic foundations, envy of Jewish business successes, but in the main it was theological. The Jews, having rejected Christ, were accursed; baptism would wash away the curse and make the Jew, now a Christian, equal. Modern anti-Semitism became "racial," allowing no escape for the Jew, even by conversion to Christianity.

But German anti-Semitism had a specific characteristic. It was a response to the perceived political weakness of the German nation compared to the powers of Europe, such as France and England. Germany had long been split into a multitude of small and weak states. It had been conquered by Napoleon. Romanticism, a movement that placed emotion over reason and included a yearning for the past, had replaced the Enlightenment. The Germans were gripped by Romanticism. The population, chafing under German powerlessness, looked back to the Middle Ages when the German Empire supposedly had been the most powerful nation in Europe. At that time the Jews had been excluded from society, now their influence had grown. They were held responsible for German weakness; their subversive influence had caused it. The remedy lay in the creation of a *völkisch* (nationally homogenous German) society, bound together by race, common emotion, and Christianity. The Jews would, by necessity, be excluded from it, and might best be eliminated from it. Johann Gottlied Fichte (1762–1842), a founder of the University of Berlin, declared that even conversion to Christianity could not change the corrupt character of the Jew. From his club, Christians, whose grandparents had been Jews, were excluded. This was pure racism.

Germany became a united country under Prussian leadership only in 1871. A latecomer among the great powers, it suffered from an inferiority complex and saw itself constantly as a potential victim of forces from abroad and subversion from within. Only the *völkisch* spirit, could assure its strength. Among the leaders of the movement was, among others, the imperial Court Preacher Adolf Stoecker. In the universities, it cast deep roots not only among the student fraternities but also the professors. The highly respected German historian Heinrich Treitschke coined the slogan, "The Jews are our misfortune." It was widespread in the population. In 1881 a petition signed by a quarter of a million persons was submitted to the government, demanding the closing of the frontier to Jewish immigrants, the elimination of Jews from all administrative positions, and a special registry for Jews. There was an anti-Semitic party in the German parliament. In 1882 the first international congress of anti-Semites was held in Dresden.

This German anti-Semitism had a profound impact on the rest of Europe, especially Eastern Europe and above all Russia. It was felt that Germany, land of thinkers, would not have embraced anti-Semitism were it not justifiable. Austria had an anti-Semitic party in its parliament and Vienna installed an anti-Semitic mayor, Karl Lueger, who became Hitler's role model.

In spite of the widespread prejudice among Christian Germans, the German Jews felt that if they excelled as good citizens the Germans would recognize them in their true character, and prejudice would disappear. German Jews became fervently patriotic and rejected Zionism, which would have directed their concerns to another land (and which, according to Hirsch, was against Jewish law as well, for only in God's own time and with the coming of the Messiah was the Land to be redeemed; premature action was not permissible). Insecure themselves, they set themselves apart from their Eastern European brethren assisting them financially and educationally without associating with them socially. At the same time, a considerable number of German Jews were well educated in Judaism and faithful in observance of Mitzvot, although some groups became outright assimilationists.

Since the civil service and the university professorships were closed to them they went into free professions, medicine, law, merchandising (creating the department store), banking, journalism, the arts, especially music and the theater. This exposed them to the claim that their practices and publications were designed to corrupt the German spirit. The majority lived in the cities. Rural Jews eked out a living by being cattle dealers and owners of small stores.

The years after World War I were troublesome. The German economy broke down. Ill-equipped to understand democracy and live by it, Germans degraded their new government. The heavy war reparations brought poverty to the middle class and embittered it. It was a fertile period for demagogues. Hitler gained popular support by promising the Germans greatness, power, and wealth through becoming a *völkisch* union. This, as they did not consider, was in exchange for freedom. The Jews were a useful scapegoat for the ills that had befallen Germany. They were held out as a source of destructive capitalism, and had gained their supposedly great wealth by exploitation of the people. At the same time, they were branded as "communists," undermining the national spirit of the people. The people did not see the contradiction in these claims. The immediate tangible goal for the Nazis was the expropriation of the property of Jews, and the population acquiesced.

With the Germans the Jews shared a belief in law and order, a love of education, and thrift and ambition. The prophetic message, reinforced by the rabbis, had instilled into generations of Jews aversion to and condemnation of violence. By the teaching of their leaders, they had come to accept the idea that society was improving (moving toward a Messianic age). They had frequently been made scapegoats in the years since the Emancipation, but considered these incidents holdovers from a tragic past, which education and time would eventually help to overcome. It was inconceivable to them that the constitution, the basic law of the land, could be overthrown. They had become acculturated and could not fathom the possibility of a whole nation turning against them at the behest of a few maniacs. Dwelling in all sections of the German cities they had Christian friends among their neighbors. They had no emotional preparation, physical training, or even opportunity for united action. Gathered in the ghetto, their forebears in Germany had taken up arms against their attackers during the Crusades. Now they were in neither physical nor psychological position to do so. The heroes of the Warsaw ghetto would eventually, after long hesitation, do so when their cup of misery was finally running over. All of this conspired against them when Hitler came to power in 1933.

From 1933 on, their lot deteriorated rapidly. It began with a state-ordained boycott of all Jewish stores and offices on April 1, 1933, then grew with the elimination of all Jews from public institutions. In 1935, radical racial laws were promulgated completely, excluding Jews from the cultural, economic, and social life of the country. They were placed outside the law, subjected to all its restrictions—which were rapidly increased for them—but excluded from its protection. Concentration camps were established. In 1938, the synagogues were burned down and Jewish property looted. Jews were taken to concentration camps, which had been well prepared. I was one of the prisoners. This was the beginning of the Holocaust.

The population rejoiced in its newly found spirit of unity, "One Empire, One Folk, One Leader," and in its growing prosperity. Prosperity was the result of Hitler's rearmament, which was illegal under international treaties. The new spirit rested on his promise of world domination for Germany. His "Third Empire" (after the mediaeval German Empire and the Prussian-led second one) would last for a thousand years. By its strength and power it would redeem the weakness of the past. In their intoxication, even decent Germans—with some exceptions—felt hardly any concern with the fate of their Jewish fellow citizens.

The History of Anti-Semitism: An Evolution of Hate

Hitler's extermination of millions of Jews was the culmination of a spirit of contempt and hatred that had been planted and deliberately nurtured for centuries. We shall better understand the Holocaust by briefly following the stages of anti-Semitism.

In *Roman Days*, Jews enjoyed citizens' rights, their religion was licit, special privileges such as exemption for military service due to their Sabbath observance were accorded them. But they were looked at by many Romans with antipathy because they would not accept the Roman gods and frowned at the libertinism of Roman society. They could invite Romans for dinner in their homes, but they would not eat in Roman homes on account of their dietary laws. They were considered lazy for their observance of the Sabbath. They engaged in widespread missionary activities, making converts among leading citizens who were looking for spiritual guidance which Roman religion could not give. In short, the Jews were a nuisance. By their ideas and life they held up a mirror to a dissolute Roman society and tended to subvert it, and they were gaining adherents. Christianity would build on these foundations of Jewish missionary work.

Medieval Christianity held the Jews responsible for the death of Christ, and thus considered them rejected by God. It explained their survival as a divine decree, that by their misery they might be the witnesses of the triumph of the Church. This was theological anti-Semitism, based on a doctrine which was declared false by the Ecumenical Council in 1965. Yet it was taught for centuries and built into German consciousness by Luther's anti-Jewish teachings. The hatred of the Jews as unbelievers and deicides led to their exclusion from agriculture and all trades except money lending, which was forbidden to Christians by the Church. Through it, however, the Jews earned the additional accusation of being usurers, shrewd and dishonest business manipulators. Since the Church saw them as a condemned people, they were an international, accursed enemy of humanity.

The Enlightenment saw no reason for theological anti-Semitism, and in its spirit Jews were emancipated. The age of science weaned many from adherence to theological dogmas and further weakened anti-Semitism. Yet there were, even then, "enlightened" thinkers such as Voltaire, who agreed with the principle of the Enlightenment that all human beings were equal. But to him the Jews were not "human beings."

Romanticism followed the Enlightenment as the age of emotion and nostalgia for a past considered better than the present. With it came a strong outburst of nationalism. Looking back on the supposed glories of the past, the Germans found that only a *völkisch* Germany, united by race, would be strong again. The Jews were subverters of the Germanic spirit. Contaminated by anti-Jewish teachings, the Germans became prey to demagogues: Why not make the Jews the scapegoats for all that had gone wrong? They were the enemies of the national state and, it was claimed, were actually an international conspiracy. The Russian forgery, *The Protocols of the Wise Men of Zion*, supposedly the plan of Jewry's international leaders to destroy the nations and assume world domination, was put into circulation. It served its purpose of fanning hate all too well, right up to the present. Additional hate literature swamped the country.

As science became the ultimate authority, replacing faith and dogma, a new, pseudo-science was put to work by the already prejudiced, the Science of Race. It was introduced to prove that the Jews were, scientifically speaking, a rotten, destructive race. There is no justification for such a "science" nor any vestige of scientific truth to the fact that the Jews are even a race, but "science-minded" anti-Semites took up the idea, planting the seed that was to produce a harvest of terror.

Hitler merely went one step further. He eradicated the last vestige of ethical conscience at the notion of exterminating human beings. The Jews were not human, they were poisonous vermin. There was no reason to have any qualms in "liquidating" them. The extermination of the Jewish race was now not a means to a goal (as were the atom bomb over Hiroshima and the bombardment of Dresden as means to winning the war), it was *the* goal. It turned out to be Hitler's only "victory."

A Jewish Renaissance

Before and during the Nazi regime, a Renaissance of Judaism took place in Germany. Jewish learning increased; books in Hebrew and German were published in increasing numbers, and adult academies of Jewish learning were organized in every larger community. In adversity, German Jewry had one of its moments of greatness. It produced thinkers, scientists, artists, writers, musicians, industrialists, physicians, and politicians, some of whose contributions transformed the thinking of humanity, among them a number of Nobel Prize winners. Only a few examples of steadfast Jews shall be mentioned. ALBERT EINSTEIN revolutionized our image of the universe with his Theory of Relativity, as did SIGMUND FREUD with our psyche. The stories and novels of FRANZ KAFKA appear like a vision of the tragedy that was to befall Jewry. In one we find a man transformed overnight into a beetle, as Jews were overnight transformed into "vermin" by the Nazis. An innocent man is accused of a capital crime, never told of the crime he allegedly committed, is tried before a court he never is permitted to face, is convicted, and executed. This was exactly the fate of European Jewry before the satanic "court" of Hitler and his ilk. Max Liebermann was the greatest impressionist painter of Germany. The poet Nellie Sachs gave expression to the inexpressible of the Holocaust, "O the Chimneys," and asked humanity: "If the prophets came back, ear of humanity would you listen?"

As if in preparation for the hour of need, German Jewry produced Jewish thinkers, schooled in German philosophy but filled with a profound love and knowledge of their heritage. That some of them were *Baale Teshuvah* (Men of Return) from the fringes to the core of Judaism makes their work even more significant for modern Jews. They grappled with the problem of God–Torah–Mitzvot–Land. Each saw the essence of Jewish survival in a different one of these elements without eliminating the others. To these thinkers and leaders who gave the Jews spiritual strength, belong HERMANN COHEN (1842–1918), FRANZ ROSENZWEIG (1886–1929), MARTIN BUBER (1878–1965) and LEO BAECK (1873–1956). They will be discussed later.

CHAPTER 7

The American Destiny

WHEN FREDERICK JACKSON TURNER read his epoch-making paper "The Significance of the Frontier in American History" before the American Historical Society in 1893 he was not thinking of the Jews. He could, however, have cited their destiny as a prime proof for his hypothesis. Challenged by the frontier, immigrants from many European lands created a new society of Americans in a distinct American spirit, a "democracy born of free land, strong in selfishness and individualism . . . pressing individual liberty beyond its proper bounds." This society had its dangers as well as its great advantages.

JUDAISM IN A NEW LAND

Early Struggles

In 1654 twenty-three Jews arrived in the port of New Amsterdam. They had been preceded by a few Jewish individuals who had settled along the Atlantic seaboard. Their arrival marked the end of an odyssey for these Jews that had extended over generations.

In 1492 the Jews of Spain were expelled by King Ferdinand and Queen Isabella. In the same year, possibly on the very day of the Jews' forced departure, Columbus set sail on his voyage of discovery. It has been claimed that he chose this day because he had Jewish sailors among his crew who were being put out of Spain that day. Columbus wrote movingly about the plight of Spanish Jews, whose rickety ships he passed as he left port. He opened a new home for them.

Jewish refugees from Spain settled in many countries, including Holland. Some were permitted to find new homes in Portugal, but this hospitality lasted but a short time. King Manuel of Portugal, who came to the throne in 1495, had to promise his bride's parents, the Spanish rulers Ferdinand and Isabella, that he would get rid of the Jews. In December 1496 the Jews were given ten months to depart. Actually, Manuel, who was aware of the economic benefits the Jews had brought him, did not wish them to depart. In 1497 he had large numbers of Jews, especially children, baptized by force. Many Jews became *marranos*, underground Jews (see Chapter 4).

The opening of the New World gave the Portuguese Jews an opportunity to escape. They settled in Brazil, which was under Portuguese rule. There, many of them openly returned to their Jewish faith. This made them heretics to the Church, since they had once been baptized. Soon the Inquisition was established in Brazil. It pursued heretics and delivered them to death.

Now Holland entered the contest for colonies in the New World. In 1624 the Dutch, having defeated the Portuguese, began to establish themselves in Brazil. Numerous Jews, former refugees from Spain but now Dutch citizens, went to the new colony to develop it. In 1645, however, the Portuguese began to reconquer Brazil, and by 1654 they had won it back completely. Some of the Jews returned to Holland, others scattered throughout Central and North America, where the Dutch had established the colony of New Amsterdam.

In August 1654, a Dutch citizen named Jacob Barsimson was the first Jew to arrive at New Amsterdam. One month later, he was followed by twenty-three others, also Dutch subjects and fugitives from Brazil. They were destitute, having been raided by pirates at sea. The funds they had expected from Amsterdam to pay for their passage had not arrived, and the master of the ship that had brought them obtained a judgment against all their property in payment for his services.

The governor of New Amsterdam was Peter Stuyvesant, a harsh master and religious bigot. In letter after letter to Amsterdam he demanded the right to expel the members of this "deceitful race." The Dutch West India Company, who held the charter of the colony, overruled him; Jews were shareholders in the Company, and could not be antagonized. The Jewish settlers had to give a solemn pledge, however, that their poor would never become a burden to the Company or the community but would be supported by their own people. Jews have held to this principle ever since.

The newcomers were not satisfied with merely being tolerated. They immediately demanded the right to purchase land for a cemetery (July 1655), and in other ways kept petitioning the Company for rights and recognition. They obtained the right to build a synagogue. When the colony was under attack by Indians, they requested and received the right to bear arms and join its defenders. (Bearing arms was a privilege of citizens, and Jews originally were excluded and had to pay a tax instead.) These rights were but a step toward full citizenship. On April 21, 1657 the Jews of the colony, already Dutch citizens, were admitted to full citizenship in the colony. In 1664 the British took New Amsterdam from the Dutch and renamed it New York. The colony became British, but the status of the Jews did not change.

In contrast to New York, the Massachusetts Bay Colony admitted no Jews. It was ruled by the Puritans and persecuted non-Puritan Christians. But Roger Williams, Governor of Rhode Island, opened the gates of the colony to them.

Citizens of the United States

By the time of the American Revolution only about two thousand Jews lived in the country. Their overwhelming majority fully embraced the spirit of American freedom. They were prepared to give their all—life and property—to the

American cause. (A few of them, like some colonists, felt conscience-bound to maintain their allegiance to the British crown.)

In contrast to their European fellows, they could count on the support of the Founding Fathers. BENJAMIN FRANKLIN was first on the list of subscribers to the synagogue built in Philadelphia. THOMAS JEFFERSON insisted that Christian theology be eliminated from the compulsory subjects at his University of Virginia so that Jews could study there and gain entrance into society. JOHN ADAMS expressed the hope that all prejudice against Jews would vanish from the earth through the example of the United States. JAMES MADISON was the determined advocate and fighter for the separation of Church and State, and explained in a letter to Mordecai Manuel Noah that freedom of religion and freedom of opinion were to him the basic values of society. In Maryland, THOMAS KENNEDY, a Scotch Presbyterian, spoke out powerfully for the rights of Jews because, although he knew no Jews, he felt justice demanded it.

The greatest support, however, came from GEORGE WASHINGTON, who, in a letter to the Jewish congregation of Newport, Rhode Island, made it clear that "happily the government of the United States, which gives to bigotry no sanction, to persecution no assistance, requires only that they who live under its protection shall demean themselves as good citizens in giving it on all occasions their effectual support." He concluded by saying, "May the children of the stock of Abraham, who dwell in this land, continue to merit and enjoy the goodwill of the other inhabitants, while everyone shall sit in safety under his own vine and fig tree, and there shall be none to make him afraid" (Morris U. Schappes, *A Documentary History of the United States,* New York, 1924, pp. 68ff.) This was assurance and challenge. Jews became patriots without giving up their faith.

The French nobleman ALEXIS DE TOCQUEVILLE, who in the 1830s traveled throughout the United States, has given us a most penetrating analysis of the American character and society in his book *Democracy in America.* He saw the roots of Americanism in family life, religious traditions, and the guarantees of freedom. The local communities were the cells of the wider political community, and the participation of the citizens in local politics prepared them for political action on a wider scale. De Tocqueville also coined the term "individualism" as *the* characteristic of Americans. By such criteria the early Jewish settlers were typical Americans and by their lives they established the patterns for American Judaism. They had escaped discrimination and persecution, had gone from exile to a homeland. They quickly embraced the spirit of America as men of the frontier, that place where the old pushes forward toward the new. Above all, these Jews were individualists.

AARON LOPEZ (1731–1782), a former *marrano* who now breathed freely, saw the opportunities his new country offered. He became one of the largest shipowners in America. But he was also aware of his obligation to serve his community and country. During the War of Independence he fitted his ships with guns to serve as armed frigates. Able to associate with his Christian neighbors as an equal, he struck up friendships with leading citizens and was lavish in his charity for the poor. Under his leadership as president of the Jewish congregation of Newport, Rhode Island the synagogue (in neo-classical style) was built. Its services attracted Christians as well as Jews. In the end he died a poor man, having given his entire fortune to the American cause. His close friend Ezra Stiles, president of Yale, wrote him a moving obituary, pointing out that he was revered by the entire community for his character and generous charitable gifts.

HAIM SOLOMON (1740–1785) was Lopez's contemporary and a Lithuanian Jew. He also grasped the opportunities of his new country and became a highly successful banker and broker. Aware of the obligations his freedom imposed on him, he placed his entire fortune at the disposal of the new government, which was always deeply in need of funds. He kept it running, and died destitute.

JUDAH TOURO (1775–1854) embodied the spirit of American fellowship that transcended religious differences. He was wounded while fighting the British in the battle of New Orleans. A bachelor, he found a home within a Christian family. As a patriot, he paid one-fifth of the cost of the Bunker Hill monument, and in the spirit of interfaith cooperation, he left his great fortune to both Jewish and Christian institutions.

URIAH P. LEVY (1792–1862) illustrated the opportunities open to Jews. He reached the highest rank in the United States Navy, that of commodore, but always had to combat anti-Semitism. (It would never have occurred to a European Jew of that period even to aspire to a military career. In peacetime European Jews could not even serve in the armed forces, for this was an honor reserved for Christians.) Levy abolished flogging in the Navy. In gratitude for Thomas Jefferson's fight for religious liberty, Levy bought Jefferson's deeply indebted property, restored it, and donated it to the nation. The Jewish chapel of the Naval Academy at Annapolis now bears his name.

MORDECAI MANUEL NOAH (1785–1851) reveals the freedom of thought, action, and promotion enjoyed by Jews. He held numerous public offices, including that of United States Consul at Tunis. Later he devised a plan to establish a Jewish state as part of the United States, around Buffalo, New York, there to gather the persecuted Jews. The cornerstone was dedicated in solemn ceremonies attended by Christians of all social strata. The cornerstone is all that is left, however; Noah's plan failed because Jews did not come. So he advocated rebuilding Palestine, if this was the place the Jews preferred. He was an early "Zionist."

GERSHON MENDES SEIXAS (1745–1816), a rabbinic official and representative of the Jews, became a pillar of society. American-born and with an excellent general and Jewish education, he became spiritual leader of New York's Shearit Israel congregation. A fervent patriot, when the British came he moved to Philadelphia where he acted as rabbi of the congregation. His appeal as a preacher made a new synagogue building necessary. After the war he returned to New York, and regularly invited his Christian friends and clergy to his services. He stood at the side of George Washington at the first presidential inauguration, and at the ratification of the Constitution he joined the parade in Philadelphia and marched arm-in-arm with the Christian clergy. He then joined his fellow Jews at the table with kosher food that had been especially provided for them. In 1787 he became a trustee of Columbia College, an honor hitherto reserved for Anglicans, and his name appears in its incorporation certificate. All this was possible, not only because he was an exceptional man, but because America responded.

In these personalities we find role models for American Jews and for Americans of all religions. There were others we could mention. Jews served in the Revolutionary War both as privates and as high officers. They loved their country and fought for their country and for their rights.

A New Society: The Hegemony of German Jews

The German Jews were the first to arrive in the United States in large numbers. They left Germany to escape the intolerable conditions of civil repression that, in the backlash after the defeat of Napoleon, had been imposed on them. In Bavaria, for instance reactionary princes imposed a quota on Jews permitted to get married. Other Germans arrived after the failure of the Revolution of 1848 and found a ready haven in the Midwest, where Christian Germans had settled. Among them were not only Jews, but also many non-Jewish defenders of democracy who had found it necessary to escape retributions in Germany. By 1860 the Jewish population had risen to about 150,000.

Some of the German Jews who arrived brought some means with them, many were poor. Many settled on the eastern seaboard, others in the interior of the country. They brought with them their skills, the German talent for organization, and, in many cases, a liberal outlook schooled on the principles of the Enlightenment. They were capable of rapid acculturation that led to economic success. Those who had settled in the frontier regions became significant contributors to the opening of the frontier. Beginning as peddlers, they provided merchandise and communication with the outside to isolated farmers. Eventually they were able to open general stores and small but growing banks that offered these farmers much needed credit. By 1875 the American Jewish community had reached a total of 250,000, mostly of German origin. They were prosperous and happy; they had found their niche.

The following examples of successful German immigrants illustrate some of their collective characteristics. Their ingenuity and spirit of adventure brought them success. They were conscious that America had been good to them, however, and showed their gratitude by going into public service and generously sponsoring the arts and sciences. They affirmed their Jewishness and were concerned with the welfare of the Jews at home and abroad. Thus they became role models for those who followed.

LAZARUS STRAUS, starting as a peddler in Georgia, eventually became the owner of Macy's, and served twice as American ambassador to Turkey where he was advocate for the Jews. His son co-founded another department store, Abraham & Straus. MEYER GUGGENHEIM also started as peddler. He became a multimillionaire in mining, and expressed his gratitude to America by founding and endowing the Guggenheim Museum in New York and the Guggenheim Foundation for the Promotion of the Sciences and Scientists. LEVI STRAUS arrived in San Francisco from Germany with a load of heavy canvass, intending to make tents for the miners in the Gold Rush, but the rush was over. He used his material to make "Levi's" instead; his firm remains one of the most socially conscious in the country.

The LEHMAN BROTHERS (who were relatives of mine from Bavaria) began their career at Montgomery, Alabama and later established the banking house Lehman Brothers. Their descendants dedicated themselves to public service, among them HERBERT LEHMAN, governor of New York and subsequently United States Senator. He was a man of highest personal ethics and an advocate of social justice. ADOLPH OCHS acquired *The New York Times* and made it one of the most distinguished newspapers in the world. The outstanding personality among the German Jews was JAKOB SCHIFF, who arrived as a youngster from Frankfurt to join the bank of Kuhn & Loeb. He financed enterprises such as ATT, Westinghouse, U.S. Rubber, Anaconda, and the Union Pacific. In the war between Japan and Russia he supported Japan against the anti-Semitic Russians. He treated presidents as his equals when it came to the defense of his people, and spent millions supporting Jewish immigrants. He characterized himself as one-third German, one-third American, and one-third Jewish.

These Jews and others formed a close-knit autocratic society. They held themselves responsible to be advocates, supporters, and educators of their co-religionists, and, in turn, expected them to accept their leadership.

The Civil War and Its Sequence

The Civil War had Jews on both sides. JUDAH P. BENJAMIN served in Jefferson Davis's cabinet, and was subjected to defamation even though he had broken all contact with Judaism. In the border regions, widespread smuggling was common. Under the influence of anti-Semitic adjutants, Ulysses S. Grant, the commanding general of the Federal forces, singled out the Jews and, in December 1862, issued "General Order Number 11" expelling the Jews of the border districts within twenty-four hours. It was the only official measure ever taken against Jews and was immediately rescinded by President Abraham Lincoln. Grant felt shame for the rest of his life.

In the decades after the war, anti-Semitism made inroads. German Jew-haters came to the United States to implant hate. The war had brought great wealth to Christian entrepreneurs, and these formed an aristocracy of newly rich, but they were scorned by the old aristocracy. They had to form their own caste. Afraid that the prosperous German Jews might wish to crash their new society, they excluded them from their enterprises and society. In 1877, when Joseph Seligman arrived by private train at the fashionable spa of Saratoga he was denied admission to the suite he had reserved. It was the beginning of a period lasting for decades, during which the Jews were forced into a "gilded ghetto." They were excluded from certain hotels, vacation spots and clubs, from fashionable city districts, banks, business concerns and industrial firms, and from fraternal associations. Universities instituted a quota system against them. They went into politics, civil service, law, the arts, and founded new enterprises.

Immigration from Eastern Europe— America As a Center of Jewry

Beginning in the 1880s immigration from Eastern Europe became a torrent. Two million Jews eventually escaped the intolerable conditions in Russia. Observing the arrival of these masses of Jewish immigrants "yearning to breathe free," the Jewish poetess Emma Lazarus wrote the poem now affixed to the Statue of Liberty.

Huddling together on the lower east side of New York in overcrowded, vermin-infested tenement houses, desperately poor and surrounded by crime, dirt and disease, they were aided by the German Jews, but essentially had to make it on their own as street vendors who would graduate to pushcarts and eventually become small shop owners. Many others began as laborers. Men and women toiled in the sweatshops of the garment industry, working under the most inhuman conditions. Of those who flocked to the needle trades, some had been tailors in the old country. A good many entered this trade because the owners, themselves Jews from an earlier migration from Eastern Europe, permitted them to observe the Sabbath, exploiting them in return during the rest of the week. In this environment emerged the Yiddish-speaking society of the Lower East Side, the little Eastern European town, the *shtetl*, transposed to America. The immigrants shared trials and poverty, and became involved in conflicts.

For the newcomers, life in the United States spelled the transition from the Old World to the New, from a homogeneous Jewish society guided by Jewish religion in all its aspects to a heterogeneous one composed of many groups, and from life in the *shtetl* to urban sweatshops. A number of these immigrants had been drawn to socialist ideas; from them some of the leading union organizers and leaders were to emerge.

Embarrassed by their "lack of culture," the established Jewish community did not absorb them. True to the pledge of the first settlers, the German Jews, under the leadership of Jakob Schiff, generously aided the newcomers, and organized a crash program to assimilate them quickly to American life and ways. What they failed to see was that the immigrants needed the shelter of their ethnic surroundings as a psychological defense against the overpowering influences of the new and, later on, as a transitional stage toward acculturation. The newcomers thus refused to adjust in line with the hopes of the settled Jewish community; they maintained their Orthodox congregations (each group having its own congregation), continued to speak Yiddish among themselves, and preserved their old traditions. The result was an antagonism between the German and Eastern European Jews that only time has begun to heal.

German Jews had joined and promoted the Reform congregations and saw the Jewish community as simply a religious one. To the Eastern European immigrants the Jews were simply a people. Oppressed in Eastern Europe, denied a secular education both by the opposition of their rabbis and parents and by the czarist state, these people were frequently self-taught. Many of them were deeply religious. Others were not religious but were "cultural Jews" who affirmed the culture of Judaism if not its religious character. They were committed to the Jewish spirit of social justice, which many of them found in socialism and Marxism. (In Russia they had organized a strong socialist labor organization, the *Bund*, Yiddish for "Union." Faced with the hostility of non-Jewish socialist parties and repression by the czarist government, the Bund had nevertheless grown among the Jewish masses. The communist regime eventually liquidated it.) Among these idealistic Jews were the founders of the State of Israel.

Those who came to America brought this ideology and ideals with them. In 1888 they founded the United Hebrew Trades, eventually establishing twenty-two unions in New York City, mostly in the needle trades. In 1909 twenty thousand female workers in shirtwaist factories went on strike in New York, and in 1910 workers in the cloak and suit industries struck. The general public sided with the strikers. Both employers and employees were Jews, and both were entreated to avoid the then-common violence in order not to harm the reputation of the Jews. After long negotiations, the strikers won their demands. There were other strikes and conflicts, and some progress was achieved. The issue of whether unions should be ideologically committed raised violent controversies. The emerging Jewish labor leaders opposed any ideological commitment. They and their successors in the American labor movement were to have a lasting influence on its nonideological character. SAMUEL GOMPERS (1850–1924) gave the union movement in America its character. A Jewish cigar maker of British descent who became the founder of the American Federation of Labor, Gompers saw the unions as simply a tool for improving the workers' living conditions; ideology had no place in them. Eventually the unions rejected ideological commitment.

Cultural Jews did not accept religious practices and beliefs, as they were in conflict with scientific thought and American ways of expression, yet they remained Jews, feeling strongly that survival was assured by maintaining Jewish peoplehood and culture. They had an additional example in the development of the Land of Israel, where a nonreligious Judaism was emerging. Religion thus was not regarded as essential; Zionism, folkways, and culture (ethnic identification) were sufficient. Eliminating God, they identified Torah with education in general. Mitzvot meant working for social justice, similar to the manner in which the Social Gospel movement interpreted the message of Christianity. The Land of Israel (then being reclaimed by the Jewish pioneers) added another strong force for Jewish survival.

Some Outcomes of Eastern European Jewish Immigration

Several significant consequences emerged from the Jewish mass immigration. First, the mass immigration of people from various "primitive" countries—such as Jews, Slavs, Italians, and Asians—frightened the settled Americans. The White-Anglo-Saxon-Protestant establishment saw in it a threat to the basic character of America; among labor there was the fear of cheap competition. Anxiety over the intrusion of foreign ideologies was combined with apprehension that immigration of "undesirables" would breed criminality; racial animosity came into play. A popular anti-immigration wave swept the country and resulted in the enactment of an ever-more restrictive quota system for immigration from these countries. The German-Jewish leaders tried in vain to stem it. Greatly reduced quotas adopted by Congress in 1924 closed the doors to innumerable Jewish refugees during the Nazi period.

Second, the apprehensions of the German-Jewish elite proved unfounded. Amidst their poverty and at great sacrifice Eastern Jewish immigrants determined to give their children an education, possibly at the university, with startling results. Among the well-known representatives of the new generations are numerous members and senators of Congress, governors and cabinet members, and presidents of leading universities, including the ivy leagues. A large percentage of professors were Jews, as were chief executive officers of great corporations.

Jews also left their imprint on the arts. Our list of artists is selective and merely serves to demonstrate the ascent of Jewish immigrants from Eastern Europe, and includes only some of those who remained tied to their Jewish heritage and gave expression to its ideals.

The American musical which, in contrast to the European operetta, holds a social message, owes its existence and character to Jewish composers and lyricists such as KERN, ROGERS, HAMMERSTEIN, HART, HAMLISCH, and SONDHEIM. LERNER and LOEB, in "Fiddler on the Roof," brought the life in the shtetl to the world. AARON COPELAND described rural America and wrote "Fanfare for the Common Man." GEORGE GERSHWIN, in his opera "Porgy and Bess," brought the life of the blacks to public attention (and insisted that only black singers be given the roles). Conductor and composer LEONARD BERNSTEIN dealt with specifically Jewish subjects in his "Kaddish Symphony" and "Chichester Psalms." In "West Side Story" (for which Sondheim wrote the lyrics) he dealt with one of the burning social issues of the day: the conflict between Whites and Puerto Rican Latinos. Among opera singers, JAN PIERCE and RICHARD TUCKER, both former cantors and very Orthodox, brought some of the Jewish heart to the operatic stage. ISAAC STERN, the violin virtuoso and deeply religious Jew, saved Carnegie Hall from the wrecker's ball.

SAUL BELLOWS, a Nobel prize-winning writer, understood the Jew as the universal "Faust" searching for his soul. BERNARD MALAMUD made a blood libel against a Jew the subject of one of his novels. Actress BARBRA STREISAND produced "Yentel" at her own expense, in honor of her heritage. EDWARD ASNER was a social activist and committed interpreter of Judaism. JACKSON POLLOCK gave painting new directions. BETTY FRIEDAN became the mother of the feminist movement and GLORIA STEINEM was its zealous exponent.

The whimsical humor of the Jews in the face of their destiny may have been the root from which many Jewish comedians sprang, among them the MARX BROTHERS, JACK BENNY, and others. GEORGE BURNS could even tastefully portray God in film. Comedian DANNY KAYE received the Nobel peace prize for the work of UNESCO, which he directed.

Among movie producers, STEVEN SPIELBERG has held a special position. To make amends for being ashamed of his Jewishness in his childhood, he produced *Schindler's List*, which is based on a true story and depicts in gruesome detail the horrifying brutality of the Nazis as well as the deep humanity of one Christian, Schindler, who saved 1,200 Jews. His explanation of the reasons for his film was a ringing affirmation of his Jewish heritage. The proceeds of the film go to Holocaust research.

Third, American Zionism derived its specific character from the leadership of LOUIS D. BRANDEIS (1856–1941). He was a brilliant lawyer with a deep social conscience, who became a U.S. Supreme Court Justice. Earlier in life he had drifted to the periphery of Judaism, but when he became arbitrator in the labor conflicts mentioned, he was impressed by the mutual empathy of employers and workers and their desire to avoid violence in order not to harm the reputation of the Jews. He rekindled his love for the Jewish people, which transformed him into a leading Zionist. His concept of American Zionism took root: American Jews were to support Israel with all their being, without envisioning emigration, for America was their home.

American Jewry thus came to consider itself as either a religious group or an ethnic group—or as is more often the case, a religious-ethnic group. The traditional respect for learning has made it acceptable among Jews to be considered "intellectuals." In American society, intellectuals have come to form a subgroup that cuts across ethnic lines. Members of this group are naturally attracted to each other and feel free to follow the conclusions of their own individualistic reasoning. Many Jews have felt free to marry members of other religious or ethnic backgrounds.

Depression and War

The post–World War I years began with an hysterical chase after Bolsheviks, which brought suspicion upon many Jews. The poison of anti-Semitism had its effects. Henry Ford had "The Protocols of the Wise Men of Zion" published in his newspaper, the *Dearborn Independent*. Agitators arose. Under the impact of the Great Depression, foreign elements came to be viewed with distrust. With the rise of Hitler German embassies and consulates became centers of anti-Semitic propaganda. "The German American Bund," a Nazi movement, whose members wore uniforms and engaged in rallies, recruited among the people and caused riots.

As war broke out in Europe, America split. The "America First" movement advocated strict isolation, and many of its followers may have watched the disaster striking European Jewry with equanimity. In the State Department, anti-Semites advised the consulates to restrict Jewish immigration even within the permitted quotas. Only after the pogrom night of 1938 did President Franklin D. Roosevelt direct his consulates fully to utilize the existing quotas. When the extent of the Holocaust came to be known it was not initially believed and therefore kept secret. The quota system, however, continued to be implemented with severity. In 1942 the steamer *St. Louis* was chartered by German Jews for passengers who had received their visas to Cuba. Upon arrival they found the visas rescinded and had to return. Slowly the captain steamed along the shores of Florida, hoping the government would relent and admit the Jews. It did not, and the Jews were returned to Germany . . . and exterminated. President Roosevelt promised that the criminals would be punished, but with the reservation that this would be done after victory had been won. The railroad tracks to Auschwitz were never bombed to prevent the transports.

After the War

With German inhumanity now clearly revealed, the victory over the forces of evil called for renewal. Exclusions of minorities through restrictive covenants between sellers and buyers, renters and employers who barred Jews were made illegal. Above all, competition called for "meritocracy," the employment of persons irrespective of race or background but simply on the basis of their merit.

The Supreme Court decision of 1954 and subsequent legislation grounded the equality of African-Americans in law. Prejudice had not disappeared against African-Americans, women, or Jews. Vigilance and active struggle remained imperative, but barriers were beginning to fall. American Jewry entered its most propitious period.

THE EMERGENCE OF A PLURALISTIC JUDAISM

In the American environment, a society built upon the Enlightenment, the European form of the synagogue, its worship, and its customs eventually came to appear as an anachronism. There were no ordained rabbis in the United States until the middle of the nineteenth century, so some immigrants, slightly versed in Judaism, would be appointed to lead the service, teach the children, and perform religious functions. The lay leader (already significant in medieval Jewish life) became all-powerful in individualistic America. As a man of success in life, he often assumed dictatorial powers in his congregation, which he directed as president. Frequently religiously nonobservant in their own lives, the majority of these leaders insisted on a strict (pre-Mendelssohnian) pattern of religion in the synagogue, and they were supported by the new arrivals. These Jews found psychological shelter from the onslaught of the new world in the synagogue of old-time religion. Their children, however, were exposed to the pull of American life; they saw no link to life in this form of faith and attempted to reform it. Many Jews were attracted by the lure of the West. In most cases they set immediately to establish new congregations as soon as they had found a sufficient number of coreligionists. In many of these the majority of the members soon tended toward religious reforms. In some cases Jews were swallowed up by the vastness of America. Being far from Jewish community life, they weakened in their religious observance and some lost their faith.

Under the impact of the frontier, a new community emerged. Some of its impact can still be found in American Judaism. Among it are the clash of individuals, the power of leaders prominent in the world without necessarily being religious, the independence of congregations, each going its own way. Torah and Mitzvot might serve as psychological defenses against the overpowering experiences of the new environment or might become a mechanical performance. Emotion might be the primary link to Judaism. The universal affirmation by these Jews of their belonging to the House of Israel therefore stands as a positive element. They wanted to be full-fledged Americans, inobservant but determined to be Jews.

Early Reform Attempts in Orthodoxy

From the beginning, the openness of the United States in spirit as in physical dimensions, favored reforms, even among those who had been Orthodox in the old country. The first one to undertake the task was Isaac Leeser (1806–1868). An immigrant from Germany, he showed such profound knowledge of

Judaism that, although he was not a rabbi, he was appointed spiritual leader of the congregation in Philadelphia. He used his position as a base from which to affect all of American Jewry. Leeser was strictly Orthodox and deeply influenced by Mendelssohn: The Mitzvot must be upheld; at the same time, people must be educated to understand Torah. Leeser translated the Bible and the prayer book into English, published a periodical, and traveled widely. His hope was to equip strictly Orthodox Jews to live in two civilizations, as Mendelssohn had done. He was not a theoretical theologian like the German rabbis (the American leaders were not primarily concerned with philosophical considerations), but was pragmatic in his approach, for the spirit of America was pragmatic. Later religious leaders were to follow his approach. Leeser's hope of developing a strict Orthodoxy in worship and life that would be meaningful and also aesthetically appealing to Americanized Jews, was to bear fruit in later years. As a result Orthodoxy took two divergent directions.

Some communities chose to be led by rabbis of the "old" type: men without academic training, living a pre-Mendelssohnian life. They were not Orthodox, in the sense of forming a denomination, they were simply "Jewish," as they had been in the *shtetl*. On the other hand, there were communities whose members felt that separation from the world could not be maintained. Academically trained rabbis were needed to bring the people into the new era and maintain them, guiding them to face modernity without compromising Torah, Mitzvot, and traditional Jewish observances. To produce such men, the *Yeshivah* (Orthodox rabbinical seminary) in New York was expanded into a university. Similar schools emerged. These men, strict in their interpretation of the divine Torah and the binding force of Mitzvot, tried to adopt a philosophy akin to that of Samson Raphael Hirsch. But, whereas Hirsch maintained that Jewish law prohibited Jews from actively engaging in the upbuilding of the Land of Israel, American Orthodoxy became universally Zionist.

Orthodoxy has strongly and successfully reasserted its presence and viability on the contemporary Jewish scene in America. To stem the movement of Jews into other Jewish denominations, Orthodoxy has tried to strengthen its theological foundations, which accounted for the increased use of Hirsch's works and the theology of Rabbi Joseph Soloveitchik. It has extended its school system. In the Young Israel Movement, it has developed a system of Neo-Orthodox synagogues and institutions, and has successfully promoted the establishment of *Kashrut* (kosher laws) in communal affairs and kosher eating facilities at numerous universities.

Orthodoxy also gained momentum from the immigration of entire communities from Eastern Europe, especially the Hasidim, after World War II. They settled as units, surrounding the rabbi who had led them here. As noted before, the community of the Lubavitcher Rebbe (the late Rabbi Menachem M. Schneerson) has become a significant influence in Jewish and American life. Pre-Mendelssohnian in character, it insists on the wearing of the Orthodox Jewish garb of the shtetl and rejects worldly ways and education. For the joy of Jewish living, the members have willingly sacrificed opportunities for advancement in society, and many are poor.

Orthodox Judaism has benefited from the general trend in America toward religious conservatism. Many of its adherents are men and women of achievement in the intellectual and business world. And in turn, Orthodoxy has influenced the move toward greater traditionalism in all branches of religious American Jewry.

At the same time that Orthodoxy has witnessed a resurgence, inner conflicts persist. A group of "left-wing" Orthodox rabbis has been pressing for changes within the framework of halakhah, and some have been willing to enter a dialogue with non-Orthodox Jewry. Orthodox women have fought for greater rights within the synagogue and have even instituted their own prayer services, being careful not to violate halakhah, but nevertheless meeting frequent opposition from the rabbinate. In general, and in principle, the antagonism to non-Orthodox Jewry still exists and has been strengthened by the fact that the state-supported chief rabbinate in Israel is regarded by Orthodox Jewry as the central authority. To Orthodoxy, there is only one true Judaism, a "Torah-true" Judaism; all other forms are aberrant. Since the chain of tradition is regarded as a transmission from a greater past to a less distinguished present, the decisions of previous rabbinical authorities, including those of Russia and Poland, cannot be overruled by moderns. New and more indulgent interpretations of halakhah can only relate to minor issues not to basic ones. Conservatism and Reform, therefore, cannot be "true." The result has been a deepening split of Jewry along denominational lines.

In recent years, an effort to build bridges between the different movements of American Jewry has been made by the Orthodox Rabbi Irving (Yitz) Greenberg, who has founded an organization, CLAL, an achrostic of the movement's name and meaning "The Community (of all Israel)."

American Reform

Reform Judaism has had the difficult task of ever-adjusting to changing times. German immigrants were less excluded from general society and were acquainted with the reform endeavors in the old country. They were determined to rise quickly in America and did not necessarily need the shelter of old-time religion. They joined the Reform movement, frequently became its sponsors, and, as leaders of American Jewry, set a trend. Actually, they were not forced to make a fundamental religious adjustment, because American Reform was a direct offshoot of the German Reform movement. Most of the rabbis who arrived early in the United States came from Germany and were influenced by Abraham Geiger. They were immigrants themselves, and German was for a time the language in which they preached. These architects of American Reform Judaism were enchanted by America. Here Jews lived in full freedom, the congregations were new and malleable, and not supervised by the state. Together with many other German-Jewish immigrants they desired their Jewishness to be typically American. Actually, American Reform went way beyond the revisions Abraham Geiger had been able to achieve in Germany.

ISAAC MAYER WISE (1819–1900), who came from Bohemia, was the father of the Reform movement. His fervent love of liberty compelled him to leave Europe. Under his guidance, Reform became a movement and acquired structure and organization. Wise held the hope and ambition of creating a united and integrated American Judaism. He started out as a Conservative, choosing a middle road which he hoped would rally American Jewry, but he came into conflict with Orthodox leadership.

Still striving to find a common ground for all American Jews, he inspired the formation of the Union of American Hebrew Congregations by a group of distinguished lay leaders. It was conceived as an umbrella organization for all types of congregations that would not interfere in their internal affairs. The Orthodox group refused to join. Wise then developed a rabbinical seminary, the first in the Western world, called the Hebrew Union College in Cincinnati. It was intended to train rabbis for all religious groups. Again Wise was rebuffed by the Orthodox.

His final hope for unity was pinned on the organization of a rabbinical body in which rabbis of all persuasions could hold membership. It led him to found the Central Conference of American Rabbis. The Orthodox rabbis refused to join; they wanted none of his spirit of even moderate reform. In his middle position, Wise suited neither the radical reformers nor the Orthodox traditionalists. If he wanted any kind of organization without surrendering his hopes for some kind of unification, he had to shift to the liberal wing. Thus he turned to Reform. Eventually, his organization was to grow into one of the powerful wings of American religious Jewry, Reform Judaism. Yet Wise's original dream was to be fulfilled in a fashion. American Jewry became organized, not in one but in several groups, and each group followed Wise's organizational plan.

During its early stages the Reform movement became radical. The moving force behind it was the brilliant David Einhorn, whose views were so extreme that he could not see any rabbinical career in Germany. Geiger's most extreme ideas were translated into reality. Beyond that, many innovations were approved (e.g., the elimination of requirement to cover one's head in worship). Torah was no longer binding except in its ethical pronouncements; Mitzvot were equated with ethical conduct. The Land of Israel was regarded as of no concern to free American Jews. The Messianic hope was no longer anticipated in the future; it had been fulfilled in America.

These positions were promulgated in the "Pittsburgh Platform," hammered out during a conference of fifteen rabbis in that city in November 1885. The guiding spirit was KAUFMANN KOHLER, Einhorn's son-in-law, a rabbi and scholar who was to become president of the Hebrew Union College. In his youth, Kohler had been a disciple of Samson Raphael Hirsch. We find in him the same extremism and unreserved allegiance to state and society, though otherwise the two men were on opposite sides. Kohler's break with Neo-Orthodoxy was the result of his university studies.

The platform, Kohler's "declaration of independence," proclaimed among other things that

> It will not do to offer our prayers in a tongue which only few scholars nowadays understand. We cannot afford any longer to pray for a return to Jerusalem.

It is a blasphemy and lie upon the lips of every American Jew. . . . We accept as binding only its [Scripture's] moral laws, but reject all such as are not adapted to the views and habits of modern civilization. . . . We hold that all such Mosaic and rabbinical laws as regulate diet, priestly purity and dress originated in ages and under the influences of ideas entirely foreign to our present mental and spiritual state. (Ismar Elbogen, *A Century of Jewish Life;* Philadelphia: Jewish Publication Society, 1946, pp. 344ff.)

So great was the prestige of the fifteen rabbis who worked out the platform that it came to be regarded as the philosophy of Reform Judaism, even though the platform was never officially adopted by the Central Conference of American Rabbis or the Union of American Hebrew Congregations.

After the platform had been adopted by the conference, Isaac Mayer Wise, the presiding officer, asked the question: "What are you going to do with this declaration of independence?" It was a fateful question. The term "declaration of independence" is so fraught with meaning for Americans that, in this context, it came to mean for many Jews that Reform wanted to pursue its way independent of the rest of Jewry. Even those who looked with favor on reforms but did not wish to sever with tradition entirely felt there was no room for them in Reform Judaism. In the rest of Jewry the Pittsburgh Platform evoked an image of Reform Judaism that was totally assimilationist, denying Jewish peoplehood, hostile to Zionist aspirations, and scornful of tradition. Reform Judaism has had great difficulties in living down this image. Fortunately, it saw and continues to see itself not as reformed in one complete act, but rather as given to reform. Thus, Reform was to move back into the mainstream of Jewish living.

The "Columbus Platform" of 1937 revealed the evolution of Reform Judaism under the imperative of changing conditions. By that time, Jews from Eastern Europe, who carried with them the sense of Jewish peoplehood and an attachment to tradition, constituted the majority of American Jewry. In Germany, the Nazis had come to power and the Jews were in deep distress. The Land of Israel had been designated by the powers as a "Jewish Homeland." Jews rebuilt it but were stymied in their efforts by the British government, the mandate power over the land. No longer could American Jews live in splendid isolation. They had to recognize their kinship—the Jews were a people. The new platform recognized the need for a return to traditional concepts and commitments, it affirmed Jewish peoplehood and the duty to support the rebuilding of the Jewish homeland.

Judaism is the historical religious experience of the Jewish people. . . . The Torah, both written and oral, enshrines Israel's ever-growing consciousness of God and of the moral law. It preserves the historical precedents, sanctions and norms of Jewish life. . . . Being products of historical processes certain of its laws have lost their binding force with the passing of conditions that called them forth. But as a depository of Israel's spiritual ideals the Torah remains the dynamic source of the life of Israel. Each age has the obligation to adapt the teachings of Torah to its basic needs in accordance with the genius of Judaism. . . . Judaism is the soul of which Israel is the body. . . . In the rehabilitation of Palestine . . . we affirm the obligation of all Jewry to aid in its upbuilding as a Jewish homeland. . . . In Judaism religion and morality blend into an indissoluble unity. . . . Religious practice: the religious life . . . the home . . . the synagogue . . . education . . . prayer. . . . Judaism as a way of life requires in addition to its moral and spiritual demands, the preservation of the Sabbath, festivals and Holy Days, the retention and development of such customs, symbols and ceremonies as possess inspirational value, the cultivation of distinctive forms of religious art and music and the use of Hebrew, together with the vernacular, in our worship and instruction. (Central Conference of American Rabbis *Yearbook*, Vol. 18, pp. 97–100; © 1937 by CCAR)

Thus the unity of Torah–Mitzvot–Land was restored. Some of the most ardent fighters for the restoration of the Land of Israel have come from the Reform rabbinate.

By 1976, the extent of the Holocaust had become known. Israel was now a sovereign state, but the Jews in the communist world still suffered under severe discrimination and persecution. In connection with the American Bicentennial in 1976, the Central Conference of American Rabbis at its San Francisco Convention issued a statement: "Reform Judaism, A Centenary Perspective," embodying the most recent thinking of the Reform rabbinate. "The Holocaust shattered our easy optimism about humanity and its inevitable progress. The State of Israel, through its many accomplishments, raised our sense of the Jews as a people to new heights of aspiration and devotion." The Conference declared:

The affirmation of God has always been essential to our people's will to survive. . . . We ground our lives, personally and communally, on God's reality and remain open to new experiences and conceptions of the Divine. . . . *The Jewish people* [italics added] and Judaism defy precise definition because both are in the process of becoming. . . . Jews, by birth or conversion, constitute an uncommon union of faith and peoplehood. . . . Throughout our long history our people has been inseparable from its religion with its Messianic hope that humanity will be redeemed.

The Torah: Torah results from the relationship between God and the Jewish people. . . . Lawgivers and prophets, historians and poets gave us a heritage whose study is a religious imperative and whose practice is our chief means to holiness.

Religious practice was therefore an obligation; it was to be combined with Jewish ethical responsibilities.

Judaism emphasizes action rather than creed as the primary expression of the religious life, the means by which we strive to achieve universal justice and peace. Reform Judaism shares this emphasis on duty and obligation. Our founders stressed that the Jew's ethical responsibilities, personal and social, are enjoined by God. The past century has taught us that the claims made upon us may begin with our ethical obligations, but they extend to many other aspects of Jewish living, including: creating a Jewish home, centered on family devotion; life-long study; private prayer and public worship; daily religious observance; keeping the Sabbath and the holy days; celebrating the major events of life; involvement with the synagogue and community; and other activities which promote the survival of the Jewish people and enhance its existence. Within each area of Jewish observance Reform Jews are called upon to confront the claims of Jewish tradition, however differently perceived, and to exercise their individual autonomy, choosing and creating on the basis of commitment and knowledge.

The State of Israel was seen as imposing obligations as well.

We are privileged to live in an extraordinary time, one in which a third Jewish commonwealth has been established in our people's ancient homeland. We are bound to that land and to the newly reborn State of Israel by innumerable religious and ethnic ties. We have been enriched by its culture and ennobled by its indomitable spirit. We see it providing unique opportunities for Jewish self-expression. We have both a stake and a responsibility in building the State of Israel, assuring its security and defining its Jewish character. We encourage Aliyah (emigration to Israel) for those who wish to find a maximum personal fulfillment in the cause of Zion. We demand that Reform Judaism be unconditionally legitimized in the State of Israel.

At the same time that we consider the State of Israel vital to the welfare of Judaism everywhere, we reaffirm the mandate of our tradition to create strong Jewish communities wherever we live. . . . The State of Israel and the Diaspora, in fruitful dialogue, can show how a people transcends nationalism, even as it affirms it, thereby setting an example for humanity which remains largely concerned with dangerously parochial goals.

The "missionary ideal," calling on Jews to be "a light unto the nations" by their commitment to ethics (which both Hirsch and Reform had stressed) was thereby given a new dimension. By embracing both their homelands in the Diaspora and Israel, Jews demonstrated to the world the necessity and possibility of growing beyond parochial nationalism that had brought so much ill to humanity.

At the same time the statement recognized a change in Jewish duties to humanity. Early Reform Jews saw the major duty of Jewry as serving universal goals. Their outlook was based on a belief in the growing universalism in the world. Newly admitted to society, these Jews felt that they had the primary obligation to work for a world in which the spirit of America, "liberty and justice for all," would be universal. This left no room for a pluralistic society and world, and a specific concern for the Jewish people. It had to be corrected. Neither the principle of universal concern nor that of concern with the Jewish people could be abandoned. The tension between the two had to be accepted.

In recent years we have become freshly conscious of the virtues of pluralism and the values of particularism. . . . Until the recent past our obligations to the Jewish people and to all humanity seemed congruent. At times now these two imperatives appear to conflict. We know of no simple way to resolve such tensions. We must, however, confront them without abandoning either of our commitments. A universal concern for humanity unaccompanied by a devotion to our particular people is self-destructive; a passion for our people without involvement in humankind contradicts what the prophets have meant to us. Judaism calls us simultaneously to universal and particular obligation.

The statement concluded with a call to sober hope:

Previous generations of Reform Jews had unbounded confidence in humanity's potential for good. We have lived through terrible tragedy and been compelled to reappropriate our tradition's realism about the human capacity for evil. The survivors of the Holocaust, on being granted life, seized it, nurtured it, and rising above catastrophe, showed humankind that the human spirit is indomitable. The State of Israel, established and maintained by the Jewish will to live, demonstrates what a united people can accomplish in history. The existence of the Jew is an argument against despair; Jewish survival is a warrant for human hope.

We remain God's witness that history is not meaningless. . . . (Central Conference of American Rabbis *Yearbook*, Vol. 85, San Francisco, California, 1976, pp. 174–78; ©1977 by CCAR. Used with permission.)

The draft of "Ten Principles for Reform Judaism" circulated in 1998 went further. Reform Judaism integrated itself in Jewish tradition. As this book went to press, it was amended. A form of the draft may or may not be adopted by the conference.

Preamble: As Reform Jews we are open to the entirety of our tradition.
Principle 1: Created by the Holy One we are seekers after God: Reform Judaism embraces the story of the Jewish people, which tells of three great encounters with God: Creation, our redemption from Egypt, and our standing together at Sinai. These encounters, re-enacted throughout the Jewish year, lead us to seek our relationship with God . . . that will enable us to praise, thank, celebrate, petition, sing to, argue with, and cry out to the Ribbono Shel Olam, the Great One who presides over all time and all space.
Principle 2: Having stood at Sinai, we respond to the call of Mitzvot amid modernity: . . . Through study we become aware of God's Mitzvot, commandments that call to us even though we live in a modern society. . . .We respond to the call of Torah: out of the ever-growing body of interpretation by Kenesset Yisrael, the eternal community of the Jewish people, and of our individual understanding of what is holy in our own time. . . . Such responses will help us transform a life too often lived exclusively in a state of *chol*, ordinariness, into a life filled with *Kedushah*, holiness . . .
Principle 3: We were redeemed from Egypt to help repair the World: . . . Mindful of our own redemption from Egypt we commit ourselves to help redeem the new century . . . to transform it into a realization of Israel's great messianic hope for the establishment of truth and justice, for moral and spiritual disci-

pline, compassion and integrity, and at long last, a world repaired, a world at peace.

Principle 4: We are committed to Shabbat, which elevates our work and frees us from it: We commit ourselves to observance of the mitzvot of Shabbat, which our tradition has seen as *mey-eyn olam ha-ba*, a foretaste of the world to come. . . . Shabbat . . . offers us the opportunity to participate in the sanctity of our synagogue community and to sanctify our homes . . .

Principle 5: We are committed to learning and seasonal celebration: An informed response to the call of the mitzvot requires a disciplined commitment at every stage of our lives to learn Torah in the widest sense—biblical, rabbinical, medieval, and modern texts, history, philosophy, art music and dance; and to encourage our children and our friends to learn and interpret them with us . . .

Because Torah needs to be studied in an environment of *kedushah* [holiness] we commit ourselves to steer the course of our lives by creative celebration of the seasonal festivals . . . delighting in the special foods and observing the somber fasts. . . . We will celebrate the seasons of our personal lives as well. . . . The *brit* [induction into the Covenant eight days after birth] . . . for girls and boys, at stages of children's maturation, at marriage, at other milestones . . . at time of healing and when faced with death . . .

Principle 6: We are open to expanding the itzvot of reform Jewish practice: We renew our classic devotion to *chinuch*, to Jewish education, some of us sending our children to Jewish day schools, others to supplementary schools. . . . We renew our commitment to *Zedakah*, setting aside a portion of our earnings to provide justice to those in need, and to engage in *gemilut chasadim*, showing our caring presence our love for those in pain. . . . In the presence of God we may each feel called to respond in different ways: some by offering traditional or spontaneous prayers, others by covering our heads, still others by wearing the tallit or tefillin for prayer. . . . Some of us may observe practices of kashrut. . . . Others may wish to utilize the mikvah . . . not only for conversion but for periodic experiences of purification . . .

Principle 7: We are members of a holy people, from whom we learn, whom we teach: . . . We wish to strengthen the ties with Jews from all the movements in Israel. Reminded that we all stood once together at Sinai, we seek to work together in mutual respect, aware of our many serious differences. . . . While our solutions may radically differ, we all face common problems. If we can only listen to each other we can learn much. Perhaps our greatest common concern is the consequences of the successful integration of Jews into our society. While this often seems an invitation to assimilation, our Reform commitment . . . leads us to see this integration as a challenge to expand individuals' knowledge and practice of Jewish tradition. . . . We are cheered . . . that Jewish life has been reborn throughout Europe. We pledge to help provide Progressive congregations around the world with rabbinic service. . . . We promise to be vigilant in helping Jews around the world protect ourselves against renewals of anti-Semitism and other forms of discrimination . . .

Principle 8: Members of a Holy People, we are rooted in a Holy Land, Eretz Yisrael: The Land of Israel represents an historic triumph of the Jewish people and of Zionism which created. . . . The State of Israel. We wish to create a State which promotes full civil, human and religious rights for all its citizens, and in which no religious interpretation of Judaism takes legal precedence over another. We wish to help the State unceasingly for a mutual atmosphere of peace, justice and security with Palestinians and other Arab neighbors. . . . We encourage Reform Jews to make *aliyah*, immigration to Israel, settling the Land of Israel in a manner consistent with our Reform commitments. We call Reform Jews everywhere to dedicate their energies and resources to strengthening an indigenous Progressive Judaism that can help transform *Medinat Yisrael.*

Principle 9: Members of a Holy People, we are heirs to a holy tongue: . . . We believe that God endowed the Hebrew language with a particular measure of *kedushah* . . . Hebrew binds us to Jews in every land and in particular to our brothers and sisters in the State of Israel. We shall read it, to let it help us articulate our prayer and inform our study, to speak it. The more Hebrew we use in our prayer and our study, the more we shall share in the holiness of our people's heritage.

Principle 10: We are committed to the equality of all the people of God: . . . Jewish women and men alike have been strengthened from the admission of women to the rabbinate. . . . We affirm that all people, regardless of gender, age, belief, physical condition and sexual orientation, are all created in the image of the Holy One. In whatever ways we can, we shall strive to help all the children of God and all the peoples of God fulfill their divine potential to contribute to a world transformed, the world of our people's storied dream.

Ken yerhi ratzon—May this be God's will.

Reform Jews thus stand under a double tension: They feel the universal obligation to be fighters for social justice in the world. At the same time they are committed to the Jewish people and the State of Israel. They feel increasingly bound by tradition and Mitzvot as the compelling forces making for survival and *kedushah*, holiness. At the same time they are equally committed to the spirit of individual autonomy, which lies at the root of Reform thought. This difficult decision is perennial.

Hebrew Union College was later to be merged with the Jewish Institute of Religion, a rabbinical school founded in New York by Rabbi Stephen S. Wise (not related to the founder of the Reform movement), a champion of Zionism and social justice. In consummating this merger, Hebrew Union College acquired an additional campus in New York City. As its new name, Hebrew Union College–Jewish Institute of Religion, indicated, it accepted some of Stephen Wise's spirit as well. Wise was an ardent Zionist. He envisioned Jewry as one people, and his rabbinical school was to equip rabbis to serve all branches of Judaism. By incorporating his school, Hebrew Union College widened its scope ideologically as well as regionally. An additional campus was established in Los Angeles and an Institute for Archaeology was founded in Jerusalem; it was eventually developed into another campus and, since 1970, every rabbinical student is required to spend one year of study there. At this campus a number of Israelis have been ordained to serve Reform congregations in Israel. Synagogues and schools were established and a *kibbutz* founded. The link to the Land was affirmed.

Hebrew Union College–Jewish Institute of Religion became a pioneer. Such a pioneering step for Judaism has been the school's ordination of women as rabbis (since 1972) and the investiture of women who are educated in the cantorial school of the institution as cantors. This step has been strongly attacked by Orthodox Jewry. In 1983 the Convention of the Central Conference of American Rabbis, recognizing the realities of American life, including the increase in interfaith marriages, resolved to regard the children of a Jewish father and a non-Jewish mother as Jews—if they had been brought up as such. Since *halakhah* determines the faith of a child by that of his or her mother, this action has been severely censured by Conservative and Orthodox Jewry.

True to Reform tradition, the Union of American Hebrew Congregations, its rabbis, and congregations have been active on behalf of national and international social justice, and have forcefully spoken up for the rights of minority groups. At the same time the movement has shown deep concern and been most active in strengthening Jewish life and consciousness. Camps have been established in many parts of the country where young people and adults live a life of Torah and Mitzvot for varying lengths of time in a total Jewish environment. In the past, Jewish education for children was confined to "Sunday School," conducted one day a week. Numerous congregations have expanded it to three-day instruction. Hebrew is stressed in all schools. A serious concern for an integrated curriculum of Torah and life is shown in the emerging trend of establishing Jewish day schools. Liturgical and educational materials have been issued, including gender-neutral ones; affiliated brotherhoods, sisterhoods, and youth groups are expanding; and excellent theologians have emerged. Reform Judaism is deeply concerned with the dangers faced by Judaism because of intermarriages, but cannot forbid its rabbis to solemnize them, since rabbis have the freedom of following their own consciences. On this issue the Reform rabbinate is split.

The Reform Movement, as a group, is a member of the World Zionist Organization. It has founded and maintains *kibbutzim* and schools in Israel. Its rabbis and congregations in Israel are not recognized by the state, which stands under the influence of a rabbinate, militantly hostile to non-Orthodox Judaism. Obtaining recognition and state support as granted Orthodox congregations remains an uphill struggle.

Conservatism

In the latter part of the nineteenth century a new generation, descendants of the Eastern European immigrants, came along that was ready to move into the mainstream of American life. But it was unwilling to accept Reform Judaism, which it saw as too extreme, too formal, too cold. Reform lay leaders were the first to provide this generation with the means of establishing a religious movement that would synthesize American ways of life and the convictions of tradition-bound Eastern European Jewry. These Reform Jews felt that they were living up to the American ideal of unity in diversity. JACOB H. SCHIFF (1847–1920) was their leader. He provided the funds for the Jewish Theological Seminary, helped organize it, became one of its overseers, and promoted its growth. The seminary became the fountainhead of Conservative Judaism.

Conservative Judaism in America is based on the principle of positive historical Judaism expressed by Zacharias Frankel. SOLOMON SCHECHTER (1850–1915), president and guiding spirit of the Jewish Theological Seminary, maintained that the development of Torah and Mitzvot is squarely placed by God in the hands of the Jewish people, who by unspoken consent adjust and evolve it. Schechter developed institutions for Conservative Judaism similar to those Wise developed for Reform, but he reversed the order of their creation. First came the Jewish Theological Seminary, bearing the same name as Frankel's seminary at Breslau, then came the Rabbinical Assembly, and finally the United Synagogue, the congregational organization. The seminary thus held the central authority and, organizationally at least, the key position.

The Character and Development of Conservative Judaism

According to Conservative doctrine, halakhah, based on the decisions of Torah, Talmud, and Codes must be followed and Mitzvot must be practiced, except as the people change them. The rabbinical leaders and the seminary generally authorized only those changes which had been universally adopted. These changes varied, however, due to the autonomy of individual congregations, even in the evolution of Jewish practices. Some congregations, for instance, used organ music in their services; others rejected it. But this approach, pragmatic and, as such, typically American, failed to provide strong support to individual rabbis and communities while changes were being debated by their own membership.

Originally, all basic decisions were made and handed down by the seminary. In recent decades the movement and its rabbis have been given greater influence. The power of the local rabbi as *More d'Atra*, authoritative "teacher of the community," has been strengthened. The Committee on Jewish Law and Standards of the Rabbinical Assembly has handed down some bold decisions, all of them within the framework of halakhah, but giving it new and innovative interpretations (e.g., the Pilgrimage Festivals may be observed on one day only or on two days, depending on the resolution of the congregation and the approval of the local rabbi). Most incisive were the resolutions on the status of women, beginning with the permission to count women in the *minyan* and call them to the Torah and culminating in the ordination of women.

The Ordination of Women

The developments surrounding the ordination of women mirror the process of decision making in Conservative Judaism. First, intensive halakhic analysis by experts at the seminary had led to the opinion that women's ordination could be accommodated within halakhah. After lengthy debate, the resolution permitting the ordination of women was passed by the Rabbinical Assembly at its 1980 convention. The issue was then submitted to a cross-section of Conservative congregations whose opinion was generally favorable.

Those favoring ordination held that, ethically, it should be granted in the spirit of equality of the sexes. It was wasteful to dispense with the full contribution of half of the Jewish people to Jewish life. It was decidedly unfair to allow women participation in the full rabbinical program but deny them ordination. Many women dedicated to Judaism as their life's vocation had since childhood gone through all the stages of Jewish studies, organizational life, and commitment only to find that at the end of their training and development they were denied ultimate fulfillment. If they wished to fulfill their desire, Conservative women had to transfer to one of the Reform or Reconstructionist seminaries that ordained women. As a result Conservatism would be impoverished.

Halakhically, as the chancellor of the Jewish Theological Seminary explained, the rabbi's function in modern days was different from that of earlier times. Notice had to be taken that in Antiquity women were permitted to read publicly from the Torah, lead prayers, and perform other duties. Eventually they found themselves deprived of these rights. While some restrictions might be imposed on women, there was no reason for them not to function as preachers, counselors, teachers, guides, and pastors—the main functions of the contemporary rabbi. The Commission for the Study of the Ordination of Women as Rabbis, in its the final paper concluded, "There is no direct halakhic objection to the acts of training and ordaining a woman to be a rabbi, teacher, and preacher in Israel."

The opposition pointed out that ordination of women was so basic a departure from tradition that it would create cleavages between Conservative congregations and within them and between Conservatism and the Israeli rabbinate, and would increase the chasm between Conservatism and Orthodoxy. Against this, it was argued that Conservative congregations would adjust. Moreover, Conservatism was a great and vital movement and should not be overly anxious about the opinions of other groups in Judaism. If ordination of women was acceptable under Conservative principles, the movement should go ahead, as it was ethical to do so.

After finally approving the ordination of women, the convention left implementation of the resolution to the faculty of the Jewish Theological Seminary, which has the authority to grant ordination. After long hesitation the resolution was implemented and the first woman ordained in 1985. The investiture of women as cantors followed.

Other Contemporary Issues

Divorce. Halakhah grants the right to divorce to the husband only. If he refuses or deserts, the woman remains *agunah,* "anchored," to him and is not permitted to remarry. Conservative Judaism has written safeguards in the *ketubah,* the Hebrew marriage contract. On the talmudic principle that "every marriage is done in accordance with the rabbis' opinions," it has instituted a rabbinical court that can annul marriages if needed.

Patrilineal Descent. Recognition of persons with non-Jewish mothers and Jewish fathers as Jews was rejected, since it would break the unity of the Jewish people. Conversion to Judaism had been made much less difficult, and solves all problems.

Gays and Lesbians. After much debate the Committee on Law and Standards, and subsequently the convention, ruled that open homosexuals and lesbians should not be admitted to the rabbinate or cantorate, but with the consent of the individual congregation, could serve in other Jewish positions. An ordained rabbi who came out into the open after years of service and was seeking a new pulpit was also granted the aid of the Placement Committee, with the proviso that the congregation be informed. The same committee was also empowered to aid gay or lesbian synagogues in their search for a rabbi. Rabbis were forbidden to solemnize the bond between two men or two women.

Emet Ve-Emunah—Statement of Principles of Conservative Judaism

In 1988 a "platform" under the title *Emet ve-Emunah*, "Truth and Affirmation," was published. It is divided into three sections: "God in the World" deals with theological issues, "The Jewish People" addresses issues of the community, and "Living a Life of Torah" concerns the conduct of life. In line with positive historical Judaism the statement declared in principle: "We reject relativism which rejects any objective source of authoritative truth. We also reject fundamentalism and literalism, which do not admit a human component in revelation, thus excluding an independent role for human experience and reason in the process" (p. 20). Halakhah remained open for evolution: "Halakhah is . . . what the Jewish community understands God's will to be" (p. 21).

The platform accepted the traditional view of God as "a supreme supernatural being with the power to command and control the world," but also allowed a view of God as "not a being to whom we can point" but "a presence and a power that transcends us." This opinion was held by Mordecai Kaplan (see below). The traditionalist and the modernist were thereby legitimized in their thinking.

The platform affirmed the chosenness of Israel . It underscored the requirement that Mitzvot, expecially Sabbath and kashrut observance must be emphasized and strengthened. It pointed out that Torah included the equality of women. It asserted that Israel and Diaspora stand in creative polarity as centers of Jewish life.

The Conservative Jew is called to learning and striving, resulting in the decision to "refract all aspects of life through the prism of one's Jewishness." The Jew must be striving because "what is needed is an openness to those observances one has yet to perform and the desire to grapple with those issues and texts one has yet to confront. . . . as modernity and tradition inform and reshape each other the Jewish person becomes whole" (pp. 56–57). The emphasis on striving pointed to Franz Rosenzweig's thinking, as we shall see below.

This was the first platform Conservative Judaism had presented. In enunciating its basic principles, it also revealed its ambiguities.

Fissures within the Movement

When the ordination of women appeared to be certain, a split developed (1984) within the Conservative movement between those who endorsed ordination and those who regarded it as halakhically inadmissible and were generally dissatisfied with the prevailing trend. They organized the Union for Traditional Judaism, which came to be joined by a substantial number of rabbis and congregations. To them, tradition has principal authority, and whatever evolution may be permitted must rest on rabbinic decisions, not popular consensus.

Conservative Judaism has developed a wide organizational network, including men's and women's groups, youth camps, and youth groups, and it issues educational material and prayer books. The Jewish Theological Seminary, headquartered in New York, also has campuses in Los Angeles, called the University of Judaism, and in Jerusalem. The movement as a group is affiliated with The World Zionist Organization. Conservatism has grown into a very strong movement. Both its strengths and its weaknesses are still with us.

The Masorti Movement

The movement, in spite of being halakhically grounded, remained totally unrecognized by the Israeli State Rabbinate and was subjected to unceasing attacks and grave disabilities. Unlike Orthodox congregations it received no state support and its rabbis were denied the right to carry out rabbinical functions in Israel. A number of Conservative synagogues emerged, but essentially the Israeli population, knowing little about it and seeing it as an American institution, kept aloof. Conservatism had to affirm itself as an independent but traditional movement and had to develop within Israeli society. In 1979, the *Masorti*, "Traditional," movement was created in Israel. It established settlements, summer camps, programs at universities, and public schools that accepted it and, above all, *Bet Midrash L'Limudei Ha-Yahadut*, "The Seminary of Judaic Studies" at Jerusalem that has ordained Conservative rabbis.

Reconstructionism

Reconstructionism is a philosophy of American Jewry that rests on the American experience, the unity of Judaism, the impact of science, the significance of Israel, and above all the centrality of the people. It sees Judaism as an evolving religious civilization, not a revealed religion but the creation of the Jewish people. The Jewish people received its God-concept and its religious forms out of its own needs.

Started as a school of thought, Reconstructionism reached wide circles ideologically. Becoming a denomination it was able to give unity to its followers. While numerically a small movement, Reconstructionism has influenced the thinking of a great many rabbis, especially non-Orthodox ones.

Its founder was MORDECAI M. KAPLAN (1881–1983), a man distinguished not only by the most profound scholarship but also by his love and concern for Judaism and for individuals. Kaplan was deeply disturbed that many Jews had become alienated from Jewish religion because it clashed with the insights of science, and he endeavored to "reconstruct" Judaism.

Kaplan was profoundly influenced by the ideas of the French Jewish sociologist EMIL DURKHEIM (1885–1917), who, in his work *The Elementary Forms of Religious Life*, expressed the theory that any organic community develops the consciousness of "something beyond itself, greater than ourselves with which we stand in communion." In this manner, out of its own *elan vital*, the Jewish people, according to Kaplan, has found the God idea and the commitment to ethical nationhood. Additionally, Reconstructionism as an American movement was influenced by the philosophies of William James and John Dewey, and was imbued with the spirit of American democracy. Finally, it articulated the image many Jews in America held of themselves.

Started in the 1930s, Reconstructionism is found today primarily in the United States and Canada. In 1968, Reconstructionists opened their own rabbinical school, The Reconstructionist Rabbinical College at Wicote, Pennsylvania. It organized graduates in a rabbinical organization and its member congregations in the Federation of Reconstructionist Congregations and Fellowships. It has published its own prayer books that attempt a gender-neutral form and instructional materials.

Innovations of Reconstructionism in halakhah include recognition as Jews those whose fathers are Jewish but not their mothers, provided the child has been brought up within the Jewish faith and has received a Jewish education. A similar break with tradition was the 1980 provision for egalitarian divorce procedures, which allowed wives to divorce their husbands through the instrumentality of Jewish law. Reconstructionism also ordains women as rabbis.

For a full comprehension of Reconstructionism, a basic understanding of Mordecai Kaplan's theology is required. We will discuss it in Chapter 15.

AMERICAN JEWRY TODAY

The life of American Jews is wholly different from that of their old-world ancestors. In their overwhelming majority they are native-born and have become fully acculturated and assimilated, belonging generally to the middle class of society. By their very acculturation and prosperity their religious life has suffered. They affirm their belonging to Judaism, grounding it in emotion, the memories of the shtetl, the tragedy of the Holocaust, and the commitment to Israel. They express it through dedication to universal social justice, but not necessarily in response to the commanding voice of God. This may pose a danger. Memories and attachments may fade, social justice is a universal challenge. Neither of them holds a long-range assurance of Jewish survival.

Jews have moved to the suburbs among Christian friends and neighbors, live well, and have a low birthrate. Their children go to college. In tune with the American way they have founded congregations, every one of which is fully autonomous. They have built splendid synagogues, most of which are lacking in attendance much of the year. The majority is affiliated with a congregation (though a sizable minority is not), but there is no great religious fervor as might be expressed in regular attendance at worship, home observance of Mitzvot, and extensive study of Torah. Although most children are sent to religious schools and are made Bar Mitzvah or Bat Mitzvah, their knowledge is minimal and in daily life there is little Jewish content.

The parents hope their children will find Jewish mates, but have had to acquiesce when they do not. Here lies the gravest threat for the future of American Jewry. Approximately half of the Jews who married between 1985 and 1990 chose non-Jewish partners. Only 28% of their offspring were brought up exclusively as Jews while 21% were raised as Christians, 20% self-identified with some combination of Judaism and Christianity, and 31% had no religion at all. This means that in 1990 there were 700,000 children under the age of 18 in Jewish families who were not raised as Jews (*Sh'ma* #24/458, October 1, 1993).

Countermeasures

Aware of this grave danger to the future, the religious bodies have taken action, whose ultimate results remain to be seen.

Outreach. Reform Judaism, recognizing the danger early, resolved to accept children of non-Jewish mothers as Jews, as long as they are brought up as Jews. Additionally, it has actively reached out to non-Jewish partners of Jews, in an effort to win them to Judaism by showing them the beauty of Judaism and its rich integrated way of life. By printed material, radio and video programs, lecture courses, personal visits, and in similar ways, it has striven to bring them into the fold of Judaism and has welcomed them, even before or without conversion, into its congregations, their worship, and activities. Conservative Judaism has followed suit.

Conversion. Traditionally made difficult, conversion has been made easy. It has in fact brought many thousands into the Jewish fold. These "Jews by Choice," as they wish to be known, have frequently shown a deep love for their new faith and become the backbone of congregations. Brought up to consider public worship an essential part of the religious life, they have strengthened synagogue attendance.

The Universities. A most auspicious recent development has been the flowering of Jewish scholarship at numerous universities and colleges. Chairs for Judaic studies have been established and courses on Judaism introduced. These courses have attracted Jewish students interested in learning about Judaism in an "unbiased," scholarly setting. It has also resulted in ecumenical dialogue, affecting both religious and cultural Jews.

The Havurot. An internal, spontaneous development is the *Havurot*. Families find each other in informal groupings, to assist each other, to celebrate together and to pray together in small informal circles. They frequently have developed their own highly selective and creative ways of worship. Reform, Conservative and Reconstructionist congregations have supported the havurot, and the congregational rabbis will counsel and guide them on demand.

Orthodoxy and Hasidism. Some young Jews have been drawn to Hasidic groups, which to them represent an undiluted Judaism and the security offered by a fundamentalist outlook.

Israel. Young Jews of all groups have been increasingly dedicated to the cause of Israel and have spent summers there. They have come to the support of Jews still oppressed in many lands or subject to anti-Jewish propaganda.

JEWISH ORGANIZATIONS

There exists a feeling that one must work for Judaism, and this urge to do something (in typically American pragmatic style) has led to a proliferation of charitable, social, and service organizations that are sharply competing with each other for membership and recognition.

In 1843 a number of Jews organized the Order of *B'nai B'rith*. Its name is revealing: "Sons of the Covenant." When an incipient anti-Semitism led to the exclusion of Jews from a number of the general fraternal orders, they decided to establish their own, emphasizing the Covenant that unites. This was well in the spirit of American self-reliance and initiative. The order was to provide fellowship and offer assistance; for instance, an insurance program gave group protection to the members against calamity. These programs have been expanded and new ones added to them. The Anti-Defamation League of B'nai B'rith (founded 1913) has combated prejudice on a wide front. Educational activities have been stressed. The Hillel Foundations sponsored by B'nai B'rith at universities provide Jewish centers for students; and youth groups initiate youngsters into their obligations as Americans and Jews. Membership is not dependent on synagogue affiliation but the member has to be a Jew. B'nai B'rith lodges were frequently founded in small Jewish communities not yet able to organize congregations, and then became the nucleus of new congregations. Eventually, the order spread throughout the world. The pragmatic, action-directed spirit of America can be clearly recognized in B'nai B'rith.

The American Jewish Committee (founded in 1906), was originally an elitist organization of German Jews regarding themselves as advocates of the community. It remained active in many fields, especially the interfaith dialogue. In the 1920s, when the fraudulent pamphlet "The Protocols of the Elders of Zion" was given wide publicity by Henry Ford in the United States, he was forced to issue an apology. In contrast to the Committee, the *American Jewish Congress* (which held its first meeting in 1918), was established as a democratic organization, to serve the causes of Jewish defense, interfaith dialogue, and social justice in general. *The World Jewish Congress,*(1933 reorganized 1936) was an extension of the American Jewish Congress, in response to the Nazi atrocities. Subsequently it devoted itself to the defense and rights of Jews throughout the world. A great deal of defense work had to be done; in some ways it had to be continued. In 1996 it was discovered that Swiss banks had held on to the money deposited by Jews that were eventually murdered in the Holocaust. The World Jewish Congress initiated the attack that forced these banks to compensate the descendants of these Jews.

Jews in the armed services have been served by the *Jewish Welfare Board* (founded 1917), which is also the sponsor of Jewish community centers similar to those run by the YMCA. *The Jewish Veterans* are organized in the Jewish War Veterans of the United States of America, founded after the Civil War, to counter the falsehood Jews had shirked their duty. It is now the oldest veterans' organization in the United States, has been chartered by the United States Congress and has many "Posts." *Jewish Community Federations* exist in every larger community. Their common element is philanthropy. The Federation appeals to all Jews, irrespective of ideology, serving as the unifying bond between the groups and "denominations." In philanthropy, American Jewry responded sacrificially to the demands of every new arising emergency. It has provided funds for Israel, made possible the rescue and resettlement of thousands of Jews both refugees from the Nazis and, more recently, émigrés from Russia, and it has supported charitable and educational Jewish institutions in the United States. In 1948, following the practices of many churches, Jews established a university open to students of all races and creeds, *Brandeis University*, in Waltham, Massachusetts.

There are many other organizations, such as the *Zionist Organization*. Its very active women's branch, *Hadassah*, was instrumental in founding Hadassah Hospital near Jerusalem, now the teaching hospital of the medical school of Hebrew University. There are fraternal orders, charitable organizations, book clubs, and many others, a sign of the diversity of interests among Jews, and perhaps also of the power drives of individuals and the resulting lack of unity. Lay people and lay organizations, rather than rabbis, are generally the spokespersons for American Jewry. But this is historically conditioned.

CONTEMPORARY CHALLENGES AND SOCIETAL ISSUES

The condition of the Jews has never been so good in any country as it is in the United States. Jews feel at home in America. Generally, there exist no obstacles to a completely free and integrated life for American Jews. George Washington's hope for "the children of Abraham" has been fulfilled. But there remain significant challenges.

The devastation of Jewish life throughout the world began with Hitler's extermination program. It continues to this day wherever civil war exists. The persecution of Jews in the former Soviet Union resulted in the emigration of masses of Russian Jews when the Soviet system collapsed. American Jewry was confronted by a twofold challenge: It had to provide homes and a new start for the multitude of refugees not only in the United States but also in other parts of the world, and it had to give help on the widest scale to the impoverished Jewish communities in many lands, assistance to young settlements that sprang up as a result of migration, and aid to the upbuilding of Israel. These challenges were accepted. *The Joint Distribution Committee* has extended its activities worldwide. Israel, the communities in Europe, and the fast-growing Jewish communities of South America owe their emergence and development to American Jewish aid. The Land of Israel could not have been redeemed, nor could its institutions have been developed in such unique fashion, without the support of American Jews.

Yet American Jewry, having come of age so suddenly, finds itself faced with a further challenge. It must provide spiritual guidance and leadership. It must develop a Jewish theology and forms of Jewish life that will sustain the spirituality of the Jewish people in the midst of these years. It must serve as a role model for all of Jewry. This demands from every Jew a commitment to the Jewish heritage and to living a truly Jewish life. This has not yet been achieved.

Anti-Semitism, though far from extinct, is not threatening, and yet vigilance is called for. Societal unrest, economic reverses in the country, demagogues, or subversion may lead to flare-ups. Jewish "defense organizations" maintain this vigilance. The individual Jew stands under Micah's prophetic summons to "do justice, love mercy, and walk humbly with your God."

American Jewry and Israel

The rabbinical leadership of all branches has recommended *aliyah* (immigration to Israel) for those Jews who feel they can fulfill their lives as Jews only in the Holy Land. The wars of 1967 and 1973 revealed the full identification of American Jews with Israel. In need and in danger, ideological barriers quickly collapsed and unity among all parts of Jewry was restored. The Israelis in turn came to recognize the Jewishness and importance of American Jewry. The bonds between American Jews and Israel have since become even stronger. Israel is recognized as a great spiritual force in Judaism and the Yishuv is held in deep affection. Israel hoped that large numbers of American Jews would settle in the Land. *Aliyah* developed but remained small. For American Jews America is home. For many years American Jews felt that the spirit of unity forbade any criticism of Israel and its politics. This has changed. Criticism on some of Israeli policies is not illegitimate and does not break the bond. Tensions exist. Israel has an Orthodox state rabbinate that has denied non-Orthodox Jewish movements the right to exist. The overwhelming majority of American Jews is non-Orthodox. It regards religious diversity as permanent. It has therefore called for recognition of Jewish religious plurality in Israel. It has insisted that rabbis ordained by non-Orthodox rabbinical seminaries be given full authority to carry out all rabbinical functions. It has demanded that State and society of Israel recognize as Jews, the "Jews by choice" brought into the fold by these rabbis. American Jews of all denominations have nevertheless strongly affirmed the bond of Covenant that binds them to Israel.

Tensions between Jews and Blacks

In recent years tensions have developed between certain groups of blacks and the Jews. This has surprised and disturbed the Jewish community. Jews had been advocates of social improvement for all Americans even when it entailed sacrifices for themselves. They had internalized the teachings of the prophets (see Amos), and drawn the lessons of their own experiences as a minority. Therefore they strongly supported blacks in their struggle for complete political, societal, and economic equality. The NAACP (National Association for the Advancement of Colored People) was cofounded by Jews. Two young Jews—together with a black man—were brutally murdered while volunteering in voter registration among the blacks in the South. Abraham Heschel walked with Dr. Martin Luther King, Jr. in the protest march to Montgomery, Alabama. Many rabbis joined him. Dr. King in turn emphatically called for a fully integrated society of "blacks and whites . . . Jews and Gentiles."

The Jews could not understand and were appalled to find that blacks had turned against them. It turned out that militant demagogues among the blacks were at work, blaming the Jews for the hardships suffered by non-white communities. By stereotyping the Jews, this leadership offered a simplistic explanation for the ills affecting the blacks at the hands of the white establishment. Therein lay a danger for America.

We can offer only some guesses about some of the reasons that made some blacks listen to these leaders. Suffering might have spawned envy, which looked for a scapegoat. The Jews, immigrants arriving after blacks had been brought to this country against their will, had been successful and found "the good life." Moving to the suburbs they had left the inner city where blacks now lived often under appalling conditions. All Jews could now be stereotyped as exploiters. In earlier years Jews had found in the civil service an escape from discrimination in the private sector. By holding tenure they blocked blacks and other minorities from taking the same route. Jews drawing on their own experiences may have assumed a paternalistic attitude in trying to help the blacks which may have led to resentment by the minorities who wished to go it alone.

Essentially, the Jews saw it as scapegoating in an effort to attack the non-Jewish white majority and effect black separation from whites. A minority of blacks turned to Islam in remonstrance against Christianity, seen as an oppressive religion of the white establishment. Some groups formed adaptations of Islam, such as "The Religion of Islam," whose leaders—in contrast to Dr. King—called for the separation of blacks from whites in society. Louis Farrakhan, Minister of Islam, called Judaism a "gutter religion." A pretext for the slander of the Jews was found in a resolution of the United Nations General Assembly on November 10, 1975, declaring Zionism to be racist. It was introduced and promoted by the USSR and Arab nations. In 1991 it was rescinded on the initiative of the United States and with the cooperation of Russia. After the Holocaust, "anti-Semitism" had become a proscribed word. It was replaced by "anti-Zionism," which conveyed the same hostility against Jews as a whole. It seemed incongruous for minorities to be anti-Jewish, but an anti-Israel and anti-Zionist position could camouflage this attitude. Dr. King saw this clearly. Seymour Martin Lipset, then professor of government and social relations at Stanford University, related a remark Dr. King made to black students at Harvard: "One of the young men present happened to make some remarks against the Zionists. Dr. King snapped at him and said, 'Don't talk like that! When people criticize Zionists, they mean Jews. You're talking anti-Semitism'" (*The Left, the Jews, and Israel*, Anti-Defamation League of B'nai B'rith, 1969).

Agitation combined with unemployment caused violence, particularly in the cities. Poorer Jews, in large numbers still city-dwellers, became its victims and felt insecure. In the Crown Heights section of New York City, blacks and Lubavitcher Hasidim lived together. When the driver of the car of the late Lubavitcher Rebbe accidentally ran over a black child in 1991, riots developed among the blacks and a yeshivah student was murdered.

Fortunately, the restless ones formed only a minority within the African-American community. By 1995 over two-thirds of African-Americans earned between 65% and 90% of the income of whites and close to one-third of well-educated blacks had been able to move to the suburbs. Yet a majority of the blacks remained convinced that racism remained a problem and many remembered the racism they faced on their way to success. Severe prejudices existed in society and needed to be remedied (*Time*, Vol. 150, No.10, November 7, 1997, pp. 60–63). Like the Jews, these African-Americans had found an escape through education. They recognized that the methods of education and the funding of schools, especially in the inner cities, needed to be greatly improved. Both Jews and blacks have strongly promoted these reforms. Joining forces among themselves and with fair-thinking whites they have striven to eradicate racial animosity by whites and blacks. All Americans had to transform their inner selves and commit themselves to racial healing.

Both sides have realized that in the battle for the souls of all Americans and in the struggle against discrimination, minorities should sustain rather than fight each other. Both sides have made efforts to mend the misunderstandings and to eliminate tensions where they exist. Individual friendships were maintained on both sides, and both groups could count on mutual support when one or the other needed it.

Neo-Nazi Ideologies

Neo-Nazi ideologies were equally revived. Skinheads engaged in riotous activities. Militant enemies of American democracy prepared themselves for the overthrow of democracy by armed force. These groups attempted to transform America into a racially oriented state and society under a "leader," like Hitler. They were marginal groups and, when needed, were dealt with by the police. Under the constitutional guarantees of freedom of speech and assembly the public demonstrations of groups like the Skinheads could not be forbidden. From their printing presses hate literature has appeared and been exported abroad. In recent years, anti-Semitic "revisionist" historians have even tried to prove that the Holocaust never happened. These writers deliberately turned their backs on the overwhelming documentation of the Holocaust and its victims. Facts did not matter. The Holocaust was "a Jewish lie." Small and insignificant as these groups may appear, vigilance is required. Hitler, too, started as the leader of a "marginal group."

CHAPTER 8

Zionism and the State of Israel

THE SIGNIFICANCE OF ZION IN JEWISH CONSCIOUSNESS

The modern term *Zionism* denotes the striving of Jews for the Land of Israel as their own. The term was well chosen. *Zion* as reality, hope, and ideal has been deeply rooted in Jewish consciousness ever since biblical times. Zion, a holy hill in the city of Jerusalem, has been the symbol of Jerusalem, the Temple, the Land, and its people. As such it is found more than 175 times in Hebrew Scriptures. From the words of prophets, singers, and poets we may almost weave a tapestry of Jewish history. A few examples may illuminate the significance of Zion.

Zion and Jerusalem are Israel's capital. "The king [David] and his men set out for Jerusalem against the Jebusites. . . . David captured the mountain stronghold of Zion, it is now the city of David" (2 Samuel 5:6, 9). From this day on, Zion-Jerusalem was the capital of Israel. Here King Solomon built the Temple (1 Kings 7), making it the spiritual center for the Jews. From there God's word was to go out to the world and lead the nations in His way.

Israel fails God and prophets predict doom. None of the nations have found their way to God, not even Israel. Therefore, "the Lord roars from Zion, sends out His voice from Jerusalem" (Amos 1:2) condemning the nations of the world, including Israel.

Israel in exile. Israel was punished for its lack of faith: Jerusalem fell and the Temple was destroyed by Nebuchadnezzar. In bitter lamentation Jeremiah cried out at the suffering of his people, whom he called Zion's daughter,

> Zion's roads mourn. . . . From Zion's Daughter all her splendor has vanished. . . . Woe, in His wrath my Lord has beclouded the Daughter Zion's, has hurled from heaven to earth the majesty of Israel. . . . God resolved to demolish the walls of Zion's Daughter. . . . To the ground sank, made moot, the elders of Zion's daughter (Lamentations 1:4, 6; 2:1, 8, 10).

But, looking into the future, Jeremiah offered hope: "Your iniquity, Daughter Zion's, is gone away, He will exile you no more, He will account it to your iniquity, Daughter Edom's [symbol of Israel's tormentors]. He will uncover all your sins" (Lamentations 4:22).

The Jews in exile. The exiled Jews in Babylonia were in utter despair. "By the rivers of Babylon, there we sat and we wept, as we recollected Zion. . . . For there our captors demanded of us words of song, our torturers a song of joy, 'Sing us something from the song of Zion.' How can we sing a song of God on alien soil?" (Psalm 137:1–4).

God's judgment and Israel's restoration. But God removed the dross from Israel as the people repented, "Zion will be delivered through justice, her repentant ones through righteousness" (Isaiah 1:27). God will judge and punish the nations of the world for all the crimes they have committed against Israel. For the Jews, "on Mount Zion will be escape, it will be holy and the House of Jacob shall inherit its inheritance anew. . . . Liberators will ascend Mount Zion to pass judgment on Mount Esau [symbol of Israel's persecutors] and the kingship will be God's" (Obadiah 1:21).

Going Home. "When God lets come home the home-comers Zion's, we shall be as in a dream. Our mouths shall be filled with laughter, our tongues with jubilation" (Psalm 126:1).

The end of days. The prophet Zechariah gives us a picture not only of the immediate future as he perceived it, but also of the ultimate fulfillment: "Thus speaks God: I have returned to Zion and I will dwell in the midst of Jerusalem, and Jerusalem will be called City of the Truth, the Mountain of the God of Hosts, the Holy Mountain" (Zechariah 8:3). In the end the nations of the world will give up their resistance to the word of God. Zion will be the spiritual center of all humanity. "In the end of days the Mount of the Lord's house shall be firmly established at the head of the mountains . . . And people shall go there in multitudes and shall say: 'let us go and ascend to the Mountain of the Lord, to the House of Jacob's God, that He may instruct us in His ways and we may walk in His paths.' For from Zion Torah shall go forth and God's word from Jerusalem" (Isaiah 2:2–3). Whenever the Torah scroll is taken out of the Ark for reading, the congregation sings this verse.

Later development. In his "Ode to Zion," Judah Halevi addressed Zion as a person, "Zion wilt thou not ask for the welfare of those who seek thy peace . . ." Martin Buber speaks of Zion "as aim and as task." Zion symbolizes Israel's life under God in freedom and as light unto the nations. It is the aim and striving for it is the task. It is the yearning of the Jewish people and the fulfillment of this yearning. The movement of the nineteenth century could have found no term more hallowed, more filled with meaning, and more challenging than *Zionism.*

In 1969 the late Richard Cardinal Cushing of Boston spoke with deep insight of the feelings that move Jews in regard to Israel:

The State of Israel is not just a refuge for a people the world has abused—it is for the Jews the fulfillment of prophecy . . . the realization of the Covenant, the answer to the prayers of generations of the Chosen People. . . . Of course, only a portion of the Jews of the world will ever settle in Israel, but some part of every Jew belongs there; some portion of his heart, if we may say it, watches and waits upon its fortunes.

The Cardinal's insight may explain the perspective of this chapter. I have earnestly attempted to present the events objectively but may veer toward a Jewish point of view of the history leading up to the creation of the State of Israel and its subsequent evolution. I am cognizant of the sufferings of the Palestinians and empathetic with their aspirations. But as a Jew who has lived through the years of struggles and rejoiced in Israel's achievements, my emotions might unconsciously affect my objectivity, and therefore ask the reader for understanding and forbearance.

BACKGROUND AND BEGINNINGS

The emergence of the State of Israel was the result of a chain of events— of ideas and ideals, theology, history, and human action. Throughout the Diaspora, Jewry remained linked to the Land. Returning to it and establishing self-government were envisioned for Messianic days (e.g., Obadiah 1:19–21; Micah 4; Zechariah 7:9–15). This hope for the coming of the Messiah was real, its fulfillment was expected at any time, in accordance with God's will. It served as a life-sustaining force during Jewry's dark ages. The hope for the restoration of a Jewish commonwealth was expressed in daily prayers; in grace after meals; and in the rites surrounding birth, marriage, and death. The totality of life was permeated by this expectation. During the nineteenth century several divergent views emerged.

Orthodoxy was divided. There were those who held that Jews were not permitted to work for the return to Zion, but had to wait for the day of divine dispensation; they were only permitted to pray for this day. Others believed that it was permitted and even imperative to promote the day of independence and to work for it politically and by actual return to the Land. This migration to Palestine, now Israel, has been called *aliyah*, "ascent," a term that denotes its spiritual character.

Eastern European Jewry, suffering from endless persecutions, leaned toward the second point of view; Orthodoxy in Western Europe, where Jews were reasonably secure, tended to follow the principle of waiting and praying without eliminating from its theology the concept of return and independence. Liberal Judaism believed that the "Messianic Age" had arrived with the Emancipation, that Western European countries were the final destinations for those Jews who were their citizens. The same process would eventually take place in the East as well. In addition, they feared that any concern with Palestine as a Jewish homeland would create suspicion of their loyalty in the eyes of the state and society. Cultural Jews were again split. One group saw the creation of a universal socialist society as the answer to all problems, including discrimination against Jews. Another group strongly believed in an independent Jewish state as the only lasting solution. Palestine was originally settled largely by this latter group.

ZIONISM

Russian Jewry was suffering agonies throughout its history. The thought stirred, in line with the emerging nationalism of the nineteenth century, that only a return to the Land could provide freedom. *Auto-Emanzipation*, "self-emancipation" was the slogan of LEON PINSKER (1821–1891), a Jewish physician and leader. He saw anti-Semitism as an incurable affliction of the world, and therefore, it was futile to expect the nations to grant emancipation to the Jews. Jews had to emancipate themselves. The only cure lay in national independence.

Cultural Zionism: Ahad Ha-Am

Cultural Zionism regarded the Land as a needed home for persecuted Jews, but it also went further than that. Political independence was not the ultimate goal, Jewish culture had to be liberated and revived as well. This could be done only through a free Jewish society in Palestine. The main exponent of "cultural Zionism" was ASHER GINZBERG (1856–1927), who wrote under the pen name *Ahad Ha-Am*, "One of the People." He, like Pinsker, was a product of the Enlightenment movement *Haskalah* that had taken hold within some Eastern Jewish circles. He also believed in the Jews as a people. But no people can be creative, he felt, unless it has a spiritual and cultural center in a land of its own. Let Palestine be restored as the center of Jewish life and Judaism will be reborn.

In *The Jewish State and the Jewish Problem*, Ahad Ha-Am maintained that both Jews and Judaism had come out of the ghetto and joined the world. Previously, self-isolation had preserved the people, but these walls had fallen. With their inevitable entry into the wider society, the Jews had lost their protective shelter. Their future was endangered. By returning to their own land and forming their own society, Jews would be able to reshape their future. They would be able to live a natural life as a national body. Out of their collective experience they could organically develop their own culture. Through it, they could interact with Diaspora Jewry and make a contribution to humanity. Ahad Ha-Am desired the right of self-government for the Jews in their land, but he did not insist on full sovereignty for a Jewish state.

Early Settlements

The yearning for liberation from intolerable pressure and a hopeless fate in Russia expressed itself in a number of efforts to resettle on the Land. Organizations were founded such as the *Hovave Zion*, "Lovers of Zion," and student groups exchanged classrooms for the backbreaking work demanded by the cultivation of arid soil. For the new immigrants, the French Baron Rothschild established colonies in Palestine as early as the 1870s. Migration was difficult, however, since the Turkish government in whose domain Palestine lay placed great obstacles in the way of a large-scale aliyah. The Turkish rulers had no desire to increase the numbers of non-Muslims in their empire. Since the nineteenth century they had had much trouble with them, especially Christians. To succeed in opening Palestine to mass immigration and making it a homeland for the Jews Zionism would need an experienced and determined leader. That leader was Theodor Herzl.

Political Zionism: Theodor Herzl

Ahad Ha-Am recognized the twofold problem faced by modern Jewry in its quest for survival: the internal problem of searching for meaning and spiritual vitality and the external problem of the need for escape from intolerable persecution. Ahad Ha-Am placed major emphasis on the first without neglecting the second.

By contrast, THEODOR HERZL (1860–1904) looked for a purely political solution to survival. "We are a people, *one* people," he stated. His was the age of emerging nationalism. By becoming an independent nation on their Land, the Jews could find freedom from persecution. At the same time they would develop their cultural powers and spiritual endowments to the benefit of humanity. With all Jews leaving their diaspora countries, anti-Semitism would disappear because the majority in these nations no longer had a minority against which it could be directed.

Born in Budapest and raised in the Austrian-Hungarian empire, Herzl was the son of a family strongly assimilated to Western surroundings and life. Handsome, charming, and brilliant, he nevertheless had to cope with anti-Semitism in his student years. He became a successful playwright and novelist but chose to be a newspaper correspondent. His paper, *Die Neue Freie Presse* of Vienna, sent him to Paris to cover one of the most sensational trials of the century, the Dreyfus trial. Alfred Dreyfus, a Jewish captain and the only Jewish member of the French general staff, was accused of having submitted secret documents to the Germans (1894). His accusers knew he was innocent; the German emperor knew the identity of the traitor who had surrendered the documents, but Dreyfus the Jew was made the scapegoat. Witnesses were forced by threats to perjure themselves, and Dreyfus was convicted and sent to Devil's Island. The trial led to severe anti-Semitic outbursts in France. In 1906 Dreyfus was exonerated thanks largely to the efforts of dedicated and courageous non-Jews, including the French novelist Emile Zola and the statesman Clemenceau.

For Herzl the trial was an eye-opener. If this could happen in France, mother of democracy in Europe, then Jews were not secure anywhere. The only answer was a free and internationally recognized homeland. In his 1896 brochure, *Der Judenstaat*, "The Jewish State," Herzl proposed its creation. He then organized a *Jewish Congress*, which met in 1897 in Basel, Switzerland to create "a Jewish, internationally recognized homeland in Palestine." The congress outlined the steps to be taken toward the achievement of its goal. This was *political* Zionism.

The burden of implementation fell upon Herzl. His job was twofold. First, he had to convince his fellow Jews in Western Europe that his plan was not only feasible but desirable. He met with a great deal of opposition among those who felt secure in their surroundings. They had constructed their thought and life on the assumption that they were to be and always remain full-fledged citizens in the countries to which they had given their emotional and physical allegiance. At the same time, Herzl had to plead with princes, potentates, and governments to get a hearing and gain support for his project. The task was immense. Here was an individual, backed up by no power, representing a mass of powerless and oppressed people, venturing into the arena of power politics where might alone spoke. In the pursuit of his mission Herzl wore himself out completely. He died prematurely at the age of forty-four, exactly forty-four years before his hope became a reality.

His work was taken up by his disciples, among them CHAIM WEIZMANN (1874–1952), a brilliant chemist living in England who placed the high reputation his scientific work had given him in the service of his people. He was to end his life as the first president of the State of Israel. Among the early champions of Zionism in America were LOUIS BRANDEIS (1856–1941), the advocate of human rights, and RABBI STEPHEN S. WISE, defender of social justice.

FROM BLUEPRINT TO REALITY

Early Developments in Palestine

To Herzl, awakened by the Dreyfus affair, it was initially immaterial where the Jewish homeland was to be established. He was prepared to accept Uganda, which the British government offered him, but he ran into unalterable opposition from the representatives at the congresses he convoked: Palestine was the land promised the Jews in Torah and inscribed in their hearts and prayers. From Abraham to the present, Jews had always lived there. It became clear to Herzl that no other country would be acceptable to the Jews.

Beginning with the return of the Jews from the Babylonian Exile, the Land of Israel was called "Judaea." After the defeat of Bar Kokhba, the Romans renamed it "Palestine," Land of the Philistines, who had held it in the distant past. By this change of name the Romans wished to destroy any association between Land and Jews. In the course of subsequent history Palestine then stood under many powers. Since the fifteenth century, the Turkish Ottoman Empire—Muslims but not Arabs—held possession of the entire region, including present-day Saudi Arabia, Syria, Iraq, and Jordan. Jews and Arabs lived on the soil, with neither holding sovereignty. The land had become poor, having lost its fertility through neglect, and was now a barren desert, forgotten except for its holy city. Both Arabs and Jews lived in poverty, the latter supported by charity from abroad. The new Jewish settlers therefore believed that the Arabs would welcome them, as together they could reclaim the soil and make a better life for both of them.

In World War I the Turks were allies of the Germans. To weaken the Ottoman Empire from within, the British promised independence to all the territories held by it if their inhabitants cast their lot with Britain. In 1917 Great Britain also gave the Jews a solemn pledge known as "The Balfour Declaration." In it Britain committed itself to provide "the establishment in Palestine of a national home for the Jewish people, provided that the rights of the non-Jewish inhabitants of Palestine and the political status and rights of the Jews outside of it were in no way affected." Unfortunately, the conflicting territorial claims of the various new states were not clarified.

At the time of the Balfour Declaration the war was still in progress on many fronts, but on December 10, 1917, General Allenby of Britain was able to enter Jerusalem, which he had taken from the Turks. In order to help the British win complete victory in Palestine, the Jews organized a Jewish brigade. By furnishing these five thousand volunteers who came from Palestine and the United States, the Jewish community wished to show its appreciation and its claim in action.

At a conference of the Allied Powers at San Remo in 1920 Great Britain was entrusted with administrative authority over Palestine. This power was approved by the newly formed League of Nations in 1922. But Britain was not to own Palestine, but merely govern it as a mandate of the League. Under the terms of the mandate, a "Jewish Agency" was to be formed to develop the Jewish homeland. Its membership included both Zionists and non-Zionists who were willing to support the upbuilding of the homeland.

After the Balfour Declaration had been issued, immigration immediately increased. It grew as Eastern European Jews found themselves under increasing pressure. From 1917 to 1929 the number of Jews in Palestine grew from 56,000 to 175,000. The "Jewish Agency" bought more land from its Arab owners. In April 1925, The Hebrew University was opened in Jerusalem.

The dismantlement of the Turkish empire led to the establishment of the Jewish homeland and the emergence of new and sovereign Arab states such as Saudi Arabia, Jordan, and Iraq. In attaining sovereignty, these Arab states sparked a spirit of nationalism among all Arabs. The Jewish homeland was a foreign element within the Arab world. The Arab countries had political strength, natural wealth, especially oil, and offered economic promises. The British were therefore concerned with strengthening their friendship with the Arabs. Britain began to whittle down the intentions of the Balfour Declaration. While Arabs were given public land, Jews had to buy it. Under various interpretations of the Balfour Declaration, Jewish immigration was more and more restricted. Britain's partiality may have helped foster the animosity between the two peoples. The development of the Land had been conceived as a cooperative enterprise of both Arabs and Jews in a spirit of mutual friendship. It now became a source of hostile confrontation.

Tensions developed and attacks on a number of settlements occurred. In 1929, aged Talmud scholars were massacred in Hebron; these old men had been spending their lives in sacred pursuits near the graves of the patriarchs buried there. A day of fasting, prayer, and repentance was ordained throughout the Jewish world. I, too, as a youth, joined in the fast.

With the ascent of the Nazis in Germany, increasing numbers of Jews sought refuge in Palestine. Britain tightened its restrictions on Jewish immigration. Jews in flight to save their lives were brought in "illegally." Their acceptance by the *Yishuv* (the settled Jews) led to confrontations with the British armed forces.

Before the Nazis had come to power, HENRIETTA SZOLD (1860–1941), a distinguished American Jewish woman and founder of *Hadassah*, the Zionist Women's Organization in America, had made aliyah. During the Nazi period, her prestige and unceasing appeals gained her permission to organize a Youth Aliyah. It enabled her at least to rescue children otherwise destined for extermination.

During World War II Arab sympathy lay with the Germans, and the spiritual leader of Jerusalem, the Grand Mufti, spent his later years in Germany as a guest and advisor of Hitler. Arab threats that they might join the Germans induced Britain to ever-wider concessions. The end of the war found Arabs and Jews aligned against each other. After debates extending over years, the United Nations saw but one solution: divide the territory into an Arab and a Jewish sector. The latter was much smaller than originally envisioned. This sector became the State of Israel in 1948.

A New State and Continuing Conflicts

By resolution of the United Nations the British were to evacuate Palestine by August 1, 1948. To open the road for the Arab armies they had trained, they decided to withdraw on May 15 before the Jews could organize a defense force against Arab attack. But the Yishuv had, more or less secretly, trained a defense force, the *Hagganah*. Certain of an immediate attack by its neighbors, but trusting in "The Rock of Israel," Israel declared its independence on May 14. DAVID BEN GURION, "father" of the state and its first prime minister, read the Declaration. CHAIM WEIZMANN became president. President Harry S. Truman was the first head of state to grant it recognition on behalf of the United States. In 1952, with the consent of the USSR, Israel was admitted to the United Nations.

From the day of the United Nations resolution Arabs began to attack the Jewish settlements. At the moment Israel declared its independence, the armies of five Arab states under Egypt's leadership declared war against the new State of Israel. After many bitter battles it ended in an armistice arranged by the U.N. The positions of the armies which had been created by the ebb and flow of military action became the temporary border lines. It was intended to adjust them later, but they came to be regarded by the Arabs as permanent borders. Jerusalem became divided, the sacred Jewish shrines falling into Arab hands. Henceforth the Jews had no access to their shrines in Jerusalem or their age-old cemetery on the Mount of Olives. They found out later that its stones had been used for latrines and buildings and its sacred soil been transformed in part into a road. They discovered that ancient synagogues, monuments of history, had been destroyed. The territory was badly cut up, leaving indefensible Israeli borders. Beginning in 1948, a United Nations force, stationed at the borders between Israel and its neighbors Jordan and Egypt, shielded the antagonists from each other.

During the war the Arab population feared the advance of the Jewish units and began to flee their homes. The flight became a mass exodus after Jewish forces attacked the village of Deir Yassin, where many women and children were killed. Those who remained became Israeli citizens. Those who fled were settled by the Arabs in refugee camps, where they had to live under great hardships and be supported by the United Nations. Egypt and other Arab states in turn expelled the Jews. These refugees were accepted and supported by Israel. Israel's transformation into a state with an eventual majority (about sixty percent) of Third World peoples began.

The Arab states imposed a boycott on all firms trading with Israel. American firms were forbidden by law to accept its terms. Armed and terrorist attacks on Israel continued. In 1956, Egypt expropriated the Suez Canal, financed, built and hitherto owned jointly by France and Britain. The canal was an international waterway, that was to be open to shipping by all nations, but from whose use Israel had been blocked. Britain and France went to war against Egypt. Israel joined them, both to free itself of constant terrorist attacks originating in Egypt and to gain use of the Suez Canal. The USSR now threatened to intervene on the side of Egypt. The United States, therefore, pressured for the withdrawal of Britain and its allies, and President Eisenhower assured Israel that the canal would be opened to it. The withdrawals came about, but the canal remained closed to Israel.

The Six Day War

In 1967 Egypt and its Arab allies were ready for a war that would annihilate the State of Israel. They demanded and obtained the withdrawal of U.N. border guards. Taking preventive initiative, Israel in a lightning attack destroyed the Egyptian air force on the ground. In what became known as the Six Day War, the Israeli armed forces under the command of Yitzhak Rabin drove deeply into the Sinai peninsula and the West Bank of the Jordan River. They took the Golan Heights, a hill commanding the entire northern area of Israel from which Syrian guns had repeatedly shelled Jewish settlements in the valley. They also united Jerusalem.

There was no question that the Arabs had mobilized and aligned their forces for war against Israel; yet the United Nations, taking a legalistic position, declared Israel the aggressor. The USSR, Egypt's chief supplier of arms, broke diplomatic relations with Israel. So did many Third World nations, though some retained their Israeli agricultural advisors. These countries needed oil for their development and were very poor; they may have hoped for special consideration from the Arab oil producers. In addition, they were strongly influenced by communist power and propaganda hostile to Israel.

Holding a greatly enlarged territory with an Arab population imposed burdens on Israel. The Palestinians did not suffer economically, their condition actually improved. Making their living by working for Jews, their wages were much higher than in the surrounding countries and they had certain social privileges. The bridge to Jordan was kept open for commuting workers, trade, commerce, and personal visits. Nevertheless, the Palestinians naturally felt defeated, deprived of land that had been theirs and subject to Israeli authority. They remained largely antagonistic. Restlessness and frequent insurrections continued. The State of Israel suppressed demonstrations and uprisings with harsh actions.

After the 1967 war Israel agreed to "the withdrawal of armed forces from territories occupied in the 1967 conflict to secure recognized and agreed boundaries to be determined in the peace agreements." This resolution, made under

U.N. auspices, continued to be the subject of contention. Many Arab states and groups denied Israel's right even to exist. Those Arab states who had in principle recognized Israel's right to exist demanded a return to the armistice lines of 1948. Israel demanded a settlement that would give it defensible borders.

The Conflict Grows

In 1964 the Palestine Liberation Organization (P.L.O.) was founded, and in 1969 Yasser Arafat became its head. Its goal was the eradication of the State of Israel. Terrorism continued; in 1972 eleven Israeli Olympic athletes were murdered at the games in Munich. The United Nations was ineffective in the crisis. It merely passed a resolution condemning violence on all sides.

For geopolitical reasons, the USSR gave increased support to the Arabs, hoping to establish its own hegemony in the region. For the same reasons, but also motivated by moral concerns, the United States aided Israel. America could not afford to have this region fall under communist control, and it did not wish to see another Holocaust. At the same time, the United States also remained concerned with the welfare of the Arab lands and peoples.

In the meantime a new power had emerged in the region, Colonel Muammar al-Qaddafi, a charismatic man who became absolute ruler of Libya in 1970. Qaddafi returned to the most extreme interpretation of Islamic scriptures, and ruthlessly pursued opponents to his regime among his own people both at home and abroad. Qaddafi devised the plan to withhold oil from those nations opposed to him and for the next decades engaged in terrorist activities. He is said to have supported terrorist movements in many parts of the world. Perhaps unable to accept a non-Muslim sovereign state within the heartland of Islam, he proposed a "holy war" against Israel. Some Islamic theologians supported a holy war against Israel, but most did not.

The Yom Kippur War and Subsequent Developments

In 1973, while peace efforts were under way at the United Nations, Egypt and Syria, perhaps in part motivated by Qaddafi, jointly went to war against Israel. Although Israel had observed troop concentrations at the Suez Canal, it took no action to mobilize. On October 6, 1973 (which was Yom Kippur, the holiest day of the Jewish year) the Egyptians and Syrians struck from two sides and with great force. The Arab states declared war on Israel. The military aid by the USSR to the Arabs and an Arab oil embargo against the West led to American involvement and raised the crisis to worldwide proportions. Israel prevailed but suffered great losses. Eventually an armistice was put in effect on January 18, 1974. The United Nations issued a resolution calling upon Israel to withdraw from the territories it occupied. Israel was willing to withdraw to defensible borders, but the Arabs insisted on complete withdrawal to the 1948 borders.

In the years following the war, Arab power grew and Israel became more isolated. The Arabs had a powerful resource: oil. They used it politically, and the threat of withholding it created tremors in the industrial world. Pressure on Israel increased. The oil-rich Arab countries gave their support and funds to the P.L.O., and recognized it as the sole representative and speaker for the Palestinians. The USSR also gave its support to the P.L.O. Invited to speak before the United Nations General Assembly, P.L.O. leader Yasser Arafat offered the palm branch to the Jews in Israel if they accepted the establishment of an Arab state on the soil of Israel. The Jews would be permitted to live undisturbed in this state; otherwise, they would face the sword. As the influence of the P.L.O. grew, the Arabs refused to negotiate with the Israeli government, declaring that only the P.L.O. spoke for them.

A coalition of Arab states, the USSR, and Third World nations succeeded in gaining passage of a resolution in the United Nations General Assembly on November 10, 1975, which they all knew to be false. It declared that Zionism was racism. A new propaganda tool had been created. The resolution was rescinded in 1991 by U.S. initiative and with the support of the new Russia. In the meanwhile it had done great harm.

Among the terrorist acts at this time was the high-jacking of a French airplane with many Jews aboard to Uganda, which was ruled by the cruel dictator Idi Amin. In a sensational maneuver at Entebbe, Uganda's airport, Israelis rescued the Jewish hostages.

Peace with Egypt

The war of 1973 did have one lasting positive result. President Anwar Sadat of Egypt had come to feel that Arab performance in the Yom Kippur War offered the opportunity for negotiating with Israel from strength and decided to establish personal contact with Israel. In November 1978, he traveled to Jerusalem to address the *Knesset*, the Israeli parliament. The Jews welcomed him enthusiastically as a peacemaker. Sadat did not compromise in his demands for Palestinian rights under Israeli rule, nor in his demands for a return of the territories taken in the wars. But the dialogue had begun.

President Jimmy Carter saw in Sadat's visit and his warm reception by the Israelis an opportunity to bring peace between the two countries. In the spring of 1979, under constant pressure from Carter, President Sadat and Israeli Prime Minister Menachem Begin hammered out a peace treaty that was signed at Washington, D.C. Israel returned the Sinai Peninsula to Egypt and made economic and strategic concessions. Sadat's initiative and the peace were condemned by Arab powers. Egypt was expelled from the council of Arab states and Sadat was subsequently assassinated as a traitor to the Arab cause. Under his successor, Hofni Mubarek, Egypt was readmitted to the council of Arab states. Relations with Israel cooled, but the peace has held.

In 1980 the United Nations demanded the return of the old city of Jerusalem to the Arabs. The resolution was declared void by President Carter as far as the United States was concerned. It was rejected by Israel, which instead legally designated Jerusalem as Israel's capital, which it had been since the days of King David. This also reflected world Jewry's overwhelming sentiment. The Jews of the world remembered that, contrary to pledges made, Jordan had refused to grant Jews access to their holiest places, when the old city was in Jordanian hands. Israel also incorporated the Golan Heights in the state as being vital for its security.

Years of Violence

Turmoil in the Middle East increased during the following decades. After a revolution that brought the fall of the Shah of Iran in 1979, the Ayatollah Khomeni assumed leadership of the country. He restored Shi'ite fundamentalism as the state religion and became the spearhead of fundamentalist Islam which made inroads throughout the Islamic world. An outspoken enemy of the West, Khomeni saw the United States as Satan, and Israel its tool. He had the staff of the American embassy in Tehran imprisoned for 444 days. Iran, under the Shah friendly to Israel, joined the ranks of Israel's enemies and became a moving force of terrorism.

Lebanon, the only sovereign nation in the area besides Israel not wholly Islamic, now became a battlefield. A power struggle between Christians and fundamentalist Muslims devastated the land. The U.N. sent a peacekeeping force including a contingent of American Marines. In a terrorist attack on the American Embassy in Beirut the Marines suffered great loss of life. The P.L.O. had its headquarters in Lebanon. Southern Lebanon had long been a staging area for raids on Jewish settlements in northern Israel. To end these raids Israel invaded Lebanon and gave assistance to Lebanese Christian forces who had asked for it. The occupation of Lebanese territory was a violation of international law, for which Israel was condemned by the United Nations. When the Lebanese Christian forces massacred Palestinians at the Sabra and Shatila camps in 1982, Israeli troops stood idly by. This massacre of innocent people, which Israeli troops might have prevented, brought condemnation from the world and massive Israeli antiwar demonstrations.

Eventually Islamic Syria became Lebanon's "protector," thereby realizing the aim it had pursued from the beginning of the conflict. Raids into Israel continued, and Israel retaliated with reprisal raids. Syria was declared a "terrorist nation" by the United States. The P.L.O. moved its headquarters to Tunis.

Worldwide terrorism became a means of war. Airplanes were set on fire on the ground and Israeli as well as European airports were attacked. Explosives were smuggled on an airplane which blew up over Lockerby, Scotland, causing heavy loss of life. Qaddafi's refusal to extradite the terrorist to be brought before a court of justice led to United Nations sanctions against him in 1992. An Italian luxury cruiser, the "Achille Lauro," was pirated by terrorists on the high seas, and a handicapped Jewish passenger killed and tossed into the sea. Acts of terror were carried out against synagogues in Turkey and France, a Jewish restaurant in Paris, the Israeli embassy in Buenos Aires (1992), etc.

Israel's conservative government of the *Likud* party was determined not to yield an inch of the territory that "God's Torah had granted to the Jewish people." More and more Jewish settlements were established on the West Bank, especially by Orthodox Jews who held that the coming of the Messiah depended on the possession of all of Eretz Yisrael by the Jews.

The Palestinians became ever more desperate. From the West Bank and Gaza they opened the *Intifada* in 1987. It was a new form of militant action within cities. It began with constant surprise attacks spearheaded by children with rocks and stones, and grew in gravity. Israeli forces answered with harshness, lives were lost on both sides. Stones hurled by Palestinians from the hill of the Mosque of Omar on worshipers at the Western Wall below brought excessive Israeli police action that killed numerous Palestinians.

In 1990 Saddam Hussein, president and dictator of Iraq, attempted to annex Kuwait, an independent Islamic country. Warned by the United Nations under America's leadership to withdraw or face war, he failed to yield and war ensued in 1991. Led by an American command a coalition of Western and Islamic countries defeated him decisively. Apprehensive that the Islamic allies would withdraw if Israel joined the war, the United States obtained a promise of neutrality from Israel. Saddam, however, attacked Israel's population centers with SCUD missiles. Fearing poison gas or biological warfare, Israelis donned gas masks and went into sealed shelters whenever sirens sounded. In accordance with their pledge, the Israeli government and people refrained from any defensive measures. American "Patriot Missiles," manned by Americans, shot down later missiles. In a sense Israel, years earlier, had contributed to the victory by bombing an Iraqi nuclear weapons plant then under construction, thereby incapacitating Iraq from launching nuclear attacks. Israel's action was condemned by the United Nations.

Saddam Hussein was permitted to retain power and continued to be a threat to the region. He maintained secret manufacturing plants for nuclear, biological, and strategic weapons. Experts sent by the U.N. against Saddam's objections discovered some of them and had them destroyed. Saddam's unknown ultimate designs have kept Israel and the world in apprehension His refusal to abide by his signed commitment to the U.N. and to allow continued U.N. inspections led the U.S. and Britain in December 1998 to conduct air raids on plants suspected of manufacturing weapons of mass destruction.

During the war the P.L.O. and Jordan sided with Sadam, and many Palestinians living in Kuwait also sided with Iraq. The Kuwaiti government therefore expelled Palestinians after the war. The joy demonstrated by Palestinians at the attacks on Israel reinforced the Israeli government's refusal to negotiate with the P.L.O.

Changed conditions, however, offered the opportunity for negotiations. The collapse of the USSR had made the United States the undisputed leader of the world. By liberating one Islamic country and removing the fear of attack from others, it had now gained the trust of the Arab nations. States such as Syria, which had hitherto depended on the USSR for arms, had to lean toward the U.S. Jordan and the P.L.O. felt they had to mend their fences, other Arab states, such as Saudi Arabia, might be expected to be less resistant to negotiations. Yasser Arafat, having lost prestige, became fearful of being supplanted by even more radical groups, such as the extremist *Hamas*. In Israel a long-existing peace movement gained momentum. It furthermore became clear that an Israeli state, comprising all the territories acquired in 1963, had the choice of either granting all its Arab inhabitants full citizenship, which would in time give them the majority and deprive the state of its character as a Jewish state, or deny them these rights and cease to be a democratic state.

Conferences, the Oslo Accord, and New Challenges

Under these circumstances President George Bush made peace in the Near East a primary goal of his foreign policy. He called for a peace conference between the Arabs, Palestinians and Israelis. Both parties eventually accepted. The conference convened at Geneva in October 1991 and was opened by Presidents Bush and Gorbachov. This was acceptable to Israel as the relationships between Israel and Russia had been normalized.

Israel's prime minister, Yitzhak Shamir, was opposed in principle to any surrender of territory. He maintained that only the establishment of new settlements on the West Bank could convince the Arabs of the urgency of peace negotiations and border adjustments. He refused to impose even a moratorium on settlements in the West Bank, and was supported by Orthodox Jews, especially a militant ultra-Orthodox group, *Gush Emunim* (Block of the Faithful). These groups held that Israel's claim to the land was based on the Torah and was therefore not negotiable. He was opposed by the "Peace Now" movement pushing for compromise solutions and for concessions.

In the general election of 1992, Shamir and the Likud party were defeated, a coalition headed by *Hitdradut*, the Labor Party, came to power and Yitzhak Rabin became prime minister. He had been the commanding general in the Six Day War, but now was a committed advocate of peace. The desire of Israelis to obtain peace even at the expense of territory had become manifest.

Conferences were held in Madrid, Moscow, and Washington. It became evident that the parties were far apart and the negotiations would be slow, tedious, and extended. The Arabs insisted that the P.L.O. was the only representative of the Palestinians; the Israelis rejected it. But a beginning had been made. Israel's foreign minister, Shimon Perez pushed on in his determined quest for peace. Secret negotiations were initiated. With the help of the Norwegian government these negotiations between Israel and the P.L.O. took place in Norway during the spring and summer of 1993 and succeeded.

Before a startled and happily surprised world, the "Oslo Peace Accord" between Israel and the P.L.O. was signed at Washington on September 13, presided over by President Clinton. Israel granted the Palestinians land and self-government. It began with the transfer of the city of Jericho and the Gaza strip to them. Future transfers of territories were to be negotiated. Yitzhak Rabin, the general who had won the Six Day War for Israel, and Yasser Arafat, whose aim had been Israel's extermination, shook hands. A peace treaty with Jordan followed. The accords were ratified by the Knesset, the Israeli parliament, by the P.L.O. and by the Jordanian parliament. Subsequent conferences took place between Perez and the crown prince of Jordan, and between Rabin and Arafat. Both parties envisioned a close cooperation. Jointly they would develop the natural and economic resources of the area and bring new prosperity to the whole region.

The accord presented great and immediate challenges to Arafat. He had to create an administration and police force in the Palestinian sections. Above all, the economic conditions had to be stabilized, the resources developed to assure a decent standard of living for the Palestinians. Ways had to be found to keep these territories from becoming staging areas for new raids on Israel. The world community set aside two billion dollars for that purpose. Israel expressed its readiness to render whatever development assistance would be asked of it, and various Third World countries established or renewed official relations with Israel.

Long-range problems could be foreseen, especially in the adjustment of borders. Jerusalem, dear to Muslims and Jews, was Israel's capital, and equally chosen by the Palestinians as the capital of their state. Old Jerusalem with its Jewish and Muslim shrines became a difficult issue. The Israelis also desired that the Arab territories acquire internal authority without becoming an independent state that might eventually threaten Israel. The Palestinians envisioned an independent state. Syria stood aloof from the peace process. Even a personal visit by President Clinton could not move Syria's President Assad to join the peace process unless his conditions, especially the return of the Golan Heights, was met. This posed a dilemma because peace could not be fully achieved without Syria's participation. Surrender of the Golan Heights *before* the peace negotiations had even started was not possible for Israel. The Heights commanded its whole northern region and exposed it to shellings.

The accord with the P.L.O. roused strong minority opposition on both sides. Muslim extremists stepped up their terrorist activities in order to sabotage the agreements; Orthodox rabbis protested in the name of Torah, maintaining that no government had the right to dispose of land given Israel by God. By the end of 1993, fundamentalist Arabs and fundamentalist Orthodox Jews, both hoping to scuttle the accord, began to engage in increasing violence. Orthodox Jewish settlers of the West Bank facing eventual resettlement resolved to resist. It was their God-given right, they claimed, to live within the biblical borders of Israel. Hebron saw repeated battles mostly between Orthodox Jews and Palestinians. In a surprise attack, one of these Jews massacred Moslems at prayer in the Hebron mosque. Some Orthodox rabbis solemnly invoked divine curses upon Rabin, the "traitor" who was prepared to give away sacred Jewish soil. The overwhelming majority of the Israelis however supported the "Peace for Land" efforts. On November 4, 1995 tens of thousands assembled in the main square of Tel Aviv to express their full endorsement of Yitzhak Rabin's peace policy. They sang a song of peace, and he, a reticent man, for the first time joined them in song. As he stepped from the platform to his car, he was assassinated point blank by a young fundamentalist Orthodox Jew who claimed to have acted on God's command to kill the traitor. The entire world was gripped by shock. Leaders of great and small powers, including Arab countries, attended Rabin's funeral.

Shimon Peres, Rabin's close collaborator, became prime minister and pledged to carry the peace policy forward. Additional territory was turned over to Palestinian rule. But there was uneasiness among the population that Perez would make too many concessions. The division in Israeli opinion became evident in the general election of 1996. The conservative Likud party gained just enough votes to form a government in coalition with the irreligious parties. Benjamin Netanyahu became prime minister. The position of the Israeli government toward the Palestinians hardened.

A new housing project was started outside Jerusalem. The Arabs, who also claimed the land, saw this as a provocation. Ensuing Arab acts of terror surpassed in number and ferocity all previous ones and claimed many innocent lives. Among them was the bombardment of busses at terminals and explosions caused by suicide terrorists in central markets and shopping malls during business hours. To what degree Arafat might have been able to stem these acts, or even contributed to them, became debated. In September 1997, U.S. Secretary of State Madeleine Albright, visited the area for discussions with Arafat and Netanyahu. She was critical of both sides but especially of Arafat. In her judgment Arafat appeared to lean toward *Hamas*, the Muslim terrorist organization. Mrs. Albright returned home only with the hope that true negotiations might take place some time in the future. In the Congress of the United States Arafat was criticized for his responsibility in the deaths of so many innocent people. Terrorist activities against Jews became more frequent and destructive than they had been before the Oslo Accords. But the conviction prevailed within the leadership of both sides that the peace process would have to continue and would eventually lead to success.

On the Road to Peace

One of the great achievements of these years has been the peace with Jordan. It has been a peace truly initiating friendship and mutual cooperation. King Hussein completed the work of his grandfather, Emir Abdullah. The Emir had welcomed close relationships with Israel seeing in them benefits for both countries. For this he was murdered by Muslim extremists on his visit to the Temple Mount for prayer. His grandson had to witness the deed. Visitors from Israel have now been invited, joint enterprises have begun. In 1999 King Hussein died. It is anticipated that a cordial peace will endure under Abdullah, his son and successor.

On October 23, 1998 a peace accord was signed in Washington between Israel's Prime Minister Benjamin Netanyahu and the head of the Palestinian Authority, Yasser Arafat. Israel yielded more land, granted free movement to Arabs in Israel traveling between their territories, agreed to release Arab prisoners, and granted access to an airport in Gaza. Arafat pledged to wipe out Arab terrorism and bring Palestinians to trial for crimes committed in Israel and against Israelis. Above all he committed himself to have his Legislative Council (a form of parliament) eliminate the provisions in the PLO's charter that made exterminating Israel a fundamental principle.

In December President Clinton visited both Israel and the territories under Palestinian rule. In his presence, the Palestinian Legislative Council rescinded the provisions in its charter calling for Israel's annihilation. Many issues remained unresolved, but a peace agreement had been reached. Its stability would rest on the sincerity of both parties and their determination to negotiate in good faith. As cooperation replaced violence a new chapter in history opened. Peaceful collaboration of Israel and the Palestinians could bring great prosperity to the region. This is to be hoped for.

Main credit for this achievement has to go to President Clinton. He kept the negotiators together and acted untiringly as honest broker until they had hammered out the agreement. The issue of a sovereign Palestinian state remained open. To assure enduring peace, living conditions and standards of the Palestinians had to be improved. President Clinton pledged development aid from the United States, some of which was transferred subsequently. At the same time he emphasized anew the unique and deep bond between America and Israel.

SOCIETAL ISSUES IN ISRAEL

From the beginning, Jews in Palestine engaged in important social experiments, the most significant among them being the *kibbutz*. It is a cooperative whose members hold everything in common and govern themselves democratically. Members surrender all possessions and assets are held in common. In turn the kibbutz sustains members as long as they are affiliated with it. The community assigns members duties. Admission is by membership vote and affiliation is completely voluntary. Without this common effort the barren soil of the land could not have been developed. Settlers have equally shared their knowledge and experiences with emerging Third World nations.

Israel's founders came from Europe, had a scientific outlook, and were highly educated and inspired by the examples of Western democracies. Under their leadership Israel developed agriculturally, industrially, culturally and societally as a Western country. It established universities, technical schools, research institutions, modern hospitals, theater, and music. The dynamics of its society may have contributed to the conflict between Israel and its Arab neighbors, who were used to extremely gradual developments. They also created tensions with the Sefardic Jews, immigrating from non-Western countries. Their lifestyle and lack of Western education set them apart from the Ashkenasic leadership. Steps have been taken to integrate them and prepare them for leadership in Israel whose population is sixty percent Third World.

Most of the founders were socialistic and non-religious, but granted the rabbinate great power especially in connection with family law. The rabbinate is strictly Orthodox and rejects Western culture. The power of Orthodoxy has grown to new heights under the Netanyahu government. Unlike Western states Israel has not eliminated small splinter parties. Small "Religious Parties" are represented in the Knesset and in coalition governments can hold the balance of power. In this manner they succeeded in maintaining the will of the rabbinate under law. Many Israelis did not wish to accept this form of Orthodoxy, but did not know any other form of Judaism. They have turned from religion to secular nationalism. Others, who are religious but not Orthodox have found themselves in grave difficulties. The Conservative and Reform movements have been under constant attack by the established rabbinate. Their rabbis have been denied recognition, and converts whom they brought into the fold, have not been fully recognized as Jews. Both movements have nevertheless made inroads, and are jointly challenging the rulings of the State Rabbinate. Christians and Muslims have no religious restrictions and receive government subventions.

In spite of the heavy burden it imposes, the State of Israel has urged and welcomed aliyah, especially from the West. The response from Western countries has not been overwhelming, but some Western Jews have felt that they could live a full Jewish life only in Israel and so have moved there. Jews in distress have found a heartfelt welcome and became citizens on arrival. Israel has made every effort to liberate those who were held abroad against their will. It has been enriched by the large-scale immigration of Jews from the former Soviet Union, finding among the immigrants many highly educated persons. Like all immigrants they had to be settled, learn Hebrew and the basic elements of Judaism, adjust to the cultural and social life, and find employment. Their new jobs were not always in line with their previous professions. Some immigrant groups have had difficulties with acculturation. To the Jews of Georgia in the Russian Commonwealth, Israel was too secular a state, others married to non-Jewish women had difficulties with the rabbinate. Many found the freedom of expression, including their grievances, a hallmark of democracy, puzzling. Even going to a supermarket was for many a new experience. The need to provide them with housing has been partially responsible for the new settlements on the West Bank.

In the 1980s Ethiopian Jews subjected to thousands of years of persecution, starvation, and eradication, were rescued by Israel and absorbed in its society. They faced problems with the rabbinate. Non-Jews, including a number of Vietnamese boat people, have been absorbed and feel at home.

Relationships with Arabs who were citizens of the state has been tense and may improve. Represented in the Knesset, they were not permitted to serve in the armed forces. The Druse, a Muslim sect that cast its lot with Israel, enjoy complete equality. Their full acceptance may serve as a model for the complete incorporation of Arab citizens in the state.

Aliyah has strained the Land's capacity. Military service has been compulsory for both men and women. Israel's bureaucracy has been ponderous and officious, and corruption has been discovered in government and other circles. Slum problems exist. Israeli Jews have emigrated to other countries, perhaps temporarily. Heavy defense costs have led to inflation.

Still Israel hopes for more immigrants. The socialist outlook of the founders led them to fashion a socialist state and society. It proved to be economically unsuccessful and led to a transition to a free market economy. The changeover brought strains. Some critics held that Israel, instead of being an agricultural country, should develop as an industrial country such as Holland or Belgium. It would allow it to sustain a large population in a small area. The change has been under way. Israel's exports in many fields have grown. Among them have been inventions in technology, in pharmaceutics and other areas.

Some Editorial Comments by the Author

Israel is a new state, built by men and women who had no experience in building a state. They might have chosen a form of dictatorship, but they chose democracy, placing themselves at the will of the electorate. They built a society generally permeated by the principles of social justice. The *Histadrut*, the national labor union, encompasses all: management, labor, and professionals. The founders built in the midst of wars and pressures and yet developed high cultural institutions. Mistakes are to be expected of any state, new or old; the government of Israel has made many and serious ones. For every one of them it has it has been criticized from within by the people and from without. That such an internal criticism has been considered the people's right reveals the state's democratic principles.

Israel is not perfect and should not be measured by absolutes. No nation should be measured by absolutes as long as other nations are not so judged. The vision planted by the prophets has not vanished; it only awaits the day of peace for its full realization. Measured by the standards of nations, Israel has not done so badly.

The population, has shown a remarkable calm in the face of danger, as its reaction to the SCUD attacks revealed once again in 1991. Up to now Israeli society as a whole has lived in a pale, as did Russian Jewry once: close to $4\frac{1}{2}$ million Jews in a small space. We should not be surprised at the great pride they take in their land and their achievements under the most difficult conditions, nor at their toughness. For almost two thousand years, Jews throughout the world tried to be good. Unwarlike, they were derided by their non-Jewish neighbors as cowards and weaklings. In the end they were almost completely exterminated. The Holocaust has been seared into the soul of Israelis. "Our ancestors loved peace and were exterminated, we also love peace but will be tough enough not to be killed like sheep." The living memory of the Holocaust may help to understand Israel's at times harsh actions.

ISRAEL AND THE WORLD

Israel is a small country in the Middle East. Having no natural resources, it is insignificant. Its location constitutes its problem. Thus it has been the pawn in the political and economic power struggles of totalitarian and imperialist nations and individuals, and the victim of propaganda. Israel is "the Jew writ large," the scapegoat, victim of anti-Jewish prejudices and barometer of humanity's conscience. Herzl's expectation that anti-Semitism would disappear with the emergence of a Jewish state has not been fulfilled. Israel itself has been subjected to it.

The war of 1948 created the refugee issues: The problems of dispossessed Arabs, it is hoped, will be solved as a result of the accords entered and to be arrived at. Jewish refugees from Arab lands have long been absorbed by Israel and are no issue.

Religious traditions are unquestionably a factor in the relationship between the world and Israel. Dialogue between Jews and Muslims is imperative; it can lead to true conciliation and cooperation. Islam is a highly ethical faith. In dialogue, Muslims and Jews will get to know each other and eliminate misconceptions and the stereotypes many of them entertain of each other.

Israel is "like a stump picked out of the fire" (Amos 4:11) of Hitler's Holocaust. Its outward posture of strength should not deceive us. It appeals to the conscience of humanity in its will to survive, to prosper, and to create a society built on social justice.

World Jewry and Israel

Israel has given Jews throughout the world new self-assurance and self-affirmation, new pride in their heritage, and a renewed will to live. To many it has been a powerful witness to God's intervention in history. Having hidden His face during the Holocaust, He revealed it at the restoration of the Jewish state. The Covenant endures. I remember the day when Israel declared its independence. I felt like a new person, I had been reborn. The wars of 1967 and 1973 revealed the bonds that bind world Jewry to Israel and its Yishuv. Reform Jews by that time had come to regard Israel as essential in Judaism. Pilgrimage to Israel has become common for those American Jews who can in any way make it possible. Rabbinical students of the Reform Hebrew Union College–Jewish Institute of Religion have to spend one year of their rabbinical studies at the school's Jerusalem campus. The Jewish Theological Seminary has a center there.

In times of peace, divergences in thought have emerged between Israeli and world Jewry, and were noticeable in the political situation of the early 1990s. They were disagreement between brothers and sisters. They did not break the bond. The Yishuv has equally come to embrace Diaspora Jewry for its Jewish creativity, its contribution to the upbuilding of the state, and simply as valuable members of *Bet Yisrael*, the house and family of Israel.

It was agonizing for Jews during the years from 1948 to 1967 not to be permitted to visit their holy places located in the Jordanian sector. Jewry is presently in agreement with the government and people of Israel that Jerusalem shall remain united, and all nations and creeds shall have access to it. In contrast to Catholicism and Islam, the Jews have only one holy city, Jerusalem. In Catholicism, Jerusalem takes second place to Rome, in Islam it takes second place to Mecca. To the Jews, Jerusalem, whose three thousandth anniversary as Israel's capital they celebrated in 1996, is the one and only center. The words of the late Richard Cardinal Cushing, which we cited at the beginning of this chapter show in deep empathy what the State of Israel means to Jews.

The greatest good fortune that could come to Israel and the whole region would be for Arabs and Jews to recognize that they are kin, to establish true peace and friendly relations between individuals and communities, meet each other, engage in common projects and celebrations, learn from each other and with each other, try to understand each other's feelings and hopes, agree, and in friendship permit one another to disagree. This consummation must be envisioned as the goal, to be actively pursued. There is hope that it may be attained.

CHAPTER 9

The Holocaust

THE HOLOCAUST RADICALLY IMPACTED contemporary Jewish history; its effects had to be mentioned in our presentation. Nevertheless, as the force of absolute evil, it required a separate chapter, even at the risk of repeating some events already mentioned.

The word *holocaust* denotes a sacrifice, a total consumption by fire. The term has come to refer to the extermination of six million Jews under the direction of Adolf Hitler and his cohorts. It evolved in stages, from repressive measures designed to force Jews to emigrate from Germany to the "final solution" of exterminating them. Hitler immediately enforced repressive measures upon assuming power in 1933. The devilish design of total annihilation ended only when Germany was defeated in 1945 and Hitler committed suicide.

The Holocaust, in Hebrew *Shoah*, "the Catastrophe," was the apocalyptic climax of centuries of anti-Semitism—theological, economical, pseudo-scientific, and racial. But only in the twentieth century did it reach proportions of genocide. There was no escape for a Jew caught in Hitler's sphere of power, even for a mere "racial" Jew. In all earlier persecutions, Jews had been given an escape hatch; namely, baptism. The Holocaust also constituted a reversal of the recognition hitherto given to human beings as inviolate by virtue of their humanity.

A LONG SILENCE ENDS

For about thirty years following World War II there was virtual silence about the Holocaust. The agonizing pain of its victims made them moot. But getting older, the victims felt compelled to talk. Time had given them perspective. Furthermore, there was the danger that, after the eyewitnesses were gone, the Holocaust might simply become a paragraph in history books. This the survivors could not permit, for the Holocaust changed humanity as a whole. Psychologists found that not only the rescued victims themselves were scarred for the rest of their lives, but their children, too, could be psychologically damaged; perhaps talking about the events might lead to catharsis.

Recent years have seen a host of books published: documents of governments, memoirs of survivors, diaries, and oral histories of victims. Courses have been instituted at universities, lectures have been offered, and television has brought the Holocaust—at times fictionally—to life for millions of people all over the world. Documentaries such as "Shoah" revealed the extent of the horror. In 1993, when Steven Spielberg released *Schindler's List,* he told his cast, "We're not making a film, we're making a document." The movie chronicles one of the most horrendous crimes in human history. Spielberg made his film so that humanity never forgets but forever learns from it. Receipts of the film have gone to Holocaust studies (see *Time,* Vol. 142, No. 25, November 13, 1993).

I was arrested in Oldenburg, Germany during the *Kristallnacht* on November 9, 1938. That night my synagogue was burned down, as were all the other Jewish houses of worship in Germany. The following day I was taken to Sachsenhausen concentration camp, where I remained for approximately three weeks. By that time the Chief Rabbi of the British Empire, Dr. Herman Hertz, had provided me with a visa to England. In 1938 Jews were released from the concentration camps if they could prove they were able to emigrate immediately. Thus, compared to what happened later, conditions were "good." But even then I witnessed events that make me realize that film and television portrayals have been frequently toned down. Even documentaries that portray the actual stark-naked terror cannot fully reveal the emotions of the victims exposed to the reality of torture and the expectation of certain and cruel death.

The sudden transition from freedom to absolute captivity, degradation and physical humiliation, the complete uncertainty in anticipation of a horrifying fate were shocks that affected my whole life. Subsequently my mother and many relatives were murdered in the extermination camps. For many years I could not speak about it. Grateful to have been spared, I, as many other survivors, have felt "guilty" having been saved while so many others, including those dearest to me, perished. I tried to repress the experience.

THE ROAD TOWARD THE HOLOCAUST

In his book *Mein Kampf,* written as early as 1923, Hitler made his designs clear. Initially, he did not plan to exterminate the "demonic Jews" but to expel them. His acts were directed toward this aim. When he assumed power in Germany in 1933, one of his first acts was the state-ordained boycott of all Jewish businesses and offices. By the time of the boycott, however, violent actions against Jews had already occurred. Concentration camps were constructed and Jewish isolation and degradation was systematically and progressively enforced. Jews were forcibly retired from public service, excluded from trades and professions (or pushed out of their businesses, thereby losing their livelihood), denied admission to universities, and forced out of public schools.

Under the Nuremberg Laws of 1935 Jews were deprived of their citizenship and the protection of the courts. They were placed under police supervision, especially the dreaded Secret State Police called *Gestapo*. Sexual relationships between Jews and Aryans were considered "rassenschande" (defiling the Aryan race) and penalized with years of imprisonment. Aryans were those of "pure Germanic or Nordic" descent, which was meticulously investigated by the state authorities. On release, these Jews were arrested by the Gestapo and confined in a concentration camp for the rest of their usually short life. Aryan women under forty-five could not serve as domestics in Jewish homes; according to the Nazis they might be sexually misused. Jews were excluded from all general culture, including cinemas, theaters, and concerts, and eventually were forbidden to have automobiles, radios, telephones and newspapers. They were barred from public parks and from all contacts, both business and social, with Aryans. They were pressured to sell their property at ridiculously low prices—and even this compensation was kept by the government. Many cities placed signs on their approaches stating "Jews not wanted." Storm troopers kept watch in front of marked Jewish stores and noted any Aryans who entered them.

The Nazis were determined to increase step-by-step the humiliation, harrassment, degradation, and torment. Nazi laws grew in brutality and led to elimination from society, government service, schools, business, the application of the laws of 1935, loss of property, the forced imposition of Jewish names, sequestration and ultimately deportation and extermination. All were "penalties." The "crime" of the Jews consisted in being. Aryan legislation made careful distinctions among Jews with four Jewish grandparents, three Jewish grandparents, and down the line. Their application rested on the degree of the person's racial "impurity," as spelled out in detailed ordinances.

I remember the psychological pressure laid on us. No one was sure they would not be accosted in the street or torn from bed at night by the Gestapo and taken away. Gestapo men attended every service of mine in the synagogue and noted down the words of my sermons. Even an innocent word could be interpreted as subversive. It is impossible for me to tell all the details within the compass of this work. I attended court trials for *rassenschande* to bring the defendants assurance that the Jews were with them. I visited them in prison. I had the sad task of visiting a distinguished Jewish man confined to prison for criticizing the regime. He died in a concentration camp. I had to organize a Jewish school for the children exposed in public school to derision and attacks. We provided food and shelter to the starving and dispossessed, and helped them in their difficult task of finding visas to Palestine or other countries. We had to comfort those whose dear ones had been taken to concentration camps and try to sustain them when the death notification arrived. It was usually in the form of a statement saying, "So and so is dead. If you wish to have his ashes, pay twenty marks."

In 1936 overt anti-Semitism actions were somewhat reduced. Germany, as host of the Olympic Games, wished to make a good impression on the world. In 1938, however, the pressure was resumed. Jewish congregations lost their corporate rights, and individual Jews had to report all their property, domestic and foreign. Jews were permitted to give their children only listed Jewish names, and adults had to add the name "Israel" or "Sarah" to their given names. It was a way to humiliate them and single them out.

From the beginning of Hitler's anti-Jewish campaign, there were mass demonstrations by American Jews, and a boycott of German goods was proposed. The Nazis declared they were holding the Jews in Germany as hostages against any action directed against Germany. The rest of the world either did not believe the reports of what was happening in Germany or was unconcerned or not displeased with the displacement of Jews from society. In the summer of 1938 an international conference was held at Evian, France to effect the resettlement of the Jews under Nazi domination; none of the great powers, however, was willing to accept Jews in any substantial number. Hitler now knew he could not get rid of the Jews by forced emigration. He also saw that there would be few repercussions for his anti-Jewish actions.

In October 1938 Poland declared all its citizens that resided outside its borders to be stateless by November 1. This was an act directed against Jews, many of whom resided in Germany. Polish Jews were rounded up by the Germans, put on trains, and dumped at the Polish border homeless and helpless. Herschel Greenszpan, a young man who lived in Paris but whose parents were among the deportees, shot and killed an attaché at the German Embassy as an act of protest. This offered a welcome pretext for the Nazis to put into effect a well-planned pogrom. On November 9 the synagogues were put to flames while fire brigades stood idly by. Homes were raided, the furniture smashed and thrown out the windows, and the Jewish occupants assaulted. The night was designated by the Nazis as the *Kristallnacht*, "night of the flying glass," after the windowpanes broken as Jewish stores were looted. Male Jews were rounded up and taken to concentration camps, which were ready and waiting. I shared this fate. Together with the men of my congregation I was marched through the streets of Oldenburg, past the burned-out synagogue to prison, and on the next day was put on the train that took us to the concentration camp. From my experiences there I can state that most of what is represented in film are understatements.

The "Final Solution"

In 1938 Hitler annexed Austria, whose population received him with jubilation. He immediately started pogroms. Hitler invaded Czechoslovakia the following year. The German invasion of Poland later that year led to war. Germany was victorious on all fronts, overrunning Poland where multitudes of Jews lived, as well as Holland, Belgium, France, Denmark, and Norway. In all of these countries as well as those in Eastern Europe that aligned themselves with Hitler, the "Jew laws" were immediately introduced and storm troopers put in charge. Denmark and Bulgaria saved its Jews. In Holland many Christians hid them. In this manner Anne Frank and her family hid for years until finally they were betrayed and Anne died at Bergen Belsen concentration camp. In France there was widespread collaboration with the Nazis.

In 1941 Hitler declared war on the USSR. The conquest of large Eastern territories brought millions of Jews into the grip of the German armies. The Nazis decided to deport all Jews and exterminate them. This "final solution" was perfected in all its technical and organizational details at a conference at Wannsee, a fashionable suburb of Berlin, on January 20, 1942. Emigration was now forbidden. Preceding their deportation, Jews were herded into ghettoes, or "Jew houses," forced to wear a yellow star, restricted in their movements, prohibited from buying food except some staples (white bread, meat, and milk were among the forbidden "luxuries"), and then only during a few hours, when the supplies were exhausted.

Nazi policies were carried out by a bureaucracy said to be "only following orders." The chemical plants improved their poison gas, Nazi doctors developed experiments they were to carry out on living human beings, the delivery system to the extermination camps was coordinated by the railroads. It was all done scientifically and efficiently by scientists and civil servants with professional detachment, knowing exactly what they were doing.

The Jews were squeezed into cattle cars and made to stand without food or water for the long ride to the extermination camps. Under a Nazi law of 1941, Jews leaving Germany had to pay a special tax for fleeing, lost their nationality, and their remaining belongings were confiscated by the state. As soon as the deportation trains crossed the German borders, this law took effect, for it did not matter under what circumstances the Jews had crossed. Their mistreatment had become legal in Germany.

By the time the trains arrived many had died, the rest passed review. Major Joseph Mengele, a physician based at Auschwitz, is now infamous as the "angel of death" at the extermination camps. By a flick of his hand he ordered the arrivals one by one to the left or the right—one group destined for immediate death, the other for temporary survival as slave workers or medical guinea pigs. Resisters were publicly tortured and hanged. In the end, slave workers also perished.

Although what happened in the camps has been amply documented, it defies description. Victims had their heads shaved. Then they were herded in front of gas chambers, made to undress and place their clothing carefully on various piles: men's shoes, women's shoes, children's shoes, and so on, nicely separated. Then they were squeezed into the gas chambers, tightly pressed together. Cyclone gas entered from vents in the ceiling. The victims died in agonizing pain. The chambers were then opened by Jewish attendants who were forced to perform the task and "rewarded" by being permitted to live a short time longer.

Pulling the bodies out by hooks, the attendants extracted crowns and gold fillings from the deceaseds' teeth. These and the women's long hair were used for commercial use. They stacked the bodies like cordwood and then piled them into the ovens of the crematoria that burned day and night, blanketing the region with the acrid smell of burning human flesh. Deportations to the camps proceeded on schedule. Because the number of victims arriving at the camps surpassed the capacity of the gas chambers to kill them, they had to wait their turn, meanwhile they were forced to exist on a starvation diet until they were transformed into living skeletons. At Auschwitz, Birkenau, and similar camps the Nazis pursued a twofold policy: Jews were to be murdered, but before they were, they were stripped of all human self-respect and dignity. The Nazis succeeded in the murders, but not in their design to demoralize their victims. Millions of Jews died *al Kiddush Ha-Shem*, "in sanctification of God's Name," their dignity untouched.

Terms like "final solution" belong to euphemisms used by the Nazis to disguise their true actions. "Extermination" was used to prepare executioners for their task; they were indoctrinated to think that they were not murdering people but exterminating contagious vermin, a job to be done with complete detachment but absolute ruthlessness.

The records of the murdered Jews are kept in Jerusalem in the archives called *Yad Va-Shem,* "Monument and Name" (see Isaiah 56:5). The interior of the memorial erected there is utterly simple: in one corner of the dark room burns an eternal flame and on the floor are inscribed the numerous camps where Jews were put to death.

Jews in Desperate Struggle to Escape

As long as emigration was still possible, Jews made every effort to escape; after 1938 the scramble turned into a torrent. However, the nations of the world refused to open their gates. The United States strictly held to its immigration quotas. Great Britain, which had mandate power over Palestine, forcefully expelled those beyond the imposed quota. They arrived instead clandestinely as illegal immigrants in rickety ships. If a ship was discovered, it was turned back by armed force. Jews watched their brothers and sisters drown at the shores of freedom. Had the State of Israel existed at the time, millions would have been saved.

Jewish Community Life during the Final Years

In the meantime, the Jewish communities in Europe had to be administered. Nazis assigned this task to Jewish administrators and counselors. In Germany, Rabbi Leo Baeck was made head of the Jewish community. One of the most outstanding rabbis, he had received many calls to congregations and seminaries abroad but refused all of them, preferring to go with his people and suffer with them. He survived the concentration camp named Theresienstadt, and is recognized as one of the great witnesses to the Jewish faith. He died in England in 1956. Under Baeck and other leaders, Jewish life and cultural activities were maintained among starving Jews in their ghettoes. Services were conducted and holy days observed at risk, for all these activities came to be forbidden.

The Jewish counselors in various communities were victims of a deep dilemma: should they tell their people, many of whom expected merely to be resettled, the fate that awaited them, or should they allow them a bit of hope for survival? These men were given the task of determining who should go on a transport and who should remain behind. It was a power over life and death. Some tried to postpone the deportations, warned the Jews, and even helped them to escape and join the resistance. Others favored their families and close ones, condemning others to their death. A number of them committed suicide. There were unscrupulous men among them, as there were brutal Jewish policemen in the ghetto towns. The fate of individual Jews rested to a considerable degree on the decency of those in charge.

The Uprisings: The Warsaw Ghetto

There were leaders that stood up to the Nazis, which was a hopeless but courageous cause. Ghetto uprisings occurred in a number of cities. The most important uprising took place at Warsaw, where the Jews armed themselves with smuggled weapons. It began on January 18, 1943, when Jews destined for deportation fired on their guards and escaped. Nazis decided to wipe out the ghetto. Entering in force on April 19, they met with determined resistance. The Germans moved from block to block and, in the end, brought in flamethrowers and heavy guns. The resistance lasted for five weeks. The Jews knew from the beginning that it was hopeless but wished to die as heroes in the spirit of Masadah. The day of the Warsaw ghetto uprising is remembered worldwide by Jews.

The German People: Response, Doubts, Fear, Resistance

The majority of Germans were intoxicated by Hitler's promises of power and wealth and eagerly followed him. There were those who were happy to get rid of Jewish competition in business or the professions, others expected advancement from joining Hitler's party. Some saw the inhumanity of the Nazis but lacked the courage to oppose it: They "followed orders." The working classes were often more resistant to it than the intellectuals. Many intellectuals and professionals immediately fell in line. I remember one professor with the Jewish sounding name "Wechssler" who, in April 1933, authorized his students to obtain certificates of his Aryan lineage from Nazi headquarters. I heard another well-established professor, Woerner, lecture that Hitler's *Mein Kampf* had greater literary value than all of Goethe's works. Goethe had hitherto been regarded as the greatest literary genius Germany had produced. The Medical Association, in its regular bulletins, compared the Jews to the tuberculosis bacillus that had to be completely eradicated to restore the body it had invaded.

Germans were also subjected to incessant propaganda and indoctrination. From the beginning, the media were conscripted for propaganda purposes, Jewish owners were expropriated. The hideous *Stürmer*, a pornographic hate sheet, could be read in boxes constructed on the streets.

The churches were under pressure. Among the Catholics there were some prelates who cautiously advocated human concern, at least regarding Christians of Jewish descent. Some bishops, however, were outspoken Nazis. Protestants were split. Their majority joined the Nazi "German Church." A minority founded the Confessional Church committed to the gospel of Christ. It protested the coercion of faith by the Nazis. But even this church never passed a resolution in support of the human rights of Jews. The great theologian Karl Barth later regretted not having submitted such a resolution to the founding synod of the church. In his memoirs he added, however, that "a text of this kind would certainly not have been acceptable in 1934, considering the state of mind of the 'confessors.' " There were individual clergymen who aided Jews at great personal risk. Churches were hostile or remained silent. What they might have achieved by open protest is difficult to say. When the Catholic Church protested the extermination of non-Jewish "undesirables," such as the mentally retarded, Nazis suspended action.

There were courageous Germans who, at the peril of their own lives, hid and rescued Jews and publicly opposed Hitler. Their number was small, but their names deserve to be remembered in honor. Among them was Berhard Lichtenberger, dean of the Catholic Cathedral of Berlin, who prayed publicly for the Jews and died on the way from one concentration camp to another. The brother and sister Scholl who together with the philosopher Huber at Munich organized and called their small group "The White Rose." They produced and disseminated pamphlets condemning Nazi inhumanity and were executed for it. Protestant pastor Spitta asked his congregation for donations of food which he personally brought to starving Jews in Oldenburg. By order of the Nazis he was drafted as a private and sent to the front in Russia where he fell. I knew an old lady, Mrs. Gerschütz, from Bavaria, who together with her husband sheltered and saved two Jewish women. When I asked her why she had done so she simply replied, " I am a Christian and have only done my human duty as God commands." The assassination attempt of Hitler by high army officers, led by Count Stauffenberg, should be mentioned. They all were executed under horrible tortures. There were more, but most of them did not wish to be honored after the war for "simply having done their human duty." Their names ought to be remembered as heroic examples.

LESSONS OF THE HOLOCAUST

The magnitude of the Jewish slaughter startles the mind. Centers of Jewish life and piety were destroyed. Upon the rest of Jewry now fell an unparalleled responsibility. In the words of Emil Fackenheim, Jews are not permitted to give Hitler a posthumous victory. They had to replenish their ranks, their spirit, learning, and piety. They had to return into history and dialogue. Jews have been fearful that the message of the Holocaust may be forgotten all too soon. For humanity's sake as well as their own, they have been dismayed at the hate literature that claims it never happened. Having faced the unspeakable in Germany, the most "enlightened" of the Western nations, Jews have felt deeply the insecurity of the age. They have closed ranks about Israel. If Israel has been uncompromising in negotiating with others, the Holocaust may be one important reason. Israel feels that it must secure its borders; there must be no second Holocaust. World Jewry agrees.

The Holocaust teaches us that all prejudice must be wiped out both by law and by education that changes attitudes. It mandates a constant, living dialogue between all groups on all levels, based on mutual respect. It holds a warning against "following orders" in blind obedience to authoritarian government, which was the grievous fault of the German people. It calls for the kind of courage shown by non-Jews who stood with Jews. It calls on governments to stand up for right as against expedient solutions, and to act forcefully against hate groups.

There is no rational or theological explanation for the Holocaust, but a commanding voice goes forth from it. Humanity must heal and renew itself. The question, asked by Nellie Sachs, poetess of the Holocaust, remains: If the prophets came again [to call for social justice], would humanity listen?

Holocaust Museums

The powerful impact of the Holocaust on American Jewry is reflected in the creation of Holocaust Museums in Los Angeles and New York. The main museum is in Washington, D.C. The United States government provided the land and the Jewish community the means. Its cornerstone was laid by President Reagan, and President Clinton presided at its dedication in 1993. It is to rekindle Jews' emotions, remind all Americans of the absolute evil to which humans can descend, and call all humanity to commit to democracy and social justice. From the beginning, the number of visitors to the museum from all circles of society has been so large that it taxes the facility, an indication of Americans' interest and concern with social justice.

CHAPTER 10

Jews outside Israel
and North America

JEWISH POPULATION FIGURES are difficult to ascertain with exactitude. In the Diaspora only those Jews affiliated with congregations can be counted. These figures have been in constant flux. In many countries, such as the United States, the population has decreased, in others, such as Israel and Germany, it has increased. Among the reasons for the decrease are a low birthrate and interfaith marriages, where the children are no longer Jews. In other countries emigration is the main cause. The Jewish population in Israel and Germany has increased largely because of the influx of immigrants from the former USSR. These trends may change. The estimates below are tentative and may soon be out-of-date.

In 1995 there were slightly more than 13 million Jews worldwide. Nearly half of them, about 6,160,000 lived in the *United States* (5,800,000) and *Canada* (360,000). *Israel* had a Jewish population of over 4.5 million. Thus, the leadership of world Jewry had fallen on these two countries.

Central and South America had a Jewish population of about 511,000: Argentina 250,000, Brazil 130,000, Mexico 40,000, Venezuela 35,000, Uruguay 30,000, Chile 17,000, Panama 7,000, Columbia 6,000, Peru, 5,000, Costa Rica 2,500, Puerto Rico 2,500, Cuba 1,500, Paraguay 1,200, Ecuador 1,000, Guatemala 800, Bolivia 700, Panama 4,500, the Virgin Islands 400.

Europe had approximately 2.6 million Jews: France 600,000, Great Britain 300,000, Hungary 80,000, Germany 70,000, Belgium 40,000, Italy 35,000, The Netherlands 30,000, Sweden 18,000, Switzerland 18,000, Latvia 15,000, Spain 15,000, Romania 14,000, Austria 8,000, Denmark 8,000, Poland 8,000, The Czech Republic 6,000, Slovakia 6,000, Lithuania 6,000, Greece 5,000, Bulgaria 3,000, Estonia 3,000, the former Yugoslavia (including Bosnia and Herzegovina) 3,000, Norway 1,500, Finland 1,200, Ireland 1,000, Monaco 1,000, Portugal 900, Luxembourg 600, the former USSR 1,075,000 (of these, 550,000 lived in Russia, 400,000 in the Ukraine, and 175,000 in the other states).

In *Asia*, outside of Israel, about 25,000 Jews lived in Turkey, 6,000 in India, 2,000 in Japan, 300 in Syria, and small numbers in other countries.

Africa had about 150,000 Jews: South Africa 114,000, Zimbabwe 1,000, and Kenya 450. The number of Jews in Ethiopia and the Islamic countries of North Africa had greatly decreased due to emigration, mainly to Israel: Morocco 6,500, Tunisia 2,000, and Ethiopia 500.

Australia and *New Zealand* together counted about 105,000 Jews among their population.

The post-Holocaust destiny of Jews outside of America and Israel deserves brief attention.

THE POSTWAR FATE OF THE JEWS

Europe

Continental European Jewry has not recovered from the losses of World War II, either in numbers or in leadership; it lives on the soil that was the theater of the Holocaust. Its older generation consisted of immigrants in search of peace and a livelihood. They did not trust the world or its governments and kept their suitcases packed. Emotionally they were linked to the Jewish life of the past. The younger generation is native-born, integrated, and future-oriented. Generational tensions have therefore arisen.

The older generation held fast to Orthodoxy. It hired rabbis educated in the "old countries" or in Israel. These men have been very strict. Their feeling may have been that the Emancipation was a failure, and only complete commitment to tradition could give the Jews strength by separating them spiritually and in life patterns from the world. The younger generation is divided. Many among them are looking for forms of the religious life that are more in tune with the world in which they live; others agree with the beliefs and life patterns of their fathers and mothers. Numerous congregations have split over these issues. Of course, there are those who simply wish to enjoy life while it lasts. The shortage of trained leadership has resulted in inadequate education for many young people, especially Russian Jewish immigrants. They know almost nothing about Judaism and require loving guidance and Jewish education. All Jews have close emotional ties to the State of Israel. It is their source of strength.

France

French Jews live in security but are not without apprehensions. With a population of about 600,000, French Jewry has become the largest in Western Europe and is aware of the spiritual leadership this entails. It is hierarchically organized in Consistories (central, congregational bodies) created by Napoleon I. Its rabbinical seminary is in Paris. There also exist numerous yeshivot.

The character of French Jewry has changed since World War II. Before the war, French Jews were mostly Ashkenazic. They generally belonged to the middle classes and followed a rather complacent religious Conservatism. This

Jewry was largely wiped out, and in its place came Sefardim who had lived in the formerly French provinces of Northern Africa, such as Algeria, and were French citizens. Becoming independent, these countries instituted Muslim rule. The Jews moved to France and resettled throughout the country They were small merchants and artisans who were exposed to the hazards of unemployment, old age, and disease. They belonged to Orthodoxy, and placed its imprint on the French congregations they revived.

The French people, who were forced to absorb them, exhibited an ambiguous attitude toward them. The Nazis had reawakened lingering anti-Semitism. Marshal Petain, head of the Vichy Government in the country's unoccupied, free southern section, implemented Nazi edicts with rigor. French police willingly collaborated with the Nazis in rounding up Jews for deportation and extermination. Animosity against "foreigners" among the "little people" came to the fore in the postwar period, when large numbers of non-whites settled in the country. Many of these immigrants were French citizens from former French colonies.

A radical right-wing party made the expulsion of the foreigners—especially Africans—its goal. It was also sternly anti-Semitic. The party made inroads at various elections. Propaganda, also from Arabic interests, fanned anti-Israel and anti-Semitic sentiments. Outbursts occurred in which Jewish stores were ransacked, people killed, synagogues attacked, and cemeteries desecrated. These atrocities should not be seen as reflecting the outlook of the majority of French people. Christians repeatedly joined Jews in massive protests against the atrocities. Jews realized that they had strong support in the population, but were equally burdened by a sense of insecurity. This may have stimulated a numerically small, but nevertheless significant, aliyah of French Jews.

In recognition of its new leadership role, French Jewry has been creative in producing leaders in Jewish thought. Since 1955, some French universities have maintained chairs in Judaism, thus placing it in the stream of academic thought. Jewish university professors became its spokespersons. JACQUES DERRIDA and EMMANUEL LEVINAS belonged to the leading French philosophers. Levinas equally stood out as teacher of the Jews and defender of their tradition. He felt and explained that Judaism could give spiritual and practical guidance to all of humanity (see Chapter 16).

Britain

The Jewish population of about 300,000 in Britain has become fully integrated in the life of the nation. The Jews have been active in communal affairs, Parliament, government, industry and commerce, and the life of the country. Every year, a number of Jews have received honors from the Queen, among them the now-retired Chief Rabbi, DR. IMMANUEL JAKOBOVITZ, who was elevated to the peerage.

The majority of British Jews are Orthodox. The United Synagogue, hierarchically organized, is the official religious body. Its spiritual head is the Chief Rabbi, a position held since 1991 by Dr. Jonathan Sacks. He also oversees the theological seminary called Jews' College. The United Synagogue has been Neo-Orthodox in its character, but strong right-wing Orthodox congregations have also been developed and have influenced it. Conservative and Reform congregations (communities) and synagogues (houses of worship) also exist and have attracted members in increasing numbers. Under a rabbinical council, the non-Orthodox movement has operated a rabbinical school, the Leo Baeck Rabbinical College, that has attained a high standard. It provides non-Orthodox rabbis for Europe. RABBI LOUIS JACOBS is a member of its faculty. He may be regarded as the leading scholar and theologian of English Jewry. He was formerly head of Jews' College, but was expelled for some mildly Bible-critical statements. British Jewry is united in its attachment to Israel and its deep concern with the plight of Russian Jewry.

Germany

Democracy has become firmly rooted in Germany. The Jews are treated with respect and urged to integrate fully into German society. Some have been elected to public office. The government takes action against any violations of Jewish rights. By law it has also instituted a Holocaust Memorial Day. Among the vast majority of Germans there exists a great deal of goodwill. Interest in Judaism and the history of the German Jews has grown. Even small communities have published the history of the Jews who once lived there. Jewish museums are widely visited by Christians. Lectures and workshops are conducted even in small communities and are well attended.

Much care is accorded Jewish antiquities. Jewish cemeteries are well maintained, sometimes by Christian volunteers or high school students. Synagogues have been restored even in places where Jews can no longer be found. There they serve as memorials and interfaith meeting places. Monuments or at least tablets remind all of formerly existing Jewish places of worship. A dedicated interfaith movement seeks to promote fellowship and dialogue. Unfortunately there are too few Jews left who are knowledgeable in Judaism and willing to engage in dialogue. The churches have publicly repented their guilt, have sought dialogue with the Jews, and have ordained the establishment of Jewish studies in their seminaries.

The Jewish will to survive found expression in the establishment of the *Hochschule für Jüdische Studien*, Graduate School of Higher Jewish Studies (1979) as a department of the University of Heidelberg. It was designed to train teachers and social workers for Jewish communities, but the majority of its students consists of Christian students wishing to get acquainted with Judaism. Other universities have established departments or, at least, courses in Judaism, and numerous scholarly works by Christians and Jews appear regularly. Many public schools now teach the Holocaust as part of the curriculum.

Numerous cities have invited their former Jewish citizens to visit their old homesteads in order to rekindle the relationship. The number of Germans visiting Israel surpasses that of many other countries. Surprisingly, a proportionally large number of Gentile Germans have wished to convert to Judaism, and those accepted have lived as committed Jews. Heroic Germans who saved Jewish lives have become known. Their numbers were larger than anticipated, but they regarded their actions to be in no way exceptional but merely a fulfillment of their human and Christian duties. The young generation wishes to know what happened, and is showing concern and a sense of responsibility for human rights. There is reason for hope.

It is not possible to guess how much anti-Jewish sentiment still exists in the hearts of the older generation and among those who insist that the time has come to "bury the past." Those Germans who say they did not know may well have known. Those who have admitted their lack of courage by failing to stand up for the Jews during the Hitler years have looked for ways to make amends. However, anti-Semitic ideology is still alive in some circles. It was revived in part by Skinheads and Neo-Nazis inspired by hate pamphlets smuggled in from the United States and Sweden. It was also imported from the former East Germany, then a satellite of the Soviet Union, which filled its youth with anti-Zionist ideology. It was fed by discontent with the large numbers of foreigners, both guest workers formerly used for the upbuilding of Germany and large numbers of political asylum seekers. All of the asylum seekers were now housed and supported at government expense. In some circles, growing unemployment and housing shortages came to be attributed entirely to foreigners.

Anti-Semitic terror acts included burning the dwellings and synagogues of foreigners, murder, and vandalism. Synagogues and community centers had to be placed under constant police protection. Visitors and worshipers were frisked at the entrances. These movements are small but their crimes made news. They are not representative of the character and thinking of the German people; the overwhelming majority of Germans, together with the media, expressed their revulsion through powerful protests. Marches of hundreds of thousands took place, and the government took strong measures. Vigilance was required, and is being applied. In general, there is hope for Jews in Germany.

German Jewry, numbering about 70,000 and growing, has shown signs of revival. The prewar generation is gone. The Jewish immigrants who came after World War II had little affinity with German culture. They are being replaced by a new native generation and by immigrants from various countries, including Iran, but above all Russia and even Israel. The Central Council of the Jews in Germany is recognized by the state as the representative and fiscal agency of German Jewry. It is governed from the top and is overwhelmingly Orthodox. But there are not enough rabbis to staff the pulpits. Most of those who officiated originated from Orthodox yeshivot abroad, especially Israel. They are frequently not in tune with the needs of the new generation, so their congregations are in ferment. New non-Orthodox congregations are slowly emerging. The Jewish congregations have been supported by the government and, like the churches, are empowered to impose taxes. Beautiful synagogues have been built or restored. The immigration of Russian Jews promises numerical and spiritual replenishment, provided German Jews have the strength and will to reeducate them.

Smaller Communities

Ireland has been friendly to the Jews, Dublin even elected a Jewish mayor. HAIM HERZOG, former President of Israel, was a native of Ireland. His father was chief rabbi there. In Israel's War of Independence, Irishmen volunteered their services in its armed forces; they felt that they understood the Jews from their own experiences with Great Britain. The Jewish community of about 1,000 is dwindling due to emigration. *Scandinavian* communities adhere to an Orthodox or Conservative form of Judaism. Sweden's 18,000 Jews have been guided by American Conservative rabbis for a number of years. Its former chief cantor, Leo Rosenblüth, a distinguished composer, has made valuable contributions to contemporary liturgical music. Sweden also has an Orthodox community. The Swedish diplomat Raoul Wallenberg, a Christian, saved thousands of Hungarian Jews from deportation by the Nazis by granting them visas to his country. When the Russians overran Hungary, he was arrested by the Russians and has never been heard from again. The Russians claimed that he died; the United States, at the time assuming he might still be alive, made him an honorary citizen.

Denmark has 8,000 Jews. The heroic rescue efforts of the Danish people, who saved their Jews during the time of Hitler, will always be remembered by world Jewry. When the roundup date for the Jews was leaked, Danish fishermen, at greatest risk of life, transported them under cover of night and fog in their small boats through the German patrol ships to neutral Swedish soil. Nearly all Danish Jews were saved. The Danes were inspired by the example of their king, Christian X, an outspoken foe of the Nazis. He used to ride daily through Copenhagen to give courage to his people. Sadly, one day he was mysteriously thrown by the horse he had ridden for years and killed. He is counted preeminently among the "Righteous of the Gentiles," each of whom has a tree planted in a grove at Jerusalem.

Norway was invaded by the Nazis and its Jews hunted. It now has only 1,600 Jews. *Finland* has 1,200. Finnish Jews were sheltered from extermination during the war. The courage of the Finns is gratefully remembered by the Jews.

Holland was the only country whose labor unions went on general strike to protest the Nazi atrocities directed at the Jews. The number of Dutch people who gave shelter to Jews during the Nazi years was high, though many of the Dutch have felt too modest to talk about it. But there were also collaborators, like the woman or policeman who betrayed Anne Frank and her parents, hidden by a Christian family. Holland has renewed its kindly concern for its Jewish citizens. Its 30,000 Jews have taken part in the life of the country. Historic synagogues of Amsterdam have been restored. The main trend in religious life has been Orthodox, but a liberal movement has also been growing. Anne Frank's house remains a shrine.

Belgium has a Jewish population of 40,000, the majority of whom are Orthodox. Many Jews are engaged in diamond cutting and trade, making Antwerp one of its centers in the world.

Spain has accorded its 15,000 Jews full equality. The edict of 1492 expelling the Jews and prohibiting them from ever setting foot in the country was rescinded in

1969. A beautiful synagogue was built in Madrid. In March 1992, the five hundredth anniversary of the edict, a solemn service was held in the synagogue. It celebrated the formal revocation of the edict of 1492 and gave recognition to the invaluable contributions of the Jews to Spanish culture. It was attended by King Juan and Queen Sophia of Spain and President Haim Herzog of Israel. Other larger cities also have synagogues. Jewish antiquities are reverently preserved, and streets named after great Spanish Jews, such as Judah Halevi and Maimonides, to whom a statue was erected in his birthplace of Cordova. The synagogues of Toledo were at one time transformed into churches, and are now museums. They give evidence of ancient glory.

The late Generalissimo Francisco Franco was a ruthless dictator of Spain, but he saved the lives of thousands of Jews in Hitler's days. He refused to ally his country with Hitler during the war or to surrender those Jews who had found refuge in Spain.

Switzerland has approximately 18,000 Jews. Never too friendly to the Jews, it insisted that a "J" be stamped by Germany in the passports of Jews during the Nazis' time. They could thereby be recognized as Jewish fugitives and turned back at the border. This measure was thereupon introduced by the Nazis for all Jews. Switzerland did, however, save a number of Jews. Jews are integrated into Swiss life. Internally they face the problem of Orthodoxy versus liberalism. In 1996–7 it was discovered that Swiss banks had held on to funds deposited during the Nazis' time by Jews subsequently murdered. The banks were forced to reveal these assets and make restitution.

Austria was a center of anti-Semitism even before World War I. In the 1880s Georg von Schönerer developed the program for a pan-Germanic empire with a racially pure population. Karl Lueger, mayor of Vienna made use of it to gain power. Adolf Hitler, Austrian by birth, was their disciple carrying their ideas to their horrifying consummation. He was jubilantly welcomed by the populace when he entered the Austrian cities after annexing the country to Germany in 1938. Pogroms were immediately started which surpassed the German ones in brutality. After World War II, Kurt Waldheim, gravely suspected of complicity with Nazi atrocities, was elected president of the country. A nationalistic party attempted to gain power. Austrian Jewry of approximately 8,000 has restored its organizations as far as possible, but is exposed to a substantial anti-Semitism among the population.

Jews in *Italy* gained from the influx of Lybian Jews who left after Qaddafi overthrew the king and established his rule in September 1969. Numbering about 35,000, it has a rabbinical seminary and all institutions. Even before Vatican II, the friendship between the rabbi of Venice, Leone Leoni, and the then archbishop of the city, later pope, John XXIII, is said to have been strong. Since then, Italian Jewry has gained by the spirit of ecumenism. The visit of the synagogue of Rome by Pope John Paul II for a joint prayer service in 1978 was a symbolic act of worldwide significance for the relationship between the Catholic Church and Judaism. It was the first time in history that a pope visited a synagogue to pray with Jews, thereby acknowledging the abiding importance of Judaism. The Vatican recognizes the State of Israel and diplomatic relations have been established between both. The projected visit of Pope John Paul II to Israel in the year 2000 is anticipated by the Israelis with great enthusiasm.

The Jewish population of *Greece* has dwindled to about 5,000. The community consists mainly of elderly people. The centers of Jewish scholarship exist no more.

These population figures are in flux due to the vast migration taking place. In 1991 the number of Jews in transit was estimated to be around 30,000.

THE FORMER USSR AND COMMUNIST COUNTRIES

Historical Developments

Czar Nicholas II had planned new and severely regressive laws against the Jews after World War I. He did not live to implement them. The Bolshevik Revolution gave the Jews hope for it outlawed anti-Semitism, but it also outlawed religious distinctions so the Jews could not be regarded as a religious group. Eventually they were designated a national group. Their identification cards, which every Russian had to carry, were stamped with a mark signifying Jewish status. Hate of the Jews was repressed but alive. In World War II, it prompted many Ukrainians to assist the Germans in capturing hidden Jews for their deportation and extermination. Anti-Semitism survived the war. Stalin, the cruel dictator of the Soviet Union, was a rabid Jew hater. He found anti-Semitism useful to rally his people and use the Jews as a scapegoat. The lot of the Jews was hard from the beginning and got worse when Stalin sided with the Arabs against Israel, hoping to establish Russian hegemony in the region.

The Russian Jews came to be regarded as members of a "subversive nation." Access to universities, employment, and society were restricted or barred. They could not escape their Jewishness, nor could they find strength and solace in their own religious and cultural heritage, which was dismantled by the state. Synagogues were closed. Prayer books had not been printed since 1917, and the offer of the American rabbinate to provide them was rejected by the Russian government. Even Yiddish newspapers were eliminated under Stalin's government. Jewish education was forbidden by law. Many Jews had no knowledge of Judaism, which resulted in a large number of intermarriages. Stalin, revealing an ever-more rabid anti-Semitism, made far-reaching plans for the extermination of the Jews. Jewish writers were accused of subversion, Jewish doctors of having plotted to poison Soviet leaders; all were executed. Only Stalin's death frustrated his designs for their elimination. The Jewish writers and doctors were posthumously exonerated.

Emigration was surrounded by grave obstacles. In applying for an exit permit the applicant declared that Israel, and not Russia, was his homeland, which amounted to treason. He immediately lost his rights as citizen, his job and his apartment. He had to wait for years for the government's reply that frequently denied the request. In the meanwhile he had to be housed and fed by relatives or friends. Rallies in Western countries, vigils in front of USSR consulates, and other protest actions eventually moved the USSR to permit a trickle of emigration, amounting to about 100,000 over a period of fifteen years (1965–79). The Jews were trapped. They were, in the words of Elie Wiesel's moving account, *The Jews of Silence.* Yet there were *Refusniks* who maintained Jewish life in their homes and taught their children. It was dangerous. Anatoli Shcharansky, one of the Refusniks was arrested immediately after his wedding on trumped-up charges. He was imprisoned for many years under harshest conditions and eventually exchanged for a Russian spy. Reports from Christians, including clergy, who had visited the USSR, confirmed the plight of the Jews that surpassed that of other religious groups. In contrast to other religious groups, who were permitted to stay in touch with their religious bodies abroad, the Jews were not granted this right. They were destined for spiritual genocide.

In 1975 an international conference at Helsinki, Finland, drew up an international charter of human rights. The USSR signed it but gave it only lip service. A group of courageous non-Jewish Russians, under the leadership of the Nobel Prize winner ANDREI SAKHAROV, now formed a Committee on Human Rights. They were severely punished. Sakharov was exiled to Gorki, a small town in the interior, and allowed back to Moscow only after the collapse of the USSR.

The Turnabout of Russian Policy and the Dissolution of the USSR

Beginning in 1985 the policy of the USSR was reversed. Michail Gorbachov, President of the Supreme Soviet—and then President of the USSR, recognized that the communist regime had bankrupted the nation economically and societally. He undertook the dismantling of the existing structure with the aim of gradually transforming the USSR into a democratic state. The Soviet Union collapsed. Gorbachov was pushed out by Boris Yeltsin, who was elected to the presidency in 1990. Under these men diplomatic relations with the State of Israel were restored. The Russian Jews could freely practice their religion or emigrate if they so chose. Many Jews now felt secure in the new Russia. But hundreds of thousands decided to emigrate. They remained apprehensive that anti-Jewish prejudice, so deeply instilled in the Russians, would continue. They saw no assurance that the new regime would endure. They also hoped for a better life for themselves and their children. Their apprehensions were not unjustified.

After the collapse of the communist regime the whole country was in deep distress, famine threatened, and the West had to provide emergency help. Feeding on the discontent, armed insurrection erupted in 1993 led by a coalition of hard-core communists and neo-Nazi nationalists, both vicious anti-Semites. It was put down by the armed forces, who were loyal to Yeltsin. Yeltsin had won. For the Jews, everything had been at stake in Yeltsin's victory. On the evening before the armed confrontation, an armed band invaded the great synagogue of Moscow, shouting anti-Semitic threats. Had these forces won, pogroms might have ensued.

Subsequent elections revealed the anti-Semitism in Russian society. Vladimir Zhirinovsky had founded the ultra-nationalistic Liberal Democratic Party of Russia. In the parliamentary campaign of 1993 he voiced his rabid anti-Semitism. The party gained twenty-five percent of the votes. The communists, anti-Semitic by indoctrination, also gained substantially. In the presidential election campaign of 1996 Zhirinosky, a leading contender, praised Hitler, called for attacks against the West, and declared concerning the Jews, "deport this small troublesome tribe" to some remote outpost. Zhirinovsky did not win. These campaigns revealed that a large percentage of the Russian people were either outspoken Jew haters or silent ones. The situation resembled the rise of the Nazis in the German Republic. Yeltsin won the presidency. By 1998 Russia was in shambles both politically and economically. The currency had been deflated, the people were starving. Yeltzin, now aged and sick, had proven himself incompetent. The Jews of Russia had reason for their apprehension. Again many Jews considered it prudent and urgent to leave the country.

According to recent estimates, 1,200,000 Jews lived in the territory of the former USSR (550,000 in Russia, 400,000 in the Ukraine, 45,000 in Uzbekistan, 40,000 in Moldavia, 24,000 in Belarus, 25,000 in Azerbaijan, 13,000 in Georgia, and the rest in the other states). Even with a continued emigration, the Jewish population in Russia is likely to remain substantial. The natural increase through births will compensate for the migration. The Jews in the free world therefore have felt themselves called upon to make certain that free emigration remained an option for those who wanted to leave. They had to keep a watchful eye on any forms of anti-Semitism. At the same time they had to assist the Russian Jews in rebuilding their religious and cultural life. Russian Jews needed everything, from synagogues and prayer books to instruction, teachers and religious functionaries. These had to start with the very rudiments of Jewish life and tradition. To meet the need Reform, Conservatism and Orthodoxy have established congregations, synagogues, schools, and yeshivot.

Jews in the Former Satellites of the USSR

The breakup of the communist empire affected the Jews in various countries that had been satellites of the USSR.

Poland was the only country where a pogrom was staged after World War II, at Kielcze in 1946. After the war, 200,000 Jews, a remnant of the once-flourishing community of three million, returned . . . and found themselves unwelcome. Most of them left the country after the pogrom, only 25,000 remained. In 1968 students and intellectuals rose up to protest the repression. In response the communist government fomented anti-Jewish hysteria by blaming the few remaining Jews for the country's misery. The majority of Jews still living in the country emigrated in a hurry, only about 4,000 elderly persons remained. In 1981 the leadership of the emerging union movement "Solidarity" condemned the communist leaders of 1968 for their persecution of the Jews. When Poland achieved its independence from USSR domination, Lech Walessa, the leader of the Solidarity movement, became president. In his election campaign he made hints playing to popular anti-Jewish sentiments, a fact which he later glossed over. The Jewish population has since grown to approximately 10,000.

Among the Poles who showed true humanity and friendship to the Jews was Pope John Paul II, before his election as Primate of the Catholic Church in Poland. As a devout Catholic he had experienced persecution as a youth. He also had Jewish friends. As pope he had to intervene repeatedly in statements deprecating Jews which his successor as Primate made. Among the actions revealing contempt for the Jews was the establishment of a convent and the setting up of a huge cross on the grounds of the Auschwitz extermination camp, to the Jews a sacred memorial to their six million martyrs. Anti-Semitism in Poland—in spite of the fact that there were hardly any Jews left in the country—called for continued vigilance. Its elimination depended on the obedience of clergy and people to the orders of the Catholic Church issued in the resolutions of the second Vatican Council.

In the *Czech Republic* (now separated from Slovakia), the hatred of its former Soviet oppressor was clearly evident throughout the land. From its beginnings after World War I it was a pillar of democracy and human rights. In World War II Czechoslovakia was conquered by the Nazis, and after World War II it came under the knout of the USSR. After a "democratic spring," it was in 1968 overrun by its armies. Immediately anti-Zionist trials were held against some intellectuals. In 1970, on the occasion of the seven hundredth anniversary of the Old-New Synagogue at Prague, no delegates from the Jewish community abroad were permitted to attend and no government officials were present. The country's return to its democratic tradition was led by Vaclav Havel, a poet who as a defender of freedom, had been repeatedly imprisoned by the communists. Havel became the country's first president.

Prague had been designated by the Nazis as the location of a museum-center, exhibiting the artifacts of "a now extinct race." The city has Jewish treasures from all the countries conquered by the Nazis. The ghetto, synagogue, Jewish city hall, cemetery, and Jewish museums with their amassed treasures belong to the great tourist attractions of Europe.

The existing Jewish community numbering about 6,000 seemed to have acquired some new vitality, but emigration continued. About 6,000 Jews live in *Slovakia,* once a center of Jewish life and learning. They have established a new Jewish community. It was not certain that anti-Semitism had been removed from the minds of all the people in these countries.

Hungarian Jewry has a population of 80,000. Many of them owe their lives to Raoul Wallenberg. They live a fairly normal life and have participated in the restoration of the country. Its conservative Jewish Theological Seminary was the only one in Eastern Europe kept open even during the communist period. The great synagogue at Budapest, considered the largest in Europe, has been restored and draws large numbers of worshipers; the attached museum contains precious exhibits. Numerous synagogues throughout the land testify to the community's ancient glory.

In *Romania* the situation was in flux. Nicolae Ceausescu, whose terrorist rule became known after his fall and execution, retained diplomatic relations with

Israel and permitted the Jews to emigrate. He saw in the Jews a kind of "hostage" for his own recognition in the world, and treated them with less harshness than did his neighbors. Emigration among the Jews continued after the dictator's demise; 18,000 remained.

The former *Yugoslavia* gave its Jews fair treatment under Marshal Tito's rule. Upon the dissolution of the USSR, Yugoslavia became embroiled in civil war, due to the Croat and other constituents' desire to attain independence. The war brought devastation to large sections of the land and caused many thousands of deaths. Religious hatred of Christians against Muslims led to ethnic cleansing (another term for racism) that was carried out with great brutality. The small Jewish community of 3,500 suffered in the civil war, although it was not singled out. The Jews of Serajevo established in their Great Synagogue a storehouse for medicine and food sent from abroad and supplied the whole population. In 1999 government terror engulfed the ethnic Albanians in Kosovo. NATO took action; Jews fled to Israel.

Lithuania had once been so distinguished a center of Jewish life and learning that it was compared to the Jewish community in the Holy Land during Temple times. Its capital, Vilnius (Vilna), used to be called "the Jerusalem of Lithuania," and was a summit of piety and scholarship. Now only 6,000 Jews are left and the great yeshivot have disappeared. *Latvia* has 15,000 Jews and *Estonia* 3,000. These Baltic states, the *Ukraine*, and other states attained their independence after the breakup of the USSR, and officially affirmed the equality of the Jews. The head of the Russian Orthodox Church also committed himself to the fight against anti-Semitism. *Bulgaria* never surrendered its Jewish population into Hitler's hands; about 3,000 Jews now reside there. In all these countries emigration to Israel remained a source of hope in the midst of insecurity.

SOUTH AMERICA

Two factors distinguished South American Jewry and its destiny. One was the volatile political situation in these countries that led to apprehension about the future of Jewry (e.g., in Chile and Argentina); the Jews were fearful of being made scapegoats during changing power structures and revolutionary warfare. The other factor was the anti-Semitism that made some of these countries places of refuge for Nazi leaders after World War II.

Argentina experienced years of terror under the dictatorship of the military. The Jews were exposed to exceptional persecution. This ceased under the democratic government. Jews have participated in the political, cultural, and economic life of the country. The Jewish community of 250,000 has two rabbinical seminaries: One is Orthodox, the other (*Seminario Rabinico Latinoamericano*) is affiliated with the Conservative movement in America. *Mexico* had a prosperous Jewish community of 40,000. In *Cuba* Jewish life has recently experienced a revival.

Anti-Semitism has lately been combated under the leadership of the Catholic Church in the spirit of Vatican II. South American Jewry gained by the influx of Jewish refugees from Hitler, which included rabbis, but its potential has as yet not been realized, due partly to a dearth of rabbis and partly to internal conflicts. To find their recreation within their own community, South American Jews have developed large and lavish community centers for sports and social and cultural activities.

The concerns of South American Jewry include Israel, Russian Jewry, and the internal problem of strengthening Judaism through education.

OTHER PARTS OF THE WORLD

Africa

In *South Africa* a flourishing Jewish life exists. The country has about 114, 000 Jews, well organized and strongly Zionist, but split between Orthodox and Reform. Interestingly, the racist government's policy of apartheid did not result in any anti-Jewish orientation. Among South African Jewry were strong and articulate opponents to apartheid. In a Passover message in 1992, Nelson Mandela, leader of the National African Congress, and president of the Republic, acknowledged with gratitude the Jewish contribution to the liberation of the native black majority and called for future cooperation.

In general the Jewish community confined itself to maintaining Jewry. South African Jews have taken a leadership role in world Jewish affairs. Their bond with Israel is very strong. The future of South African Jewry rests on the development of state and society, now that the black population has finally attained full citizenship rights, and the white population has become a permanent minority. Jews frequently send their children abroad, but for the present, there was little apprehension.

Ethiopia once had a sizable Jewish community called the Falashas. They had settled there before the destruction of the first Temple in Jerusalem and had lost contact with the evolving Jewish tradition, but, in spite of ruthless extermination attempts, held fast to Judaism. The remaining 20,000 were rescued by Israel and resettled in the Jewish state; 500 Jews remained. The majority of the pious Jews of *Yemen* also were rescued and resettled in Israel; 800 remained. Emigrants from these countries were generally forced to leave most of their belongings behind.

The Jewish community in *Zimbabwe* dwindled from approximately 5,000 to 1,000 (due to emigration, mainly to Israel) after the country gained independence.

Islamic Countries

In Islamic countries the Jewish remnant felt very insecure due to the hostility of these countries toward Israel and the rise of Islamic fundamentalism.

Iraq had about 200 Jews, now there are even fewer. In 1969 nine Jews and five Muslims and Christians were accused by the Iraqi government of espionage for Israel and were publicly hanged. In *Iran* the Jewish community, which is thousands of years old, found itself in dire straits when the Shah was overthrown and an Islamic theocracy established in 1979. The majority took flight, most finding shelter in Israel. The future of the 25,000 that remained is insecure. Emigration is no longer permitted. Iran has become an outspoken enemy of Israel and has prosecuted and executed prominent Jews as Zionists, and therefore enemies of the state. *Syria*, Israel's most hostile neighbor, long prohibited the emigration of its 4,000 Jews, holding them hostage under strict police supervision. According to a promise made by the Syrian government in 1993, most were permitted to emigrate. Only 300 remained.

Under Islamic law, "nonbelievers" cannot be granted full citizenship rights. The small Jewish community in *Afghanistan* had to pay a special tax. By the time the country was invaded by the USSR in 1980, almost all of them had emigrated. Jews have not been permitted to enter *Saudi Arabia*, and there are no Jews in *Lybia*.

Egypt, for thousands of years a center of Jewish life, only has at most 200 aged Jews remaining. The majority were expelled when the State of Israel was proclaimed. The lot of this remnant has improved since peace was made with Israel. *Morocco* had approximately 7,500 Jews and *Tunisia* about 2,500, whose situation was precarious as Islamic fundamentalism grew.

The Rest of Asia

India's 6,000 Jews are the remnant of a once-large Jewish settlement. They have always been treated well; the ancient synagogue at Cochin was depicted on a postage stamp that the government issued. The majority, however, decided to go to Israel because they saw no Jewish future in India.

Japan has only 2,000 Jews, among them were several distinguished converts, such as the late Professor Kosuji, who was once the teacher of the present emperor. The main Jewish congregation is in Tokyo and its rabbis are provided by seminaries in the United States. The relationship between Japan and Israel has been tenuous. Although cooperative enterprises were carried out, Japan had not recognized Israel, perhaps in deference to the Arabs, on whose oil it depended. Japanese tolerance of all religions served to stay anti-Semitism. In recent years, however, anti-Semitic material has been published in the country and found readers, which is surprising, since there are so few Jews in Japan. It is also dangerous, for the Japanese readers have no other sources to acquaint themselves with the character of the Jewish people. Economic interests and conditions could influence the relationship with the State of Israel and the Jews in Japan.

China had a Jewish community even in antiquity. These Jews were not in touch with the mainstream of Jewry and its members became indistinguishable from the rest of the Chinese population. They lived in various cities, and have left works of arts and literature. The synagogue and congregation at Kai-fung-fu was discovered by a group of Jesuit missionaries toward the end of the sixteenth century. There are hardly any Jews left in China, but a few Chinese still claim to be descendants of these Jews.

During the Nazi period, China was one of the few countries to open their doors to Jewish refugees, and a sizable community sprung up at Shanghai. These Jews suffered severely under the Japanese occupation, since Japan was an ally of

Germany, but they survived and subsequently emigrated. The Chinese revolution under Mao Tse Tung transformed China into a communist state. Israel recognized it and hoped for good relationships, but China remained hostile to the Jewish state. No diplomatic relationships existed in 1998. However, a certain thaw in business relations has been observed in the last few years.

There were other, small Jewish communities in *Hong Kong* (2,000), *Singapore* (300), and *Thailand* (200).

Australia and New Zealand

Australia had a Jewish population of about 105,000 and Jews in *New Zealand* numbered 5,000. The communities were prosperous, secure, and well integrated in the life of the countries. They were organized in competing Orthodox and liberal congregations.

These population figures reveal the spread of Jews worldwide. They dispersed, at times in search of a better life, mainly in escape from intolerable persecution. At times they were expelled. In all the countries in which they lived they heeded the admonition of the prophet Jeremiah (29:4–7). They cast roots and earnestly sought the welfare of the peoples with whom they had identified. The Jews also became racially mixed.

These figures also reveal the ravages of the Holocaust and the effects of religious intolerance. Flourishing centers of Jewish life have disappeared. Jews have found out that minorities can live at peace only in democratic countries that respect human rights. In spite of being so widely dispersed, Jews have retained their sense of belonging to the Jewish people. It rested ultimately on a consciousness, sometimes deeply hidden, that Torah was their bond. The State of Israel has been a liberator for millions and will have to fill this function in the future. The rebuilding of Jewish life in Israel and some Diaspora countries after the Holocaust testifies to the will to live and the vitality of the Jews.

CHAPTER 11

The Restored Christian-Jewish Dialogue

JUDAISM AND THE MONOTHEISTIC RELIGIONS

The Jewish Position

JEWS HAVE NOT BEEN UNANIMOUS in regard to their view of Christianity. They hold firmly that the Messiah has not come. Belief in the incarnation and divinity of Christ is strictly forbidden to Jews. However, some outstanding Jewish masters have explained that the Christian belief in the divinity of Christ, in the sense of being God's "partner," was compatible with monotheism.

RABBI JACOB BEN MEIR, one of the great masters of the French-German school, himself a victim of the persecutions in France in 1147, rose above his own suffering to declare that "in our time the mind of Christians is indeed directed toward the Creator of Heaven, though they use the Name of Heaven in conjunction, or partnership, with another, a matter not prohibited under Noahide commandments" (Talmud Sanhedrin; Tossafor: Assur, Sanhedrin 63). And teaching at the beginning of the modern era, RABBI JACOB EMDEN (1697–1776) declared:

> The founder of Christianity has given the world a twofold blessing: He strengthened the Torah of Moses by emphasizing its eternally binding power; in addition, he brought blessings to the heathens, as he removed idolatry from their midst and imposed upon them the higher moral obligations that are contained in the Torah of Moses. There are many Christians of highest qualities and outstanding morality. Would that all Christians lived by their own commandments. They are not obligated, as are the Jews, to fulfill the law of Moses, nor do they commit a sin, if they associate other beings to God as His partner, in worshipping the triune God. They will receive their reward from God for spreading the faith in Him among peoples that never before had even heard of His Name, for He looks into the heart.

For centuries Orthodox Jews have recited the philosophical poem called "The Royal Crown" on Yom Kippur eve. Written in the eleventh century by Solomon ben Judah Ibn Gabirol, it says, "You are God! All creatures are Your servants, serving You in worship. Your honor is not diminished through those serving another next to You, for all seek to attain to You."

Maimonides, however, shows the reasons for Jewish ambiguity. He sees a divine design in Christianity and Islam and recognizes their importance in spreading monotheism throughout the world and leading it to messianic times. But he regards their teachings to be in error and condemns them for their Jewish persecution. Ascribing the later teachings of Christianity to Jesus he writes,

> Has there ever been a greater stumbling block than this? All the prophets affirmed that the Messiah would redeem Israel, save them, gather their dispersed, and confirm the commandments. But he [Jesus] caused Israel to be destroyed by the sword, their remnant to be dispersed and humiliated. He was instrumental in changing the Torah, causing the world to fall into error and serve another besides God.

Yet he also sees a divine dispensation in the emergence of these two great religions:

> But it is beyond the human mind to fathom the designs of the Creator, for our ways are not His ways, nor our thoughts His thoughts. All these matters, relating to Jesus of Nazareth and the Ishmaelite, who came after him [Mohammed], only served to clear the way for the King Messiah, to prepare the world for the worship of God with one voice. (Zephaniah 3:9f) Thus the messianic hope, the Torah and the commandments have become familiar topics, topics of conversation even [among peoples] of the far away islands, and among many people uncircumcised in heart and flesh. These discussions, though filled with error, will prepare the people for the time when the Messiah will come and correct their errors. (Mishneh Torah: Judges–Kings, Ch. 11)

Maimonides had previously pointed out that to acclaim a man as the Messiah during his lifetime was not against Jewish law. Rabbi Akiba had so designated Bar Kokhba, hoping that he would bring the prophesied freedom to the Jews. Having died without fulfilling the prophetic prediction, that man receives the heavenly rewards for his striving but is deprived of his messianic claim. But Jesus had set a stumbling block for his people and was regarded as the Messiah *after* his death, although he had not met the requisites of the prophets. To maintain this claim his followers were compelled to change the Torah. This had actually happened in Christianity. In order to win the Jews to this new faith they had to be led astray from Torah, to force their conversion they were subjected and "destroyed by the sword, their remnant dispersed and humiliated." (Mishneh Torah: Judges–Kings, Ch. 11)

Maimonides pointed his finger at the root of the problem: conversion of the Jews. By their ruthlessness pursuit of this aim, the majority religions confirmed the Jewish conviction that the Messiah, the bringer of peace, had not yet come. Beyond that, persecution in the name of Christ struck such terror in the hearts and souls of Jews that they could not calmly mention the name of Jesus, who was held to be the cause of all the cruelty meted out to them. Religious persecution has disappeared, but targeting Jews for conversion has not, as we shall see.

Those Jews that followed the teachings of Rabbi Jacob Tam and Rabbi Jacob Emden have regarded Christianity and Islam as divinely accepted roads to God for *their* faithful, who surely belong to "the righteous of all the nations of the world [that] have a share in the world to come" (Tosefta Sanhedrin 13:21). They also might have acknowledged all ethical religions (e.g., Buddhism) that regarded love of fellow human beings and social justice as integral parts of the duties of each person and society. To the degree that all religions accept the principle of religious pluralism, recognize religions other than their own as a way to God, and grant all of them equality in law and life, Judaism may enter dialogue with them.

There is no doubt that there are things common to all Jews, Christians, and Muslims, especially the belief in God as the Creator of the universe, from which all else flows (see Maimonides, *Guide for the Perplexed*, 1, ch. 71).

THE NEW DIALOGUE

On the Jewish Side

Speaking to his own people, without mentioning any other religions, the saintly chief rabbi of Israel ABRAHAM ISAAC KOOK (1865–1935) declared that the mature human mind will recognize all expressions of the spiritual life as one organic whole. Maturity in spirit will overcome the conflict between different religions and create out of their multitude one "ensemble of faiths." Speaking to the world, Martin Buber proclaimed that out of their respective patterns of faith, Christianity and Judaism "would have something unsaid to say to each other and a help to give one another—hardly to be conceived at the present time" (*Two Types of Faith,* New York: Harper, 1951, p. 174). Franz Rosenzweig we shall see actually saw Christianity and Judaism as complementing each other, and therefore, dependent upon each other.

On the Protestant Side

Reinhold Niebuhr was among those leaders who opened the road to dialogue. Rejecting any Christian missionary activity among Jews, he pointed out that

If we measure the two faiths by their moral fruits the Jewish faith does not fall short. . . . [Missionary] activities among Jews . . . are wrong . . . not only because they are futile and have little fruit to boast for their exertions. They are wrong because . . . the two faiths, despite differences, are sufficiently alike for the Jew to find God more easily in terms of his own religious heritage than by subjecting himself to the hazards of guilt feelings involved in a conversion to a faith, which, whatever its excellencies, must appear to him as a symbol of an oppressive majority culture. (*Pious and Secular America*; New York: Charles Scribners Sons, 1958, pp. 107ff.)

Our time has witnessed the restoration of a meaningful Christian-Jewish dialogue. Actually, it is a new form of dialogue. The so-called disputations during the Middle Ages had to arrive at the foregone conclusion that God had sent Christ the Messiah, chosen Christianity, and rejected the Jews. The new dialogue has been conceived on the basis of mutual respect, love, and recognition. We see in it one of the true achievements of our age, a decisive step initiated by the Catholic Church.

On the Catholic Side

World War II, from Auschwitz to Hiroshima, powerfully disclosed a rejection of both Christianity and humanism as ethical guides. The spread of communism, as ideology and political force, revealed to all religions the threat of antireligious materialism. Secularism had grown in society. Pope John XXIII held the conviction that the Church could counter the forces that challenged it only if it updated its teachings and practices and healed the divisions that weakened it. In 1962 he convoked a Church Council to address these momentous issues.

The pope was equally troubled in conscience by the terrible ordeal the Jews had been made to endure, as well as the historical responsibility the Church bore on account of its teachings regarding the Jews and the complete absence of a dialogue with them. When he convoked the Ecumenical Council, Vatican II, he specifically included in its agenda a statement on the Jews. It was designed to eradicate long-established misconceptions about them; to eliminate opinions, beliefs, and practices which had done them harm; and to initiate dialogue. Pope John XXIII died before a statement on the Jews could be promulgated. His successor, Paul VI, officially issued the decree in the fall of 1965, and subsequent popes reinforced it. After its first words it is called *Nostra Aetate*, "In Our Age."

To affirm the brotherhood between Christianity and Judaism as two living religions, Pope John Paul II met with Jewish representatives in all the countries he visited on his extensive travels. In 1987 he joined in common worship with the Jews at the synagogue of Rome, something hitherto unprecedented. In 1993 the Vatican established diplomatic relations with Israel.

The statement on the Jews, the result of extended debate within the Council, established a new spirit of mutual respect and dialogue between Catholics and Jews in discussion and life. The decree, "Declaration on Relations with Non-Christians," consisted of five sections, of which only the fourth dealt specifically with the Jews. The first section outlined the purpose and underlying philosophy of the decree. The next two dealt with the contributions of various religions, such as Hinduism, Buddhism, and Islam, some of whose insights the Catholic Church considered valuable for itself and for all humanity. The Catholic faithful should engage in prudent dialogue and collaboration with adherents of these religions. The final section was a call to universal love; it reproved all discrimination on account of race, color, condition in life, or religion.

The fourth section, on the Jews, was the longest and most involved. The most salient points are condensed here: "The Church acknowledges the spiritual ties binding it to the Jews through Abraham, the Patriarchs, Moses, and the prophets; it holds them to be the beginning of her own [the Church's]." This bond is confirmed in the words of St. Paul "theirs [the Jews'] is the sonship and the glory and the covenants and the law and the worship and the promises, the fathers and Christ according to the flesh" (Romans 9:4–5), and the fact that disciples and apostles sprang from the Jewish people. The decree declared that "Jerusalem did not recognize the time of its visitation." Only a few accepted the gospel and many opposed its spreading, "yet God holds the Jews most dear for the sake of their fathers, for God does not repent His gifts or the calls He issues." On the basis of the common patrimony, the Council recommended and wished to foster understanding and respect based on biblical and theological studies and from a fraternal dialogue.

The following declarations are of fundamental importance. They wipe out the conviction hitherto held by Christians that all Jews were guilty of the passion and death of Christ and, therefore the Jewish people have been rejected by God. Jewish authorities, the statement pointed out, pressed for the death of Christ, but

> what happened in Christ's passion cannot be charged against all Jews, then alive without distinction, nor against the Jews of today. Although the Church is the new people of God, the Jews should not be presented as rejected and ac-cursed of God, as if this followed from the Holy Scriptures. All should see to it that in catechetical work or in preaching nothing be taught that does not con-form to the truth of the gospel and the spirit of Christ. (*Nostra Aetate*, section 4)

There follows a condemnation of all forms of anti-Semitism and Jew-hatred:

> Rejecting persecution against any man, mindful of the patrimony shared with the Jews, moved, not by political reasons but by the gospel's spiritual love, the Church decries hatred, persecution, and displays of anti-Semitism directed against Jews at any time and by anyone.

The final paragraph asserts the abiding belief of the Church that Christ un-derwent his passion and death freely, because of the sins of humanity and out of infinite love, in order that all might reach salvation. It is, therefore, the burden of the Church's preaching to proclaim the cross of Christ as the sign of God's all-embracing love and as the fountain from which every grace flows.

Jewish Reactions

Jewish reaction to the Vatican II decree was generally positive. To those most deeply concerned with dialogue, the document offered a great deal of hope. The affirmation of Jewish corporate innocence in the death of Jesus was an act of long overdue justice. It proclaimed what the Jews had maintained all along. The same applied to Christian belief that the Jews were accursed and rejected by God. The declaration actually rebuked anyone holding it henceforth. The call for friendship and brotherhood was recognized as genuine and was welcomed. The statement rebuking anti-Semitism was a help; if even one soul were kept from harm by it, it was worth it.

However, one question remained unanswered. The decree of 1965 had not mentioned the religious dimensions of the State of Israel. This omission was eventually remedied but only after a period of tension.

There were some Jewish reservations. Future statements of the Church and the relationships established in life proved them to be unfounded. Some Jews held that the decree was of small import, because twentieth-century anti-Semitism rested on social, political, and economic factors, not theological considerations. To a degree they were right, but facts have also refuted this contention. In the Islamic world, religious beliefs have deeply affected political considerations and actions. In Western Christianity, too, the influence of religious teachings has been decisive. Results of a long-term study on anti-Semitism, undertaken by the Survey Research Center of the University of California and released in 1966, reinforced this fact. The study indicated that the majority of Christians who are anti-Jewish base their attitude on religious teachings of their churches learned in childhood. It was found that this attitude, once instilled at an early age, could never be entirely eradicated. One of the primary sources of anti-Jewish attitudes was the teaching that the Jews were guilty of Christ's death. African nations were building their societies, and large numbers of their populations accepted Catholicism. They would enter their new faith without learning prejudices. South American countries, largely Catholic, could be weaned from anti-Jewish sentiments hitherto justified by religion. The declaration of the Vatican Council was therefore considered as being of great importance as a weapon against anti-Semitism.

The decree was promulgated as an internal document guiding the Catholic faithful. It had to take into account the total theology of the Catholic Church. To Jews, the gospels are not holy; to Catholics they are holy "gospel truth," and allowed no challenge to the text itself. But reinterpretation of anti-Jewish statements was now ordained. The survival of Jewry did indeed pose a serious theological problem to Catholics. They had hitherto held that the Christian revelation canceled out Judaism, and Jews were regarded by the Church as the remnant of a cursed people holding stubbornly to an outworn faith that had long been superseded. Their eventual conversion was the only reason for their survival under conditions of misery. Now Christians had to affirm Judaism as a living faith, beloved by God, and with a continuing function given it by God. The decree's position constituted a radical change.

Furthermore, the decree on the Jews is meaningful in the context of other decrees, particularly the "Declaration on Religious Freedom, on the Right of the Person and of Communities to Social and Civic Freedom in Matters Religious." In it, the Council declared that the right to religious freedom had its foundation in the very dignity of the human person, as this dignity was known through the revealed word of God and by reason itself. It is also stated that "Religious communities have the right not to be hindered in their public teaching and witness to their faith, whether by the spoken or by the written word." The significance of this proclamation in connection with the declaration on the Jews was great. There were countries in which the free profession of faith in open affirmation had been hampered by problems, laws, suspicions, and misunderstandings.

Implementations and Guidelines

As Church authorities began to interpret the decree, they recognized that some statements lacked a clear articulation. These efforts showed the intention to lay to rest apprehensions of Jews. They also revealed the earnest desire to establish brotherly relations with the Jews.

Changes were made on a practical level in liturgy, preaching, and catechetical instruction. Derogative statements about Jews in textbooks were eliminated, and, most important, New Testament references hostile to Jews were given new interpretation. Directions were issued to clergy, laity, and Catholic school authorities. This was done in guidelines. The Archdiocese of New York was the first to issue such guidelines, in 1969, followed by a committee of French bishops in 1973. Worldwide guidelines were handed down by the Vatican itself in December 1974. A working paper entitled "Basic Theological Issues of the Jewish-Christian Dialogue," which was issued by the German bishops, followed in 1979. We will consider some of these statements in greater detail below.

The Six Day War in 1967 between the Arab states and Israel made it clear to the Jews that the decree of 1965 had totally ignored the religious dimensions of the Land of Israel for Jewry. The Vatican decree did not mention Israel. The silence of the Church at a time when Israel was in mortal danger, as well as the omission of any mention of the State of Israel by name in papal speeches, created persistent apprehensions in Jewish minds. This fear was mitigated somewhat by Episcopal pronouncements that acknowledged the restoration of Israel on its soil as a basic element of the Jewish faith. With the Vatican's recognition of the State of Israel in 1993, the fear was dispelled.

Guidelines for the Advancement of Catholic-Jewish Relations

The statement issued by the archbishop of New York and the bishops of Brooklyn and Rockville Center in 1969, framed with the cooperation of rabbis and Jewish community leaders, dealt with both practical and theological issues. It reaffirmed that "proselytizing was to be carefully avoided in the dialogue," strongly condemned anti-Semitism, called for expurgation of anti-Semitic statements from textbooks, invited scholarly studies, and rejected the historically inaccurate notion that Judaism at the time of Christ—especially Pharisaism—was a decadent formalism and hypocrisy. The life of Jesus and the primitive church were to be studied in their Jewish setting; a full explanation of the use of the label "the Jews" in various New Testament references needed to be given, and Catholics were to acknowledge the living and complex reality of Judaism. The election of Israel under special Covenant with God was permanent and had not been abrogated with the election of Christianity. All these matters were to be incorporated into Catholic teaching.

Councils of Catholics and Jews were also to be formed on every level, mutual invitations were to be extended and accepted, and a spirit of reciprocity was to prevail. Participation in some forms of common worship was also approved. Rabbis were to be accorded respect, were permitted to speak at church services before and after the Mass, Jews and Catholics could be attendants in wedding services of the other faith, and so on.

The Statement of the Committee of French Bishops

Although never adopted as official policy, this statement was the most advanced and comprehensive of all guidelines, and appears to have influenced subsequent ones. It revealed both a profound knowledge of Judaism and a deep empathy with Jewish self-perception. A wise and bold document, it showed how far the Church could go without compromising its own integrity. The statement could serve as a resource to all who wished to base their relationship with Jews on official pronouncements. For this reason large excerpts have been added in the Appendix.

The statement regarded the decree of Vatican II as "more of a beginning than as an achievement," and regretted the "slow course of Christian conscience." The document opened with the statement that the history of the Jewish people, its survival amidst the most horrendous trials, and its return to the Land of Israel constituted a divine mystery which would help Christianity—being bound to Israel—to find meaning for its own vocation under God's plan. This was the first Church document that saw in the return to Israel a divine dispensation (Appendix 1).

By God's will the Jewish people are eternal and will be for all time witnesses to God and teachers of God's will. By its very existence, it had been an exacting partner and challenger of Christianity, which had to come to grips with this divinely willed fact, and had to do so with respect. Every Jew, therefore, had to be recognized both as a human being and as a member of the Jewish people. As human beings Jews were entitled to all human rights, as members of the Jewish people they also required recognition "on the level of faith." Christians had to recognize the Church's Jewish roots; Judaism must not be regarded as simply one of the many religions on earth, nor as a relic of the past. According to biblical revelation, God Himself had constituted the Jewish people, sealing with it an eternal Covenant (Genesis 17:7). They had a special place in God's dispensation. Nor had their mission in the world come to an end. Through it monotheism became the common good of Judaism, Christianity, and Islam (Appendix 2).

The bishops called all Christians to love the Jews and warned against any form of stereotyping Jews. Then they added a significant point not mentioned in the Vatican decree: admission of Christian guilt for failing to extend esteem and love to the Jews. Because Christians failed to love the Jews, they too were guilty in the tragic fate of Jews throughout the ages (Appendix 3).

From this love had to spring the battle against anti-Semitism. Christians had to recognize that anti-Jewish actions and feelings of the past frequently had their roots in pseudo-theological arguments, above all, holding the Jews guilty of Christ's death. These had to be cast out (Appendix 4).

Christians held a number of misconceptions about Judaism. These had to be eradicated. There was the contention that the election of Israel had been canceled. There existed the erroneous idea that Jewish religion was based on fear, in contrast to Christianity which was the religion of love. There were misjudgments of the character of the Pharisees and their successors, the Masters of the Talmud. Jesus associated with the Pharisees, and his harsh rebukes were directed only at certain Pharisees. This was in accord with the judgment of the pharisaic masters themselves on some unworthy members of the group.

The recognition given the masters of the Talmud was of special significance coming from the French bishops, as it was in France that the Talmud had been publicly burned during the Middle Ages. The bishops' statement became an acknowledgment of a wrong committed by the Church.

In order to acquire a "just comprehension of Judaism," Christians had to gain a true knowledge of Jewish tradition and self-perception. They had to be cognizant that the Old Testament was "the root and source, the foundation and the promise" [of the New Testament] and was relevant for the Christian community. They should never forget that Jesus himself, a Jewish man, was faithful to Torah.

Speaking of Israel's vocation, the bishops explained that it was "the Sanctification of the Name." This sanctification expressed itself in the fulfillment of divine commandments. Contrary to Paul who saw in the commandments a "yoke," the bishops understood Jewish thinking, which sees in Mitzvot a divine gift. The bishops, equally spoke of the Jews' "building time" and referred to the Sabbath (Appendix 5). Obviously they were influenced by Abraham Heschel, who explained that through deeds (observance of Mitzvot) the Jew sanctifies time and cited the Sabbath as example.

"Sanctification of the Name" was also the reason for Jewish exile-existence. Jews in their suffering testified to God before the whole world. The suffering of the Jews was an effect of their prophetic condition. Keeping this in mind, Christians must resolutely combat anti-Semitism, because anti-Semites rationalized that a people so relentlessly persecuted must be evil. The bishops used as prooftext the "Suffering Servant" (Isaiah 53), as the Jews understood it. In Christian tradition these words had been regarded as a prophetic description of the passion of Christ (Appendix 6).

The bishops were aware of the problems faced by the State of Israel, and yet were inclined to see in its restoration a divine dispensation. Both the dispersion of the Jewish people and their return to their land, given them by God, were to be understood as the Jews, in the light of their own history, had come to understand them. Justice, however, demanded that the other inhabitants of the land be given their rights.

With great insight the bishops touched on a point not mentioned in any other declaration: the variety of Jewish experiences. Jews followed different schools of thought, religious movements, forms, and rites to express their Jewishness, but their variety did not affect their fundamental unity. Christians had to admit that there could be different fashions of being a Jew. They were to make no distinction between Jewish adherents of one thought or movement and another. They had to respect every Jew, irrespective of the manner in which he expressed his Jewishness, and the rites that were dear to him.

In Christian-Jewish dialogue each partner was to give full testimony of his faith without being suspected of any missionary intents. The respect owed the other's religion forbade targeting people for conversion. It was legitimate, however, to assist an individual who sought conversion based on personal conviction (Appendix 9).

Addressing themselves specifically to the priests, the bishops pointed out that the Covenant with Israel was eternal, and actually had made the Covenant with Christianity possible (Appendix 10).

Finally, the statement addressed itself to "The Church and the Jewish People." Christians had claimed that with the coming of Christ there was no longer any continuing function for Judaism in the world. The bishops pointed out to them that the function of the Synagogue was eternal. This was also a rebuke to the medieval portrayal of the Synagogue as blindfolded with a broken staff and the Church triumphant. Actually, the bishops proclaimed, Church and Synagogue would forever stand in a reciprocal contest, making each other "jealous." The bishops referred to Paul. But Paul had only held that the Jews would have to become "jealous" of the Church, but not the Church of the Jews. The bishops boldly reinterpreted his words. In contrast to Paul, they proclaimed that the Church must become just as "jealous" of the Jews as the Jews were to be of the Church (Appendix 11).

In conclusion, the bishops expressed the hope that the enmity between Christians and Jews would yield to mutual acceptance and offer promise of a world under God. Both Judaism and Christianity were eternal. The bishops' statement influenced later pronouncements, including the guidelines issued by the Vatican, to which we shall now turn.

Guidelines and Suggestions for Implementing the Conciliar Declaration

The guidelines issued by the Vatican rested on the pronouncements of the bishops and the experience of ten years of interfaith dialogue. They set the stage for the future and clarified those points that had created apprehensions among Jews. For instance, Jews had felt that "deploring" anti-Semitism was too weak after all that had happened in the Holocaust. The guidelines straightforwardly condemned it: "The spiritual bonds and historical links binding the Church to Judaism condemn all forms of anti-Semitism and discrimination." (All guideline quotes are from a pamphlet issued by the Commission for Religious Relations with the Jews, Rome, 1974.)

The links and relationships between Judaism and Catholicism made better mutual understanding and renewed mutual esteem obligatory. On the practical level, Christians were told to strive to acquire a better knowledge of the basic components of Jewish religious tradition. They must strive to learn by what essential traits the Jews define themselves in the light of their own religious experience.

On Dialogue. The section on dialogue took cognizance of the tragic conditions of the past, when dialogue in reality was Christian monologue. They also revealed an awareness of the suspicion still existing among Jews in regard to the Church's intent in engaging in dialogue. Not triumphalism but care was to be the hallmark of the Christian attitude. Dialogue must rest on the respectful desire for mutual acquaintance.

While the Church was duty bound to teach and witness to Jesus Christ, Catholics must at the same time show strictest respect for religious liberty. Regarding the Jews in particular Catholics must understand the difficulties Jews justifiably have "when faced with the mystery of the Incarnate Word" namely the incarnation. Christians must be aware of their historical responsibility, "inspired by an unfortunate past," for the widespread suspicion in which Jews have been held even in present days. They must see to what extent the responsibility is theirs and must remedy the causes. Common study, and, as far as possible, common worship is encouraged.

> In addition to friendly talks, competent people will be encouraged to meet and to study together the many problems deriving from the fundamental convictions of Judaism and of Christianity. In order not to hurt (even involuntarily) those taking part, it will be vital to guarantee, not only tact, but a great openness of spirit and diffidence with respect to one's own prejudices.

On Liturgy. The common elements in the liturgical life of Christianity and Judaism are to be recognized. Both are living faiths. These common elements are based on Scripture. The Old Testament is to be given greater study and attention.

Regarding the relationship of the Old and New Testaments, the Guidelines instructed:

> The Old Testament and the Jewish tradition founded upon it must not be set against the New Testament in such a way that the former seems to constitute a religion of only justice, fear and legalism, with no appeal to the love of God and neighbor (cf. Deuteronomy 6:5; Leviticus 19:18; Matthew 22:34–40).

Regarding the New Testament it was pointed out that some utterances in it had in the past become a powerful source of anti-Jewish indoctrination, had caused loathing, and brought much suffering to the Jews. To erase hostility against the Jews, these passages were to be interpreted in the correct light. This applied to preaching, prayer, biblical translations, catechetical instruction, and education.

> Thus the formula "the Jews," in [the Gospel of] St. John, sometimes according to the context means "the leaders of the Jews," or "the adversaries of Jesus," terms which express better the thought of the evangelist and avoid appearing

to arraign the Jewish people as such. Another example is the use of the words "Pharisee" and "Pharisaism," which have taken on a largely pejorative meaning. (Footnote on p. 4 of the guidelines.)

Teaching and Education. Christians needed to know certain basic facts about Jewish religion and history, and then act upon this knowledge. To further this aim scholarly studies (especially on the level of higher education), cooperation with Jewish scholars, and the establishment of chairs of Jewish studies were recommended.

The guidelines repeated that Jesus was born of the Jewish people, as were his apostles and a large number of his first disciples. Jesus rested his teachings on the Old Testament. It also repeated that the Jews could not be held responsible for the death of Christ. With regard to the trial and death of Jesus, "what happened in his passion cannot be blamed upon all the Jews then living, without distinction, nor upon the Jews of today" (*Nostra Aetate,* 4). Perhaps with an allusion to the Talmud, but surely in contrast to former teachings, the Guidelines stated that the "history of Judaism did not end with the destruction of Jerusalem, but rather went on to develop a religious tradition . . . rich in religious values." These instructions were to be followed at all levels of Christian instruction, education, and information. Among sources of information, special attention should be paid to the following: catechisms and religious textbooks; history books and the mass media (press, radio, cinema, television).

On Joint Social Action. The best way for people to know and respect each other was to join in common endeavors for others. This was recognized in the section on joint social action. In the spirit of the prophets Jews and Christians should work willingly together, seeking social justice and peace at every level: local, national, and international. Jewish and Christian tradition, founded on the Word of God, was aware of the value of the human person, the image of God. Love of the same God must show itself in effective action for the good of mankind.

Implementation of the guidelines was entrusted to the bishops. They were to create commissions or secretariats on national or regional levels, or to appoint suitable representatives to implement the mandate of the council.

On October 22, 1974 the pope instituted for the universal Church a Commission for Religious Relations with the Jews, and attached it to the Secretariat for Promoting Christian Unity. At the Council, the section on Judaism had been removed from the proposed inclusion in the section on "Christian Unity" and inserted in "Relations with Other Religions." Now it was affirmed that relations with Judaism was an aspect of Christian unity.

The German "Working Paper: Basic Theological Issues of the Jewish-Christian Dialogue"

The German "Working Paper" followed the papal guidelines. As Germans, the authors of the paper had to address themselves to the Holocaust and the State of Israel. The document did not mention the responsibility of theological anti-Semitism for the tragedy. The paper revealed the influence of Franz Rosen-zweig, who was referred to by name. Rosenzweig had held that Christianity and Judaism were by God's will dependent on each other. The bishops, therefore, held that Jews and Christians were responsible for each other, they had a God-given, living interrelationship. The paper addressed both Christians and Jews about their mutual obligations. It was somewhat "magisterial."

In accord with the theology of Rabbi Emil Fackenheim the bishops affirmed that there could be no theological answers to the Holocaust, only an action re-sponse. Christians and Jews had to be joint witnesses to God in the world. This applied specifically in regard to several fundamental questions raised by the Ho-locaust and the restoration of the State of Israel:

> How, in the face of the mass murder which has been committed against the Jews and the attempted destruction of the Jewish people, is it still possible to believe in God? How is it possible to bear guilt and suffering in the presence of God, instead of suppressing or fixating them? What meaning is there for Jews and Christians, and for their mutual encounter, in the systematic extermination of large segments of European Jewry, and in the founding of the State of Israel? How, in the face of the founding of the State of Israel as a central event in recent Jewish history, is it possible to combine the millennial Jewish hope in God's salvation with concrete political action in the present, without advocating either a religiously grounded ideologizing of politics or a politicization of religion?
>
> What is the meaning of the fact that, in a world which is as polytheistic as ever before (it is simply that the gods are given different names today), Jews and Christians believe in the One God? Is it not possible, indeed, is it not man-datory for Jews and Christians, on the basis of their revelation, jointly to de-velop a critique of ideology—in a world which still fights wars which essen-tially are wars of religion (which becomes clear when we substitute the word "ideology" for the word "religion")?
>
> Do not Jews and Christians have the common obligation, in the face of world conditions which threaten the survival of humankind, to demonstrate and to show through personal example what the Bible understands by righ-teousness and liberty? The basic demand of biblical Revelation, common to Jews and Christians, is the absolute respect for the life of another human being. They should jointly specify the consequences which follow from this today for the maintenance of human dignity and human rights. In particular, they should, for example, together develop an ethic of the sciences, of technology, and of a concern for the future. (People who live after the year 2000 are also our "neighbors.") What concrete consequences can be drawn from the conviction, common to Jews and Christians, that man has been created in God's image? What obligations follow from the commandment, common to Jews and Chris-tians, of unrestricted love? (cf. Leviticus 19:18 and Mark 12:30ff.)

The emphasis on concrete goals of life gained significance as it emerged from the Germans.

The Catechism of the Roman Catholic Church of 1992

The Catholic Church has used Catechism to bring its dogmas, doctrines, and practices to the grassroots level. Written simply, it serves the clergy as an authoritative guide. It is taught to children from early age and often memorized by them. The Catechism issued in 1992 is a massive work, designed to strengthen the faith of Catholics and ground their lives in the affirmation of its divine calling. Its pronouncements on Judaism, mirroring the resolutions of Vatican II, evidence the Church's new position.

Within the framework of the divine New Testament, the relationship of Jesus to the Jewish people and its leaders, especially the Pharisees is sympathetically presented. The abiding connection to Judaism is shown and emphasized. Misconceptions are corrected. Disagreements and differences are not glossed over. The Jewish submission to the Torah are explained. By his divinity Jesus was the only person able to fulfill the Torah in all its integrity. But the Pharisees also insisted on the integrity of the law not only in letter but also in its spirit, and all Jews know that no human being can fulfill all the commandments of the law; they therefore ask forgiveness for their transgressions on the Day of Atonement. Jesus' animosity, as told in the Gospels, was not directed against all Jews or all Pharisees, but against some of them. Actually, Jesus dined with Pharisees and "confirmed doctrines held by this religious elite of the People of God." He confirmed pharisaic doctrines, among them the resurrection of the dead, forms of piety (charity, fasts, prayer) and the mode of addressing God as "Father." He emphasized the centrality of the commandment to love God and neighbor.

Jesus revered the Temple as God's dwelling place on earth and made regular pilgrimages. Veneration for its holiness moved him to eject the money changers. He also predicted its destruction. This destruction came to be seen by Christians as God's punishment on the Jews for having rejected Christ; it was clear evidence that the covenant with the Jews had been abrogated. The Catechism provides a new interpretation that eliminates the "guilt" of the Jews. Jesus declared that henceforth, in consequence of the new dispensation beginning with his physical death, the Temple had lost its function. The Body of Christ was the New Temple. The Catechism had to balance the necessity of the death of Christ for salvation and the responsibilities of the Jewish court condemning him. It characterized their actions as a tragic misunderstanding in the face of an unprecedented situation. The personal guilt of even those who condemned Jesus (Judas, the Sanhedrin, Pilate) was known only to God. Jesus himself pardoned them on the cross (Luke 23:34).

In spite of the cry of a manipulated mass, "Let his blood be on us and on our children" (Matthew 27:25), one could not attribute the responsibility to the whole Jewish community in space and time. The catechism repeated the declaration of Vatican II: "what happened in Christ's passion cannot be charged against all Jews, then alive without distinction, nor against the Jews of today. . . . the Jews may not be presented as rejected and accursed of God, as if this followed from the Holy Scriptures." The faithful are urged to acquire a better knowledge of the faith and life of the Jews. It was pointed out that the Liturgy of the Word had its origin in Jewish prayer. The Prayer of the Hours and other texts and liturgical formulations rested on it; above all, the formulations of most venerable prayers such as "Pater[noster]" had their parallels in Judaism.

Relationships as well as differences were also visible during the great festivals of the liturgical year, such as Passover. The offering of wine and bread were traced to the Jewish past, especially on Passover. The designation "son of God" was traced to the Hebrew Scriptures, where angels and the Chosen People were so designated. It indicated their adoptive sonship of God. Jesus' sonship surpassed it. Prayer, above all, the Psalms, were accorded a broad treatment; we shall quote from it in the next chapter. As old as creation, prayer permeated the whole Old Testament and called for a change of heart and an ever-renewed search for God.

The people of God under the new Covenant are bound to the Jewish people "to whom God spoke first." The Jewish faith, in contrast to other non-Christian religions, was already a response to the revelation of God in the old Covenant. "The People of God of the Old Covenant and the People of God of the new Covenant aimed toward analogous ultimate visions: the expectation of the coming of the Messiah" (*Catéchisme de l'Église Catholique*, Mame/Plon 1992; translation mine).

From Pronouncement to Action

As the "Working Paper" concludes and the Catechism reveals, "the Jewish-Christian dialogue must no longer remain the monopoly of a few interested specialists, it must engage all; clergy, educators, pastoral workers, the media—both Christian and Jewish," and the people. Subsequently, an office for Catholic-Jewish relations was established at the Vatican and a U.S. Secretariat for Catholic-Jewish Relations in the United States. Many dioceses created offices dealing with Catholic-Jewish relations. Official statements have faced the problems that may impede the dialogue. Among them were the conflicting and yet justified claims of both Arabs and Jews in the State of Israel; an understanding approach was needed. Numerous Catholic universities have provided courses in Jewish studies, and high schools have invited local rabbis to present Judaism to Catholic youth. Curricula have included the Holocaust. Conferences and lecture series have been common. Texts have been subjected to scrutiny in order to eliminate items derogatory to Jews. Cordial personal contacts have developed or deepened.

We have dwelt at great length on the pronouncements of the Catholic Church for several reasons. By its organization, the Church is able to make pronouncements for all its faithful and give directions with a certain assurance that they will be implemented. By its size and its impact on Christianity as a whole, it can influence other Christian denominations with which it has an ongoing ecumenical relationship.

PROTESTANTISM

Protestant churches of various denominations, their leaders, and many scholars have also spoken out on relations with the Jews. FRANKLIN LITTELL, a leading Protestant theologian and formerly president of Iowa Wesleyan College, was deeply committed to confronting Christianity with its past. He called for an acknowledgment of its guilt and for its active renewal. PAUL VAN BUREN, the late Professor of Religious Studies at Temple University, published a three-volume work, *A Theology of Jewish-Christian Reality*. To him, Jewish reality, including the Holocaust and the State of Israel were basic elements in the reconstruction of Christian theology, since both were called upon jointly to complete God's unfinished work of creation.

During the tensions of 1967, when Israel was in grave danger and Jews throughout the world were terrified at the possibility of another Holocaust, the churches were silent and questions arose in Jewish minds about whether the Church was even concerned. Was it tied to the concept of the Jews as homeless wanderers? Was it afraid that its missionary activities in the Third World might be jeopardized by any support for Israel? Two Christian theologians, A. ROY ECKHARDT and ALICE L. ECKHARDT, in their joint work, *The Silence of the Churches*, accused the churches of dereliction. Other church leaders disagreed with them. They pointed to the work the Church had done during the crisis. The controversy itself proved to be beneficial. The dialogue might have come to an end; instead, the crisis called for a maturing of expectations and of conscience on all sides. It compelled an increased awareness and renewed effort on a deeper level of understanding and cooperation.

The Mormons, in the words of Joseph Smith, proclaimed this theology as early as 1843. In 1969 the Reverend Robert C. Dodds, Director of Ecumenical Affairs of the National Council of Churches, pointed out that contact with Israel would help Christians to recover the full authenticity of their own faith. For the first time they would come to understand Jews of a generation that had not known the humiliations by the Christian majority; namely, the youth of Israel.

One fact has become clear even by the few examples we have cited: The basic principles of theological dialogue had to be carried into the arena of human events.

Synodal Ordinance toward Renewal of the Relationship between Christians and Jews

In 1980 the Evangelical Synod of the German State of Rhineland, the official governing body of the Lutheran Church of that state, issued an ordinance binding on all its affiliated churches. *Renewal* was the key term. The ordinance clearly admitted that age-old teachings of Christianity were the basis of "Christian co-responsibility and guilt in regard to the Holocaust, the degradation, persecution and murder of the Jews" in Hitler's Germany. The Holocaust, in fact, constituted a crisis in civilization, culture, politics, and religion, all of which contributed to it.

In addition, Christians in Germany live "under the curse that Hitler's policies of "Judenreinheit" (cleansing from the Jews) [that] have been almost fully realized." The church must repent actively. The Synod prayed that Jews may be willing to join with Christians in the work of renewal.

Because both Jews and Christians were witnesses to the One everlasting God, Christian missionary activity among Jews was to be rejected as contrary to the will of God, who has ordained Jewish survival and loves Israel. The New Testament must not be presented as standing in contrast to the Old; Christians were advised to speak of the "Hebrew Bible" rather than "Old Testament," which was a pejorative term. Statements hostile to Jews and Judaism in the New Testament must be reinterpreted. Jesus must be recognized as a Jew. Christians must know that for both Christianity and Judaism God is the God of both love and justice.

The restoration of the State of Israel was a "sign of God's historical faithfulness to His people" revealing His abiding concern. Referring to the Holocaust and the State of Israel it was stated that the question of a theodice (a justification of God's actions) existed for Christians as for Jews. There could not be a satisfactory explanation for God's actions, but there could and had to be a common affirmation of God in the world.

Christians and Jews were bound together in love as one people. In different ways, they had received God's mandate. Jointly they had to explore God's word, as found in Scripture, and carry His mandate as His witnesses in the world. Practical ways of cooperation were outlined, including committees for common study and work on the local level and the establishment of a program of Judaic studies at universities. The Synod's statement invoked the spirit of Karl Barth, who declared that ecumenism is possible only if the Jews are part of it.

Realities

The pronunciations of the Catholic Church and some of the Protestant churches have been excerpted in greater detail because of their fundamental importance. Theological anti-Semitism was a cause of the endless sufferings inflicted on the Jews. Later forms of anti-Semitism were grafted on it and then existed independently. In order to fight it and do justice to the Jews the churches changed doctrines that had been held for centuries.

The Holocaust had left its imprint on their consciences. But these pronouncements reached only those prepared to obey them. Modern society had become widely secularized. Social and economic forces determined its attitude. Selfishness, and ideologies, be it communism or neo-Nazism had become "gods" as the German bishops recognized. In spite of the overwhelming evidence to the contrary "revisionist historians" tried to prove that the Holocaust never existed, in order to rekindle the hate of the Jews. The pronouncements of the churches had no impact on them.

But certain church bodies also refused to change old attitudes. Fundamentalist churches did not adopt the principle that Judaism and Christianity were equally beloved of God and assured of life eternal and resurrection. In 1996 the

Southern Baptist Convention, America's largest Protestant denomination, declared that it had the obligation of targeting the Jews for conversion. It was reported that Richard Mouw, President of Fuller Theological Seminary, the leading seminary of Evangelicals, had declared in an editorial in *Christianity Today* entitled "Witnessing to the Jews," that he held "a nonnegotiable commitment to evangelism—and this includes witnessing to Jewish people about my firm conviction that Jesus is the promised Messiah" (*Jewish Bulletin*, San Francisco, California, Vol. 101, Number 33, August 27, 1997, p. 19).

Churches and cults committed to missionary work among the Jews looked for targets among young American Jews, whose ties with the religious community were often tenuous, and among immigrant Russian Jews, who frequently knew nothing about Judaism. The evangelist Dr. Billy Graham declared that he would not target Jews specifically but felt committed to approach "all men concerning personal faith in Jesus Christ," including the Jews. Maimonides's apprehensions were still justified. When the Jews of Yemen were under severe persecution to convert, he called them to steadfastness. He pointed out that in history, nations had used two methods in their attempts to wean Jews away from Torah. One was the sword. Better educated and more intelligent nations resorted to arguments, disputes, and polemical writings. Maimonides urged his fellow Jews to resist both. (See *Epistle to Yemen*.)

Liberation theologies called for the liberation of all oppressed from subjection and deprivation. They were in part based on the principle that Jesus Christ had liberated the world from the narrow formalism and selfishness of the Jews. The Jews were then a class of exploiters. Even the German bishops asked the question how it was "possible to combine the millennial Jewish hope in God's salvation with concrete political action in the present, without advocating either a religiously grounded ideologizing of politics or a politicization of religion?" They thereby revealed a lacking understanding of Jewish millennial hopes. To the Jews, the Messiah will in fact create in Israel and the world "religiously grounded" democracies. Millennialists did not ask the question and simply put Judaism in contradiction to Christianity's ultimate hope.

Jewish Orthodoxy generally rejected the religious dialogue as pointless. Jews who accepted Maimonides's idea that Christians were in error, saw in incarnation and Trinity an adulteration of pure monotheism. They also were aware of the continued attempts of churches to proselytize among them. The late Rabbi Joseph Soloveitchik, who in the twentieth century ordained generations of Orthodox rabbis, additionally explained that the faithful of a religion could understand the fullness of their faith only because they had been fashioned by its doctrines, traditions, and practices from earliest childhood. They had made them part of their innermost being. Religious dialogue could not convey the depth of a religion to any person outside of it and was therefore useless and futile.

But neither the Fundamentalist nor these Orthodox Jews excluded mutual cooperation on societal issues, such as social justice. Additionally, both Jews and Christians had many internal tasks. Dialogue between them necessarily took second place in the total program of instruction and education. Widespread laxity among Christians made strengthening the faith the first priority of the leadership. Jewish leadership had to devote efforts to the same task. It became more complicated for Jews since they lived in a Christian environment. As Franz Rosenzweig stated, the Jew who drifted out of Judaism moved not into a neutral sphere but into a Christian one. The efforts by the Christian Coalition to make America a "Christian state" raised apprehensions in Jews of being relegated to a *de facto* second-class citizenship.

Ambiguity concerning Israel was sometimes a source of tension between Christians and Jews. Liberal Protestantism appeared to favor the Arabs in the name of equal justice, whereas fundamentalist churches were supportive of Israel, seeing in the return of the Jews to their homeland a prelude to the second coming of Christ.

The pronouncements of the churches helped dispel anti-Semitism in wide circles of the population. The Christian-Jewish dialogue has made the greatest progress in the Western countries, especially the United States. In Germany, it suffered from the absence of a numerically strong and spiritually creative Jewry. In Israel, times and conditions had as yet not permitted a true concern with it, although the Hebrew University through a number of its professors, had become a center of studies of other religions. To many of the Third World nations, especially in Africa, who had accepted Christianity, Judaism was an unknown faith. They identified it with what they heard of Israel in a political context, often very hostile.

The Church could become an advocate of understanding and tolerance. Much has yet to be done to eliminate slander and hate against Jews and to grant Judaism full recognition as an equal. But the declarations of the Catholic and some of the Protestant churches have paved the way and may stand as one of the redeeming achievements of the twentieth century.

DIALOGUE WITH ISLAM

Islam was long neglected by the West, which mistakenly felt that there was nothing to learn from it. Islamic religious leaders saw no need for a dialogue either since, for Muslims, the Quran contains the entire truth. Jewry saw dialogue with Christianity, in whose lands it had spread, as a significant task. Real dialogue with Islam has scarcely begun, although there may be indications of a beginning interchange of ideas. (I participated in a workshop of Christian, Jewish, and Muslim scholars and was elected moderator.) Much can be learned from Islam—such as the cohesion of its faithful, their piety guiding every aspect of life, the absence of racial and ethnic discrimination among its adherents—which makes an interchange of ideas highly desirable.

However, there are also problems with a Muslim-Jewish interchange. Above all, dialogue requires reinterpreting sacred scriptures, which in Islam is very difficult. Some Muslim scholars, among them a number who teach in the West, have begun to attempt it, but their investigations, coming from a Western environment, do not carry much weight elsewhere.

Dialogue between the Muslims and "the people of the book" is of vital importance. Islam has one billion adherents and is the fastest growing religion today. As dialogue expands, fellowship and peace may be promoted. As Mohammed stated, "None of you is truly faithful as long as he does not desire for his brother what he himself loves."

CONTACTS WITH EASTERN RELIGIONS

Judaism used to give little attention to the religions of the East. Jews have had little occasion to relate to them as there were few Jews in the regions where these religions prevail. In India the small Jewish community seems to be phasing itself out by emigration. A Jewish community in Kaifeng, China died out in the nineteenth century after existing for almost one thousand years. Contact between these Jews and the rest of Jewry was scant. Jesuits discovered the Chinese Jewish community in the seventeenth century and explored it in the belief that these Jews owned Torah scrolls so old that they were written before the rabbis supposedly had expunged prophecies relating to the coming of Christ from the Hebrew Scriptures. No such references were found, but Christian missionaries described the life of these Jews and have given us a picture of their ways.

Anti-Jewish sentiment generally did not develop in the East because, unlike Christianity and Islam, Eastern religions did not emerge out of Judaism, so they had no reason to disparage their mother religion. Being unrelated to Judaism, they generally have a greater tolerance for other beliefs. Intolerance flared up in contemporary Japan, although it had hardly any Jewish population.

Eastern religions such as Hinduism and Buddhism essentially call on humanity to get away from the illusions of the world by withdrawing from it. In contrast, Western religions taught their faithful to enter the world and make it better for humanity. Some observers have seen in the Eastern attitude reason for the lack of social progress in these countries. The West can therefore influence the East through Western religious tradition, and lead it toward ever greater awareness of human social duties. At the same time, the East can teach the West that the frantic search for achievement, status, power, and goods of consumption is futile and brings no happiness but causes much suffering. Studying Eastern faiths can also encourage the faithful of Western religions to find deeper values in their own traditions. Contact with these religions deserves to be deepened. Buddhist teachings and practices have already attracted many Westerners, including Jews. Many feel that this will not compromise Judaism.

Initial contact was made when the Dalai Lama, exiled from his land after China invaded Tibet, called upon Jewish leaders to help him. Jewish experience, he felt, could show him ways of survival for his faith and people now in exile. He invited Jewish representatives to his residence in India. The Jews were profoundly impressed by his spirituality and humility. Since then the Dalai Llama has lectured in the West, addressing Jewish gatherings and conferring with Jewish thinkers. A bond of affection has formed between Jews and this great spiritual leader.

APPENDIX: QUOTATIONS FROM
THE FRENCH BISHOPS' STATEMENT

1. The present existence of the Jewish people, its frequently precarious condition in the course of its history, its hopes, the tragic trials which it has known in the past and primarily in modern times, its partial ingathering on the land of the Bible, constitute more and more for Christians a given situation which might facilitate for them a better comprehension of their faith and enlighten their lives.

2. Even if for Christianity the Covenant has been renewed in Jesus Christ, Judaism ought to be looked upon by Christians not only as a social and historical reality but primarily as a religious one; not as a relic of a venerable and completed past, but as a living reality through the ages.

3. The Jew merits our attention and our esteem, often our love. It is that, perhaps, that was missing most and where Christian conscience is most guilty.

4. Anti-Semitism is a heritage of the pagan world but is still reinforced in a Christian climate in pseudo-theological arguments. It is a theological, historical, and judicial error to keep the Jewish people indistinctly guilty of the passion and death of Jesus Christ. . . . If it is true that historically the responsibility for the death of Jesus was shared on various grounds by certain Jewish and Roman authorities, the Church maintains that . . . Christ . . . submitted Himself to His Passion and to his death so that all receive salvation.

5. We should present the particular vocation of this people as the "sanctification of the Name." This is one of the essential dimensions of synagogal prayer by which the Jewish people, invested by a sacerdotal mission (Exodus 19:6), offers all human activity to God and glorifies Him. This vocation makes the life and prayer of the Jewish people a benediction for all nations of the earth. It would be underestimating the precepts of Judaism to consider them only as restrictive practices. The rites are gestures which break the daily routine of existence and remind those who observe them of the sovereignty of God. Faithful Jews receive as a gift of God the Sabbath and the rites which have as their purpose to sanctify human action. Beyond their literalness, they are for the Jews light and joy on the path of life (Psalm 119). They are a manner of "building time," and to render grace for the entire creation. All of existence has to refer to God as Paul told his brethren (1 Corinthians 10:30–31).

6. If Jewish tradition considers the trials and exile of its people as a punishment for its infidelities (Jeremiah 13:17, 20:21–23), it is nonetheless true that since the letter addressed by Jeremiah to the exiles of Babylon (Jeremiah 29:1–23), the life of the Jewish people in dispersion has also had a positive sense; across the trials, the Jewish people have been called upon to "Sanctify the Name" amidst the nations of the world. . . .

Christians ought constantly to combat anti-Jewishness . . . which consists in regarding the Jewish people as accursed, under the pretext that it has been obstinately persecuted. On the contrary, according to the testimony of the Scriptures (Isaiah 53:2–4), to be subjected to persecution is often an effect and reminder of the prophetic condition.

7. It is, at present, more than ever, difficult to pronounce a serene theological judgment on the movement of return of the Jewish people to "its" land. In this context, we cannot forget as Christians the gift once made by God to the People of Israel of a land where it was called to be reunited (see Genesis 12:7, 26:3–4, 28:13; Isaiah 43:5–7; Jeremiah 16:15).

All through history Jewish existence has been constantly divided between life among the nations and the wish of national existence on this land. The aspiration poses numerous problems even to the Jewish conscience. In order to understand this aspiration and the debate which results from it in all dimensions, Christians ought not let themselves be carried away by explanation that would ignore the forms of communal and religious life of Judaism or by a political position that might be generous but nonetheless hasty. They must take into account the interpretation which Jews give to their ingathering around Jerusalem, which, in the name of their faith they consider as a benediction.

By this return and its repercussions, justice is put to a test on the political plane. There is on the political level confrontation of various exigencies of justice. Beyond the legitimate divergencies of political appeals, universal conscience cannot refuse to the Jewish people, who were submitted to vicissitudes in the course of history, the right and the means of political existence. Also, this right and possibility of existence cannot be refused to those who, following the local conflicts resulting from this return, are now victims of grave situations of injustice. So let us turn our eyes with attention toward this land visited by God and let us have the lively hope that it will be a place where can live in peace all its inhabitants, Jews and non-Jews. It is an essential question faced by Christians in the same manner as by the Jewish people, to know whether the reassembly of the dispersal of the Jewish people, which took place under the constraint of persecution and by the play of political forces, will finally be, in spite of so many dreams, one of the ways of God's justice for the Jewish people and at the same time for all the peoples of the earth. How can Christians remain indifferent to what is actually happening on this land?

8. The first condition is that all Christians have always respect for the Jew, whatever his manner of being Jewish. That they seek to understand the Jew as he understands himself, instead of judging by their own ways of thoughts. They should esteem his convictions, his aspirations, his rites, and the attachment to them. They should also admit that there can be different fashions of being a Jew or to recognize oneself as Jewish without detriment to the fundamental unity of Jewish existence.

9. The second condition is that in encounters between Christians and Jews there should be recognized the right of each to give full testimony of his

faith without being suspected of trying to detach a person in a disloyal manner from his community and to attach it to his own.

10. The reason is that the Jewish people are a people of an "Eternal Covenant" without which the new Covenant could never exist. Also, far from envisaging the disappearance of the Jewish community, the Church recognizes itself in search for a living bond with it.

11. The Jewish people are considered as having received through its particular vocation a universal mission with regard to the nations. The Church, for its part, estimates that its own mission can only be inscribed in the same universal message of salvation.

Israel and the Church are not complementary institutions. The permanence of the vis-à-vis of Israel and the Church is a sign of the incompletion of God's design. Jewish and Christian people are thus in reciprocal contestation or, as the apostle Paul said, of "jealousy" in view of unity (Romans 11:14; see also Deuteronomy 32:21).

CHAPTER 12

Tanakh

IN THE INTRODUCTION we discussed the internal forces that have shaped Judaism. Then we sketched in bare outline the basic currents of Jewish history. History and the various environments in which Jews have lived became the stage for the dramatic unfolding of Jewish ideas interacting with those of the surrounding world.

In the following chapters we shall discuss Judaism's spiritual and literary creations that emerged out of the genius of the people and its heritage—above all, Torah, both written and oral. This will enable us to understand the creative tensions and the blending of internal ideas and external forces, as well as the emerging new forms and theological concepts held by all or some of the Jews in the contemporary world.

Although the Jews have made many contributions, they are best known for having given to the world the Holy Scriptures of the Bible. Christians call them the Old Testament; Jews, who do not use the New Testament, simply call it the Holy Scriptures or look at it as the Bible. In ecumenical dialogue discerning Christians have come to refer to them as the Hebrew Scriptures. The Hebrew word for this work is *Tanakh,* an abbreviation of the three words—*Torah, Nevee-im, Ketuvim*—which make up the three sections of the Holy Scriptures. *Torah,* in this specific connotation, stands for the Five Books of Moses, the Pentateuch. *Nevee-im* (Prophets) contains the messages of the great prophets of Israel, but also the history leading up to and surrounding their ministry. *Ketuvim* (Collected Writings) is an anthology of a variety of works, including Psalms, Job, Proverbs, and the "Five Scrolls" of Song of Songs, Ruth, Lamentations, Ecclesiastes, and Esther.

This chapter will show how the Tanakh became the source of Jewish theology and orientation. By revealing to Jews the divine origin of the universe and humanity, it led them to the duties that emerge from these facts. Tanakh discloses to the Jews the meaning of Jewish existence, it makes the Covenant manifest, and keeps alive within them the spirit of *emunah*, "trust in God." It is the source of wisdom and the ladder of ascent in prayer.

For this reason, Tanakh has become the Jew's companion and is read to the congregation in worship. We have included in this chapter the selections appointed for special occasions of the liturgical year and the reasons that prompted their choice. We have also included some commentaries, both ancient and modern, and interpretations given by Jews to demonstrate how the Tanakh revealed ever-new meanings to the searching mind. We have consciously omitted the results of biblical criticism in this context, as they have not affected Jewish thought throughout the ages.

TORAH

The Torah, or The Five Books of Moses, is the basic source of Jewish law and ethics. It is the guidepost for thought and conduct and for the relationships between God and humanity and among people. Hence it is read to the people regularly during the cycle of the year, on Sabbath days, holy days, and every Monday and Thursday (these were once market days when farmers came to town and could receive instruction in conjunction with their business). It is recited from a handwritten parchment scroll, which is stored in the Holy Ark and removed for the recital of its message. The congregation stands in reverence as it is carried to the reading desk.

Genesis

Bereshit (Genesis) is the first book of Torah, dealing with creation and the lives of the patriarchs and matriarchs. Bereshit is the Prelude. Here the destiny of the people as people of the Covenant is anticipated and founded. The story of creation emphasizes the divine origin of the universe, and humanity's stewardship in it.

The first few chapters establish the principle of human equality: All humanity descended from Adam (literally "earth creature") who was created in God's image as male and female (Genesis 1:27). All human beings are therefore in God's image, equal before God, and must treat each other as such. All human relations must be fashioned in this spirit.

The first commandment is given: Adam and Eve are not to eat from the tree of knowledge. They do so and are sent out from the shelter of the paradise. Thus are the significance of law and commandment as tools for moral decision clearly demonstrated. Adam and Eve had two sons, Cain and Abel. Immediately, the human condition at its worst is laid open. In the desire to serve God, both offer a gift: Cain offers from his fruit, Abel offers from his sheep. When Abel's offering is received and Cain's is rejected, Cain cannot suppress his envy at his brother's success. He seeks revenge. God warns him: "Sin crouches at the door, its urge is

Torah Scroll, open to Leviticus 19 which includes the commandment "You shall love your neighbor as yourself." (Photo is of author's Torah scroll and was taken by the author.)

toward you, but you must master it" (Genesis 4:7). Cain is so enraged that he cannot master his envy and kills his brother. Human history is the human struggle to master the urges of selfishness and hate. History begins with brother murdering brother, but it also reveals the power of repentance. After the deed has been done Cain confesses to God, "my sin is too great for me to bear" (Genesis 4:13), and the divine punishment is mitigated.

In subsequent generations only Noah recognizes this obligation to moral living under God's law. He is therefore rescued when the Great Flood destroys a wicked and unrepentant society. As he emerges from the Ark after the flood, God makes a Covenant with him, the sign of which is the rainbow. Noah, as an individual, has been found worthy of the covenant on account of his obedience, God includes all of Noah's descendants—namely, all of humanity—in the covenant (Genesis 9:9). Thus, individualism and universalism are joined in Jewish thought.

The Patriarchs as Role Models. Noah's descendants are gripped by the drive for power. They build the "Tower of Babel" that is to reach heaven and will permit them to dethrone God. In punishment they are dispersed over the earth and their single language, that has fused them together, is converted into many. But God will not destroy humanity again. Instead He provides it with role models. The patriarchs appear on the scene.

The first patriarch is Abraham. His homeland is in "Ur of the Chaldeans," a country with a highly developed civilization. But its people adore national and family idols. Abraham alone turns to the one God. He is commanded to leave his native land and migrate to a land God will show him. He obeys and becomes a sojourner in Canaan. He loses the rights and privileges of citizenship and has to subject himself immediately and exclusively to God's kingship. Only in Melchizedek, ruler of Salem (*Shalem* in Hebrew) does he find a personality of equal commitment. Melchizedek, as the name indicates, is a "Righteous King," even a priest of God, the Supreme Ruler. Abraham receives Melchizedek's blessing. Even in Abraham's time Salem is the center of devine worship and blessing goes forth from it. *Shalem*, in popular etymology, came to mean the city of Shalom, "peace" (Genesis 14:18–20), from which comes *Jerusalem* (*Jerushalaim* in Hebrew).

God makes a Covenant with Abraham: "*I have given* this land to your offspring" (Genesis 15:18); the fact *is accomplished*, the Land belongs to Abraham's offspring. But Abraham is also told that his descendants will have to endure centuries of persecution, slavery, and marytrdom before the Promised Land will be theirs. Their survival will depend entirely on their trust in God and God's promise. In return, circumcision is the seal his descendants affix to themselves—*B'rit Milah*, the Covenant of Circumcision (Genesis 17); it cannot be eradicated.

Then Abraham is tested. He is to sacrifice his son Isaac. The sacrifice does not take place because after Isaac is bound by his father, God stays the knife in Abraham's hand; Abraham passes the test. In Jewish tradition, the *akeda*, "binding," became symbolic of Israel's fate, for in every generation Jews have been willing to give their lives and their children's in expression of their love of God.

A second element of the story is equally remembered. Abraham, like his contemporaries, believed that God actually called for human sacrifices. In rejecting the sacrifice, God taught him that He demands the response of the living, respect for life, and love; He does not call for death. A new level in humanity's God-awareness had been reached. Hence the congregation pleads "that God who desires life, may grant life." Many have died at the hands of those who showed no such reverence; let the test be over.

Abraham is the role model of heroism and initiative born of trust in God. The guiding principle of his life is response to God, *hineni*, "here I am" (Genesis 22:1, 11). He leaves his homeland for an unknown destination. On his travel he already makes converts to his God, takes them with him, and attaches them to his clan (Genesis 12:5). He takes up arms to liberate his kinsman Lot, captured by enemies (Genesis 14:1–16). He has the courage to circumcize himself as an old man (Genesis 17:24–25). He offers generous hospitality to dusty wayfarers who appear at his door and whom he does not know (Genesis 18:1–8). He argues even with God in behalf of the city of Sodom, destined to be destroyed by God for its wickedness. A just God must spare it if there be but ten righteous persons in it (Genesis 18:22–32). He raises the knife over his son Isaac, willing to sacrifice him on God's behest (Genesis 22:1–19).

Isaac became a symbol of the Jew who is willing to suffer that the tradition of his people be carried from generation to generation. He is the meditator (Genesis 24:63) the passive sufferer. Even his wife Rebecca is chosen for him by his father. (Genesis 24:1–9 ff.). In old age he loses his eyesight (27:1). Deceived into giving his blessing to Jacob rather than to Esau, the elder son he loves, he acquiesces

Ark open, Temple Emanu-El, San Francisco. Each of the three Torah scrolls has a crown, breastplate, and pointer. On the mantle are the letters "KT," for Keter Torah, the Torah is a crown. On the breastplates are the windows for insertion of the plaque indicating the occasion for which the scroll is rolled. The mantle on the center scroll is white in preparation for the High Holy Days. Its embroidered inscription states: "It [Torah] is a tree of life to them that hold on to it" (Proverbs 3:13). (Photo by the author, reproduced courtesy of Congregation Emanu-El and Rabbi Joseph Asher.)

(Genesis 27:33; 28:1–4) into what he has done. He has realized upon consideration that Esau was unworthy and Jacob was worthy. He feels that his service lies in acceptance of the divine burden laid on him. As a young man he had willingly permitted himself to be bound on the altar to be the sacrifice. The experience had shaped his life and guided the Jews ever since. The story of the binding (Genesis 22: 1–19) is read on Rosh Hashanah, the Jewish New Year's Day. It calls the people to pledge their fullest measure of submission to God, as Isaac did. Many penitential prayers have been written elaborating on the subject and the submission by Jews during the centuries. They are called *Akeda*, the binding, and

Torah Ornaments. Torah crowns (rimmonim) (Padua, nineteenth century), breastplate, and pointer (silver). Note the small window on the breastplate with the plaque showing the occasion for which the scroll has been set. (Photo by Kathie Minami, reproduced courtesy of Judah L. Magnes Memorial Museum, Jewish Museum of the West, Berkeley, California.)

during the penitential days the plea is repeated: "Remember the Covenant with Abraham and the binding of Isaac, and bring back the remnant of the children of Jacob, and deliver us for Your Name's sake."

Jacob is a role model for the typical human being. In his character the elements of nobility and vulgarity are mixed. He buys the dignity and responsibility of being the firstborn from his elder twin Esau for a pot of stew. He cheats his brother out of the father's blessing by guile. He does so upon the request of his mother. He is faced with a basic dilemma. If he listens to his mother, he will deceive his father, but in order to obey his mother he has to deceive his father. He obeys his mother. Threatened by his brother with assassination he flees, leaving everything behind. On his flight he has a dream, he sees a ladder reaching from the ground to heaven. From there God gives him assurance. The dream reveals Jacob's character. He is firmly planted on the ground, but his head is in heaven. He never forgets it in the severe trials of his life. He remains a realist without ever losing sight of his ideals and of God, who sustains him.

He falls in love with Rachel, his uncle Laban's daughter, and pledges to serve her father for seven years to gain her hand. During the wedding night he finds out that he has been deceived and given her sister Leah instead. He is ready to serve another seven years for his beloved. When the time is over he works for his father-in-law for a share of the flock. Again he faces deception, but increases the share of the flock to go to him by superior breeding methods. Returning home with his family he decides to make peace with Esau by sending him lavish presents. Esau is going to meet him, accompanied by a large, armed guard.

Jacob is afraid of being wiped out. He divides his family into two camps, that at least a part of it may escape. In the night before the meeting he has a wrestling match with an unknown dark stranger, a divine force. He will not let him go before he has beaten him and received his blessing. The stranger changes Jacob's name to Israel, "for you have striven [*sarita*] with forces divine and human and have prevailed." (*Sarita*, "you have striven," constitutes the first part of the name, and *El*, God the second.) But then the stranger wrenches Jacob's hip and henceforth he limps (Genesis 32:23–33). The new name is subsequently confirmed by God (Genesis 35:9)

Jacob's struggle characterizes all his descendants. They fought with the forces in themselves and those of the surrounding world, would not admit defeat, and always emerged scathed. The meeting with Esau is peaceful. Jacob continues homeward. At a resting place his daughter Dinah is seduced by a son of a local chieftain, who is prepared to marry her. Jacob's sons Simeon and Levi take brutal revenge on the whole tribe, and Jacob now has to fear the vengeance of his neighbors. Then his beloved Rachel dies giving birth to her second son, Benjamin. At home Jacob spoils Rachel's elder son, Joseph, inciting the jealousy of his brothers. When they have the opportunity they sell Joseph as a slave and give their father the impression that a wild beast has torn him. The old man is inconsolable. Only after many years will he meet his son again, in Egypt. There Jacob settles and dies. He adjures his sons to return his body to the sacred burying place of his fathers in the Holy Land. Jacob is *the* Jew, tried and tested, victorious and wounded, idealistic and weak.

Knowing that Canaan is the place where his seed was to grow into an organic society, Abraham and his successors actually spent large portions of their lives abroad. The Land can exert its influence even as an idea, once its spiritual significance is recognized. Abraham does however buy a burial place, the cave of Makhpelah at Hebron. He wishes to be physically present to his posterity. Isaac is buried there. His son Jacob and Jacob's son Joseph, dying abroad, are aware of the symbolism of their own lives for their descendants, and request to be buried "with their fathers." These men are individualists; they had to be in order to stand their ground against the society in which they dwelled. They hear God's call, and, in individual response, act upon it. However, with individualism inevitably goes human error, and these people show themselves all too human on many occasions.

The greatness of the patriarchs rests in the fact that they had *emunah*, trust in God, though they had no tangible evidence that He would keep His promise. "He trusted in God, and He accorded it to him as merit" (Genesis 15:6). Said of Abraham, it also applies to Isaac and Jacob. In this manner "the deeds of the fathers became the guideposts for the children," the Talmud points out.

The story of Joseph, dramatically told, explains the transition of Jacob's clan from Canaan to Egypt. It equally tells us of sibling rivalry, but above all, in the person of Joseph, unfolds the growth of a human being through adversity, from being a spoilt youngster to becoming the sustainer of the Egyptian people in times of famine, a man of maturity, compassion and forgiveness—all under the guidance of his faith in God.

Equally great were the "mothers," Sarah, Abraham's wife who shared her husband's *emunah* and established herself as the undisputed authority in the home. She saw Ishmael, Abraham's son through his concubine Hagar, to be unworthy "to share in the inheritance with my son Isaac" (Genesis 21:10). God confirms her decision. To a deeply distressed Abraham God gives the assurance that Ishmael will be made into a great nation. But Sarah must be obeyed. "Whatever Sarah tells you, you must do as she says" (Genesis 21:9–13). Rebecca, Isaac's wife, had more vision than her husband and, using deceit, saw to it that Jacob, her deserving son, received the father's blessing, against the wild Esau. Rachel, Jacob's wife, who died as the family returned from exile, is revered as intercessor for all Jews in exile and distress (see Jeremiah 31:14–15). Leah, given to Jacob in marriage by her deceitful father, bore most of his children. Paying attention to the advice and guidance these men received from these women we find that their influence made their husbands great.

Exodus

The second book of Torah, *Shemot* (Exodus), presents the transformation of the small clan of Jacob into the collective experience of an emerging people. They are molded within a hostile environment in Egypt, where they have been made slaves; they are tested in their perseverance. They are to be a collective individual, composed of individualists. They are shown the differences between God-centered individualism, which leads to salvation, and human-centered, selfish individualism, which leads to destruction. Moses and Pharaoh are the two great protagonists: Moses speaks in the name of God; Pharaoh, an absolutist, considers himself divine. Pharaoh is defeated, and the people are redeemed to find their way back to the Land of Promise. They cross the Red Sea, which God miraculously parts, and sing a hymn of praise to God. Miriam, Moses' sister, recognized as a prophetess, leads the women in song (Exodus 15:20–21).

No people can live without law, and as a God-centered people, they receive a God-given law. The Ten Commandments form the core of this law, encompassing the relationship of humanity to both God and fellow human beings.

1. I the LORD am your God who brought you out of the land of Egypt, the house of bondage. [God is to be worshiped as God of history and time, creative, dynamic. Therefore . . .]

2. You shall have no other gods beside Me. You shall not make for yourself a sculptured image, or any likeness of what is in the heavens above, or on the earth below, or in the waters under the earth. You shall not bow down to them or serve them. For I the LORD your God am an impassioned God, visiting the guilt of the fathers upon the children, upon the third and upon the fourth generations of those who reject Me, but showing kindness to the thousandth generation of those who love Me and keep My commandments. [Recognition of other gods denies divine omnipotence; graven images render God as static. The image is also stationary, a representation of gods linked to a locale, to space; but God is everywhere, He goes with Israel.]

3. You shall not take in vain the name of the LORD your God; for the LORD will not clear one who takes His name in vain. [This person denies His all-knowingness and desecrates His majesty.]

4. Remember the Sabbath day and keep it holy. Six days you shall labor and do all your work, but the seventh day is a Sabbath of the LORD your God: you shall not do any work—you, your son or daughter, your male or female slave, or your cattle, or the stranger who is within your settlements. For in six days the LORD made heaven and earth and sea, and all that is in them, and He rested on the seventh day; therefore the LORD blessed the Sabbath day and hallowed it. [God's creatorship is thus affirmed; He owns the universe and may enjoin people from work on it. The equality of humanity is also established; no one under another's influence may be compelled to work; all are entitled to rest from toil.]

5. Honor your father and your mother, that you may long endure on the land which the LORD your God is giving you. [Having brought you into the world, they are next to God.]

As we turn to the second half of these commandments, we note that they apply to human relations in terms parallel to those of the first five relating humanity to God.

6. You shall not murder. [Even as God is unique and His living presence inviolate, so is every human person unique, and his life is inviolate and holy.]

7. You shall not commit adultery. [As God may not be compromised by worship of other gods, even so is the creative unity of humans holy and may not be diluted.]

8. You shall not steal. [It would mean considering other people's possessions to be expendable; the name attached to their possessions may not be taken away in vain, even as the name of God, owner of the world, may not be taken in vain.]

9. You shall not bear false witness against your neighbor. [As Sabbath rest makes you a true witness of God's omnipotence as creator, so must evidence against fellow human beings be true.]

10. You shall not covet your neighbor's house: you shall not covet your neighbor's wife, or his male or female slave, or his ox or his ass, or anything that is your neighbor's. [Both the fifth and tenth commandments go beyond visible actions and appeal to thought, intent, and ethical principles. Honoring parents may express itself in outward forms, but ultimately it is a matter of the soul's commitment. The prohibition of envy appeals equally to thoughts.]

The Ten Commandments are found twice in the Pentateuch, in Exodus 20:1–14 and in Deuteronomy 5:6–18. The versions differ slightly, but those differences are significant, especially in regard to the Sabbath commandment. In Exodus, the reason given for the observance of the Sabbath is religious: "for in six days the Lord made heaven and earth and sea and all that is in them." In Deuteronomy, the reason given is social: "so that your male and female servant may rest as you do. Remember that you were a slave in Egypt and the Lord your God freed you from there." Religious observance that does not grow into social justice is without meaning; social action that is not based on the religious concept of human dignity under God will easily go astray.

In connection with the revelation of the Ten Commandments, a Covenant is made with the people: "Now then, if you obey Me faithfully and keep My covenant, you shall be My treasured possession among all the peoples. Indeed all the earth is Mine, but you shall be to Me a kingdom of priests and a holy people" (Exodus 19:5–6). It is worth noting that this Covenant was not made in connection with a special dispensation of grace or of obligations, but in conjunction with commandments that were universal. Israel's position then was established as the priestly servant of all humanity, all of which is God's possession. The rabbis actually told the legend that God offered the Ten Commandments to the peoples of the world first, entrusting them into the care of Israel only after all the others had rejected them for reasons of expediency. The revelation took place in no-man's land (Mount Sinai), the rabbis explain, to show that it belongs to all and is not connected with any country or nation. Jews have thus seen themselves as missionaries, not of their religion, but of the Ten Commandments.

The Ten Commandments are incised by God on two tablets of stone and handed to Moses. In practically every synagogue two stylized tablets grace the holy Ark where the Torah scrolls are kept. They remind the people of their duties.

Archaeology has not verified the event at Sinai, and biblical scholarship has shown that the religion of Israel took centuries to mature. Yet Sinai was a great religious experience. To the Jews, Sinai has been the moment when the people and their faith were fashioned as one. They therefore are one. To Jews, Sinai has always been a living experience. It has been true. Encompassing God and humanity, action and thought, law and ethical motivations, the Ten Commandments are the core of Torah.

Exodus gets into case law, leading up to ethical conduct: You must assist your enemy, you may not discriminate against the stranger. As eternal reminders of your relationship to God and your fellows, you shall observe specific festivals throughout the year.

Individualism, doubt, and uncertainty led the people astray. Moses, their visible representative of God has tarried on the mountain. Will he ever return? As a visible sign of God in their midst they make themselves a golden calf, and thus turn their backs on God. Yet God forgives and, in forgiving, reveals to Moses the attributes of His Being: "The Lord! the Lord!, a God compassionate and gracious, slow to anger, rich in steadfast kindness, extending kindness to the thousandth generation, forgiving iniquity, transgression and sin; *yet* He does *not* remit all punishment" (Exodus 34:6–8).

Seeing in these attributes guidelines for human conduct in imitation of God, the rabbis omitted the italicized word in liturgical use. God does remit punishment. Moses is bidden to make a sanctuary, a visible sign that God dwells within the people. Centered around the sanctuary, the people's life has meaning.

Leviticus

Vayikra (Leviticus), the third book of Torah, sets up the sacrificial service entrusted to the priests, the descendants of Aaron. They are to be assisted by the Levites, who are given secondary functions. The ceremonies at the consecration of both the sanctuary and the priests are described, including a terrible tragedy: Nadav and Avihu, Aaron's older sons, present an offering that is not prescribed and are devoured by fire from God. Having been elevated, they may have seen in their office as a stepping stone to power and a means to unbridled individualism. It destroyed them. Priests and people must learn that their distinction lies only in serving and obedience. Dietary laws are also handed to the people, who partake of the "royal table," and the priests are specially entrusted with the service of healing and of isolating communicable diseases and their bearers. Sexual purity is enjoined.

Then Leviticus turns to a second command: You shall become holy. How can they become holy? By careful attendance to universal commands, by attuning their hearts as well as their actions to the will of God:

> You shall revere each his mother and his father, and keep My Sabbaths. . . . Do not turn to idols. . . . When you reap the harvest of your land, you shall not reap all the way to the edges of the field . . . you shall leave them for the poor and the stranger. . . . You shall not steal; you shall not deal deceitfully or falsely with one another. You shall not swear falsely. . . . You shall not coerce your neighbor. You shall not commit robbery. The wages of the laborer [being due him at night] shall not remain with you until morning. You shall not insult the deaf, or place a stumbling block before the blind. . . . You shall not render unfair decision: do not favor the poor or show deference to the rich; judge your neighbor fairly. Do not stand by when your neighbor bleeds. You shall not hate your kinsman in your heart. Reprove your neighbor that you incur no guilt because of him. You shall not take vengeance or bear a grudge against your

kinsfolk. You shall love your neighbor as yourself: I am the Lord. (Leviticus 19:1–17)

You shall rise before the aged and show deference to the old. . . . When a stranger resides with you in your land, you shall not wrong him. The stranger who resides with you shall be to you as one of your citizens; you shall love him as yourself, for you were strangers in the land of Egypt: I am the Lord. You shall not falsify measures of length, weight or capacity. You shall have an honest balance, honest weights. (Leviticus 19:31–36)

The neighbor may never be aware of any deceitful acts; he may be "deaf," "dumb," or "blind" to them, but God knows. Hate, grudges, the search for vengeance must yield to concerned guidance. "You shall love your neighbor as yourself " is augmented by "You shall love the stranger as yourself." This observance of God's unchanging, universal law makes human beings holy. Through absolute honesty in weight and measure and in compassionate concern for the equal treatment of the stranger, the spirit of holiness is universally revealed and individually implemented.

Holy days are again explained. Finally, the law of the jubilee year is proclaimed. At the beginning of this year all agricultural property was returned to its original owner, and all the bondsmen went free. In purchasing crop land during the fifty-year period, the purchaser paid in accordance with the years left in the cycle. If he bought in the fifteenth year, for instance, he paid for the thirty-five remaining years (Leviticus 25:8–17). While keyed to an agricultural society, the regulation holds a basic principle for all societies: It strikes a balance between free enterprise and social planning. The wealthy may acquire the Land of a needy seller and utilize it for their own gain and profit, but only for a limited period. Eventually, the Land returns to its original owner, the bondsman is free. Exploitation on a permanent basis is curbed.

The clarion call for freedom, connected with the proclamation of the year of the jubilee, came to be inscribed on America's Liberty Bell: "Proclaim liberty throughout the land unto all the inhabitants thereof" (Leviticus 25:10). "For the children of Israel are servants to Me, they are My servants whom I freed out of the land of Egypt, I am the Lord their God" (Leviticus 25:55). As the rabbis explain, "My servants and not servants to other servants" (B. Kiddushin 22b).

The people are finally warned: obedience to these laws and principles spells prosperity, and disobedience leads to punishment and disaster. But even though they may be dispersed to the lands of enemies, it will not be forever. The Covenant endures.

I will remember My Covenant with Jacob, and My Covenant with Isaac and My Covenant with Abraham will I remember; and I will remember the Land. . . . And even then, when they are in the land of their enemies, I will not reject them nor spurn them to destroy them, breaking My Covenant with them, for I, the Lord, am their God. I will remember in their behalf the Covenant with their ancestors, whom I freed from the land of Egypt in the sight of the nations, that I should be their God; I the Lord. (Leviticus 26:42, 44, 45)

Numbers

The fourth book, *Bamidbar* (Numbers), starts with the assumption that the people are now ready for their march into the Promised Land. The multitudes are numbered; the marching orders are given. The solemn blessing which the priests are to pronounce in God's name is exactly formulated. They may not bless on their own terms or "adjust" their blessings to their individual preferences, but must invoke God's name upon the people; God—and not the priest—blesses them. This blessing has become universal:

> The Lord bless you and keep you;
> The Lord make His face to shine upon you and be gracious unto you;
> The Lord lift up His face upon you and give you peace. (Numbers 6:24–27)

The princes of the twelve tribes are now permitted to present their gifts to the sanctuary. They must all be identical so that there may be no envy and distinction, and, as a symbol of their equality and the equality of the tribes they represent, all the gifts are recorded in detail, though they are all alike.

Spies are sent out to scout the Land. One man is chosen from each tribe, twelve in all. They are men of distinction but small faith. Ten are convinced that even God cannot sufficiently sustain the people in battle against the fortified cities of the mighty enemy. In endorsing their views, the people prove that theirs is still the spirit of fainthearted slaves; they are not yet ready to enter the Land. A whole generation must remain in the desert (a total of forty years) until all the fainthearted have died. A new generation, under the leadership of the two men of faith, one of whom was Joshua, will enter the Land.

The people become restive under their enforced leisure and homelessness. Rebellion breaks out against Moses. Korah, a member of the tribe of Levi like Moses, joined by friends accuses Moses of self-centered love of power. Moses had to be vindicated or else his whole ministry as God's servant will remain misunderstood by the people. The earth opens up and swallows the mutineers.

Slowly the years pass. The people begin to move again. The conquest begins. Then, Balak, King of Moab, fearing them, devises a plan. He invites Balaam, a heathen prophet, to curse the people and destroy them. Yet Balaam's curse turns to a blessing in his mouth as he looks down from the mountain heights upon the people in the valley. He cannot curse what God has blessed, and the people, by the purity of their lives, have deserved God's blessing. Thus did the Jews learn that God is indeed a mighty fortress, and obedience to Him is a bulwark against the forces of destruction from without.

They saw it even more clearly after they had fallen for another ruse. They had yielded to heathen orgies, weakening themselves in sexual license by joining the rites of those whom they had beaten. Their inner decay led many to defeat and death and weakened the very fabric of the nation. It was Phineas who redeemed them by his passion for God. There was no leadership; thus, in true individualism, he went ahead and stabbed the licentious couple who had set the pattern. A covenant is made with him and his descendants: "Behold I give to him my covenant of peace . . . the covenant of priesthood" (Numbers 26:12–13).

The rabbis dwell on the greatness and inspiration granted to Balaam, a seer and diviner; it approached that of Moses himself. But Balaam misused his power, being a man of hate. God's spirit and the gift of prophecy was not granted to Israel alone, the rabbis point out; it was given equally to all nations and all faiths, in order that all humanity might find its way to God, follow His commandments, and be a blessing (Bamidbar Rabba 14).

In preparation for entry into the Land, the festive offerings are once more explained. All seems to be ready; Moses views the Land from a distance and apportions it. A census of the new generation is taken. Aaron and Miriam have already been called to their rest, and Moses knows he, too, must soon die and leave his people. On God's behest, he ordains Joshua as his successor. A new era is about to begin.

Deuteronomy

Devarim (Deuteronomy), the fifth book, has been judged by biblical criticism to be of later date, but Jewish tradition has seen it as Moses' great farewell speech to his people. He relates to them their whole past, not glossing over his own shortcomings. He impresses upon them that they must not let the past fade from their minds and must never make graven images or worship idols. Once more he reviews the Ten Commandments for them.

His great affirmation, which has remained central in Jewish life and worship, is significant in every word:

Hear, O Israel! The LORD our God, the LORD is One. Love the LORD your God with all your heart and with all your soul and with all your might. Take to heart these words with which I charge you this day. Impress them upon your children. Recite them when you stay at home and when you are away, when you lie down and when you get up. Bind them as a sign on your hand and let them serve as frontlets between your eyes; inscribe them on the doorposts of your house and on your gates. (Deuteronomy 6:4–9)

This divine plea for love calls for an emotional response (all your heart), a total commitment even of life (all your soul), and a consecration of every act and human possession (all your might). Thus in every performance of Mitzvah, there must be found not merely the action in itself but the attunement of the heart. "God the All-merciful wants the heart," is the conclusion the rabbis draw (see also pp. 323–326). Love cannot be commanded; it can only be a plea of one who, in turn, is full of responding love. It is made clear to the people that God loves them dearly and tenderly and unconditionally. This love did not result from their strength and numbers, but is truly God's freely extended gift. Out of this love, we can understand God's "jealousy." He does not want His love to be diluted. Out of this love, we understand the blessing He will give the people, if they will but respond; the penalties He imposes in an effort to lead them back if they have gone astray; and His readiness to pardon graciously and fully when they return. In this love is enshrined the variety of forces which have fashioned Israel (Deuteronomy 11:13–21).

God–Torah–Mitzvot–Land form an indivisible unit, safeguarding survival. As the text shifts from a general appeal to the people as a whole to a direct plea to each individual, the collective future of the people becomes the responsibility of every single person. Yet they assure themselves of their own survival only as they remain linked in duty, obligation, and kinship to the whole.

As children of God, the people are warned against self-mutilation. Once more they are told to abide by dietary laws. The human body is God's most perfect work of art and must not be defaced. It is the vessel of the divine spirit and has to be sustained in purity. As part of serving Him, they are to tithe themselves, not just their possessions. Also they must remit debts owed to them every seven years to allow debtors to make a new start in life on equal footing with others.

The festivals are again reviewed, and the organization of government and proceedings in court are outlined, followed by a most significant statement: In all disputes, the people shall be guided by decisions of their magistrates, duly appointed at any given time (Deuteronomy 17:8ff.). The rabbis saw in this injunction the basic justification for the evolution of Torah. Bound by conscience and tradition, ordained leaders had the right and duty to adjust Torah to the conditions of the times. Torah could not become ossified; by being keyed to life, it kept the people alive.

The king, if there was one, was to read the Torah throughout his life, that he might not rule by his own whim or regard his position as a tool for autocratic government. Later follows the command that the king read the Torah to all the people once every seven years, so that they would know what the law is and that the ruler would not deviate from it. Arbitrariness and self-centered individualism were thereby excluded.

Laws of war are enunciated. No action may be taken without a preceding offer of peaceful settlement (Deuteronomy 20:10). Emphasis, however, is placed on laws of peace and relationships among the people. The concern is shown in such details as, "When you build a new house, you shall make a parapet for your roof, so that you do not bring bloodguilt on your house if anyone should fall from it" (Deuteronomy 22:8), and, "You shall not turn over to his master a slave who seeks refuge with you from his master" (Deuteronomy 23:16). The latter was a source of controversy between North and South in pre-Civil War America because United States marshals were authorized to catch fugitive slaves in the anti-slavery North and return them to their masters in the South. Torah forbade such action.

Moses is emphatic as he says to his people, "You stand this day before the LORD, your God . . . your children, your wives, even the stranger . . . to enter into the Covenant of the LORD to lead you into the land. . . . Not with you alone do I make this Covenant but with those who are standing here with us today before the LORD our God and with those who are not with us" (Deuteronomy 29:9–14). The Covenant was to safeguard them and the Land. And as the rabbis explain, "those not with us" are the coming generations, not yet here, but included in the Covenant, in the people.

Before departing from his people, Moses blesses them. Like Jacob before him, he has an individual benediction for each of the tribes based on his deep knowledge of their abilities, shortcomings, and potential. Each of them is given a specific task. Each is to make a specific contribution to the whole.

Then Moses goes up on Mount Nebo to glimpse the Promised Land which he will not enter, and is called to his rest. God Himself buries him so that no one will know where his grave is located; Israel is not to make saints of anyone, even Moses. The living spirit is the monument.

The rabbis find an additional message in this final story. Torah begins with charity, as God Himself fashioned clothes to cover Adam and Eve's nakedness, and it ends with charity, as He buries His servant Moses. All of Torah is thus wrapped in the spirit of divine charity. In seeking God through Torah, humanity must imitate Him.

NEVEE-IM

Nevee-im (Prophets), the second section of the Tenakh, is divided into two basic parts: *Former Prophets* and *Later Prophets. Former Prophets* includes the Books of Joshua, Judges, 1 and 2 Samuel, and 1 and 2 Kings. They relate the historical events in the life of Israel. The prophets stand out providing leadership, serving as magistrates, and offering counsel, admonition,reprimand, and hope to the people and their leaders. We learn of their actions and hear their words as spoken at specific occasions. The literary ability of these prophets is not revealed. (The exception is Deborah, see Judges 5.) *Later Prophets* consists to a large degree of the preserved records of the messages presented to the people. These men were literary geniuses, often poetic artists. Their messages transcend their time.

Only portions of these writings are regularly used in the worship of the synagogue. On holy days and special occasions, a portion of Prophets is read after the reading of Torah. It is called *Haftarah,* and its subject matter is chosen either in relation to the Torah portion or to convey the special significance of the day. For instance, on the Sabbath day when the story of the death of Jacob is recited from the Torah scroll, the Haftarah deals with the death of David. On the Day of Atonement, the meaning of the fast is explained in the words of Isaiah 58. Social action is the message of the fast: "to loose the fetters of wickedness, to undo the bands of the yoke. . . ."

Former Prophets

This part of the Tanakh contains the historical books, whose events we have discussed. They cover the period from the people's arrival in the Land of Canaan through the destiny of the two kingdoms. The struggle the people must engage in is twofold: with the nations they have to conquer and enemies they have to repel, *and* with themselves. We are told that they arrive before the walls of a still mighty Jericho and make them fall without raising a hand in battle. They simply process around the mighty fortress (preceded by the Ark which contains the Ten Commandment tablets), invoke the name of God, sound the shofar, and then watch the fortress walls tumble. The conquest is so related that it might be a symbol to them: when the people march behind the Torah and sound to Him as their King, they prevail. Soon the symbolic message fails. The unity of the people breaks down under the strain of self-centered antagonism, and their spirit erodes as they yield to the culture of their neighbors and adopt their idolatrous and licentious practices.

Martin Buber sees in the events during the times of the Judges and in the conflict between prophets and kings one basic issue. To him, it is a struggle between the people's concept of their destiny and God's design for their existence. Buber explains that, under the Covenant of Sinai, God desired to be the people's only King. To transmit His demands, God might appoint messengers and leaders who would disappear from the scene when their mission had been accomplished, but He was opposed to any monarchy under which one man would acquire personal power, hold on to it in his own right, and bequeath it to his descendants. God made it quite clear: "You shall be unto Me a kingdom" (Exodus 19:6), or, in Moses' words, "He was King in Jeshurun" (Deuteronomy 33:5).

The unity of the people rested in God. But in the days of the Judges, the people's unity under God's rule dissolved. Internal conflicts arose and enemies from without overpowered the people. Instead of returning to God the people believed that a monarch and royal dynasty would give them unity and strength. They clamored for a king (see Buber, *Kingship of God*, pp. 121ff., 136ff.). Samuel, their prophet and leader, grieved that the people had rejected him as God's appointed, but God enlightened him, saying, "They have not rejected you, but have rejected Me, that I should not be King over them" (1 Samuel 8:7).

In the end, Saul, Israel's first king, initially overcame the people's oppressors. But as he came to regard himself as absolute and ceased to see his function as only the executor of the divine will, he forfeited his claim to rulership. He and the people suffered complete defeat.

In David, the struggle of a man with himself parallels that of a king against his enemies. David overcame his external enemies, expanded his realm, and made Jerusalem capital of the nation and seat of the national sanctuary, all as a result of his inner regeneration. During his lifetime he committed grievous sins, but he always found the strength to admit them and repent sincerely. In distress as in triumph, he acknowledged God in song. David became Israel's ideal king.

Solomon is described in Scripture as the "wisest of men." Wisdom, *Sophia*, came to be seen as a divine power. To the writers of the Tanakh, "wisdom" meant Torah. By their obedience to Torah, the message of written text and prophetic utterance, kings are judged. After Solomon's rule, decay sets in once more, resulting in political and spiritual division of the kingdom and in weakness, defeat, and destruction. The people fail to see that the Land is to be a laboratory of the spirit; feeling settled is to be a challenge. Their failure means not that they are worse than other nations, but that they are no better. They desire to be simply a nation when they are supposed to live as a holy nation.

Attention also must be given to the few women mentioned in Scripture. They stand out by their ability and their spirituality. Among them was Deborah, who was judge of Israel, victorious general in battle, and a poetess who praised God in song. She saw her greatest distinction in being a "mother in Israel" (Judges 5:7), guiding her people with loving wisdom as a mother guides her children. She gave the Land forty years of tranquillity.

Hannah is a childless woman. (Having children was the only fulfillment for ancient women [see Genesis 30:1–13]. Hannah was taunted by her husband's other wife for being childless [1 Samuel 1:1–8]). On pilgrimage to the national sanctuary at Shiloh, she silently pours her heart out to God. Eli the priest believes she is drunk because he sees her lips moving but no words spoken. Hannah has to teach him that her silent prayer, coming from the heart, reaches God as surely as noisy appeals. Her prayer is granted, Samuel is born. The text says she "lends" him to God, and gives thanks in hymnic praise (1 Samuel 1:1–2:11). In contrast to Abraham, who believed he had to sacrifice his son, and in contrast to Jephthah, a judge and victorious general who felt he had to sacrifice his daughter to redeem an oath (Judges 11), Hannah dedicates her son to the service of God. Samuel would become the people's leader and guide.

The Character of the Former Prophets

This period is distinguished by the emergence of the prophets. They, not the kings, are God's messengers, and they have therefore given their names to these books. The movement started as a kind of school, as people banded together, linked to each other by a certain spirit of ecstasy. To the people of the time, the prophets were just diviners who could foretell the future. But out of their bands there emerged individuals who rejected the narrow scope of the organization. They did not wish to be "fortune tellers." They had a message to deliver, a burden placed upon them by God. They stood out in their strength and indomitable courage.

The Hebrew word for "prophet" is *Navee* which, from its Accadian source, means "the one who is called" by God (William F. Albright, *From the Stone Age to Christianity*, New York: Doubleday Anchor, 1957, p. 303). Prophets thus receive their call from God. They have to rebuke the people and warn them; they call for rebirth of spirit, repentance, and return. They are also comforters. They assure the people of the ever-present love of God and His everlasting willingness to receive them back into His grace.

In this spirit, SAMUEL faces the people who want a king, warning them against dependence on human leadership and advising them to place their faith in God. He yields when God tells him to heed their demand. The people have not rejected Samuel, but God acquiesces in the fact that they have rejected Him by desiring an earthly king (1 Samuel 8:4–9). They are to be warned of the burdens kings impose on their subjects (vv. 9–22). Samuel tells them that only if their king and people be servants of God will it go well with them, otherwise God will strike them (12:13:15).

Emboldened by his divine mission to rebuke when necessary, the prophet NATHAN approaches David at the height of the king's power and accuses him to his face of having committed a shameful crime deserving death (2 Samuel 11–12). (David had seduced his neighbor's wife, Bathsheba, and sent him to certain death in battle.)

In the period of the divided kingdom the prophet ELIJAH predicts doom to King Ahab, the sinful king of Israel, and has to flee from his wrath. Yet Elijah returns to face all of Israel, including the king. The people, smitten by a drought, have made their appeal to both God and Baal (an all-powerful and cruel deity worshiped by Israel's heathen neighbors). It was a compromise of expedience that went directly against the Commandment not to have "other gods before" Him. There can be no compromise, Elijah makes clear: "How long will you keep hopping between two opinions? If the Lord be God, follow Him; but if Baal, follow him!" (1 Kings 18:21). For the people in their weakness, Elijah provides a visible sign of God's power. But the prophet himself learns that it is not in storms or quakes that God makes Himself manifest, but rather in the still, small voice of conscience and inner vision that God is revealed, and this voice people must follow (1 Kings 19).

The vision of the divine may be granted more poignantly to the prophet, but it is granted to all humanity. The prophet, like the midwife, releases that which lies implanted in every human being, placed there by God Himself. This will be evident in the Later Prophets, whose utterances we possess, at least in part. We have no verbatim record of the speeches of the former prophets.

Later Prophets

Traditionally we count three major prophets and twelve minor ones. Those of whose works significant portions have been preserved are called *major* prophets; they are Isaiah, Jeremiah, and Ezekiel. The *minor* prophets are of equal significance but only small portions of their works exist. They are Hosea, Joel, Amos, Obadiah, Jonah, Micah, Nahum, Habakkuk, Zephaniah, Haggai, Zechariah, and Malachi. The Book of Daniel, being quite late, is included in the third portion of the Tanakh (see below, *Ketuvim*). We know that some of the books ascribed to these men, such as Isaiah, were actually written by several authors. We also know that some of the names were not the true names of the authors (for instance, Malachi simply means "My Messenger"). We shall be concerned only with some of their major ideas, as they interpret, adapt, and evolve Torah.

These prophets came from all strata of society. Isaiah came from the ranks of the highest nobility, Amos was a lowly farmer, Hosea belonged to the middle class of comfortable burghers, and Jeremiah and Ezekiel were priests. In a side comment we learn of a woman prophetess, HULDAH (2 Kings 22:14ff). The northern as well as southern kingdoms were their spheres of action. And like Ezekiel, they served as pastors to the people in Babylonian exile.

AMOS (750 B.C.E.), compelled by the urgency of his call to lay down his plow, applies farmer's logic to his message: "As you sow so shall you reap." If you plant righteousness, your harvest will be good; if you sow wickedness, evil will grow up around you. This is a universal fact and Amos knows it. The providence of the universal God of all time and space rests equally upon all the farmers' toil throughout the world. Equally, it extends to all His children in all their ways, regardless of their race. "Are you not unto me like the children of the Ethiopians?" (Amos 9–7). He speaks of dark-skinned Ethiopians and lighter-skinned Philistines and Israelites in the same terms. Humanity is one. If Israel holds any special place, it is to set an example of true living under God and to assume higher responsibility for which it will be held to account. "You only have I known of all the families of the earth; therefore will I visit upon you all of your iniquities" (Amos 3:2). The "chosenness" of the Jew does not spell privilege, for all humanity is equally privileged before God; rather, it demands higher performance. In this sense, every nation is chosen to contribute in fullest measure of its strength those goods which by endowment and education it is best equipped to give to humanity.

The prophets' opposition to a self-serving establishment is revealed in Amos' encounter with the high priest Amaziah of the royal sanctuary of the northern kingdom. Amos interrupted a solemn service at the royal sanctuary, crying out in God's name, "I hate, I despise your feasts . . . nor will I look upon the peace offerings of your fatted beasts. . . . But let justice roll down as waters, and righteousness as a mighty stream" (Amos 5:21–25). Otherwise the sanctuary will be destroyed and Israel will fall (3:14–15). Amos' demonstration created a scandal, and the prophet was expelled from the sanctuary and the northern kingdom. Yet he was proven right.

HOSEA (ca. 745 B.C.E.) was equally severe in his rebukes, but he also emphasized divine love. On divine behest the prophet takes back his errant wife after she has had many exploits. This act of forgiveness symbolizes God's never-ceasing love for His people, though they may go astray. His call to repentance (Hosea 14) is read in the synagogue as Haftarah on the Sabbath between Rosh Hashanah and Yom Kippur, the period of repentance: "Return, O Israel, unto the LORD, for you have stumbled in your iniquity. Take with you words, and return unto the LORD. Say unto Him: Forgive all iniquity, and accept that which is good, and we will render instead of bullocks [the words of] our lips" (Hosea 14:2–3). Prayer, the words of the lips, is better than animal sacrifices; thus has Judaism interpreted the verse.

FIRST ISAIAH (742 B.C.E.), comprising chapters 1–39 in the Book of Isaiah, and MICAH (740 B.C.E.) are concerned with social injustice. In scathing words Isaiah condemns ritual that is merely empty performance of rites and is not undergirded by social justice. If it is carried out by the very same people who oppress their fellows, then ritual turns into blasphemy, blessing into a mockery of God. He will have none of it. Isaiah demands not only repentance, but to "wash yourselves clean; remove the evil of your doings from before My eyes; cease to do evil, learn to do good; seek justice, correct oppression, defend the fatherless, plead for the widow" (Isaiah 1:16–17). Only then will the prayer of contrition have meaning. Micah has the same message.

The whole tenor of Isaiah's prophecies appears already in the account of his call:

I saw the Lord sitting upon His throne, high and lifted up, and His train filled the Temple. Above Him stood the seraphim. . . . And one called to another and said: "Holy, holy, holy is the Lord of hosts, the whole earth is full of His glory." And the foundations of the thresholds [of the Temple] shook at the voice of Him who called, and the house was filled with smoke. (Isaiah 6:1–4)

God is not just in the Temple; He is in the whole earth. The actions of society have to proclaim His holiness. It is vain hope to assume that Temple ritual will be meaningful to Him without social responsibility. The same theme is taken up at the very end of the second Isaiah:

Thus says the LORD: Heaven is My throne and the earth is my footstool; what is the house which you would build for Me, and what is the place of My rest? . . . This is the man to whom I will look, he that is humble and contrite in spirit, and trembles at My word. . . . He who sacrifices a lamb [is] like one who breaks a dog's neck. (Isaiah 66:1–3)

The true response is for humanity to offer itself, to unite under God's kingship, to establish peace and justice. Then God will choose His priests from among all nations. The whole world will have become a kingdom of priests, a holy people; only thus can ritual—the symbolic expression of true worship—be meaningful and acceptable. This world will be realized in the time of the Messiah. It is foretold by both Isaiah (2:2–4) and Micah (4:1–5):

And it shall come to pass in the end of days, that the mountain of the LORD's house shall be established as the top of the mountains, and shall be exalted above the hills; and all nations shall flow unto it. And many peoples shall go and say: "Come, let us go up to the Mount of the LORD, to the House of the God of Jacob; and He will teach us of His ways, and we will walk in His paths." For out of Zion shall go forth Torah, and the word of the Lord from Jerusalem. And He shall judge between nations, and shall decide for many peoples; and they shall beat their swords into plowshares and their spears into pruning hooks; nation shall not lift up sword against nation, neither shall they learn war any more.

As this time is not yet, Israel has the task to prepare for it by example: "O House of Jacob come let us walk by the light of the Lord" (Isaiah 2:5). All this will take place simply as the result of humanity coming to its senses. No miracles are needed, only simple awareness on the part of individuals and nations that God is the center, justice is humanity's best weapon in the struggle for survival, and peace is the most precious goal and treasure. Yet it may bring about a complete transformation of habits, practices, and attitudes. It will be like the wolf dwelling with the lamb, as national jealousies depart. Thus it will come to pass under a truly chosen ruler.

Isaiah finds him in thinking of David:

But a shoot shall grow out of the stump of Jesse [David's father] . . . and the spirit of the LORD shall alight upon him, the spirit of wisdom and insight, the spirit of counsel and valor, the spirit of devotion and reverence for the LORD. . . . He shall judge the poor with equity. . . . Justice shall be the girdle of his loins. . . . The wolf shall dwell with the lamb . . . the lion, like the ox, shall eat straw . . . a babe shall play over a viper's hole. . . . In all of my sacred mount nothing evil or vile shall be done; for the land shall be filled with devotion to the LORD as the water covers the sea. In that day the stock of Jesse that has remained standing shall become a standard to peoples; nations shall seek his counsel, and his abode shall be honored. (Isaiah 11:1–10)

In such manner is the Messiah seen and the messianic age conceived; there will be no obstacles to Torah and Mitzvot in their widest meaning. There will be universal peace in justice. This portion of Isaiah is traditionally recited as Haftarah on the very last day of Passover, the festival of redemption from bondage. It makes the march through history a pilgrimage of free people toward universal freedom, and it releases the Jew from holy days to daily rounds with a challenge and obligation.

In a similar spirit, Isaiah 58 has become the Haftarah in the morning service of Yom Kippur, the Day of Atonement.

Is such a fast I desire, a day for men to starve their bodies? Is it bowing the head like a bulrush and lying in sackcloth and ashes? . . . No this is the fast I desire: to unlock the fetters of wickedness, and untie the cords of the yoke to let the oppressed go free; to break off every yoke. It is to share your bread with the hungry, and to take the wretched poor into your home; when you see the naked, to clothe him and not to ignore your own kin. Then shall your light burst through like the dawn. . . . Then, when you call the LORD will answer (Isaiah 58:5–9).

Not in chastisement, or in one-day prayer can God be fully worshiped, or even in the house of worship, but only through social justice.

Micah, voicing God's concern, puts it in terms of a litigation. God reminds the people of His liberating acts by bringing it out of Egypt and giving it role models, among them Miriam, the woman. "He has a suit against Israel. My people! What wrong have I done you? What hardship have I caused you? Testify against me. In fact, I brought you up from the land of Egypt, I redeemed you from the house of bondage, and I sent before you Moses, Aaron and Miriam" (6:2–4).

His command extends to all humans, creatures of earth. Their response must be, "With what shall I approach the LORD. . . . Shall I approach Him with burnt offerings? . . . He has told you, "Adam," you creature of earth, what is good, and what the Lord requires of you: Only to do justice, and to love goodness, and to walk modestly with your God" (Micah 6:6–8). The theme is carried through all the prophets.

JEREMIAH (626–587 B.C.E.) tells the people in no uncertain words how meaningless the Temple really can become, how its existence holds no magical power of survival; that power lies in the conduct of the people (Jeremiah 7). In spite of terrible persecutions, Jeremiah never gives up his faith in the regenerative powers that lie within the people, and neither do the other prophets. Jeremiah has to face trials much more severe than the others and, in the end, witnesses the destruction of the Temple, which he foresaw. But he transforms defeat into victory: Exile may be the challenge which will bring about regeneration; hence his letter to the Jews in Babylonia.

> Thus said the LORD of Hosts, the God of Israel, to the whole community which I exiled from Jerusalem to Babylon: 'Build houses and live in them, plant gardens and eat their fruit. Take wives and beget sons and daughters; take wives for your sons, and give your daughters to husbands, that they may bear sons and daughters. Multiply there, do not decrease. And seek the welfare of the city to which I have exiled you and pray to the LORD in its behalf, for in its welfare [peace, *shalom*] you shall have peace.' (Jeremiah 29:4–7)

EZEKIEL (593–573 B.C.E.) is the preacher of individual and mutual responsibility. The Temple has fallen and can no longer unite the people or atone for their sins. Henceforth each is responsible for his own destiny, yet accountable for the conduct of those whom he may influence. Ezekiel synthesizes individualism and collective destiny. He also reminds the exiled of the eternal Covenant: "I will remember My Covenant I made with you in the days of your youth, and I will establish it with you as a Covenant for all eternity" (Ezekiel 16:60).

Ezekiel is a visionary and has powerful revelations in Babylonia, as if to say, God's glory indeed fills the whole earth; He reveals Himself everywhere. His overpowering vision of the heavenly chariot (Ezekiel 1) is called *Maase Merkavah*, the Events of the Chariot, and is read as Haftarah on *Shavuot*, Festival of Revelation. In another vision he is shown how the spirit of God revives dead bones Through the spirit of God, the dead bones of a decayed society can be made alive again; the hopeless can restore their trust, and even the Land can be restored to them (Ezekiel 37:1–15). This chapter is recited as Haftarah on Passover, the festival of regeneration. Humanity can gain rebirth by guiding itself by His spirit.

SECOND ISAIAH (c. 540 B.C.E.), responsible for chapters 40–66 of Isaiah, is a prophet of hope. He says, "Comfort ye, comfort ye my people, says your God" (Isaiah 40:1). The chapter is recited as Haftarah after the mournful fast of Av, commemorating the fall of the Temple. Israel is God's witness in the world (Isaiah 43:10–12), "a light to the nations to open eyes that are blind" (Isaiah 42:6–7). This witness entails suffering, as the servant of God, despised, disfigured, and mocked, upholds his ideals. May the people's hearts be strong, for God will redeem them, and the entire human family will benefit (Isaiah 53). True to his belief that the Jews serve the world community, Isaiah welcomes converts who have joined the people and cleave to God; they, too, have a share in the future of Israel (Isaiah 44:5–56:3).

HAGGAI is the gadfly to the people returning from exile. He wants a second Temple to be built, as a symbol of the people's willingness to offer sacrifices to God. May they give of their substance, even though it hurts, to restore a visible center of divine presence. May they also not be dismayed at the smallness of the new building, for its true glory may surpass the splendor of the ancient one.

ZECHARIAH reminds the people that victory comes "not by might, nor by power, but by My spirit" (Zechariah 4:6). Zechariah no longer shares the hope that reason alone will lead humanity to unity, as did Isaiah. Wars and cataclysmic events will break forth on the "Day of the Lord," the evildoers be punished, and then eternal peace be established. "On this day God will be king over all the earth" (Zechariah 14:9). Here we find one of the eschatological prophecies. Yet victory and peace are assured those who fight with God (Zechariah 14:1–21), and Israel will dwell in safety amid a reborn humanity. This portion is read on Sukkot, the festival which symbolizes God's protection.

MALACHI points the way, the goal, and the guide. The way is by faithfully serving God amidst trials, even while seeing the arrogant happy. In the end, "You shall come to see the difference between the righteous and the wicked, between him who has served the LORD and him who has not served Him" (3:18). The goal is attained with the coming of the prophet Elija, herald of deliverance. He shall reconcile fathers with sons, and sons with their fathers" (3:24). Even the natural conflict of the generations will have ceased.

The guide is Torah: "Be mindful of the Torah of my servant Moses, whom I charged at Horeb with laws and rules for all Israel" (3:22). Before redemption, there will be conflict; nations will be arrayed against each other. There will be devastation. But the Land of those abiding by Torah will not be destroyed. "For you who revere My name a sun of victory shall rise with healing on its wings" (3:20).

For JONAH, we have no historical background. The book's author places his mission before the seventh century B.C.E., since the setting is Nineveh, the capital of Assyria, when Assyria was still a mighty power. (Nineveh was destroyed in 612 by the Babylonians.) God tells Jonah to call the Assyrians to repentance but Jonah refuses; redeeming Nineveh would mean restoring Israel's enemy. After many "adventures" (including three days in the belly of a great fish), Jonah agrees to do God's will. He calls for repentance. The king and people of Nineveh listen, have a change of heart, and the city is saved.

Jonah's only transmitted prophecy is to non-Jews. This is significant as it shows the way in which Jews are and have come to think even of their enemies and of God's concern for non-Jews. All are His children and deserve a second chance, especially those "who know not their right hand from their left hand" (Jonah 4:11). It is the Jews' task to extend their help, insight, strength, and life to them. If the Jews have the power to influence others for good but refuse to use it, God will see that it is done through them anyway.

The story is recited as Haftarah on the afternoon of Yom Kippur. It reminds the Jews that they are not singularly chosen for God's special attention and mercy, which He extends to all. Jews must consider themselves the world's servants, though they suffer in serving. Judaism's concept of God and humanity is universalistic.

Divine Pathos, Prophetic Sympathy

Abraham Joshua Heschel, in his classical work *The Prophets,* has given us a new perception of the prophets. Some of his thoughts may guide our understanding. He opens by stating his book was "about some of the most disturbing people who have ever lived, the men whose inspiration brought the Bible into being—the men whose image is our refuge in distress, and whose voice and vision sustains our faith" (*Prophets,* p. XIII). The prophets of Israel are no philosophers. They do not wish to be. To philosophers such as the Deists, God is detached, to Aristotle God is the unmoved mover, pure form, eternal, wholly actual, immutable, immovable, self-sufficient, and wholly separate from all else. His activity is in Himself. (*Prophets,* p. 234) God does not relate to His creation. The prophets reject this calm, intellectual definition. To the Bible, God has "pathos" and the prophets are in sympathy with God's pathos. "Pathos" means being emotionally moved and affected, something happens to a person. God is affected by human actions, because human beings are relevant to Him.

> In contrast to the *primum movens immobile* [the immovable prime mover of the philosophers], the God of the prophets cares for His creatures and His thoughts are about the world. He is involved in human history and affected by human acts. It is a paradox beyond compare that the Eternal God is concerned with what is happening in time. . . . The grandeur of God implies the capacity to feel emotion. In the biblical outlook, movements of feeling are no less spiritual than acts of thought.
> . . . The idea of divine pathos has also anthropological significance. It is man's being relevant to God. To the biblical mind the denial of man's relevance to God is as inconceivable as the denial of God's relevance to man. This principle leads to the basic affirmation of God's participation in human history, to the certainty that the events in the world concern Him and arouse His reactions. It finds its deepest expression in the fact that God can actually suffer. At the heart of the prophetic affirmation is the certainty that God is concerned about the world. (*Prophets,* p. 259).

God is in search of humanity. Humanity brings grief to God by failing Him. It fills Him with joy by raising the standards of ethical conduct toward absolute social justice. Without this striving, human ritual in worship of God becomes meaningless and actual mockery to Him.

The prophet sympathizes with God's pathos. He feels what God feels, and "discloses divine pathos not just a divine judgment" (p. 24). He wishes to bring the world in divine focus. "How else could the prophet perform such a fateful task if not in overwhelming sympathy with the divine pathos?" (p. 92). Confronted, in the same way as is God, with the spiritual and moral plight of the people, "the prophet may react in the same mode as God, in sorrow or indignation, in love or anger" (p. 314).

From the prophet's sympathy with the divine pathos spring his great and overpowering emotions. God has infused the prophet with divine inspiration.

This inspiration compares to the poetic inspiration granted the poet, but transcends it. The prophet is a God inspired poet. (see p. 367) Standing under divine compulsion the prophets do not speak in generalities, as poets may do. They address themselves to concrete situations, rebuke people for failing to live up to the highest ideals of ethical conduct. They call on Israel to be holy, which means setting an example. They rebuke Israel not for being worse than other peoples, but for being no better than the rest. They castigate Israel for serving God in ritual alone not linked to social justice. Israel was created to be God's foremost coworkers in the world. For this it will endure and, in God's time, find its reward.

Setting for all humanity the highest ethical goals and speaking in language of supreme grandeur, the prophets have remained the world's greatest and, in fact, only heralds of the truly good society under God, a society in which conviction will overcome expediency. They do not abrogate Torah and Mitzvot; they clarify their purpose.

KETUVIM

Ketuvim (Collected Writings) constitutes the third portion of the Tanakh. As the title indicates, it is composed of a variety of different works, including Psalms, Proverbs, Job, Song of Songs (Song of Solomon), Ruth, Lamentations, Ecclesiastes, Esther, Daniel, Ezra, Nehemiah, and 1 and 2 Chronicles. These are used in Jewish worship at a variety of occasions, which we shall mention in connection with the works themselves.

The Psalms

The Psalms are a collection of 150 poems, some of them lengthy, others quite short. A good many of them have attached to them the names of the supposed authors, ranging from Moses to the sons of Korah and Solomon; the majority are ascribed to David. A number of them have musical annotations, including which instruments were to accompany them when they were recited in public worship in the ancient Temple.

Several poetic forms are employed in the Psalms. Parallelism is used frequently (as it is in other Hebrew poetry), which is the technique of paraphrasing the first verse in the second. For example, Psalm 15:1 notes,

"Lord, who shall sojourn in Your tabernacle?
Who shall dwell upon Your holy mountain?"

The alphabetic acrostic is also frequently employed. Each verse begins with a letter of the alphabet (e.g., Psalms 34 and 145). In Psalm 119, each letter is used eight times. Some psalms are arranged for antiphonal responses (e.g., Psalm 24). The Psalms of Ascents (120–134), as the title indicates, were sung when the people ascended in solemn procession to the hill on which the Temple stood.

In content, the Psalms range from glorification of God to outcry and lamentation, from meditation to jubilant praise, from individual prayer to choral hymn. They speak of encompassing "foes," and, since the foe is not characterized, one may insert personal need and distress for the "foe" when the psalm is offered as prayer. They may be framed in the first person, yet the "I" may stand for an individual or for the people as a whole.

The Psalms have been guide and comforter, a source of strength and renewed faith for Jews and Christians throughout history. They have upheld the people in sickness, distress, and trial; instructed in the way of God; and expressed the deepest yearning of their hearts. Only supremely gifted poets could have formulated all these emotions to such perfection. In Hebrew, the Psalms are called *Tehillim* (Praises), for even the outcry directed to God affirms Him as ever-present and ever-powerful to rescue; it affirms human trust in Him, that He does right, even though the individual cannot understand the reasons for His actions. Thus Psalms are praises, in affliction and in victory.

Jewish tradition has divided the Psalms into five books, corresponding to the Five Books of Moses. They are a human response to Torah, witnessing to the fact that the Jews have understood it, accepted it, and made it their own.

In the ancient Temple, a special psalm was assigned for choral presentation every day of the week. (They are still used in the worship.) Psalm 92 is sung on the Sabbath. It reflects on God's work of creation, too deep for human beings to understand, yet culminating in the victory of the righteous, who shall be planted in the house of the Lord. On holy days, Psalms 113 through 118, called the *Hallel* (Praise), are recited in synagogue worship. God is recognized as God of nature and of nations; He rescued Israel from Egyptian bondage; may all people give thanks to His Name. Calling on Him in distress, petitioners shall always find rescue; hence they need not fear the devices of enemies. As humans move in His direction they shall be blessed from His House. Therefore, "Praise the Lord for He is good, His goodness endureth forever" (Psalm 118:1, 29).

Jewish worship always opens with Psalms, and the Sabbath is especially welcomed with them. The affirmation of God as Sustainer is expressed daily by reciting Psalm 145. The Scroll of Torah is removed from the Ark and returned to it as Psalms rise in glorification of its Giver. Psalm 6 expresses the spirit of contrition and hope in Him; it is prefaced in daily prayer by the words "Merciful and compassionate God, I have sinned before You."

In prayer for the sick, the name of the afflicted is presented to God as those verses of Psalm 119 which spell the person's name are being recited. Verses of the Psalms are woven into the prayers of the liturgy. Millions have turned to the Psalms in time of need and of joy. In opening their hearts to God, they found comfort in the knowledge that "the Lord is my shepherd, I shall not want" (Psalm 23).

The Psalms have sustained the Jews, their faith and their hope, even as they are one of Judaism's greatest gifts to humanity. They form a bond between Judaism and Christianity. This is revealed in the insights expressed in the Catholic catechism of 1992. Some excerpts are cited here:

The Psalms nurture and make manifest the prayer of the People of God, joined in assembly, as on the great festivals at Jerusalem and on every Sabbath in the synagogues. This prayer is indivisibly both personal and communal; it concerns those who pray and all humanity; it rises from the Holy Land and the communities of the Diaspora, but it embraces all of creation; it calls to mind the saving events of the past and extends itself up to the consummation of history; it reminds us of God's promises already realized, and it awaits the Messiah who will fulfill them definitively.

The Psalter is the book in which the Word of God becomes the prayer of humans. In the other books of the Old Testament "the words proclaim the works" (of God for humans). . . . In the Psalter the words of the psalmist, express, in song to God, His works of salvation. The same spirit inspires the work of God and the response of man.

The multiple forms of expressing prayer in the Psalms give form to faith in the liturgy of the Temple and in the heart of man. Whether hymn, or prayer in distress, or in response to manifestation of grace, supplication of the individual or of the community, royal or pilgrimage song, or meditation on wisdom, the Psalms are the mirror of God's miracles in the history of His people and in human situations as lived by the psalmist. A Psalm may reflect an event of the past, but it is of such discretion that it can in fact be prayed by humans under all conditions and at all times.

Throughout the Psalms we find certain constant traits: simplicity and spontaneity of prayer, God's own longing for His entire creation, and all that is good in it; the anguish of believers, whose love moves them to choose the Lord, but who find themselves exposed to a host of enemies and temptations, and placing their dependence on the dispensations of a faithful God, are upheld by the certainty of His love and his own restoration to His will. The prayer of the Psalms is always undergirded by praise; therefore the title of this collection is adequately chosen for its contents "The Praises." As appointed for public worship it calls for affirmation of the appeal of prayer and to song with the response "Hallelu-Yah" Praise the Lord." (Catechism 2586–2589)

Proverbs, Ecclesiastes, and Job

Proverbs, Ecclesiastes, and Job offer worldly wisdom or philosophical discussion and therefore are called Wisdom books. Wisdom (*Hokhmah*) is actually personified at times. Wisdom is equated with Torah; Torah is wisdom, and all wisdom, as Jews have seen it, is an extension of Torah and enshrined in it. *Proverbs* is a collection of short maxims that afford guidance in life. *Ecclesiastes* is a pessimistic reflection on life's vanity, and is redeemed only by the last sentence (which was added later): "The sum of the matter, when all is said and done: Revere God and observe His commandments! For this is being human (12:13).

Job is a book that has fascinated philosophers, theologians, poets, and writers throughout the ages. We do not know who wrote the work. The rabbis disagree about whether Job was a Jew or a Gentile. Some rabbis hold that the whole poem is just a fictional dialogue which serves as a work of instruction and that Job never lived.

Job is a good man, a simple man, who renders daily thanks to God who has blessed him. Unbeknownst to him, a wager takes place between God and Satan: Will Job remain righteous even under severe affliction? God believes he will. Job is tested. In his agonies, he cries out in protest against God who has chastised him without reason. But he also proclaims, "Though He slay me, yet will I trust in Him" (13:15). His friends come to "comfort" him with the rationale that he must have sinned, for why else would God punish him so severely? But against their strongest arguments Job maintains that he has not sinned, hence his suffering is not the wages of sin.

Job also affirms that God must have willed his suffering. He rejects the suggestion that the world and humanity might be subject to a purely accidental chain of events. Job turns in violent rebellion against God. The rabbis, however, sought to excuse him and claim he never weakened in his affirmation of God. In the end, God appears to Job. This is dual vindication: It proves that there is a God; it also proves that Job has not sinned, for God does not reveal Himself to sinners. Job has to learn, however, that the ways of God are hidden to people, whose life span is too short to comprehend God's overall design and the tests He inflicts. One rabbinical interpretation is that Job prays for his friends (43:10), and his fortunes are restored as he makes up with his adversaries.

The Five Scrolls

The Five Scrolls, or *Megillot* (plural of *Megillah*), were each originally written on separate scrolls for public reading at various times during the liturgical year. In traditional congregations they are still recited at these occasions, but from the festival prayer book and silently. Only the Book of Esther is still read publicly from a handwritten, separate scroll; it has come to be known as "the *Megillah.*"

The first Scroll, Song of Songs (*Shir ha-Shirim*), is a fervid love song. It has been interpreted as symbolic of God's love for Israel. It is recited on Passover, the festival of spring. Nature, like a bride in all her beauty, forecasts rich blessings; God is the groom. Should not Israel and all humanity equally prepare themselves, link themselves to God's love, and bring to fruition the blessings He has implanted within them? For Franz Rosenzweig the Song of Songs is the core of Judaism, which is love.

Ruth, the second Scroll, is recited on Shavuot, the festival commemorating the revelation at Sinai, the giving of Torah. It is an idyllic story. Ruth, a Moabite convert and the childless widow of a Jewish man she married in Moab, cleaves to Torah and to the people of Israel. No adversity can weaken her commitment to her Jewish mother-in-law: "Wherever you go I will go." A desperately poor immigrant from abroad, she is eventually permitted the peaceful life of the happy farmer's wife in the Land, but this is only one part of her reward. Marrying a man of distinction, she becomes the great-grandmother of King David. Ruth's faith in adversity becomes a shining example of how to cling to Torah. A woman, by her love and spirituality, becomes the role model for the people she has made her own.

The third Scroll, Lamentations (*Ekhah*), ascribed to the prophet Jeremiah, is recited on the Fast of Av, commemorating the fall of the Temple. It expresses the numb terror and despondency as well as the hope that springs eternal within the people, even as disasters grow to unbearable proportions. Whenever the Torah is returned to the Ark after being read to the people, the congregation sings the concluding words of "Ekhah": "Take us back, O Lord, to Yourself, and Let us come back; Renew our days as of old" (5:21).

Ecclesiastes (*Kohelet*), the fourth Scroll, is also one of the Wisdom books, as we have seen. It is recited on Sukkot, and reflects and mitigates the sense of frustration and pessimism at the approach of a bleak winter's season. It concludes with counsel: "Obey His commandments," it says, "for this is the meaning of being human."

Esther, (*Ester*), the fifth Scroll, is recited on Purim. It is a strange, rather fantastic book and quite a thrilling story. It never mentions the name of God. Perhaps it was performed as a religious stage play, hence God's name could not be mentioned. Perhaps it means to tell that God works everywhere, though we may not be aware of His presence. The scene is laid outside Palestine, in Persia. Haman, viceroy of King Ahasuerus, has concocted a vicious plan to exterminate the Jews. Unwittingly, the king approves. Actually, without knowing it, he has taken a Jewish woman, Esther, as his consort. She becomes the story's chief protagonist, its true heroine. She combines her womanly charm with supreme diplomatic skill and sacrificial devotion to her people. Risking her life, she approaches the king unsolicited and successfully pleads her people's case. Haman is hanged, and Mordecai, Esther's foster father and mentor, is given Haman's position. Esther inspires the Jews' deeper commitment to God. The book gave hope to many in modern extermination camps, for they knew that though they might perish as individuals, the Jewish people would surely survive. Ruth and Esther are the two books in the Tenakh named after women.

Daniel

The Book of Daniel is found in Christian Bibles among the prophetic books, and in the Hebrew Bible among the Ketuvim. This in itself indicates the difference in status accorded the work in the two traditions. Its narrative is placed in the period of Nebuchadnezzar, which is the time of the Babylonian Exile of the Jews (sixth century B.C.E.). Many biblical scholars believe, however, that the book is of much later origin, possibly of the period of the Maccabean revolt (second century B.C.E.). During both of these periods Jewish religion was under great pressure, and might have come to extinction had it not been for the faith and courage of dedicated leaders. The Maccabees furnished such leadership, and Daniel is depicted as a man prepared to give his life for his faith. The book was designed to give hope and guidance to Jews in difficult times; it showed them how previous generations had faced and overcome serious problems, and it armed them for the problems that lay ahead in their own time. The wisdom of Daniel is extolled. He is set up as a role model. Even at a time when prayer to God was forbidden by the ruler on penalty of death, he prayed three times a day, facing Jerusalem. For this he was cast into a lion's den. God rescued him. Daniel was rewarded for setting God and His commandments over the edicts of worldly powers.

Several characteristics reveal the work to have originated at a time much later than the narrative would have us assume. First, portions of the book are written in Aramaic, a language closely related to Hebrew. Second, the Book of Daniel contains significant apocalyptic portions dealing with eschatology. (The term "apocalyptic" will be explained in detail in the section on Jewish Apocalyptic literature [see page 255].) Apocalyptic utterances are usually cryptic and enigmatic, and deal with symbolic forms of statement. Eschatology deals with the end of times and the cataclysmic events that will bring it about.

In order to understand why the Book of Daniel was placed differently in the Christian and Hebrew Bibles, we have to know that the Hebrew Bible was ultimately edited and authorized by the rabbis of the Mishnah. They decided which books of the many then current should be admitted and which should be excluded. This was a lengthy undertaking. Most likely, the rabbis felt that the Book of Daniel had sufficient merit to be included, for it told of Daniel's faith and could inspire the Jews never to abandon their holy tradition. Also, there were among the rabbis men who were interested in apocalyptic literature. At the same time, however, it was a recent book. And, above all, it was apocalyptic and eschatological. Its study might lead to "calculations of the end," of which the rabbis disapproved as a subject of general study. If these calculations were proven wrong, they might weaken the faith. (In spite of the rabbis' warnings against eschatological speculations, these continued to have a place among many Jews.) Also, in contrast to the clearly understandable language of the prophets, Daniel spoke in symbolic terms; such language would allow for interpretations that might be subversive. The rabbis finally compromised and included the book in the canon, but not among the prophetic books.

Among Christians, however, the book assumed great importance. Daniel's remarks dealing with cataclysmic eschatological events have inspired many Christians to speculate about the ultimate future, not shared by Jews. For Christians, the Book of Daniel assumed an importance that warranted its inclusion in the prophetic section of Christian Bibles. It could be regarded as a forerunner to The New Testament's Book of Revelations, which contains similar speculations, and may have been influenced by Daniel. Daniel will be mentioned further in the section on Jewish apocalyptic literature.

Ezra and Nehemiah

Ezra and Nehemiah relate the trials of the people as they rebuild their land and Temple after the Babylonian Exile. Surrounded by the dangers of cultural and religious contamination, Jews withdraw from contact with the world to renew their Covenant with God and Torah and Land.

1 and 2 Chronicles

1 and 2 Chronicles review the historical events described in the Books of Samuel and Kings. They emphasize the chain of tradition that had come down through the generations and the religious significance of the events of Jewish history. An idealized picture of David and Solomon is drawn and presents details not found in other books. The kings' negative traits are left out, instead they appear as pillars of faith. The importance of the Temple and the priesthood are emphasized and Israel's history is revealed as sacred history.

THE APOCRYPHA

The books of the Tanakh were collected, edited, and approved by the Pharisees. The Hebrew Bible is what these men decided it should be. Some of the material the rabbis considered was excluded from the canon because they thought it repetitious or felt that its message was not significantly in line with the educational objectives of Torah. Some of it was excluded simply because it was of too recent origin.

But the people had used these books for inspiration. The Septuagint had translated some of them for the use of Diaspora Jewry who spoke Greek. The books had, therefore, acquired a degree of popular acceptance and could not be destroyed. They remained but were withdrawn—hidden—from use in public worship. They were called *Genuzim*, "hidden books," or *Apocrypha* in Greek. In this manner, a distinction could be made between the portions of the fixed canon, designed for use in public worship, and works not to be read in public worship and therefore of limited distribution. They were not, however, explicitly forbidden reading.

The works had been written in Palestine and Egypt during the period of the Second Temple and shortly afterward. Some of them were in Hebrew or Aramaic, others in Greek. We shall mention only a few of them.

Maccabees I (written between 135 and 65 B.C.E.), is a reliable report of the Maccabean uprising. *Maccabees II* (composed between 125 and 25 B.C.E.) covers much of the material of Maccabees I, but with a strongly religious overtone. These two books are a primary source for the events surrounding the festival of Hanukkah.

Ecclesiasticus, or *The Wisdom of Jesus (Joshua) ben Sirah*, was written by a deeply religious author in 180 B.C.E. It offers practical ethical wisdom and prayers. Ben Sirah's grandson translated the work from Hebrew into Greek. *Judith* (written about 150 B.C.E.) is fiction. It may have been inspired by the story of Jael, who cut off the head of the enemy Sisera, found in Judges.

Other works expand the biblical texts. *Esdras (Ezra) 1*, a fragment of a Greek translation (around 150 B.C.E.), offers variations to the Ezra-Nehemiah reports in the canon. *Esdras (Ezra) II* is an apocalyptic work. Chapters 3–14 are assumed to have been written in Hebrew or Aramaic near the end of the first century C.E.;

chapters 1, 2, 15, and 16 are regarded as being composed by Christian authors. *Esdras III* and *IV* were added from existing sources to the Bible in Jerome's translation, the Vulgate. Here we also find apocalyptic sections.

The Wisdom of Solomon was written by two authors. One wrote Chapters 1–9, in Hebrew; the other translated the first part into Greek and added the rest. It is conjectured that the work was composed late in the first pre-Christian century. The work praises wisdom, calls for faithful adherence to God, and offers a review of history, showing Judaism as superior to paganism. *Tobit* is a fictional work that tells of the trials and tribulations of a deeply pious and charitable man and his son, Tobias, who are exiled to Niniveh.

The Catholic Church includes the Apocrypha in the canon. Luther regarded them as useful reading. Parts of the Apocrypha, particularly the *Book of Enoch*, contain eschatological speculations and prophecies that have had a significant impact upon Christian theology and Jewish mysticism. For scholarship tracing the events in the period between the Hebrew Scriptures and the Christian Scriptures, the apocryphal books have been a rich source of knowledge and continue to be. In Judaism they have held a generally minor place.

Pseudepigrapha, or "False Titles," are books (such as *The Testament of Abraham*) that wished to give the impression of having been written by biblical personalities, and therefore have false titles. Unlike the Apocrypha, which were admitted into the Greek version of the Bible, these works were not admitted to the Hebrew or Greek versions. Written before the final canonization of the Tanakh they were deliberately excluded. Only modern scholarship has explored them.

JEWISH APOCALYPTIC LITERATURE AND ITS IMPACT

"Apocalyptic literature" refers to works that originated after prophetic revelation had ceased. These works began to appear in the second pre-Christian century, although there are apocalyptic sections in the prophetic writings as well. Some rabbis were interested in apocalyptic pronouncements. They admitted the Book of Daniel into the canon.

We can discern two major forms of apocalyptic writing: descriptions of heaven and hell, the realm beyond our world, and predictions regarding the future, specifically, the end of time. The prophecies are couched in highly symbolic and allegorical form.

Among Jewish apocalyptic works are The Book of Enoch, The Fourth Book of Ezra, The Testament of the Twelve Patriarchs, The Abraham Apocalypse, The Barukh Apocalypse, and several chapters (chapter 3, and possibly 4 and parts of 5) of The Sibylline Oracles.

As we can see from the titles of the works, they were ascribed to earlier personalities: patriarchs and prophets. This was done in order to give them greater value. They may have been written to meet the need of the people, now deprived of prophetic guidance. They wished to show them that the events of their time and its outcome were foreordained and stood under divine providence. At the same time, there was a greater distance between God and His creatures.

Apocalyptic literature deals with visions heretofore not made known, secrets of the world beyond. God is surrounded by a heavenly court of angels, whose names and functions are described. The Messiah was created from the beginning and dwells with God. This "Son of Man" (as we find in Enoch), will be sent to earth when the time has come. There are fallen angels who have plunged into hell. They are also seen as demons who roam and afflict humanity with sickness and destruction. Human beings dwell between heaven and hell. After death they will be assigned either to paradise or to *Gehinnom* (*Gehenna*; namely, purgatory; Gehinnom was a valley near Jerusalem), depending on their actions.

Apocalyptic literature also deals with eschatology, the end of days and the events surrounding this end. Cataclysmic, cosmic wars will engulf humanity and the universe before the end. The terrors that are the signs of the end are symbolically described. Then the messianic age will come about, and the dead will be resurrected.

These concepts deeply affected both Jews and Christians, especially in the struggle against Rome in the days of Jesus, and in the thinking of the early Church regarding Jesus. They continued to have an impact on Jewish and Christian thought and belief. They came to be incorporated in the Midrash—which means that the rabbis selectively adopted and adjusted them.

The period of the Second Temple marks the beginning of some Jewish mystical and apocalyptic literature that unfolded for over a thousand years and laid the foundation for later Jewish mysticism. The *Hekhalot* (Heavens) works describe the passage of the mystic through the heavens to the ultimate contemplation of God's Glory, the *Markabah* (Chariot) literature, based on Ezekiel 1:1, deals with the heavenly chariot. Concepts found in them have also been retained in popular and even officially ordained traditional belief.

TRADITION AND BIBLICAL CRITICISM

The Torah is the word of God, but was it actually dictated by God and written at the time, or close to it, when the events described occurred? Did the prophets whose names are attached to various books really write all the books ascribed to them? Sometimes they lived long before the events to which they refer, at times their language shows traces of later usage, or their messages do not seem consistent.

Orthodox Jews and fundamentalist Christians have firmly maintained that the text as we have it is God's literal word in every aspect. The "scientists" among Bible scholars have felt differently. They called for critical analysis of texts and for historical evidence to sustain the events related in Scripture. In their enthusiasm, nineteenth-century Bible critics went far in dismembering Scripture. However, twentieth-century archaeology has proven the Bible accurate on many points previously considered fiction or legend.

It must be remembered that the Bible is essentially a message and not an historical work; facts are frequently adjusted to sustain the message. Furthermore, a great deal of the written material was transmitted by word of mouth for a long time before it was put into writing and so was subject to embellishment. It is widely held that oral tradition was essentially accurate and generally trustworthy. This applies to both the Hebrew Scriptures and the Gospels. However, ideas and even stories and poetry from other sources did find their way into it, and at times individual biases influenced the final versions.

The reader must realize that "older" parts of Scripture often were actually written later than the "newer" ones. The epistles of Paul in the New Testament precede the Gospels. The prophets precede parts of the Five Books of Moses.

Biblical criticism tells us that the Book of Amos was written by several people, with material added later. This conclusion is based on inconsistencies and contradictions in the various ideas expressed, and on the forms of the writings. The Book of Isaiah had several authors; it may, in fact, be an anthology of writings. It is certain that chapters 40–66 were written by a different author from the one who wrote the first part, but there is grave doubt that all the earlier chapters were written by one man. It is also doubtful that all the chapters in Second Isaiah were written by one man. The order of the chapters may have been changed as well, as they were by different hands and in wrong sequence. The "utopia" of "the end of days" (Isaiah 2:2–4; Micah 4:1–5) is found in Isaiah and in Micah but was probably written by neither; the chapter of "the suffering servant" (Isaiah 57) is said to belong to another author. The Psalms are also an anthology; even the names attached to some of them may not be the authors' names but those of the choral groups to whose repertoires they belonged. The Book of Daniel was written in retrospect and after the success of the Maccabean uprising which proved God's redeeming help; this places the book around 165 B.C.E. We are merely citing examples. Biblical scholarship has encompassed the entire two Testaments, and its work continues.

Most important has been research into the Pentateuch, based in part on the critical analyses by two Protestant scholars of the nineteenth century, Graf and Wellhausen. The two men were puzzled by the use of two terms for the name of God in the earliest chapters of Genesis, namely *YHVH* and *Elohim*. In addition, the creation story is given twice and with different slants in Chapters 1 and 2. To the critics, this indicated several authors, not only for Genesis, but for all of Scripture. They arrived at the conclusion that there was one author who used the term *YHVH* for "God" (or, in German, *JHWH*); they called him the "J" author. Another author, using the term *Elohim*, was called "E." Another author, concerned with priestly functions and privileges, was called "P." The Book of Deuteronomy was written by still another author, "D," who reflected the ethics of the prophets.

It is now assumed that a "redactor," ("R") combined the "J" and "E" traditions into one manuscript, "RJE." The "J" manuscript originated approximately in the tenth or ninth century B.C.E.; the "E" manuscript approximately the ninth or eighth century B.C.E. The "RJE" manuscript combined both.

"D," the author of Deuteronomy, actually wrote more than this book. Deuteronomy was composed only in part by him; some parts were written after the Babylonian exile. "D" was concerned with showing that the entire world is God's, who acts in behalf of Israel. He places his major emphasis on ethics, as the prophets had done. The books from Deuteronomy through Kings reflect his spirit and authorship.

Finally, there came "P," around the sixth or fifth century B.C.E. Its author wrote an entire manuscript of his own, and then incorporated the edited elements of "J" and "E" without changing them. This has led to contradictions in the text. "P" was concerned with law, both religious and civil, and his influence is noted in the first four books of the Pentateuch. In order to present his viewpoint, "P" wrote Chronicles as a balance to the "D" books of history. He also wrote Ezra and Nehemiah. The tenor of the writings serves as clues to authorship. We note, therefore, that parts of Deuteronomy were written before Leviticus. One effect of this is that the holiest day of the Jewish Year, Yom Kippur, mentioned in Leviticus, would be of the most recent origin among the festivals.

We would now have to arrange final versions of the historical books of Hebrew Scriptures thus:

P: Books 1, 2, 3, 4 of the Pentateuch, Chronicles, Ezra, Nehemiah

D: Book 5 of the Pentateuch, and the rest of the historical books

How deeply did these results of critical research affect Jewish life? In some ways, they have affected it in modern times. The divine spirit of the Torah is acknowledged by all Jewish schools of thought. But Reform saw no need for the observance of all the details of Mitzvot, as they had simply emerged in the course of time and need not be considered the literal command of God. Conservative Judaism saw in the variations the key to its religious outlook: It retained that which the people had accepted and declared holy, but it emphasized the evolutionary process that may still go on. Orthodoxy rejected biblical criticism. The division in religious Jewry is, to a large degree, based on critical Bible research.

On the other hand, research did not affect Jewish life. Yom Kippur may have been introduced late in biblical times, but it is universally observed and regarded as the holiest day of the Jewish year. Isaiah and Micah's "utopia" may rest on other sources. But the very fact of its incorporation in the messages of two prophets indicates that it was either a widespread tradition or a highly regarded tradition or both. This increases its value instead of diminishing it.

Finally, Jewry through most of its Diaspora was Orthodox. Many modern Jews have been more deeply influenced by their heritage than by scientific analysis of Scripture. The impact of biblical criticism must be seen in the perspective of the evolution of the Jewish people and its contemporary results.

CHAPTER 13

Of Oral Torah

BACKGROUND

THE DOCTRINES, PRINCIPLES, AND PRECEPTS OF JUDAISM rest on Written and Oral Torah. Written Torah consists of the Tanakh within which the Five Books of Moses hold the primary authority. Oral Torah is instruction and explanation, which by tradition was revealed by God in conjunction with Written Torah and is based on it. Resting on both, the rabbis assumed the authority to reconstruct Jewish Life after the fall of the second Temple (70 C.E.). This was essential if Torah, Judaism, and the Jewish people were to survive under wholly changed conditions. (For example, the sacrificial service and the role of the priests had ceased. The masters of the Talmud discovered in the Written Torah that prayer was of the same efficacy as the sacrifices.) After being handed down by word of mouth for generations, the teachings of the rabbis were eventually written down. This is the Talmud. In it Judaism attained its normative expression. Normative Judaism rests on sources that existed long before Christianity; it is, however, not a forerunner but a contemporary of Christianity. Nor is Judaism identical with biblical Hebrew religion. This religion existed before the Talmud, and was not guided by its instruction.

The Talmud consists of Mishnah and Gemara. The *Mishnah* is the concise edition of the laws and ordinances arrived at through debate and decision by the Rabbis of Palestine, the *Tannaim*. Begun around 100 B.C.E. and originally transmitted by word of mouth (Oral Torah), it was eventually put in writing around 200 C.E. *Gemara* contains the ongoing discussion of the Mishnah by the Rabbis of Palestine and the Rabbis of Babylonia, the *Amoraim*. The "Palestine" or "Jerusalem Talmud" was edited in the second half of the fourth century, the "Babylonian Talmud" was edited toward the end of the fifth century C.E.

The Talmud is the "Compendium of Learning" and reflects the full spectrum of life. It is a stenographic transcript of the words spoken in debate. It includes jest and banter, and frequently follows free association. It includes opinions of men who were farsighted and wise as well as those who were narrow and legalistic or petty and superstitious. Seen as a whole the Talmud is an instruction in ethics through ethical action, and as such has formed the Jews. We shall here emphasize this side of the Talmud.

Although most of the Talmud originated after the fall of the second Temple, it contains extended debates and regulations about Temple worship, sacrifices, and the Land, all of which had already been taken away from the Jews. The hope for a return was never abandoned; the Messiah might come at any time, so they must be prepared. In the pages of the Talmud it was as if the Temple still existed and Israel dwelt on its own soil as a sovereign nation.

The Talmud transported the Jews into another world, far away from the exile in which they lived. Through the centuries, study of the Talmud became both a form of worship and an escape. Jews who immersed themselves in the Talmud were removed from the trials of daily life and given the will to survive. The command of Joshua 1:8, "Let not this book of Torah cease from your lips, meditate on it day and night," became the watchword. Jewish men came to regard the study of the Talmud as their vocation. It also sharpened their intellect.

The medieval Church attacked the Talmud on the grounds that it supposedly contained anti-Christian statements. (Anti-Semites, even down to Hitler's times, have maligned it as a blueprint for depravity.) In the thirteenth century all copies that could be found by the authorities in France were burnt. Why this hatred of the Talmud? It does not contain any significant disparagements of Christianity (although a few remarks could be found and were excised by the Christian censors without affecting the work as a whole). The Hebrew Scriptures could not be attacked—they were part of the Christian heritage—but the Talmud was Jewish. It proved that, under God's guidance, Judaism had not ceased to be creative and had continued to evolve, that it was alive. The Talmud affirmed the Messiah yet to come and the return to the Land. Scholars and laypeople, both Christians and Jews, recognize it as one of the great achievements of the human spirit. It was a weapon of resistance, a denial of Christian triumphalism, and it disparagers were aware of this.

Written and Oral Torah

The rabbis held that Moses received from God both a Written Torah and verbal instructions to be transmitted orally, Oral Torah. Written Torah offered hints that an oral tradition accompanied the written word. A clear instance could be seen in the verse of Torah, "you shall slaughter any of your cattle or sheep . . . as I have instructed you" (Deuteronomy 12:21). There were no instructions regarding the slaughter of animals in Written Torah, so the verse must refer to an orally given commandment. Torah was thus transmitted from generation to generation: "Moses received the Torah from Sinai and transmitted it to Joshua, and Joshua to the elders, and the elders to the prophets, and the prophets transmitted it to the Men of the Great Assembly" (Avot 1:1).

The relationship of Written and Oral Torah is explained in a simple parable found in a medieval Jewish work, *Seder Eliyahu Suta* (82). To a doubter of the validity of Oral Law, the rabbi answers:

> Both were given at Sinai, as a king presents a gift to faithful servants. Once there were two servants, a wise one and a foolish one, and both received from their king a measure of wheat and a bundle of flax. The foolish one put them away in a chest, that they remain forever unchanged; the wise servant spun the flax into a cloth and made precious bread out of the wheat. Placing the bread on the cloth, he invited the king to be his honored guest.

Thus, human concern, wisdom, and love of the Supreme King transform divine gifts of Torah into *Shulhan Arukh*, "a well-prepared table." Without Oral Torah evolution is impossible, and God is not served.

According to rabbinic teaching, prophecy came to an end with the Book of Malachi at the time of Ezra in the mid-fifth century B.C.E. Ezra is regarded as the founder of the Great Assembly, whose members founded the rabbinic tradition. It was carried forward by the masters of the Talmud, the Pharisees, and their successors, who saw themselves as entrusted with the divine task and felt sustained by the presence of God's holy spirit.

The rabbis did not consider themselves equal to the prophets but as legitimate heirs in the unfolding of tradition. They found their authority in the words of Deuteronomy 30:12–14: "This Torah is not in the heavens . . . [it] is . . . in your mouth and in your heart to observe it."

Method of Interpretation

To the rabbis, Written Torah is literally the word of God and therefore timeless and unchangeable. No single word or even nuance may be regarded as superfluous. In order to arrive at the full meaning of the Written Torah, the rabbis pay attention to every nuance of the written word. They note spelling, grammar, and contradictions, as well as compare similar statements in various sections. The late Professor Harry L. Wolfson of Harvard noted that they employ a "hypothetico-deductive method," which is used in scientific work, but they apply it to the sacred word. They also consider the practical needs of the people. The following example may help explain the rabbinical method.

We read in the Ten Commandments "Honor your father and your mother" (Exodus 20:12). The Hebrew text reads "kabed *et* avikha *ve-et* imekha." The *et* is grammatically superfluous, but it is used twice. The rabbis explain that the first *et* is introduced to include the father's wife, even if she is not the mother; the second *et* is to include the mother's husband, even if he is not the father; the *ve* is included to extend the duty of rendering honor to the elder brother, who has certain responsibilities in the upbringing of the younger children. They all must be given their due honor and respect (B. Ketuvot 103a).

That commandment also says to "*Honor* your father and your mother." Torah also says that "Everyone shall *respect* his mother and his father" (Leviticus 19:3), and the rabbis note that, while previously the father was mentioned before the mother, now the mother is mentioned before the father. There must be a reason for the difference. They explain:

Children are wont to love and *honor* their *mother* more than their father for all her kindnesses to them. The first verse (in Exodus) places the father first, because you may be inclined to honor him less than your mother, so you must make an effort to honor him more than your inclination inclines you, in order that both be equally honored. The second verse (in Leviticus) deals with the equally strong inclination of children to *respect* their *father* more than their more yielding mother. Therefore, you must transcend your inclination and respect her as you do your father. Thus the rabbis find that the two verses indicate that both are to be *equally* honored *and* respected (B. Kiddushin 31a).

MASTERS OF THE TALMUD

The task of evolving Torah calls for integrity, humility, knowledge and wisdom, and a deep love of God and humanity. The Pharisees, their disciples, and the rabbis of the Talmud possessed all of these; theirs is indeed the spirit of the prophets, whose successors they are in both time and spirit. We recognize this spirit in the teachings and maxims of their lives. As it says in B. Shabbat 88b:

The Rabbis taught: Those that accept humiliation without ever humiliating others, hear their disparagement without retorting, act always out of love, and joyfully accept chastisement, of them Scripture says: "They who love Him are like the sun as he rises in his might" (Judges 5:31).

Hillel's love of God and humanity came to be proverbial:

Be of the disciples of Aaron, loving peace and pursuing peace, loving all creatures and leading them to Torah.
He who aggrandizes his name destroys it; he who does not grow [in knowledge and wisdom] decreases; he who does not wish to learn deserves death [he withers away]; and he who puts the crown [of Torah and position] to selfish use shall perish.
If I am not for my self [doing the work, if need be alone], who will be for me? If I am for myself only, what am I? [My work is without meaning.] And if not now, when [will it be done]? (Mishnah Avot 1:12–14)

Rabbi Eleazar places a good heart above all other qualities, for all of them are included therein (Avot 2:13), and counsels: "Let the honor of your fellow man be as dear to you as your own; don't be easily angered; return [to God in repentance] one day before your death [that is, every day]" (Avot 2:15). Rabbi Gamaliel warns against selfish ambition as he pleads for civic responsibility: "May all who work in behalf of the community work *with them* for the sake of Heaven" (Avot 2:2). His son, Rabbi Simeon ben Gamaliel, advises, "The decisive thing is not study but the deed" (Avot 1:17). He also pointed out that "The world rests on three things: truth, justice, and peace" (Avot 1:18).

Shammai, Hillel's intellectual antagonist, proclaimed as the rule for his life: "Make your study of Torah a well-appointed practice, say little and do much, and receive every person with a cheerful face (Avot 1:15). Yet the decision in all religious matters follows the School of Hillel: "A heavenly voice was heard at Javneh: "The words of both are the words of the living God, but the decision must follow the School of Hillel."

In talmudic discussion it was asked,

> "If both are the words of the living God, why was the decision accorded to the School of Hillel?" The answer was: "Because they were kindly and peaceful, always studied both their own views and those of the School of Shammai, and even presented the words of the School of Shammai before their own, which teaches that he who humbles himself, God raises him up, and he who looks for aggrandizement, God humbles him. He who chases after recognition finds it running away from him; he who strives to avoid it, finds it following him. He who pushes his objectives will find himself pressured by them, he who puts them aside finds himself aided by destiny. (B. Eruvin 13b)

Life, as the rabbis saw it, must be imitation of God.

> Rabbi Hama, son of Rabbi Hanina, said: "Follow none but the Lord your God" (Deuteronomy 13:5). But can man follow God? It means that we must follow God's acts. As He clothes the naked, so shall you clothe the naked (Genesis 3:21); as the Holy One—Blessed be He—visited the sick (Genesis 18:1), so shall you visit the sick. As He . . . comforts those who mourn (Genesis 25:11) so shall you comfort those who are in mourning. As the Holy One . . . buries the dead (Deuteronomy 34:6) even so shall you bury the dead. . . . The Torah begins with deeds of kindness as God made clothes for Adam and Eve—and it ends with kindness, as it is written: "He buried [Moses] in the valley." (B. Sota 14a)

The Rabbis' Rank and Title—Ordinances and Preachments— In Search of Meaning / *Tannaim* and *Amoraim*— *Halakhah* and *Aggadah*—Midrash

These were the principles held by the men who developed the Talmud. The masters of the Mishnah are called *Tannaim* (teachers), those who carried their discussions forward in the Gemara and made the decisions laid down in it are called the *Amoraim* (speakers). By their ordinances they erected the fence around Torah; by their preachments they conveyed ethical teachings.

The normative legal decisions that direct the Jews' path in life are called *Halakhah,* walk. The preaching, ethical sayings, philosophical wisdom, and meditations and admonitions became known as *Haggadah* or *Aggadah*, which means preaching. In Mishnah and Gemara, both are interwoven, but we find Aggadah also in separate works arranged as a commentary to Scripture, called *Midrash*, or the "search" for meaning.

Law and ethics, Halakhah and Aggadah, cannot be separated. Judaism, as a religion of action, has always seen the law as an instrument of ethics and as an ethical ideal to be pursued. The Torah does not say, for instance, "You shall love your enemies." It says instead, "If you see the ass of your enemy lying under its burden and would like to refrain from raising it, you must nevertheless help him to lift it up" (Exodus 23:5). This is not a general injunction to love but a concrete, specific act, which, in turn, cannot help but promote love among two former enemies. As a piece of general legislation, it will eventually create a society whose members feel an inner obligation to help each other, thus overcoming animosities.

Aggadah lays the ethical foundations, halakhah is practiced ethics. Mitzvot become Torah; namely, instruction. Judaism denies the often-heard argument that we cannot legislate morality. The road to ethical conduct may actually have to start with legislation. Out of its observance, disagreeable as it may appear at the beginning, a new spirit may emerge. Halakhah fortified by Aggadah may achieve it.

The statement "the words of both Hillel and Shammai are the words of the living God" cannot be understood by Greek logic. If the words of one are God's words, then those of the other cannot be. Thus Judaism does not hold with this principle of Greek logic. Opinions need not exclude one another. As a matter of practical halakhah, Hillel's decisions were adopted since he was more lenient and understanding of human needs. If we translate this into the field of religions for instance, Judaism can say that both it and other religions are "true" in the sense that they lead people to God. They give evidence of their abiding value by the kindness and humanity they extend to all human beings.

ORGANIZATION OF THE TALMUD

The Talmud is divided into six orders. Each order consists of a number of tractates. The tractates are subdivided into chapters and paragraphs. An individual Mishnah constitutes a paragraph, and is simply called *Mishnah*.

1. The first order, *Zeraim* (Seeds), deals with the laws of agriculture. Since it is a duty to give thanks to God for the gifts of nature, the order opens with the Tractate *Berakhot* (Blessings), dealing with worship in general.

2. The second order, *Moed* (Appointed Times), discusses the rules and regulations pertaining to holy days. Among its tractates we find *Shabbat* (Sabbath), concerning the observance of the Sabbath; *Yom Tov* (Holy Day), dealing with the rules regulating the other holy days; and several tractates laying down Halakhah regarding specific holy seasons, such as *Yoma* (The Day of Atonement), *Sukkah* (Festival of Sukkot), and *Pessahim* (Feast of Passover).

3. The third order, *Nashim* (Women), contains marriage and divorce laws. Among its tractates are *Kiddushin* (Sanctification of Marriage), *Ketuvot* (Civil Laws of Marriage), and *Gittin* (Laws of Divorce).

Talmud, open. The opened page gives the text analyzed in this chapter (tractate Berakhot 10b, 11). Note Rashi's commentary on the inner margin, Tosafot on the outer margin, and references, etc., on the sides. (Photo by the author from Vol. 1 of his own 18-volume Vilna edition, 1896.)

4. The fourth order, *Nezikin* (Damages), forms the code of civil and criminal law. These were public laws when Israel was a nation. During the Middle Ages, when Jews had their own internal civil jurisdiction, the rabbis applied these laws within their congregations.

5. The fifth order, *Kadashim* (Holy Things), deals with laws of Temple sacrifices in times of old and also lays down the dietary laws (*Hullin*).

6. The sixth order, *Taharot* (Purifications), states the laws of ritual purity whose observance was required as prerequisite for entry and service in the Temple of old.

In opening one of the heavy tomes of the Talmud we find first of all that, regardless of the edition, its pages are numbered identically. Otherwise we could never find an indicated quotation or discussion. At the beginning, we shall find the Mishnah; it is followed by the Gemara, which discusses and analyzes it, and in turn is followed by another Mishnah. This text is found in a column in the center of the page. It is surrounded on the inner margin by the commentary of Rashi and, on the outer, by *Tosafot* (the additions made by Rashi's successors). Supercommentaries and cross-indexes may be found on the side or bottom of the page.

Rabbis and their Functions

Oral Torah did not come to an end with the compilation of the Talmud. It led to further commentaries and to codes, such as that of Maimonides, the Turim (see p. 267), and the Shulhan Arukh. On the basis of the accumulated material and precedents, the Orthodox rabbi has to decide individual cases brought to him. Throughout the ages, a number of these decisions, called *Responsa*, were collected; they serve rabbis the same way court decisions guide judges and attorneys. The authority to hand down these decisions is granted rabbis by their ordination. Modern rabbis are trained in many fields and serve in many areas of life, being teachers, preachers, and counselors. Ancient and medieval rabbis were simply scholars and teachers and, above all, the vested authority of Jewish law. Traditional rabbis still fulfill this function. The Israeli rabbinate operates almost exclusively as judicial authority in religious law. In some Diaspora countries as in the United States and in England, several of the various religious movements have appointed a central *Beth Din* (court of law). It consists of a group of rabbis who are specialists in Jewish law, and deals with the more difficult cases.

COMMENTARIES AND CODES

To understand the use of the rabbinical commentaries and codes, we shall follow the development of one small item of law from its source to its codes, looking for the sources from which the rabbis drew their conclusions to see how they did it, understand their controversies on the basis of different readings of the sources, follow their mutual critique based on logic, and end with the final practical decision by the codifiers. Our procedure will follow five steps: (1) find the source in the Written Torah and study it; (2) study Rashi's commentary to the verse in Written Torah; (3) turn to the Talmud and first study the Mishnah; (4) follow the comments of the Gemara. At each of these steps, Rashi's commentary will aid us. We may also study additional commentaries, such as Tosafot.

Finally, we will (5) turn to the codes, which give us the accepted decisions. (It is not always necessary to consult all of the codes. In easy cases, it may be sufficient to turn to the *Shulhan Arukh*, or even to one of the digests written later. In difficult cases, however, a rabbi may consult other codes and commentaries as well.) We can choose the code written by Maimonides, his *Mishneh Torah*. We may follow it by the *Tur*, the code of Rabbi Jacob ben Asher, who arranged the law in the four "Rows," or *Turim*. We shall certainly consult the Shulhan Arukh by Rabbi Joseph Karo, which is the authoritative code for traditional Jewish practice. Following the Tur, Joseph Karo arranged the code in four sections: (1) *Orah Hayim* (The Way of Life), containing laws of worship and holy days; (2) *Yore Deah* (The Teacher of Knowledge), dealing with dietary laws; (3) *Eben ha-Ezer* (The Stone of Help), containing the rules of family relationships, marriage, divorce, and so on; and (4) *Hoshen Mishpat* (The Breastplate of Judgment), dealing with civil laws and similar items.

Interpretation of the Sh'ma

Our selection deals with the recital of the Affirmation of Faith, beginning with the words, "Hear, 0 Israel! the Lord our God, the Lord is One." The first word, *Hear*, is the Hebrew *Sh'ma*; hence the whole paragraph is called the *Sh'ma*.

Our source in Written Torah is Deuteronomy 6:4–9, quoted here with the usual verse numbers to aid in the discussion:

(4) Hear, O Israel! The Lord our God, the Lord is One. (5) Love the Lord your God with all your heart and with all your soul and with all your might. (6) Take to heart these words with which I charge you this day. (7) Impress them upon your children. Recite them when you stay at home and when you are away, when you lie down and when you get up. (8) Bind them as a sign on your hand and let them serve as frontlets between your eyes; (9) inscribe them on the doorposts of your house and on your gates.

Rashi explains, citing midrashic and talmudic sources:

"You must love" (Verse 5): Do His bidding out of love, for he who acts out of love cannot be compared to him who acts [only] out of fear. . . . "With all your heart": With both your inclinations (toward good or evil), or another explanation: do not act half-heartedly in relationship to God. "And with all your soul": Even if He takes your soul [life]. "And with all your might" (citing Tractate Berakhot): With all your substance or money. There are people to whom their money is more precious than their person, hence it is stated: "and with all your substance" [after the surrender of life is demanded]. Another explanation: With all your capacities. . . . And how does this love express itself? "These words . . . take them to heart" (Verse 6); through it, he recognizes God and cleaves to His ways. . . . "Recite them" (Verse 7): Your basic talk shall be about them. Make them your basic concern and not merely a side issue. "When you lie down": I might have thought even if he lies down in the middle of the day [he would have to recite them], hence Torah says: "When you get up." I might have thought, even if he rises up in the middle of the night, hence Torah says: "When you stay at home and when you are away." The Torah speaks of the customary usage, the usual time of lying down and the usual time of rising up.

As we turn to the Talmud, we find the Mishnah in the Tractate Berakhot, Chapter 1, Mishnah 3. This is followed by the Gemara. The Mishnah and the following discussion of Gemara are found on pages 10b and 11a in all editions of the Babylonian Talmud.

In Tractate Berakhot, Chapter 1, Mishnah 3, we read:

The School of Shammai teaches: In the evening one must recite the Sh'ma in a reclining position, and in the morning standing up, for it is said: when you lie down and when you get up. The School of Hillel teaches: One may read it in any position, for it also says: When you are away [literally, when you walk on the way]. [Torah simply says, you must recite it wherever you are and whatever you do.] Why does [Scripture] say: When you lie down and when you get up? This refers to the hour of the day when people lie down, and the hour when they rise up. Rabbi Tarphon told: "Once, when on the road, I reclined to recite the Sh'ma in accordance with the teaching of the School of Shammai, and I was almost attacked by robbers." They retorted: "You deserved to get into trouble, having transgressed against the words of the School of Hillel."

And in the Gemara we find:

> The School of Hillel has indeed explained its reason and refuted the School of Shammai; but why, then, did the School of Shammai refuse to yield? It could argue [from the verse]: Scripture should have stated "in the evening and in the morning" [then the School of Hillel would be right]; but it states "when you lie down and when you get up." It must mean that at the time of evening rest a leaning position is required, and at the time of getting up, a standing position is required.
>
> The Rabbis taught: The School of Hillel says: one may recite it leaning, or standing, or sitting or reclining, or while walking on the way, or during one's work. Once, Rabbi Yishmael and Rabbi Eleazar, Son of Azariah, were together. Rabbi Yishmael was reclining, Rabbi Eleazar standing. When the time for Sh'ma came in the evening, Rabbi Eleazar reclined and the Rabbi Yishmael stood up. Rabbi Eleazar said to Rabbi Yishmael, "Brother Yishmael . . . while I was standing you were reclining, now that I am reclining you stand. [Why?]" He answered, "Because I followed the decision of the School of Hillel [which permits the recital in any position; therefore I stood up, even in the evening]; you followed the opinion of the School of Shammai. Furthermore [had I not stood up], the disciples might have observed it and established Halakhah in that manner." What did he mean by the second statement? According to the School of Hillel, one may recite the Sh'ma while reclining, provided that one finds himself in a reclining position. Until now, you were standing, then sat down and reclined [to recite the Sh'ma]. [I was reclining, and had I continued to recline, the disciples would have seen both of us reclining, and] therefore they would have believed that both of us followed the decision of the School of Shammai. Noticing it, the disciples might have fixed Halakhah permanently [according to Shammai]. [Hence I stood up.] (10b–11a)

In other words, one of the rabbis had been reclining already, and the other sat down before reciting the Sh'ma. According to Hillel, the first one could have remained in his position, but this might have created the wrong impression that both followed Shammai; hence Rabbi Yishmael stood up. Now the disciples knew that the Sh'ma could be recited in any position.

The overriding issue was the principle. There must be no doubt in the disciples' minds that the School of Hillel must always be followed because this principle had implications in numerous fields of Halakhah. In addition, the masters were aware of their obligation to teach not only by their words, but equally by their actions. Conduct is instruction; teaching and practice must go hand in hand. Example is more important than preachment. The disciples would recognize in the performance of their masters that they took in utter seriousness not only the act of reciting the affirmation of faith and of love of God, but the meaning of their affirmation, as well, in preparation and in recital, in adjustment of body and direction of heart. The two rabbis knew that in the presence of their disciples their action spelled out both a legal precedent and an inspiration in faith. Seen in this manner, the concern of these men is not a dwelling on trivialities and hairsplitting, but an act of guidance. No one ever knows how deep the impression of his actions may be, though they may appear insignificant to himself. It is only in this manner that we can fully understand the great concern of the rabbis with the exact performance of every Mitzvah.

Now, in Maimonides's *Mishneh Torah*, Book 2, we find the following:

> Twice a day one must recite the Sh'ma, in the evening and in the morning, as Scripture says, "when you lie down, and when you get up," at the hour when people lie down, namely at night, and at the hour when people rise up, namely at daytime. (Chapter 1, Par. 1)
>
> He who recites the Sh'ma without directing his heart [to God] . . . has not done his duty. (Chapter 2, Par. 1)
>
> Everyone may recite it in his prevailing position, standing or walking or sitting or riding on an animal. Yet it is forbidden to recite the Sh'ma stretched out, facing downward or upward; but he may recite it resting on his side. If he is obese or sick and cannot turn on his side, let him turn a bit sidewise and recite it. (Chapter 2, Par. 2)
>
> If he is walking, he shall stop during the first verse; the rest he may recite walking. If he is asleep . . . one must wake him up. (Chapter 2, Par. 3)
>
> He must wash his hands before he recites it. (Chapter 3, Par. 1)

The regulations regarding the Sh'ma are found in the Orah Hayim section of Tur and Shulhan Arukh. In the Orah Hayim we read:

> He shall recite it in awe and attunement to God . . . everyone shall consider it a new royal proclamation, newly issued, whenever he recites it. . . . It is God's proclamation. Thus do we find it in the Midrash . . . when a king of flesh and blood issues a proclamation to his provinces, all the people receive it standing up . . . but the Holy One . . . said to Israel: . . . "I will not burden you by commanding you to stand up when you recite it . . . you may do so even while walking on the way, but must do so in awe and reverence."
>
> He may read it either walking or standing or sitting down, but not lying down on his back, as Maimonides points out [here Maimonides is quoted]. Anyone who wishes to impose upon himself a special burden by standing up when he had been sitting down does wrong, and is actually called a sinner.
>
> [Commentary by Joseph Karo] For in daytime he transgresses against the decision of the School of Hillel and appears to be following the School of Shammai . . . and at night he follows neither school. He is called a sinner, for we find in [Tractate] Shabbat [40a] that he who transgresses against the rulings of the Rabbis is called a sinner. (Chapters 61 and 63)

Again, we read in Chapters 61 and 63 that

He must recite the Sh'ma with attunement to God, in awe and reverence. "Which I charge you this day" [is mentioned in Scripture] to tell you that it must be new to you every day, and not be like something often heard and habitual. It has been a custom to recite the first verse aloud, in order to arouse the "Kavanah" [attunement].

It has been a custom to place the hands over the face during the recital of the first verse, in order that he may not be distracted from his Kavanah by extraneous impressions.

He shall prolong the pronouncement of the letters of the word "One" in reflection on God's Kingship in heaven and on earth and to call to mind that God is One and Only in the universe, ruling over its entire expanse. After the first verse he shall recite: Blessed be His Name, His glorious Kingdom is for ever and ever. [This sentence is not part of the verses in Deuteronomy.]

After these first verses he shall pause for a brief instant [before continuing "and . . . love . . ."] to indicate [and reflect on] the distinction between "Acceptance of the Kingdom of Heaven" [contained in the first and second verse, which are the foundation of Jewish life and all its Mitzvot] and the Mitzvot ["love," which derive from it]. He may recite it walking, or standing, reclining, or riding on an animal, but not lying stretched out, facing downward or upward; yet he may recite it lying on his side [note: if he is lying down already, and it would be a burden for him to get up]. If he is obese and cannot turn to his side, or sick, let him turn a bit to the side and recite it.

He who wants to make it hard on himself and stands up after he has been sitting, to recite it standing up, he is called a sinner.

If he is walking and wants to recite the Sh'ma, he shall stop at the first verse. If he is asleep one must wake him up, even if it troubles him.

In these developments, we see the respect for Written Torah—every word in it is regarded as significant. Fluid interpretation at the beginning of the development yields to terse regulation at the end. We should remember that Hillel and Shammai lived at a time when the Land constituted a unifying force. Maimonides balanced strictness in observance by free speculation in philosophy, as Torah permitted. The Shulhan Arukh, at the end of the development, was written to unite the people and strengthen their will to live through Mitzvot. Immersion in Mitzvot gave the people the sense of closeness to God and to one another. The elements of God–Torah–Land–Mitzvot are all there, yet emphasis is placed differently, as outward conditions weakened the Land, the living soil of a people, and as persecution drew them ever more deeply into the shell of minute performance.

A Midrashic Section

The following excerpts are from the Tractate B. Makkot, pages 23b/24. I have added the commentary of Rashi wherever appropriate. I have also added some observations of my own, which are introduced with the initials "LT."

Rav Simlai taught: 613 Mitzvot were told to Moses, 365 prohibitions corresponding to the days of the sun year, and 248 duties of performance, corresponding to the limbs of the human body.

RASHI: Every day he is thereby admonished not to transgress.

LT: The figures given reveal the ethical character of Torah and its commandments: Every day of the year demands anew that the Jew keep desires in check. At the same time, every limb of the human body must be placed in active service to make God manifest in the world.

Rav Hamnuna said: Which verse in Torah points to this [the 613 commandments]? It is: "Moses charged us with Torah as the heritage of the congregation of Jacob" (Deuteronomy 33:4). The numerical value of [the letters of] word "Torah" is 611, and the commandments "I am the Lord your God, who brought you out of the land of Egypt" (Exodus 20:2) and "You shall have no other gods beside Me" (Exodus 20:3), we heard from the mouth of the Almighty. [This brings the total to 613.]

RASHI: 611 came from Moses, therefore it is written: "Torah" (611) did Moses charge us, two came out of the Almighty, a total of 613.

LT: The Rabbis did not count the commandments; they gave the figure of 613 as an ethical guideline, as we saw. Now Rav Hamnuna looks for text in Scripture as reinforcement. He finds it by adding the numerical value of the letters in the word *Torah* [each Hebrew letter has a numerical value] and arriving at 611. Now we find in Exodus 20:15–16 that the people fell back; they were overpowered by the voice of God and pleaded with Moses to speak to them and give them God's word. By tradition, this happened after the first two commandments had been spoken by God Himself. The first two they heard from God's mouth directly. Thus Moses wrote *Torah*, 611, and God spoke 2, for a total of 613. This play with numbers reinforces the rabbinic statement. We have to assume, however, that the number 613 came first and was based on the addition of the days of the year and the limbs of the body (as known to the rabbis), to teach the lesson of faith symbolically. Then came the "proof." (Maimonides gives a list of the 613 commandments.)

The text continues,

Then came David and reduced them [the 613 commandments] to 11; as we read: "A Psalm of David. Lord who may stay in Your tent, who may reside on Your holy mountain? (1) He who lives without blame, (2) who does what is right, (3) and in his heart acknowledges the truth, (4) whose tongue is not given to evil, (5) who has never done harm to his fellow, (6) or borne reproach for [his acts toward] his neighbor, (7) for whom a contemptible man is abhorrent,

(8) but who honors those who fear the Lord; (9) who stands by his oath even to his hurt; (10) who has never lent money at interest, (11) or accepted a bribe against the innocent; the man who acts thus shall never be shaken (Psalm 15)."

(1) "He who lives without blame": This is our father Abraham, of whom it is said: "[God said to him] 'Walk in My ways and be blameless'";

(2) "who does what is right": as for instance Abba Hilkiyahu, a man of scrupulous integrity (B. Taanit 23a/b);

(3) "and in his heart acknowledges the truth": as for instance, Rabbi Safra;

(4) "whose tongue is not given to evil": This is our father Jacob, as it is written: [when his mother Rebecca ordered him to put the fleece of a lamb on his arm to appear like Esau at the touch of his blind father Isaac, and receive the blessing destined for Esau, he said] "if my father touches me, I shall appear to him like a trickster and bring upon myself a curse, not a blessing" (Genesis 27:12). [He therefore did not want to do it.]

(5) "who has never done harm to his fellow": He does not cut into the business of his neighbor [undercutting him];

(6) "or borne reproach for [his acts toward] his neighbor": He brings close those near to him [coming to their aid];

(7) "for whom a contemptible man is abhorrent": This is King Hezekiah, who dragged the bones [even] of his father on a rope ladder. [He set an example of the fate awaiting the sinners even after death; his father Ahaz was very evil and even sacrificed a son to the idols; he was abhorrent to Hezekiah; see 11 Kings 16 for all of Ahaz's evil deeds.];

(8) "but who honors those who fear the Lord": This is Yehoshafat, king of Judah; when he saw a disciple of the wise, he rose from his throne, embraced and kissed him and called him: My father, my master, my teacher;

(9) "who stands by his oath even to his hurt": as, for instance, Rabbi Johanan, who said once: 'I shall keep my fast until I get home'" [a pledge that was not binding, but, having once made it, he kept it];

(10) "who has never lent money at interest": even to a heathen [which Torah permits (Deuteronomy 23:20–21)];

(11) "or accepted a bribe against the innocent": as, for instance, Rabbi Ishmael ben Yose.

As Rabbi Gamaliel came to the verse, "The man who acts thus shall never be shaken," he wept. He said, "[Only] he who does all of these will not be shaken [a task beyond the capacity of a human being], but he who does only one of these, will be shaken. " They [his colleagues] replied: "Is it stated 'He who does all of these'? In fact, he who does but one of these, will not be shaken."

RASHI
(excerpts):   *"David reduced them to 11"*: In the beginning they were all Zaddikim [flawlessly Righteous], and could take upon themselves the yoke of many Mitzvot, but later generations were no such perfect Zaddikim, and if they were to observe all of them, no one would be able to be meritorious; hence David came and reduced them, in order that they might gain merit by observing these 11 Mitzvot, and thus, as generations get less distinguished, one reduces them [the number of Mitzvot]. *"or accepted a bribe against the innocent"*: Even when it was permissible to do so, as, for instance Rabbi Ishmael ben Yose, whose tenant farmer brought him what he owed him ahead of time, and he did not wish to accept it, as he might be his judge [in some future litigation, and then feel biased in his favor].

LT: The passage reveals the intent of the rabbis. It is not the number of Mitzvot that counts, but the spirit. No generation has to carry more than it can. Following God means not simply remaining within the letter of the law, but going beyond it, in spirit and in action toward the human neighbor, Jew or non-Jew. Even one such action establishes the person, makes the person human and thus beloved by God.

The text continues in the same manner, and the essence of Torah is further distilled.

Then came Isaiah and reduced them [the commandments] to six, as it is written: (1) He who walks in righteousness; (2) speaks uprightly; (3) spurns profit from fraudulent dealings; (4) waves away a bribe instead of grasping it; (5) stops his ears against listening to infamy; (6) shuts his eyes against looking at evil—such a one shall dwell in lofty security (Isaiah 33:15–16).

Then came Micah and reduced them to three: "He has told you, 0 man, what is good and what the Lord requires of you: (1) only to do justice, and (2) to love goodness, and (3) to walk modestly with your God; then will your name achieve wisdom" (Micah 6:8–9).

(1) to do justice: establishing justice

(2) to love goodness: doing good deeds of loving kindness to others

(3) to walk modestly: burying the dead and providing for a bride.

Then came Isaiah and reduced them to two, as it is stated: "Thus said the Lord: (1) observe what is right and (2) do what is just, for soon My salvation shall come" (Isaiah 56:1).

Then came Amos and reduced them (the commandments) to one, as it is said: "Seek Me, and you will live" (Amos 5:4).

Here we recognize the rabbis as teachers of ethics, establishing the ultimate meaning of Mitzvot. They arrive at the number of Mitzvot not by counting them but by the primary concern that Mitzvot be understood as guides for every day of the year, teaching self-discipline and motivating the use of every limb of the body to promote God's will in the world. After arriving at their conclusion, they link it up with scriptural pronouncements. To the rabbis the ultimate measure of a good Jew is not simply the performance of laws but the spirit, the ethics, that go beyond the laws. In performance, the spirit of the laws is made manifest. It should be noted that most of the actions that establish a good Jew are deeds of kindness and concern for fellow human beings. The rabbis help us to understand that the "yoke of Torah" is adjusted to the capacities of each generation, but the principle is not affected.

The rabbis used several methods in their interpretations. *Gematria* is the counting of the numerical value of the letters of a word for interpretative purposes. *Kal va-homer,* one of the hermeneutic principles, is a conclusion drawn *a forteriore* from a less involved to a heavier, or more involved, situation (for example, if theft is a crime, then theft plus murder is a crime, the latter situation being "heavier").

We recognize the power the rabbis assumed for themselves as interpreters of the divine word of Torah. In principle they wished to "build a fence around Torah." When conditions made making new solutions imperative, the rabbis struggled to find them. They based their decision upon the word of Torah, reading it into its text, making *it* the basis for their ruling. Of course, this was not always possible. The rabbis demanded respect for their decisions, and at the same time were aware of their human frailty and inadequacy. Rabbi Gamaliel wept out of the sense of his own shortcomings, and his colleagues comforted him in compassion. In choosing examples of perfect living, they did not confine themselves to personalities of the past, but drew from the lives of men living at their own time, as if to say that Jewish living, in the true spirit of Torah, is possible even today.

Note

1. Throughout these chapters "B." indicates "Babli" or "Babylonian Talmud" (e.g., "B. Ketuvot 103a" means Babylonian Talmud, Tractate Ketuvot, page 103a); "J." indicates "Jerushalmi," the "Jerusalem, Palestinian Talmud"; "M." (or no special letter, followed by Tractate, chapter, and paragraph) indicates "Mishnah."

CHAPTER 14

Definitions and Symbols: God, Humanity, and Eternity

GOD: CONCEPTS AND THEOLOGICAL ISSUES

THE SCRIPTURE USES many names for God. We have seen that the names *YHVH* and *Elohim* served the various schools of higher biblical criticism as they investigated the origin and authorship of various sections of the Bible.[1] A quotation from Scripture may guide us toward an understanding of the various names and ways of God.

> Moses drove the flock into the wilderness. . . . He gazed, and there was a bush blazing in fire, yet the bush was not consumed. . . . And God called him out of the bush . . . and He said: "I am the God of Your fathers, the God of Abraham, the God of Isaac, the God of Jacob. . . . I will send you to Pharaoh to lead my people, the children of Israel, out of Egypt." And Moses said, "When I come to the children of Israel and say to them, 'The God of your fathers has sent me to you,' and they ask me, 'What is His name?' what shall I say to them?" And God said to Moses, "Ehyeh-Asher-Ehyeh," and He said: "You shall say to the children of Israel, 'Ehyeh sends me to you.'" (Exodus 3:1–14) And God spoke to Moses, He said to him: "I am YHVH. I appeared to Abraham, Isaac and Jacob as *El Shaddai,* but I did not make Myself known to them by My name YHVH" (Exodus 6:2)

The names for God in this passage are left untranslated; they will now be explained.

Ehyeh-Asher-Ehyeh has been variously translated "I Am That I Am," "I Am Who I Am," "I Will Be What I Will Be," and "I Am Who Brings into Being." The root of the word is *hayah,* meaning "being." The name *YHVH* is derived from the same root and is related to the definition God gives Himself. Basically, the

276

term speaks of God as Being—absolute, unchanging Being. Human beings—along with all of nature—change. From the day of birth to the day of death, cells are created and cells die. God, in contrast, says of Himself that He is Absolute Being. He is What He is, always; He does not change or age and is not limited by time or space.

Yet in God, "Being" does not mean that He remains unmoved. Aristotle taught that God, being perfect Being, had to be the "Unmoved Mover," detached from the world. Abraham Heschel, disagreeing with Aristotle but in tune with Jewish tradition, explained that God has pathos. God is moved by what His children do, rejoices if they go in His ways, grieves when they go astray, and is comforted when they find their way back to Him.

God is beyond human comprehension. The Jews have therefore refrained from pronouncing the word YHVH, which expresses something unfathomable. Were they to pronounce it they might drag the name of God down to the level of human comprehension, and thus diminish His Being. Therefore, the word is pronounced *Adonai*, "the Lord." This means Jews know there is only *one* Lord, and no one, divinity or human being, could possibly be mistaken for the Lord. This is as far as human comprehension can go. Since God is Being, there can be only One God; He is not subject to change. God cannot be said to ever assume human form, because this would limit His Oneness and His absolute Being.

What about the beings in the world, stars and stones and humans? They could not have any being independent of God; therefore God is *He who Brings Into Being;* He is the Creator. What about time? There cannot be time that is outside of God. God is the Creator of Time and the God of History. Isaiah states: "I am the first and I am the last and there is no God but Me (44:6)." What about space? There cannot be any space outside God. "Holy, holy, holy is the Lord of hosts, the whole earth [universe] is full of His presence" (Isaiah 6:3). As every place is God's, the rabbis used the term *Makom*, Place, as a name of God.

God is, therefore, incomparable. "To whom then can you liken Me, to whom can I be compared? says the Holy One" (Isaiah 40:25). There is nothing but God (Isaiah 45:6). (This should not be confused with pantheism. Pantheism states that the totality of nature is God; Judaism states that God created the totality of nature and fills it. He is more than this totality, He transcends it. This is Panentheism.)

God is a person. At the burning bush, God talks with Moses. (Mordecai Kaplan does not conceive of God as a person, see p. 307.) We must understand, however, that this does not mean God has a body. He is a person in the sense that He acts freely and relates freely, something the forces of nature cannot do. Maimonides warns against ascribing to God any physical attributes and maintains that terms such as "the arm of God" and "the voice of God," which we find in the Bible, refer only to the effect of God's action that was perceived by human beings. God as a person is a unique person; there is no other person like Him. As the God of history, God also knows of human frailties. He is the God of compassion.

In Exodus, God states to Moses that He revealed Himself already to the patriarchs as *El-Shaddai*. This is a dual term. We shall turn first to *El*.

The Canaanites knew a deity called El; hence Abraham may have called God by this name. Generally, the term has been used in a different form: Elohim, a plural to which the verb is always affixed in singular form when speaking of God. *Elohim* also means "judge." The term thus means God is the sum total of power and justice (hence the plural *Elohim*). He unites all power and justice into One (hence the singular verb). He metes out judgment and enforces it.

God, as One, combines power and majesty with graciousness and kindness, and judgment with mercy. In any other being, this would be a contradiction; in God's Being it is not. "I am, nothing beside Me: Who forms the light and creates the darkness, Who makes peace and creates woe, I, the Lord am doing all these" (Isaiah 45:6).

There are no contradictions in God's being. Noting the terms *Elohim* and *YHVH*, found in the Genesis story of creation, the rabbis have given their use a meaning quite different from that applied by biblical criticism. They say that in the beginning God decided to rule the world by strict justice (Elohim), but He realized that it could not exist when judged by the absolute standard of justice. He added the attribute of His compassion, prepared to permit mercy to mitigate justice—hence the two names, YHVH Elohim. Ultimately, He found that even tempered justice was too much for humanity and world, and He based His rule entirely on mercy (YHVH).

We find, therefore, that in the pronouncement of His attributes (Exodus 34:6–7) the term *El*, God of justice, is intimately linked to *Rahum*, a term derived from *Rehem*, "mother's womb." He is concerned with justice, but He is abundantly compassionate, sheltering His people in absolute loving security. In an attempt to understand some facets of God's Being, Rabbi Johanan says in B. Megillah 31a of the Talmud,

> Whenever you find the greatness of God expressed in Scripture, you equally find expressed His humility. Thus it is recorded in Torah, repeated in Nevee-im, and again, for the third time, in Ketuvim. In Torah we read: "For the Lord your God, He is God of gods, and Lord of lords, [meaning supreme] the great God, the mighty, and the awesome, who shows no favor and takes no bribe . . . but upholds the case of the fatherless and the widow, and befriends the stranger, providing him with food and clothing" (Deuteronomy 10:17–18). In Nevee-im, Prophets, we read: "For thus said He, who high aloft dwells in eternity, whose Name is Holy: I dwell on high in holiness; yet with the contrite and lowly in spirit, reviving the spirit of the lowly, reviving the hearts of the contrite" (Isaiah 57:15). Repeated a third time in Ketubim (Psalm 68:5–6), it reads: "Sing to God, chant hymns to His name, extol Him who rides the clouds, The Lord is His name" followed by, "the father of orphans, the champion of widows."

The Jew, recognizing the holiness and absoluteness of God, is confident that God's power is but the instrument of His mercy. This synthesis is expressed in the designation of God as "our Father." A father has power and dominion, which is exercised in behalf of his love. "Blessed art you, 0 Israel," exclaims Rabbi Akiba, "for He who cleanses you of all your sins, and before Whom you cleanse yourselves, it is your Father who is in heaven" (B. Yoma 85b).

On the Days of Awe, the great prayer of petition (in which Jews ask for a year of health, sustenance, forgiveness, and blessing) appeals to God as "Our Father, our King." Trusting in Him as "our Father," secure in His eternal love, their appeal is directed to Him as "our King," all-powerful to supply all needs. As King, He must judge all humanity, for without justice the world could not endure. As Father, He suffers when His children go astray, He waits for them, urges them to repent and return to Him, and never ceases pleading with them to the moment of their death that they may return. And if they do repent, He immediately receives them in affection as His beloved children. Even in judging, He is aware of human frailties and deals with humanity kindly, as the Father who has given life and knows the weaknesses of His children. Therefore, Jews have realized that divine love is never withdrawn from them in prosperity or in adversity; they praise Him even in moments of deepest sorrow and distress.

In their awareness of God's closeness, Jews have the liberty of even "arguing" with God. Abraham is pleading for God to spare the city of Sodom if there were but ten righteous persons found in it (Genesis 18:22–32). In the same manner have Abraham's descendants spoken up to God, doing so with deepest reverence and full acceptance of the Father's will. They have been certain of His understanding.

The patriarchs knew God as *Shaddai*. The etymology of the term is not clear. Some scholars of biblical criticism explain the term as meaning "God of the Mountains." Jews have given it a different etymological derivation. Maimonides explains the term as *Yesh* lo *day*—He was self-sufficient in creating the world; He needs no other force and no assistance as Creator. Benno Jacob, a German rabbi and biblical commentator, held that Shaddai stands for "God who goes with His people wherever they may be." The patriarchs, strangers in a land not yet their own, wandering abroad from time to time, found strength in this God-awareness. This Name of God is also affixed to the *Mezuzah*, which designates Jewish homes throughout the world. It may have been the source of Rabbi Benno Jacob's interpretation that God as Shaddai is with the people and their dwellings wherever they are.

The term *Shekhinah* has been used to signify God's presence, His resting, dwelling among the people and in the world. "They shall make me a sanctuary and I shall dwell (*shakhanti*) in their midst" (Exodus 25:8), "I shall dwell in their midst forever" (Ezekiel 43:9), etc. Jews have also applied to Him the term *Shalom*, implying Absolute Perfection; *shalom* means "peace," which is the sum of perfection.

In Jewish thought the concept of God has continued to occupy the minds of mystics, theologians, or more currently, Jewish women. Against Maimonides, who severely censured those who ascribed a body to God, the medieval rabbis of the Provence and Germany firmly maintained it. The mystics speculated on the inner unfolding of the Godhead. Modern Jewish women have voiced grave objections against the portrayal of God exclusively in masculine terms (with the exception of *Shekhinah*, which is feminine). This objection has substance but poses problems, as the sacred texts refer to God as masculine. (Finding a gender-neutral pronoun for God has been impossible, at least for me. Committed to women's equality I nevertheless had to use the masculine pronoun for God in this book.)

All these approaches and conjectures in defining God are legitimate, since Judaism recognizes the inability of human beings to fathom God. To see God in terms other than absolute unity, or to hold that He assumed human form is not legitimate in Judaism.

HUMANITY

Rabbi Akiba used to say, "Beloved is man, as he was created in the image [of God], and an even greater love was accorded him in being made aware that he is created in the image of God" (Avot 3:18). All human beings are created in the image of God, all are equal and all are God's coworkers in the world. The creation of but one man and woman underscores this fact: No one can say that his ancestors were better than those of his neighbor (B. Sanhedrin 4:5). All people are products of the earth to which they must return. They are weak, frail, and insignificant. But they have also been created in the image of God, and have been endowed with a divine soul. Human beings, therefore, have worth and dignity beyond any other work of God's creation. This dual character is expressed by the Psalmist:

> When I behold the heavens, the work of Your fingers, the moon and the stars which You have established; what is man that You are mindful of him, and the son of man that You take account of him? Yet You have made him but little lower than the angels, and have crowned him with glory and honor. You have made him to have dominion over the works of Your hands. (Psalm 8:4–6)

Man, the human being, thus is the "son of man," but he is also the "son of God" (Deuteronomy 14:1); the choice is ours. The rabbis point out that we bear the features of our animal character but also those of divinity. Like any animal, the human being eats and drinks, excretes, multiplies, and dies. As a divine being, the human being stands erect, speaks, reasons, and sees straight. If worthy, the human being stands *higher* than the angels, and not *a little lower,* as the Psalmist had thought. If the human being is unworthy, every insect may offer the reminder, "I was created before you and take precedence over you."

The first questions addressed to a person appearing before God in final judgment of the conduct of life are these:

> Have you dealt faithfully with your fellowman; have you appointed regular periods for [the study of] Torah [that it be a guide to conduct]; have you brought children into the world; have you looked forward to redemption . . . ? If the fear of God is his treasure, it will be well with him, otherwise not. (B. Shabbat 31a)

The work of human beings in the world should be a striving for redemption, and their actions in their daily rounds a service in behalf of God. This assures a life of worth. Not in Mitzvot toward God, but in those toward our fellows do we primarily earn our salvation. This entails a decent love for one's own self. Of Hillel it is said that he considered the care of his body a Mitzvah. Judaism has not believed in the merits of asceticism and has even stated that every person must account for the decent joys in life which God has placed in his or her way and which they declined (J. Kiddushin 4). Joined to this self respect must be humility. Moses was deigned worthy by God to receive the Torah because he was humble (Numbers 12:3; B. Shabbat 67a).

These principles entail also an unconditional love of neighbor, even of enemies. We must help them and not bear any grudge against them (Exodus 23:4–5; Leviticus 19:17). We must consider the dignity of all and may never put anyone to shame. Only in secret may we give support to the poor, lest they feel embarrassed. Charity in Hebrew is called *Tzedaka*, "righteousness"; it is simply right living that we support those with whom destiny has dealt harshly:

> Better than charity is the loan given to the needy, which helps set him up; better even a partnership with him, that allows him to draw on your experience as well as your resources. (Abot de-Rabbi Nathan 41:66a)
>
> Let the honor of your fellow man be as dear to you as your own; and let the property of your fellow man be as dear to you as your own. (Avot 2:15, 17)

This applies not only to Jews, but to all people, regardless of faith or race or color. All of them are created in the image of God. According to Torah, God made a covenant with Noah and with nature and all humanity (Genesis 9:8–17). This covenant, according to Judaism, commits every human being to "Seven Noahide Laws." They are basic rules of morality:

1. Civil justice; the establishment of just legal systems and just courts;
2. the prohibition of blasphemy; which includes being a false witness;
3. the prohibition of idolatry; namely the worship of any human being or human creation as god;
4. the prohibition of degenerate sexual acts;
5. the prohibition of murder;
6. the prohibition of theft;
7. the law against cutting limbs from living animals to eat them; meaning cruelty in any shape, even to animals. (Sanhedrin 56a/b)

Those who abide by these laws are assured of "salvation."

The rabbis can therefore proclaim in the name of Judaism

> I call heaven and earth to witness that on every person, be he Jew or non-Jew, man or woman, or servant, the divine spirit rests on him according to his deeds. The heathen is your neighbor, your brother, to do him wrong is a sin. (Tanna debe Eliyahu 207, 284)

The Jew, therefore, respects the right of all to find their way to God in their own fashion. Judaism did exclude the heathendom of old with its immoral practices, violating the Noahide laws, but solemnly declares that "the righteous among the peoples of the world will have a share in the world to come" (Yalkut Shimoni to Prophets 296). "The just among the peoples of the world are priests of God" (Eliyahu Sutah 20).

Judaism accords respect to all ethical faiths and, finding that they all lead to salvation, does not engage in missionary work. Nevertheless, Judaism would consider it unfair to deny to any person the right to join the faith and destiny of the Jewish people. If, in full conviction, a person feels that Judaism gives him true spiritual fulfillment, he or she has a right to find it. Having thus affiliated himself or herself, the convert becomes a full-fledged member of the Jewish people, beloved by God and the newly found community in faith.

In Judaism, not one soul is considered expendable. God is the Father, and every human being is a child of God in whom the Holy Spirit, the spirit of holiness, rests. Only through sin may the Holy Spirit depart from him or her, as King David found out. Involved in grievous sin, he cried out, "Do not take Your Holy Spirit—the spirit of Your holiness—from me" (Psalm 51:13). In Teshuvah, returning to God through repentance, we find this spirit restored to us.

Why People Sin

Every human being is endowed by God with a soul. This soul given to us is pure. Daily prayer affirms "The soul which You, God, have given me is pure." Nevertheless we sin. Sin is the rejection or evasion of God's command. Human beings sin when they transgress against those ordinances that relate them to God; they sin more grievously when they wrong their fellow human beings. In the latter case, they both thwart God's will *and* hurt their neighbor. The human intent determines the severity of a sin: We may sin inadvertently, for "there is no man who does not sin" (1 Kings 8:46); we also commit sin deliberately.

There are various terms in Hebrew connoting sin. The term *Het* means "missing the mark" that Torah has established or failing it; an error in judgment or lack of determination may be the causes. The term is used in the confession on Yom Kippur, when sins against others are repentantly admitted before God. *Averah* means "transgressing," stepping out of the boundaries God has set.

As to why we sin or why God gave human beings the capacity to sin has been a difficult question for the rabbis. God is all powerful; nevertheless, "all is in the hands of Heaven (God), except the fear of Heaven" (B. Berakhot 33b). God placed the inclination to do evil into all of His creation, including human beings. It is called *Yetzer ha-Ra,* or simply *Yetzer*, "the Drive," as in "The drive of man's heart is evil from his youth" (Genesis 8:21). This Yetzer was already in Adam and prompted him to transgress against God's command in the Garden of Eden. By his transgression, Adam brought death into the world.

But people do not die on account of Adam's sin; they die on account of their own. "Adam sinned and died, Elijah did not sin, therefore he did not die"

(Pesikta 76a). A Midrash tells that God caused all future generations to appear before Adam accusing him, "You have caused us death!" When Adam was deeply disturbed at being the cause of all death, God comforted him: "They do not die on account of your sin, but all on account of their own!" (Tanhuma, Bereshit 29). Judaism holds that all sin *as* Adam sinned and not *because* Adam sinned. We are told in the Talmud that Adam's physical beauty was taken from him after his transgression (Bereshit Rabba 12:6), but his state of ethical awareness did not undergo any change; it resides in humanity as it did in the first progenitor. In this sense, there is no "original sin" in Judaism.

The Midrash states that God was sorry He created the Yetzer; but the rabbis also said God saw it as very good (Bereshit Rabba 9:17). Without the Yetzer—understood, for instance, as the sex drive—there would be no procreation. Thus, sex within its rightful confines is good. The Yetzer, a force released in us by outside temptation, can equally release in us the will to conquer it, and in so doing, we grow in our humanity. "Surely, if you do right, there is uplift. But if you do not right sin is the demon at the door, whose urge is toward you, but you can be his master" (Genesis 4:7). The power to do evil is a condition of our freedom to do good and of our responsibility. The tragedy in yielding to the Yetzer lies in the fact that one sin begets another "until it becomes permitted in [the sinner's] eyes" (B. Kiddushin 40a). With every act, the sinner unknowingly removes himself further and further from the presence of God and the fellowship with others. We are armed against sin in two ways. One is *Teshuvah*, "repentance," literally, returning to God's domain from which we have strayed. It is better to avoid sinning. Torah is the way.

Torah can be compared to a remedy; like a man who has hit his son and wounded him, and then gives him a plaster for his wound, telling him: "My son, as long as the plaster is on the wound you may eat, drink, bathe, and have no fear; but if you remove it, you will get infected." Even so God speaks: "My children, I have created the Yetzer ha-ra, but I have created Torah as its antidote; occupy yourselves with Torah and you will not fall into its hand . . . but if you do not occupy yourselves with Torah, you will be delivered into its hand" (B. Kiddushin 30b).

SUPERNATURAL BEINGS

According to Jewish tradition, the work of human beings in the service of God can be aided or impeded by supernatural beings, specifically angels and satanic forces. Humanity's struggle will culminate and be resolved with the coming of the Messiah, who is not a supernatural being but is sent by God and filled with God's spirit. The individual's striving in life will find its reward in the World to Come. We shall briefly discuss these forces that interact with human beings during their lifetimes, and the hope held out for the future that gives human beings direction now.

Angels

The Hebrew term *Malakh* simply means "messenger" (as does the Latin *angelus*). Whoever carries God's message in the world becomes His angel. Significantly, the last of the prophets is called Malachi, which means "My messenger," or "angel." Angels as supernatural messengers of God are therefore frequently called "men." Three angels disguised as men appeared to Abraham to predict, among other things, the birth of Isaac (Genesis 18). Samson's mother, to whom an angel predicted a son who would rescue his people, recognized him simply as a man of God (Judges 13:2–6).

Angels came to be considered special creatures, surrounding God as a heavenly court. *Seraphim,* Fire Beings, stand about the divine throne rapt in constant adoration, saying, "Holy, holy, holy! The Lord of Hosts! His presence fills all the earth!" (Isaiah 6:1–3). Cherubim were the bearers of the divine majesty, God's "throne" (see 1 Kings 19:15; Isaiah 37:16). They are described in Ezekiel's mystical vision (10:1–22). The Ark of the Covenant, which is the seat of God's glory on earth, was surmounted by golden replicas of two Cherubim facing each other, their wings protectively spread over the Ark and touching. From here God's voice was heard as He spoke to Moses (see Exodus 25:17–22; Numbers 7:89; also 1 Samuel 4:4; 1 Kings 6:25–30).

Serving as special messengers of God, the angels perform functions specifically entrusted to them by God Himself. The names given them are evidence of their functions: *Raphael* (God heals), *Uriel* (God is my light), *Michael* (Who is like God). It is an angel who relays God's message to Abraham, telling him not to sacrifice his son (Genesis 22:11 ff.). In later writings, the idea of guardian angels is developed. Michael is Israel's guardian angel, who will lead Israel in the conflict with the enemies of God during the battle at the end of days (Daniel 12).

While Jewish thought recognizes angels, their role is a minor one. Angels have no free will; they must perform their mission exactly as they are commanded. Humans have choice to submit by their own volition to the will of God. In this sense humans stand above angels. To God alone they offer prayer, and from Him alone do they expect help. The Psalmist says, "For His angels will *He* put in charge over you to guard you . . . because he has set his love on Me, *I* [God] will deliver him" (Psalm 91:11–14).

Satan

The concept of Satan entered Jewish beliefs from Persian thought. The Persian philosopher Zoroaster believed in a conflict between light and darkness, good and evil, which would continue throughout the ages. At the very end, God, the light of the world, would triumph over the forces of darkness and evil. God was surrounded by a heavenly host of angels; His adversary, Satan, (from *sata*, "pulling down") was surrounded by his minions of evil.

Such dualism came under attack. The second Isaiah makes it clear that God alone creates light and darkness, fashions peace as well as evil (Isaiah 45:7). Satan was demoted and became a kind of prosecuting attorney, as in the Book of

Job. He levels his accusation against Job and is given the right to test him. From then on, he no longer appears in the book. It is God who settles the issue and determines Job's fate. Yet even as the accuser doing his duty, Satan is rebuked. Has he no compassion for the remnant of Israel, "a brand plucked out of the fire" (Zechariah 3:1ff.).

Belief in Satan and his power can be traced through Jewish history to the present. Fear of demonic forces led to widespread use of amulets (protective devices worn or affixed at walls or doors) among common folk, especially in Eastern Europe. It was thought that the gaze of another person could bring "the evil eye," especially upon children, and bring them harm. Satan could disturb the worshiper's concentration or prevent the sounding of the shofar. Magical formulas were used to dispel him.

While recognized, Satan was never God's equal adversary. God could always repel him. In Conservative, Reform, and Reconstructionist Judaism, Satan plays no role. Even in those circles of Orthodox Jewry where the concept may still be held, it is affirmed that to God alone belongs the ultimate power. He alone, providentially watching over humanity as a whole and over every individual, is their merciful and living shield, protector, and guardian; He may chastise, but only in love, and He will redeem. Satan is also seen as personification of Yetzer, and then the accuser. God eventually will wipe him out.

THE MESSIAH, RESURRECTION, AND ETERNAL LIFE

In Daniel we find a "secret message," revealed to him confidentially (Daniel 12:4). It is addressed to the prophet in connection with the "end of days." It mentions Michael as the guardian angel, speaks of the time of trouble before the consummation of history, and predicts the resurrection of the dead.

> At that time, the great prince Michael, who stands besides the sons of your people, will appear. It will be a time of trouble, the like of which has never been seen since the nation came into being. At that time, your people will be rescued, all who are found inscribed in the book. Many of those that sleep in the dust of the earth will awake, some to eternal life, others to reproaches, to everlasting abhorrence. (Daniel: 12:1–3)

These events were the precursors of the coming of the Messiah.

The Messiah

The Messiah, or the messianic age, has been the Jews' basic concern and longing. They have seen history as an ascent toward his arrival. The ideal has inspired Jews' dedication to social justice.

Plagued by adversity, setbacks, and disappointments, and subjected to tyranny, the Jews remained convinced that God, Master of History, would lead the world to redemption. They came to envision the day when, after terrifying wars and upheavals, peace and fellowship would reign throughout the world. Then no further obstacles would prevent them from fully enjoying the Land and wholeheartedly responding to the divine call in Mitzvah. This was the day of the Messiah. As David once had been Israel's ideal king, so would his descendant establish a perfect society. Isaiah's utopia—the time when the lion and lamb would dwell together, and the "shoot of the trunk of Jesse" would rule in righteousness (Isaiah 11)—was transposed into the future as both goal and challenge.

According to Malachi's forecast, this Messiah, God's anointed, would be preceded by Elijah the prophet, who had never died but had gone bodily to heaven (2 Kings 2:11–12). Elijah had been the foe of compromise, the champion of integrity. He would arrive as messianic herald "before the awesome, fearful day of God," to prevent the world from being struck "with utter devastation." He would create the unity of love between the generations which would assure the coming of the messianic age (Malachi 3:23–24).

According to Daniel, the arrival of the Messiah was to be preceded by a period of cataclysmic events and worldwide ordeals, especially for the Jews, "the birthpangs of the Messiah." This has given them the will to endure. It is not surprising that many Jews have seen the twentieth century, possibly the most barbaric in human history, as such a period. The victims in the extermination camps went to their death with the song, "I believe with perfect faith in the coming of the Messiah; though he tarry, he will surely come." In recent years, Hasidic Jews affixed their expectations on posters and automobile stickers, "We want Moshiah now!" Some believed that the late Lubavitcher Rebbe actually was the Messiah, but not permitted to reveal himself as the world was not worthy.

When will the Messiah come? He will come either when the world has become so corrupt that only the intervention of a divinely ordained human person can set it right; or when humanity, by its own will and effort, has attained universal peace through ethics. Then he will but confirm and firmly anchor human achievement (B. Sanhedrin 97–98). When will this be? "Today, if you will hearken to my voice," quote the rabbis (Psalm 95:7). Maimonides warns against any eschatological predictions. The times calculated for the end of days, Maimonides points out, will pass without fulfillment; the end is concealed, speculation regarding it prohibited by the rabbis. "For the vision is yet for the appointed time. . . . Though it tarry, wait for it; because it will surely come, it will not delay" (Habakkuk 2:3).

Thus the messianic age is not a subject for calculations, but an eternal task and challenge to grow toward it. What will this end be? Again, Maimonides answers:

> The world will not change its accustomed order, but Israel will dwell secure, and humanity will find that true faith which will prevent them from making war and carrying destruction. Israel will not become exalted over humanity, or wield power, but will be undisturbed to follow Torah, study it, perform its Mitzvot. No longer will there be war in the world; all humanity will enjoy peace and prosperity; and all will search for that wisdom which God alone can give. (Mishneh Torah XI, XII)

Orthodox Jews believe in a personal Messiah, a man who will come. Many Reform Jews, by contrast, see in a messianic age to come, the symbol of a future in which all humanity will be united. The modern philosopher Hermann Cohen, as a liberal Jew, eliminated the belief in a personal Messiah yet considers the Messiah idea the most powerful lever in history and Judaism's most significant contribution to the vision of the future. As Cohen puts it,

> The future, which the prophets have painted in the symbol of the Messiah, is the future of world history. It is the goal, it is the meaning of history. It is humanity itself which has to bring about this age of the Messiah. Men and cultures must learn to think and hope for the ideal of human life, the ideal of individuals and nations, the future of the Messiah as something in the future of the human race. The realization of morality on earth, its tasks and its eternal goal, this, and nothing else is the meaning of the Messiah for us.
>
> The Kingdom of the Messiah is the kingdom of God. Not a personal ruler is this Messiah, not a hero, but the spirit of God rests upon him and he brings justice to the peoples. (*Jüdische Schriften* III, p. 173ff.)

The contemporary liberal theologian Eugene Borowitz establishes as one principle of Jewish living under the Covenant:

> . . . though the Jewish self lives the present out of the past [necessitating a concern with and commitment to Jewish history] it necessarily orients itself to the future. . . . For the Jewish self, then, Covenant means Covenant-with-Jews-yet-to-be, especially the Messiah. (*Renewing the Covenant*, Philadelphia: The Jewish Publication Society, 1991, p. 292)

The significance of the messianic idea in Judaism can hardly be overemphasized. It differs from the Christian idea, as it is directed exclusively to the future. The world is not yet redeemed but is redeemable. The messianic hope has sustained Jews in times of trials and inspired them to work and to suffer for the kingdom of God on earth, not for themselves but for all humanity.

Resurrection

Many pious and devoted workers for the great fulfillment of history will die before the event happens. Should they not be rewarded? These considerations may have prompted the belief in resurrection, which we find in Daniel. Daniel is the only one who speaks of resurrection and judgment. The idea is not found in the Five Books of Moses, but the Pharisees believed so firmly in the resurrection that they interpreted the Song at the Red Sea (Exodus 15:1) to refer not only to the rescue which Israel had just experienced but also to the future. "Then sang Moses and the children of Israel" can also be grammatically construed as, "Then will Moses . . . sing." (This rests on a grammatical ambiguity.) According to rabbinic comment, this refers to the day of their resurrection.

But Jews have not been preoccupied in daily living with the question of resurrection. Reform Jews denied it at one time. As far as punishment is concerned,

Hillel said that Jews maintain that God is altogether too merciful to impose eternal punishment for the temporary aberrations of weak human beings during their lifetime. He will be gracious to all humanity. While the idea of a temporary punishment or purgatory—the Gehinnom—can be found in Judaism, that of eternal damnation, although expressed by Daniel, would run counter to the Jewish concept of an all-loving God. Gehinnom expiates the sins of humanity's temporary stay on earth, but even it is severely limited in time, and sinners will find rest every Sabbath. "The punishment of the wicked in Gehinnom lasts for twelve months; for it has been written: 'It will be from month to [the same] month [of the following year] (Isaiah 66:23)'" (Mishnah Ediyot 2:10).

The World to Come

As Judaism firmly believes in the God-given soul, bestowed pure on every man and woman, it also maintains a firm faith in *Olam Haba*, the world to come. This is not the same as the time of the Messiah or the resurrection. It is the sheltering of souls in God's eternal dwelling forever. There they will share the joys of their closeness to the divine Glory. The Talmud warns against any particular formulation or imagery: "All the prophets have prophesied only regarding the days of the Messiah; concerning Olam Haba [it is stated]: 'No eye has seen it, O God, but Yours (Isaiah 64:3)'" (B. Berakhot 34b; B. Sanhedrin 99a).

Judaism does not devote excessive thought to the question of the "salvation" of souls. "All of Israel will have a share in the world to come" (Sanhedrin 10:1); "All the righteous of the peoples of the world have a share in it" (Tosefta Sanhedrin 13:1). The task is here and now. Jews are to devote themselves to it and leave to God the ultimate determination of the future.

> Rabbi Jacob used to say, "This world is like an antechamber of the world to come; prepare yourself in the antechamber that you may enter into the chamber." He also used to say, "Better is one hour of repentance and of good deeds in this world than the whole life in the world to come; and better is one hour of bliss in the world to come than all of life in this world" (Mishnah Avot IV: 21–22).

Our great moments of giving of ourselves fully are experiences that surpass even the world to come, yet the anticipation of the bliss in the world to come may lead us on in life.

SOME SYMBOLS

A symbol is a visible object or an act that conveys a message greater than itself. Every Mitzvah is, in a sense, a symbol. It stands for the presence of God, to whom response is rendered, and it links every Jew to the community of Israel, past, present, and future. It speaks of Torah, upon which it is based, and reveals the sanctity of life. A few special symbols will be mentioned here.

The Menorah

The menorah is the seven-branched candelabrum which was once the lamp in the Tent of Meeting and the Temple (as ordained in Torah, Exodus 25:31–40; 37:17–24). It became a widely recognized symbol of the Temple, and appears as such in early synagogal art and in the Arch of Titus. It is now the coat of arms of the State of Israel. Zechariah saw a seven-branched menorah in a vision and was told, "Not by might, nor by power, but by My spirit [will you prevail]" (Zechariah 4:6). The seven branches reflect the seven days of the week or the seven "planets," as these were understood in antiquity (Mercury, Venus, Sun, Moon, Mars, Jupiter, Saturn). All of them are to be illuminated by the light of the Holy Spirit. The windows in the Temple of old were so constructed that the light did not fall into its precincts from the outside, but was shed abroad from the menorah within. The menorah thus stands for the illumination that shall go forth from Zion. It represents Israel's function as a light to the nations; it envisions the day when all will walk in God's light. It assures Jews that guided by God's light they will prevail against the forces of adversity. (The Hanukkah menorah has nine branches and should be distinguished from the one in the ancient Temple. It will be explained in Chapter 20.)

The Magen David

As a symbol, the Magen David, the Shield of David, emerged later than the menorah. The Shield of David is a six-pointed star (although we do not know if David's shield actually had this form). The synagogue in Capernaum (second century C.E.), features the menorah prominently and the Magen David only incidentally. It may have been a charm, repelling evil spirits, even as the five-pointed star was used in the Middle Ages. The explanation that Franz Rosenzweig offers holds a great deal of poetic meaning (see Chapter 15).

The Jews were forced to wear a yellow star under the Nazi oppression so that they could be easily recognizable and subject to derision and mob attack. Written on it in black was the word "Jew." (The Nazis chose yellow from the yellow badge the Jews had to wear in some Islamic countries and later, during long periods of the Middle Ages, in Europe.) The star thereby became a symbol of Jewish suffering, pride, endurance, and survival.

The Magen David has become the emblem on the flag of Israel. There, in the form of blue bars, it is superimposed on a white background with blue, horizontal stripes. The white and blue colors are derived from the colors of the Tzitzit, ordained in Torah, as will be explained in Chapter 20.

The Head Covering

Wearing a head covering is a late symbol. For many centuries, the practice was fluid. It might signify the fact that "the glory of God resides above and I humbly cover myself before it," indicating the limitations of the human mind (B. Kiddushin 31a). Yet it may also have come to stand as a symbol of Jewish self-respect and hope. Paul declared: "Every man praying or prophesying having his head covered, dishonors his head" (1 Corinthians 11:4). At that time, in Jewish custom men might or might not cover their heads (B. Nedarim 30b). It might have hardened as a distinctive feature of Judaism as opposed to Christianity. The world forced a grotesque, horn-like hat upon the medieval Jew to symbolize his demonic character: The Jew, son of the devil, wore horns. But the Jew, never doubting the love of God and convinced of his redemption in the day of the Messiah, wore it proudly. First he wore it only during worship, then always. At the time, royal princes were distinguished at court by wearing head coverings in the presence of the king. Abused by the world, the Jew affirmed that he was a prince in God's sight and, like a prince, might let his head remain covered in the pres-

Interior of Temple Emanu-El, San Francisco, California. Note the dominant position of the Ark, reached by steps on each side. Above it is the eternal light. The Ark is placed under a canopy, or huppah. *The Torah is read from above. Below on the platform is the reading desk of the cantor, flanked by two seven-branched candlesticks. (Photo by the author, courtesy of Congregation Emanu-El and the late Rabbi Joseph Asher.)*

ence of the King of Kings. To the degree that degradation increased, the wearing of the hat became universal. As a symbol of self-respect, it was truly Mitzvah, enshrining God's presence, Torah, and commandments, and a permanent reminder of redemption.

The custom has had a deep emotional hold on Jews. Today, the head covering in the form of a skull cap, in Hebrew *kippah,* also called "yarmulke," is recognized in general society as the distinguishing mark of the Jew in worship. Reform Judaism ruled that heads need no longer be covered in worship since times, symbols, and customs have changed. At one time, covering the head was prohibited in Reform synagogues although they were heatedly attacked for this ruling. Today it makes the wearing of a skullcap optional, and the number of Reform Jews wearing it is growing. Over time, Jews, especially in non-Orthodox Judaism, have quietly discarded many laws of the Torah, but the head covering has remained as an expression of Jewish self-affirmation.

Note

1. According to biblical criticsm, the development of the Jewish concept of God came out of Egyptian, Canaanite, and Mesopotamian sources. To pursue this unfolding offers a fascinating study, as does the origin of the Jewish festivals and rites of passage. The scope of our text does not permit such a discussion here, however several works dealing with these subjects are listed in the bibliography under "Bible" and "Biblical History."

CHAPTER 15

Theological Issues

THEOLOGY IS THE SYSTEMATIC STUDY of God, humanity, and the meaning of human existence under God. The Scripture deals with theological concepts. For instance, the Book of Job asks: Why do the good have to suffer; how can a loving God permit it? The prophets spoke of God and what He demands of humanity, but theirs is not systematic theology but sympathy with the divine pathos. Fulfilling God's Mitzvot was "living theology." The Talmud points out that, "[If there were a choice,] better they forgot Me [says God] but kept my Mitzvot" (J. Hagigah 1:7), for in Mitzvot He is made manifest. God and Mitzvah are linked inseparably as call and response. Halakhah is living theology. Those who respond cannot forget the Caller.

Jewish theology derives from Written and Oral Torah. Throughout much of their history the Jews did not engage in systematic theology. It emerged from the confrontation with various non-Jewish philosophies or historical events. These tended to create questions in the minds of the faithful regarding God and divine actions and demanded explanation.

In the following section we shall briefly consider a few Jewish philosophers and theologians who have left a lasting impact on the shaping of the Jewish mind. Our treatment of Jewish theology will become more extended as we reach the present, culminating with the Holocaust and postmodern theologians.

EARLY THEOLOGIANS AND PHILOSOPHERS

The impetus for philosophic thinking came to Diaspora Jews from the Greek philosophy to which they were exposed. Plato, Aristotle, and the Stoics became increasingly known, and challenged Jewish thinkers of the hellenistic and medieval periods to confront Jewish tradition and Greek reason and logic.

PHILO OF ALEXANDRIA, a deeply religious Jew and leader of the Jewish community of Alexandria, Egypt, lived in the first century C.E. While his contribution to Jewish theology has not been significant, his work does reveal the relationship between Christian theology and Jewish thought. We shall mention three elements of Philo's thought.

First, Philo had to come to grips with Hellenistic thought. Just as Greek thinkers interpreted Homer's great poems, the *Iliad* and the *Odyssey*, symbolically and allegorically in order to make them meaningful for their own time, so did Philo for Torah and Mitzvot. By so doing he may have succeeded in keeping some of his contemporaries devoted to the Jewish faith, and also created an audience sympathetic to Judaism among philosophically schooled non-Jews.

Second, Philo's concept of the *Logos*, or Word, came to have fundamental significance in Christian thought. Philo held that God fashioned an intermediary, the Logos, in creating the universe. This Logos shaped the world to spare God contact with its finite inadequateness. Philo does not explain clearly whether this Logos was in God, or was a divine creation, or both. His idea is reflected in the first verses of the Gospel of John: "In the beginning was the word [Logos], and the word [Logos] was with God and the word [Logos] was God. He was in the beginning with God. All things were made through him" (John 1:1 ff.). This formulation became the basis for Christian theological understanding of the triune God. (Some similarities to Philo's thought can be found in Jewish mystical writings: the Torah is God's companion and consultant, with her as adviser He creates the world.)

Third, Philo took a new approach to philosophy, which we shall also find in all medieval philosophy: Jewish, Christian, and Islamic. For the Greek, philosophy was the exercise of the independent human mind, which was free to follow whatever direction the conclusions might take him. Philo saw philosophy as the handmaiden of revelation; that is, he subjected it to the truth made manifest by revelation and limited by it. The "scholastic" philosophy of the Middle Ages attempted the square philosophy with revelation.

THE GAON SAADIA (882–942 C.E.) claimed Judaism as a religion of reason. To Saadia, nothing in Torah was beyond reason. Whereas Christianity's great theologian Thomas Aquinas held that some of the divinely revealed truths will forever remain beyond human understanding, Saadia posited that even divinely revealed truth is entirely based on reason. God merely revealed it in advance, in order that humanity might live by divine truth while still searching for its understanding. The laws of Torah are, therefore, partially understandable by human reason, partially guidelines for human action in anticipation of eventual understanding. He compared humankind to children, whom the teacher gives the answer to a problem in order that they may apply it in daily life while trying to reason it out for themselves, which eventually they will do.

God can be proven by the fact that everything finite, such as our world, must have a beginning, which, by necessity, must reside in an infinite being, God. God created the world that it reflect divine wisdom and to bring happiness to His creatures. He gave them commandments as a gift to permit them the experience of happiness through self-motivated obedience, which is greater than that enjoyed as a gift of grace. For this reason He gave humans freedom of will, although He knows ahead of time how humans will decide.

The suffering of the righteous and the bliss enjoyed by the wicked rest on divine justice. The righteous are purged here for the sins they have committed, to receive their full reward in the world to come; the wicked are rewarded here for their few good deeds, and suffer punishment for their evil deeds after death. This means also that the soul is immortal. In the resurrection of the dead the Creator of the world will bring the pious back to life to rejoice in the restoration of Israel at the hand of the Messiah.

JUDAH HALEVI (1080–1140) stressed the singularity and uniqueness of the Jewish people. They were chosen by God out of all the peoples of the world. In each generation from Adam to Jacob, God picked *one* person, who was endowed with the most perfect soul and highest intellect. This special gift descended on *all* of Jacob's progeny, the entire Jewish people. They were given God's chosen Land on earth and were granted the abundance of Mitzvot by which they were to live. But this special election did not make them masters but servants of humanity.

Halevi saw Israel as "the heart of humanity," the first organ to be afflicted by the disorders in the body. Whenever Israel is afflicted, it is a symptom of disease in the entire organism of humanity. Jews as a whole have not followed this almost biological concept of hereditary election, but they have learned from Halevi to regard themselves as the "barometer" of human conditions: Throughout the ages, persecution of Jews revealed deep-seated ills in society.

Another point that emerged from Halevi's thoughts was that the Jewish people are unique and so is its contribution to the world, given in unique fashion. But the world, from early times to the present, has judged and evaluated the Jews by its standards and concepts, not by Jewish self-perception. Jews are "good" in terms of meeting the expectations of the non-Jewish world. Halevi held that Jews must be seen and judged by what they are themselves. Being themselves, they can in their unique way serve as humanity's heart.

MOSES MAIMONIDES (1135–1204) was both codifier of Jewish law and philosopher. To Maimonides, the study of philosophy was a duty, the highest rung on the ascent to God. His philosophical work *Guide of the Perplexed* was written in response to a letter by one of his disciples who claimed that the compelling logical arguments of Aristotle forced Jews to make a choice: they could either accept Aristotle's thoughts and thus become unfaithful to their tradition or they could reject his conclusions and abide by their faith but become untrue to their intelligence. In order to guide the perplexed who did not know which of the two to follow, Maimonides attempted to harmonize philosophy and revelation. In line with Saadia he wished to prove that revelation and reason were not contrary but essentially identical. Religious faith was essentially a form of knowledge. Jewish traditional teaching had not revealed this unity, only the philosopher could.

Maimonides started with God. God is One, but His Oneness surpasses any human concept of oneness. When we speak of one thing, we nevertheless can conceive that two of the same kind may possibly exist or that the one thing, such as a body, is composed of many parts. None of this can be held of God. We, therefore, can say nothing of God. While we know *that* God exists, we shall never know *what* He is. This has been called *negative theology*. Human limitations are absolute. When the Bible uses anthropomorphisms, such as the "hand" of God or the "voice" of God, or God's "anger" it merely speaks of the effect God had on human beings, as if His guiding hand had led them or His voice spoken or His anger been aroused. The Bible uses these terms because "it speaks the language of simple human beings," and wishes them to understand.

Aristotle posited that God was "the Unmoved Mover" who neither could nor did interfere with the world. Being unmoved, He could not have been the Creator God, therefore the world must have existed eternally. Maimonides proved Aristotle wrong. The world cannot have existed for all eternity, as Aristotle held. Our world is finite. Anything finite must have a starting point. The infinite God started the world. The laws of nature and time itself had to be created by God. Aristotle had made the mistake of applying conclusions from conditions existing after creation to pre-creation.

To explain, Maimonides used the example of a youth who has been stranded on a deserted island and has never seen a woman. To him, based on his experience, it is impossible to believe that the human being in gestation could dwell for nine months without air. This was Aristotle's situation. He drew conclusions based upon his experiences in the created world in which he lived. He did not consider the conditions before its creation. The creation of the world out of nothing is different from the natural creation of things in it.

Our argument against Aristotle is reinforced by our holy traditions. In Torah we find that God created the world and created time in which it unfolds. Before creation neither time, nor nature, nor the laws of nature existed. Since creation the world follows the laws of nature and unfolds in time. Why God did so and why He chose a certain moment to create the world is beyond human capacity to understand.

Maimonides was convinced that natural law guides the world. This gave him difficulty when explaining the miracles related in the Bible. Whenever he could he explained them metaphorically—such as the serpent in paradise—or sees in them experiences of poetic fantasy. Of others, such as Balaam's speaking ass, he claimed they were not fashioned *ad hoc,* but built into creation from the very beginning to take place at a certain time and place and in a certain manner.

Divine Providence must be explained. Maimonides accepted general providence for the world, but not individual one for its creatures, except for human beings. For the human being there is individual providence. But it means that God warns the human being of the dangers facing him. God does not change events. But since the human spirit is connected with the divine, the providential warning is placed in the interior of man.

Who is a prophet? For the prophet the active intellect is higher than that of the average person. The prophet is also philosopher, but the prophetical inspiration goes beyond and transcends philosophy. The prophets stand above the philosopher because the prophet receives knowledge by intuition. But even among the prophets, Moses is unique because Moses was wholly removed from the sphere of the natural and was entirely filled with the supernatural revelation of God. Therefore Jewish religion, which Moses transmitted, has a special position in the world. Religions may be revelations, but the Jewish one is unique.

Judaism teaches morality and also transcends it. Human morality serves a social function only. Moral perfection, as Judaism teaches it, serves the ultimate goal in leading to spirituality; the divine law is not only concerned with human welfare but the perception of truth.

Toward this truth we must strive. All our knowledge can and should be a way toward God. The knowledge of nature leads on the way to perception of

God. Since truth streams to man only out of God, it therefore becomes the bond between God and man. Study gives humans the happiness of direct connection with God, the love of God and His nearness (but never mystical union with God). Those who study recognize God as *the* moral being and take God as guide. They build their lives on Mitzvot, theory becomes ethical practice. The ultimate blessing of communion with God is found in life eternal. But not only elitists, dedicating their lives to study and contemplation, but even average Jews who see God in anthropomorphic terms have a share in life to come. Maimonides is a talmudist, a rabbi. But in his philosophical work he places Talmud study beneath philosophical study.

Torah and Mitzvot serve the purpose of improving the physical and spiritual condition of man. The moral laws of Torah provide for the societal and spiritual perfection of the Jewish people. The spiritual importance of the Sabbath and the festivals—next to their physical one—is obvious, that of the Tzitzit (see Chapter 17) is already given in Torah. They are to be constant reminders that "you do not go astray" (Numbers 15:37–41). These Mitzvot are perpetual reminders that Jews are to live a spiritual life. For other Mitzvot, Maimonides gives an historical explanation. At times, he sees in divine commandments a divine concession addressed to the Jews in antiquity. Sacrifices were such a concession. They were permitted because all the other nations offered them—but could be presented in only one place, the Temple. Prayer which is the true service of God, is permitted everywhere. Maimonides's scientific justification of Judaism led to a profound transformation of its religious content.

Philosophical Ideas Clash with Traditional Beliefs

After Maimonides's death, violent arguments about his work tore Jewish communities apart. At times his work was banned. Could Torah be put under the judgment of reason? The prophets had surely received revelations that surpassed human understanding. Maimonides's rejection of anthropomorphism was attacked. God, according to the Tanakh resided in heaven and had a body. Maimonides and his disciples were accused of having allegorized personalities and events related in Torah. He was charged with seeing in Mitzvot mere guides to moral living, and was taken to task for not mentioning the resurrection in his work (although he had declared it a basic principle of Judaism in his Mishnah tractate), and so forth. The split was deep. The Church joined in. Thomas Aquinas, who had learned much from Maimonides, considered him an atheist on account of his negative theology and had his books burned. Ashkenasic Jewry rejected philosophical pursuits for hundreds of years. Not until the period of the Emancipation did they take up philosophy to any significant degree.

THE AGES OF REASON AND ENLIGHTENMENT

The thinkers of the Age of Reason established Reason as the supreme judge of all thought, institutions, and action. Religion had to justify itself before

Reason's seat of justice. Its harshest judge was Benedict Spinoza; most of the others felt religion could stand the test if it became "enlightened."

BENEDICT (BARUKH) SPINOZA (1632–1677) severed the link between revelation and philosophy. He affirmed the latter's independence, seeing in it a critical evaluator of sacred scriptures and the truths proclaimed in them. When he severed the bond, Spinoza was read out of Judaism and, most likely, approved of this breaking of ties.

Spinoza was the son of Marranoes who had settled in Amsterdam and returned to Judaism. He had been given a thorough Jewish education and studied Maimonides. Now he carried Maimonides's ideas to a point which would have horrified the master. Like Maimonides he held that natural law guides the world. Unlike him he maintained that there is no God behind it. The whole of the universe with its laws constituted the one God. God and nature were one (*deus sive natura*) and were guided by the one law that natural science discovered. This was Pantheism. God, therefore, was neither person nor lawgiver, neither Creator nor Sustainer. The only way to love God was to explore nature intellectually (*amor dei intellectualis*). When Spinoza was excommunicated from the Jewish congregation at Amsterdam for these ideas he turned resolutely against Judaism. He declared that it was merely the outworn creation of Moses designed to keep his folk together. Judaism did not lead to "blessedness."

Spinoza criticized the Bible from the point of view of science. In his philosophy he felt free to subject religion to the standard of his own thinking.

MOSES MENDELSSOHN (1729–1786) showed a boldness similar to that of Maimonides. The ethical principles by which humanity is to live, he held, were placed by reason in the mind and soul of every human being. For those Torah was not needed. At Sinai, witnessed by 600,000 persons, God gave the Jews not dogmas but divinely ordained law. Obedience to the law was mandatory upon Jews but their minds were otherwise free to speculate.

Mendelssohn held that religion had no power to enforce obedience; it could only persuade. The power of coercion rested exclusively with the state, but only regarding those actions of the citizens that affected the public welfare. Religious convictions and acts did not affect the common weal and lay outside the powers of governance granted the state. This was a philosophically undergirded call for full emancipation of the Jews as Jews. (See also p. 109ff.)

SAMSON RAPHAEL HIRSCH (1808–1888), founder of Neo-Orthodoxy, was close in spirit to Maimonides, although he criticized him strongly for living in two equal worlds, namely Torah and Greek philosophy. He was also profoundly influenced by Mendelssohn, who had brought Jewry into Western culture. Hirsch actually lived in both worlds.

Originally, the Jews were commissioned to establish in their own land a commonwealth wholly governed by God's word. But they failed. They were, therefore, sent into Diaspora, with a divine vocation. Individuals and societies were motivated by greed, power drives, and self-indulgence. The Jews were to set for these persons and societies a model of ethical living under God's mandate. They were humanity's teachers of ethics. To fulfill this task they had to be absolutely faithful to the divine Torah in all its detailed commandments. But Torah also enjoined a complete immersion in and identification with the state of which Jews were citizens and the culture in which they lived. This emerged from the letter which Jeremiah had written to the Jewish community in Babylonia. Furthermore Torah committed the Jew to go out of his way to extend love to his "non-Jewish brother," sustaining and supporting him in every way. Living up to Torah meant being absolutely true to all Mitzvot *and* fully immersed in the secular state. It called for a reaching out to all neighbors. In this manner the Jew would rise to become *Jisroel–Mensch,* "Jew–Human," a paradigm of humanity through Jewish living.

Quoting a statement in the Sayings of the Fathers that the "good [way of life] consists in study of Torah combined with worldly occupation" (M. Avot 2:2), Hirsch reinterpreted it as the "good consists in Torah combined with worldly culture." The Jew is bidden to partake of general culture as long as it does not conflict with Jewish law. Since these obligations rested on Torah, only the "Torah-true" Jew could be regarded as a truly loyal citizen. This appears to be the tenor of his thought.

On this foundation Hirsch created Neo-Orthodoxy. A Hegelian at heart, he may have seen in Neo-Orthodoxy a synthesis between old-time Judaism—true to Torah but hostile to worldly culture (thesis) and Reform—committed to Western culture hostile to halakhah (antithesis).

TWENTIETH-CENTURY THEOLOGY AND PHILOSOPHY

In the twentieth century the situation of Western Jews was similar to that in Spain during the Middle Ages; Western thought and life attracted and permeated Judaism. We have chosen some representatives whose thoughts have abidingly influenced Jewry.

HERMANN COHEN (1842–1918), a Kantian, founded the Neo-Kantian school at Marburg. To Kant, God was unknowable, "thing-in-itself" due to the structural limitations of the human mind. To Cohen, God was forever removed from our grasp. But, as a stone thrown into a pond forms ever wider circles in the water, so does every partial knowledge of God lead us toward new knowledge of Him, endlessly.

Cohen proudly considered himself a disciple of Maimonides. "The Rambam [an abbreviation of Maimonides's Hebrew name, *Rabbi Moses ben Maimon*] will be satisfied with me," he pridefully declared. His final work, *Religion of Reason out of the Sources of Judaism,* reveals by its title that he affirmed the rational character of Judaism and saw in it a foundation of a universal religion grounded in reason.

Cohen sets out to prove the existence of God and of one God as a necessity. Logical thought requires the idea of God and of one God. It is manifest by the interaction of nature and moral conduct. Nature and morality are two different realms and yet they are keyed to each other. This has been achieved through the idea of One God. Nature and ethics find their focus in one single idea, namely God. Through this God-idea the world of nature can become the stage of ethical action. As this one focal point, God must be both one and unique. According to Cohen we must strive for a world where perfect moral action corresponds to the perfection of nature. This is contained in the concept of the Messiah—the symbol of the future for which we must ever strive. It symbolizes the ideal of humanity-society and nature in perfect attunement. Today we can recognize how true this is, as through ethical acts we preserve nature, and, as we act upon it, nature reacts and allows us to exist.

Ethics gives us the road toward this future in general, universal terms. But it does not supplant religion. Actually, religion holds a higher place than ethics. Religion evokes the spirit of individual compassion. Compassion is the hallmark of religion. This brings Cohen to the function of Jews and Judaism in the world. They are especially necessary for the world. Being a small minority in the world, Jews offer humanity an opportunity to show compassion with the weak and numerically small in its midst. Jews are humanity's challenge to be religious by being compassionate, and to be human by striving for the messianic future. Jews must retain their identity by performing the Mitzvot in response to God. In his final work, Cohen explains the Mitzvot in the light of reason.

Judaism thus found, teaches and lives "ethical monotheism." This living leads to "correlation," of individuals with each other and with God. By this correlation, my fellow human being becomes *Mitmensch*, human-being-with-me, instead of being merely being *Nebenmensch*, human-being-proximate-to-me. Through this interaction I get to know myself better and, together with my *Mitmensch*, build an ethical society. In his later years, according to Franz Rosenzweig, Cohen came to see God not merely as idea but as the living partner of humans.

Hermann Cohen guided and reflected the thinking of German Jewry. His influence on many thinkers was profound, especially on Franz Rosenzweig, his most influential Jewish disciple, but also on Martin Buber, whose "I and Thou" is in reality the same as correlation. Buber claimed to have arrived at his concept of "I and Thou" without knowing of Cohen's thought.

Along with German Jewry Cohen fell into a fateful error. Committed to reason, he believed that reason would guide humanity and that Germany, a nation of thinkers, might lead the movement. He was to be disappointed in his own life, and German Jewry was grievously to suffer for its error. Sigmund Freud was closer to the mark when he posited that human beings are motivated not by reason but by subterranean irrational passions. Such passions swept German and European Jewry away, and Cohen's philosophy reflects the noble "weakness" of German Jewry.

FRANZ ROSENZWEIG (1886–1929) remains one of the most significant influences on Christian and contemporary Jewish theology. He was Cohen's disciple, and was influenced by Hegel, who held that history is in a constant process of unfolding. But he turned from Hegel, who had looked for the "essence" of the universe, which was reflected in our experienced world. By his own logical reasoning Hegel found this essence in a spiritual element, the Absolute (God). This Absolute unfolds to ever greater spiritual heights, and uses the world, history, and all the human beings in it to realize its purpose. Humanity, and certainly the individual person, are but pawns in this evolution. Their ambitions, fears, and anxieties are not just their own but are formed by the "cunning of history."

Rosenzweig disagreed with Hegel. The individual human being is not an insignificant tool serving the grand design. Each person is unique in his of her needs and emotions, hopes and fears, especially the fear of death. This human being must be our point of departure and concern. Rosenzweig arrived at this insight as a result of what he called "new thinking." To him, actual thinking had to be based on good common sense—in contrast to the way philosophers were wont to think in their ivory towers.

> All philosophy inquired about "essence." By this question it takes leave from the unphilosophical thinking of good human common sense. Because this [common sense] does not ask, what a thing "really" is. It is satisfied to know that a chair is a chair. It does not ask if in reality it might be something different. But that is exactly what philosophy asks when it asks for the essence. The world, by no means, may be just world, God, by no means, just God, the human being by no means, just human being, for all must "in reality" be something else." (*Das neue Denken, Kleinere Schriften*, Berlin, Schocken, 1937, p. 377 translation by me)

Our thinking cannot dwell in the philosopher's ivory tower of the abstract but must take place in the reality of life as it is lived. It must be "speech thinking"; that is, the speaker or writer must always consider the discussant. My discussant may always say something which had not occurred to me and so force me to change my view in light of his argument. Thought develops out of correlation with another. Thus, Rosenzweig turned his back on "modern" philosophy, from Descartes to Hegel, that looked for the "essence" behind the obvious reality. He moved us into the postmodern age, and has found many disciples.

God–World–Man–Creation–Revelation–Redemption

What does common sense reveal to us? It tells us that there exist three elements: God, world, and man. It also tells us that there are three roads by which these elements stand in correlation: *creation, revelation*, and *redemption*.

Creation, for Rosenzweig, does not refer to the story of Genesis, it means that the world is being created every day anew, and humans (Rosenzweig uses the term man) are constantly recreated. Man becomes conscious that God constantly reveals His will to him. God enters man's life. By this revelation God recreates him to meet new challenges of world and life in conformity with the divine will. By his recreation through revelation, man is redeemed from his former way of existence.

Revelation is, therefore, already enshrined in creation. It is also perennial. Man [the human being] finds himself [or herself] addressed by God, who teaches man his task. This task is to love. The Song of Songs is, for Rosenzweig, the core of revelation. With this revelation man has been recreated and has found redemption from his [or her] previous state. Such revelation takes place in the world.

Redemption is the result of this love. Man, as steward of the world under God's command, brings about the unity of all, namely redemption. It is, therefore, enshrined in creation and revelation. The love we extend to every person is a revelation which brings about his recreation. It brings redemption to our fellow human beings and to ourselves. In the course of history this means that we bring redemption to the world.

History is a process taking shape among the peoples of the world. In it the three elements—God, man, and world—are linked together by the three roads of creation, revelation, and redemption. All become one organism, and constantly reveal their oneness. Ultimately, God Himself is redeemed. History is humanity in the world moving toward God. The ultimate goal of history is the union of all the elements and roads. At present humanity is still on the road.

A schematic presentation may help clarify these ideas. The first triangle represents the elements of the universe. God is at the apex and world and man at the base of a triangle are facing each other. The dynamic forces constitute the opposing triangle. Creation is God fashioning the world, revelation is God teaching man his task, and redemption is man as steward of the world under God's command bringing about the unity of all.

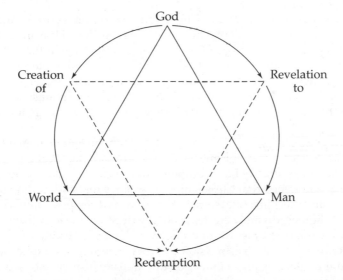

Now we can understand why Rosenzweig called his work "Star of Redemption." Written as a general work of philosophy, it rests on Judaism. But Rosenzweig wished to convey more. The people of the world are still on the road toward redemption; this is history. The Jewish people, however, have completed the journey. The Jews have traversed the entire course of history, they have stepped out of history. The Jewish people (but not the individual Jew) is at the goal, it is with God. In the liturgical year alone do the Jews repeat the road.

The Sabbath takes the Jew from creation on the eve to revelation in the morning to redemption in the evening hours. In the Kiddush of the evening, creation is remembered: "And the heaven and the earth were completed" (Genesis 2:1ff.). In the morning Torah, God's revelation to His people, is read in public. At dusk the Jew pierces into the future of ultimate world redemption. The festivals equally lead from creation to redemption. *Pessah* celebrates creation; on it the Jewish people were created. *Shavuot* is the festival of revelation at Sinai. *Sukkot* anticipates redemption. The Sukkah shelters the Jew in divine protection and forecasts the day of redemption when all humanity will be so sheltered. During the Yamim Noraim, especially on Yom Kippur, the Jew steps entirely out of the world and is with God. Judaism witnesses to the world that the attainment of the goal is possible. The Magen David, Star of Redemption, is its symbol.

From here Rosenzweig takes a second and rather revolutionary step. All humanity is to come to God "the Father." The Jewish people exist to show humanity that it can come to God. The Jewish people have come to God, they are already with Him. Therefore, the rest of the world can come to Him also as Judaism has done. The task of bringing humanity to the "Father" has been entrusted to Christianity. How can Christianity be certain that its efforts will bring humanity to God? Perhaps God cannot be reached at all? It requires the assurance from Judaism.

Rosenzweig sees Judaism and Christianity as complementary. Judaism has come to God, thereby proving that human beings can reach Him and find shelter in Him. This knowledge is to inspire Christianity to engage in the arduous task of bringing the rest of humanity to God, where the Jewish people already dwell. Rosenzweig finds a source for this interpretation in Jesus' statement, "No one comes to the Father, except through me" (John 14:6). He explains: no one comes to God except through Christ, the Son. This provides the challenge for Christians to bring the rest of humanity to God through Christianity. But then Rosenzweig continues, no one comes, but he who already *is* with the Father, namely the Jews, they need no longer come. This means the Jews do not need Christ, as their pilgrimage to God has already been completed. The rest of humanity needs Christ. Rosenzweig maintained that Christianity must move forward leading the world, but Judaism must rest inactive, showing the goal and the possibility of reaching it. The two religions, divinely created, actually depend on each other.

Here, for the first time, we find a Jewish thinker speaking of the need for Christianity to exist and do its missionary work. Rosenzweig did not foresee Judaism emerging once again from its isolation outside history and returning into history, especially with the creation of the State of Israel.

Rosenzweig's greatest impact on contemporary non-Orthodox Jewry rests on his own life. In hard, thoughtful self-examination he had found the road from the periphery of Jewish life to its core. The way was through the performance of Mitzvot. He felt that each Mitzvah had to be a "revelation" of God, a divine command, to him personally, in order for him to respond to God in observance. He did not observe any Mitzvah which he did not so understand, but he strove to understand it, in order to observe it. He did not stand idly by, waiting for the Mitzvah to grip him, he attempted to meet it.

. . . this is not selection . . . there is little choice in it. The "waiting" nowadays so highly valued, will not do. One must have the will part-way to meet the "internal must." As one has the will and looks about and lives with others (of both past and present), grasps opportunities, in short is not lazy and sometimes satisfied with being capable of doing—one arrives at "something" natural, natural to one's own, particular self—for where the capability exists the necessity can easily join it, and then, one day, one simply can do no other. (*Briefe*, Berlin, Schocken 1935, p. 427)

Two facts distinguish Rosenzweig from Orthodoxy. For Orthodoxy, Torah is literally the word of God. For Rosenzweig it is the word of God and of man; the pure, divine revelation at Sinai ended with "God descended" (Exodus 19:20) and the human element entered with "God spoke" (Exodus 20:1). The people had to bring their own language in order to understand God's word.

For Orthodoxy, the fulfillment of Mitzvot, literally ordained by God, is mandatory in their entirety. For Rosenzweig, as we have seen, it is not. Asked whether he was putting on Tefillin every morning, he replied "not yet." This "not yet" has guided many Jews and in large segments of liberal Jewry brought about a return to the practice of Mitzvot. It has particularly influenced the direction taken by Reform Judaism toward greater, more meaningful traditionalism.

MARTIN BUBER (1876–1965) has influenced Christian thought as much as Jewish thought. In his fundamental work, *I and Thou*, he grounds all life on "correlation." As he explained, he came to this concept independent of Hermann Cohen. The work opens with the following statement:

The world has for the human person a twofold aspect, depending on his twofold attitude. This attitude of the human person is twofold depending on the twofold character of the root words he can speak. These root words are not single words but pairs of words. One of the root words is I-Thou. The other root word is I-It. . . . Therefore the I of the human being is equally twofold. For the I of the root word I-Thou is another as that of the root word I-It. Root words are spoken with our entire being. When Thou is spoken, then the I of the word pair I-Thou is spoken with it. When It is spoken then the I of the word pair I-It is spoken with it.

The root word I-Thou can be spoken only with our whole being. The root word I-It can never be spoken with our whole being. (*Ich und Du* in Martin Buber, *Das Dialogische Prinzip*, Heidelberg, Lambert Schneider, 1973, p. 7, translation from the German is mine)

When I say "I," the meaning of this term is rooted in relationship. I can relate to my fellow being as an "It," using the other as my tool, examining his character, qualifications, and usefulness, employing and at times exploiting him. My own self is determined by this relationship, I remain detached. I can also relate to the other as a Thou. The other is now a subject, equal to me, influencing me, engaging me in dialogue in which both he and I will grow. In this dialogue I will myself be another person. I-Thou is the genuine relationship.

The "dialogue," however, is not confined to words. The need of the other, the Thou, calls me to personal response in action. I do not know in advance what this need may be, or when it may arise. I shall know it only at the very moment when it arises, and then I am the only one who can respond.

Every human being is a "Thou" which makes all people equal. This equality rests on the presence of an "Eternal Thou," namely God. Why do I need God? Only through God can I know that all humans are alike. God has revealed that every human being is to Him a Thou. Therefore every human being is equal to me because he or she is equal before God. At every moment I must listen to whatever God has to say to me. He will tell me how He wishes me to relate in "action dialogue" to my fellow human. As I act in true I-Thou fashion toward my neighbor, I am in dialogue with God as well, because God enters every I-Thou relationship. The most direct way to God, therefore, leads one through society.

This is the only true way of relating to God. Studying theology makes God into an It, the object of investigation. Theology will not lead to a live commitment to God. Buber once related to me that he told Ben Gurion, then Prime Minister of Israel, "If I had studied God theologically, I would have become an atheist, but I talk *with* Him."

Buber regarded Judaism as a necessary paradigm of the I-Thou spirit in the world. To be able to fulfill this task, Israel must dwell on its own land, forming its own society dedicated to the vision of the future. Here he follows Ahad Ha-Am.

Paradoxically, Buber saw in the fulfillment of Mitzvot—in fact of all ritual—a wall of separation between God and man; the dialogue was no longer immediate, it had been replaced by ordained ceremonial. This denial of Mitzvot has been hard for Jews to understand. Ernst Simon, an outstanding thinker and educator and a deeply observant Jew, was Buber's colleague and dedicated disciple for many decades. He has permitted us a glimpse at Buber's motivations:

> I told him [Buber] of my personal experience with the Jewish form of life. In spite of the objective danger of its ossification and the subjective danger of compulsion neuroses, it had yet become for me a daily opportunity to serve God, in which I placed my confidence. "Exactly this confidence is what I lack," was Buber's reply. At that we have then left it. (*Entscheidung zum Judentum*; Frankfurt am Main: Suhrkamp Verlag, 1980, pp. 154–155; translation mine)

Buber was deeply influenced by Hasidism, and saw with the realization of the I-Thou between humans and God, as every moment and every action became a dialogue with God and one another. While Buber's basic concept of I-Thou, his Zionism, and his search for peace between Arabs and Jews have deeply influenced modern Jewish thought, his rejection of Mitzvot has created problems.

LEO BAECK (1873–1956), an heroic leader of German Jewry during the Holocaust, rests his thought on that of Cohen, Buber, and Rosenzweig. Baeck was a leading rabbi in Berlin. Under the Nazis he assumed the heavy task of leading and defending German Jews. He rejected repeated calls from abroad in order to remain with his people. He was taken to the Theresienstadt concentration camp, which he miraculously survived. He spent his last years in England with frequent visits to America.

We can recognize two stages in Baeck's development. In his early work, *The Essence of Judaism,* he deals with what Judaism *is.* In his final work, *This People— The Meaning of Jewish Existence,* he speaks of the Jewish people as it lives and why it lives.

His emphasis was on the Covenant: God made a Covenant with nature, with man, with Israel. The Bible is the Book of the Covenant. Noah is under the Covenant and with him humanity (Genesis 9:9–13), Abraham is under the Covenant (Genesis 17:1–11), the Covenant with Israel is established at Sinai (Exodus 31:16–17), and it is repeated throughout Torah. Nature, subjected to natural law, is compelled to follow the Covenant. Humanity is brought under the Covenant by God commanding "You shall, you shall not." But humans are free to abide by the Covenant or to reject it. God, therefore, saw the need to create a people that would serve as an example to humanity. (This resembles Hirsch's theology.) Mysterious in His Being and actions, He created the Jewish people. These people are to find the reason for their existence in living under the Covenant, in obedience to God's commands. Jews are "this people which I formed for Myself that they might tell of My praise" (Isaiah 43:21). Jewish history reflects Jewish striving toward fulfillment of this special mission, its backsliding, and its return to its task. By its character and function, it is often at odds with a self-centered society, and therefore subjected to derision and persecution. But the Jewish people must live. Set apart, Israel serves humanity. Faith for the Jew means the decision of will and deed to respond to God's command.

The awareness of B'rit—the covenantal character of Judaism—has been given a central position in current Jewish thought. As Baeck had explained, Jews live as the paradigm of the Covenant.

ABRAHAM JOSHUA HESCHEL (1907–1972) was a Jewish thinker who has also found widespread response among Christian theologians. A descendant of a dynasty of great Hasidic Rebbes, he was permitted to go to Berlin where he got his doctorate at the university, and his ordination at the liberal Hochschule. I first met him at this time. Buber made him his successor as director of the Jewish education program in Nazi Germany. Together with other Polish Jews, he was deported to Poland in October 1938 and opened an Institute of Jewish Studies in Warsaw. Soon he was called to the faculty of the Hebrew Union College in Cincinnati, and from there to the Jewish Theological Seminary in New York. He also lectured widely, taught at Christian institutions as visiting professor and developed close bonds with some of their leading theologians. He was the Jewish advisor to Cardinal Bea in the preparation of the Vatican II Resolutions on the Jews.

A master of English, Hebrew, German, and Yiddish, Heschel went back to his experiences in the now lost environment of the Jewish communities of Eastern Europe. Life in Torah and Mitzvot filled the Jews of Eastern Europe with an awareness of God. They did not ask if there was a God; their hearts and emotions answered their quest for God. Life was a response to God's call. The whole world was filled with God's glory and testified to Him. Torah revealed Him in its sacred pages, and Mitzvot made Him manifest in life. It was a true I-Thou relationship with the Eternal Thou.

Heschel saw three trails that lead to God: We must sensitize ourselves to God's presence throughout the world in all things, we must feel His presence in the Bible, and we must experience His presence in our performance of sacred deeds.

In his *depth theology* Heschel holds that our experience of God is preconceptual, which means that it precedes our thinking. To arrive at this awareness, we must sensitize ourselves. We must awaken "radical amazement." For example, when we see a flower, we can examine its shape and color, as the artist or florist does, or the mechanism of its procreation as the biologist does, but this is inadequate. We must develop amazement not only at the flower's existence as such, but at our ability even to see it. This radical amazement will, at least at great moments, lead us out of the commonplace existence in our daily lives, and move us on to the experience of the sublime and ultimately the ineffable, namely God.

This God is not the apathetic God of the philosopher, but a living God who has "pathos." God is in search of humans, concerned with them, and influenced by them. We have shown this in our discussion of the prophets. The Bible then, as Israel perceived it, is a report on how God sees and experiences the human beings He has put in the world. It is God's anthropology. We have no proof of God descending at Sinai, but we know that something must have happened there to the people.

We meet God in prayer, and, above all, in sacred deeds. We must take the "leap" into *halakhah,* the body of Jewish law, in response to God's call. Heschel goes beyond Rosenzweig: the Jew must have the immediate will to meet halakhah, to live by it. Then it will reveal itself and we can do no other.

The Mitzvot confirm the Jewish people as the chosen people. While the world sanctifies space, from great cathedrals to the exploration of outer space, Jews are called to sanctify time. They hallow the Sabbath, as Heschel described, and consecrate every moment in performance of Mitzvot. In moving language, Heschel guided Jewry toward an actual experience of Judaism as he knew it in his childhood. The Land of Israel, promise and reality, is an intimation that the Messiah and his time can come.

The insights gained from sensing God in nature, Scripture, prayer, and deeds are not granted to Jews alone; they must serve as directives for all peoples of all times. All are called to respond to the living God. Then the living God who speaks out of the Bible and speaks today can show us the way in our troubled world and give us, as His children, true human dignity. Heschel held out a challenge to Jewry: While remaining fully in touch with Western civilization, the Jews are to evolve their way of life out of their own inner forces.

Feeling called to sacred deeds, Heschel was extremely active in movements of social justice and in interfaith dialogues. He walked alongside Martin Luther King Jr. on the march to Montgomery, Alabama. He also opposed the Vietnam War. Christians as well as Jews have acknowledged him as a teacher.

MORDECAI KAPLAN (1881–1983) has influenced all of non-Orthodox Jewry. His school has developed into a full-fledged Jewish "denomination," with its own rabbinical college and its congregations. It is called Reconstructionism.

Kaplan saw the Jews as a people not in any way chosen but simply imbued with the will to live and contribute to the welfare of its members and of humanity. Each people develops a civilization, resting on its endowment, community, history, and common experiences. A civilization expresses itself in a totality of forms—in language, literature, art, music, even cuisine. It never stands still but constantly evolves. It enhances the lives of its members, making them more meaningful.

In this manner the Jewish people have also created and evolved a civilization, including all its forms. Woven into it as an intrinsic element is Jewish religion. It is impossible to remove religion from it as religion is expressed in every one of its facets. Judaism is, therefore, the evolving religious civilization of the Jewish people.

Kaplan was an original thinker. In placing the root of the Jewish God concept in the Jewish people, rather than seeing the Jewish people as constituted by God, he brought about what he called a "Copernican revolution." In *The Elementary Forms of the Religious Life*, Emile Durkheim, a French thinker of Jewish descent to whom Kaplan felt indebted, defined religion as

> a unified system of beliefs and practices relative to sacred things which unite into one . . . single, moral community . . . all those who adhere to them . . .
>
> Before all, it is a system of ideas with which the individuals represent to themselves the society of which they are members, and the obscure but intimate relations they have with it . . . for it is an eternal truth that outside of us there exists something greater than us, with which we enter into communion. (New York: Free Press, 1965, pp. 62 and 257)

A society is therefore more than the sum of its individual members, more than the soil upon which it lives. There exists in it "something greater" than the individual, a collective spirit which it has fashioned and fosters. Every member of society "enters into communion" with this spirit and, in turn, by "its intimate relations . . . with it," shapes and evolves it. This spirit emerges from the collective ideals of a given society and the values it holds. These pull the members of society toward higher ideals. Pursuing values, the members transcend themselves and society evolves.

Kaplan accepted these principles and pointed out that values come into being as a result of an organic society that is closely united. Values are not facts, but they are factors. The value of a dollar, in the economic realm, is based on the agreement of the American society that a piece of paper (in itself without value) can be exchanged for a certain amount of goods and services. The value of the currency is based on societal agreement regarding the means of meeting its economic needs.

By partaking of the spirit of society the individual achieves self-transcendence. The spirit of the Jewish people discovered behind nature a force that brings about harmony in the universe. This force is God. God is not identical with nature (Kaplan rejected pantheism); God is transnatural. God is the force we recognize as shaping nature's balance. In the human realm, Israel, out of its own spirit, made another discovery: God is the force creating harmony among peoples and nations, He is the God of ethics. This God, YHVH, became the people's challenge, calling for "ethical nationhood." The essence of Judaism is the striving for ethical nationhood. We cannot say that God created the people; rather we must say that the people, out of its collective spirit, discovered God. God then becomes a force that exerts a constant pull. Kaplan pointed out that we have to distinguish between that which is, that which ought to be, and the means that bring the ought to fruition. We all have reason; it reveals to us what the world is like. We ought to have wisdom to lead a life of meaning. The instrument that leads us from reason to wisdom is intelligence. Wisdom, *hokhmah*, enabled the Jewish people to discover God. The eternal law of nature and of humanity was understood by Jews as B'rit, as Covenant. The striving for self-transcendence was expressed by Jews as striving for holiness. "You shall be holy [transcend yourselves], for I, the Lord your God am holy [transnatural]" (Leviticus 19:2).

How is the collective spirit of a people created and maintained? It unfolds out of folkways as well as shared history and heroes, teachings and laws, celebrations and observances. The Mitzvot are folkways. Kaplan calls them *sancta*, holy symbols. The Mitzvot are sancta. For Americans, the American flag is a sanctum, a holy symbol. The same applies to Mitzvot as sancta. If a Mitzvah loses its character as a sanctum, it can be discarded; new sancta may equally emerge out of the people's spirit. The Jews, therefore, find fulfillment within the confines of an organic Jewish people.

At the same time, American Jews have to immerse themselves fully in American civilization. American democracy was to Kaplan the closest approximation of ideal ethical nationhood. It rests ultimately on the statement made in the Declaration of Independence, the "truth . . . that all men are created equal . . . endowed by their Creator." This principle has its roots in Hebrew Scriptures. American Jews must live in two civilizations, American and Jewish. Each must mutually influence and strengthen the other. The evolution of ethics in the American civilization has led to the recognition of the right of women to full equality. This, in turn, compels Judaism fully to grant these rights to women in the religious life.

The Jews must strive to promote ethics in human society. The Jewish concept of salvation, as Kaplan sees it, is not a salvation in a hereafter, but a salvation of society here. Thus, the Sabbath is a sanctum, bringing to mind the duty of every Jew to fight for the human rights of everyone, such as the right to rest from work and the opportunity for recreation.

The State of Israel and its people can collectively promote the ideal of ethical nationhood. Israel, therefore, is important, it is central. From Israel insights go out to the Diaspora, and from the Diaspora similar insights come back to Israel. It is a two-way street.

The Jewish people are not a chosen people, but a people like others, with an individual insight, just as others have individual insights. They make a contribution to the world. Jewish religion emerges from the totality of Jewish civilization. Since Judaism is an evolving religious civilization, all Jews who in some manner identify with this civilization, regardless of denomination or even secular outlook, are to be regarded as living a legitimately Jewish life: they contribute to the civilization.

Torah is never completed; every generation adds to it and enlarges it out of the total experience of the Jewish people. But Torah must be demythologized. Its literal meaning is not accepted today and ought to be abandoned. Prayer is to call forth the power within worshipers to recognize ultimate values and to release within themselves the power of self-transcendence. It is to call forth the divine that leads them from the is to the ought. It must lead to a commitment to ethics and humanize the people.

Kaplan developed his theology to give modern, intellectual Jews a form of Judaism that did not compel them to renounce their reason and insights based on science. It is grounded in sociology. In the process he eliminated the personal God, replacing it by the impersonal "Power." Mitzvot become folkways. The election of the Jewish people is denied. Torah is demythologized in tune with modern insights. The value of this theology lies in its appeal to intellectuals. But it deprives the individual of a personal God to whom he or she can turn in need and distress.

Kaplan also fought for women's rights. He advocated creativity in liturgy and Jewish practice. He recognized any survivalist Jew, even those not religious; he promoted American patriotism among Jews; at the same time, he urged them to be Zionists. His thoughts echoed the sentiments of many American Jews. While disagreeing with Hermann Cohen, he nevertheless stood under his influence, speaking of a "correlation" of nature and ethics.

The saintly RAV ABRAHAM ISAAC KOOK (1865–1935) became the first Chief Rabbi in the City of Jerusalem and was an eminent talmudist and mystic. His was a loving heart. To him ultimate unity-in-harmony resides in God alone. The universe and humanity were created by God to come ever closer to the divine by forming one great unity and harmony. Our love must therefore be extended to all human beings and to nature. The truly religious person is filled with this awareness and strives ever to renew it.

Similar to Judah Halevi, Rav Kook was convinced that a special spirit of holiness rests on the Jewish people. It has found its full flowering in the Land of Israel. There alone has the spiritual search come to be fused with physical activity, renewing in the Jew the unity of body and soul. It has found full expression in the *halutzim*, the pioneers, who, in reclaiming the land, build the sanctuary of God for His people.

RABBI JOSEPH BAER SOLOVEITCHIK (1903–1993) in his lifetime was considered the greatest halakhic authority in America. He was equally at home in worldly culture. He ordained generations of Orthodox rabbis, who called him the *Rav*, Master. Scion of a family of talmudic scholars in Russia, he had obtained his doctorate from the university of Berlin with a dissertation on Hermann Cohen's philosophy.

In his work *Halakhic Man*, Rav Soloveitchik gave a "metaphysic" of halakhah. He set up various types of human beings. "Average man," conscious of his loneliness and frailty, seeks escape in society. "Religious man" is torn by internal conflicts as he wrestles with his conscience in seeking God. "Halakhic Man," the Jew rooted in halakhah, has no such problems. He is free. God has revealed the Torah to Israel at Sinai, made a Covenant with Israel, making the Jew coworker with God, and has given it the divine halakhah. Halakhah provides every Jew with unfailing knowledge and direction. Whether seeking the basic principles guiding the universe or the relationship with other humans, he finds true guidance in Torah, and orients himself by halakhah. All of life in all its facets must therefore be based on halakhah. Then God is included, for halakhah is divine ethics in action. Actually halakhah sets up an ideal, like a Platonic "Form," which the Jew, knowing himself to be a coworker with God, seeks to understand in study and to approximate in life. If he falls short, halakhah itself provides the way to healing, namely Teshuvah.

Halakhah is a special gift of God only to the Jewish people. Therefore, any cooperation with other religions is possible only in secular efforts to improve society, not in the area of religion, with which no outsider can have full empathy anyway.

Rabbi Eugene B. Borowitz (1924–) has for decades been Professor of Education and Jewish Religious Thought at the Hebrew Union College—Jewish Institute of Religion and has also taught at Harvard and other universities. Keenly aware of his obligation as an educator of Jews, he has in many works investigated Jewish life in America, evaluated the position of contemporary Christian theologians in regard to Judaism, and in 1970 founded the biweekly "Sh'ma—A Journal of Jewish Responsibility" permitting all Jewish views to be heard. In his work *Renewing the Covenant—A Theology for the Postmodern Jew,* which appeared in 1991, he offered his theology. At the same time he wrote a guidebook for the non-Orthodox Jew to authentic Jewish living by living under the Covenant.

EUGENE B. BOROWITZ: EVOLUTION IN HISTORY— THE PROBLEM OF THE CONTEMPORARY JEW

From its beginnings in biblical times, the Jewish people lived in the certitude that it stood under a special Covenant with God which separated it from the world and subjected it to the divinely ordained Mitzvot. The Emancipation weakened this conviction. It led the Jews into the world and made them depend on general culture.

After the Holocaust all of contemporary Jewry found itself in a dilemma. It realized the bankruptcy of reason, which had brought on the Holocaust, but it could not turn its back on reason. The Age of Reason had established democracy, emancipated the Jews, and given them equality.

Many Jews looked for new foundations on which to build their Jewish lives. Among them was fundamentalism. It called for submission to higher law by which they would be judged and required the habitual performance of Mitzvot.

Non-Orthodox Jews saw absolute foundations in *yiddishkayt*, not halakhah, but Jewish folklife. Others found them in the State of Israel, the Holocaust, or in kabbala. Again, others saw these foundations in the emotional or esthetic response Judaism elicited within them. Some Jews felt that Judaism simply meant being good human beings.

But all of these are inadequate and insufficient because the Jew needed one specific absolute, unchanging, transcendent foundation for being a Jew. This is given in the Covenant with God. The non-Orthodox Jew was now faced with a dilemma. Non-Orthodox Jews have held the conviction that God has given to all human beings, including the Jews, a certain amount of freedom to legislate for themselves. God has placed them under the Covenant, but at the same time allowed them certain freedoms in regard to halakhah, as long as they remained within the Covenant. The non-Orthodox Jew had to find a middle ground between obedience to God's command and human autonomy. Judaism had to be understood as a Covenantal partnership between God and the people as a whole, which would allow for individual autonomy.

Living under the Covenant

Living under the Covenant entails several imperatives, especially for the non-Orthodox Jew. Every Jewish person must live personally and primarily in involvement with the one God of the universe. The Jew is committed to humanity under the covenant with Noah, but, beyond that stands under the Covenant of Israel. The Jewish people are especially chosen to form a community upheld by the self-discipline of its members under the Covenant.

The imperatives are these. First, *God, a commanding God, demands a life of Torah.* The yardstick of the Jewish faith is action. Judaism rests not on theology but on duty, obedience, halakhah. This has not changed in non-Orthodox Judaism although this Judaism has reinterpreted the halakhic obligations. Second, *God made the Covenant with the entire people.* The Jew under the Covenant is, therefore, inextricably linked in multiple ties to land, language, history, traditions, fate, and faith. Third, *the Jew is commanded by God to establish the sacred society.* This society includes the local as well as the worldwide Jewish community of the Jewish people. God is God of history as it is lived. The Covenant therefore commits the Jew to link himself to his entire historical past, being guided by its wisdom, Bible, Talmud, and the Jewish classics. Combined with it he has the compelling duty to orient himself to the entire Jewish future, especially the "forward thrust to the Days of the Messiah." This orientation to messianic fulfillment will sustain him or her in times of trials.

The Jew must do more than append Judaism to the fringes of his or her general human personality. Judaism must permeate the totality of one's being. Living as a Jew may no longer mean living as a decent human being with Judaism as an appendage, but living all of life in and through Judaism. This Jew, according to the liberal Borowitz, is also conscious of the autonomy God has granted. Therefore, this Jew will examine every halakhah and practice, accepting those deemed necessary for a life under the Covenant, declining or postponing the others.

The yardstick of authentic Jewish living then will not be how many Mitzvot a Jew observes, but how determined he is in his efforts to root Jewish life in the Covenant and to acknowledge God as the absolute foundation of all his values. This will give him distance from the stresses of daily living. In regular performance of his daily duties toward God he will make his entire life spiritual. Similar to Rosenzweig, Borowitz holds that people may not wait for personal spiritual experiences that may never come. They must strive toward them through Mitzvot.

Borowitz voices a hope similar to the one once expressed by Franz Rosenzweig. Rosenzweig once stated that in the past all Jews followed one path, halakhah; but now they are united only by a common landscape, with many paths. They must not lose sight of each other.

CHAPTER 16

Attempts at Holocaust Theology

HOLOCAUST THEOLOGY is a difficult undertaking. Theology tries to interpret God's ways by means of human reason, but the Holocaust is so unique in human history that any endeavor to explain God's "reasons" fails. Therefore, attempts must be seen as tentative. Such attempts can truly be made only by Jews trying to understand the event from their inner perception of God. All dialogue with other religions must happen against the backdrop of six million martyrs and the recognition of the State of Israel as a theological fact. Its possession is an integral part of God's Covenant with Abraham and his descendants (see Genesis 17:1–14; also 13:14–17; 15:7, 18-21). In this spirit, a new generation of Jewish theologians has tried to come to grips with the events in Jewish history, both shattering and reviving. They have followed in the existential footsteps of Buber, Rosenzweig, and Baeck or the naturalist footsteps of Kaplan.

Emil Fackenheim

Emil Fackenheim (1916–) was born in Halle, Germany, and received his rabbinical education and ordination at the liberal *Hochschule für die Wissenschaft des Judentums* in Berlin. In 1938 he was confined to the Nazi concentration camp at Sachsenhausen. After his release, he studied in England and Canada. Upon completing his distinguished career as professor of philosophy at the University of Toronto, he settled in Israel. His life has been shaped by his experience of the Holocaust and the rebirth of the State of Israel. Among his Jewish works are *In Quest of Past and Future, Encounter between Judaism and Modern Philosophy, God's Presence in History,* and *Jewish Return into History.*

Auschwitz, Fackenheim points out, has shaken Jewish existence to its core. The believing Jew is confronted by the question: Has God abrogated His Covenant with Israel? The unbelieving Jew must ask if liberalism has failed; seeing humanity as the measure of all things, liberalism started out as a benevolent humanism and ended up by making one man, Hitler, the measure of all things. Will the secular city lead in the same direction, since it does not demand that humanity be accountable to a transcendent God? Perhaps God is dead and religion is only an emotion? In response, the emergence of the State of Israel gives evidence to the Jews' unparalleled will to live in the face of the most concerted effort ever made to exterminate them. The victory of this will points to a God who sustained it and brought it to fruition?

Reason offers no answer to these questions. However, existentially they must be answered, for the sake of the Jews who must retain their emotional and spiritual balance and be a light to the nations; must be answered for the sake of humanity who must come to recognize and implement the divine command for universal social justice. The answer can only be an existential affirmation of God. He is not dead, although He may have gone into eclipse, may have hidden Himself, as Buber maintained.

The existential affirmation of God rests on several existential needs. *Were the Jews to deny God, they would be giving Hitler a posthumous victory.* This may not be. Also, the world as a whole cannot expect to find its way without God. Self-transcendence is not enough, since no person or society can truly go beyond that which it is. Jews and all peoples must consider themselves accountable to a transcendent God of justice. Such an affirmation does not resolve the perplexity of the Jews, who have to face up to the two soul-shaking events that took place within one decade and to their juxtaposition. But the Jews are stabilized in the knowledge that the living God has willed them, even though His reasons are incomprehensible. As God lives, the events created by Him have meaning.

Along with the affirmation of the living God for existential reasons goes obedience. God has spoken and God speaks, demanding response and obedience. Jews must subject themselves once again to Mitzvah. The body of Mitzvot should be seen not as law but as command. Law is an impersonal force, but command, Mitzvah, points to a *Metzaveh,* a commander. It creates the relationship between the person who issues the command and the person who obeys it. This was Franz Rosenzweig's position.

The Jews are called to be a witness to the living God. Their will to live in the face of Auschwitz, resulting in the rebirth of Israel, testifies to their trust in God. But Jews must exhibit it consciously. They must inject the living God into the secular city and be a witness. Otherwise this city, humanity, may lose itself again in nihilism.

Auschwitz defies attempts at "explanation." Such attempts would be blasphemy. But a commanding voice goes forth from it. The talmudic rabbis enumerated 613 commandments binding on the Jews. In response to Auschwitz, Fackenheim postulates a 614th: survival.

> Because after the Nazi celebration of death life has acquired a new dimension of sanctity. . . . Because insanity had ruled the kingdom of darkness, hence sanity, once a gift, has now become a holy commandment. Why hold fast to mere Jewishness? Because Jewish survival after Auschwitz is not "mere" but in itself and without any further reasons or theological justifications a sacred testimony to all mankind that life and love, not death and hate, shall prevail.

Why did the surviving Jews seek the dangerous life in the State of Israel, rather than live in peaceful forgetfulness in other parts of the world? Because

> the state of Israel is a collective testimony against the groundless hate which has erupted in this century in the heart of Europe. Its watchword is: Am Yisrael Chai, "the people Israel lives" (*The Jewish Return into History*; New York: Schocken, 1978, pp. 96–97).

American Jews in particular face contradictions. Narrowly removed from Auschwitz, they enjoy great freedom. They see many of their fellow Jews subjected to persecution and suffering, and they live in a world in which the exaltation of human autonomy has brought about both human betterment and deepest human suffering. The Jews have to live with these contradictions. They have to live in the world and for the world, they may not despair of it. On account of what has happened to them, they must reopen the question of Jeremiah and Job. But while asking "why," they must not despair of God or the world. Out of their existential confrontation with the living God, the Jews must do their share as Jews, witnesses and workers, to bring about humanity's renewal. The world must come to a direct confrontation with God, recognizing Him in action. The Jews aware of the encounter, must once again see Sinai as a real meeting point of God and humanity and accept its imperative, the commitment to the Covenant.

Fackenheim's thoughts have been seconded by a number of his colleagues in the liberal rabbinate, such as Eugene Borowitz and others who have issued the call to a restoration of Covenant-consciousness and a return to Mitzvot and Halakhah. But they have also been criticized. To Fackenheim, Auschwitz becomes almost a new Sinai, a commanding voice, and as such, the ground of Jewish survival. This has been challenged, as Borowitz has pointed out. The Jewish people may not find the rationale for its existence in an outside pressure. The Jews must not survive in order to deny Hitler a posthumous victory, but as the people of the Covenant of Sinai, which was put to an unparalleled test at Auschwitz, but through it was reconfirmed.

Richard L. Rubenstein

Richard Rubenstein had to find his way painfully. He came from a home where Jewish tradition was deliberately belittled. After studying at the Jewish Theological Seminary at New York (where he was a disciple of Mordecai M. Kaplan) and at Harvard, he served as rabbi in Hillel Foundations, the Jewish student foundations at universities, and for many years as a university professor of Jewish studies.

As the title of his work, *After Auschwitz*, indicates, he too sees in Auschwitz and also in the restoration of Israel the key elements of Jewish destiny in our time. Believing, with Mordecai Kaplan, that the Jewish God concept is the result of the collective Jewish people's consciousness, he arrives at conclusions completely at variance with Kaplan's optimism—and with Fackenheim's call for a return to God. For over two thousand years the Jews had held to a basic normative belief. The Jewish God was the God of history, and the Jewish people were placed in the world to promote its progress toward an ethical future. According to Rubenstein, Auschwitz proved that the concept was erroneous and the experiment of improving human ethics a failure. Jews should therefore realize that with the restoration of Israel the end of their historical function has been reached; it is "realized eschatology." Humanity cannot be improved: The lesson of Auschwitz is that it remains savage.

Israel therefore abandons its self-assumed missionary task and returns from a religion of history to a religion of nature. Peasants live by the cycle of the year, as nature provides it; their view of life is cyclical. This is "paganism," in contrast to traditional Judaism and Christianity, which live by the timeline of history. Jews must return to this archaic paganism; as a matter of fact, they have already done so in Israel. There the festivals of Judaism are observed with new forms; namely, as festivals of sacred moments throughout the seasons of the year.

Jews, like the pagans of old, are to follow the cycle of the year from spring through summer, fall through winter, and then start over again. They step out of history, "The straight line of Jewish history has become the circle of eternal return" (*After Auschwitz*, Indianapolis: Bobbs-Merrill, 1966, p. 142). Israel has come home, and the joy at the Western Wall, the last remnant of the Temple, was the joy of homecoming after nineteen hundred years of Diaspora.

But turning from the God of history to the God of nature does not entail the elimination of traditional ritual; it actually reinforces it. In traditional ritual, the archaic and mythic elements of Judaism are contained, and in their observance the link with the ancient past of the people is forged.

> The European catastrophe marks the death of the God of History. . . . an insightful paganism, utilizing the forms of traditional Jewish religion, is the only meaningful religious option remaining to Jews after Auschwitz and the rebirth of Israel. (*After Auschwitz*, p. 130)

By "insightful paganism," Rubenstein does not call for a return to pagan gods and goddesses but rather seems to call for recognition of some pagan insights. He states:

> In the religion of history, only man and God are alive. Nature is dead and serves only as the material of tool-making man's obsessive projects. . . . In the religion of nature, a historical, cyclical religion, man is once more at home with nature and its divinities, sharing their life, their limits, and their joys. (*After Auschwitz*, p. 136)

Perhaps Rubenstein thinks of *deus sive natura*, God as nature, in ways that are reminiscent of Spinoza. That way he can maintain that the Jews must accept nature and the world without illusions, knowing that, being of the earth, they must be true to it and will return to it. People cannot hope for survival; birth and death are the boundaries of their existence. With the God of history, all messianic hope, even that of seeing in the Messiah simply the symbol of a humanity at peace (as held by Hermann Cohen) has to be given up. Only death releases people from toil and trouble, only death is the "Messiah."

In a later work, *The Cunning of History*, Rubenstein assesses history and the future of humanity in light of the Holocaust. Throughout the ages, people always found ways to exterminate the unwanted. The Nazi brought to this process of population control a hitherto unknown efficiency, and, above all, a wholly detached and highly effective bureaucracy. It is horrifying to contemplate what may be done in the future to get rid of the undesired and superfluous. Having learned the methods of the Nazis, people can improve on them by use of computers. Had computers existed during the Nazi period, no Jew could have escaped by going underground, and slave labor would have been enforced more "scientifically," as would have been their exploitation unto death. These "improvements" may be expected by future exterminators.

It is fallacious to assume that civilization reflects growth of rationality and humanitarian spirit. Civilization is an organic process of unfolding in which reason, beauty, love, and compassion on the one hand, and cruelty, destructiveness, and savagery on the other are necessarily found; this is the thesis and antithesis in the unfolding of civilization.

Judeo-Christian tradition holds no assurances either. In fact, this very tradition may be implicated in the events. Judeo-Christian tradition established the division between the elect, who will receive life, and the damned, who deserve extermination. The Nazis simply carried these theological ideas into the secular world and created a caricature of the biblical idea of the "chosen people," proclaiming themselves as *Herrenvolk*, the master race. They alone had the right and duty to survive, which meant extermination of the "damned."

The tenor and impact of Rubenstein's thought is deeply pessimistic. He has found no following, but he reveals the deep wounds inflicted by the Holocaust on earnest Jewish seekers. By his assertion that the Jewish God concept emerges out of the people he shows the influence of Mordecai Kaplan. They once found the God of history out of their collective experience. Now they are compelled and legitimized to find the deity of nature out of the experience of the Holocaust. Yet Kaplan disavowed Rubenstein's thoughts, with his pessimism and his denial that Judaism has a significant function in history. Fackenheim's view stands in total opposition to Rubenstein's. To him the commanding voice going out from Auschwitz calls for a renewal of the Covenant with the God of history, into which the Jewish people has entered again.

Elie Wiesel

Shortly after his Bar Mitzvah, Elie Wiesel (1928–) was taken from a tightly knit, traditional and love-filled life in his hometown of Sighet in Transylvania and endured various Nazi concentration camps until the liberation. Afterward he became a writer and journalist in Paris. He subsequently came to the United States, where he has served as professor of humanities at Boston University, as a writer and lecturer. Wiesel became an untiring defender of human rights and an outspoken critic of powers and governments. In 1986 he received the Nobel

Peace Prize for being a "messenger to humanity." As chairman of the President's Commission on the Holocaust, he evolved the concept of the Holocaust Museum at Washington, D.C. and took part in its dedication.

Wiesel's numerous books, including thrilling novels, give us a panorama of the Holocaust. They are regarded as midrashic since they try to convey the deeper meaning of the tragedy. For instance, he writes of the hanging of a young boy and two adults by the Nazis in Auschwitz, which the entire prisoner population had been summoned to witness.

> All eyes were on the child. He was lividly pale, almost calm, biting his lips. . . .
> The three victims mounted the chairs together. The three necks were placed in
> the nooses. "Long live liberty" cried the two adults. But the child was silent.
> "Where is God? Where is He?" someone behind me asked. At a sign from the
> head of the camp, the three chairs tipped over. . . . I heard a voice within me
> answer . . . : "Where is He? He is hanging on this gallows." (*Night*, New York:
> Avon Books, 1972, pp. 75ff.)

Later, Wiesel was to say to François Mauriac, "I knew Jewish children every one of whom suffered a thousand times more, six million times more, than Christ on the cross. And we don't speak about them" (*A Jew Today*, New York: Vintage Books, 1979, p. 22).

He also asserted that "Holocaust literature there cannot be. Auschwitz negates all literature as it negates all theories and doctrines; to lock it into philosophy means to restrict it. . . . The concept of a theology of Auschwitz is blasphemous for both the non-believer and the believer" (p. 234).

Yet the memory of Auschwitz must be kept alive for humanity's sake. Judaism must be alive; the Jewish people must live, and Israel must live. The theological contradictions are insurmountable. But life holds the answer. As the epigraph of *A Jew Today*, Wiesel uses something he was told by a wise man in 1944: "You are Jewish, your task is to remain Jewish. The rest is up to God."

Both Fackenheim and Wiesel hold on to the God of History and see their function in promoting justice in the world. Rubenstein's is a lonely voice. In his pessimistic view, Nature has given, Nature will take. To it Jews have to return and to submit.

Eliezer Berkovits

Eliezer Berkovits (1908–1993) was rabbi in one of the Berlin synagogues, then professor of philosophy at the Hebrew Theological College at Skokie, Illinois, and after his retirement a resident of Israel. He represented an Orthodox position.

Berkovits argued that those who have not suffered at Auschwitz, including himself, are at best "Job's brothers," and are forbidden to pass judgment on the faith or the abandonment of faith of the sufferers. God's absence at Auschwitz, His choosing to "hide His face," is the fundamental problem of the post-Auschwitz generation. But it is not a new problem. Resting on Isaiah's words,

"Verily You are a God that hide Yourself, God of Israel, Savior!" (Isaiah 45:15), he sees God's hiding as an attribute of the divine being, that makes God the Savior. At issue and vital for the quality of Jewish survival is our capacity to understand the mystery of God's absence, especially at Auschwitz, as an element of His salvation.

God's hiding is in no way to be regarded as either divine indifference to human suffering, or as divine punishment for human sinfulness. It is a mystery. And because the God who hides is the God who saves, Isaiah could say, "I will wait for the Lord that hides His face from the house of Jacob and will hope for Him (Isaiah 8:17).

God has created humanity as coworkers, allowing humans to choose freely between good and evil. He tested Western humanity and it failed miserably. Out of a deep concern with humanity, God chose Israel to be His witness in history. "You are My witnesses, saith the Eternal . . . that you may know and believe Me, and understand that I am He. Before Me there was no God formed, neither shall any be after Me" (Isaiah 43:10).

Reading the verse with great care, Berkovits points out that Israel is not called upon to be witness *because* it knows God, but *in order* that it may come to know and believe in God through the experience of witnessing. This was put to the test throughout Jewish history and at no time more severely than at Auschwitz. The horrible fate of the Jews in the extermination camps certainly revealed the fact that the Jew is witness, whether he knows it or not. Even those who had long abandoned Judaism, were murdered. It is now up to us to recognize it and return to a conscious witnessing in faith.

The Jews were also witnesses to the hidden God by waiting through millennia of their history for the restoration of the State of Israel, which God had promised. They are now witnesses in their land that God, no longer hidden, has fulfilled the promise. But in their land they are to be witnesses and coworkers with God in a new task. They are called to bring to fruition the divine plan of universal peace and harmony, when "nation will not lift up sword against nation" (Isaiah 2:4). "From Zion shall go forth Torah," (Isaiah 2:3) and God's blessing will embrace all of humanity symbolized in the words, "Egypt [will be] My people and Assyria the work of My hands and Israel My inheritance" (Isaiah 19:25).

The Holocaust does not preempt the entire course of history. It strongly reinforces it. Its commanding voice is simply the divine commanding voice addressed to Israel throughout its existence. The mystery of Auschwitz-Israel remains. God may decide to reward the sufferers for the pain they have borne, but He is not committed to grant such a reward. He has done so in allowing the restoration of Israel.

Jews accept the hiddenness of God, although they do not know its duration and severity. They do not doubt His providence. But this does not exonerate God for having created a world in which humans have the freedom to shape history. Humanity misused this freedom and throughout history brought immeasurable suffering to the innocent. Jews believe in absolute faith that the ever-present God will bring redemption to all suffering in a dimension beyond history. They cannot, however, forgive even God for the cries of the victims within history.

Grounded in this faith, Jews maintain that God is indebted to His people for the untold sufferings He has inflicted upon them. Did He wish to test them to the utmost? Berkovits's question springs from his faith.

God remains indebted to his people; He may be long-suffering only at their expense. This was hardly ever as true as in our own days, after the Holocaust. Is it perhaps what God desires: a people, to whom He owes so much, who yet acknowledge him? As His children, they have every reason to condemn His creation. Yet they accept the Creator in the faith that in the fullness of time the divine indebtedness will be redeemed. Then the divine adventure with man will be approved even by its martyred victims?" (*Faith after the Holocaust*, New York, Ktav Publishing House, 1973, pp. 136–137).

Emmanuel Levinas

Emmanuel Levinas (1906–1995) belonged to the leading philosophers of France. His philosophical work, widely taught and discussed in Europe, is becoming known in America. Only some of his Jewish thoughts shall be discussed here.

Levinas was born at Kovno. At the age of fifteen he went West and studied philosophy at Strasbourg and Freiburg under Husserl and Heidegger. In 1930 he became a French citizen, and during the war he wore the French uniform, which saved him from extermination. He survived in a prisoner-of-war camp; his wife was sheltered by non-Jewish friends but his family in Russia was murdered. After the war he directed a Jewish teachers' seminary, then shifted to university teaching, and eventually became a professor of philosophy at the Sorbonne. He was possibly the most creative Jewish philosopher of his time. He credited Buber and Rosenzweig with having helped him to "part with Husserl and Heidegger."

The foundation of Levinas's thought is, not "Being" and the "All," but the concrete life in relationship to "the Other." Speaking of "Being" of "the All" the philosopher makes universal statements without considering the actual, individual person, who remains isolated. In fact, the other person, by his or her very being, his needs, her questions intrude upon me in challenge. The isolation of the individual person is to be replaced by the link to "the other" in ethics, love and duty. God enters our daily life and actions. God is revealed in sacred history. Theoretical reasoning does not awaken moral consciousness, but relating to "Being as the Other Person" does. Pointing to Rosenzweig, who speaks of the elements of God *and* world *and* human being, of creation *and* revelation *and* redemption, Levinas emphasized that God is for the world and humans, and humans are for God and world. This must be understood as a living relation, not as a philosophical construct, as is Hegel's thesis-antithesis-synthesis. It is to be carried on in the *saying*, the living dialogue rather than the *said*, the written text. It means turning the *face* to the other. The beginning of philosophy is ethics.

Levinas, a strictly Orthodox Jew, saw himself as representative of Judaism, on which he has lectured widely and published numerous works. Judaism, in the title of one work is *Difficile Liberté*, "Difficult Freedom." His intention was to translate "Greek language" into "Hebrew language"; that is, types.

Greek language formulates universal concepts. It has become the common language of Western culture; it is the language of the university, of philosophy developing concepts. "Greek language" deals with abstractions (Plato's ideal state), it is disengaged. Philosophers in their ivory towers build systems. Standing outside and above the actual human life, they may overlook or even deny the actual human condition. Philosophy has, therefore, not prevented humanity's violence. "Hebrew language" enters history. It takes humanity where it is. It forces it not to deny but to confront the actual human condition of war, crimes, hatred, etc. It places itself within this condition. It adjudicates all human transactions, material, economic, social, not from the point of view of interested acts but from that of the order of justice. It recognizes that humanity cannot save itself without law and gives it law. Levinas affirms Jewish law. Jewish law has led history in a positive way; it has guided humanity to avoid the violence. Philosophy has not equipped humanity to overcome violence and has perhaps even supported it by its abstractions. "Hebrew language" is found in the Bible and the Talmud.

Levinas says, "For us the world of the Bible is not a world of figures but of faces. They are entirely there and in relation with us." The Bible speaks to modern people calling them to action. The Talmud with its debates is a saying; discussants turn their faces to each other and to us. It is practical and always ethical. Levinas considers himself both Greek and Jewish.

The Talmud with its debates gives contemporary humanity ideas and ideals found nowhere else. Levinas has interpreted talmudic texts in modern context. In these "Talmudic Readings" he wishes to give us access to the "Hebrew Language," and to set an example of reading it. In doing so he reveals his own deeply ethical vision, grounded in Judaism. He addressed Jews. After the outrages Jews have suffered, Jewish consciousness must again become certain of the worth, dignity, and mission of Judaism. He addressed non-Jews. To him, "all those who recognize their duty toward the physical needs of their neighbors are rightly 'Israel,' heirs to Abraham." (An English translation is available by Annette Aronovicz, called *Nine Talmudic Readings*.)

Levinas summed up the commanding voice that goes forth from the Holocaust by telling a fictional but revealing story, entitled "To Love the Torah More Than God." It is based on a talmudic saying in which God says, "[If need be and you are placed before the choice] rather forsake Me but keep My Torah" (J. Hagigah 1:7). Yossel ben Yossel Rakover of Tarnopol sets down his thoughts in the night before the last uprising in the Warsaw ghetto. He has lost everything and expects to be killed by the Nazis the next morning; He writes, "Now I know that You are my God, because You would not know how to be the God of those whose acts are militantly the most horrible expression of an absence of God. . . . I love Him, but I love His Torah even more . . . and even if I were disappointed by Him and downtrodden, I would nevertheless observe the precepts of the Torah." God conceals Himself, and now the Jew has to do the ultimate: preserve the Torah and its ethics. Yossel argues with God, but is prepared to die for Him.

The implication is a firm belief in messianic redemption. The world may reject the Torah now, but it will come back to it in messianic days, when God and His Torah will triumph, and the sacrificial death of the martyrs will be vindicated. When God is absent then the Jew, all by himself, has to safeguard the Torah in action and, if need be, suffering and death. He becomes God's "protector." As guardian of Torah he is everlastingly linked to God, even when He has turned His face. Torah creates the intimacy between the Jew and God. Levinas has not given us a theological reason for the Holocaust—which is impossible—but revealed, as did Fackenheim, the command that goes forth from it.

CHAPTER 17

Prayer and the House of the Lord

LIFE AS MITZVAH

THE TERM *MITZVAH* is so broad that it allows diverging emphases in observance. Orthodox Jewry has seen in Mitzvah essentially the observance of religious commandments, whereas Reform Jewry has laid stress on social justice and social action as Mitzvah. Neither, of course, has disregarded the total aspect of Mitzvah. Ideally, in traditional perspective, the totality of life is to be a witness to God, an all-encompassing Mitzvah through which God will be made manifest and the people of Israel sustained.

The *Shulhan Arukh* states it clearly:

Man shall make himself strong as a lion as he arises in the morning to serve his Creator. (Note by Rabbi Moses Isseries: "I have set the Lord always before me" (Psalm 16:8) is one of the basic principles of Torah; it is one of the virtues of the righteous who walk before Him at all times. . . . Let man take to heart that the Great King, God—whose glory fills the whole earth—stands over him and watches over all his actions. . . . This awareness will immediately fill him with reverence, humility, and awe before Him, Blessed be His Name. . . . May he never feel ashamed before those people who make mock of him on account of his service to God, His Name be Blessed). (Orah Hayim 1:1)

If he cannot study without an afternoon nap, let him take a nap, but not drag it out. . . . Even in as small a matter as that, may his intentions be not to give pleasure to his body, but to return his body to the service of Him whose Name be Blessed. The same applies to all the enjoyments in this world; not pleasure be his intention, but service to his Creator, Blessed be He, as it is written, "In all your ways recognize Him" (Proverbs 3:6), to which our sages have

323

commented: "May all your actions be for the sake of Heaven" (Abot 2:12). Even his unregulated actions, such as eating and drinking, walking and sitting, standing, intercourse, talk, and all the needs of the body, every one of them should be directed to the service of his Creator, or as a means leading to service unto Him. Thus, if he be hungry or thirsty and eats or drinks simply for his enjoyment, his acts are not praiseworthy; rather shall his intention be to eat and drink for the preservation of his life, in order that he may serve his Creator. . . . The same goes for intercourse, the marital duties ordained in Torah. If he performs them to appease his desires or for the enjoyment of his body, he should be ashamed; even if his intentions are to have children who may eventually help him and ultimately take his place, that too is not praiseworthy. His intention shall be to have children who will serve his Creator; or better yet, his intention shall be to fulfill the commandment of marital duty like a man who pays a debt. The same applies to talk. . . . All in all: He must turn his sight and heart toward his road, weigh all his actions on the scales of his intellect. If he sees something leading him to an opportunity of serving his Creator, Blessed be He, let him do it; otherwise, may he not do it. He who conducts himself in this fashion serves his Creator always. (Orah Hayim 231:1)

We may readily admit that such a life is impossible for the average person, even if he be Orthodox. Many Jews lead committed lives without being bound by all these rules. By the time the *Shulhan Arukh* was written, Mitzvah had become the pillar of Judaism; we may see in this statement a guideline and goal affecting every action, and affording a yardstick by which daily routine may be measured. We note that nothing is excluded from being a Mitzvah; there is no dualism of spirit and flesh. All depends on the intent. Sex may be a Mitzvah, while simple rest, under certain circumstances, may not be.

Since everything from enjoyment to suffering must be given a meaning in God's plan, it is essential that we be aware of our actions as we perform them; then they will become Mitzvah.

THE BERAKHAH (BENEDICTION)

All of life ideally should be Mitzvah. The rabbis of the Talmud ordained, therefore, that every act be preceded by a spoken affirmation that it is done "for the sake of Heaven." Every pleasure must be savored in adoration of its Creator. Thus the unit of prayer was formulated in order that Jews might clothe the promptings of their hearts in a structured garment. This unit is *Berakhah*, the Benediction. The Psalmist used it: "Blessed are You, O Lord, teach me Your statutes" (Psalm 119:12). And the Talmud teaches:

Over fruit growing on trees one says [before eating them]: "Blessed are You, God our Lord, King of the Universe, He who creates the fruit of the tree." . . . Over wine one says: "Blessed . . . who creates the fruit of the vine." . . . Over fruits of the ground one speaks: "Blessed . . . who creates the fruit of the ground." Over bread one pronounces: "Blessed . . . who brings forth bread from the earth." Over anything which does not grow from the earth one says: "Blessed . . . by whose word all was created." After a meal everyone shall say grace. (Mishnah Berkhot 6:1, 3, 6)

Over comets, earthquakes, thunder, storm, and lightnings, over mountains, hills, oceans, rivers, and deserts [a blessing is pronounced by the beholder]. . . . Over rain and on getting happy news one says: "Blessed . . . Who is good and is doing good." On receiving evil tidings one recites: "Blessed . . . the true judge." . . . It is man's duty to bless God for the ills that befall him holding hidden good, even as he gives blessing for the good that comes to him, though it hold hidden ills. . . . Has he built a new house or bought new clothes, he shall pronounce praise: "Blessed . . . who has kept us alive, has sustained us, and has brought us to this time." (Mishnah Berakhot 9:2, 3, 5)

Our thoughts thus revolve constantly about God. The world is truly the Lord's, and the fullness thereof. What we own may be legally ours; ideally, it is God's. The Berakhah is our request for permission to use it, joined to our pledge to make use of it for God's glory, in order that God may be made manifest. The totality of life thus becomes worship; it is Mitzvah. Understanding the character and purpose of Berakhah, may give us an understanding of Jewish prayer in general, which is built on Berakhah.

PRAYER AND ITS STRUCTURE

The Hebrew term for prayer is *Tefillah*, from the verb *palal*, meaning "to judge, plead, concentrate." Prayer is concentration on the abiding. The late Ernst Simon, a leading contemporary thinker, has given us the traditional view of prayer in general and Jewish prayer in particular. He points out that prayer in general is based on three suppositions: the belief in a personal God, our faith that this personal God cares for His children, and our conviction that we may turn to God with praise and thanks without wishing to flatter Him and approach Him with our supplications without wishing to force Him to do our bidding ("On the Meaning of Prayer," in *Tradition and Contemporary Experience*, New York: Schocken, 1970; pp. 269–73).

Jewish prayer has four additional features. First, it is communal prayer. The Jews were the first to introduce communal prayer, and peoplehood occupies a legitimate place in the Jewish faith. Second, it is formulated prayer. Judaism knows individual, spontaneous prayer, but a person is both an individual and a part of a community, the Jewish people; communal prayer must be formulated prayer. Third, it employs a multitude of external symbols: the tallit, tefillin, phylacteries, shofar, and others. These are designed to visualize the sanctity of life in acts; to promote constant awareness of God's presence; to discipline our thoughts, emotions, and actions; and to link us with our people. Finally, study and worship are equated. Both are prayer. In praise, Jews turn to the God of creation; in supplication, to the God of compassion and justice; and in study, to the God of revelation. And they listen to what God has to say.

Prayer must therefore be offered not as routine, but with *kavanah*, attunement of heart (M. Berakhot 4:4). It must acknowledge that God's will be done, not ours. Many prayers begin with the words "May it be Your will." Formal prayer is to be preceded by meditation, bringing the worshiper in tune with God's will.

Formal prayer accompanies all of life. For every day of the week, Jewish law has appointed three orders of prayer: *Shaharit*, the morning prayer, *Minhah*, the afternoon prayer, and *Maariv*, the evening prayer. On holy days, a special prayer, *Mussaf* (Additional Prayer) is added. It reflects on the significance of the day. These prayers are uniform throughout the year, as far as their core is concerned; morning, noon, and evening prayers are the same for every day. This is significant. Structured prayer, first of all, expresses our feelings better than we could in our own words. It offers the vehicle for our own thoughts, as we fill the familiar words with ever-renewed meaning. It links us to the community.

The repetition of identical prayers actually corresponds to the eternal course of time, which is always the same, from sunrise to sunset, yet ever renewed. The worshiper who endows the unchanging words with ever-new meaning is thus drawn to the fact that, though life is uniform, it may not be routine. Day follows day, but each day is a new creation. Each day is a challenge to renew ourselves in spirit and in action, and never to lose our wonderment at the miracle which is evident in the orderliness of nature. This finds clear expression in one of the Berakhot that is part of every worship:

> We gratefully acknowledge unto You that You are the Lord our God, and the God of our fathers unto all eternity. You are the Rock of our life, shield of our salvation from generation to generation. We give thanks unto You and declare Your praise for our lives committed unto Your hand, for our souls entrusted unto You, for Your miracles that are with us daily, Your wondrous deeds and acts of goodness that are with us at all times, evening, morning, and afternoon. You are good, for Your mercies never fail; compassionate, for the acts of Your loving kindness never cease. We hope in You forever. For all this Your name be blessed and exalted, You, our King, always and forever. May all the living offer laud unto You, and praise Your Name in truth, God of our salvation and of our help. Blessed are You, O Lord, "The Good" is Your Name, and to You it is proper to render thanks. (Daily Amida, eighteenth benediction)

Under God, every moment of life becomes a miracle. He is God of time (history) and space. The knowledge that He *is* gives hope. All that live express His praise, being witness to His creative power.

Of the three prayers, the morning and evening prayers have their source in the Sh'ma. It bids us to rehearse the words of God's unity and the call to love every morning and every evening. Morning prayer prepares for the road in life; evening prayer calls to account. The afternoon prayer, at the time when the afternoon offering was once presented in the Temple, calls for pause and reflection: How much has been achieved? What may yet be done to transform the work of the day into a Mitzvah?

We may compare the worshiper's appearance before God to an audience before a king. Its structure reflects this thought.

The Daily and Additional Prayers for the Festivals

Shaharit (Morning Prayer)

1. On arising, the individual, grateful for reborn strength, prepares oneself for the meeting. Putting on one's clothes, one is aware of God's beneficence in clothing, feeding, and giving bodily vigor.

2. In meditation and psalm, the worshiper puts oneself in tune with the occasion.

3. Individuals form a group to meet the King. Public worship opens with the call to worship, "Bless the Lord to whom all blessing belongs." The congregation responds, "Blessed be the Lord to whom all blessing belongs, unto all eternity."

4. The people affirm God's greatness, love, and majesty. The order of the Berakhot follows the rules laid down in the Mishnah:

   > In the morning two [Berakhot] are to be recited before [the Sh'ma], and one after [the Sh'ma]; in the evening two before [the Sh'ma] and two after [the Sh'ma and preceding the Amidah]. (M. Berakhot 1:4)

   a) God is the Creator of day and night, the Lord of nature.

   b) He is the source of all wisdom, who, in His love has given his Torah to His people. The Sh'ma Yisrael is recited.

   c) He is the God of history, who has rescued Israel from all enemies, and will help all humanity.

5. Trusting in God, the worshiper offers petitions to Him, asking for wisdom, health, forgiveness of sins, daily bread, and restoration. But he begins and concludes with praise. This prayer is recited standing and is called *Amidah*, Prayer offered while standing. (Another term for it is *Shemoneh Esrei*—the Eighteenth—Prayer, because the weekday prayer originally consisted of eighteen Berakhot.) The Amidah is first offered in silent devotion and then publicly repeated by the reader (during morning and afternoon worship). During the repetition *Kedushah*, the sanctification, is sung responsively by reader and congregation: "Holy, holy, holy is the Lord of hosts, the whole earth is full of His glory."

   The wording of the final petition closely resembles the affirmation of faith in its wording. The affirmation had started with: *Sh'ma Yisrael, Adonai Elohenu*, "Hear, O Israel, the Lord our God." The petition begins with: *Sh'ma kolenu, Adonai Elohenu,* "Hear our voice, O Lord, our God . . . and accept graciously our petition." The same rhythm that proclaims Him expresses the plea, for petition emerges out of recognition and simply evokes reciprocal love.

6. The individual confesses his sins in awareness that he is truly unworthy to petition, much less to receive the divine mercies for which he has asked. (Confession is omitted on the Sabbath and Festivals.)

7. The word of the King is heard. The Torah is read on appointed days of the week and on special days.

8. With a final affirmation, *Alenu,* and *Kaddish,* the remembrance of the departed (that their memory be a guide), the congregation takes its leave.

Minhah (Afternoon Prayer)

The afternoon prayer is short. Since the recital of the Sh'ma is not ordained, it is omitted. Psalm 145, which speaks of God's goodness to all, creates the mood of worship. It brings to mind that God is the Sustainer whether the day so far has been successful or a failure. On the Sabbath and Fast Days the Torah is read. The Amidah is recited and repeated. Confession of sin follows. (It is omitted on the Sabbath and Festivals.) Final affirmation and Kaddish conclude the worship.

Maariv (Evening Prayer)

Parallel to morning worship, the evening worship, after an introductory psalm, starts with the call to worship. Then two Berakhot are offered as Mishnah ordains. God is praised as (a) Creator of night and (b) author of Torah, source of all wisdom. Then the Sh'ma is recited. In accordance with the rules of the Mishnah two Beralkhot follow, (c) God is revered as Master of history, (d) a special prayer for protection throughout the night is added. The Amidah is recited silently. Affirmation and Kaddish complete worship. A prayer at bedtime concludes the day.

On Sabbath and holy days, all petitions are omitted. Sheltered in God's peace, Jews should forget their cares on these days. Confession of sin is also omitted; nothing should dim the joy of God's day, not even the knowledge of sinfulness. On festivals of joy, the *Hallel* (Psalms 113–118) are recited by the people in gratitude for God's special dispensations of help.

Mussaf (Additional Prayer)

To commemorate the special festive occasion and in remembrance of the ancient sacrificial service in the Temple, a special prayer is added on holy days, *Mussaf,* Addition. It is recited after the reading of Torah and keynotes the special occasion and its sacrifices in the Temple of Jerusalem. (Reform Judaism has eliminated it.)

The Structure of the Amidah

The structure of the Amidah reveals the design of the obligatory prayers, which is uniformity and variation. God and God's world are uniform. Praise must therefore be uniform throughout the year. Human needs vary. This is reflected in the Amidah. The three opening and closing Berakhot are the same throughout the year. The intermediate Berakhot vary with the special occasion. This table below will clarify it. The first three Berakhot are uniform: (1) God has been the shield and redeemer of the patriarchs throughout all generations, (2) God is Sustainer in life and revives the dead, and (3) God is holy. The following Berakhot vary:

On Weekdays	*On Sabbath and Holy Days*	*Mussaf on Rosh Hashanah*
Human needs are spread out in 13 Berakhot: They include pleas for knowledge and understanding, for forgiveness of sins, redemption from suffering, healing of the sick, sustenance, restoration of the people, ingathering of the dispersed, true judges, against heretics, for the righteous and proselytes, restoration of Jerusalem and the kingship of David's descendant. Plea for acceptance of prayer.	Sanctification of the Sabbath or the holy day (1 Berakhah). The introductory sections to the Berakhah vary.	Proclamation of God as King and sounding the shofar. Proclamation of God Who remembers in love and sounding the shofar. Proclamation of God as Redeemer and sounding the shofar (3 Berakhot).

The three concluding Berakhot are uniform: (1) May God be pleased with His people and their worship, (2) Thanksgiving for God's everlasting goodness, and (3) Prayer for peace, including the priestly benediction.

Liturgical Music

The prayers are not simply read, but are rendered in the form of a recitative which is very old. The reading of the Torah and Haftarah follows a prescribed pattern of modes, which the reader must know. While every Jew with ability and moral character may serve as "the congregation's messenger," leading them in prayer, Jews have always had a great love for music. They looked for a well-trained *chazzan* (cantor) with a good voice, who might endow the words with added meaning, expressing in song the yearning of the heart and conveying in music the message of a special day. Thus, over the years a great body of liturgical music has developed. Each holy day has its own theme song. Compositions were frequently influenced by the musical taste of the general environment. Today, leading Jewish composers are writing liturgical music in modern idiom.

The Prayer Book

We have seen that the content and formal arrangement of the order of worship go back to the Mishnah. Tradition traces the origin of its key skeletal portions to Ezra and his contemporaries and immediate successors, a body of unidentified teachers called the Men of the Great Assembly. The Prayer Book is the second oldest literary work still in constant use in the Western world, the oldest being the Bible (both are of Jewish origin). Actually, only its structure and the content of the Berakhot were established by the Rabbis of the Mishnah. The precentor was permitted to give the content his own formulation. Only in the ninth century was the actual wording of the prayers edited and canonized. Editions with slight variations appeared throughout the centuries.

The *Siddur* (prayer book) reflects the evolution and destiny of the Jewish people. The fate of Sefardic and Ashkenazic Jewry is mirrored in the variations in the Siddur used by either group. Yet the variations are small and do not prevent a worshiper brought up in one tradition from following easily in the prayer book of the other, or in fact from feeling at home in either worship. While the basic core always remained unchanged, poets and singers throughout the Middle Ages were free to add poetry of their own, especially for worship on holy days, the *piyyutim* (singular *piyyut*). Thus was variety in uniformity achieved, the new tied in with the old. It was the printing press that gave the Siddur its unchanging character; prayers and poems included in the printed Siddur found the widest acceptance and, once printed, could not easily be changed.

Throughout the ages, the Orthodox prayer book has hardly undergone any change, although modern translations have been produced, and a number of additional and optional readings have recently been included in some editions. Reform, Conservatism, and Reconstructionism, however, effected certain basic revisions.

Classical Reform was the most radical. Realizing the inability of the people to understand Hebrew, it emphasized prayer in the vernacular, leaving only a few basic Hebrew prayers. It also arranged the book to read from left to right, following the English practice, rather than from right to left, which would have acknowledged the primacy of Hebrew. (Hebrew is read from right to left.) The editors of the Reform prayer book firmly believed that the Emancipation had brought full freedom for all Jews in the countries where they lived. The prayers for the Land of Israel and for restoration of Zion were therefore eliminated. The Mussaf, dealing with the sacrifices of ancient times, was abolished. In recent years, however, new editions of the Reform prayer book have become quite "conservative." Hebrew has once more been emphasized, prayers for the Land of Israel and for Zion and numerous traditional portions have been included. Congregations have the option of using a book reading from left to right or right to left.

The Conservative prayer book shows only slight changes in the Hebrew text. The hope for the rebuilding of the Land of Israel is powerfully expressed, but the sacrificial service in the Temple, as of old, is presented merely as a recollection of the pattern of worship which once prevailed. Alternative services, some of them entirely in English, serve the outlook of various congregations. A great many English responses are added to offer variety in the service and permit it to be keyed to special religious as well as civic and national American observances.

The Reconstructionist prayer book, following basic Conservative principles, has adjusted the text to naturalistic Reconstructionist theology. References to the "chosenness" of Israel are omitted, and the link to the Land of Israel and to Hebrew is as strongly maintained as in the Conservative Siddur.

Non-Orthodox Jewry has taken on the difficult task of revising prayer books to make them gender-neutral and to include and recognize historical women in the prayer text. The Reform movement has issued such a prayer book, adjusting the gender, however, only in the English text. One of the difficulties lies in the fact that *Adonai*, "Lord," is masculine. The Reconstructionists have replaced *Adonai* by the biblical *Yah*, which is neutral. The opening prayer of the Amidah (with the changes set in italics) now generally reads in non-Orthodox prayer books: "Blessed are You, *Eternal* our God and God of our *ancestors*, God of Abraham, God of Isaac and God of Jacob, *God of Sarah, God of Rebeccah, God of Rachel and God of Leah.*"

Numerous efforts have been and are being made to key the Siddur to the needs of the people and to modern philosophy. None has fully succeeded. In all of the prayer books, however, the basic pattern, hallowed by tradition, has remained. Still, it cannot be denied that the use of different prayer books has split Jewry. Yet there is still sufficient uniformity transcending the differences to make the prayer book a unifying element among the Jewish people.

The Congregation

Prayers may be offered by every individual in private. Yet it is better if they rise from a united congregation. The congregation is a symbol of the people, a united society before God. It forecasts a united humanity under God. In addition, the congregation sustains the individual; each worshiper prays for, aids, upholds, and strengthens the next; selfishness departs; responsibility grows. The Jewish prayers are formulated in the plural form.

To constitute a congregation for the purposes of public worship, a quorum of ten, or *minyan*, is required. Why ten? The ordinance goes back to ancient times and gives us an insight into the interpretation of Torah by the rabbis of the Talmud. Twelve men were sent by Moses to scout out the land; ten came back with an evil report, and only two were confident that God's help would permit Israel to overcome the enemy. Referring to the people led astray by the ten, who had conspired for evil, God calls out in indignation, "How long shall I bear with this evil congregation?" (Numbers 14:26—B. Berakhot 21b). Once ten formed a congregation of rebellion; now ten can form a congregation of faith and obedience.

Orthodox Jewry insists on a minyan of ten males who are Bar Mitzvah. Reform and Reconstructionism do not insist on the minyan, but consider it desirable, and count women among the minyan. The Conservative rabbinate regards the minyan as required but also counts women as part of the quorum. These movements have granted women equality. In addition to being part of the minyan, they may form a minyan, lead public worship in all its facets, and assume spiritual and educational leadership in accordance with their personal qualifications.

Physical Reminders

The Tallit

The Lord spoke to Moses saying: Speak to the Israelite people and instruct them to make for themselves fringes—tzitzit—on the corners of their garments through their generations; let them attach a cord of blue to the fringe at each corner. That shall be your fringe; look at it and recall all the Mitzvot of the Lord and observe them, so that you do not follow your heart and eyes in your lustful urge. Thus you shall be reminded to observe all My commandments and be holy unto your God. (Numbers 15:37–41)

The ancient Jews, like the Bedouins of today, used to wear a large, four-cornered robe, which they wrapped about themselves. Torah commanded that they place fringes, like tassels, on the corners of the garment. Swaying at every step, these would remind the wearers of God's presence, and keep them from going astray in their daily pursuits. The wearers would remember and do all of God's Mitzvot and become holy unto God.

In our time, we no longer wear such a garment, but it became the tallit, a four-cornered robe with tassels (tzitzit) on it. It is worn in worship during day hours (the time of day when it is possible "to look at them," the tzitzit in natural light, as Torah commands). It may be a big garment, which may cover the worshiper entirely and which he may even draw over his head when he wishes to commune with God in complete concentration and absorption, or it may be simply a stole, or prayer shawl. The stole in Christian worship derives from it. The cantor or leader at worship will wear it even at nighttime. He approaches God, symbolically wrapped up in Mitzvah. Orthodox Jews wear a small four-cornered garment beneath the suit. Some permit the tzitzit to be visible. The tallit is the garment symbolically clothing the worshiper in the robe of responsibility. Life, in every step, must be walked in God's presence.

As a duty of performance linked to a certain time of day, women were not obligated to its performance and restrained from it. In non-orthodox Judaism, women wear the tallit.

The Tefillin

"Bind them as a sign on your hand, let them be for frontlets between your eyes." These injunctions contained in the Sh'ma (see p. 237) simply mean that mind and actions must be guided by the love of God. Yet the commandment was

Tallit and Tefillin. Note the tassels on the tallit's corners (the fringe along the side is not required). The tefillin for head and arm consist of the cubes containing the parchment scrolls and leather straps. (Photo by the author from his own collection.)

also taken literally, and has led to the tefillin, or phylacteries, as visible symbols. A small leather container in the form of a cube, containing several selections from Torah, is attached to a leather strap and placed on the left upper arm, opposite the heart; the remainder of the strap is wrapped about the arm and hand. Another container is similarly placed on the head. Thus are head (seat of the mind), heart (traditionally the source of will), and hand (the instrument of action) encircled by His word and His love. The word of God sets our limitations and lifts us up.

Each cube of the tefillin holds four sections of Torah, including the Sh'ma (Deuteronomy 6:4–9; Deuteronomy 11:13–20; Exodus 13:11–16; Exodus 13: 1–10). Every one of these selections contains the injunction to place God's word on hand and head.

The selections speak of God's deliverance, His providence, and His promise to return Israel to its Land. They also spell out the duties of humankind to make Him manifest through the word of education and the example of a life dedicated to Him.

The tefillin are a visible sign of covenental love that binds God and Israel. They are worn during the morning service on weekdays. On Sabbath and holy days, the tefillin are not worn. These days, in themselves, are reminders of God's nearness; to add more symbols might obscure their true meaning as guides to ideas.

As a duty of performance linked to a certain time, the day, women were not obligated to its performance and restrained from it. In non-Orthodox Judaism women wear the tefillin.

The Mezuzah

"Write them on the doorposts—*mezuzot*—of your house and upon your gates" (see p. 237). A small scroll, the *mezuzah* (singular of mezuzot), containing several of the same selections as the tefillin, including the Sh'ma (Deuteronomy 6:4–9; 11:13–20), is placed on doorposts of Jewish homes and its rooms. Thus the Sh'ma is the last greeting and admonition to those who leave the house; may their lives be guided by its ideals. The Sh'ma is also the first welcome home; may

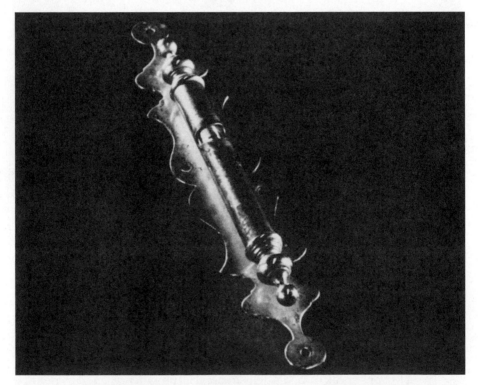

Mezuzah (India, nineteenth century). The scroll itself is enclosed in the silver container, which can be attached to the doorpost. (Photo by Kathie Minami, reproduced courtesy of Judah L. Magnes Memorial Museum, Jewish Museum of the West, Berkeley, California.)

home, and all thoughts and actions within it, stand under the instruction of God's Torah. On the back of the scroll, visible when it is rolled up, is written the word *Shaddai*: God who is everywhere with the people in all their habitations. The word *Shaddai* can also read as an acrostic of the sentence "*Sh*omer *d*elatot *Y*israel, [God is] Guardian of the doors of Israel." The mezuzah has come to be popularly regarded as a protective device for the home.

The scroll of Torah and the scrolls in tefillin and mezuzah must be handwritten on parchment. Pious men dedicate their lives to this holy art. They also make the containers and straps of the tefillin, following special regulations. No special rules apply to the container in which the mezuzah is kept, and many artistic designs have been fashioned for it.

THE HOUSE OF THE LORD

In Chapter 2 we saw that Jews in ancient times were the first to transform the small dwelling place of the deity into a meeting place where people assembled in the presence of God. The religious meeting house is a Jewish invention. Originally, it was called *proseuche*. The term *synagogue* stood for a gathering of the people rather than for a building. Eventually the term was applied to the building. It thereby subtly reminded the congregation that it is the people who give it meaning and purpose. The term *temple* came to be used in modern times under the influence of Reform. It indicated that, for the emancipated Jews, the individual synagogue had now once and for all assumed the place of the ancient Temple. Over the years, however, the term lost this denotation, and we find *temple* and *synagogue* used interchangeably without any real difference between the terms.

In antiquity, during and after the period of the Second Temple, we find synagogues in the Land of Israel and the Diaspora. They held the people together. The synagogue was the House of Prayer (*Bet Tefilah*). It was also the House of Study (*Bet Midrash*). The ancient synagogue of Capernaum in Israel shows a large educational annex attached to the central sanctuary. Finally, it was the House of the people (*Bet Am*), their assembly hall. This threefold function has been retained and has actually been strengthened in modern times. All synagogues have religious school facilities, and most of them are equipped for social gatherings in a religious atmosphere.

Structurally, the synagogue translated some of the features of the ancient Temple into its different character and purpose, while diverging from others. At the same time, individual traditions and general taste have made for variety of design in various countries. The ancient Temple had three sections: the court where the people assembled, the sanctuary where the menorah and other holy vessels were found, and the holy of holies, separated from the sanctuary by a curtain. During the period of the first Temple the holy of holies contained the Ark with the Tables of the Ten Commandments. This area was only entered once a year by the high priest. The synagogue, too, has three sections: the people's pews; the pulpit; and the Ark (*Aron hakodesh*, the Holy Shrine), which is often adorned with an artistically embroidered curtain. In it the Torah Scrolls are kept.

The differences are equally significant. In ancient and many contemporary Orthodox synagogues, the elevated reading pulpit for the Torah, *Bimah* (also called *Almemar* from the Arabic) is found in the center. The sacred scroll is carried there in solemn procession before the reading and returned to the Ark afterwards.

When Ezra convened the people after their return from the Babylonian Exile, they gathered around a "wooden tower" from which he read the Torah to them. They surrounded Torah, as they did when it was first bestowed upon them at Mount Sinai. So they do today. Modern synagogues have placed the bimah in front of the Ark, partly to save space. With the Emancipation in the spirit of adaptation to the Protestant church, additional changes were introduced: decorum,

Ark closed, Temple Emanu-El, San Francisco. This freestanding Ark is unique in synagogue architecture. It is inspired by the Ark of the Covenant of the ancient Temple, although it does not follow that design. On its sides, it has the symbols of the twelve tribes of Israel. The Hebrew inscription means "Know before Whom you stand," an admonition to the worshipers to remind them that they stand before God. This inscription is found in most synagogues. (Photo by the author, reproduced courtesy of Congregation Emanu-El and Rabbi Joseph Asher.)

the rabbinical robe, the reintroduction of the sermon, now in modern form, and so on. Traditionally, the reader of the service faced the Ark and stood on the same level as the people. He was not a priest but one of them, their "messenger." Standing in their midst, he offered their prayers. In Conservative and Reform congregations, he generally faces the people to be better heard. Some modern synagogues have two reading desks in front. One is used for reading of the Torah, while the other is used by the reader leading the congregation.

The Ark, reached by steps and the elevated Bimah are the centers of worship. They are frequently combined into one in modern synagogues. As it once was in the Temple, an eternal light burns in the sanctuary to signify the presence of God and the eternal illumination going forth from His word. A menorah,

Torah Curtain (India, nineteenth century). The embroidery features the letters "K–T" in Hebrew, an abbreviation of **Keter Torah**, *"Torah is a crown." (Photo by Kathie Minami, reproduced courtesy of Judah L. Magnes Memorial Museum, Jewish Museum of the West, Berkeley, California.)*

slightly altered to show the difference between Temple and synagogue, may also be in use. But there is another, invisible, worship center. Synagogues should be so oriented that the worshiper faces Jerusalem in prayer. God–People–Torah–Mitzvah–Land thus are fused into an indivisible unit, their oneness symbolically expressed.

Synagogues are generally set in a courtyard, allowing people to meet before and after worship. Here weddings were solemnized during the Middle Ages. It leads to the entrance hall, designed for the people to put themselves in a reverent mood. In traditional synagogues, a wash basin and water pitcher may be found there for worshipers to cleanse their hands symbolically before entering the sanc-

A breastplate of German manufacture, showing two "lions of Judah" holding the Tablets. (Photo by Kathie Minami, reproduced courtesy of Judah L. Magnes Memorial Museum, Jewish Museum of the West, Berkeley, California.)

tuary. (This is not holy water, although the holy water font in the entrance area of Catholic churches may be derived from it. Perhaps it may also be an adaptation of the laver in the court of the Temple where the priests purified themselves. In Jewish worship the water is poured over the hands, and once used may not be used again.)

From this hall, steps would sometimes lead down into the synagogue proper (we do not usually find these today). It signified how "Out of the depths I call upon You, O Lord" (Psalm 130:1). These steps were also needed to give synagogues greater internal height. The governments forbade the building of synagogues that rose above the surrounding houses. They were therefore built below street level to heighten their interior, and steps led down to them. The synagogue has to have windows. It is not to be removed from the world, but must be a place from which instruction goes forth into the world.

In line with a practice emerging during the time of the Mishnah, it became customary to separate male and female worshipers by placing the women in a gallery which was also curtained off. The purpose was to eliminate worldly temptations during worship. Conservative and Reform synagogues have seen a greater value in keeping families together in worship and have instituted mixed seating. Orthodox synagogues have retained the women's gallery and have come to place increased emphasis on the *mehitzah* the veil or grate of separation as requisite of an halakhically acceptable synagogue.

While the rabbis ordained quiet and grave decorum in the synagogue, their advice was frequently not followed. This was the people's place, their second home. Here they celebrated the joyful events of life and reflected on their afflictions, here they gathered for many purposes, and, above all, here the voices of children and adults could be heard in study, recital, and discussion. To this day, a synagogue is called a *Shul*, a school. Consequently, conduct was rather informal, and some of it has remained so.

By Jewish law, the synagogue must rise above the roofs of the houses in the town. During the Middle Ages, as we saw, this was specifically prohibited by the Christian authorities. As a symbol, therefore, Jews sometimes attached a high pole to the roof of their house of worship, surmounting it by the Star of David, a practice which may have brought the star into widespread use. There are no specific rules regarding synagogue architecture. Old synagogues frequently followed the general style of the time. Often we find Moorish architecture used to distinguish synagogues from Christian houses of worship. In modern times, this freedom from restrictions has inspired architects to fashion buildings in a modern style, some of them of great beauty and daring design.

CHAPTER 18

The Mitzvah of Physical Consecration: Dietary Laws

AS DAILY WORSHIP AND STUDY OF TORAH bring mind and soul into attunement with God, the dietary laws consecrate the body. Judaism has never made the distinction between body (as weak and human) and soul (as strong and divine). Both must serve God because both are holy.

The dietary laws may well have emerged from numerous taboos of antiquity or from health considerations; their hygienic character is in many instances self-evident. Pious Jews have looked at them in a different light. Truly devout Jews see them simply as God's law: He has commanded their observance to "sanctify us by His commandments," and He knows their purpose. Yet these laws may also be considered a means of preserving Israel's uniqueness, linking the members of the Household of Israel to closer unity. Jews could and would associate only with those who shared the practices of life and table and were barred from primary contact with those who did not. These laws may also be viewed as symbolic of belonging to a group, binding the members in fellowship (as a handshake binds members of a fraternal order), reminding them of their tradition, history, and aspirations.

Depending on the emphasis placed by individual Jews on these various points of interpretation, patterns of observance have varied among modern Jews. Orthodox Jews make the greatest sacrifices, denying themselves many contacts with friends in order to strictly observe the God-ordained rules. Others wish to honor their basic principles, as unifying bonds to God and fellow Jews, without being concerned about minute details. Many Jews observe them in their homes, in order that any Jew may join their table, yet feel free to disregard them when eating out. Their homes must be hallowed; in the home, Israel's eternity under God must be expressed, symbolized, and transmitted. Some Jews observe a few of the laws as a matter of discipline and a symbol of belonging; for instance, they may refrain from eating pork. Finally, there are those who see no purpose or spiritual meaning in the dietary laws and do not feel bound by them in any way. They cannot accept the doctrine that Torah was literally dictated by God and see no spiritually sustaining symbolic power in the dietary regulations. Of course, there are many who are simply lax in any observance, but to millions of Jews, the dietary laws are precious; they will deny themselves food rather than break them, even under difficult conditions, and will cheerfully accept the many sacrifices they entail, including comparative isolation in society.

PROHIBITED FOODS

There is no prohibition against vegetables. However, regarding animal food, Torah sets definite rules (Leviticus 11; Deuteronomy 14).

1. It permits whatever animal that "has true hoofs, with clefts through the hoofs, and that chews the cud" (Leviticus 11:3), and lists among the permitted ones ox, sheep, hart, and gazelle (Deuteronomy 14:4–5). If either of these two characteristics is missing, however, the animal may not be eaten. This forbids the pig, which has clefts through the hoofs but does not chew cud, and the rabbit, which appears to chew cud but has paws rather than hoofs.

2. It prohibits a number of birds. Since the exact meaning of the ancient Hebrew terms for the birds is not known, only those birds which have traditionally been eaten may be consumed. Thus, chickens, ducks, geese, pigeons, and turkeys are "clean."

3. Fish must have fins and scales (Leviticus 11:9; Deuteronomy 14:9), thus excluding all shellfish as well as eel.

4. "Swarming things" are prohibited, from mice to crocodiles to most insects. Certain locusts and grasshoppers were once scripturally permitted, but today no insects are permitted, as the identity of those mentioned in Scripture is no longer clear (Leviticus 11:20–23, 29–30).

Thus all animals that live by destruction of others are excluded, as are birds of prey a reminder, perhaps, to strive for peace.

RESTRICTIONS ON PERMITTED FOODS

Even permitted animals may be consumed only under certain conditions. The following are prohibited: animals that have died on their own (Leviticus 11:39; Deuteronomy 14:21), animals that have been torn by others (Exodus 22:30), all blood (Leviticus 7:26), certain animal fats (Leviticus 3:17), and certain sinews (Genesis 32:33). None of these restrictions, or any of those following, apply to fish.

Preparation of Meat

Any animal slaughtered by a method not approved by Jewish law or found diseased is not suitable for consumption.

1. Animals must therefore be slaughtered by a man trained in Jewish law, a *shohet*. Using a very sharp knife which may not have any nicks in it, he must cut the animal's throat, severing arteries, veins, and windpipe in one continuous stroke without exerting downward pressure. This is the act of *Shehitah*. In this manner, the brain is so rapidly drained of blood that no pain sensation occurs. (It takes some time to feel pain, as we know when we cut ourselves with a very sharp knife. Physiological research has shown that the Jewish method of slaughter is the most humane. Rapid drainage of blood also makes the meat better fit for preservation.) After the slaughter, the shohet must examine the animal for disease, and if he finds damage in the lungs, an ulcerated stomach, or discoloration of the brain, the animal may not be eaten.

2. The Jewish butcher, who must be an observant and knowledgeable Jew, then removes the sinews. Since those of the hindquarters are difficult to remove, this part is frequently not used unless the butcher has special, certified skill in preparing it.

3. Elimination of the blood is the task of the homemaker. The meat must be fresh; if it has been stored for three days, the blood has congealed to the point where it cannot be removed and the meat cannot be used (unless it has been soaked once in water during this period to keep it soft). The homemaker soaks the meat in water for about one-half hour, then covers it with salt on all sides, leaves it in the salt for about one hour to draw out the blood, and then washes off the salt. Another method is to broil the meat over an open fire, permitting the blood to flow out freely; this method must be used for liver. After this procedure, the meat is *kasher* (kosher), which means it is "all right."

4. Kitchen utensils that have been used in connection with forbidden foods cannot be used in a kosher household. Neither can foods that have admixtures of non-kosher ingredients. Soap containing animal fats cannot be used for washing dishes; detergents, being inorganic chemicals, may be used. The Union of Orthodox Congregations has a service of certification. On many products regularly obtainable in food stores, a circled "U" certifies that they can be used in kosher households. Other Orthodox certification services use a variety of certification marks.

Meat and Milk

At three different places in Scripture we find the injunction: "You shall not seethe the kid in the milk of its mother" (Exodus 23:19; 34:25; Deuteronomy 14:2). This was interpreted as containing three prohibitions: eating meat and milk products together, cooking them together, and using any mixture of them. These products may not be served together; for example, butter and milk may not be found at a meal that offers meat. After eating meat, a person has to wait several hours before eating milk products. Furthermore, separate utensils must be used for meat and for milk. This requires a kosher family to have two complete sets of dishes, silverware, and cooking utensils. (A third set for neutral food, such as fruit, may also be found in the home.) If these become mixed up, they may occasionally be cleansed by either boiling or burning out the food by bringing the utensils to red heat. Otherwise, the utensils become useless. The decision in this matter rests with the rabbi, whom the family will consult. In addition, the kosher family needs two other complete sets of dishes for Passover, when those having come in touch with leavened food during the year may not be used.

The laws of *kashrut* (kosher laws) call for thoroughly trained rabbis to supervise and decide problems, learned *shohetim*, conscientious butchers, and vigilance and devotion from homemakers. (Actually practices become second nature over the years). The laws of *kashrut* set God always before the Jews. They provide discipline. Obedient Jews will deny themselves certain pleasures of food and even its life-sustaining gifts. This is Mitzvah, a daily and constant response to God with body as with soul. It promotes inner strength.

CHAPTER 19

Sabbath, Day of Re-creation

DAILY OBSERVANCE IS THE HEARTBEAT which supplies Jews their lifeblood of the divine. The Sabbath re-creates them, giving them strength for meaningful daily living. It is linked to God's creative act itself (Genesis 2:1–4). God rested from His work and hallowed the Sabbath. It is the only holy day ordained in the Ten Commandments, both in Exodus (20:8–11) and in Deuteronomy (5:12–15). But God needs no rest; the meaning of the term lies below the surface meaning. God ceased from making the world all by Himself; henceforth people must be His coworkers. As Creator, God is the world's owner and may ordain rest for those who toil in His domain. In obeying this command, Jews acknowledge God's ownership of the world and constitute themselves not its masters but its stewards.

The Sabbath places its imprint on the entire week. "Six days shall you labor" reads the commandment. Every person is to become aware that he or she is called to carry on God's work during the six days of labor. This task has two distinct features: First, nature and all its produce must be utilized for beneficent purposes. We may not harm nature, or squander its riches, or selfishly claim them all for ourselves. Hence the commandment emphasizes that God is nature's Creator. Second, society and every one of its members are God's; all human beings have dignity as God's children. Servants, too, must be allowed to rest. This is further emphasized in the version of the Commandments found in Deuteronomy, "Guard the Sabbath. . . . that your servants may rest as well as you." Even the domestic cattle must be given rest. It is a universal law, applying to home-born and stranger alike. The meaning of the Sabbath synthesizes the religious and social elements, spiritualizes daily work and promotes humanity's basic rights. Judaism considers one without the other to be meaningless.

To Jews, the Sabbath has become not merely a day of rest but of spiritual re-creation for the tasks of the week's labor. As such, it has given the Jews strength, hope, and confidence. Truly, human beings, so charged with divine duty, are dear to God. The Sabbath became a Covenant between God and Israel (Exodus 13:12–17); its desecration spells denial of God and His creatorship (Numbers

15:32–36). It guarantees Israel's eternity, for the servant's life has meaning as long as the Master's work needs to be done, and this work is eternal. It has given Jews the strength to endure and preserve their mental balance. In the terms of the German Jewish poet Heinrich Heine, a dog during the week, the Jew is restored to his true character as a prince of God one day a week. If he must, he can return to the degradation the world may impose upon him for he knows his true identity. According to the rabbis, the Sabbath thus provides Jews with "a taste of the world to come." The Sabbath gives them "an additional soul." Sagely they remark, "As Israel has kept the Sabbath, the Sabbath has kept Israel alive."

PROHIBITION OF WORK

The meaning of *rest* had to be defined, lest a person rationalize that his work, or that imposed upon his servants, could not really be called work. A simple yardstick was used in this definition. As God's servant, Israel once built a sanctuary in the desert, the Tent of Meeting. It was a small symbol of His presence, because all of God's world is His sanctuary. All types of work once connected with the building of the Tent of Meeting in the desert were therefore prohibited on the Sabbath. In this manner, the people were taught that the sanctuary they built was to be the model for the great sanctuary; namely, world and humanity as a whole. In its construction, a weekly day of rest is the basic right of every human being. From it springs all other social legislation.

This led to the prohibition of thirty-nine basic kinds of work, arranged in several general categories: (1) growing and preparation of food (eleven prohibitions); (2) clothing in all its processes (thirteen prohibitions); (3) leather work and writing (nine prohibitions); (4) building shelter (two prohibitions); (5) the use of fire (two prohibitions); (6) completion of work, the final hammer stroke (one prohibition); and (7) transportation (one prohibition). Around these primary prohibitions, the rabbis added secondary ones to prevent violation of the basic ones. Thus the Sabbath became a day of complete spirituality. The toil of daily living fell away, and thoughts and preoccupation with daily events were completely banished. A truly divine peace settled upon those who fully observed it.

OBSERVANCE OF THE SABBATH

The Jewish Day of Rest always starts with the preceding evening. Torah states: "It was evening and it was morning" (Genesis 1), putting the night before the day. This is a natural arrangement for the farmer and artisan, whose days end when the sun sets; their thoughts then turn to the morrow. All Jewish holy days begin with the preceding evening.

Friday evening thus becomes a night of solemn observance. The food is prepared during the day, the body beautified, a festive table is laid out. The mother, guardian of the home, kindles the Sabbath lights, blessing God and invoking His blessing upon her household. There must be at least two candles on the table—a double portion, compared to the single dim light that was once the only illumination during the week. Traditionally, the father attended worship accompanied by only the male members of the family. The mother stayed at home with the female members and the infants. This gave her an hour of relaxation and meditation after strenuous Sabbath preparations, and refreshed her for the Sabbath meal that was to follow. Today, women frequently accompany their husbands to worship and the family prays together. It is also hoped that the men in the family assist the women in the Sabbath preparations.

After the opening Psalms, the welcome hymn to the Sabbath Bride is sung and, following the habit of the mystics, the congregation turns to the door, welcoming the "Bride" (see p. 105). Sabbath Psalms (Psalms 92, 93) follow. The evening prayer is offered, followed by the Kiddush.

According to tradition the father is accompanied by two angels on his return home. The family welcomes the Sabbath angels in song. Both parents bless their children with the biblical blessing (Numbers 6:25–26) and bestow upon them their Sabbath kiss. The father praises his wife as a "woman of valor" (Proverbs 31:10–31). He knows that their joyful family Sabbath is her work.

On the table stands the cup of wine and beside it two loaves of *hallah* bread covered by an embroidered cloth. The loaves under the cover are a reminder of the double portion of manna allotted Israel every Friday when they wandered in the desert; they were to rest on the Sabbath, and not look for their bread on the holy day. The cloth replicates the layer of dew that covered the manna (Exodus 16:14–27).

The head of the family raises the cup, blessing God for the Sabbath. This is the *Kiddush*, the sanctification of the Sabbath. Every family member shares in the wine. The hallah is cut, God is praised for bread, and each member partakes of it. The festive meal follows. The celebration is concluded by songs and grace.

The following morning, the family attends worship, which includes the reading of Torah, a special section for each week. Seven people are "called " to follow the reader, who recites from the sacred scroll. Each offers a blessing of thanksgiving for the gift of Torah. An eighth person reads the *Haftarah*, the prophetic selection of the day. The service may also include a sermon, an interpretation of Torah.

The family then returns home for Kiddush and a joyful meal. The rest of the day belongs to the people, as the morning belonged to God. Torah study may be included. An afternoon nap after the midday meal has become an accepted folk habit. A leisurely stroll in nature can also be part of the observance.

The afternoon prayer calls the worshipers back to the synagogue. Torah is read again—the first section of next week's portion. In this manner, a bridge is built across the hardships of the week; a new Sabbath beckons before the present one has departed.

The Third Meal, between the afternoon and evening prayers, was for the mystics a time of immersion into the eternal. It has been adapted in Israel and among some Jewish groups elsewhere as an hour of song, praise, and fellowship.

Evening worship commences at nightfall, when three stars have appeared in the sky (generally, the Jewish calendar gives the exact time). *Havdalah* follows the evening prayer. It formalizes the "separation" from the holy day. It is celebrated in the synagogue and, again in each family. A cup and special plate on which it stands, a spice box, and a twisted candle are needed.

Havdalah

The cup is filled to overflowing and a portion of the wine is caught in a plate beneath it symbolically expressing the hope that happiness may overflow during the week. The twisted candle is lit; it is held high by the youngest in the family. The head of the house begins the Havdalah with quotations from the Tanakh that express trust and confidence in God. He (or she) speaks the blessing over the wine. He then takes the box filled with spices—often in the form of a

Havdalah Set, including Kiddush cup, spice box (seventeenth century, Germany) in the form of a tower, and twisted candle, on a plate for the overflow of the wine. (Photo by Kathie Minami, reproduced courtesy of Judah L. Magnes Memorial Museum, Jewish Museum of the West, Berkeley, California.)

tower. It symbolizes that God is the tower of salvation. He sniffs the sweet-smelling contents, and passes the box around so that each member of the family may take a last whiff of the Sabbath aroma into the week. Then he speaks the blessing over the flame of the candle. This is the beginning of the first day of the week, when God created the light (Genesis 1). God is praised for the light. After giving thanks, he makes use of this light by watching the play of light and shadow on his hands. The actual Havdalah Berakhah follows. It ends with the words: "Blessed are you, God. . . . Who makes separation between holy and secular." On conclusion of the Havdalah, the candle is extinguished in the overflow of the wine. The wine is shared.

The greeting of the Sabbath is *Shabbat Shalom*, or, in Yiddish, *Gut Schabbes*. After Havdalah, the wish expressed in greeting is *Shavua tov*, or, in Yiddish, *A gute Woch*, both meaning "good week." A short repast is offered, to "accompany the Queen (Sabbath)" on her retreat. Pleas for divine protection during the week are rendered to God. May Elijah, guardian of Israel, accompany the members of the family on their chores and soon herald the arrival of the Messiah.

In medieval times, Jewish families had a special "Sabbath lamp," only lit on the Sabbath, which could be lowered and raised. This led to a common saying: "As the lamp is lowered [on Friday], sorrow rises and vanishes; as the lamp is raised [after Havdalah], sorrow descends again."

The best expression of the essence of the Sabbath is perhaps found in the following paragraph from the Mussaf prayer: "They who observe the Sabbath and call it a delight rejoice in Your kingdom. The people that hallow the seventh day are all sated and given delight out of Your goodness. For upon the seventh day You poured out Your grace and hallowed it; You called it the most precious of days, in remembrance of the works of creation."

Variations

Having described the traditional observance at its most complete, we should note that there are several variations in Sabbath celebration and observance. For instance, many American congregations have instituted a late Friday night service for those who cannot observe the Sabbath in the home, followed by *Oneg Shabbat*, a fellowship hour. Reform Jews do not consider themselves bound by work prohibitions.

Of Bread and Wine

Bread and wine are widely used in Jewish observances. Bread and wine, together with meat, were part of the Temple sacrifice. They are now used—together with the meat of the Sabbath meal—to commemorate the sanctification of the day in the Temple. Bread and wine are "living," they grow and change through leavening and fermentation. Perhaps this was the reason why they were used in the Temple. They are also the result of the partnership of God and human beings. God gives the grain, human ingenuity transforms it into all kinds of bread and pastry. God makes the grape ripen, people transform it into wine.

Wine depends on divine blessing of the grape and the wine maker's art. It symbolizes life with God. Therefore it is used at many special occasions in Jewish life, including weddings. At these, *kos*, the cup (of wine) is raised. *Kos* is derived from *kosas*, to measure out. It stands for the gifts God has measured out, be they plentiful or scanty, pleasant or sorrowful. As Jews raise the cup, they give thanks for all of them.

PERSONAL REFLECTIONS

I have described the Sabbath as I experienced it in my childhood, and recognize with sadness that its observance has been widely neglected. While it was "father-centered," it gave every member of the family the sense of being indispensable and loved. Gathered around the festive table on Friday night the family became a sacred union filled with joy. The Sabbath reinforced the foundations of family life. It was the root of strength and of moral principles. It revived our resilience, enabling us to meet the worries of daily and business life. During the Nazi period it provided the strength to endure amidst fear and degradation, for it cast throughout the entire week of trials, a ray of anticipation into the darkness of our lives. It gave us and ever restored to us the psychological equilibrium we vitally needed.

Being deprived of the Sabbath was for me one of the agonies of the concentration camp. This denial of the day of rest was inflicted by deliberate design of the Nazis. It made the days of the week into an endless sequence of hopeless suffering and cruelty without any ray of light. It was a scheme to deprive the enslaved of their humanity that rests on hope. At that time, I came fully to recognize the revolutionary change the Jewish Sabbath brought to humanity. In the cultures of antiquity the slave had to work without hope for rest and re-creation. Judaism was the sole exception. Through the Sabbath it gave everyone rest, and, during the week, the hope of forthcoming rest and, with it, humanity.

CHAPTER 20

The Jewish Calendar and Holy Days

OVER THE COURSE OF THE YEAR, the seasons of nature and the events of Israel's historical march from slavery to freedom under God are remembered and given meaning in the observance of holy days. To understand how these days of remembrance are fixed, we must briefly look at the Jewish calendar.

THE JEWISH CALENDAR

Counting the Years

The Jewish years are numbered from the date of creation, which the ancients arrived at by adding up the years of the generations in Scripture (see Genesis 5). While we know that the report of Torah does not coincide with scientific knowledge of the world's origin, there has been no change in the numbering; it recalls God's creatorship. Thus, the year 2000 of the general calendar is equivalent to the year 5760 in the Jewish one, except that the Jewish year starts in the fall.

Adjusting the Lunar and Solar Years

The months of the Jewish year correspond to the cycle of the moon, beginning and ending with the new moon. The Jewish year is lunar oriented. In order for the festivals to fall at their appointed seasons of the year, the lunar cycle had to be adjusted to the annual cycle of the solar year.

The Jewish calendar was permanently fixed by Hillel II (about the middle of the fourth century C.E.) and has worked well through the centuries. It is based on a combination of solar and lunar years, in order that all festivals should occur during the same season of the year. The lunar year has only 354 days, 10 days fewer than the solar year. Consequently, unless adjusted, lunar-oriented dates would recede and festivals would run through all the seasons. To adjust the two calendars, 7 leap years of 30 additional days each (one whole month) were included in every cycle of 19 years. (Nineteen moon years of 354 days equals 6,726 days; add to it 7 times 30 days, or 210 days, and we arrive at 6,936 days, or the approximate equivalent of 19 sun years. Other minor adjustments take care of the variations in the sun year, including its leap years.) Thus, Jewish holy days may move back and forth within the span of 30 days of the sun year, but they always fall in the same season.

The Second Day of the Festivals in the Diaspora—Variations

Previously, while Israel dwelt in its own land and under its own inner autonomy, the Sanhedrin solemnly proclaimed the beginning of each month. Witnesses would testify that the first sliver of the moon had appeared in the sky. Messengers were then sent out to all communities to give them the exact date. This was important for the observance of holy days on their correct dates. But these messengers could traverse only the land of Israel before the festivals; the Jews in the Diaspora had no certification. These Jews, therefore, observed two days for each holy day, to be certain that one of them was correct. To this day, Jews in Israel observe only one day of festivals, whereas Orthodox Jews observe two, even though we have a firm calendar and know the exact dates. Reform Judaism observes only one day of every festival. Since 1969, Conservative Judaism has made the observance of the second day optional, and so coordinates its holy day observances with those of Israel.

Rosh Hashanah falls on the New Moon. Because messengers could not reach even the communities within the land, it has always been observed for two days, even in Israel. The second day of Rosh Hashanah remained compulsory for Israel and the Diaspora. A number of Reform congregations also observe it. To help us in our discussion of the festivals, a table has been provided at the end of this chapter.

The Days of Awe

In the fall of the year, when the harvest is gathered, the farmers ponder: If the harvest is poor, where have they failed to sow and irrigate? If the harvest is good, how can they apply the same procedures again, and in other parts? They judge themselves, make their accounting. Translating this approach into spiritual terms, Judaism has appointed special days in the fall, *Yamim Noraim*, Days of Awe, as days of divine judgment and human reflection. As the accounting at harvest time is a universal task, so is spiritual judgment.

The Days of Awe open with the festival of *Rosh Hashanah*, the Beginning of the Year, which is followed by a week of repentance. Jews are bidden to put the resolutions they have made into action. The period culminates in *Yom Kippur*, the Day of Atonement. On this holiest of holy days Jews spend a full night and day completely separated from the world so that they may commune exclusively with God. They confess their shortcomings and ask for forgiveness. Where they have transgressed against their fellows they must make up with them before

God will grant His pardon. Then they can return to daily living with new confidence and purpose. This period of ten days has been called *Aseret Yemei Teshuvah*, the Ten Days of Return.

ROSH HASHANAH

Rosh Hashanah is the Jewish New Year's Day. "On the first of Tishri the calendar year begins" (Mishnah Rosh Hashanah 1:1). The opening period of the year is a time of great solemnity, sober judgment, and awesome awareness of God's power. It is a period of repentance, returning to God, and renewal. Pious tradition linked this moment of renewal with the supposed date of the world's creation; it must be a creative moment in the building of a better world.

The Preparation

For an entire month preceding the festival the shofar, ram's horn, is sounded in daily worship. It is the oldest musical instrument in use at any worship service in the Western world. It awakens the faithful from the slumber of unexamined living. On the days preceding Rosh Hashanah, special services of intercession called *Selihot,* prayers for forgiveness, are held at early morning. On Rosh Hashanah itself, however, no confessions are heard because it is the day of God's affirmation. Pleas and confessions follow on the subsequent days. On Rosh Hashanah God is proclaimed Sovereign, Judge, and Redeemer of all humanity, and the shofar is sounded in His honor.

The Eve

Evening services are simple. Upon returning to the festive meal in the evening, Jews find several symbols on the table in addition to the usual burning candles, wine, and bread. The hallah may be round, in the form of a wheel, for a wheel goes through the world. By God's will those who are on top may be down before long, and those who are low may be raised soon: May all put trust in Him rather than in their own strength. A sweet apple is dipped into honey and consumed by the members of the family: May the year be sweet.

The Morning

Early in the morning the people return to worship. Curtains, Torah covers, and pulpit coverings are all white to symbolize purity. In Orthodox synagogues the men wear the white garments in which they will some day be buried, as a reminder of human frailty and equality; before God, all are alike, weak mortals, and yet their very weakness evokes divine mercy and must lead them to be tolerant with one another.

The morning prayer, *Shaharit,* concludes with a litany, *Avinu Malkenu,* "Our Father our King." It is a plea to God for a year of blessings, health, sustenance, and forgiveness and peace. This litany is offered in all morning and afternoon services during the entire Ten Days of Repentance, except on Sabbath. It ends with the words that are basic for the Jewish understanding of the relationship with God: "Our Father, our King, be gracious to us and answer us, for we have no deeds to justify us; grant us your kindness and mercy and save us."

Torah reading follows. It tells of Abraham, prepared to give his son in obedience to God's will. God set aside the sacrifice. It is a call to humanity to do its utmost in obedience to God. It is equally a reminder that this obedience demands the preservation and support of all human life, and that humanity is forbidden by God to destroy any human life.

The Sounding of the Shofar

The shofar's voice is heard. Its sound is strange, primitive, like the outcry of the human heart. In its piercing sound is enshrined the full message of the day. Maimonides explains it:

> Wake up, sleepers, from your sleep; and you that are in a daze, arouse yourselves from your stupor. Reflect on your actions and return in repentance. Remember your Creator. Be not as those who forget truth in their chase after shadows, wasting their year wholly in vanities which neither help nor bring deliverance. Look into your souls, and mend your ways and deeds. Let everyone forsake his evil ways and worthless thoughts. (Teshuvah 3, 4)

Four signals are sounded in succession: *Tekiah*, a long-drawn sound; *Shevarim*, a three-times broken sound; *Teruah*, a whimpering, nine-times broken sound; and

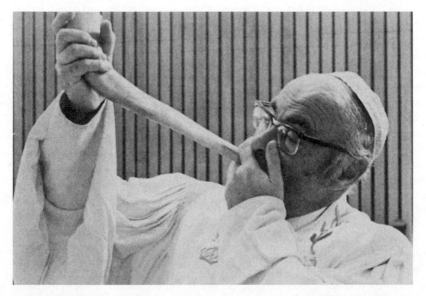

Author sounding the Shofar. Note the white robe. (Courtesy of Robert McKenzie, Napa, California.)

Tekiah again. As the rabbis point out, Tekiah is the wakening call; Shevarim the sobbing of the contrite heart; Teruah the weeping of a heart aware of its guilt; and Teklah the straight, awakening sound again.

Samson Raphael Hirsch has elaborated on the meaning by comparing the sounds to the signals alerting the people during their wanderings in the desert. Tekiah called them to attention in their daily routine, and thus it calls again. Shevarim and Teruah were signals commanding the people to break up camp; they become a call to break with the past and its errors. Tekiah once again called the people to start marching in a new direction; it enjoins change of direction in life toward holier goals (see "Choreb," *Versuche über Jisroels Pflichten*, Altona, 1837, pp. 182ff.).

Mussaf

The Mussaf prayer brings the affirmation to its climax. Before the congregation chants the *Kedushah*, "Holy, holy, Holy," it leads up to it with a majestic hymn, *Untenate tokef*, which compares God's power, judgment, and compassion to human frailty. The hymn was cast in its present poetic form by Kalonymus ben Meshullam of Mainz of the eleventh century (although he ascribed it to one of the earlier medieval martyrs of faith[1]).

> Let us speak of the great holiness of this day, for it is indeed a day of awe and dread. On it Your kingdom is exalted, Your throne established in mercy, and You are enthroned upon it in truth. In truth, You are judge and prosecutor, knower and witness, recorder and sealer. . . . You remember long forgotten deeds. You open the book of memories, and it tells its own story, for the seal of everyone's hand is set to his acts. The great Shofar is sounded, and a still, small voice is heard. The angels themselves are dismayed and gripped by fear and trembling. They affirm: "See, the Day of judgment that summons the whole heavenly host to judgment"; for in Your judgment not even they are flawless. . . . And all that live You let pass before You as a flock of sheep. . . . On Rosh Hashanah the sentence is inscribed, on Yom Kippur it is sealed: how many shall pass away, and how many shall be born; who shall live and who shall die. . . . But Repentance, and Prayer, and Works of Goodness annul every severe decree . . . for . . . You do not desire the death of the guilty, rather that he turn from his way and live. To the very day of his death You wait for him. If he returns You will right away receive him. In truth, You are their Creator, know their urges, that they are but flesh and blood. After all, man's origin is dust, and his end is dust . . . but You are King, the Living, Everlasting God. . . . as it is written by the hand of Your prophet: "and one called the other exclaiming, 'Holy, holy, holy the Lord of hosts, the whole earth is filled with His glory.'"

The *Mussaf* then moves to a threefold proclamation of God, using appropriate verses from Torah:

Malkhiot: God is King, Sovereign: "Sh'ma (Hear, O Israel)" is acknowledgment of His Kingship. Then the shofar is sounded in royal proclamation.

Zikhronot: God is the Judge who mercifully remembers all His creatures even while judging them This He has done from Noah's days to ours. The Covenant God made with Noah, Abraham, Isaac, and Jacob is brought to mind. The section concludes with the words: "Praised be You, O God, Who remembers the Covenant." The shofar is again sounded to God who Remembers.

Shofarot: God is Redeemer. By the sound of the shofar He once gave His Ten Commandments and by the sound of the shofar He will redeem humanity. The shofar is sounded once again, to God the Redeemer.

In the afternoon, following *Minhah*, a custom is observed, which may stem from Christian usage. Petrarch tells us of having observed it on New Year's Day among the population in Cologne. There the people went to the Rhine, cast flowers and straw into it that its waves might sweep all misfortunes to the sea. The Jews go to the river reciting verses from Micah: "And You will cast their sins into the depths of the sea" (7:19). May God do so unto the penitent, who symbolically express their desire to abandon sin to the waves.

The Week Following Rosh Hashanah

This is a week of implementation. Selihot are offered every day early in the morning. The day immediately following Rosh Hashanah is a day of fasting, when no food or drink may be consumed. It is called the Fast of Gedaliah. Gedaliah was the Jewish governor placed in charge of the community in Judaea by the Babylonians after the destruction of the first Temple. He was murdered by some Jews who were jealous of his position and held him responsible for their unhappy fate (Jeremiah 41:1–3 ff.). This deed brought fear of the wrath of the king upon the people, and motivated them to give up their homeland. The message is obvious: People must not blame others for their troubles or try to find scapegoats for their fate, for the consequence of such an attitude is disasterous.

YOM KIPPUR, DAY OF ATONEMENT

As Jews approach the holiest day of the year—Yom Kippur, the Day of Atonement—they must make up for the wrongs done to others. Without reconciliation between people there can be no forgiveness from God. The rabbis ordain that all people must seek out their enemies again and again and the offended parties must show generosity in forgiving and forgetting, fully and graciously. Then both are ready for Yom Kippur.

Preparation and Observance

A festive dinner in the afternoon is obligatory. Before departing for the synagogue, the mother lights the holy day candles and speaks the blessing. The parents bless their children with a special blessing. A twenty-four-hour candle will shed its gleam upon the returning family later that night. Yom Kippur, though a fast, is a festival, a day of spiritual rejoicing.

For twenty-four hours no food or drink may touch the lips of the Jew, no earthly concerns enter the mind as the Jew stands before God. In token of castigation, Orthodox Jews wear soft shoes instead of leather ones. Memorial lights are lit so that the memory of the departed may be an inspiration to their descendants. The men stand in their white garments of death.

Yom Kippur lacks the drama of the Shofar; it is all inward. All prayers during the twenty-four-hour period include the confession of sin. It is recited privately for God alone to hear. It is also repeated in unison to acknowledge mutual responsibility one for another. The confession thus renews the spirit of the responsible kinship of all people. *Avinu Malkenu* is repeated during the evening and the day.

The Eve: *Kol Nidre*

In the synagogue all the lamps burn bright, memorial candles flicker. The people are dressed in white and wear the tallit. They stand in awe as they face the white curtained Ark. *Kol Nidre,* which has given its name to the evening celebration, opens worship. It is known for its haunting melody. In itself, the prayer is simply a declaration of dispensation from ascetic vows to be made and then not kept. The tune, however, expresses the longing for God, the agony of those who pledged their lives to Him yet found it cut short in martyrdom. Immediately, the outcry finds God's answer, "I have forgiven."

Maariv, the regular evening service is offered, *Selihot* are followed by public confession of sins and the plea to "Our Father, Our King." It is a long service. Some will remain in the synagogue for most of the night, to recite the Book of Psalms in antiphon, followed by various meditations on God's greatness.

Morning. The morning service, *Shaharit,* starts early. Its theme is Selihot. The early hours of the day are seen as the time when God judges. They are therefore the most auspicious time for confession of sins and the plea for divine forgiveness. The Torah is read. Its prophetic portion, the Haftarah, includes the following passage from Isaiah, clarifying the message of the fast: "Is not this the fast that I have chosen, to loose the fetters of the wickedness, to undo the bands of the yoke, to let the oppressed go free, and to break every yoke? Is it not to share your bread with the hungry, and that you bring the poor that are cast out to your house; when you see the naked that you cover him, and that you hide not yourself from your own flesh?" (Isaiah 58:5–7). The message fits in well with the confession of sins. In the formal confession the transgressions against God are not mentioned; only those toward humanity are mentioned.

Noon. The theme of the Mussaf prayer is the recollection of Avodah the service in the ancient Temple. The people identify with their ancestors. *Avodah* once denoted the sacrificial service in the Temple. Now, however, it denotes *Avoda she b'lev,* Avodah of the heart; namely prayer. During the ancient service in the Temple the High Priest made confession for himself and his family, the priestly community and the people. As it is retold, the congregation repeats the confessions and applies them to themselves, their dear ones and religious leaders, and all of Israel and humanity. In this confession the High Priest pronounced the ineffable name of God and the people prostrated themselves before God. This name of God is never pronounced, but the congregation kneels and proclaims, "Praised be His Name, His glorious Kingdom is forever and ever." During the year, Jews do not kneel, for the action might be misunderstood: Are they kneeling before God, or is the burden of life pressing them down? Now, in solitude before Him, away from the world, they do. The congregation perceives itself as the symbol of a humanity unitedly bending the knee before Him.

Afternoon. The Torah is read again. As *Haftarah* the book of Jonah is recited. It makes it clear that God's love and forgiveness are not reserved for Jews but are given to all humanity. All are God's children, as Jonah learns. God says to him: "Should I not have pity on Nineveh [says God], that great city, in which there are more than a hundred and twenty thousand people who cannot discern between their right hand and their left hand, and much cattle, too?" (Jonah 4:11). The *Minhah* prayer follows. Its theme is Jewish martyrdom. Throughout the year Minhah is to give pause for reflection on the course of the day so far. On Yom Kippur, it brings to mind those whose lives had been lived truly to the fullest, the martyrs. Together with a memorial service for the departed, which is part of the Yom Kippur service, it extends the link from past to future. From the past the march toward a future can be charted. The individual Jew is a link in an eternal chain.[2]

Twilight. The closing prayer, called *Ne'eelah,* during the fading hours of the day is a special prayer for Yom Kippur. Its theme is the fervent plea to gain divine absolution and to enter the gates of God's love.

> Open unto us the gate, at the time that the gate is being closed,
> as day has almost waned.
> The day is waning, the sun is setting fast,
> let us enter Your gates!

In all pleas that God may *inscribe* the petitioners in the books of blessings the term is now *seal* us in these books. (See Unetane tokef: "On Rosh Hashanah it is inscribed, on Yom Kippur it is sealed.")

Nightfall. As the stars rise in the sky and the day is completed the congregation stands in silence. This is the moment of affirmation, the moment of the vision of God's kingdom. The Ark is opened. Slowly, word by word, the people recite once: "Hear, O Israel, the Lord our God, the Lord is One!" Then they recite three times: "Blessed be His Name, His glorious Kingdom is forever and ever!" Finally, they recite seven times: "The Lord, He is God!"[3]

The Ark is then closed. Now, for the first time on Yom Kippur, the shofar is sounded—Tekiah! Onward into life! Finally, Havdalah is recited. The road leads directly to Sukkot, the Festival of Thanksgiving for harvest and shelter that God has bestowed. Sukkot follows five days after Yom Kippur.

SUKKOT: COVENANT OF NATURE AND SOCIETY

The spiritual stocktaking of the Days of Awe has served as preparation for an accounting of the physical blessings in a spirit of gratitude rather than simply in economic terms; hence *Sukkot* immediately follows, a festival of joy before God who has blessed and "will bless all your crops and all your undertakings, and you will have nothing but joy" (Deuteronomy 16:15).

The Symbols of Sukkot

The Festive Bouquet is the first symbol of the festival. Scripture ordains that a bouquet of four plants be brought to the sanctuary—citron (*etrog*), a branch of the date palm (*lulav*), myrtles (*hadassim*), and willows of the brook (*aravot*) (see Leviticus 23:40). These four represent the variety of the produce of the earth: citron, an edible fruit of pleasant taste and smell; date (the branches of which are presented), an edible fruit tasty without smell; myrtles, tasteless but of sweet smell; and willows, which have neither taste nor fragrance but are of use. All of these varieties are essential for life; without any one of them, the bouquet is worthless.

The rabbis saw in them a symbol of humanity. There are those who have both intelligence and human kindness (taste and smell), others who have but intelligence nourishing society without fully relating to their neighbors (taste but no smell); some whose kindness sweetens the atmosphere about them though they be far from brilliant (smell but no taste), and those who are in no way distinguished (neither smell nor taste) yet are needed in the framework of our society. No human being is expendable.

These four plants are brought to the synagogue, and during the recitation of the Psalms of Thanksgiving (Psalms 113–118, the *Hallel*). With the recital "Praise the Lord for He is good, His goodness endures forever" they are weaved and slightly shaken in six directions (the four directions of the compass and above and below). This expresses symbolically that God is found in all the directions of the universe.

Human beings must gather the gifts of God to make good use of them on their way through life. This human function is expressed at the end of the Mussaf service. Now, preceded by the Scroll of the Torah, the congregation processes with the bouquets of the four plants in hand through the sanctuary, as they once surrounded the altar in the Temple. (Guided by Torah, they take in hand the gifts of the world in procession through days and years.) The congregation intones, "Hoshanah, Save us, O God, we beseech You." (It is Jews and humanity on the move, invoking God's help that their work be accomplished.)

The Sukkah is the second symbol of the festival. As God must be Mover, He equally provides shelter and rest. This is expressed in the Sukkah, a small hut or booth covered with a roof of branches and leaves, in which the family takes its meals during the holiday, if the weather is good. Originally a shelter in the harvest fields, the Sukkah was endowed by Torah with a deeper meaning: God

Lulab and Etrog. Whimsical handblown glass figurine by Gianni Toso of Venice. Note the additional plants (myrtles and willows) attached to the lulav (palm branch), held in the right hand, and the etrog (citron), held in the left. (Photo by the author.)

made the people dwell in booths, *sukkot*, when He took them out of Egypt (Leviticus 23:42–43). He gave them protection on their march toward the future. As long as twigs and branches form the roof, revealing the stars as witnesses to God's power, they provide hope for peace, something concrete shelters implicitly deny.

Rabbinic wisdom explains that Jews go into the Sukkah in the fall, when others return to their homes, to show that they do so not for the sake of comfort in summer's heat but in obedience to Mitzvah. How well this expresses the fate of the Jews, so often homeless and driven about when others dwelt secure, yet feeling protected by God.

Two elements are combined in the twofold lesson of Sukkot. In ancient days, humanity's greatest enemy was nature. It might withhold sustenance; failure of crops, storms, and natural disasters might lead to famine; epidemics might strike. In the festive bouquet, thanksgiving is expressed for harvest and, with it,

Traditionally every Jew brings the Arba Minim *to the synagogue for the festival prayer service. The Talmud notes that even "a child who knows how to shake the lulav is obligated to do so." Women are also obligated. Note the men wearing the tallit in various ways. (Photo by Phyllis Friedman.)*

for the preservation of life amid the natural hazards. In modern times, humanity has largely mastered nature, the Western world has abundant food, enough to feed the hungry in other countries. Through research and technology it has defeated many diseases. But a new danger has arisen as a result of its technological progress: human beings themselves.

Distances have shrunk and communications become instantaneous. Wars rooted in hatred are becoming more frightful and all-encompassing. Locked in conflicts and armed with the latest weapons of world destruction, nations can hurl missiles of mass destruction at one another. Humans are greatly to be feared. Inventions pose dangers for nature and humankind. The Sukkah makes it clear that humanity can and must live together in an open society, finding shelter in the spirit of love, which is imitation of God. Then it will dwell secure. The Jews are to maintain humanity's hope by their steadfast endurance throughout their historic wanderings. Sukkot serves as a contemporary reminder to preserve nature and humanity.

Yet the vision of the future may lead to skepticism: Can it ever come to pass? The people may well argue, "We have heard the message, but in a few days the

Family celebrating the Sukkot Festival in the Sukkah (pewter, seventeenth-century Germany).
Note the roof made of branches and decorations, including the Sabbath lamp, Inscription on
the rim: "You shall dwell in Sukkot for seven days" (Leviticus 23:42). (Photo by Kathie
Minami, reproduced courtesy of Judah L. Magnes Memorial Museum, Jewish Museum of the
West, Berkeley, California.)

festival will be over, and we will be back to the eternal, hopeless round of dreary toil and suffering." Fall and the onrush of winter, together with the events of the day, may speak more loudly than Torah and Mitzvot and holy days could. With psychological insight, the rabbis permitted the people to express these thoughts. On Sukkot the Book of Ecclesiastes is read: "Vanity of vanities, all is vanity," all is hopeless. As the feelings are given vent, an answer is also provided: "The sum of the matter, when all is said and done; Revere God, and observe his Mitzvot! For this applies to all mankind: that God will call every creature to account for all their conduct, be it good or bad" (Ecclesiastes 12:13–14).

Shemini Atzeret and Simhat Torah

In Orthodox congregations Sukkot ends with two days of celebration, *Shemini Atzeret*, the "Eighth Day, Feast of Conclusion" and *Simhat Torah*, the Rejoicing in Torah. Non-Orthodox congregations may celebrate only one day. On *Simhat Torah* the annual cycle of Scripture readings from the Torah Scroll is completed and the new cycle started immediately. The end is always linked to an ever-new beginning, each generation to a new one to follow. The scrolls are carried in procession. The children, bearers of hope, accompany the procession with little flags in their hands. They receive sweets. The last passages of the fifth Book of Moses are followed by the first passages of the first book. In Hasidic congregations there is exuberant dancing with the Torah.

"Torah is the tree of life, life for all, for in You [God] is the fountain of life" (Hymn for Simhat Torah). With the Torah in their arms (literally), the Jews step out of the holy day season into the winter and the new year.

ROSH HODESH: THE BEGINNING OF A MONTH

By biblical command, *Rosh Hodesh,* the beginning of a month, is to be celebrated (Numbers 10:10; 28:11–15). It was festively observed (Isaiah 1:13); today it is a very minor holy day but is celebrated in worship. The cycle of the moon, ever renewing itself, has been seen as a symbol of the Jewish people. It has also been regarded as the symbol of woman, whose power to conceive life is renewed every month. Contemporary Jewish women have therefore adopted it as their own, meeting in celebration among their sisters. Rosh Hodesh is announced on the preceding Sabbath with a prayer for divine help. Only a few minor festivals occur during the winter.

HANUKKAH

In midwinter the festival of Hanukkah is observed for eight days. It is a minor holiday, the only traditional one that has no biblical source. It is based on the story found in Maccabees, one of the Apocrypha. In 167 C.E., Antiochus IV (175–164) became king of the Seleucidian empire (to which Judah belonged). He was deeply imbued with Hellenism, and introduced the worship of Greek gods as the state religion. Calling himself "Epiphanes," God made manifest, he ordained for himself divine recognition, desecrated the Temple placing in it a statue of Zeus, and prohibited the exercise of Jewish religion. Jewish aristocrats and their followers fascinated by Hellenistic culture were willing to obey or strike compromises. A small band of heroic fighters recognized that Jewish survival was in gravest danger. Led by Judah the Maccabee, they rose up against him, prepared to give their lives for their faith. As far as we know, this was the first time in history that men rose in a concerted, organized, popular movement in defense of religious freedom. They overcame the enemy and rededicated the Temple. Hanukkah means "Dedication."

This observance celebrates the victory of arms by men motivated by the spirit. The rabbis chose to de-emphasize the military victory over its spiritual elements. They tell the story that when the Maccabees entered the Temple they found the menorah unusable; they took their spears and fashioned out of them a makeshift menorah, transforming the weapons of war into the implements of peace. They also found that there was left only one small cruse of oil, still bearing the seal of the high priest, sufficient to light the menorah for only one day. It would take eight days to prepare new pure oil, as Torah prescribed (Leviticus 24:1–4; see also Numbers 8:1–4). Miraculously, the oil burned for eight days, until a new supply had been prepared (B. Shabbat 21). It was then ordained that every year in every home the light be lit in memory and as inspiration.

Observance

A nine-branched special Hanukkah menorah is used. (In Israel it is called Hanukkiah.) In some types of menorah oil is used, but candles are permitted and usual. The center light, set apart, is the *shamash*, serving light, with which the others are kindled. Every evening, an additional candle is lighted, beginning with one and eventually reaching eight, even as the miracle grew day by day. The spiritual aspect of the feast is brought out in the Haftarah of the Sabbath during Hanukkah: "Not by might nor by power but by My spirit [will you prevail]" (Zechariah 4:6).

Hanukkah menorah (brass, seventeenth-century Dutch). The menorah shows in stylized form the cups and calyxes that were hammered out of the seven-branched menorah of the Tabernacle (Exodus 37:17ff.). (Photo by Kathie Minami, reproduced courtesy of Judah L. Magnes Memorial Museum, Jewish Museum of the West, Berkeley, California.)

The festival is minor and there is no work prohibition. While the candles are burning, the family might engage in work which really is not work, such as playing cards. Children play with a dreidel (a little top, from the German *drehen*, "to turn, spin"). Four letters are engraved on it: *N* (which gives a child *n*othing), *G* (which allows him or her to *g*et all out of the kitty), *H* (which yields *h*alf), and *S* (at which a nut or a chip or a penny is to be *s*et into the kitty). But the letters also form the initials of the sentence: *Nes Gadol Hayah Sham*, a Great Miracle Happened There. The children might get a few coins to play the game. This was the extent of gifts.

Hanukkah has become a much more important holiday in America. The house is decorated and the children receive gifts every night of the feast. This "upgrading" of Hanukkah is significant for several reasons. Jewish practices evolve and change in accordance with popular consensus among Jews, a testimony to the character of Judaism as a living and unfolding civilization. Hanuk-

Hanukkah menorah, in form of a wall plaque for decorative use during the year (brass, nineteenth-century Dutch). The shamash (serving light) is elevated above the plaque with the Hebrew inscription "For Mitzvah is a lamp, Torah a light" (Proverbs 6:23). This menorah burns oil. (Photo by Kathie Minami, reproduced courtesy of Judah L. Magnes Memorial Museum, Jewish Museum of the West, Berkeley, California.)

kah unquestionably assumed a greater significance due to its proximity to Christmas. Both occur at roughly the same time; both are festivals of light. The increased emphasis on Hanukkah reflects a desire of many parents to give their children an occasion for celebration that is similar to that of their Christian friends. This change reveals the influence of the surrounding culture on the development of Jewish ways, and the ability of Judaism to absorb these influences into its own structure.

Hanukkah also testifies to Jewish self-affirmation. The Talmud ordains that the Hanukkah candles be placed in the window "to proclaim the miracle" to all the world. Inspired by a call of the Lubavitcher Rebbe, Jews in recent years have placed giant Menorahs in the center squares of great cities, from San Francisco to Paris, and Melbourne to Moscow. The lights are kindled every night and the Berakhot, preceding them, broadcast by loudspeakers over the entire area. This has contributed to making Hanukkah a universally acknowledged festival. In 1996 the United States Post Office issued a special Hanukkah stamp.

The renewal of light at the winter solstice goes back to ancient pagan rites. It was given expression by Christians in the Christmas tree and by Jews in the Hanukkah menorah. Christians and Jews have adopted and adjusted it. Each is to celebrate the light of spiritual renewal in its own traditional way. Thus a unity-in-difference was created and made manifest. It will be of value to the adherents of both religions in their individual expressions and in their common endeavors of promoting human spirituality and social justice.

Hanukkah reveals another side of Jewish religious practice as well. By permitting card playing and games at an appointed time, the rabbis built them into the structure of the faith itself, thus decreasing the temptation which a blanket prohibition might have incited. We shall see this again in connection with Purim, the Feast of Lots.

OTHER DAYS OF OBSERVANCE

The Tenth Day of Tevet, a fast day, commemorates the siege of Jerusalem. It may also serve to remind the card players that the time has come for a return to their duties.

The Fifteenth of Shevat, New Year's Day of Trees planting season in Israel, is observed by giving children various fruits, while the youth in Israel go out to plant new trees. Many religious schools in America have laid out gardens with biblical and Israeli plants. The link to the Land of Israel is thus made.

The Fast of Esther is a day of reflection before the merrymaking of Purim.

Purim

Purim has its source in the Book of Esther. She was the consort of King Ahasuerus, and no one knew that she was a Jew. The king appointed Haman, a ruthless Jew hater, as his viceroy. With his power Haman was determined to destroy the Jews. Upon Esther fell the duty to plead her people's case to the king. She had to go to him in his throne room, unbidden (which could cost her life). In prayer and fasting she prepared herself. With courage, she approached the king and was graciously received. By her diplomacy she brought deliverance to her people. Haman was subsequently hanged. We have no historical evidence that the story ever happened, but Esther's spirit deserves emulation. Purim means "lots." The Feast of Lots received this name because Haman cast lots to ascertain the best day for the massacre of the Jews. Since Purim falls during the Christian carnival season it has acquired many of its characteristics.

In the evening and morning, the Book of Esther is recited from a special scroll, the *Megillah*. Children are armed with noisemakers and are permitted to rattle them whenever the name of Haman is mentioned. This permission may perhaps be in allusion to the words of the Psalm: "From the mouths of infants and sucklings You have founded strength on account of Your foes to put an end to enemy and avenger" (Psalm 8:3).

The morning is given over to the exchange of gifts. Esther commanded that all send gifts to their friends and to the poor. Deliverance was to be celebrated through benefactions. The poor cannot reject the gifts. They receive them not because they need them, but because they are friends. No one can feel ashamed.

The afternoon brings a sumptuous banquet and merrymaking. Masquerades were introduced during the Middle Ages. In Israel, there are great carnival parades. Purim is specially set aside as a day when getting drunk becomes a Mitzvah: "He shall drink until he no longer knows whether Mordecai [who planned the rescue with Esther] is to be blessed or cursed, or whether Haman [the villain] is to be cursed or blessed" (*Shulhan Arukh*).

In Israel, the feast is therefore also called *Ad delo Yada*, "Until he no longer knows." Again, we note the psychological insight of the rabbis. By permitting drunkenness on one day they eliminated the temptation of alcohol. Jews have always used alcohol in moderation, accompanying it with a Berakhah. The taking of a drink was transformed into a Mitzvah. It is accompanied by a toast, *l'hayim*, may it be unto life.

PESSAH (PASSOVER): THE BIRTH AND COVENANT OF FREEDOM

Pessah, the festival of spring, comes one month after Purim and marks the rebirth of nature in renewed strength and promise. In the Land of Israel it is the season of the beginning harvest: The grain has grown, the lambs have developed to usefulness for human needs. From the earliest times, people have marked this moment in celebration, rejoicing in the harvest of early grain. Farmers linked their feasting to that of the shepherds, who saw their flock blessed. Pessah has remained a festival of nature, of gratitude for the land and for its yield, but Torah gave it an additional meaning. It has become the festival of freedom, commemorating the divine deliverance of Israel from Egyptian bondage. The fusion of these ideas into the unity of God–Torah–Land–Mitzvah is most clearly expressed in Deuteronomy 16:1–4:

> Observe the "month of the green corn," and prepare a Passover unto the Lord your God, for in the month of green corn did the Lord your God lead you out of Egypt by night. [Note the linking of agriculture to a historical event.] Offer a Passover sacrifice of the flock and the herd in the place which the Lord will choose for His Name to reside there. [The shepherd's thanksgiving is fused with Mitzvah, a response to God.] You shall not eat leavened food with it; for seven days shall you eat matzot [unleavened bread], the bread of affliction; for in great hurry did you go forth from the Land of Egypt. [The historical significance of the feast is added to its agricultural and pastoral one.] Thus shall you remember the day of your departure from Egypt all the days of your life. [The event in all its implications calls for a commitment.] And there shall not be seen any leaven in all your domain for seven days. . . .

The Message

Pessah makes God manifest as the God of nature and of history. Freedom is the principal message of Pessah. Pessah and the exodus from Egypt are therefore the key events and challenges to the Jews. The Ten Commandments establish God as He "who brought you out of the Land of Egypt, out of the house of bondage." The Sabbath and holy day *kiddush* includes the words "in remembrance of the Exodus of Egypt." Daily worship contains this remembrance as well. The Exodus revealed God as Master of history. He made humanity His coworkers, in order that freedom might extend to all. "The stranger . . . you shall love him as yourself, for you were strangers in the land of Egypt: I the Lord am your God" (Leviticus 19:34).

Matzah

It was too easy to forget this, and quite common for the poor, having become affluent, to wish to forget and think only of themselves. This may not be. On the festival of deliverance and harvest joy, the Jews are not permitted to feast on leavened bread and pastry; they may only eat *matzah*—unleavened bread. Matzah consists simply of flour and water baked quickly into a flat cracker, for it must not rise. Any admixture of salt and spices, which wealth can provide, is forbidden. Matzah is the "bread of affliction"; in Egypt slavery permitted no time to prepare decent bread. But matzah is the bread of liberty as well, symbol of freedom "because they were thrust out of Egypt and could not tarry" (Exodus 12:39) to bake real bread. Remembrance of enslavement was to provide the incentive to promote liberty. By linking God–Torah–Mitzvah–Land, Judaism has made of a nature and historical festival a powerful call to freedom and righteousness.

Removing Leaven

In preparation for the festival, all leavened items must be removed, "you shall remove leaven from your houses" (Exodus 12:15). Leaven, *hametz*, includes a great many varieties of bread and pastry, products made with starches, and grain alcohol. No hidden traces may be left. This called for a complete spring housecleaning. Through it Jews may well have promoted their health during the Middle Ages. The general population permitted dirt to accumulate and become a breeder of epidemics.

On the night before Pessah, "one must search for hametz by the flame of a light" (B. Pessahim 1:1). It is a custom still observed. The family joyfully marches through the house and the children gather small pieces of hametz (left on purpose). To them it is a happy opportunity to share: they learn the meaning of the feast by doing. The next morning all hametz is burned in a big bonfire. Since the dishes used throughout the year have become permeated with hametz, traditional Jews will replace them by special ones. They are used only during the holiday and stored throughout the year.

The Seder

Ordination of the Seder

So significant is the message of Pessah that observance in removal of hametz and in the worship of the synagogue is not sufficient. "When, in the future, your son asks you, saying 'What does this mean?' you shall tell him: 'It was with a mighty hand that the Lord brought us out of Egypt, the house of bondage'" (Exodus 13:14).

Torah ordained a specific family celebration on the eve of the holiday. It is based on the family gathering preceding the exodus (Exodus 12:1–14). During that night God *passed over* the homes of the Israelites while He punished the Egyptians, hence the name Passover. At that moment the Israelites, fully prepared for departure, were to hold a family service in their homes and eat a lamb roasted over the fire "with unleavened bread [*matzot*], and bitter herbs [*maror*]. . . . This day shall be to you one of remembrance: you shall celebrate it as a festival to the Lord throughout the generations; you shall celebrate it as an institution for all times" (Exodus 12:8, 14).

In Temple days each family slaughtered its paschal lamb in the Temple. During the evening meal, the family ate it together with Matzot and Maror. Sacrifices are no longer offered in Judaism, but otherwise the Seder or "order" of the family service, outlined in the Mishnah (Pessahim), has remained.

Celebrating the Seder

The Symbols on the Table. To make the meaning clear to the child, symbols are used:

Seder Plate (silver, German, nineteenth century). The open doors reveal the three tiers for the matzot; the condiments and symbolic items are placed on top and in the ornamental containers. (Photo by Kathie Minami, reproduced courtesy of Judah L. Magnes Memorial Museum, Jewish Museum of the West, Berkeley, California.)

1. At each seat is a little book containing the story in its right order; it is called *Haggadah*, the story.

2. At each place there is a cup, which will be filled with wine four times. Four promises of freedom are found in Exodus (6:6–7); four times the cup of deliverance is therefore passed. God says, "I will bring you out from . . . Egypt; I will deliver you from their bondage, I will redeem you. . . . And I will take you to Me for a people."

3. In anticipation of the future an additional cup is placed at the hand of the leader, who conducts the Seder. This cup points to a fifth promise "I will bring you into the land, which I swore to give to Abraham, Isaac, and Jacob, and I will give it to you for a possession, I the Lord" (Exodus 6:8). To the Jews this promise predicts the time of the Messiah and of ultimate redemption for Israel and humanity. The arrival of the Messiah will be heralded by Elijah (Malachi 3:22–24; 4:4–6, according to the King James Version). The cup is therefore called the "Cup of Elijah." It is not drunk

but used only as a reminder and a hope. Elijah's coming is expected at any time and with it the coming of the universal day of peace.

4. At the head of the table three matzot are placed, symbol of the three groups in Israel's community who were liberated: Priests, Levites, and common folk Israelites. They were all redeemed equally and must all be mindful of the message of the matzah. These three matzot are covered.

5. On the "Seder plate" several symbolic foods are placed:

   a. a roasted shankbone is a reminder of the Pessah offering of old (the Passover lamb). It is not eaten; there are no more sacrifices.

   b. an egg, symbol of nature's awakening, is placed next to it. It also commemorates ancient Temple sacrifices. It, too, is not eaten.

   c.–d. a dish of green vegetables (parsley) and a dish of salt water come next; the beauty of nature once was made bitter by the tears the slaves shed in their toil. It was also utilized and made glorious as, by God's help, they marched dry-shod through the salty waters of the Sea of Reeds (the Red Sea).

   e.–f. bitter herbs, *maror,* including horseradish and *Haroset,* a dish containing a brownish-colored mixture of nuts, apples, wine, and cinnamon. Both are reminders of slavery; one brings its bitterness into the mouth; the other serves as a reminder of the mortar which ancient Jews had to make for Pharaoh.

The Service. Opening Ceremonies

Candles are lit as on every festival. The members of the family recline in comfort; the Kiddush, sanctification of the day, is recited over the first cup of wine. Then parsley is dipped into salt water and distributed; it is a symbol of wealth, ancient banquets would always start with an aperitif. But woven into it is both the idea of spring and redemption and the memory of enslavement, the salty water of tears.

The head of the house breaks the middle matzah, putting aside one portion for later use, as a poor person would reserve some bread for the future. The leader then shows the other part of the broken matzah to the family: "This is the bread of poverty our fathers ate in the land of Egypt." Immediately, the celebrant draws the relevant conclusion: "May those who are still cast out in the street come and join us in our celebration." The family is to exhibit the spirit of hospitality which will make humanity free.

The Events of the Past

Now the child asks the questions of the day: "Why is this night different from all other nights? Tonight we eat only matzah and no leavened bread; tonight we eat bitter herbs; tonight we dip herbs in condiments; tonight we sit in special comfort." The actual story is a response to these questions. The past is reviewed. It is briefly interrupted by an admonition to the adults. There are four different kinds of children, bright ones and wild ones, average ones and simple ones. All children have to be individually raised in accordance with their personality and abilities. Then the past will become relevant to future generations and tradition will be preserved through the spirit of the family.

Returning to the story of divine rescue in days gone by, the leader tells the story of God's redemption from slavery, including the Ten Plagues, and explains the meaning of the symbols. The Seder is to be a present, existential experience, emphasizing the unity of the people throughout the generations.

"Not our ancestors alone did God redeem from Egypt, but us as well."
"In every generation each person must look at himself, as if he had been freed."
(Haggadah)

The first part of the Seder concludes in thanksgiving. The second cup of wine, praising God for help in ages past, is consumed.

The Present

The present enters. The matzah, whose meaning has by now been explained, is shared by all. The bitter herbs are dipped in haroset and consumed. Following the practice of Hillel, a sandwich is made of matzah and bitter herbs. The custom offers an opportunity of bringing to mind Hillel's way of life and his teachings. He saw the essence of Torah in love of neighbor, and that is the essence of this celebration.

The festive meal follows, concluded by the sharing of the matzah previously put aside, the *afikomen*, a reminder of the ancient paschal lamb. Previously the children have been permitted to "steal" the afikomen, perhaps to keep them entertained during the long recitation, perhaps to indicate that they should "steal" the spirit of matzah from their elders and carry it into the next generation. They will now receive a small reward for returning it. After grace, the third cup is drunk, in gratitude for God's manifold gifts of the present.

The Future

Now the thought turns to the future, the task ahead. The door is opened to welcome Elijah, symbolically expressing ultimate rescue. In the Middle Ages, this served an additional, tragic purpose. Jews were accused of using Christian blood for the Seder. This was a calumny once directed by pagans against Christians. These pagans did not comprehend the idea of the Mass, and accused Christians of using the blood of pagan children in the Mass. Now Christians, forgetting that they too had been outcasts, leveled it against the Jews, and the Jews looked outside to watch if there were any evil spies or a corpse had been laid at their doorsteps.

The Seder then returns to hope for the future in song and praise and even children's charades. It concludes with the fourth and final cup of wine, a toast to the future "next year in Jerusalem!"

Morning Worship

Morning Worship follows the regular order and contains special poetry for the festival. But beginning with the third day of Passover, sections of the Psalms of Praise, Hallel (Psalms 113–118), are omitted. In this way compassion for the Egyptians is expressed. They suffered also; therefore joy is diminished. "Rejoice not when Your enemy falls," says Torah (Proverbs 24:17). The rabbis put the admonition into God's mouth. When the angels wished to break out in song at Pharaoh's destruction in the waves of the Red Sea, God rebuked them sharply, "The works of My hands [the Egyptians] are drowned in the sea and you want to sing?" (B. Sanhedrin 39b).

The Song of Songs, which is recited on Pessah, strikes the positive note of thanksgiving. It is a fervid love song, and has been understood by Jews as an expression of God's eternal love for His people.

THE PERIOD OF COUNTING

On the second day of Passover a measure, an *omer*, of barley was offered in the Temple of old. From this day on the days to the festival of Shavuot are counted, " . . . you shall keep count until seven full weeks have elapsed" (Leviticus 23:15). This has been called the *Omer* period. Passover spelled deliverance from slavery; Shavuot, commemorating the giving of the Ten Commandments, placed the Jew under the freedom of obligation. The people counted the days leading to the freedom under God's "constitution," the one and only true guarantee of abiding liberty.

The period between Pessah and Shavuot is considered a time of mourning. Tradition has it that the disciples of Rabbi Akiba died of a plague during this period, stricken as a result of their feuding, in spite of their knowledge. The Talmud mentions 12,000 disciples (B. Yevamot 62b), suggesting to scholars that these disciples were actually slain in the Bar Kohkba rebellion against Rome. They may have had too many "leaders" with individual strategic plans. This is also the period of the great massacres of German Jewry during the Crusades of 1096.

MODERN DAYS OF POPULAR OBSERVANCE

Yom Ha-Shoa ve-Ha-Gevurah (Holocaust and Resistance Day). In World War II, during the last days of Pessah, Jews in the Warsaw Ghetto rose up against the Nazis. They knew that they could not win but wished to show their resistance and die with dignity. The battle was fierce and ended only after the Germans cut off the water supply to the ghetto and brought in flamethrowers. But the myth of

German invincibility had been destroyed; no longer did the uniform itself invoke fear. The twenty-seventh of Nissan has therefore been chosen for general remembrance of Holocaust and Resistance. In Israel, on Yom Hashoah, all activities and traffic come to a complete standstill for one minute in remembrance of the martyrs. It is widely observed in the Diaspora. When this date falls on a Sabbath, the holiday is observed on the preceding Thursday.

Yom Ha-Atzmaut (Israel Independence Day). On May 14, 1948, surrounded by the armies of their enemies, the leaders of Israel declared the State's independence, putting their trust in the "Rock of Israel." The event brought new pride to world Jewry, and an upsurge of self-confidence and self-affirmation. The day is observed on the fifth of Iyar. If this date falls on a Sabbath, the holiday is observed on the preceding Thursday.

Yom Yerushalayim, Jerusalem Day, commemorates the reunification of the Holy City in 1967. It is observed on the twenty-eighth of Iyar, unless this day falls on the Sabbath. Then it is advanced to the preceding Thursday. From 1948 to 1967, the City of Jerusalem was divided. The "Old City" with its many shrines was in Jordanian hands. During this period, Jews were denied access to their shrines, including the Western Wall, Judaism's holiest place of pilgrimage. When the city was reunited, the Jews discovered that ancient synagogues had been blown up, Jewish cemeteries desecrated, and gravestones used for latrines. Jewish determination not to permit these desecrations to happen again may be one reason for their tenacious refusal to cede half the city once again.

Further, Jerusalem has been capital of Israel since King David's times. As such, it is mentioned repeatedly in the Bible, and is remembered in daily prayers that express the hope that it be restored to its former position. Jerusalem is thus deeply enshrined in Jewish consciousness and love. Jerusalem, particularly the "Old City," which is filled with the monuments of Jewish history, is, in a sense, a "mother" for all Jews.

SHAVUOT, COVENANT OF TORAH

The next major festival of the year is Shavuot, the Feast of Weeks, falling seven weeks after Pessah. It commemorates the giving of the Ten Commandments, and is called in the Talmud *Atzeret*, concluding festival. The march to freedom was completed only with dedication to God's Covenant of Torah. In ancient times the farmers brought their first fruits to the Temple on this day. Therefore synagogues are decorated with trees and flowers, but there are no symbols. Nothing can symbolize Torah revealed on this day.

The Torah reading is the Ten Commandments. The Book of Ruth is also recited, not simply because it tells of an event occurring during the harvest period of the year. Ruth, the Moabite who cleaved to God, becomes the great-grandmother of King David. Jews know of no distinction in races and backgrounds; they only know those who accept the divine charge of creative living and those who reject it. Those who live by it are truly worthy to bring about redemption, symbolized in David regardless of their background. Many congregations have instituted a service of confirmation on this day. Young people (usually after completion of junior high school) confirm their lives in Torah and the traditions of the Jewish people.

THE THREE PILGRIMAGE FESTIVALS— GENERAL RULES FOR HOLY DAY OBSERVANCE

Torah ordained that three times a year, on Pessah, Shavuot, and Sukkot, the men of Israel were to make a pilgrimage to Jerusalem (Deuteronomy 16:16–17). By their pilgrimage and physical presence in the Temple the people were to express the indivisible unity of the Jewish people under God. The three pilgrimage festivals, *Shalosh Regalim*, clearly represent the unity of God–Torah–Mitzvot–Land. During the festivals, the same work prohibition applies as on the Sabbath, with one exception: The preparation of food and all that pertains to it is permitted (Exodus 12:16).

Pessah is ordained for seven days, of which the first and the last are full holy days with work prohibition. The intermediate days are half-holy days, when work is allowed. Diaspora Jews observe eight days, of which the first two and last two are full holy days. Shavuot is ordained for one day, a full holy day, although two full holy days are observed in the Diaspora. Sukkot is ordained for eight days, of which the first and the last are full holy days. Diaspora Jewry observes the feast for nine days, the two first and two last days being full holy days.

Christian Parallels

The three festivals have been adapted by Christian and American tradition. Pessah and Shavuot became Easter and Pentecost; Sukkot, the secular Thanksgiving. Christian doctrine translated the societal revelations into individual revelations of universal significance. Judaism connects the Passover feast with the "resurrection" of the Jewish people from Egyptian bondage. From this rebirth it takes its task to help "redeem" humanity from injustice. Christianity at Easter celebrates the risen Christ and his redemptive work for humanity. Shavuot is dedicated to the giving of the Ten Commandments to the people; Pentecost recalls the outpouring of the Holy Spirit upon the disciples. Thanksgiving observed in America by all faiths has been turned into a secular feast. It originated with the Puritans who, well aware of the biblical holidays, may have drawn on Sukkot. The great holy days of Rosh Hashanah and Yom Kippur have no counterpart in other religions, but some of their liturgy and scriptural readings were taken over into Holy Week of Christianity.

SUMMER DAYS OF MOURNING

Two events once took place during the summer months that call for fasting and repentance. *The Seventeenth of Tammuz* marks the time when the walls of Jerusalem were breached, and the sacrificial Temple worship came to an end. Three weeks later, the ninth of Av marks the date of the destruction of both the first and the second Temple. *Tishah b'Av,* the ninth of Av, is observed in deep mourning. For twenty-four hours, the congregation fasts. All the coverings are removed from Ark and pulpit. The people, like mourners for a dear one, sit on low stools. In the evening the Book of Lamentations is recited. In the morning dirges are sung telling of Israel's tragic fate throughout the centuries.

Yet hope is expressed as well. Tradition will have it that the Messiah will be born on Tishah b'Av. An understanding of the meaning of suffering will lead to the kind of conduct which will bring humanity's salvation. Three weeks after Tishah b'Av, the shofar summons the people to prepare themselves for a new year.

VARIATIONS

It should be noted that the various groups in Judaism follow different styles of observance. Reform, as we noted, observes only one day of the festivals and its members need not feel bound by the work prohibitions. Torah readings vary in various rites. The Seder of the Passover festival is practically universally observed, but nonreligious Jews may develop their own individual "Haggadah" dealing with human freedom in general and/or Israel in particular.

Various popular forms of celebration have emerged in Israel. They may be added to the traditional ones or take their place. These, and other forms of expression and of celebration, reflect the varieties of Jewish belief among affirming Jews.

The Months and Festivals, Their Source and Observance

The table on the following page provides an overview of the festivals, which accentuate the course of the Jewish calendar year. It provides the names of the Jewish months and the days of special observance that fall within them, their length, and their biblical origin. The names of the months are of Persian derivation; Torah simply calls them "first month," "seventh month," etc., counting them from *Nissan,* the month of liberation, the beginning of Israel's freedom (Exodus 12:2). Major festivals are underlined, and an asterisk marks those that are observed for only one day in Reform Judaism and in Israel, and whose observance of the second day is optional in Conservative Judaism. The intermediate days of Pessah and Sukkot are half holidays. The days of fasting have no specific names and are simply called by the calendar date on which they fall. Each *day*

Name of month	Hebrew date	Festival	Biblical origin	Observed and obligatory in Israel and Conservatism	In Reform
Tishrei	1	Rosh Hashanah	Leviticus 23:23–25	Yes	Yes
	2	Rosh Hashanah		Yes	No
	3	Fast of Gedaliah	2 Kings 25:22–25 Zechariah 7:5; 8:19	Yes	No
	10	Yom Kippur	Leviticus 23:26–32	Yes	Yes
	15	Sukkot	Leviticus 23:33–36	Yes	Yes
	16	Sukkot	Deutoronomy 16:13–17	Yes in both, but not as major holiday in Israel and Reform	
	17–22	Sukkot		Yes	Yes
	22	Shemini Atzeret		Yes	Yes
	23	Simhat Torah		No	No
Marheshvan					
Kislev	25	Hanukkah	Apocrypha: Maccabees	Yes in both, observed for 8 days	
Tevet	10	Fast day	Zechariah 7:5; 8:19	Yes	No
Shevat	15	New Year's Day of Trees		Yes	Yes
Adar I	(additional month in leap years)				
Adar II	13	Fast of Esther	Book of Esther	Yes	No
	14	Purim	Book of Esther	Yes	Yes
Nissan	15	Pessah	Exodus 12; Leviticus 23:4–8	Yes	Yes
	16	Pessah	Deutoronomy 16:1–8	Yes in both, but not as major holiday in Israel and Reform	
	17–20	Pessah		Yes	Yes
	21	Pessah		Yes	Yes
	22	Pessah		No	No
	27	Yom Ha-Shoah: Holocaust Memorial: new		Yes	Yes
Iyar	5 or 3	Yom Ha-Atzmaut: Israel Independence Day: new		Yes	Yes
	28	Yom Yerushalayim: Jerusalem Day: new		Yes	Yes
Sivan	6	Shavuot	Exodus 19–20	Yes	Yes
	7	Shavuot	Leviticus 23:15–21 Deuteronomy 16:9–12	No	No
Tammuz	17	Fast day	Zechariah 7:5; 8:19	Yes	No
Av	9	Fast day	Jeremiah 52	Yes	Yes
Elul					

begins with the previous evening, the calendar *year* begins in the twilight of the sun year, in the fall. We shall start with the fall month of *Tishrei*, beginning between September 6 and October 4 of the solar year.

Notes

1. The hymn originated during the Byzantine period in Palestine. The Kalonymus family originating in Lucca, Italy, and in contact with Palestinian Jewry, probably brought it to Germany, when it settled at Mainz, and Kalonymus ben Meshullam gave it its enduring poetic form. At the same time a Jewish cantor by the name of Romanus, who became a Christian, brought it into the Church. It was used as a model for "Dies Irae" in the Catholic Requiem Mass, which however speaks of the Last Judgment, when the road to repentance is no longer open to the sinner.

2. In many congregations the departed are remembered after the Torah reading in the morning and the martyrs are commemorated in Mussaf. This deprives Minhah of a special theme. In the western Ashkenasic rite, the martyrs are mentioned in Minhah, and the remembrance of the departed family members frequently follows Minhah. In all rites the victims of the Holocaust are brought to mind.

3. The One God is affirmed once—God's glory is affirmed three times, as it is in the Kedushah—God, as Ruler of time and space is affirmed seven times. God is the Lord of space, symbolized in the "seven planets" and of time, symbolized in the seven days of the week. It may also be suggested that the custom may go back to the Jewish mystics. During Yom Kippur God dwelt with His people on earth, now he recedes through the ten sefirot to Heaven (1: 3 + 7 = 10).

CHAPTER 21

The Years of Life

As THE TRANSITION from season to season is marked by special observances, the milestones in human life are similarly set aside for reflection, dedication, and commitment. The rabbis of old gave clear expression to their conviction that every age group has its specific duty. Rabbi Judah ben Tema outlined it:

> At five years [the child is ready] for the study of Scripture,
>
> At ten for Mishnah,
>
> At thirteen for [responsibility in performance of] Mitzvot,
>
> At fifteen for Talmud,
>
> At eighteen [the youth is ready] for marriage,
>
> At twenty for the pursuit of a livelihood,
>
> At thirty [man reaches] strength,
>
> At forty full understanding,
>
> At fifty the ability to provide counsel,
>
> At sixty he enters his senior years,
>
> At seventy he attains old age,
>
> At eighty [his survival reflects] strength,
>
> At ninety bent in anticipation of the grave,
>
> At one-hundred he is as dead and past, withdrawn from the world.
>
> (Mishnah Avot 5:24)

The life of a Jew starts with Torah, leading to Mitzvot, reaching its first fulfillment in marriage. From then on, his duty is to those around him, the children through whom he perpetuates the household of Israel, the family whose livelihood is his responsibility, and his society, to whom he must impart the wisdom he has acquired by guidance and counsel. Old age to him is a period not of rest but of reflection, as he gives thanks to God who has permitted him to attain the span of "threescore years and ten, or even by reason of strength, fourscore years" (Psalm 90:10). Aware of his destiny to stand before his Maker, he faces death in

378

calm submission. Should he live beyond the usual span of life, he must gain the wisdom of withdrawal, letting new generations face their problems in their own way and find new solutions for their own time and needs.

Living in this fashion, he knows that his work on earth will not be without results, that he will pass on his name and achievements even after he has died. This is symbolically expressed in the fact that succeeding generations will bear his name, making a name for themselves by building upon the foundations of the past and the name their ancestors have made in the world. In the spirit of his time Rabbi Judah ben Tema speaks only of Jewish males. In general, his guiding words also address Jewish women.

THE JEWISH HOME AND JEWISH NAMES

The strength that safeguards Jewish life and survival rests on the Jewish home. The family covenanted within itself and as a unit with God and Israel is the bulwark of the future. The congregation is, in a sense, a family of families and at the same time their protector. Judaism would be threatened if the family were shattered.

This continuity is expressed in Jewish names. It is customary to give every son and daughter a Hebrew name in addition to his or her common one; by this name, the Jew will be called to the Torah, recorded in the marriage certificate, remembered in prayer after death. There were no family names in Jewish usage. A son and daughter were known by their own names and that of their father. Moses thus would be called Mosheh ben (son of) Amram. The name of the biblical Miriam would be Miriam bat (daughter of) Amram. King David is known as Son of Jesse. In our time it has become a custom to mention both the father's and the mother's names. Moses would therefore be called Mosheh ben Amram ve-Jokhebed.

It is customary among Ashkenazim to name their children after departed ancestors in order that the examples of fulfilled lives may be guides and that the eternal chain of the generations may be made visible. The Sefardim name their children after forebears who are still living in order that a child may look upon a living grandfather or grandmother as special guide and counselor in life. These names are traditionally bestowed upon boys at the time of circumcision and on girls in a special blessing in the synagogue shortly after birth. (See below for contemporary rites initiating girls in the Covenant of Israel.)

The civic name given a child may, of course, be the same as the Hebrew name, as in the case of biblical names such as David, Ruth, or Michael. It may be a translation of a Hebrew name or its meaning: Johanan becomes John; Miriam is given its latinized common form of Mary; Judah, compared in Scripture to a "lion's whelp" (Genesis 49:9), becomes Leo. Most common, though least desirable, is the practice of using alliterations, making the civic name start with the same letter as the Hebrew one; thus Aaron becomes Alfred, Samuel becomes Seymour.

Family names were introduced under civic ordinances in the Napoleonic period. Frequently they are based on the cities from which the family originated, such as Oppenheimer (from the German city of Oppenheim on the Rhine), or Posner (from Posen, now Poznan, in Poland). Names may indicate the family's descent from the priests or Levites of old—for instance, Cohen (priest) or Cahn, or Katz, an abbreviation of "*Ka* hen *Tzedek*" a righteous priest. Segal is an abbreviation of *Sega*n Levaya, overseer of Levites. Hebrew names may be translated into modern languages. Today in Israel, they are being translated back into Hebrew.

In medieval times, various homes were distinguished by signs or special features, and the people dwelling in them were remembered by these. A house with a red shield bestowed upon it the name Rothschild; one with a large flight of steps in front (a *treppe,* or *trepp* in earlier and colloquial German) resulted in the name Trepp. A great many names, however, were simply bestowed by officials upon the Jews by government decree. This led to abuses, as these officials were frequently corrupt. If a man were willing to pay well, he might get a beautiful name, such as *Blumenfeld* (a field of flowers) or *Rosenberg* (a mountain of roses); if not, some hideous name might be given instead.

Many Jews whose names might be hard to pronounce in America have anglicized their names and have become indistinguishable. Unhappily, this also had to be done to escape discrimination.

JOINING THE HOUSEHOLD OF ISRAEL

In antiquity, Judaism was a missionary faith. "Be of the disciples of Aaron, loving peace and pursuing peace, loving all your fellow creatures bringing them to Torah" said Hillel (M. Avot 1:13). This is disapprovingly echoed in the New Testament "Alas for you, lawyers and Pharisees, hypocrites! You travel over sea and land to win one convert . . ." (Matt. 23:15). Under Christian rule conversion to Judaism was punishable by death for the converter and the convert. Nevertheless it did occur. By that time, Judaism found itself surrounded not by heathens, but by worshipers of God, which made conversion no longer necessary. Orthodoxy has therefore made conversion to Judaism difficult. In principle it will and has accepted non-Jews into the Jewish faith and people.

A person becomes a member of the House of Israel either by birth or by conversion. By birth, a person is considered a Jew if the mother is a Jew, even if the father is not. Reform and Reconstructionism now recognizes the child of a Jewish father and non-Jewish mother as a Jew if the child has been brought up as a Jew and become Bar Mitzvah or Bat Mitzvah. Conversion implies full acceptance of the duties and obligations of the Jewish faith and people. The convert must fully take on "the yoke of Torah and Mitzvot" and cast his or her lot with that of the Jewish people.

Judaism has held that salvation does not depend on being a Jew. It also has maintained that it be open to those who were attracted by its spirituality and way of life. Traditionally, it has not made conversion easy. In recent years we find a readiness in American Judaism to accept converts without great difficulties, and the number of converts has grown significantly.

Preceding conversion, the candidate has to discuss his or her resolve carefully with the rabbi, for conversion must stem from conviction. The rabbi outlines the privilege of joining the Jewish faith but also the disadvantages attached to being a Jew. He explains the duties that it demands and the discrimination to which Jews have been exposed. The rabbi also points out that from the standpoint of "salvation," a non-Jew is not considered in any way inferior or less privileged than a Jew. On the contrary, a non-Jew reaches this state by simple compliance with the Noahide commandments. He merely has to live up to the principles of ethics and justice. To attain the same state, a Jew is obligated to add to the Noahide commandments all the Mitzvot of Torah. After an initial meeting the rabbi sends the candidate home to give him or her an opportunity for a clear analysis without any pressure. If the candidate is determined to convert, the postulant undergoes a period of study to learn what it is he or she is accepting. He or she is still free to withdraw. Larger Jewish communities in America conduct regular classes for postulants.

The rite of final acceptance traditionally consists of circumcision for males plus immersion in a *mikveh*, a ritual bath; for women, only immersion is required. The formal rite includes a declaration of acceptance of Judaism before a rabbinical court, a *Bet Din* of three. Reform Judaism requires only this declaration and no other rites, however, many of its rabbis follow traditional requirements, especially immersion. The convert then receives a Hebrew name. In the case of men, the name is usually Abraham, the patriarch, the founder of Judaism. At the same time he becomes a son of Abraham, who brought many converts to the One God. He is called Abraham ben Abraham. Henceforth he or she is no longer a "convert" but "a Jew by choice." He or she enjoys all the rights of a Jew and bears full responsibility for the performance of Mitzvot. A certificate testifies to the admission.

No one may ever hold it against such a Jew that once he or she was not a member of the family of Israel (B. Baba Metzia 58b). On the contrary, "having left the environment of their childhood, they deserve our special respect and kindness" (Bamidbar Rabba 8:2); "they are beloved of God." Many of the great leaders of Jewry were themselves either proselytes or the immediate descendants of converts. "He may see his grandson be high priest" (Bereshit Rabba 70). Ruth saw her great-grandson David become king of Israel. In the Amidah, "the faithful proselytes" are specifically entrusted to God's special grace.

Admission to Judaism can be and is granted to people of all races and colors by even the most Orthodox rabbis, and all these converts become full-fledged members of the Jewish people. But Orthodoxy makes conversion difficult as a matter of principle. The number of American converts to Judaism has been estimated at about 12,000 per year. They have come from all races and nationalities. Many of them have become pillars of their congregations. Interfaith marriages have also greatly increased, reaching proportions that have caused serious concern. Many congregations have instituted "outreach" programs; if the non-Jewish partner in a marriage can find spiritual meaning in Judaism, his or, above all, her conversion will benefit the unity of their family and the survival of the Jewish people. The children will be Jews.

Who, then, is a Jew? This question has become acute in our time. Problems have developed in Israel, where all family matters stand under the authority of the State Rabbinate, which is Orthodox. The rabbinate will not recognize as a Jew any person brought into the Jewish faith and people under the auspices of non-Orthodox rabbis, even when all the halakhic requirements have been met. This can mean that the child of a mother who is a Jew by choice may not be so recognized either. Non-Jews wishing to become Jews in America need to be cognizant of this fact. In America they face no problem.

For immigration purposes a person brought into the Jewish faith by any rabbi abroad will be recognized as a Jew. This allows Jewish immigrants to ask for and obtain Israeli citizenship immediately upon arrival. "The Law of Return" was enacted at a time when persecuted refugees streamed into the land. They were to be given the assurance of a home. From now on the new citizens of Israel, like all the other citizens, are subject to all the laws. In family matters, such as marriages, they stand under the authority of the rabbinate, which decides if they can be regarded as Jews. Conversions by the Israeli rabbinate have not met the demand. The rabbinate and many Orthodox Jews in Israel have been politically active to have "The Law of Return" repealed.

Also, under talmudic law a member of the Jewish people never loses his status, even if he is not religious. The Supreme Court of Israel has ruled, however, that a person who consciously adopts another faith has made a deliberate choice. By electing another "family of faith" this person has relinquished Jewish allegiance and all it entails. Jews having joined non-Jewish sects, such as Jews for Jesus, cannot claim affiliation with the Jewish people and religion.

Circumcision: The Covenant of Abraham

B'rit Milah, the Covenant of Circumcision, is the first Mitzvah to which the newborn son is led. For a long time its hygienic value was regarded as great; recently it has been subject to medical controversy. In America physicians have performed it almost routinely on all newborn boys, regardless of religious affiliation, simply as a health measure. (Some medical studies indicate that there is a much lower incidence of cancer of the penis when circumcision has been performed, and women married to circumcised men have a lower incidence of cervical cancer; other studies have found no such benefits.) To the Jew, however, it is a religious act ordained in Torah (Leviticus 12:3). The child is admitted into the Covenant of Abraham, for he was the first to enter the B'rit (Genesis 17:10ff.). Circumcision has been regarded as so important that it was to be performed in the synagogue in the presence of the congregation. It is so significant that the operation must be performed even on the Sabbath or Yom Kippur, when these days fall on the appointed eighth day after birth. Only when there is danger to a child's health may it be postponed. But according to the law of Torah it should never be performed before the eighth day. An uncircumcised

Jew is still a Jew though lacking the basic Mitzvah of life. He is called upon to remedy the situation.

Pious men, specially trained in the performance of the operation, are called to conduct it; such a man is called a *mohel*. The Conservative and Reform movements have each established seminars for mohelim, mainly physicians, acquainting them with the halakhah surrounding B'rit Milah, and granting certification as mohel to the graduates. It is an honor to be a mohel, and there are distinguished physicians or businesspeople who, to the neglect of their own affairs, dedicate themselves to this Mitzvah, naturally without pay. Lately it has become a paid profession.

Tradition calls for a quorum of ten (the legal minimum constituting a congregation) to be present. The grandmother or a close relative brings in the child, thus becoming his godmother; a close relative holds him during the operation, thus becoming his godfather. The godfather is seated on a chair next to which another chair is placed, symbolically for Elijah, guardian of Israel's Covenant with God. With a quick stroke, the mohel removes the foreskin of the penis, wipes off the blood, and secures the skin so it cannot grow back. The father speaks the blessing: "Blessed are You, O Lord . . . who has commanded us to enter him into the Covenant of our father Abraham." The people respond: "As he entered the Covenant, so may he enter into [the study and performance of] Torah, into marriage, and [the performance of] good deeds." The name is then bestowed upon the child as the mohel raises the cup of salvation in prayer that it be a cup of happiness. A drop of wine is passed to the child's lips, and the father finishes it. A festive meal completes the observance.

Today, circumcision on newborn Jewish boys is at times performed a few days after birth in the hospital. Some close relatives may be present or it may simply be a surgical procedure. This may be required by the rules of the hospital, and has the advantage that the mother can take her circumcised baby with her when she returns home. Torah is explicit, however, that the rite on a healthy child be performed on the eighth day and not sooner. A celebration on the eighth day, conducted within a circle of relatives and friends, corresponds to the commandment of Torah and may leave precious memories among the family and its guests. (Hadassah Hospital in Jerusalem has a surgical section attached to its synagogue in order that the rite may be performed under highest hygenic conditions and yet according to the traditional custom of Jewish religion.)

In recognition of women's equality, non-Orthodox Jewry has instituted a rite for newborn girls. There is, of course, no operation. The child is brought into the gathering by the godmother and held by the godfather. The parents express their thanksgiving to God, the name is bestowed upon the child, and a festive meal follows.

In Orthodox congregations, girls are named in the synagogue shortly after birth. The father is called to the Torah, recites the Berakhot before and after the reading of the portion assigned to him, and then he, the mother, and the child are given a special blessing in which the girl's Hebrew name is proclaimed. The mother may be present and watch from the women's gallery. By tradition her first going out after confinement is to the synagogue. The baby is not present.

Chair of Elijah (German-Jewish folk art, Rheda, Westphalia, Germany, 1803). This double-seated chair is used at circumcisions. The godfather, holding the child, sits on the left seat. Elijah, "guardian of the Covenant, " symbolically sits on the right. (Photo by the author, reproduced courtesy of Jack H, Skirball Museum of the Hebrew Union College-Jewish Institute of Religion, Los Angeles, California.

In non-Orthodox congregations both parents are seated together in the synagogue. Depending on the practice of the congregation, the child may also be brought. At a special blessing, the child's Hebrew and English names are bestowed. The child, if present, is personally blessed by the rabbi, who places hands on the little one's head. This applies to boys and girls equally. The naming does not replace the B'rit and is no substitute for it, but can be held in addition to give the child the English name as well.

BAR MITZVAH AND BAT MITZVAH

From infancy on the child is to be initiated into the faith. The parents, by word and example, are the natural guides and earliest teachers. Under their care the little child begins to learn the prayers, the affirmation of faith: "Hear 0 Israel, the Lord our God, the Lord is One." Father and mother reveal to the child the value of Torah. The child learns: "Moses commanded us Torah, it is the heritage of the congregation of Jacob . . ." (Deuteronomy 33:4). The spirit and celebrations in a religious home surround the child with a warm Jewish atmosphere and lead him or her to the performance of Mirzvot.

At the age of thirteen, regarded as the onset of puberty, the boy becomes *Bar Mitzvah* (responsible), Son of the Mitzvah. At this age a Jewish boy automatically enters the state of responsibility. No special celebration is required though it has been in practice throughout the ages. It is an important rite of passage: the boy knows where he stands. Still a child he is viewed as being endowed with adulthood. The first Mitzvah he performs is to give allegiance to Torah. Now that he may be counted as one of the minyan, he will be called to Torah to witness or, if he is able to read Hebrew, himself read a portion of it; to recite the Haftarah; and, above all, to pronounce the blessing which is a pledge to Him "who has given us the Torah of truth, thus planting eternal life in our midst." Today, as part of the worship service, the boy may give a short speech explaining a passage of the Torah reading and giving thanks to his parents and family. He will then be addressed and blessed by the rabbi. Finally, he is given gifts at the joyful celebration which follows.

The American rabbinate has sternly called for a correction in the form of this celebration. They have pointed out that all too often it may be far too lavish, designed more for the parents and their friends than for the boy himself. While it may well express the parents' pride in having raised a child to conscious Jewish living, it frequently is wholly secular. Worst of all, it may fail to impress the youngster that Bar Mitzvah is not the end of his training as a Jew but very much the beginning. It is the open door to responsible living.

Girls, who mature earlier than boys, attain religious responsibility at the age of twelve. There used to be no celebration. In recent years the celebration of *Bat Mitzvah* (Daughter of the Commandment) for girls has become rooted in non-Orthodox congregations. It recognizes the equality of women in our society and is identical with Bar Mitzvah or patterned after it.

Following the Christian custom of confirmation, a similar ceremony has found entrance in the synagogue. It offers an incentive for the young people to continue their Jewish education after Bar or Bat Mitzvah. They confirm their faith at the age of about sixteen when they have a greater awareness of their duties. Confirmation is held on Shavuot, the festival commemorating the giving of the Ten Commandments. It is the day of the revelation of Torah, to which these young people are to give their allegiance.

MARRIAGE

Judaism believes in early marriage yet feels that a man should be able to support his family when he takes this important step. The Talmud advises careful thought in order that both partners be matched well physically and emotionally, in background and in outlook. The rabbis advise against any marriage in which the woman is of higher social status. This has been borne out by experience. We frequently find men being jealous of their wives' superior status or education, leading to conflicts and even divorce. It is to be hoped that, in our age, men will adjust to the equality of women, and this jealousy will disappear. The support of the family often requires two working parents. Both are then equally called upon to share the chores of the household as well, and mutual recognition may result. The Rabbis see the best assurance for a blessed home in a mother who is the daughter of a "disciple of the wise" (B. Yoma 71a); she has acquired the spirit of Torah and can transmit it to the children. It may be prudent, even in our day, for young people to obtain their parents' guidance and the rabbi's counseling before they enter the holy bond of marriage.

The Traditional Wedding

In antiquity, young people were solemnly betrothed to each other one year before their final marriage vows. This waiting period allowed the future bride to prepare her trousseau and eliminated the man's fear "that someone else might get her." The betrothal ceremony has now become a part of the marriage.

Formalized in ancient Judaism, the wedding ceremony, by tradition, combines both legal and religious features. In Jewish law, a couple is married if the man gives a gift of some value to his bride with the intent of marrying her, and she accepts it in this spirit. This custom resulted in the wedding ring; hence a double-ring ceremony is not essential in Judaism. A second method of marrying was by contract, *ketuvah*, and a third by cohabitation. All these elements are present in the wedding rites. In addition, God's blessing is invoked.

The Service

By tradition, the groom is called to the Torah on the Sabbath preceding the wedding. The bride goes to the mikveh before the wedding day. They visit the graves of their parents if these are no longer living. Both fast and say confession of sins before the ceremony to impress upon themselves that, as on Yom Kippur, they stand at the threshold of a new life.

Preceding the ceremony, in the officiant's study, the ketuvah is signed by the witnesses and the groom formally agrees to its conditions. Traditionally, the groom now sees the bride and veils her, while the rabbi speaks, "O sister, may you grow into thousands of myriads" (Genesis 24:60), as a reminder of the send-off Rebecca received. Perhaps it was also instituted to assure the groom that she is indeed the one he has chosen as his life's companion. This saves him from the fate of the patriarch Jacob, who was deceived by his father-in-law, Laban (Genesis 29:16–25).

In the center of the expectant congregation stands the *huppah*, the wedding canopy. It symbolizes the home the couple is to build in twosomeness. There the rabbi, flanked by the witnesses, awaits the couple. To the strains of joyful song and music (often Psalm 118:26–29: "Blessed who enters by the Name of the Lord, we bless you out of the house of the Lord") the groom enters, escorted by his father and father-in-law. He waits for the bride, who will join him under the huppah, escorted by her mother and mother-in-law, and stand at his right side.

Upon ascertaining that the two wish to be married, the rabbi raises the first cup of wine and recites the blessings of betrothal. Groom and bride share the cup, which is put to their lips by their father and mother.

A Huppah (wedding canopy) with rabbi and couple under it in the whimsical style of the glassblower Cianni Toso of Venice. (Photo by the author.)

The groom places the ring on the index finger of the bride's right hand, saying: "Be you consecrated unto me by this ring according to the law of Moses and Israel." Willingly accepting the ring, the bride indicates her consent. The marriage contract signed by witnesses is then read by the rabbi.

Raising the second cup of wine, the rabbi invokes upon the couple the "Seven Blessings." Again, groom and bride share the cup, as they will henceforth share the cup of life together. It is now put to their lips by their in-laws. The rabbi's address and blessing are optional but customary.

At the end of the ceremony, a glass is broken as a reminder of Jewish suffering ever since the fall of the Temple. It may also serve as a reminder to the couple that love can break easily, and they must therefore treat each other tenderly. The congregation exclaims "*Mazel tov*." May it be under a good constellation.

Music has always been an essential part of the wedding celebration. It strikes up as the couple leaves the synagogue to break their fast together in solitude. Their togetherness now has an additional meaning: they might consummate their marriage. All the requirements have now been met: the gift (the ring), the contract (ketuvah), and their "coming together."

At the festive meal the Seven Blessings are recited again.

Modern Issues

Some modern practices can be built into the traditional wedding ceremony in addition to its prescribed form. The processional has been changed. The two-ring ceremony has become widely accepted. The couple may wish to speak words to each other. All this is acceptable, but not in replacement of the ordained declarations.

Other practices separate non-Orthodox weddings. In the traditional ketuvah the husband "acquires" his wife. Modern texts emphasize the mutuality of the relationship. The Conservative ketuvah authorizes the rabbinical court to act if necessary, as we shall explain below. Reform Judaism has abbreviated the wedding ceremony and issues a certificate in place of the ketuvah.

The official rabbinate of Israel does not recognize marriages solemnized by non-Orthodox rabbis as valid under halakhah.

Marriage and Divorce

Life in Marriage

The Jewish marriage ceremony is called *Kiddushin,* sanctification; in the home its spirit was truly fulfilled. The Jewish home was holy, a haven of peace, for it was a home with a purpose. The women knew that theirs was the greatest task of all, that of raising the children in Torah and Mitzvot. "Be fruitful and multiply" says Torah (Genesis 1:28), and the Talmud comments that each family should have at least one son and daughter (Mishnah Yebamot 6:6). But mutual enjoyment of marriage was equally important, and the Talmud permitted contraceptives under certain conditions, for instance, when a pregnancy would endanger either the health of the mother or the welfare of a previous child, for instance when the mother's milk would run dry too soon as a result of a new pregnancy (B. Ketubot 39a).

Artificial insemination, with the husband as donor of the sperm, has been permitted. Termination of pregnancy is mandatory in Judaism if the mother's life is at stake. Adoption is permitted, and must be in accordance with the law of the land. If the child is not Jewish, it has to be converted. The child then becomes the son or daughter of his or her adoptive parents and must observe the mourning rites for parents. In all of these cases, the advice of the rabbi is first to be sought.

Niddah

Another Jewish law may have contributed to the permanence of the home. Jewish law based on Torah prohibits intercourse during the period of menstruation and seven days thereafter. For about twelve days every month, a husband and wife may not even touch each other. She is *Niddah,* ritually "Separated." Then the wife has to immerse herself in a ritual bath of purification, a *Mikveh,* before intercourse can again be permitted. As a matter of cleanliness and hygiene, this immersion was of great value, especially in the Middle Ages, when bathing was very rare in most other cultures. This commandment is strictly observed by Orthodox women to this day. Thus, husband and wife can hardly get tired of each other physically, a factor greatly contributing to the stability of the home.

Divorce

If a marriage does not work out, divorce is permitted. While the rabbis proclaim that the altar sheds tears when a home is broken (B. Gitin 90b), Judaism has been wise enough to permit divorce without requiring the proof of "guilt" on the part of either partner.

Before a rabbinical court of three, a bill of divorcement, *get,* is written in accordance with specific detailed regulations, purposely made difficult as a deterrent to divorce. The husband, who must request the *get*, then hands it to his wife, and as she accepts it in free will, she is divorced. She may remarry ninety days later (in order to avoid questions of paternity in case of an early pregnancy in her second marriage). A woman may remarry her husband, but only if she has not been married to another man after her divorce from him.

In the United States no religious divorces may be granted until the final divorce has been obtained by the couple in the civil courts, in accordance with the law of the state. Under the talmudic law, "the law of The State is the [religious] law as well" (B. Baba Kamma 113b).

Halakhah and Modern Issues

According to halahkah set down in Torah, the husband can divorce his wife, yet she cannot divorce him (Deuteronomy 24:1–4). In ancient times the court could force him to grant her a divorce when conditions warranted. (In Israel today the husband can be imprisoned in an effort to make him yield.) This divorce law places the woman under disabilities. She cannot obtain a divorce against her husband's will. The Orthodox woman has to accept the situation. Conservative Judaism has included a provision in the ketuvah, by which the husband obligates himself to grant his wife a religious divorce should the occasion arise. As a last resort she can place the matter in the hands of a rabbinical court, which can annul the marriage. Reform Judaism requires only the legal divorce granted by the state. It has, however, instituted a Ritual of Release and issues a Document of Separation for those who desire it, making it clear that these do not constitute a halakhic *get*. Reconstructionism has provisions allowing the woman to initiate and obtain the divorce.

Halakhically, women who have obtained only a court divorce are regarded as still married. A wife whose husband refuses to grant her a *get*, or has disappeared, such as missing in action, becomes *Agunah*; a deserted wife, who may not remarry. In Israel there are at least 5,000 such unfortunate women to whom the rabbinate will not permit remarriage.

A woman, who enters a second marriage, without having a *get* is regarded by Orthodoxy as an adulteress and any child out of this marriage as a bastard, *mamzer* who may marry only another *mamzer*, down through the generations. A man who marries again on the basis of a court divorce, but without a *get* has transgressed against the ordinance of Rabbenu Gershom prohibiting polygamy (see p. 75), but not against the law of Torah, thus the children are not affected. Children born out of wedlock are not considered mamzerim. Conservative, Reform, and Reconstructionist Judaism have done away with the concept of mamzer and its implications.

SICKNESS AND DEATH

It is a Jewish duty to keep one's body in good health, a worthy instrument in the service of God. But sickness is the lot of all, and Jews must seek competent medical aid when it occurs. Jews may therefore not live in a town that has no physician (J. Kiddushin 4:12). When illness strikes they turn to God and find strength in friends, whose duty it is to visit, but Jews must also do all that can humanly be done to restore their health.

As Death Approaches

During the last stages of life as death approaches, no manipulation of the dying is permitted beyond that which is medically required. It is believed that any touch might shorten life and that we have no right to diminish this God-given span by even a moment. It is not required, however, to prolong death by artificial means.

As the patient faces death, family and friends stay with their loved one, that no one might die alone. They recite with the expiring the confession of sins, or, if the patient is too far gone, do this for the dying. They repeat the affirmation of faith, "Hear O Israel, the Lord our God, the Lord is One," making an effort so to time or repeat the affirmation of faith that the Oneness of God is proclaimed by the dying with the last living breath. These last acts of kindness are traditionally performed by the men and women of the "holy fellowship," the *Hevrah Kadishah*, a group of people distinguished by their piety, who perform this service as a voluntary act of free devotion, a true Mitzvah, for which the departed can render no thanks; only God may.

Attending to the Dead

After death the members of the Hevrah Kadishah place the deceased on the earth (as symbol of the return to dust, whence we came). Later they wash and dress the body in the simple white linen garments worn on Yom Kippur and around a man's shoulders they put a tallit. Women have similar white garments and are similarly attended by women in this ritual. The "fellows" make a simple wooden coffin and place the body in it. In Israel, Orthodox Jews will be buried in only a shroud. These rules, ordaining absolute equality and simplicity in death follow the ordinances of Rabban Gamaliel and the rabbis, who taught that

> Formerly, they used to serve in the house of mourning, the rich in crystal goblets, the poor in colored glasses. Formerly, they kept the faces of the rich uncovered, but covered those of the poor, which had been darkened from want. Since the poor were thus put to shame, it was ordered that the faces [of the departed] be always covered, out of respect for the poor. Formerly, the rich were carried out on a specially made, bed-like coffin and the poor on a simple bier; since this put the poor to shame, it was ordered that all be carried on a simple bier. . . . Formerly, the funeral of the dead was harder on his family than his death [on account of the expense involved]; then Rabban Gamaliel took action, ordering that he be treated in the plainest way, ruling that he be buried in linen garments. Thus the popular custom developed to bury the dead in linen garments. (B. Moed Katan 27a, b)

The equality of all in death is to be visibly demonstrated. The poor need not go into expensive arrangements which might be too hard on them. The message seems to be particularly significant for our time. No ostentation is allowed. The departed is to be laid to rest as quickly as possible; embalming is to be avoided unless the law requires it. Flowers need not be sent; the money can be used for charitable purposes in honor of the departed. It is the duty of all to perform the Mitzvah of *levayat hamet*, accompanying the dead on the last journey.

Funeral Service and Burial

The traditional service is simple: a psalm, a prayer, eulogy, Kaddish. Friends dig the grave. After a brief eulogy and prayer, they lower the coffin. Family and friends put the earth back. Thus does "the body return to the earth whence it came, as the spirit returns to God who gave it" (see Ecclesiastes 12:7). (Cremation is not permitted in traditional Judaism.) At the moment of their bitterest grief, the mourners tear their garments. This is often done symbolically by tearing a ribbon attached to the garment. (Judaism, in psychological insight, permits grief to be expressed freely rather than be bottled up to lead to neuroses later on.) Then the children recite the *Kaddish*. As they leave to return home they pass through the lines of their friends, who greet them with the words, "May God comfort you together with those who mourn for Zion and Jerusalem."

Mourning Rites

Upon their return the mourners receive their first meal as a gift of friends, lest, in their grief, they forget to sustain their bodies. For seven days, *Shivah*, they sit on low stools, receiving the consolations of their neighbors. A memorial light burns throughout this period, for "the soul of man is a light of God" (Proverbs

20:27). In Jewish traditional practice the house of mourning becomes a place of quiet gathering, where friends truly comfort the mourners in quiet rehearsal of the departed's virtues. During the days of Shivah, they gather for daily worship and in meditation on God's merciful justice. Grief is expressed—it must be given an outlet to restore people to healthy living—and the friendship of their fellows sustains the mourners.

On the Sabbath eve service during the Shivah, the mourners are received at the door of the synagogue by the rabbi with "May God comfort you . . ." (There is no mourning on the Sabbath, which is counted among the seven days.)

After thirty days, life must return to normal; the period of mourning is over. The one exception is the death of a parent, for whom mourning lasts a full year. Each morning and evening the children join the congregation in worship and recite the Kaddish for eleven months.

Funeral and mourning practices have been "modernized" in our time. A return to the simplicity of the Jewish funeral might be helpful to the bereaved and is in keeping with tradition. There is greatness in the uniformity of the Jewish service, its simplicity, the traditional robes for the dead, the wooden, closed casket covered by its black shroud. In simplicity lies nobility and the source from which comfort springs.

Tombstones

Mourners are advised not to visit the grave of their departed during the first year. Each visit may tear up wounds and prolong the healing process. Around the end of the year the tombstone is erected and dedicated in a short ceremony. Stones have been fashioned along the taste of the time. The older ones are entirely in Hebrew, giving the Hebrew names and extolling the virtues of the departed. Later ones have an inscription in the language of the land on the back. In more modern ones the inscription may be to a large degree or entirely in the language of the land. Two inscriptions are always found on Jewish tombstones: on top we find two Hebrew letters that state "here is buried" or "here is concealed." On the bottom we find five Hebrew letters, meaning "may his/her soul be bound up in the cluster of [eternal] life."

Yahrzeit

As the years pass, the anniversary of death is observed by the children. It is called *Yahrzeit* (from the German *Jahr*, "year," and *Zeit*, "time," meaning "anniversary"). A light is kindled for twenty-four hours. The children visit the grave of their parent and, on parting, place a small stone on the tombstone. In ancient days stone-hills marked the resting places of the dead, and each visitor placed a stone on them to maintain them. The custom has remained, though Jewish cemeteries now have regular tombstones. Children and friends thus leave their "visiting card."

They offer their prayers to God at the cemetery and throughout the day. In worship, meditation, and fasting they reflect upon the lives of their dear ones. By donations to good causes they seek to emulate their example of tzedakah (righteousness, charity). They hope that their lives reflect true honor upon those who brought them up.

The Kaddish

This is the meaning of the Kaddish, recited at the burial, during the year of mourning, and on Yahrzeit. It is not a prayer for the dead but an affirmation of faith, and as such is used in other parts of the service. How better can children demonstrate the faith and strength bequeathed unto them by their parents than by affirming God in the hour of their deepest loss? How better can they honor them than by declaring before the assembled congregation:

> "Magnified and sanctified be His Great Name throughout the world which He has created according to His will. May He establish His kingdom during your life and during your days and during the life of all the House of Israel. To this say ye Amen [so be it]."

And the people, uplifted by the faith of those who are bereaved, respond:

> "Amen. May His great Name be blessed for ever and ever."

The declaration of trust and praise continues, to conclude with the words:

> "May He who establishes peace in His universe, make peace for us also, and for all of Israel. To this say ye Amen."

And the people respond:

> "Amen."

In this prayer (likely a source of the Christian "Our Father") is enshrined the entire course of Jewish life, through days and seasons and years. The Kaddish is the motto of Jewish life: "Sanctification of the Name." It is appropriate that it conclude the lifetime of a Jew, linking it with those who follow.

VARIATIONS IN MOURNING PRACTICES

In Reform Judaism no special garments are required for the deceased and no special coffin is needed. The tearing of the garments or black ribbon is omitted. Cremation is permissible. Observance of the days of mourning is left to the individual. In non-Orthodox congregations women also recite the Kaddish. More important than the specific differences that characterize the various schools of thought and practice is the unity that undergirds Jewish life. A Jew who affirms and practices the traditions of the "denomination" to which he or she belongs is regarded as a faithful Jew.

CHAPTER 22

The Position of Women

CONTEMPORARY JEWISH WOMEN FACE TRADITION

CONTEMPORARY JUDAISM HAS witnessed the struggle of Jewish women for equal rights under religious law and life. These women insisted that gender cease to be a measure of evaluation. They claimed their right to equality as human beings and wished to be recognized by the yardstick of their inherent worth. They maintained that in Torah the position of the women was at times obscured, at times depreciated; to gain a glimpse of reality the interpreter had to pierce behind the cloud of the narrative. Thus, Torah needed a new and careful reading. This meant, in the words of Judith Plaskow, "standing again at Sinai" (also the title of one of her works).

WOMEN IN THE BIBLE

The Names of God

God has been invoked as a masculine deity. However, a careful reading of Torah permits a gender-neutral designation. God is One and Only, beyond and above sexual differences. Divine recognition actually may imply the equality of the sexes. It emphasizes the prowess of men and the wisdom and comforting presence of women. To warriors God is the "Man of War" (Exodus 15:3). For those in need of solace God says, "as a mother comforts her son, so will I comfort you" (Isaiah 66:13). Divine wisdom (Torah) is called "our sister" (Proverbs 7:4; Sota 11a). Dwelling with the people, God is spoken of as *Shekhinah*, "the indwelling," which is a feminine term.

Women in Biblical History

Israel emerged as a society for centuries torn by inner strife and exposed to wars of survival, even during its settled life on its land. Men thus had to take on a major burden in battle and women tended the home and children, maintaining the stability of society. The men's public exploits led to male dominance in public life, even after the reasons for it had disappeared: men were military leaders, priests, the teachers of Torah. Their power grew and, in the course of the centuries, gradually became consolidated. In biblical history women were accorded dependency on men, were temptresses of men, or were passed over.

Genesis contains two versions of the creation of woman. The first gives her full equality: "God created man in His image. . . . Male and female He created them" (Genesis 1:27). The second states that God created woman out of man's rib, "out of him," implying she derives her existence from him (Genesis 2:21–22). Tradition grounded itself on the second account. The Midrash held that Adam had a first wife, Lilith, who insisted on equal rights and was therefore banished to the end of the world where demons dwell (see Isaiah 34:14). From there she demonically roams the earth. Jewish feminists have seen her instead as a heroine worthy of emulation.

The position of the woman as subject to the man was reinforced by the judgment imposed by God on the first couple after their sin. When Adam and Eve sinned by eating from the forbidden fruit, Eve became the first scapegoat. Adam tries to excuse his actions by saying, "the woman You put at my side—she gave me and I ate" (Genesis 3:13). Eve's punishment is that "in pain shall you bear children. Yet your urge shall be for your husband, and he shall rule over you." Adam is cursed "because you heeded your wife [instead of God]" (Genesis 3:17). The ground for the relation of the sexes was thus laid.

The nomadic existence of the patriarchs in search of land and settlement and its hazards—wild beasts, raiders, attacks by enemy armies—called for an equal division of duties. Raising the herds and repelling these attacks was the task of men, who had to be ready at a moment's notice. Guiding the destiny of the clan was the prerogative of the women. It gave them great power, they exerted it with determination. When Abraham was asked "Where is your wife Sarah?" he answered, "There in the tent" (Genesis 18:9). This statement defined Sarah's status; in Abraham's eyes she was bound to the tent. However, we gain a new perspective when we regard "the tent" as the place of her authority. Perhaps Abraham too understood it in this manner. "In the tent," the mothers of Israel exercised a commanding power. When Sarah insisted that Ishmael, son of the concubine Hagar, be expelled as an unworthy companion to her own son Isaac, God instructed the unwilling Abraham, "Whatever Sarah tells you, do as she says" (Genesis 21:12). A principle had been established.

REBECCA decided that her son Jacob, not Esau, should receive his father Isaac's blessing. Isaac is blind (physically and spiritually), Rebecca far-sighted, and she prevails. RACHEL and LEAH, Jacob's wives, strategize how Jacob would depart from their oppressive father, Laban.

MIRIAM saved the life of her brother Moses by her presence of mind. In compliance with Pharaoh's inhuman decree that all Hebrew boys be killed, the baby was set adrift on the Nile. Miriam watched over him, and when he was discovered by the princess of Egypt, she persuaded her to have him taken to his own mother to be nursed and brought up (Exodus 2:1–10). When Israel was rescued at the Red Sea, the people sang a hymn to God. Miriam led the women (Exodus 15:20–21). At this occasion Torah explicitly calls her a "prophetess" (15:20). But when Miriam and Aaron later criticized Moses, claiming that God spoke to them as well, God expressed His indignation over this slander and presumption, for only Moses was granted God's immediate revelation. Miriam was afflicted with leprosy and was expelled from the community for the duration of her sickness; Aaron went free (Numbers 12:1–16).

DEBORAH served as a victorious general and judge of Israel for forty years (Judges 4–5). We are given her husband's name, thereby indicating his dominance. We find, however, that Barak, the general chosen by her, refused to lead the army unless she led the troops with him. She too sang a hymn of praise upon her victory, in which she pointedly states that the people had been in dire straits until she led as "a mother in Israel." Her motherlike courage and intuition rescued the people and brought peace.

Torah commanded "all males" to make pilgrimage to the central sanctuary three times a year (see Exodus 23:17; 34:24; Deuteronomy 16:16). HANNAH and the female members of the family joined Elkanah, the husband, because he permitted it. Hannah also entered the sanctuary of the Tent of Meeting. She taught Eli, the officiating priest, the meaning of silent prayer: "She spoke of her heart, only her lips moved but her voice was not heard" (1 Samuel 1:13). To Eli she seemed drunk, since silent pleas were unknown to him. But she was praying for a child; if God would give her a son, she would give him to God "all his life" (1 Samuel 1:11). Unlike Abraham, who was prepared to sacrifice Isaac, she would not sacrifice his life, but make it creative in the service of God. Mother love transcended Abraham's "fear of God." After the child, Samuel, had been granted her, she burst forth with a glorious hymn of praise.

Of HULDAH the prophetess we learn only by accident (2 Kings 22:14–20). She had given such distinguished leadership that the king turned to her for judgment concerning whether a book newly found in the recesses of the Temple was truly a divine revelation. By her ruling this book, namely Deuteronomy, came to be enshrined in Torah. It was a momentous decision of surely a great prophetess. We are however given no details about her prophetic activities or any of her speeches. Her husband's name is mentioned.

ESTHER, initially stands completely under the guidance of her guardian Mordecai, even after becoming queen (Esther 2:7). He tells her how she has to act in order to rescue her people (4:13). Esther risks her life for her people, and, by her own intelligence and superior diplomatic skill, saves the Jews. From now on Mordecai is no longer her tutor but her associate (8:7). She becomes his superior and benefactress. The institution of Purim and its rites rest on her ordinances; Mordecai is but her coworker (Esther 9:29).

In Proverbs (31:10–31) the praise of the "woman of valor" is sung. She is mistress of the house and an untiring contributor. She manages a home-industry and oversees her servants and workers with wisdom. A businesswoman with prudent foresight, "she sets her mind on an estate and acquires it . . . she sees that her business thrives." She attends to the cultivation of the land, and transacts her business in the marketplace, buying and selling her merchandise. She is wise, a loving parent and teacher to her children, and charitable to the poor. But she is not fully independent. She frees her husband from his burdens and allows him to be "prominent in the gates, as he sits among the elders of the land." But she cannot join these elders; her husband's praise is the yardstick and reward for her valor.

Women in the Assembly of Israel and the Laws of Torah

Women were included at Sinai and subsequent great historical convocations. At Sinai, God enjoins Moses to warn the people that they stay pure, abstain from sex, and wash their clothes (Exodus 19:10); Moses conveys the commandment to the people. He did not ordain that men and women not touch each other, but spoke to the men only saying, "do not go near a woman" (19:15).

Moses called the people together to enter the covenant "your tribal heads . . . all the men of Israel, your children, your wives . . ." (Deuteronomy 29:9–10). They all belong together, but a subtle distinction is made. The women, following "your children" are "your wives," they belong to the men.

After the return of the Jews from Babylonian exile, they are considered equals in intelligence and influence. Ezra convokes the people to hear the Torah read to the "men and women, all who could listen with understanding . . . he read from it . . . to the men and women and those who could understand" (Nehemiah 8:2–3). Then all of them solemnly committed themselves to the Torah. (Nehemiah 10:1–30). In the urgency of renewal the differences in status seem to have disappeared.

WOMEN AND THE LAWS OF TORAH

The laws of Torah distinguished women from men to the women's detriment. Polygamy was permitted. He could divorce her if he found something displeasing in her (Deuteronomy 24:1–4). She could not divorce him. A jealous man who suspected his wife of infidelity could force her to undergo the "divine test" of drinking the "bitter waters" (Numbers 5:11–31), which was a public humiliation.

Moses appears dubious and indecisive regarding the rights of women. When the daughters of Zelaphehad came to him claiming their father's inheritance, since he had no sons, Moses had no answer. Seeking divine judgment he was told that women were entitled to their inheritance—if there were no male heirs (Numbers 27:1–12).

Thus, in biblical and early postbiblical times we note a decreasing fluidity. Great women act—but stand under guardianship.

In the Days of the Second Temple

The second Temple, especially after its enlargement by Herod, had three courts: the court of women, the court of men, and the court of the priests. The court of women was the largest. Here the population mixed freely. When they offered sacrifices, they had to enter the court of priests, which may have included the women. On only one occasion was segregation put in effect. On the first day of Sukkot, water was offered at the altar in thanksgiving for this precious gift. As night fell an exuberant celebration with dancing and acrobatics was held in the Women's Court, the festival of water drawing. A "great need," namely levity among the spectators, led to an enactment of a rabbinical ordinance for this occasion only. A gallery was built for the women and the women shielded from men's gaze by a partition (M. Sukkot 4:9, 10, 5:1–4). This enactment was to become permanent in the synagogue.

In the Early Synagogue

Excavations in both Israel and the Diaspora have revealed that in the early synagogues men and women worshiped together without separation. We even find women holding the official title "head of synagogue" or "mother of synagogue." These may have been honorary titles but need not have been. They occupied seats of honor next to the Ark of the Torah. Women were both generous donors to the Temple and synagogues and leaders of congregations.

The Evolution of Halakhah

In early Halakhah women could perform religious functions. They were empowered to perform *shehitah* (B. Hulin 2a/b). They can no longer do so. In principle, women could be called to the Torah during worship and read a section from it to the congregation. Eventually this right was taken from them out of respect for the "dignity of the congregation" (B. Megillah 23a; Berakhot 20b). "Congregation" came to denote "men." There were men in the congregation who were incapable of reading from the Torah; they may have been disturbed finding a woman in "their congregation" who had greater knowledge than they did. The women had to be removed.

Women were and are bound to all Mitzvot of prohibition. This included all work prohibitions on the Sabbath and holy days. Women have to obey all prohibitions of forbidden food. They must comply with the prohibition of eating and drinking on Yom Kippur and other fast days. But women were released from Mitzvot of performance linked to certain times. Prayer is a Mitzvah of performance, but not linked to a certain time. Women are obligated to pray. According to Torah, the Sh'ma is to be recited in the evening and morning, it is linked to specific times. Women were released from it. This made sense (for instance, a nursing mother might not be able to say the Sh'ma at the ordained time). This dispensation did not mean that women were forbidden to perform these Mitzvot (see Rashi: B. Rosh Hashanah 33a).

Women were not obligated to hear the shofar on Rosh Hashanah, to shake the lulav on Sukkot, or hear the Megillah on Purim because all these are to be performed at specific times. Tradition holds however that they freely committed themselves to the performance of these commandments and remained bound by them. This reveals the once-existing fluidity of Jewish law under which women could assume these duties. Eventually, women were not merely relieved of time related Mitzvot of performance, they were forbidden to fulfill them. This included, among others, the wearing of tallit and tefillin. In Orthodox congregations they were forbidden to hold the Torah or dance with the Torah on Simhat Torah.[1] They could not be called to the Torah. Women have to kindle the Hanukkah lights, but only if there is no male person in the home to do so.

These issues are among those that have become matters of argument between traditionalists and contemporary women. In demanding equality these women have pointed to the historical fact that women can perform those obligations to which they commit themselves.

Studying Torah

Among the rights and duties denied women was the study of Torah, even though it was not linked to a specific time. It was held that Torah stated "teach them [the words of Torah] to your sons" [therefore, not your daughters] (Deuteronomy 11:19; B. Kiddushin 29b).

But the rabbis were not unanimous on this issue. Ben Azzai declared: "Every one is obligated to teach his daughter Torah." Rabbi Eliezer demurred, "He who teaches his daughter Torah teaches her lasciviousness" (M. Sota 3:4). Rabbi Haninah ben Teradyon taught his daughter Beruriah. The rabbi became one of the martyrs of Hadrian's persecution; he was burned at the stake. At the time of her father's execution Beruriah publicly affirmed God's greatness and love. Her father must have been proud of her during the last moments of his agonies (B. Avoda Zara 18a). Beruriah was skilled in halakhah and able to put her adversaries in place.

Beruriah was the wife of Rabbi Meir. She was able to comfort him at a moment of the couple's greatest trials. Their two sons died on a Sabbath afternoon, while Rabbi Meir was lecturing in the Bet Midrash. Beruriah did not tell her husband until he had come home at the end of the day and said farewell to the Sabbath in havdalah. She asked him, "a creditor came to demand the loan he has given us; do we have to return it?" "Naturally" replied Rabbi Meir. She said, "God who had loaned us our precious sons has come to claim them back for Himself." In his grief Rabbi Meir had been comforted by a woman who combined wisdom with empathy.

All Women Are "Temptresses" and Inferior

Rabbi Eliezer's opinion took hold. Women would use knowledge of Torah for seductive purposes. Woman was a temptress: her limbs, her voice, her hair were enticements (B. Berakhot 24a); to walk behind her, look at her, or talk to her exposed a man to temptation (Ber. 61 a/b).

In Temple days women had functioned as singers and musicians (1 Chronicles 25:5–6). The Psalmist had sung in the "processions of my God, my King, into the sanctuary, first come singers, then musicians, amid maidens playing timbrels" (Psalm 68:25–26). This was now out of question. Women had no active place in public worship.

The rabbis may have drawn on their own life. Many of them, as numerous episodes in the Talmud reveal, repeatedly had to fight against "Satan, the angel of death" of sexual temptation. They saw the power of *yetzer*, the "inclination toward evil," namely sexual temptation, as all-pervading. The righteous were more violently exposed to it. The fight against it was unending, and had to be renewed every day. The way to master the *yetzer* lay in the study of Torah. "Blessed . . . Israel, As long as they occupy themselves with Torah and good works the yetzer is in their hand not they in its" (B. Avoda Zara 5b). The Bet Midrash was the bastion against the yetzer. Women, by their very being tempting the purity of the men, could therefore not be admitted to its precinct. They could not study Torah. Their voices could not be heard in public. They had to be separated from the men and curtained off in the synagogue. They were restricted from wearing the ornaments of men, tallit and tefillin.

Eve's weakness of character and lack of judgment led to her curse, by which God placed her under man's rule and power. Men came to regard women as intellectually inferior and emotionally unstable. For this reason they could not be judges or, generally, be witnesses. They were their husband's helpers and he was their master and owner of their property. Only he, as we have seen, could give her a divorce. Their inferiority found expression in the traditional prayer book. It contains a benediction for men: "Blessed are You, God . . . who has not made me a woman." [2]

The deterioration of the Jewish woman's position may also have been caused by the impact of Christianity and Islam. In these religions the position of woman was equally inferior, if not more so, for the Jewish husbands generally surrounded their wives with dignity. Under Rabbenu Gershom's ordinance, for instance, polygamy was prohibited. Also in accordance with Rabbenu Gershom's rulings a Jewish husband could not divorce his wife against her will. Under Islamic law, polygamy was permitted and the husband could divorce his wife against her will.

Why Women Submitted

Why did women accept this inferior status for so many centuries and still accept it in Orthodox Jewry today? There may be several reasons. They believed with a firm faith that their place had been ordained to them by God. In place of the man's prayer they prayed: "Blessed . . . who has made me according to His will." In spite of their negative observations about women, the rabbis held their wives in high respect, and strongly counseled all the men to hold their wives in esteem.

> Rabbi Helbo used to say: A man must always be careful showing respect to his wife, for blessing is found in the man's home only on account of his wife, as it is said, "and God treated Abraham well on account of her" (Genesis 12:16). For this reason, Rava said to the people of Mahuza: Defer to your wives that you may prosper (B. Baba Metzia 59a).

The rabbis ascribed to women a greater sensitivity toward God's will. The wife came to be the ruler in the home and the primary influence in the upbringing of the young children. The women saw this as an equitable distribution of functions; they insisted on their rights in the home and gloried in their responsibilities. Perhaps they also realized that their husbands were frequently humiliated in the marketplace, and they wished to give them a sense of importance and power at home. In this manner, they preserved their husbands' self-respect. Many women had to become active in business, to permit their husbands undisturbed time to study Torah.

WOMEN FASHION A SPIRITUAL LIFE

Women came to fashion their own forms of religious life. In the ancient synagogue of Worms a small window was cut into the wall that separated the women from the men. Here stood a woman, a "fore-singer," who repeated the prayers she heard for her sisters. They had their own supplementary prayer books, *Tehines*, supplications, written in Yiddish. Following their text, the women expressed their thoughts and emotions in deeply personal and moving prayers. They prayed for their husbands and children, as they prepared the Sabbath meal, kindled the Sabbath lights, emerged from the mikveh, gave birth and faced death. A simple Torah commentary, with explanations and midrashim, called *Tzene-Rene*, Go out and See (Yiddish after: T'ze-enah ur-enah, "Go forth, and see, you daughters of Israel") (Song of Songs 3:11) accompanied them through the weeks of the year.

Generally, their Hebrew education was minimal. Some could read Hebrew, others had merely learned the basics of keeping a kosher Jewish home from their mothers. They attended the synagogue when their duties at home permitted it. They embroidered the curtains of the Ark and Torah mantles, finding profound satisfaction in this holy work that followed the example set by their ancestresses at the building of the Tent of Meeting in the desert (Exodus 35:25–26).

In Eastern Europe their lot became harder. The economic conditions for the Jews grew ever worse. The men spent their days in the yeshivah; studying the Talmud was their vocation. The women had to take hold of business and the livelihood for their family. They became businesswomen, toiling for pittances. At the same time they had to bring up the children and do the household chores. These women became worn and bitter. From Western Europe we possess the memoirs of the Glückel von Hameln. She was an exceptional woman, who bore her husband fourteen children and then became a widow and faced the trials of life by her own strength. Her memoirs reveal a good education and Jewish knowledge, deep piety, steadfastness in submission to God—and business acumen.

WOMEN ON THE MOVE

The Emancipation led to changes in the life of Western European Jewry. Business now lay entirely in the hands of the men, some of whom became very wealthy. Their wives had to learn to serve as gracious hostesses for Jews and

Christians. They became interested in general culture and came together to study and discuss the events in the world and in Judaism. They began to strive for equality within the Jewish faith. The women's movement began.

Orthodox Ordinances

The changes resulting from the Emancipation in Western Europe did not originate exclusively from non-Orthodox Jewry. Orthodoxy also saw the need for them. Several decisions are cited here.

In 1828 the strictly Orthodox Chief Rabbi Nathan Adler of Oldenburg, ordained equal elementary Jewish education in Hebrew, Bible and prayer for boys and girls. He also demanded the regular attendance at worship for both sexes. Rabbi Israel Meir Ha-Kahen (1838–1933), one of the great talmudic authorities of Eastern Europe, called "Hafetz Hayim" after his major work, permitted the teaching of Talmud to women. His ruling was accepted and implemented in the Orthodox girls' schools (Bet Yaakov Schools) in Israel. In the 1920s women desired to be represented on the boards of Jewish congregations. Rabbi Anton Nehemia Nobel at Frankfurt, an outstanding Orthodox rabbi and great talmudist, recognized the benefits women could bring to the governance of Jewish organizations. He ruled that halakhically women could run for office, saying "Frankfurt could have waited—Eretz Yisrael cannot." The first Orthodox woman joined the Board of the Frankfurt congregation. Nobel's vision was confirmed when Golda Meir became Prime Minister of Israel. But in *shul* she still remained relegated to the women's gallery. The Israeli rabbinate has not followed Rabbi Nobel's ruling.

Women As Leaders in the World and the Jewish Community

Beginning in the nineteenth century and accelerating in the twentieth, Jewish women joined their non-Jewish sisters to do battle for the franchise and equal rights. General society responded slowly to the ethical imperative of women's equality. The Jewish community lacked behind. Gradually, women were able to organize Ladies' Auxiliaries in congregations, found spokeswomen, and created women's federations, such as the National Council of Jewish Women in the United States. Numerous Jewish women, individually, made a mark for themselves in Jewish and general life. A few examples will have to suffice.

REBECCA GRATZ (1781–1869) became the founder of the Jewish Sunday School movement. EMMA LAZARUS (1849–1887) regularly went out to witness the arrival of Eastern European Jewish immigrants, "yearning to breathe free," who streamed into the port of New York. On this experience she wrote her poem, affixed to the Statue of Liberty.

The experience of RAY FRANK (1865–1948) was typically American. A journalist on assignment at Spokane, Washington (1890), she found that the Jews of the city had made no arrangements for services during the forthcoming High Holy Days. She encouraged them by promising them to give the sermons during the services, and used her sermons to motivate them to organize a permanent congregation. Without this first woman "rabbi," the Jews might have drifted and the founding of the congregation been postponed.

HENRIETTA SZOLD (1860–1945) combined intellectual achievement and motherly sensitivity, organizational ability and a loving heart. A rabbi's daughter, she studied for several semesters as an associate student at the Jewish Theological Seminary. Then she became executive secretary of the Jewish Publication Society, evaluating manuscripts for their worth. Inspired by Zionism, she founded Hadassah, the Women's Zionist Organization of America. Under Szold's leadership these American Jewish women undertook the creation of a modern medical establishment in Israel, and set up its medical school and hospitals. Finally, Szold organized the Youth Aliyah which brought thousands of Jewish children out of Nazi Germany to Israel. Szold refused to take second place in the synagogue. A fatherly friend offered to say Kaddish for her departed mother, since there were no sons, who, under halakhah, could do so. She graciously turned him down. She was going to say Kaddish herself.

Subsequently, more and more Jewish women rose to distinction in the world, some by virtue of their achievements became spokespersons for Judaism, such as the author CYNTHIA OZIK. Others moved into the forefront of the women's movement, as did BETTY FRIEDAN and GLORIA STEINEM.

In religious life, the Jewish women remained second-class members. They found the berakhah, mentioned above, discriminatory. They noted that the blessing invoked on the congregation on Sabbath days reads: "May He who has blessed our fathers Abraham, Isaac, and Jacob bless this holy congregation . . . them and their wives, sons and daughters . . ." It spoke of men only as "congregation"; their wives and children were appended to them. This permeated all worship and exegesis.

The Holocaust

The Holocaust revealed the urgency of granting women their full and equal share in Jewish life and learning. The irreplaceable losses the Jewish people had suffered called for a mustering of all resources the Jewish people could muster. The gifts of half of the Jewish community, the women, could no longer be wasted.

DEMANDS, ACHIEVEMENTS, AND CHALLENGES

The women essentially called for the fulfillment of certain basic requirements: restoration of those rights women had held under original halakhah, reinterpretation or abolition of those halakhic elements that were obviously derogatory to women and their rights, reformulation of the text in the prayer book, and the right to study Torah and Talmud and to complete their study with ordination. They asked for the right to be judges and deciders of Jewish law. Ultimately, they insisted on a new Jewish theology, resting on a new reading of Torah.

Progress was easier in non-Orthodox Judaism. Orthodoxy offered determined opposition. But even in Orthodox congregations women obtained the right to study Torah, based on the ruling of the "Hafetz Hayim." Against rabbinical opposition, they began to hold their own women's services, without men and within the confines of basic halakhah. Non-Orthodox Jewry has moved faster and with great determination. It began with the abolition of the women's gallery. Other changes followed: the right to be counted in the minyan and be called to the Torah; the right to wear tallit and tefillin, the right to be ordained as rabbis and cantors. Conservative Judaism instituted changes in the laws of divorce and Agunah. The adjustments in the prayer book are difficult to make. Its Hebrew language is old and venerable. Changes will involve incisive changes. A beginning has been made with the English text, for which gender-neutral forms are being found.

To the Jewish feminists these have been worthwhile beginnings, but much has yet to be done. So far, certain "rights" have been "granted." Essentially, these rights exist and need not be granted. Fundamentally, the theological and halakhic structure of Judaism has to be so transformed. *Klal Yisrael*, the community of Israel, will have to understand itself and live as an organic community of equal men and women.

Wherever women have attained equality with men, they have had to prove themselves. They have had to show that they were better than men in order to be regarded as equals. This attitude of the males is receding. Women have assumed a heavy responsibility: doing traditionally male work and being mothers. But already they have brought great intellectual gifts and a new spirituality and sensitivity into the Jewish religious life.

Their considerable if not complete success constitutes a new stage in the unfolding of Judaism, perhaps a watershed in its evolution, holding the promise of spiritual and societal benefits.

Notes

1. The explanation sometimes heard that women may not touch the Torah on account of their ritual impurity during *niddah* is incorrect.

2. The explanation is sometimes given that men give thanks only for the privilege of being permitted to perform more Mitzvot than women.

Chapter 23

Retrospect and Prospect

Jews, as individuals and as a people, are both exceptional and unexceptional. The liturgy of Sabbath afternoon reflects this: "Is there like Your *people* Israel any other *earth-tribe* on earth?" The Hebrew word used for "people," *Am*, emphasizes the exceptional in a people; the term used for *earth-tribe* (a translation adapted from Martin Buber) is *Goy*. This term is often used colloquially by Jews in reference to non-Jews; here it is applied to Jews, denoting their character as an unexceptional family of people among other unexceptional families.

AMERICAN JEWS AS "GOY"

Jews share the characteristics of average people: their strengths and their weaknesses, their joys and their sorrows. Some Jews are bright, others are average. Some are wealthy, others are very poor, even in America. Some belong to the management of corporations and institutions of higher learning, others are union members.

Jews have lived in America ever since colonial days. They have fully and wholeheartedly identified with the United States ever since its inception. In war and peace they have borne the burdens and obligations of our country's call with patriotism. There are also conscientious objectors and social rebels among them.

Jews exhibit the varieties of political and social ideas and affiliations of their neighbors. They have been affiliated with both the Republican and Democratic parties and have held high offices there. The social and economic status and the lifestyle of many Jews might suggest a greater affinity with the Republican Party. This has not been the case and may have its roots in the fact that the emancipation of the Jews was the result of liberal thinking in political theory and practical implementation by progressive states. Of course, the political affiliation of Jews may change at any time.

Generally, Jews have been free to move both economically and socially. They have moved into the suburbs. Most of their children go to college. Among the young generation, reared as equals in society, many have regarded religious barriers as minor, as have their non-Jewish contemporaries. As a consequence

405

interfaith marriages have greatly increased. Conversions to Judaism have also reached an all-time high. Common religion can give families unity and greater cohesion. We also find parents of different faiths who bring up their children as Jews.

Jews are a minority, a very small minority, and their birthrate is lower than that of the general population. Therein lies the risk that the Jewish community may lose the political clout related to voting strength. Their current strength as voters is the result of their being congregated in large cities and states that frequently hold the balance. Their minority position may have been for the Jews one of the challenges leading to intellectual achievement. They have felt that recognition can come only from the ideas and values they produce. They have felt that they have to excel. Jewish contributions in the fields of religion, ethics, literature, the sciences, the arts, and politics has been greater than the proportion of their numerical strength. Their commitment to social justice and social welfare has earned them respect. Their rapid economic rise was admired, or at least grudgingly respected; at times it was resented. American Jews are secure. Elements of prejudice exist in society, but can be dealt with. However, a minority is never totally without anxieties.

Individually, Jews are neither altogether intelligent nor rich nor ethically outstanding. As it would be an error to stereotype them to their disadvantage, it would also be unjustified to do so to their advantage. The individual Jew shares all the weaknesses and shortcomings of the rest of the human race, stands in need of the same forbearance on the part of neighbors that all human beings can claim and is entitled to it. In turn, the Jew is duty bound to accord this forbearance to non-Jews.

JEWS AS "AM"—THE NEED TO RESTORE THE COVENANT

"Am Yisrael Hai" has been the Jewish affirmation throughout the ages. I found it clumsily scratched in the base of the Arch of Titus at Rome, a monument of antiquity celebrating the emperor's victory over the Jews in 70 C.E. Defilement of monuments upsets me deeply, but this one moved me. It affirmed, 1,900 years after Titus had destroyed the Temple, that "The Jewish people in its uniqueness lives."

Jews are exceptional by the very fact of their survival. The events of the twentieth century, especially the Holocaust and the restoration of the State of Israel, testify to this fact. These events have seared history, heritage, and kinship into the very being of the Jew.

The Holocaust surpassed Titus's barbarism in extent and savagery. Designed to bring about the total annihilation of the Jews, it was scientifically organized and carried out with cold efficiency. Yet it failed. However, almost every American Jew has learned of the extermination from immediate members of their family, if they themselves do not bear its personal scars, and the pain of having lost dear ones. The twentieth century also witnessed the rebirth of the State of Israel. There are hardly any Jews at all who have not been uplifted in spirit by this resurrection, following utter devastation, and have not been involved in the destiny of the new Jewish commonwealth.

These two events have so deeply gripped Jewish emotions that for large segments of Jewry they have become the ground of their Jewish affirmation. They are the root of ethnic avowal and the spark of unparalleled generosity. American Jews have sacrificially promoted the upbuilding of Israel and the rescue of persecuted or endangered Jews worldwide. American Jewry has admirably met its historical task of being the sustainer, deliverer, and defender of Jews throughout the world.

The imperatives emerging from the Holocaust and Israel have motivated the assistance given the Jews in the former Soviet Union after its dissolution. Jewry has shouldered the burdens of relocating and acculturating the emigrating Russian Jews in Israel and throughout the world. It has brought Jewish institutions, books, rabbis, and teachers to Russia, to aid and guide those Jews who choose to remain in Russia. It has kept a watchful eye on the leaders and people in the former Soviet Union, to make sure that the full rights of these Jews be neither abrogated nor in any way endangered.

But the Holocaust and Israel are insufficient as ultimate grounds for Jewish survival. With subsequent generations the Holocaust will recede into history and by its very unnatural brutality become ever more difficult to grasp. The relationship between the Jewish state and World Jewry may change in the course of time. Unquestionably, World Jewry will always be intimately bonded to Israel. But the state may no longer find its help indispensable for its survival and development. Predictions regarding Israel's ideologic, political, and economic developments are premature. The compelling need for complete identification of Diaspora Jewry with Israel may come under discussion. Whether or not these developments will occur is not the issue. The issue is that they can be seen as potentials. Jews, therefore, have to look beyond these rationales for survival and find an unchanging one.

Jewish thinkers have called for a renewal of the Covenant as foundation of Jewish affirmation and life. This includes the centrality of God and Torah, the acknowledgment of Israel's chosenness in service to humanity, and a return to Mitzvot. It also includes the eternal remembrance of the martyrs of the Shoah and close links to the Jewish state of Israel. But it envisions Jews who see the world through their Judaism, rather than seeing Judaism as an appendage to their worldview. This affirmation will form the immutable bedrock of Jewish endurance. Its attainment will be difficult. It calls for education and commitment.

ON THE JEWISH CONDITION

Most contemporary Jews, both young and old, lack an adequate knowledge of their heritage and fall short of practicing it in their life. Earnest attempts to instill these are being made by all denominations in Judaism. The day-school movement is growing, new materials for adults and children are being published, camps and institutes are spreading, and experiments in new forms of worship are going on. Means are being sought to strengthen meaningful family observances, as-the family is the core of Jewish life. Many families have organized *haburot* (fellowships) dedicated to study, joint worship, mutual support, and life in Jewish heritage. The study of Hebrew has expanded due to the impact of Israel and pilgrimage to Israel has come to be regarded as essential by many American Jews. Some have even made Aliyah.

The availability of college courses in Judaism has motivated many to study Torah in an atmosphere that permits challenge and criticism and includes both Jews and Christians among the students. Many young Jews have turned from the nominally religious Judaism of past generations and have committed themselves to a return to Jewish learning, *halakhah*, Jewish values, and Jewish social action. Under the impact of the Chabad movement a small but significant number of Jews has returned to Orthodoxy. Among them are highly educated, "modern" Jews. All these movements wish to offer a positive resistance to a materialistic society. These Jews wish to recapture their inner autonomy by living an authentic and creative Jewish life. For those comparatively few who migrate to Israel, this step has a transforming significance: It makes them "normal," by making them into members of a majority as Jews.

Israel, in addition to being the fulfillment of Jewish prayers and hopes, has normalized the position of American and world Jews. No longer are they members of a strange group calling themselves a people and yet lacking a basic characteristic of normal nationhood, an independent country of their own. The establishment of the State of Israel remedied this situation; vicariously, it normalized Jews. Even the shortcomings of the State contributed to this normalization.

Repeatedly threatened with extermination, standing deserted in the face of overpowering enemies, Israel appealed to world Jewry for assistance. Jewry responded and, in doing so, came to feel its bonds with the Land. Even marginal Jews derive from its existence a new spirit of self-assurance and pride. Apart from its theological significance for Judaism, which has been pointed out, Israel, through fruitful exchange of ideas with the Diaspora, serves the spiritual and cultural evolution of Judaism.

American Jews, like many concerned non-Jewish Americans, feel that Israel is important for the United States. The three peace accords between Israel and its antagonists, Egypt, Jordan, and the PLO, were sealed under the moderating presence of Presidents Carter, Bush, and Clinton. It is hoped that Israel, America's trustworthy ally in democracy and a technologically leading country in the Middle East, will cause the whole region to flourish through cooperation. Jews trust that a true peace between Jews and Arabs will soon become a reality. They hope that it will not merely be organizational but will develop into friendly relationships with Arab states and neighborliness between individuals. Jews also desire to share with Islam the insights Muslim religion and Judaism have to offer each other.

OUTSIDE PRESSURES

The French philosopher Jean Paul Sartre once claimed that anti-Semitism has been the cause of Jewish coherence and survival. Jews do not agree that an outside force is their source of cohesion. It may have to be admitted however that it contributed to it. Anti-Semitism by the radical left and radical right has indeed brought American and world Jewry together in common concern.

Radical nationalism has grown in many lands and poses grave dangers. The fall of 1993 witnessed the armed insurrection of hard-core communists in Russia bent on the overthrow of democracy. Had they succeeded they would have initiated pogroms. In following election campaigns a demagogic leader evoked frightening memories of Hitler. In other countries such as France and Italy the ultra-nationalists also made inroads; the governments have taken action. The former Yugoslavia has been torn by wars initiated by leaders committed to "ethnic cleansing." Terrorism has remained a grave threat, even in the United States. The United States has declared Iran a terrorist state. In Israel, Hamas, a religiously motivated militant Islamic group dedicated to the eradication of Israel, kept the population under terrorist attacks. Ultra-Orthodox Jewish settlers, who regarded the surrender of any territory as forbidden by Torah, responded by force of arms.

Neo-Nazi movements, including the skinheads, have disrupted societal peace in many countries. In Germany they engaged in murder and arson. They set fire to a synagogue and to the Sachsenhausen concentration camp, that had been dedicated as a memorial to the Holocaust. Radical groups, resting their claim on the publications of "revisionist historians" have spread the calumny that the Holocaust never actually happened but was a cunning invention of the Jews. Their ideology has found only a very limited echo among average citizens. The national elections of 1998 in Germany brought these radicals a resounding defeat.

It should be stressed that anti-Semitism is so marginal in America that it poses no real threat to the Jewish community. But Jews, seared by the tragedies in the twentieth century, have come to be extremely sensitive. They get deeply upset by graffiti on buildings and defacements of monuments even if these are the wanton acts by delinquent youths, expressing no ideology. Jews have been particularly grieved to find anti-Semitism among minorities, above all blacks. Jews have felt that minorities have to make common cause with each other, and fight for the rights of all. Jews have done that. Essentially, Jew hatred symptomizes the weakening of abiding values in society. Their strengthening has become a first priority for America, to which all Americans have to dedicate themselves. This has been attempted by the fundamentalist Christian Right. Its members are friendly to the Jews. Actually, numerous Jews share many of the values of conservative Christians. But the movement has also filled Jews with certain apprehensions. They are concerned with the missionary activities among Jews. They are also fearful that the endeavor of certain fundamentalist groups to place state and society under the "Lordship of Jesus Christ," might *de facto* reduce Jews to second-class citizenship. American Jews have welcomed all legislation strengthening religious liberty.

THE CHALLENGE OF THE FUTURE

Jewry is thus reaching out in many directions, past and future, in America, the rest of the Diaspora, and in Israel. It strives toward self-realization and dialogue with other faiths, in thought and action. It is *Am* and it is *Goy*. It is unique.

Its cohesion is based ideally on both religious and communal association. As the people of the Covenant, Jews have to establish this synthesis. Historically we note that as one form of association undergoes stresses, the other makes itself felt more strongly. The nineteenth century saw emphasis placed on religion, leading to the evolution of Judaism; the twentieth century has witnessed an unparalleled reemergence of the spirit of communality at a time when religion was in need of reevaluation in the light of historical events.

Communality may in a sense be seen as religion, living theology. Strengthened by the Holocaust in their will to survive, Jews have embraced their faith and ethnicity in order not to give Hitler his "posthumous victory," as Fackenheim termed it. During World War II other nations were subjected to violent destruction. Their cities and populations were devastated. But their destruction, as for instance in the cases of Hiroshima, Nagasaki, and Dresden, was perceived as a "strategic necessity." There existed no such necessity in regard to the Jews. They were exterminated simply because they were Jews. As long as there is a vestige of belief among any person that Jews "deserve" to be homeless and oppressed, the world has not fully recognized its human obligation. It is still in the grip of ancient fanaticism that annihilates human beings exclusively for what they are, their "ethnicity" or "race." Hitler-like extermination for the sake of "ethnic cleansing" in the former Yugoslavia and in some African countries is the crime against God and humanity.

Jews are concerned not only for themselves but for the world, for its humanity. This means that a vibrant Jewish life in Israel and the Diaspora is vital. By bringing forth life out of death, victory out of utter defeat, the Jews performed a task for all humankind. Therefore they see meaningful dialogue between people of all faiths, backgrounds, races, and nationalities as imperative for humanity's future. Humanity is the only answer to the Holocaust.

Judaism as religion is essential, Judaism as communality is essential, the memory of the Holocaust and the inspiration of Israel are essential. But they must be synthesized to form one organic whole. This is the Covenant.

By living as the people of the Covenant, the Jews can offer the challenge of true humanity to the entire world. They can be "a light unto the nations." The Jews thus become and will remain *Am Olam*, the eternal people, and a people of and for the entire world, for all humanity.

Av, ninth of—fast day mourning the fall of the Temple of Jerusalem both in 586 B.C.E. and in 70 C.E.

Averah—transgression, sin.

Adonai—the Lord, speaking of God; replaces the tetragrammaton, *YHVH,* which is not pronounced by Jews.

Aggadah—the Story; term for the homiletic portions of the Talmud, containing legends, parables, and ethics.

Alenu—concluding prayer of worship, named after its first word: "*upon us* rests the duty to render praise."

Aliyah—going up; migration of Diaspora Jews to Israel; also being called up to speak the blessing over the Torah at its reading.

Almemor—elevated reading desk for the Torah in center of the synagogue; see also **Bimah.**

Amen—see **emunah.**

Amidah—prayer of affirmation and petition recited three times daily while standing.

Amora (pl. *Amoraim*)—masters of the Gemara in Palestine and Babylonia (approx. 200–500 C.E.).

Apocrypha—books of semi-sacred character excluded from the canon of Hebrew Scriptures.

Ashkenazim—inhabitants of *Ashkenas,* supposedly meaning *Germany;* Jews living in Germany, France, England, and later in Poland and Russia during a large part of their history who developed a set of identifying religious practices and customs. Most American Jews are Ashkenazim.

Baal Shem—master of the (Divine) Name; the name given to the founder of Hasidism (Jewish mysticism) in Poland.

Bar Mitzvah—son of Mitzvah, responsible for its fulfillment. A boy reaches this stage at the age of thirteen, when a ceremony underscores his passage from childhood to adult membership in the Jewish community.

Bat Mitzvah—daughter of Mitzvah, responsible for its fulfillment. A ceremony of recent origin underscores this passage of girls at the age of twelve from childhood to adult membership in the Jewish community.

B.C.E.—Before the Common Era; designates dates preceding the Christian era.

Berakhah—benediction, blessing, praise; the unit of prayer.

Bet Am—house of the people; *Bet Hakneset*—house of assembly. Both are terms for "synagogue."

Bet Din—rabbinical court, adjudicating cases arising from religious law (**Halakhah**).

Bet Midrash—house of higher Jewish studies.

Bimah—pulpit from which Torah is read to the people; used also for "chancel" in the synagogue; see also **Almemor.**

B'nai B'rith—sons of the Covenant; worldwide fraternal order, founded in America.

B'rit—Covenant. God made a Covenant with nature, humanity, Israel. God never abrogates his Covenant, even when the partners fail to live up to it.

B'rit Milah—covenant of circumcision or act of circumcision.

C.E.—Common Era; designates dates of the Christian era.

Chabad—worldwide organization of Lubavitcher Hasidim.

Cheder—(school) room; primary school for Hebrew study in the Eastern European education system.

Conservatism, Conservative Judaism—Jewish denomination based on tradition but believing in the evolution of "positive historical Judaism" by the people's consent; Conservative Judaism endeavors to adapt Jewish law to modern conditions by means of reinterpretation.

Covenant—see **B'rit.**

Diaspora—the dispersion or scattering of the Jews; also the Jewish community outside Israel.

Dietary laws—laws based on Torah governing food permitted and forbidden to Jews.

Ecumenical—worldwide; a movement toward Christian unity but also taking into account Judaism and other non-Christian religions. The ecumenical spirit between Christians and Jews has grown, especially since the Second Vatican Council, which concluded in 1965.

El—name of God, in Jewish tradition emphasizing God's attribute of justice. The Canaanites of antiquity used this term to designate one of their deities.

Elohim—pl. *El*, but always used with a singular verb; the One God as Sum of all power and justice.

Emancipation—elimination of civic disabilities of Jews by modern states, requiring Jewish adjustment to Western culture.

Emunah—faithfulness, trust; God's faithfulness at all times and conditions calls for humanity's trust in Him. The word *Amen* has the same root; it is an affirmation of trust, literally, "so it shall be."

Eretz Yisrael—Land of Israel.

Eschatology—discourse about the last things, dealing with the end of days, ultimate judgment, and so on.

Etrog—citron; one of the four plants used in worship on **Sukkot.**

Existentialism—a philosophy and theology encompassing various schools. Instead of asking about the essence, the universal features of all things; existentialism asks: What must I, as a concrete human being, accept and believe, in order that my life will be authentic and have meaning? Existentialism calls for the individual human decision that has to be made by each person and has to be made anew in every situation. The religious existentialist hears the voice of God, revealing Himself out of God's grace and love; the individual then responds. Since science cannot offer proof of the truths arrived at existentially and individually, the individual must take the leap into faith, to God. But without this belief his life might be meaningless and desperate. Jewish theologians, such as Franz Rosenzweig and Martin Buber, developed Jewish existentialism. Emil Fackenheim writes that the issue of Auschwitz calls for an existential answer affirming God, else Jewish existence would not be bearable.

Galut—exile; life outside the Land of Israel, in oppression.

Gaon—excellency, title of the head of academy in Babylonia.

Gedaliah, Fast of—fast day immediately after Rosh Hashanah, named for the Jewish governor of Palestine murdered by his fellow Jews at the time of destruction of the first Temple (2 Kings 25; Jeremiah 40:1).

Gehinnom—purgatory.

Geiger, Abraham—one of the founders of Reform Judaism in Germany (1810–1874).

Gemara—record of extensive discussion of the rabbis, based on the **Mishnah.** Mishnah and Gemara together complete the **Talmud,** the compendium of learning.

Get—writ of divorcement required under Jewish law.

Haftarah—portion of Prophets appointed to be read after the reading of Torah on holy days and special occasions.

Haggadah—text used at the celebration of the Passover Seder (see also **Aggadah**).

Halakhah—the path of life; law and the legal decisions of developers of Jewish law, guiding life and its activities; core of traditional observance.

Hallah—loaf of bread set on the table on Sabbath and holy days; after a blessing, thanking God for its gift, the family partakes of it.

Hallel—Psalms 113–118; psalms of thanksgiving recited on holy days of joy.

Halutz—(pl. *Halutzim*) Jewish pioneer(s) in the Land of Israel.

Hametz—leaven, and all items made with it, which must be removed from the house during Passover.

Hanukkah—midwinter festival of eight days, commemorating the reconsecration of the Temple after the victorious uprising of the Maccabees in behalf of religious freedom.

Hanukkah—nine-branched candlestick (or oil lamp) used on Hanukkah; see also **Menorah.**

Hasidism—mystical movement at various periods of Jewish life, particularly that founded by Rabbi Israel Baal Shem in Poland (1700–1760); in modern days the movement has been explored by Martin Buber and Gershom Scholem.

Hasidei Ashkenas—medieval mystical movement centering in Germany.

Haskalah—enlightenment movement among Jews in Central and Eastern Europe.

Hasmon—founder of the House of Hasmonaeans, the family of the Maccabees (see **Maccabees**).

Havdalah—prayer of separation of the Sabbath and holy days from the days of the week.

Havurah—fellowship of Jews for joint creative worship and mutual support; accords equality to women.

Hazzan—cantor, musically trained singer and leader of worship; today also frequently in charge of education.

Hazzanit—woman trained and serving as **Hazzan**.

Herzl, Theodor—founder of political Zionism (1860–1904).

Het—sin; "missing the mark" of God-ordained performance in life.

Hillel (first name)—one of the greatest among the Pharisaic masters and known for his graciousness and love of humanity. His opinions became **halakhah.**

Hillel Foundations—Jewish student foundation at universities named after Hillel. They are a division of the **B'nai B'rith.**

Hokhmah—wisdom. Divine wisdom, *sophia* in Greek, is equated in scriptural "wisdom books" and ancient Jewish philosophy with Torah.

Holocaust—genocide of the Jews carried out by the Nazis.

Huppah—the canopy under which the couple stands during the wedding ceremony, symbolically beginning their life under a common roof.

Kabbalah—tradition; specifically the mystical tradition in Judaism.

Kaddish—call to sanctification of God's Name with congregational response, expressing the hope that "His kingdom come." Used in worship and also recited by mourners as evidence of their faith in God; possibly the source of the Christian "Our Father who art in heaven."

Kahal—congregation; also communal organization of Eastern European Jewry.

Kaplan, Mordecai M.—Jewish theologian (1881–1983), founder of **Reconstructionism.**

Kashrut—kosher laws.

Kavanah—attunement of the heart to God in prayer and Mitzvot.

Kedushah—*sanctification* of God in public worship; "Kadosh, kadosh, kadosh . . . holy, holy, holy is the Lord of Hosts . . ." (Isaiah 6:3).

Ketuvah—marriage contract, setting forth the duties of the husband toward his wife.

Ketuvim—collected writings; third part of the Tanakh, including Psalms, Job, and so on, and also Daniel.

Kibbutz—cooperative settlement in modern Israel, whose settlers hold all property in common.

Kiddush—the sanctification of the Sabbath and holy days over a cup of wine; part of the traditional Sabbath and holy day observance.

Kiddush Ha-Shem—sanctification of God's Name, martyrdom in behalf of the Jewish faith.

Kiddushin—the sanctification of married life, namely, the marriage ceremony; a "setting apart."

K'lal Israel—the union of Israel, the Jewish people as a whole; used specifically in terms of religious unity.

Knesset—assembly; also name of the parliament of Israel.

Kol Nidre—declaration opening the service on the eve of Yom Kippur, and giving it its name, known for its haunting melody.

Kos—cup, from *kosas*, "to measure out." In Kiddush, Havdalah, and the wedding ceremony (during which bride and groom share the cup) it becomes the symbol of the destiny measured out by God for man and woman.

Kosher—all right, fit, proper; designation given to foods and other items signifying that they are usable under Jewish law; the term has entered general American usage standing for right, proper.

Lubavith—modern Hasidim movement (see **Chabad**)

Lulav—palm branch, one of the four plants used in worship on Sukkot.

Maariv—evening prayer.

Maccabees—priestly family who led the Jews to independence in the war against the Syrians (167 B.C.E.). Its descendants became high priests and kings (see **Hanukkah**).

Magen David—shield of David; the six-pointed star; a symbol of Judaism. It had to be worn on a yellow badge by Jews under the Nazi oppression. It is part of the Israeli flag.

Mahzor—prayer book for the festivals.

Maimonides, Moses—leading medieval Jewish philosopher, theologian, and codifier of Jewish law (1135–1204).

Makom—place; a name of God who encompasses every place and all time.

Malakh—messenger, angel.

Maror—bitter herbs eaten at the Passover Seder in commemoration of the bitterness of Egyptian slavery.

Maskil—member of **Haskalah,** the Enlightenment.

Masorah—tradition; Masoretes are the establishers and preservers of the traditional version of Holy Scriptures.

Matzah—unleavened bread; "the bread of affliction" and of deliverance, eaten at Passover instead of leavened bread.

Mazel tov—expression meaning "congratulations," "good luck" (*Mazel* means "star" or "constellation"; *Mazel tov*, "may the constellation be good!").

Megillah—scroll; specifically the Scroll of Esther, read on **Purim.**

Mehitzah—wall, or grating separating the women from the men's view.

Mendelssohn, Moses—philosopher; father of Western-oriented, modern Jewry (1729–1786).

Menorah—candelabrum; seven-branched menorah used in the Temple; the symbol of Judaism and coat of arms of the State of Israel. A nine-branched menorah is used on Hanukkah.

Messiah—the anointed one; the human ruler who is forecast for the end of days to bring peace to humanity and to rule over the perfect society.

Mezuzah—a small scroll containing selections of Scripture, including the **Sh'ma,** placed on the doorposts of Jewish homes.

Midrash—search for meaning; homiletic commentary on the Scriptures; also applied to individual exegetic portions.

Mikveh—the ritual bath primarily used to ritually purify women after their menstrual period; also used for immersion of converts.

Minhag—custom, practice (pl. *minhagim*).

Minhah—afternoon prayer.

Minyan—the quorum of ten needed for public worship.

Mishnah—review; the interpretations of Torah passed along by word of mouth (Oral Torah) and finally codified c. 200 C.E. (see **Talmud**).

Mitnagged—(pl. *Mitnaggedim*) opponents of Hasidism.

Mitzvah—commandment (pl. *Mitzvot*). Mitzvah is God's command, both religious and ethical. It is also the Jew's response to the divine call by way of action.

Mohel—a pious man who performs the act of circumcision.

Mussaf—additional service on Sabbath and holy days reflecting the significance of these days and commemorating the sacrificial service at the Temple of old.

Ne'eelah—the closing service on Yom Kippur.

Negev—southern part of the Land of Israel.

Nevee-im—(sg. *Navee*) prophets; the Books of the Prophets, second part of the Tanakh.

Neo-Orthodoxy—Western-oriented orthodoxy (see **Orthodoxy**).

New Covenant—Christianity.

Niddah—a woman maritally "separated" during the menstrual period.

Olam haba—the world to come; *Olam hazeh*—this world.

Oneg Shabbat—the delight of the Sabbath; also used for communal Sabbath celebrations outside formal worship.

Orthodoxy—traditional form of Judaism, believing in the literal truth of Torah and its absolute historicity, and the binding force of Halakhah as promulgated by ancient and later sages of Torah.

Pale—area in Russia where Jews were permitted to reside during the period of the Russian Empire.

Pentateuch—the Five Books of Moses; first part of the Tanakh.

Pessah (Passover)—festival of spring and rebirth marking Israel's freedom from Egyptian bondage.

Pharisees—sect of ancient Judaism; heirs and transmitters of the high ethical standards of the prophetic ideals; interpreters and molders of Jewish law (Oral Torah), holding Oral Torah to have been revealed at Sinai together with written Torah; believers in immortality of the soul, freedom of will, divine providence, the existence of angels, and the resurrection of the dead. Frequently misjudged in history, they are acknowledged as the masters of Judaism and revered for their sincerity of heart and soul.

Pilgrim Festivals—Pessah, Shavuot, and Sukkot, when Torah ordained pilgrimage to the national sanctuary.

Pilpul—a method of hairsplitting dialectic in the study of Talmud.

Piyutim—liturgical poems.

Proseuche—early term for the synagogue building where religious gatherings were held.

Purim—carnival-like spring feast, commemorating the liberation of Jews from extermination in ancient Persia, as related in the Book of Esther, which is read on this day.

Rabban—title of the head of the Sanhedrin in the period of the Talmud.

Rabbi—teacher; the ordained spiritual leader of a congregation. Rabbi is a "degree" obtained in America after approximately five years of postgraduate study in a Jewish theological school. Traditional ordination empowers a rabbi to hand down authoritative decisions on religious law, based on Halakhah.

Rashi—foremost commentator on Bible and Talmud (1040–1105).

Rav—master, title of the Amoraim, also applied to great rabbinic scholars.

Reconstructionism—religious movement founded by Mordecai Kaplan; explains Judaism as the creation of the Jewish people, defining it as an evolving religious civilization, and the Jewish people's ultimate concern with ethical nationhood. Reconstructionism utilizes scientific insights as tools for interpreting Judaism and sees in it a way to meet the societal issues of our time. It calls upon the American Jew to live in two civilizations, American and Jewish.

Reform—liberal movement based on the scientific study of religion. It seeks to make Judaism relevant to modern times. It does not regard Halakhah as divinely grounded and leaves its observance to the conscience of the individual. In recent years Reform has become increasingly more traditional, emphasizing the spirit of K'lal Israel.

Responsum (Hebrew, *Teshuvah*)—halakhic decision by a rabbi in response— *Teshuvah*—to an individual inquiry, often establishing a precedence case.

Rosh Hashanah—New Year's Day, an autumn festival; the beginning of a ten-day period of penitence.

Sadducees—sect of Conservatives in the period of the second Temple, centering around the priesthood (the descendant of Zadok, who anointed Solomon, hence the name Sadducees) and concerned with the perpetuation of Temple worship. Antagonists of the Pharisees, the Sadducees denied the validity of Oral Torah, the immortality of soul, resurrection, angels, and divine providence; some became worldly.

Sanhedrin—the Jewish Supreme Court and lawmaking body in the times of the Temple; administrators of the law.

Seder—order; the order of the family service at Passover.

Sefardim—Jews whose ancestors lived in Spain; now primarily Jews in Mediterranean countries, who developed their own customs in the course of history.

Sefardim constitute a significant element in Israel. Sefardic Jews have established congregations in America.

Sefer Torah—the Scroll of the Torah, containing the Five Books of Moses.

Sefirot—the ten emanations of God according the Jewish mysticism.

Selihot—prayers of forgiveness, especially those during the penitential period.

Shavuot—Feast of Weeks (seven weeks after Passover), commemorating the giving of the Torah at Mount Sinai.

Shaddai—name of God, who is with the Jews wherever they are; found on the Mezuzah.

Shaharit—morning prayer.

Shalom—peace; also name of God meaning absolute perfection, peace being perfection (root of the word); greeting between the people in the State of Israel.

Shamash—server, name for the beadle in the synagogue; also used for the serving candle in the Hanukkah menorah used to light the others.

Shehitah—slaughter of animals in accordance with Jewish dietary law.

Shekhinah—name for God, dwelling within His world, resting in the midst of the people.

Sh'ma—the first word of the affirmation of faith: "Hear, O Israel, the Lord our God, the Lord is One" (Deuteronomy 6:4–9, and also including Deuteronomy 11:13–21, Numbers 15:37–41), hence standing for the whole affirmation.

Sh'mini Atzeret—eighth day of the Sukkot festival.

Shevarim—a three-times broken sound on the shofar, signifying the sobbing of a contrite heart.

Shivah—seven days of mourning after the death of a close relative.

Shoah—Holocaust; Nazi extermination of six million Jews.

Shofar—ram's horn; sounded on Rosh Hashanah, the month preceding it, and at the end of Yom Kippur.

Shohet—man trained in Jewish law who slaughters animals in accordance with ritual requirements.

Shtetl—small, wholly Jewish Eastern European town surrounded by a non-Jewish world; developed its own way of life and its own culture.

Shul—the school; popular name for "synagogue," testifying to its character as a place of instruction.

Shulhan Arukh—"The Well-Prepared Table," written by Joseph Karo and published in 1565; the authoritative code for Orthodox Jewish practice.

Siddur—the prayer book.

Simhat Torah—Rejoicing in Torah; final day of the Sukkot festival, when the cycle of the annual Torah reading is completed and the new one begun; celebrated with joyful processions and dance.

Sukkah—a small hut or booth covered by branches and leaves in which the family takes its meals during the Sukkot festival.

Sukkot—fall festival of thanksgiving for the blessing of the harvest and protection.

Synagogue—building where the congregation meets for prayer, study, and assembly; formerly used to mean the congregation itself.

Tallit—a four-cornered garment with tassels (*tzitzit*) on it, worn to serve as a constant reminder of the presence of God; traditionally worn by the male members of the congregation during morning worship and by the leader of worship at all services; frequently in the form of a "prayer shawl." In non-Orthodox Judaism worn by women as well.

Talmud—"The Compendium of Learning" consisting of Mishnah and Gemara. Two versions of the Talmud, one in Palestine, the other in Babylonia. The latter, completed about 500 C.E., is the basic source for Jewish law and codes.

Tanna (pl. *Tannaim*)—the teachers who speak in the Mishnah.

Tanakh—abbreviation for Hebrew Holy Scriptures, arrived at by combining the first letters of the three sections that constitute them: Torah, Nevee-im, Ketuvim.

Tashlikh—"You will hurl all their sins into the depth of the sea" (Mikah 7:18–22), prayer hymn recited on Rosh Hashanah on the banks of rivers or lakes.

Tefillah—prayer.

Tefillin—phylacteries; small cubes containing scrolls with several scriptural selections, including the Sh'ma (Deuteronomy 6:4–9, 11:13–21; Exodus 13:1, 11). Scrolls and containers made of parchment are worn by men during the morning service on weekdays, placed on the forehead and left arm by means of attached leather bands. In non-Orthodox Judaism they are worn by women as well.

Tehillim—praises; Hebrew term for "psalms."

Tekiah—a long-drawn sound on the shofar "awakening the slumbering conscience."

Tereah—torn, referring to animals that are therefore not usable as food; term is generally used for food that is not kosher.

Teruah—a whimpering, nine-times-broken sound on the shofar; the weeping of a heart aware of its sinfulness.

Teshuvah—return to God; repentance.

Torah—instruction; specifically, the divinely revealed instruction of Holy Scriptures. Used to designate the Five Books of Moses (Genesis, Exodus, Leviticus, Numbers, and Deuteronomy), the first part of the Tanakh; used in wider connotation as Tanakh as a whole. In a still wider sense it includes written and Oral Torah, the whole body of authoritative teaching and instruction and its evolving tradition. Also term for the Scroll from which the scriptural portion is read publicly.

Tosafot—additions, written by Rashi's successors during the twelfth and thirteenth centuries in France to explain his commentary on the Talmud.

Tosefta—collection of material of the mishnaic period, not in the Mishnah.

Tzaddik—a righteous person; in Hasidism the master of a Hassidic group.

Tzedakah—righteousness; used as term for charity.

Tzitzit—the tassels on the four-cornered robe, the Tallit.

Yahrzeit—anniversary of the death of a family member.

Yamim Noraim—Days of Awe; Rosh Hashanah, Yom Kippur, a time of repentance.

Yeshivah—academy of advanced talmudic studies.

Yetzer—the drive, inclination: *Yetzer Ha-Tov:* inclination toward good; *Yetzer Ha-Ra:* drive toward evil.

YHVH—name of God, pronounced "Adonai," a substitute term for the unfathomable Name.

Yiddish—basically a medieval German having undergone its own development as the spoken language of Ashkenazic Jewry, including additions from other languages; used by Ashkenazic Jews throughout the world.

Yishuv—the Jewish settlement in the Land of Israel.

Yizkor—memorial service for the departed and the martyrs, held on Yom Kippur and the festivals.

Yom Kippur—Day of Atonement.

Zaddik—pronounced "Tzaddik" (see **Tzaddik**).

Zion—hill in Jerusalem, location of David's castle. In a wider sense, Temple, Jerusalem as a whole, or even all the Land.

Zionism—a movement to obtain a Jewish state and life center in Palestine. The founder of political Zionism was Theodor Herzl.

Zohar—*The Book of Splendor* (thirteenth century), a mystical commentary on the Torah, the primary work of the Kabbalah.

BIBLIOGRAPHY

This bibliography is offered merely to provide the next step for the interested reader.

UAHC stands for the Union of American Hebrew Congregations. JPS is the abbreviation for the Jewish Publication Society of America.

INTRODUCTION TO JUDAISM; JEWISH IDEAS

Baeck, Leo, *The Essence of Judaism.* New York: Schocken, 1961.

———, *This People Israel: The Meaning of Jewish Existence.* New York: Holt, Rinehart and Winston, 1964

Buber, Martin, *Israel and the World.* New York: Schocken, 1948.

———, *On Judaism.* New York: Schocken, 1972.

Cohn-Sherbok, *The Jewish Faith,* Valley Forge, Penn.: Trinity Press, 1993.

Finkelstein, Louis (ed.), *The Jews: Their History, Culture, and Religion,* 3 vols. New York: Schocken, 1970–1971.

Herberg, Will, *Judaism and Modem Man.* New York, Atheneum, 1970.

Heschel, Abraham J., *God in Search of Man: A Philosophy of Judaism.* Philadelphia: JPS, 1954.

Kaplan, Mordecai M., *Judaism As a Civilization.* New York: Schocken, 1967.

———, *The Meaning of God in Modern Jewish Religion.* New York: Jewish Reconstructionist Press, 1962.

Neusner, Jacob, *The Way of Torah: An Introduction to Judaism,* Encino: Dickenson, 1974.

Roth, Cecil (ed.), *Encyclopedia Judaica,* 16 vols. Jerusalem: Keter, 1971.

———, *The Standard Jewish Encyclopedia.* New York: Doubleday, 1959.

Steinberg, Milton, *Basic Judaism.* New York: Harcourt Brace, 1947.

Telushkin, Joseph, *Jewish Literacy,* New York: Morrow, 1991.

Trepp, Leo, *A History of The Jewish Experience: Eternal Faith, Eternal People.* New York: Behrman, 1973.

Wigoder, Geoffrey (ed.), *The Encyclopedia of Judaism.* New York: Macmillan, 1989.

HISTORY

Bamberger, Bernard J., *The Story of Judaism*. New York: Schocken, 1970.

Barnavi, Eli, *A Historical Atlas of the Jewish People*. New York: Knopf, 1992.

Ben-Sasson, H. H. (ed.), *A History of the Jewish People*. Cambridge, Mass.: Harvard University Press, 1976.

Eban, Abba, *My People—The Story of the Jew*. New York: Random House, 1978.

Flannery, Edward H., *The Anguish of the Jews: Twenty-three Centuries of Anti-Semitism*. New York: Macmillan, 1965.

Grayzel, Solomon, *A History of the Jews*. Philadelphia: JPS, 1985.

Gubbay, Lucian and Abraham Levy, *The Sephardim—Their Glorious Tradition from the Bablonian Exile to the Present Day*. Philadelphia: JPS, 1992.

Johnson, Paul, *A History of the Jews*. New York: Harper & Row, 1987.

Margolis, Max L., and Alexander Marx, *History of the Jewish People*. Philadelphia: JPS, 1927; New York: Meridian Books, 1960.

Parkes, James, *A History of the Jewish People*. Baltimore: Penguin, 1969.

Potok, Chaim, *Wanderings*. New York: Random House, 1978.

Stillman, Norman A., *Jews of Arab Lands*. Philadelphia: JPS, 1979.

Waxman, Meyer, *A History of Jewish Literature*. New York: Yosseloff, 1960.

BIBLE AND THE BIBLICAL PERIOD

The Holy Scriptures (standard translation). Philadelphia: JPS, 1917.

TANAKH, The Holy Scriptures (standard translation of the Tanakh, revised). Philadelphia: JPS, 1962–1985.

The JPS Torah Commentary, 5 volumes. Philadelphia: JPS, 1990ff.

Albright, William F., *The Archaeology of Palestine*. New York: Pelican, 1949cf.

———, *From the Stone Age to Christianity: Monotheism and the Historical Process*. Garden City, New York: Doubleday, 1959.

———, *The Biblical Period from Abraham to Ezra*. New York: Harper & Row, 1963.

Alt, Albrecht, *Essays on Old Testament History and Religion*. Garden City, New York: Doubleday, 1967.

Alter, Robert, and Frank Kermode, *The Literacy Guide to the Bible*, Cambridge, Mass.: Harvard University Press, 1987.

Bamberger, Bernard J., *The Bible: A Modern Jewish Approach*, 2nd ed. New York: Schocken, 1963.

Bickerman, Elias, *From Ezra to the Last of the Maccabees: Foundations of Postbiblical Judaism*. New York: Schocken, 1962.

Bright, John, *A History of Israel*. Philadelphia: Westminster, 1972.

Buber, Martin, *Kingship of God*. New York: Harper & Row, 1972.

———, *Moses: The Revelation and The Covenant*. New York: Harper & Row, 1958.

———, *The Prophetic Faith*. New York: Harper & Row, 1960.

———, *On the Bible*. New York: Schocken, 1968.

Cross, Frank, *Canaanite Myth and Hebrew Epic*. Cambridge, Mass.: Harvard University Press, 1973.

Glatzer, Nahum N. (ed.), *The Dimensions of Job*. New York: Schocken, 1969.

Greenberg, Moshe, *Studies in the Bible and Jewish Thought*. Philadelphia: JPS, 1998.

Heschel, Abraham, *The Prophets*. Philadelphia: JPS, 1962.

Josephus, Flavius, *The Jewish War*. Baltimore: Penguin, 1970.

Kaufmann, Yehezkel, *The Religion of Israel from Its Beginnings to the Babylonian Exile*. Chicago: Chicago University Press, 1960.

———, *History of the Religion of Israel: From the Babylonian Captivity to the End of Prophecy*. New York: Ktav, 1978.

Kittel, Rudolph, *Great Men and Movements in Israel*. New York: Ktav, 1968.

Noth, Martin, *The History of Israel*. New York: Harper & Row, 1960.

Orlinsky, Harry M., *Ancient Israel*. Ithaca and London: Cornell University Press, 1971.

Sandmel, Samuel, *The Hebrew Scriptures: An Introduction*. New York: Knopf, 1962.

Sarna, Nahum M. *Understanding Genesis*. New York: Schocken, 1966.

———, *Exploring Exodus*. New York: Schocken, 1996.

———, *Songs of the Heart, An Introduction to the Book of Psalms*. New York: Schocken, 1992.

Vriezen, Th. C., *The Religion of Ancient Israel*. Philadelphia: Westminster, 1967.

Zeitlin, Solomon. *The Rise and Fall of the Judean State*, Philadelphia: JPS, 1962–78.

POSTBIBLICAL AND TALMUDIC PERIODS

Baeck, Leo, *The Pharisees and Other Essays*. New York: Schocken, 1947.

Baron, Salo and Joseph L. Blau, *Judaism in the Post-Biblical and Talmudic Period*. New York: Liberal Arts Press, 1954.

Bickerman, Elias, *The Jews in the Greek Age*, Cambridge, Mass.: Harvard University Press, 1992.

Gaster, Theodor H., *The Dead Sea Scriptures*. New York: Doubleday Anchor, 1957.

Hanson, Paul D., *The Dawn of Apocalyptic*. Philadelphia: Fortress Press, 1975.

Josephus, Flavius, *The Jewish War*. Baltimore: Penguin, 1959.

Neusner, Jacob, *From Politics to Piety: The Emergence of Pharisaic Judaism*. Englewood Cliffs, NJ: Prentice Hall, 1973.

———, *Rabbinic Judaism: Historical Studies in Religion, Literature, and Art*. Leiden: Brill, 1975.

———, *The Study of Ancient Judaism*. 2 vols, New York: Ktav, 1981.

Russell, David S., *The Method and Message of Jewish Apocalyptic*. Philadelphia: Westminster, 1964.

Saldarini, Anthony J., *Pharisees, Scribes and Sadduccees in Palestinian Society*. Edinburgh: T & T Clark, 1989.

Sandmel, Samuel, *Philo of Alexandria*. New York: Oxford University Press, 1978.

Schuerer, Emil, *History of the Jewish People in the Time of Jesus*. New York: Schocken, 1961.

Stone, Michael, *Scriptures, Sects and Vision: A Profile of Judaism from Ezra to the Jewish Revolts*. Philadelphia: Fortress Press, 1980.

Strack, Herman L., *Introduction to the Talmud and Midrash*. Philadelphia: JPS, 1959; New York: Meridian Books, 1959.

Yadin, Yigael, *Masada*. New York: Random House, 1966.

CHRISTIANITY

Baeck, Leo, *Judaism and Christianity*. New York: Atheneum, 1970.

Buber, Martin, *Two Types of Faith*. New York: Harper & Row Torchbook, 1961.

Carmichael, Joel, *The Death of Jesus*. New York: Macmillan, 1962.

Cohen, Arthur H. , *The Myth of the Judeo-Christian Tradition*. New York: Schocken, 1971.

Davies, Alan T. *Anti-Semitism and the Foundations of Christianity*. New York: Paulist Press, 1979.

Eckardt, Roy A., *Elder and Younger Brothers—The Encounter of Jews and Christians*. New York: Schocken, 1973.

Flannery, Edward H., *The Anguish of the Jews*. New York: Macmillan, 1965.

Gilbert, Arthur, *The Vatican Council and the Jews*. Cleveland and New York: World Publishing, 1968.

Isaac, Jules, *The Teaching of Contempt: Christian Roots of Anti-Semitism*. New York: Holt, Rinehart and Winston, 1964.

Klausner, Joseph, *Jesus of Nazareth*. New York: Macmillan, 1953.

————, *From Jesus to Paul*, New York: Humanities Press, 1956; Boston: Beacon Press, 1961.

Klein, Charlotte, *Anti-Judaism in Christian Theology*. Philadelphia: Fortress Press, 1978.

Levine, Lee I., *The Galilee in Later Antiquity*. Cambridge, Mass.: Harvard University Press, 1992.

Maccoby, Hyam, *Judaism on Trial—Jewish Christian Disputations in the Middle Ages*. London: Littman, 1993

Neusner, Jacob, *Rabbinic Literature and the New Testament*. Valley Forge: Trinity Press, 1993.

Parkes, James, *The Conflict of the Church and the Synagogue*. Philadelphia: JPS, 1969.

————, *Prelude to Dialogue: Jewish Christian Relationship*. New York: Schocken, 1969.

Rubenstein, Richard L., *My Brother Paul*. New York: Harper & Row, 1972.

Ruether, Rosemary Radford, *Faith and Fratricide: The Theological Roots of Anti-Semitism*. New York: Seabury Press, 1974.

Sanders, E. P., *Paul and Palestinian Judaism*. Philadelphia: Fortress Press, 1977.

Sandmel, Samuel, *Anti-Semitism in the New Testament*. Philadelphia: Fortress Press, 1978.

————, *The Genius of Paul*. New York: Farrar, Strauss, 1958; Boston: Beacon Press, 1961.

———, *A Jewish Understanding of the New Testament.* Cincinnati: Hebrew Union College Press, 1957.

———. *Judaism and Christian Beginnings.* New York: Oxford University Press, 1978.

———, *We Jews and Jesus.* New York: Oxford University Press, 1965.

Werner, Eric, *The Sacred Bridge, Liturgical Parallels in Synagogue and Early Church.* New York: Schocken, 1970.

Segal, Alan F., *Rebecca's Children, Judaism and Christianity in the Roman World.* Cambridge, Mass.: Harvard University Press, 1986.

Simon, Marcel, *Versus Israel—A Study of the Relations between Christians and Jews in the Roman Empire AD 135–425.* London: Littman, 1996.

Stendahl, Krister, *Paul among Jews and Gentiles.* Philadelphia: Fortress Press, 1976.

Van Buren, Paul, *Discerning the Way, A Theology of the Christian-Jewish Reality.* 3 vols. New York: Seabury Press, 1980.

Vermes, Geza, *Jesus the Jew: A Historical Reading of the Gospels.* London, Collins, 1973.

Wistrich, Robert S., *Antisemitism—The Longest Hatred.* New York: Schocken, 1994.

Zeitlin, Solomon, *Who Crucified Jesus?* New York: Bloch, 1964.

TALMUD—CLASSIC TEXTS

Alon, Gedaliah, *The Jews in Their Land in the Talmudic Age.* Cambridge, Mass.: Harvard University Press, 1989.

Bialik, Hayim Nahman and Yehoshua Hana Ravnitzky (eds.) *The Book of Legends/ Sefer Ha-Aggadah.* New York: Schocken, 1993.

Bin Gorion, *Mimekor Yisrael, Classical Jewish Folktales,* 2 vols. Bloomington, Ind.: Indiana University Press, 1990, 1991.

Cohen, A., *Everyman's Talmud.* New York: Schocken, 1975.

Ginzberg, Louis, *The Legends of the Jews.* Philadelphia: JPS, 1909–1938.

———, *The Legends of the Jews* (abbreviated). Philadelphia, JPS, 1961.

Goldin, Judah (ed.), *The Living Talmud: The Wisdom of the Fathers.* New York: Mentor, 1957

Holtz, Barry W., *Back to the Sources, Reading the Classic Jewish Texts.* New York and Philadelphia: Summit and JPS, 1984.

Kadushin, Max, *The Rabbinic Mind.* New York: Blaisdell, 1965.

Katz, Michael and Gershom Schwartz, *Swimming in the Sea of Talmud—Lessons for Everyday Living.* Philadelphia: JPS, 1998.

Klagsbrun, Francine, *Voices of Wisdom.* Philadelphia, JPS, 1980.

Levinas, Emanuel, *Nine Talmudic Readings.* trans. Annette Aronowicz. Bloomington: Indiana University Press, 1990.

Montefiore, C. G. and Loewe H. (eds.), *A Rabbinic Anthology.* New York: Schocken, 1974.

Moore, George Foot, *Judaism in the First Centuries of the Christian Era: The Age of the Tannaim.* 2 vols. New York: Schocken, 1971.

Neusner, Jacob, *Invitation to the Talmud: A Teaching Book*. New York: Harper & Row, 1973.

———, *There We sat Down: Talmudic Judaism in the Making*. Nashville: Abingdon Press, 1972.

———, *Major Trends in Formative Judaism, Society and Symbol in Political Crisis*. Chico, Calif.: Scholars Press, 1983.

———, *What Is Midrash?* Philadelphia: Fortress Press, 1987.

———, *The Study of Ancient Judaism: Vol. 1: Mishnah, Siddur; Vol. 2: The Palestinian and Babylonian Talmud*. New York: Ktav, 1981; Atlanta: Scholars Press, 1992.

———, *The Talmud of Babylon: An American Translation*. (Jacob Neusner and Tzevee Zahavy, trans.). Atlanta: Scholars Press, translation ongoing.

Safrai, Shmuel, *The Literature of the Sages. First Part: Oral Torah, Mishnah Tosefta, Talmud, External Tractates*. Assen, Netherlands: von Gorcum, 1987.

Steinsalz, Adin, *The Essential Talmud*. New York: Basic Books, 1974.

———, *The Babylonian Talmud Translation and Commentary*. New York: Random House, ongoing.

Stone, Ira F., *Reading Levinas/Reading Talmud—An Introduction*. Philadelphia: JPS, 1998.

Travers-Herford, *The Ethics of the Talmud: Sayings of the Fathers*. New York: Schocken, 1969.

———, *The Pharisees*. Boston: Beacon Press, 1962.

Urbach, Ephraim E., *The Sages: Their Concepts and Beliefs*. Cambridge, Mass.: Harvard University Press, 1987.

MEDIEVAL AND MODERN PERIODS

"Jewish" Middle Ages

Abrahams, Israel, *Jewish Life in the Middle Ages*. Philadelphia: JPS, 1960.

Ashtor, Eliyahu, *The Jews of Moslem Spain*. Philadelphia: JPS, 1973–79.

Baer, Yitshak, *A History of the Jews of Christian Spain*. Philadelphia: JPS, 1961.

Dawidowicz, Lucy (ed.), *The Golden Tradition—Jewish Life and Thought in Eastern Europe*. New York: Schocken, 1990.

Foxbrunner, Roman A., *Habad, The Hasidim of R. Shneur Zalman of Lyady*. Tuscaloosa, Ala.: University of Alabama Press, 1992.

Goitein, S. D., *Jews and Arabs: Their Contacts through the Ages*. New York: Schocken, 1964.

Gubbayl, Lucien and Abraham Levy, *The Sephardim—Their Glorious Tradition from the Babylonian Exile to the Present Day*. Philadelphia: JPS, 1991.

Katz, Jacob, *Exclusiveness and Tolerance*. New York: Schocken, 1962.

———, *Tradition and Crisis—Jewish Society at the End of the Middle Ages*. New York: Schocken, 1994.

Marcus, Jacob R., *The Jew in the Medieval World*. New York: UAHC, 1938; Meridian Books, 1960.

Scholem, Gershom, *The Messianic Idea in Judaism*. New York: Schocken, 1971.

————, *Sabbatai Sevi: The Mystical Messiah 1626–1676*. Princeton: Princeton University Press, 1973.

Schwarz, Leo. *Great Ages and Ideas of the Jewish People*. New York: Random House, 1956.

Shulvass, Moses A., *Jewish Culture in Eastern Europe: The Classical Period*. New York: Ktav, 1975.

Stern, Selma, *Josel of Rosheim: Commander of Jewry in the Holy Roman Empire of the German Nation*. Philadelphia: JPS, 1965.

Stillman, Norman A. *The Jews of Arab Lands*. Philadelphia: JPS, 1949.

————, *The Jews of Arab Lands in Modern Times*, Philadelphia: JPS, 1991.

Stow, Kenneth, *Alienated Minority, the Jews of Medieval Latin Europe*. Cambridge, Mass.: Harvard University Press, 1992

von Hameln, Glückel, *The Memoirs of Glückel von Hameln*. New York: Schocken, 1977.

Weinryb, Bernard D., *The Jews of Poland: A Social and Economic History of the Jewish Community of Poland from 1100–1800*. Philadelphia: JPS, 1973.

Werblowsky, Zwi, *Joseph Karo*. Philadelphia: JPS, 1977.

Emancipation and Modern Period

Altmann, Alexander, *Moses Mendelssohn, A Biographical Study*. London: Littman, 1998.

Baron, Salo W., *The Russian Jews under Tsar and Soviets*. New York: Macmillan, 1975.

Dawidowicz, Lucy, *What Is the Use of Jewish History?* New York: Schocken, 1992.

Gay, Ruth, *The Jews of Germany, a Historical Portrait*. Philadelphia: JPS, 1992.

Glatzer, Nahum N., *The Dynamics of Emancipation*. Boston: Beacon Press, 1965.

Himmelfarb, Milton, *The Jews of Modernity*. Philadelphia: JPS, 1973.

Hirsch, Samson Rapheal, *Nineteen Letters on Judaism*. New York: Feldheim, 1960.

Katz, Jacob, *From Prejudice to Destruction–Anti-Semitism, 1700–1933*. Cambridge, Mass.: Harvard University Press, 1982.

Manuel, Frank, *The Broken Staff, Judaism through Christian Eyes*. Cambridge, Mass.: Harvard University Press, 1992.

Mendes-Flohr, R. Pau and Jehudah Reinharz, *The Jew in the Modern World*. New York: Oxford University Press, 1980.

Richarz, Monica, *Jewish Life in Germany, Memoirs from Three Centuries*. Bloomington: Indiana University Press, 1992.

Sachar, Howard M., *The Course of Modern Jewish History*. New York: Dell, 1964.

Yerushalmi, Yosef Hayim, *Zakhor—Jewish History and Jewish Memory*. Seattle: University of Washington Press, 1982.

JEWISH PHILOSOPHY AND THEOLOGY

Bokser, Ben Zion (trans.), *Abraham Isaac Kook—The Lights of Penitence, Lights of Holiness, The Moral Principles, Essays, Letters, and Poems*. New York: Paulist Press, 1978.

Borowitz, Eugene B., *Renewing the Covenant, A Theology for the Postmodern Jew.* Philadelphia: JPS, 1993.

———, *How Can a Jew Speak of Faith Today?* Philadelphia: Westminster, 1969.

———, *A New Jewish Theology in the Making.* Philadelphia: Westminster, 1968.

Buber, Martin, *I and Thou.* Edinburgh: T & T Clark, 1937.

———, *Eclipse of God.* New York: Harper & Brothers, 1952.

———, *Between Man and Man.* New York: Macmillan, 1948.

Cohen, Arthur A., *The Natural and Supernatural Jew: A Historical and Theological Introduction.* New York: McGraw-Hill, 1962.

Cohen, Hermann, *Religion of Reason out of the Sources of Judaism.* New York: Frederick Ungar Publishing, 1972.

Fackenheim, Emil L., *God's Presence in History.* New York: New York University Press, 1970.

———, *To Mend the World.* New York: Schocken, 1982.

———, *Encounters between Judaism and Modern Philosophy.* Philadelphia: JPS, 1973.

Gillman, Neil, *Sacred Fragments, Recovering Theology for the Modern Jew.* Philadelphia: JPS, 1990.

Glatzer, Nahum N., *Franz Rosenzweig, His Life and Thought.* Philadelphia: JPS, 1953.

Greenberg, Irving, *The Third Great Cycle in Jewish History.* New York: National Jewish Resource Center, 1981.

———, *Voluntary Covenant.* New York: National Jewish Research Center, 1982.

Guttman, Julius, *Philosophies of Judaism: The History of Jewish Philosophy from Biblical Times to Franz Rosenzweig.* New York: Schocken, 1973.

Haam, Ahad, *Selected Essays of Ahad Haam.* Philadelphia: JPS, 1936.

Halevi, Judah, *The Kuzari: An Argument for the Faith of Israel.* New York: Schocken, 1964.

Heschel, Abraham J., *God in Search of Man.* Philadelphia: JPS, 1956.

———, *Man Is Not Alone.* Philadelphia: JPS, 1951.

———, *The Insecurity of Freedom.* New York: Farrar, Straus & Giroux, 1966.

———, *Israel, an Echo of Eternity.* New York: Farrar, Straus & Giroux, 1969.

———, *Between God and Man: An Interpretation of Judaism. Selections from the Writings of Abraham J. Heschel,* edited by Fritz A. Rothschild. New York: The Free Press, 1959.

Husik, Isaac, *A History of Medieval Jewish Philosophy.* Philadelphia: JPS, 1958.

Jacobs, Louis, *A Jewish Theology.* New York: Behrman, 1973.

———, *Jewish Ethics, Philosophy and Mysticism.* New York: Behrman, 1969.

Kaplan, Mordecai M., *The Future of the American Jew.* New York: Macmillan, 1948.

———, *Judaism As a Civilization.* New York: Reconstructionist Press, 1957.

———, *The Meaning of God in Modern Jewish Religion.* New York: The Jewish Reconstructionist Foundation, 1937.

Kaufman, William E., *Contemporary Jewish Philosophies.* New York: Reconstructionist Press & Behrman House, 1956.

Kohler, Kaufmann, *Jewish Theology.* Cincinnati: Riverdale Press, 1943.

Levi, Hans, Alexander Altmann, and Isaac Heinemann (eds.), *Three Jewish Phi-*

losophers—*The Essential Texts and Doctrine: Philo—Saadya Gaon—Jehudah Halevi.* Philadelphia: JPS, 1960f.

Maimonides, Moses, *The Guide of the Perplexed.* Chicago: University of Chicago Press, 1963.

Rosenzweig, Franz, *The Star of Redemption.* New York: Holt, Rinehart & Winston, 1971.

———, *On Jewish Learning.* New York: Schocken, 1955.

Rothenstreich, Nathan, *Jewish Philosophy in Modern Times, From Mendelssohn to Rosenzweig.* New York: Holt, Rinehart and Winston, 1968.

Schulweis, Harold M., *Evil and the Morality of God.* Cincinnati: HUC Press, 1984.

Schweid, Eliezer, *Jewish Thought in the Twentieth Century—An Introduction.* Atlanta: Scholars Press, 1991.

Soloveitchik, Joseph, *Halakhic Man.* Philadelphia: JPS, 1983.

Twersky, Isadore, *A Maimonides Reader.* New York: Behrman, 1972.

———, *Studies in Maimonides.* Cambridge, Mass.: Harvard University Press, 1992.

JEWISH MYSTICISM AND HASIDISM

Ariel, David S., *The Mystic Quest—An Introduction to Jewish Mysticism.* New York: Schocken, 1989.

Gindburg, Elliot K., *The Sabbath in the Classical Kabbalah.* Albany: SUNY Press, 1989.

Idel, Moshe, *Hasidism, Between Ecstasy and Magic.* Albany: SUNY Press, 1994.

———, *Golem: Jewish Magical and Mystical Traditions on the Artificial Anthropoid.* Albany: SUNY Press, 1990.

Scholem, Gershom, *Major Trends in Jewish Mysticism.* New York: Schocken, 1954.

———, *On the Kabbalah and Its Symbolism.* New York: Schocken, 1965.

———, *Origins of the Kabbalah.* Philadelphia: JPS, 1987.

——— (ed.), *The Zohar: Book of Splendor.* New York: Schocken, 1963.

———, *On the Mystical Shape of the Godhead.* New York: Schocken, 1990.

———, *On the Possibility of Jewish Mysticism in Our Time.* Philadelphia: JPS, 1998.

Sperling, Harry and Maurice Simon (trans.), *The Zohar.* 5 vols. London: Soncino Press, 1984.

Tishby, Isaiah, *The Wisdom of the Zohar—An Anthology of Texts.* London: Littman Library, 1989.

Buber, Martin, *The Legend of the Baal-Shem.* New York: Schocken, 1969.

———, *Tales of the Hasidim.* New York: Schocken, 1961.

Elior, Rachel, *The Paradoxical Ascent to God: The Kabbalistic Theosphy of Habad Hasidism.* Albany: SUNY Press, 1992.

Foxbrunner, Roman A., *The Hasidims of R. Shneur Zalman of Lyady.* Tuscaloosa, Ala.: University of Alabama Press, 1992.

Jacobs, Louis, *Hasidic Thought*. New York: Behrman, 1976.
———, *Hasidic Prayer*. New York: Schocken, 1978.
Mintz, Jerome R. *Hasidic People—A Place in the New World*. Cambridge, Mass.: Harvard University Press, 1992.

HOLOCAUST AND THEOLOGICAL ENDEAVORS

Bauer, Yehudah, *The Holocaust in Historical Perspective*. Seattle: University of Washington Press, 1978.
———, et al. (eds.), *Anatomy of the Auschwitz Death Camp*. Bloomington: Indiana University Press, 1994.
Berkowitz, Eliezer, *Faith after the Holocaust*. New York: Ktav, 1973.
Dawidowicz, Ludy, *A Holocaust Reader*. New York: Behrman, 1976.
———, *The War against the Jews*. New York: Holt, Rinehart and Winston, 1975.
Fackenheim, Emil L. *Quest for Past and Future*. Bloomington: Indiana University Press, 1968.
———, *The Jewish Return into History*. New York: Schocken, 1978.
Friedlander, Albert (ed.), *Out of the Whirlwind*. New York: Schocken, 1992.
Friedlander, Saul, *Probing the Limits of Representation*. Cambridge, Mass.: Harvard University Press, 1992.
Glatstein, Jacob, Israel Knox, and Samuel Margosches, *Anthology of Holocaust Literature*. Philadelphia: JPS, 1969.
Hillberg, Raul, *The Destruction of the European Jews*. New York: Harper & Row, 1979.
Langer, Lawrence L., *The Holocaust and the Literary Imagination*. New Haven and London: Yale University Press, 1975.
Levin, Nora, *The Holocaust: The Destruction of European Jewry, 1933–1945*. New York: Schocken, 1973.
Lipstadt, Deborah E., *Beyond Belief—The American Press and the Coming of the Holocaust*. New York: The Free Press, 1986.
———, *Denying the Holocaust—The History of the Revisionist Assault on Truth and Meaning*. New York: The Free Press, 1993.
Ringelblum, Emmanuel, *Notes from the Warsaw Ghetto*. New York: Schocken, 1958.
Rubenstein, Richard, *After Auschwitz*. Indianapolis: Bobbs Merrill, 1966.
———, *The Cunning of History: Mass Death and the American Future*. New York: Harper & Row, 1975.
Sachs, Nelly, *O, The Chimneys*. Philadelphia: JPS, 1968.
Swiebocka, Teresa, *Auschwitz, A History in Photographs*. Bloomington: Indiana University Press, 1992.
Tory, Abraham, *Surviving the Holocaust—The Kovno Ghetto Diary*. Cambridge, Mass.: Harvard University Press, 1990.
Volavkova, Hanah (ed.), *I Never Saw Another Butterfly—Children's Drawings and Poems from the Terezim Concentration Camp*. New York: McGraw-Hill, 1958.

Wiesel, Elie, *Night.* New York: Avon, 1972.
———, *The Gates of the Forest.* New York: Holt, Rinehart and Winston, 1966.
———, *A Jew Today.* New York: Vintage, 1978.
———, *The Jews of Silence.* New York: Holt, Rinehart and Winston, 1972.

JUDAISM IN AMERICA

The American Jewish Year Book. Philadelphia: JPS, annual.
Cohen, Steven M., *American Assimilation or Jewish Survival?* Bloomington: Indiana University Press, 1988.
Cohen, Naomi W., *Encounter with Emancipation—The German Jews in the United States, 1830–1914.* Philadelphia: JPS, 1984.
Glazer, Nathan, *American Judaism.* Chicago: University of Chicago Press, 1959.
Glock, Charles Y. and Rodney Stark, *Religion and Anti-Semitism.* Berkeley: University of California Press, 1966.
Goldberg, M. Hirsch, *Just Because They Are Jewish.* New York: Stein and Day, 1978.
Herberg, Will, *Protestant, Catholic, Jew.* New York: Doubleday, 1955.
Hertzberg, Arthur. *The Jews in America—Four Centuries of an Uneasy Encounter; A History.* New York: Simon & Schuster, 1989.
Heschel, Abraham J., *The Insecurity of Freedom.* Philadelphia: JPS, 1966.
Janowsky, A., *The American Jew, A Reappraisal.* Philadelphia: JPS, 1964.
Karp, Abraham, *Heaven and Home: The Jews in America.* New York: Schocken, 1985.
Korn, Bertram W., *American Jewry and the Civil War.* Philadelphia: JPS, 1961.
Liebman, Charles, *The Ambivalent American Jew.* Philadelphia: JPS, 1973.
Neusner, Jacob, *American Judaism, Adventure in Modernity.* Englewood Cliffs, N.J.: Prentice-Hall, 1972.
Quinley, Harold E. and Charles Y. Glock, *Anti-Semitism in America.* New York: Free Press, 1979.
Sidorsky, David (ed.), *The Future of the Jewish Community in America.* New York: Basic Books, 1973.
Silberman, Charles, *A Certain People—American Jews and their Lives Today.* New York: Summit Books, 1985.
Stark, Rodney, James C. Foster, Charles Y. Glock and Harold E. Quinley, *Wayward Shepherds: Prejudice and The Protestant Clergy.* New York: Harper & Row, 1973.
Zborowsky, Mark and Elizabeth Herzog, *Life Is with People.* New York: Schocken, 1976.

VARIETIES OF RELIGIOUS EXPRESSION: LIFE AND LAW

Blau, Joseph L., *Modern Varieties of Judaism.* New York: Columbia University Press, 1966.

Bleich, J. David, *Contemporary Halakhic Problems* (Orthodox). New York: Ktav, 1977.

Bokser, Ben Zion (ed.), *Abraham Isaac Kook. . . Essays, Letters and Poems.* New York: Paulist Press, 1978.

Borowitz, Eugene B., *Reform Judaism Today.* New York: Behrman, 1978.

————, *Liberal Judaism.* New York: Union of American Hebrew Congregations, 1984.

Cohen, Arthur A. and Paul Mendes Flohr, *Contemporary Jewish Religious Thought.* New York: The Free Press, 1988.

Davis, Mosheh, *The Emergence of Conservative Judaism.* Philadelphia: JPS, 1963.

Freehof, Solomon B., *Responsa* (Reform), numerous volumes. New York: Ktav, 1955–1963; New York: Hebrew Union College, 1969–1974.

Gillman, Neil, *Conservative Judaism—The New Century.* West Orange, N.J.: Behrman, 1993.

Heilman, Samuel C. and Steven M. Cohen, *Cosmopolitans and Parochials: Modern Orthodox Jews in America.* Chicago: Chicago University Press, 1989.

————, *Defenders of the Faith—Inside Ultra-Orthodox Jewry.* New York: Schocken, 1992.

Kaplan, Mordecai M., *The Future of the American Jew* (Reconstructionist). New York: Macmillan, 1948.

————, *The Meaning of God in Modern Jewish Religion* (Reconstructionist). New York: Reconstructionist Press, 1937.

————, *Questions Jews Ask: Reconstructionist Answers.* New York: Reconstructionist Press, 1956.

Klein, Isaac, *Guide to Jewish Religious Practice* (Conservative). New York: The Jewish Theological Seminary, Ktav, 1979.

Meyer, Michael M., *Response to Modernity—A Hisotry of the Reform Movement in Judaism.* New York: Oxford University Press, 1988.

Nadell, Pamela S. *Conservative Judaism in America—A Biographical Dictionary and Sourcebook.* New York: Greenwood Press, 1988.

Plaut, W. Gunther, *The Growth of Reform Judaism.* New York: World Union for Progressive Judaism, 1965.

————, *The Rise of Reform Judaism.* New York: World Union for Progressive Judaism, 1963.

Siegel, Seymor, *Conservative Judaism and Jewish Law.* New York: Ktav, 1977.

Weissman Joselit, Jenna, *New York's Jewish Jews—The Orthodox Community in the Interwar Years.* Bloomington: Indiana University Press, 1990.

THE WOMAN IN CONTEMPORARY JEWISH LIFE

Baskin, Judith R. (ed.), *Jewish Women in Historical Perspective.* Detroit: Wayne State University Press, 1991.

Biale, Rachel, *Women and Jewish Law.* New York: Schocken, 1984.

Fishman, Sylvia Barak. *A Breath of Life, Feminism in the American Jewish Community.* New York: The Free Press, 1993.

Frankel, Ellen, *The Five Books of Miriam—A Woman's Commentary on the Torah.* New York: Putnam, 1996.

Greenberg, Blu, *On Women and Judaism—A View from Tradition.* Philadelphia: JPS, 1985.

Grossman, Susan and Rivka Haut (eds.), *Daughters of the King—Women and the Synagogue.* Philadelphia: JPS, 1992.

Heschel, Susannah, *On Being a Jewish Feminist.* New York: Schocken, 1988.

Lacks, Roslyn, *Women and Judaism.* New York: Doubleday, 1980.

Meiselman, Mosheh, *Jewish Woman in Jewish Law.* New York: Ktav, 1978.

Plaskow, Judith, *Standing Again at Sinai—Judaism from a Feminist Perspective.* Harper San Francisco, 1991.

Priesand, Sally, *Judaism and the New Woman.* New York: Behrman, 1975.

Umansky, Ellen and Dianne Ashton (eds.), *Four Centuries of Jewish Women's Spirituality—A Sourcebook.* Boston: Beacon Press, 1992.

Rosen, Norma, *Biblical Women Unbound—Counter Tales.* Philadelphia: JPS, 1997.

ZIONISM

Bein, Alex, *Theodor Herzl.* New York: Atheneum, 1970.

Buber, Martin, *On Zion.* New York: Schocken, 1973.

Halkin, Hillel, *Letters to an American Friend.* Philadelphia: JPS, 1978.

Hammer, Reuven (ed.), *The Jerusalem Anthology—A Literary Guide.* Philadelphia: JPS, 1997.

Hertzberg, Arthur (ed.), *The Zionist Idea.* Philadelphia and New York: JPS and Meridian Books, 1960.

Heschel, Abraham J., *Israel.* New York: Farrar, Straus and Giroux, 1971.

Laqueur, Walter, *A History of Zionism.* New York: Schocken, 1989.

Sachar, Howard, *A History of Israel from the Rise of Zionism to Our Time.* Philadelphia: JPS, 1979.

Spiro, Melford E., *Kibbutz, Venture in Utopia.* New York: Schocken, 1963.

THE JEWISH YEAR IN WORSHIP AND ART

Prayer Books and Haggadahs by the various denominational groups.

Philip Goodman has authored anthologies for every holiday, published by the Jewish Publication Society of America (Philadelphia).

Agnon, S. Y., *Days of Awe.* New York: Schocken, 1948.

Arzt, Max, *Justice and Mercy: Commentary on the Liturgy of the New Year and the Day of Atonement.* New York: Holt, Rinehart and Winston, 1963.

Elbogen, Ismar, *Jewish Liturgy—A Comprehensive History.* Philadelphia: JPS, 1983.

Frankel, Ellen and Betsy Platkin Teutsch, *The Encyclopedia of Jewish Symbols.* Northvale, NJ: Aronson, 1992.

Gaster, Theodor H., *Festivals of The Jewish Year.* Philadelphia: JPS, 1953.

———, *Passover: Its History and Traditions.* Boston: Beacon Press, 1962.

Hammer, Reuven, *Entering Jewish Prayer—A Guide to Personal Devotion and the Worship Service.* New York: Schocken, 1994.

Heinemann, Joseph, *Prayer in the Talmud.* Berlin: W. de Gruyter, 1977.

Heinemann, Joseph and Jakob J. Petuchowsky, *Literature of the Synagogue.* New York: Behrman, 1975.

Idelson, A. Z., *Jewish Liturgy.* New York: Schocken, 1967.

———, *Jewish Music.* New York: Schocken, 1944.

Kampf, Avram, *Contemporary Synagogue Art.* Philadelphia: JPS, 1966.

Millgram, Abraham, *The Sabbath, Day of Delight.* Philadelphia: JPS, 1944.

Roth, Cecil, *Jewish Art.* New York: New York Graphic Society, 1971.

Schauss, Hayyim, *The Jewish Festivals.* New York: UAHC, 1938.

Trepp, Leo, *Jewish Worship, Form and Evolution.* Stuttgart: Kohlhammer, 1992. (English translation in preparation.)

Wischnitzer, Rachel L., *The Architecture of the European Synagogue.* Philadelphia: JPS, 1964.

———, *Synagogue Architecture in the United States.* Philadelphia: JPS, 1955.

Yerushalmi, Yosef Hayimn, *Haggadah and History.* Philadelphia: JPS, 1998.

LIVING AS A JEW

Donin, Hayim Halevi, *To Be a Jew* (Orthodox). New York: Basic Books, 1972.

Geffen, Rela M. (ed.) *Celebration and Renewal—Rites of Passage in Judaism.* Philadelphia: JPS, 1993.

Klein, Isaac, *A Guide to Jewish Practice* (Conservative). New York: Ktav, 1978

Siegel, Richard, *The First Jewish Catalog—A Do-It-Yourself Kit.* Philadelphia: JPS, 1973.

Strannfeld, Sharon, *The Second Jewish Catalog—Sources and Resources.* Philadelphia: JPS, 1976.

———, *The Third Jewish Catalog—Creating Community.* Philadelphia: JPS, 1983.

Trepp, Leo, *The Complete Book of Jewish Observance.* New York: Behrman House-Summit Books, 1980.

SOME PERIODICALS

There exists an abundance of publications of which but a few will be mentioned.

The various synagogue and rabbinical bodies and their affiliates have regular periodicals for their constituents.

B'nai B'rith issues *The National Jewish Monthly,* which is popular in style and has wide appeal beyond the membership, and *Jewish Heritage,* an educational quarterly.

Commentary, Judaism, and *Tikkun* are scholarly magazines, concerned in various degrees with contemporary issues

Commentary, a monthly magazine issued by the American Jewish Committee, holds high prestige among Jewish and non-Jewish readers. *Tikkun* frequently offers radical thought. *Judaism,* published by the American Jewish Congress, has a high standard. *Hadassah* publishes a magazine by the same name. The *Reconstructionist* deals with many subjects from the Reconstructionist point of view. *Sh'ma, A Journal of Jewish Responsibility,* deals with the issues of our time from the Jewish point of view; the journal is daringly innovative. *Tradition* is an excellent quarterly issued by the Orthodox Rabbinical Council of America. The national rabbinical and congregational organizations issue scholarly and popular journals. *Moment* is a magazine dealing with all aspects of Judaism. *Midstream* is a review published by the Herzl Institute. Other groups as well as individual publishers issue magazines and periodicals. *Hadoar* is a Hebrew magazine.

The larger Jewish communities have their own newspapers, usually dealing with local Jewish affairs, but often including wider coverage; they are usually weeklies and written in English.

The *Leo Baeck Institute,* dedicated to the study of German Jewry since the Emancipation, issues an annual Yearbook with scholarly contributions and has published numerous works.

INDEX

Italicized page references indicate illustrations.